Rivers
of the
United States

Rivers
of the
United States

VOLUME IV
PART A: THE MISSISSIPPI
RIVER AND TRIBUTARIES NORTH OF ST. LOUIS

Ruth Patrick

FRANCIS BOYER CHAIR OF LIMNOLOGY
THE ACADEMY OF NATURAL SCIENCES OF PHILADELPHIA

JOHN WILEY & SONS, INC.

New York • Chichester • Weinheim • Brisbane • Singapore • Toronto

This publication is designed to provide accurate and authoritative
information in regard to the subject matter covered. It is sold with
the understanding that the publisher is not engaged in rendering
legal, accounting, or other professional services. If legal advice or
other expert assistance is required, the services of a competent
professional person should be sought.

Library of Congress Cataloging-in-Publication Data:

Patrick, Ruth.
    Rivers of the United States.

    1. Rivers—United States. I. Title.

GB1215.P29   551.48′3′0973   93-27583

ISBN 0-471-30345-3 (v. 1)
ISBN 0-471-10752-2 (v. 2)
ISBN 0-471-30346-1 (v. 3)
ISBN 0-471-19741-6 (v. 4, Pt. A)
ISBN 0-471-19742-4 (v. 4, Pt. B)
ISBN 0-471-30347-X (v. 4, set)

Printed in the United States of America.

10 9 8 7 6 5 4 3 2 1

Preface

==

This volume is the fourth in a series of books describing the functioning ecosystems in the rivers of the United States. In this volume the rivers of the Mississippi Drainage are discussed. There are many more rivers that drain directly or indirectly into the Mississippi. Unfortunately, the lack of sufficient information on the aquatic life prevented them from being included. The rivers that have been included are representative of the types of rivers, diverse as to chemical and biological characteristics, that drain directly or indirectly into the Mississippi River.

The main purpose of the book is to describe the organisms that compose the structure and function in the ecosystems in each river that make possible the conversion of waste into energy and food and hence transfer to other organisms the nutrients that were originally tied up in wastes.

At each stage of nutrient and energy transfer there are a great many species representing very different phylogenetic groups of macro and microorganisms with different life cycles and different requirements for growth. This gives redundancy to the system and ensures that the process of the conversion of waste into nutrients and energy will be maintained. The criterion for selecting habitats in a stream for description was that a natural functioning ecosystem was operative: in other words, that they have not been altered by the effects of pollution or by manmade structures. In the case of the Mississippi proper, it was impossible to find an area that was not affected by dams or pollution. Therefore, I have had to consider areas between dams where the flow of the river approached natural conditions.

In selecting an area of study, it was important to find areas that had not been adversely affected by pollution. It was impossible to study the Ohio River proper and the main course of several other rivers, because pollution was present or the natural structure of the river had been altered. However, I was able to obtain information on enough rivers and their tributaries to have representative samples of the different types of riverine systems that are part of the Mississippi Drainage.

The Mississippi Drainage extends to the far west, such as in the headwaters of the Missouri River and in the east to the Appalachian Mountains. These streams drain directly or indirectly into the Mississippi River. Rivers that have different types of physical conditions and different chemical characteristics of their waters were given preference to rivers that were very similar to each other. This was done because the scope of this book is to show how ecosystems function in very different types of rivers. For example, headwater streams in the Appalachian Mountains are found to be very low in conductivity and contain small amounts of alkaline metals. In contrast, some of the streams in the west, such as tributaries of the Arkansas River, are very high in alkaline metals and often contain other types of metals from natural sources.

It is these chemical and physical differences in rivers as well as differences in the river morphology that enable different types of ecosystems to develop. In this book I have tried to describe how the ecosystem functions in a selected river. Unfortunately, sometimes this was not possible because of lack of information. In such cases the ecosystem has been constructed by using streams that are geographically close to each other and chemically and physically have the same characteristics and water qualities.

The data in the description of many of the rivers in this book are the result of my own research and that of the team of scientists that study rivers at the Academy of Natural Sciences. To these scientists I owe a great deal because it is the data they helped to accumulate that makes this book possible. The chemical characteristics of the water usually are those that were present in a river at a given time when the biological data were collected. It is recognized that the chemical characteristics of all rivers vary and that these data are simply benchmarks for determining the characteristics of the river. For these various reasons, one cannot be sure that the species noted would occur at the present time in the river described. However, the general structure of the ecosystems should be similar if the river is in its natural healthy condition.

The taxonomic list of species used to construct the ecosystem in a given river may be from many different sources. Often, it is the result of studies of mine or those of other scientists at the Academy of Natural Sciences. In some cases they are derived from scientific papers of other workers. These taxonomic lists have been studied carefully. However, the names given by the original authors have been used and no attempt has been made to change the classification of a given taxon. The only uniformity that exists in considering these taxons is at a higher level—the class, order, or family level—so that there is consistency in the order in which the taxons are described.

In this treatment of the rivers of the Mississippi Drainage, there are many different types of water. In general, the streams that rise in the Appalachian Mountains or in the northern part of the United States have relatively low conductivity, whereas rivers to the west of the Mississippi that drain into the Mississippi have varying degrees of hardness and of sulfur and chloride concentrations. These chemical characteristics greatly influence the type of fauna and flora that are present.

The taxonomic literature on these various streams is scattered. Much of the information comes from unpublished studies made by me and by others at the Academy of Natural Sciences. A great variety of literature has been consulted. The large treatises on fish from various watersheds have been extremely valuable in determining the habits and characteristics of different species. Also very helpful has been the general literature. A systematic work of great value to us is *An Introduction to the Aquatic Insects of North America* by R. W. Merrit and K. W. Cummins.

The results of these studies have shown that natural streams have a great variety of species composing these functioning ecosystems. This is true not only for the megafauna but also for the meiofauna. In many cases, the types of species in midwestern streams are quite different from those found in eastern United States. As previous books have also done, this book emphasizes that biodiversity is essential for the functioning of the ecosystem of our planet, for it enables waste to be changed into nutrients for many species and hence into energy and growth.

The ecosystems of these streams are very complex and they differ from stream to stream. The nutrient requirements of various species of plants and animals are quite different. The stream structure—that is, patterns of current, materials that make up the substrates, depth, shade, and so on—form the variable environmental characteristics necessary for the functioning of many species that compose the ecosystem.

This series of books should be very useful to students of rivers and to people of all ages who are interested in conservation and preserving the naturalness of streams, because by understanding these systems one can better understand the reasons why it is so important to maintain the naturalness of streams both in structure and in chemical characteristics of the water. This book should be of interest not only to students of rivers but to industrialists who wish to understand the characteristics of the streams that are associated with their plant sites in developing plans to use the streams but not abuse them. Similarly, this book should be of great use to land planners who wish to understand how streams function in order that they can plan to develop the watershed in a manner that will not destroy these important ecosystems. It should also be important to those who administer our national resources, as it includes a great deal of information integrated in a manner that is unique to this series.

Acknowledgments

I wish to acknowledge the many people who have made this book possible, particularly those who have done the research that has contributed to this work. The scientists involved in the early studies were John Cairns, protozoologist; Fairie Lyn Carter, chemist; Thomas Dolan IV, entomologist; and Charles B. Wurtz, invertebrate zoologist. Other scientists who helped were William A. Daily, Matthew H. Hohn, Wilbur E. Wade, John H. Wallace, and John T. Gallagher (deceased). I also wish to acknowledge the help in the identification, particularly of chironomids, of Selwin S. Roback (deceased).

The construction of a functioning ecosystem demands information from many different disciplines. For the help of these scientists, I am very grateful. Individuals in various governmental agencies that have been particularly helpful are David Tomljanovich, Tennessee Valley Authority, and David Webb, Tennessee Valley Authority. Several state agencies have been particularly helpful in the development of the knowledge necessary to write this book. I refer particularly to the state agencies of Kansas, Missouri, and Illinois. I also want to acknowledge the help of the Tennessee River Basin Authority, which has given me much general information about the Tennessee River and its tributaries.

The writing of this book has required researching a great many papers. I particularly want to thank Dennis Murphy, who brought together a considerable amount of the data used in the writing of this book. I particularly want to thank Sue Durdu for her aid in the technical editing and typing of the manuscript. My assistant, Rita Kolchinsky, has also been helpful in gathering some of the technical information required for this book. The artist Su Yong contributed some of the art used in the book.

Many of my colleagues at the Academy of Natural Sciences have furnished pertinent information that has been very helpful. I particularly want to mention the scientists at the Stroud Water Research Laboratory and the staff of the library of the Academy, who have been very helpful in bringing together technical information that was necessary for the creation of this book.

Besides the work of colleagues at the Academy of Natural Sciences, I want to thank Dr. Philip C. Manor, Bob Hilbert, and Diana Cisek of John Wiley & Sons, Inc. for their help and suggestions in the preparation of this volume.

This book would not have been possible without the financial help of many people. I want to acknowledge the John and Alice Tyler Award and the money associated with the award. Others who have been of great assistance in providing the finances necessary to do such a large and comprehensive volume include the E.I. DuPont Company, the Phoebe W. Haas Charitable Trust, the Procter & Gamble Company, Marian B. Stroud, and Lewis H. Van Dusen, Jr.

Contents

CHAPTER 1

Upper Mississippi River

INTRODUCTION

The Upper Mississippi River, which extends from the Minneapolis–St. Paul metropolitan area to the confluence with the Missouri River near St. Louis, covers much of the north-central United States. Formerly an island-braided river with substantial seasonal changes in river stage, the Upper Mississippi has been greatly modified for navigation. These modifications culminated in the 1930s with the construction of a series of locks and dams, which have transformed the free-flowing river into a series of shallow river-lakes.

These modifications have impaired some organisms, but the creation and/or expansion of backwater habitats following impoundment has generally increased species diversity and productivity, although the kinds of species are somewhat changed. Unfortunately, the impoundments have also altered sedimentation dynamics and increased eutrophication. In addition, the stabilization of flow resulting from impoundment has encouraged the development of floodplain. Combined with the direct effects of navigation (i.e., prop wash, wave action, and increased turbidity), these navigation improvements now threaten the diversity and productivity they once engendered.

PHYSICAL CHARACTERISTICS

The Mississippi River flows about 3736 km from its source at Lake Itasca, Minnesota, to the Gulf of Mexico. The Upper Mississippi River extends 1059 km from the bottom of St. Anthony Falls in the Minneapolis–St. Paul metro-

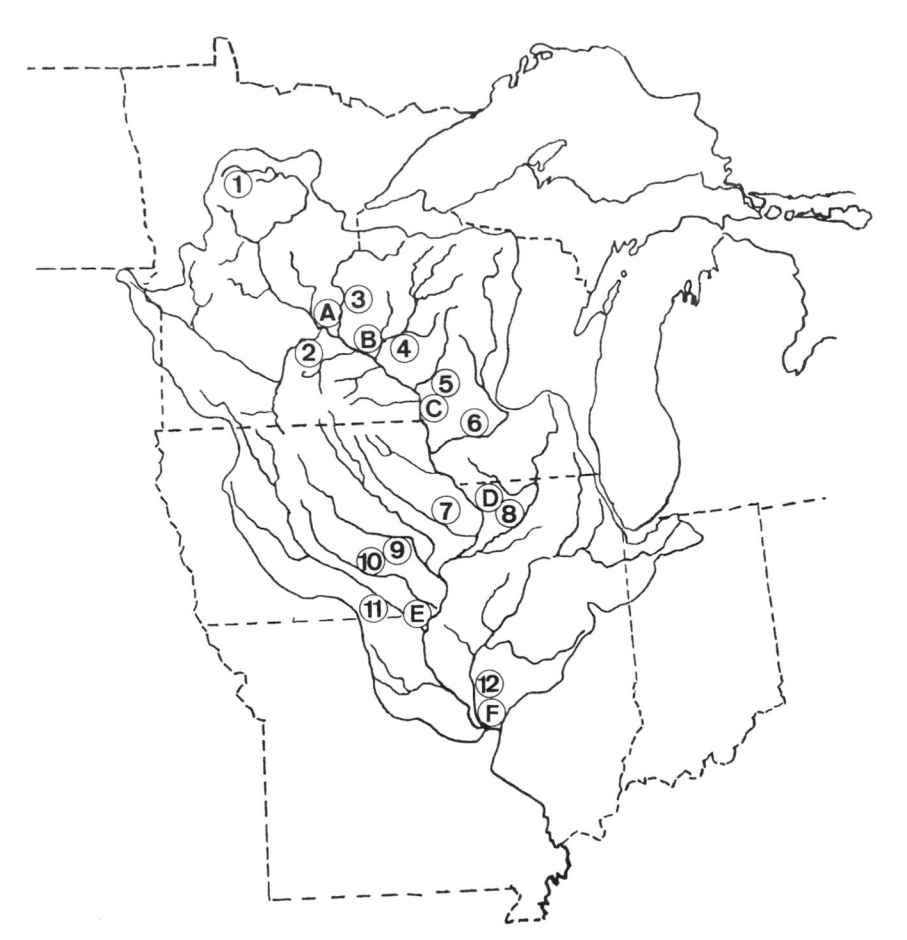

FIGURE 1.1.   Map of the Upper Mississippi River Basin. Points of interest: A, Minneapolis/St. Paul, Minnesota; B, Lake Pepin; C, Navigation Pool 8; D, Navigation Pool 13; E, Navigation Pool 19; F, Navigation Pool 26. Selected tributaries: 1, Mississippi headwaters; 2, Minnesota River; 3, St. Croix River; 4, Chippewa River; 5, Black River; 6, Wisconsin River; 7, Wapsipinicon River; 8, Rock River; 9, Iowa River; 10, Skunk River; 11, Des Moines River; 12, Illinois River.

politan region to its confluence with the Missouri River (Fremling et al., 1989). At Alton, Illinois, which lies approximately 12 km upstream from the Missouri River, the watershed area of the Upper Mississippi was 444,185 km^2 (USGS, 1975). The Upper Mississippi drains most of Minnesota, Wisconsin, Iowa, and Illinois and also drains portions of Missouri, South Dakota, and Indiana (Figure 1.1). The river is impounded by a series of 26 navigation dams situated 9.3 to 74.5 km apart. The location, size, and selected geographic features associated with these impoundments are presented in Table 1.1.

The Upper Mississippi River drains portions of the Superior Upland and Central Lowland Physiographic Provinces. Much of northern Wisconsin, as well as part of northeastern Minnesota, lies within the Superior Upland. Four

TABLE 1.1.   *Navigation Pools of the Upper Mississippi River*

Pool	km[a]	Bordering States	Length (km)[a]	Area (ha)	Comments
1	1,363.8	Minnesota	9.3	202	At St. Paul, Minnesota
2	1,311.7	Minnesota	52.1	3,932	Near Hastings, Minnesota
3	1,282.2	Minnesota and Wisconsin	29.5	2,634	Joined by St. Croix River
4	1,211.3	Minnesota and Wisconsin	70.9	9,431	Contains Lake Pepin; joined by Chippewa River
5	1,187.6	Minnesota and Wisconsin	23.7	4,737	
5A	1,172.2	Minnesota and Wisconsin	15.4	3,075	
6	1,149.3	Minnesota and Wisconsin	22.9	4,574	
7	1,130.3	Minnesota and Wisconsin	19.0	6,290	Contains Lake Onalaska; joined by Black River
8	1,092.8	Minnesota and Wisconsin	37.5	10,425	Joined by Root River
9	1,042.5	Iowa and Wisconsin	50.3	14,233	Joined by Upper Iowa River; contains Big Lake
10	989.7	Iowa and Wisconsin	52.8	8,456	Joined by Wisconsin River
11	938.0	Iowa and Wisconsin	51.7	8,043	
12	895.7	Iowa and Illinois	42.3	4,997	Bordered by Dubuque, Iowa
13	840.7	Iowa and Illinois	55.0	11,379	
14	793.7	Iowa and Illinois	47.0	4,165	Joined by Wapsipinicon River; bordered by Clinton, Iowa
15	777.0	Iowa and Illinois	16.7	1,468	Bordered by Davenport, Iowa
16	735.6	Iowa and Illinois	41.4	4,706	Joined by Rock River
17	703.3	Iowa and Illinois	32.3	3,293	Bordered by Muscatine, Iowa
18	660.5	Iowa and Illinois	42.8	4,754	Joined by Iowa River
19	586.0	Iowa and Illinois	74.5	12,329	Joined by Skunk River; bordered by Keokuk, Burlington, and Fort Madison, Iowa
20	552.2	Missouri and Illinois	33.8	2,930	Joined by Des Moines River
21	522.8	Missouri and Illinois	29.4	2,977	Bordered by Quincy, Illinois
22	484.6	Missouri and Illinois	38.2	3,274	Bordered by Hannibal, Missouri
24	440.0	Missouri and Illinois	44.6	4,469	Joined by Salt River
25	388.4	Missouri and Illinois	51.4	6,506	
26	326.5	Missouri and Illinois	61.9	7,065	Joined by Illinois River; bordered by Alton, Illinois

Source: After Fremling et al. (1989) (reproduced with permission of the Minister of Supply and Services, Canada 1996) and Rasmussen (1979a).

[a]km denotes river km, or the distance in kilometers from the Lock and Dam to above Cairo, Illinois, where the Mississippi is joined by the Ohio River. There are 505.2 km below Lock and Dam 26 and the Ohio River.

subdivisions of the Central Lowland Province are present within the basin. The Driftless Area occupies southeastern Minnesota, southwestern Wisconsin, and northeastern Iowa. The Western Lake Section occupies most of Minnesota and north-central Iowa. The Eastern Lake Section occupies the east-central margin of the basin near southern Lake Michigan. The Till Plains

Section occupies most of Illinois, while the Dissected Till Plains Section occupies most of eastern Iowa and Missouri. The Driftless Area displays no direct evidence of glaciation and is characterized by maturely dissected river valleys. Outside the Driftless Area, the bedrock is covered mostly by glacial drift and the topography is typically gently rolling (Nielsen et al., 1984).

Bedrock within the Superior Upland, which is part of the Canadian Shield, is composed of Precambrian igneous and metamorphic deposits. The Central Lowlands are underlain primarily with clastic and carbonate rocks formed by epicontinental seas. Late Precambrian and Cambrian sandstone are prevalent in the Driftless Area and extend up to the boundary of the Superior Upland Province. Paleozoic shales and limestones are thickest in Illinois and Iowa. This bedrock is buried beneath extensive surficial deposits of drift and loess, which become thinnest in the southernmost basin. Bedrock of Cretaceous shale lies within the western part of the basin (Nielsen et al., 1984).

The basin was heavily modified by Pleistocene glaciation. Two of the main effects have been the scouring of preglacial topography and the filling in of much of the remainder with glacial drift. Most of Wisconsin, Minnesota, and northern Illinois are buried with Wisconsin Drift, which is younger and considerably less weathered than the Illinoian and Kansan Drift, which covered most of the southern basin (Nielsen et al., 1984).

In addition to altering the topography and geology of the Upper Mississippi River Basin, glaciation has had major influences upon the river itself. The reach of the Upper Mississippi River extending from the Twin Cities (Minneapolis–St. Paul) through the Driftless Area apparently lies within its preglacial course. Within this reach, the river flows through a flat-bottomed river valley varying in width from 2 to 11 km and bordered by bluffs as high as 300 m. The river valley was as much as 90 m deeper than its current level because of scouring caused by overflow from the glacial lakes, Agassiz and Superior. With the retreat of the glaciers, overflow from these lakes was diverted elsewhere. Consequently, the valley aggraded with glacial outwash of sand and gravel. This aggradation continues at a much slower rate (Claflin, 1973; Fenneman, 1938; Fremling et al., 1989).

Downstream from the Driftless Area, Pleistocene glaciation apparently changed the course of the Upper Mississippi on at least two occasions. The narrowness of the gorge between Clinton and Muscatine, Iowa, suggests that the river had cut through here in relatively recent times. Two drift-filled valleys, which are known only through drilling, suggest former channels of the Mississippi. The smaller of the two buried valleys runs parallel to the west of the river and reenters the present channel in the vicinity of Keokuk, Iowa. The other runs to the southeast and leads to the bend of the Illinois River at Hennepin, Illinois. Rapids at Rock Island, Illinois, and at Keokuk are evidence of the northern and southern extent of the diversions (Fenneman, 1938). One consequence of this series of river diversions is that the river valley is less deeply incised through much of Iowa, Illinois, and Missouri than it is in the Driftless Area. For example, the bluffs on the Iowa side of Pool 19 are less than 40 m high, while on the Illinois side they gradually slope upward (Grumbaugh and Anderson, 1987).

The Upper Mississippi River has a mean gradient of only 0.07 m km^{-1} (Fremling et al., 1989). The geomorphology of this low-gradient river has been greatly influenced by north–south differences in geology and by anthropogenic modification to improve navigation. Bank erosion of extensive glacial outwash deposits has contributed substantial amounts of coarse sandy bedload to a number of tributaries in the northern basin. One of the most dramatic effects of this high bedload is the partial impoundment of Lake Pepin (between Pools 3 and 4) by the delta of the Chippewa River. Large inputs of sand from the Chippewa and other tributaries, including the Trempealeau, Black, La Crosse, Turkey, Upper Iowa, and Wisconsin Rivers, have resulted in a high degree of island braiding in the northern reach of the Upper Mississippi. Channel morphology is most complex in the vicinity of tributary confluences. Here, the main channel is typically impinged on the bank opposite the tributary's entry, islands and subsidiary channels are numerous, and the tributaries are often forced to flow parallel to the river for several kilometers (Nielsen et al., 1984).

The influence of these outwash tributaries diminishes as the Upper Mississippi River leaves the Driftless Area. Tributaries draining most watersheds in Iowa, Illinois, Missouri, and southwestern Minnesota contain sediment loads dominated by silt originating from surficial deposits of loess rather than coarse sand originating from outwash deposits. Reduced loading of the Upper Mississippi with coarse sand results in a reduction in island braiding, while increased loads of loess-derived silt promote bank stabilization and tend to fill in subsidiary channels. Consequently, while island and subsidiary channels are present in the southern reach of the Upper Mississippi, they are much less frequent than they are in the northern reach. Moreover, the more favorable soils of the Till Plains and Dissected Till Plains Provinces have encouraged intensive agricultural development. Crops such as corn and soybeans cover much of the southern basin, whereas forest and pasture predominate in much of northern basin. Intensive cropping of the southern basin has resulted in elevated suspended sediment loads, which in turn have increased the difference in geomorphology between the northern and southern reaches of the river (Nielsen et al., 1984).

Navigation Projects
Superimposed onto the effects of tributary sediments have been the effects of assorted navigation projects. Navigation in the Upper Mississippi River was impeded by ice during the winter and a variety of obstructions during low summer flows. As early as 1824, navigation improvements such as snag removal, closing of subsidiary channels, sandbar dredging, and excavation of rapids were attempted to facilitate summer navigation. A comprehensive effort to improve navigation was initiated in 1878 with the authorization of a 1.37-m (4.5-ft) channel from St. Paul to the mouth of the Missouri River. This channel

was maintained with bank revetments, longitudinal dikes, and closing dams. A 1.83-m (6-ft) channel, which was authorized in 1907, was created primarily with the construction of numerous wing dikes. The structures from both of these channelization projects promoted channelization by diverting flow into the main channel and filling in some of the backwaters. As a result, there was a general decrease in water surface area and an increase in island area. For example, water surface area in Pool 4 below Lake Pepin decreased 9.6%, while Pool 25 decreased 13.0% from 1897 to 1923 (Chen and Simmons, 1986).

The most dramatic change to the Upper Mississippi River came with the authorization of a 2.75-m (9-ft) navigation channel in 1930. Summer flows in the Upper Mississippi were insufficient to maintain a 2.75-m channel developed with conventional dikes and revetments, so a series of locks and dams were constructed. These locks and dams facilitated summer navigation by impounding water in a series of navigation pools. By maintaining minimum pool elevations at or near the sites of the dams, depths of at least 2.75 m were maintained throughout the main channel. The channels are also maintained with supplemental dredging. Twenty-four of these locks and dams were constructed during the 1930s. Two other dams were constructed prior to the authorization of the 2.75-m channel but were incorporated into the navigation project. Lock and Dam 1 (near the Twin Cities) was completed in 1917, while Lock and Dam 19 (near Keokuk, Iowa) was completed in 1913. Both serve as hydroelectric as well as navigation facilities. Unlike flood control dams, the 26 dams in the Upper Mississippi River were designed to maintain minimum flows, while high flows are allowed to recede naturally downstream (Chen and Simmons, 1986; Fremling and Claflin, 1984; Fremling et al., 1989; Grumbaugh and Anderson, 1987; Rasmussen, 1979a).

The series of locks and dams has transformed the Upper Mississippi from an island-braided, free-flowing river into a series of shallow river-lakes (i.e., navigation pools). Within the navigation pools there is a characteristic longitudinal sequence of river morphology. Three reaches are usually recognized: the lower pool, middle pool, and upper pool. The maintenance of minimum pool elevations has permanently inundated the floodplains immediately upstream of the locks and dams. Consequently, the lower pool is typically wide and, except for the navigation channel, shallow. Minimum pool elevations have also inundated many of the low-lying portions of the former floodplain in the middle pool. This has typically resulted in the expansion of existing backwaters and the creation of others, as well as an increase in the number of islands. The upper pool has been affected least by minimum pool elevations and in some ways is most like the preimpoundment river (Fremling and Claflin, 1984; Rasmussen, 1989b).

Aquatic Habitats

The Upper Mississippi River has a diversity of aquatic habitats. A number of classification schemes have been employed, but most include the following habitat types: tailwater, main channel, main-channel border, side channel, slough, and floodplain lake or pond. Tailwaters, which extend 0.8 km from each dam, are characterized by fast currents and coarse sediments (sand, gravel, and sometimes cobble). The main channel is maintained at a minimum of 2.7 m in depth and 122 m in width and is characterized by swift currents and sand to gravel substrates. The main-channel border is the shallow zone lying between the main channel and the shoreline. Currents near the main channel can be swift, but those near the shore are often negligible. Sand dominates main-channel border substrates in the upper pool, while substrates in the lower pool are characterized by silt and clay. Side channels are subsidiary channels that carry flow for most of the year. They have relatively swift currents and predominantly sandy substrates. Sloughs are subsidiary channels that maintain contact with the main river but usually receive fresh flows only during periods of high flow. Otherwise, currents are typically low to negligible. Substrates are dominated by silt, clay, and muck. Floodplain lakes and ponds are essentially lentic habitats that are connected to the main river during high flow but remain isolated from it for much of the year. Currents can be relatively high during high flows but tend to be nonexistent for the rest of the year. Substrates are typically silt, clay, and muck (Anderson and Day, 1986; Fremling et al., 1989; Rasmussen, 1979a). Dike fields (i.e., the area encompassed by three or more adjacent dikes) and littoral areas (i.e., macrophyte beds that extend outward from the shore) are important components of the main-channel border and side-channel habitats (Fremling et al., 1989).

Any scheme for classifying habitats in the Upper Mississippi River is confounded by the diversity of habitats. The difference between floodplain lakes and sloughs is usually one of degree. For example, Big Lake, a floodplain lake in Pool 9, is connected to the main channel by a number of side channels (Eckblad et al., 1977). Similarly, a subsidiary channel can possess the fast currents and sandy substrates of a side channel near its divergence from the main channel but can also become shallower and more sluggish downstream. Habitat classification is especially problematic for the main-channel border habitat. This habitat encompasses locations with swift currents and sandy substrates as well as those with negligible currents and silty substrates. Some authors (e.g., Anderson and Day, 1986) include the wide, shallow expanses of the lower pool with the main-channel border, whereas others (e.g., Fremling et al., 1989) designate the entire lower pool as the "navigation pool." Others (e.g., Rasmussen, 1979b) classify the lower pool as another type of lake.

In addition to the diversity of habitats within each pool, there are substantial differences in the relative distribution of aquatic habitats among the pools. In general, backwater habitats (i.e., sloughs and floodplain lakes) account for half or more of the total aquatic habitat area in Pools 2 to 13, while backwater habitats in Pools 14 to 26 typically range between 20 and 40%. Similarly, side channels are prevalent in many of the northern pools but not in several of the southern pools (i.e., Pools 18 to 24). Corresponding to the north–south decrease in off-channel habitats is the relative increase in the main-channel border habitat (Peck and Smart, 1986). Differences in pool morphology and the resulting distribution of aquatic habitats are also apparent with the comparisons of maps from different pools. Pool 8, for example, presents a complex maze of backwaters and islands, especially in its middle reach, which contrasts with its largely open lower pool. Pool 19, on the other hand, exhibits a much simpler morphology, although islands and side channels tend to be more extensive in the middle and upper reaches. The abundance and variety of backwater habitats present in the pools in the Driftless Area (Pools 4 to 13) are largely the result of island braiding caused by high tributary inputs of sandy sediments (Nielsen et al., 1984).

Effects of Impoundments
Impoundment of the Upper Mississippi River has resulted in the creation of extensive and productive backwater habitats. However, these same impoundments that created these productive backwaters are now threatening them via sedimentation. Mean sedimentation rates that range between 1.1 and 4.2 cm yr^{-1} have been estimated for Pools 4 to 10 and 14 for the period between 1965 and 1975 (Chen and Simmons, 1986; McHenry et al., 1984).

Although there appears to have been little significant change in the rates of sediment deposition, impoundment has altered the dynamics of deposition. Formerly, sedimentation was concentrated on floodplains and in backwaters, and it occurred primarily during high flows (McHenry et al., 1984). Following impoundment, sedimentation has been concentrated in the lower pools and in backwaters of the middle pools. Moreover, sedimentation continues for most of the year (Bhowmik and Adams, 1986; Chen and Simmons, 1986; McHenry et al., 1984; Smart et al., 1986). Barge traffic and dredging aggravate sedimentation within backwaters by transferring sediments from the main channel to areas of reduced currents (Chen and Simmons, 1986; Smart et al., 1986).

Based on current rates of sedimentation, backwater lakes will probably become marshes within 50 to 100 years, while many of the lower pools will shoal within a century or two (McHenry et al., 1984). Sedimentation has been particularly dramatic in Pool 19. This pool differs from others in the Upper Mississippi River in that the lock and dam was constructed some 50 years earlier than those authorized by the 2.75-m navigation channel. Moreover, Lock and Dam 19 was designed with surface lift gates, which are more efficient in trapping sediments than the roller gates employed in most of the other dams (Jahn and Anderson, 1986). During its first 66 years of operation, Pool 19 has lost 55% of its original impounded capacity to sedimentation. This loss in capacity is primarily the result of decreasing depths; some areas have received more than 10 m of deposited sediments. The greatest loss in capacity occurred within the 15 years immediately following impoundment (1913 to 1928). Loss rates have declined with time and it is predicted that a dynamic volumetric equilibrium will be achieved sometime near the year 2000. By this time, however, Pool 19 will have lost 67% of its original volume (Bhowmik and Adams, 1986). In another estimate, this equilibrium will be achieved by 2050 with a loss of 80% of original pool capacity (Grumbaugh and Anderson, 1989).

Originally, the primary site for sediment deposition during high flows, floodplains in the Upper Mississippi commonly exceeded several kilometers in width. Undeveloped floodplains are covered by a mosaic of alluvial forests, willow forests, and meadows (Peck and Smart, 1986). Alluvial forests in the northern pools are typically dominated by silver maple (*Acer saccharium*), American elm (*Ulmus americana*), and river birch (*Betula nigra*) (Swanson and Sohmer, 1978) while those in the southern pools are typically dominated by *A. saccharium* and cottonwood (*Populus deltoides*) (Grumbaugh and Anderson, 1989). Willow forests are typically dominated by several species of willows (*Salix nigra, S. amygdaloides,* and *S. interior*) and *P. deltoides.* Meadows were typically dominated by *Carex emoryi, C. laeviconica,* and *Phalaris arundinacea. P. arundinacea* often forms nearly monotypic stands, which were regularly harvested for hay (Swanson and Sohmer, 1978).

Impoundments, floodplain reclamation, and other modifications have greatly altered the floodplain–river relationship of the Upper Mississippi River. Permanent inundation following impoundment has removed floodplain habitat from most of the lower pool and much of the middle pool (Grumbaugh and Anderson, 1987; Junk et al., 1989). Moreover, the maintenance of minimum pool elevations has moderated seasonal fluctuations in water levels, thereby facilitating the succession of marshlands to alluvial forests (Smart et al., 1986). Floodplain reclamation via levee construction has isolated much of the remaining floodplain from the river in Pools 19 to 26; agricultural development of the floodplains is greatest within these southern pools (Peck and Smart, 1986). Although floodplain reclamation and agricultural development are less extensive in the northern pools, railroad levees effectively isolate much of the floodplain from the river (Swanson and Sohmer, 1978).

Because its large watershed area tends to average out local differences in discharge, changes in river stage in the Upper Mississippi River have tended to be relatively gradual. Flow is characterized by spring and autumn rises and low flow during summer and winter (Dawson et al., 1984; Grumbaugh and Anderson, 1987; USGS, 1975). High spring flows result from snowmelt and increased surface runoff following precipitation. Summer flows are reduced primarily because of increased evapotranspiration. Autumn increases in flow result primarily from increased surface runoff following leaf fall. Reduced winter flows are attributable to freezing in the river as well as in the watershed.

A 107-year record of daily water elevations at Burlington, Iowa (Pool 19), has made possible the study of long-term changes in the hydrology of the Upper Mississippi River. Mean elevation during the 34-year preimpoundment period was 157.27 m above mean sea level, while the mean high- and low-water elevations were 159.35 and 156.11 m, respectively. Seasonally, river flow was characterized by a spring rise, which occurred sometime between early February and early September and lasted for a mean of 209 days. A secondary rise lasting for a mean of 102 days occurred in autumn. Both the spring and autumn rises would result in extended seasonal inundation of significant areas of the preimpoundment floodplain (Grumbaugh and Anderson, 1987). Conversely, low flows during summer often resulted in the dewatering of some backwaters (Carlander et al., 1963).

Closure of the dam in Pool 19 resulted in significant increases in river stages. Mean (158.63 m), mean high-water (160.26 m), and mean low-water (157.87 m) elevations increased significantly in the 72 years following impoundment. Maintenance of minimum pool elevations eliminated low-water intervals between the spring and autumn rises. Consequently, the spring rise was shortened by a mean of 19 days and the autumn rise became undiscernible (Grumbaugh and Anderson, 1987).

Changes in Pool 19 following impoundment greatly reduced floodplain availability. One obvious effect is the permanent inundation of floodplains in the lower pool. Another effect is the reduction in the difference between high and low flows. Prior to impoundment, the difference between the mean low-flow and mean high-flow elevations was 3.24 m. Following impoundment, this difference decreased to 1.39 m (Grumbaugh and Anderson, 1987). This reduced range in river stages is a reflection of changes in stage–discharge relationships. The preimpoundment river was narrower and contained a smaller volume of water so that increases in discharge resulted in relatively rapid increases in river stage (0.05 to 0.10 m of elevation per 1000 m^3 of discharge). Inundation of former floodplains and the rising of river elevations following impoundment greatly increased the river's capacity. Consequently, the response of stage to discharge in the postimpoundment river was reduced by more than an order of magnitude (0.003 to 0.005 m per 1000 m^3) (Grumbaugh and Anderson, 1989). Even though impoundment moderated stage–discharge relationships and reduced the difference between high and low flows, floodplain inundation would still have been extensive. The mean postdam flooding would have extended 3400 m onto the floodplain opposite Burlington. However, levee construction has reduced that lateral extension to 30 m (Grumbaugh and Anderson, 1987) (Figure 1.2).

Impoundment and the construction of levees initially reduced flooding and facilitated the agricultural development of floodplains in the middle and upper reaches of Pool 19. However, as sedimentation reduces the capacity of Pool 19, the responsiveness of stage to change in discharge has increased. By the time a dynamic equilibrium in pool volume is achieved sometime around 2050, stage–discharge relationships are expected to resemble those of the preimpoundment river. Unfortunately, the increasing responsiveness of river stage to increases in discharge is coupled with higher mean annual river elevations. Together, these result in an increase in the number of days with flooding and in increases in flood stages. This increase in flooding is aggravated by the scarcity of accessible floodplains, which would normally store and dissipate

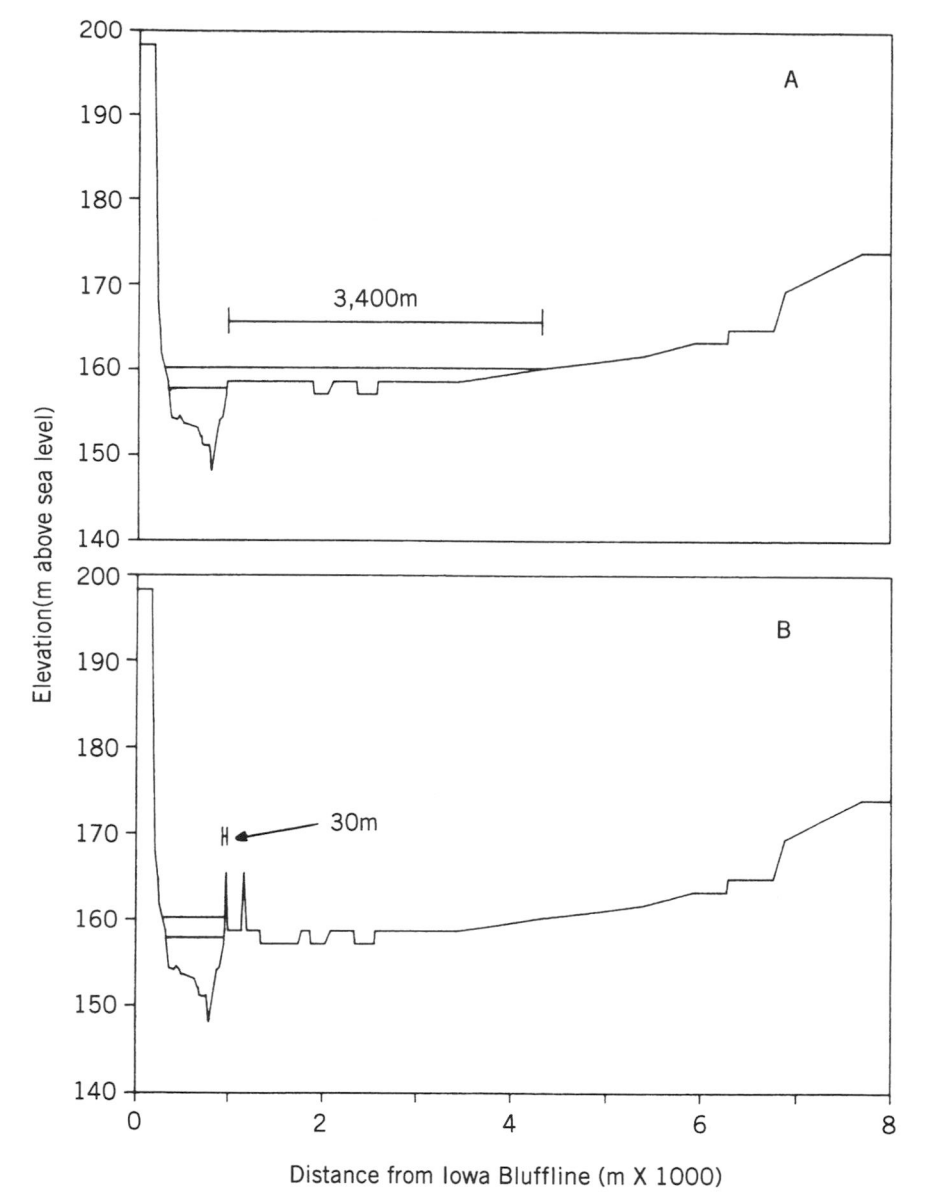

FIGURE 1.2. Hypothetical lateral extension of postimpoundment mean high flow onto the floodplain near Burlington, Pool 19, Upper Mississippi River. Profile A illustrates lateral extension without levees; profile B illustrates lateral extension with levees. Horizontal lines denote mean high and low flows. (From Grumbaugh and Anderson, 1987.)

the impact of flooding. Consequently, flooding will also increase in intensity and destructiveness (Grumbaugh and Anderson, 1989).

Other pools in the Upper Mississippi River have experienced increases in mean river stage and a dampening of the response of river stage to increases in discharge (i.e., stage–discharge relationships). They have also experienced losses in pool capacity because of sedimentation (Chen and Simmons, 1986; McHenry et al., 1984). However, the long-term changes in stage–discharge relationships following impoundment that were observed in Pool 19 have not yet been observed in the other pools. This may simply be a result of differences in age of the pools. If so, similar increases in flood frequency, flood magnitude, and flood intensity may also be in store for the other pools (Grumbaugh and Anderson, 1989).

Turbidity
Turbidity within the Upper Mississippi River varies both longitudinally and among habitats. Longitudinal differences are primarily the result of differences in local tributary inputs since trapping at the dams reduces downstream exports of suspended sediments. Suspended sediment concentrations appear to increase downstream as a result of increases in tributary wash loads in Iowa and Illinois. For example, the maximum concentration of suspended sediment recorded at Winona, Minnesota (Pool 6) was 392 mg L^{-1}, whereas the maximum recorded at Keokuk, Iowa (Pool 20), was 765 mg L^{-1} (McHenry et al., 1984).

Turbidity within pools tends to be lowest in habitats with low to negligible currents (i.e., backwaters). In Pool 8, for example, summer turbidities were lowest [8 to 9 Jackson turbidity units (JTU)] in stagnant ponds; intermediate (11 to 20 JTU) in sloughs, lakes, and main channel borders with currents less than 16 cm s^{-1}; and relatively high (19 to 37 JTU) in side channel, main channel, and main-channel border habitats with currents ranging from 21 to 72 cm s^{-1} (Elstad, 1977).

Seasonally, turbidity tends to be highest during the spring rise and lowest during winter. At a U.S. Geological Survey (USGS) water quality station at Burlington (Pool 19), turbidity during water year 1970 ranged from 62 to 100 JTU during March through June, from 16 to 24 JTU during July through October, and from 2 to 6 JTU during November through February (USGS, 1975). Turbidities are highest during the spring rise because of faster currents and greater tributary inputs, whereas low winter turbidities are largely the result of lower flows and ice cover. Turbidities from July through October are probably higher than those from November through February because of phytoplankton production and anthropogenic disturbances. Barge traffic was found to significantly increase concentrations of suspended sediments in the main channel and in adjacent backwaters. Small-boat traffic also increases suspended sediment concentrations in backwaters (Smart et al., 1986). Similarly, dredging activity increases concentrations of suspended sediments both within the channel and near dredge spoil disposal sites (McHenry et al.,

1984). Wind action can also increase turbidity, especially in shallow, open habitats (Eckblad et al., 1977; Sparks, 1984).

The Upper Mississippi River is a warm-water stream. During water year 1982, temperatures in the main channel at Keokuk (Pool 20) ranged from 0 to 27.5°C (Jahn and Anderson, 1986). Mean monthly temperatures for a 10-year period (1972 to 1981) in a main-channel site in Pool 7 ranged from 0 to 24.6°C. Means of less than 1°C occurred from December through March, while means in excess of 21°C occurred during June, July, and August (Dawson et al., 1984). Normally, one would expect that the temperature regimes in backwaters would differ significantly from those in the main channel or the swifter and deeper side channels. In a study of winter macroinvertebrates in Pool 13, Herbert et al. (1984) reported that temperatures during March exceeded 4°C in sloughs but not in lake, side channel, main channel, main-channel border, or tailwater habitats. On the other hand, summer temperatures from the more eutrophic sites (i.e., sluggish and generally shallow backwaters) in Pool 8 were similar to those recorded in the less eutrophic sites (i.e., faster currents and largely deeper main and side channels) (Elstad, 1986).

CHEMICAL CHARACTERISTICS

Throughout its reach, the Upper Mississippi River is a hard to very hard calcium–magnesium bicarbonate stream. pH ranges from circumneutral to alkaline, and total alkalinity and specific conductance are relatively high (Dawson et al., 1984; Jahn and Anderson, 1986; MPCA, 1978; USGS, 1975) (Table 1.2). From its source in Lake Itasca through its passage in north and central Minnesota, the river is hard, averaging 145 to 161 mg L^{-1} as $CaCo_3$ during 1975; noncarbonate hardness is low. Total hardness and noncarbonate hardness increase somewhat with the entry of the very hard (384 mg L^{-1}) Minnesota River, which has relatively high concentrations of sulfates (120 mg L^{-1}) and chlorides (41 mg L^{-1}). Mean total hardness in St. Paul was 205 mg

TABLE 1.2. *Selected Water Chemistry Characteristics of the Upper Mississippi River*

	Pool			
	3	12	19	21
pH	7.1–8.5	7.7–9.4	7.8–8.8	7.3–8.2
Total hardness (mg L^{-1})	162–250	132–184	154–210	132–258
Noncarbonate hardness	—	—	—	24–97
Calcium (mg L^{-1})	—	—	—	33–72
Magnesium (mg L^{-1})	—	—	—	12–21
Sulfate (mg L^{-1})	22–83	33–38	25–44	34–92
Chloride (mg L^{-1})	8–20	—	10–20	3–32
Alkalinity (mg L^{-1})	123–184	110–194	110–175	108–184
Conductivity (μS cm^{-1})	525	315–400	340–460	297–555

Source: After USGS (1975).

TABLE 1.3. *Water Chemistry from Main-Channel (MC) Sites in Pools 7 and 8 and from Lake Onalaska, Pool 7, Upper Mississippi River, 1972–1981*

Parameter	MC (Pool 7)	MC (Pool 8)	Lake Onalaska
pH			
Mean	8.0	8.0	7.3
Range	7.3–9.2	6.8–9.4	6.6–9.5
Total hardness (mg L^{-1})			
Mean	150	153	83
Range	105–192	100–219	24–158
Total alkalinity (mg L^{-1})			
Mean	133	131	76
Range	87–173	74–173	21–140
Conductivity (μS cm^{-1})			
Mean	353	347	194
Range	216–481	208–644	70–443
Nitrate-nitrogen (mg L^{-1})			
Mean	0.44	0.57	0.44
Range	0.05–1.30	0.06–1.58	0.08–0.89
Ammonia-nitrogen (mg L^{-1})			
Mean	0.44	0.40	0.29
Range	<0.05–1.80	<0.05–1.80	<0.05–0.73
Total phosphorus (mg L^{-1})			
Mean	0.51	0.36	0.42
Range	<0.05–1.50	<0.05–1.91	<0.05–0.75
Biochemical oxygen demand (mg L^{-1})			
Mean	3.2	3.3	3.0
Range	0.7–7.3	0.7–7.2	0.3–7.2
Dissolved oxygen (mg L^{-1})			
Mean	11.6	11.8	7.4
Range	6.0–15.5	6.9–16.2	1.7–16.2
Suspended matter (mg L^{-1})			
Mean	17.3	20.4	7.5
Range	<0.5–90.5	2.0–119.0	<0.5–86.0

Source: After Dawson et al. (1984).

L^{-1}, while mean sulfates were 37 mg L^{-1} and mean chlorides were 13 mg L^{-1} (MPCA, 1978).

Below the Twin Cities, the river receives medium-hard and soft waters from tributaries draining large areas of relatively inert deposits in the Superior Upland Province. For example, mean total hardness for the St. Croix, Chippewa, and Wisconsin Rivers is 84, 57, and 110 mg L^{-1}, respectively (Wis. DNR, 1973). Consequently, hardness is somewhat lower as the Upper Mississippi River flows through the Driftless Area. By the time the river reaches Pool 7, total hardness averages 150 mg L^{-1} (Dawson et al., 1984). The river continues to receive flows from medium-hard-water (e.g., the Black and Wisconsin Rivers) and hard-water (e.g., Root and La Crosse Rivers) tributaries as it passes through the Driftless Area, but the water contributed from tributaries draining the glaciated regions of Iowa and Illinois is very hard. As a result, mean total hardness has increased to 195 mg L^{-1} by the time the river reaches Keokuk in Pool 19 (Fremling et al., 1989). Downstream from Pool 19, noncarbonate hardness is increased somewhat via tributary (e.g., Des Moines River) inputs of calcium–magnesium–sulfate–chloride waters draining the western basin (USGS, 1970).

Water chemistry was monitored for a 10-year period (1972 to 1981) in the main channels of Pools 7 and 8 and in Lake Onalaska, a large, shallow inundated area located off the main channel in Pool 7. Total hardness, alkalinity, conductivity, and pH were substantially higher in the main channel than in Lake Onalaska (Table 1.3). Presumably, this is a consequence of the relative isolation of Lake Onalaska from the main channel, combined with inflow from the Black River; total hardness in the Black River averaged 62 mg L^{-1}. Seasonally, total hardness, alkalinity, and conductivity at all three sites tended to be inversely related to discharge, probably because of dilution (Dawson et al., 1984). The relationship between pH and discharge was not evident, but pH tended to be lowest during the winter (Table 1.4).

The waters of the Upper Mississippi River are eutrophic, and concentrations of nitrogen, phosphorus, and silica are generally not limiting to primary production (Elstad, 1986; Fremling et al., 1989; Huff, 1986; Luttenton et al., 1986). Anthropogenic enrichment originates from both point and nonpoint sources. Serious enrichment from point sources is localized, except for the reach below the confluence with the Illinois River and the reach between the Twin Cities and Lock and Dam 4; Lake Pepin serves as a settlement basin for nutrients and other pollutants originating from the Twin Cities (Elstad, 1977;

TABLE 1.4. *Monthly Mean Discharge, Total Hardness, and pH in Lake Onalaska (LO) and the Main Channels of Pools 7 (MC7) and 8 (MC8), Upper Mississippi River, 1972–1981*

	Discharge $(m^3 \, s^{-1})^a$	Hardness (mg L^{-1})			pH		
		MC7	MC8	LO	MC7	MC8	LO
Jan.	475.8	175	167	93	7.7	7.7	7.0
Feb.	458.8	180	172	88	7.6	7.7	7.2
Mar.	1030.8	157	156	71	7.9	7.9	7.3
Apr.	1838.0	135	137	49	8.2	7.8	7.2
May	1356.5	152	147	67	8.7	8.5	7.4
June	1056.3	158	169	72	7.9	8.2	7.6
July	818.4	157	166	86	8.2	8.4	7.3
Aug.	739.2	164	153	106	8.6	8.4	7.8
Sept.	739.2	153	155	84	8.0	8.1	7.2
Oct.	739.2	147	150	84	8.1	8.3	7.4
Nov.	713.7	164	156	92	8.3	8.3	7.5
Dec.	535.2	172	153	90	8.1	8.1	7.1

Source: After Dawson et al. (1984).
[a]Discharge from Lock and Dam 7.

Fremling and Claflin, 1984; Jahn and Anderson, 1986). Nonpoint-source enrichment occurs primarily via inputs from agricultural watersheds and is more extensive in the lower pools (Jahn and Anderson, 1986; Nielsen et al., 1984).

Deterioration of water quality often occurs at lower flow, since point-source effluents usually do not decline with declining water levels (Sparks, 1984). One of the more extreme examples occurred in Pool 19 during the record 1976 and 1977 drought. Concentrations of nonionized ammonia reached a maximum of 0.198 mg L^{-1} and commonly exceeded 0.03 mg L^{-1}. Such high concentrations may have contributed to the precipitous decline in populations of the fingernail clam, *Musculum transversum;* bioassays demonstrated that concentrations of 0.4 and 0.8 mg L^{-1} were acutely toxic to juvenile and adult *M. transversum,* respectively (Sparks, 1980).

Anthropogenic inputs of macronutrients are moderate in Pools 7 and 8, and water quality was generally acceptable. Seasonally, nitrate-nitrogen concentrations in the main channels were highest in April, relatively high from November through March, and relatively low from late spring through early autumn. Ammonia-nitrogen was high from January through March and low from June through September or October. Nitrate-nitrogen concentrations in Lake Onalaska did not exhibit an April maximum, but concentrations were relatively high from November through March and low from June through September. Seasonal patterns of ammonia-nitrogen in Lake Onalaska were similar to those in the main channel, although winter maxima were somewhat lower. Total phosphorus was generally lowest during winter and higher during summer at all three sites, but concentrations in the main channel were also relatively high during March (Dawson et al., 1984) (Table 1.5).

TABLE 1.5. *Monthly Mean Concentrations of Nitrate-Nitrogen, Ammonia-Nitrogen, and Total Phosphorus for Lake Onalaska (LO) and Main-Channel Sites in Pools 7 (MC7) and 8 (MC8) in the Upper Mississippi River, 1972–1981*

	Nitrate-Nitrogen			Ammonia-Nitrogen			Total Phosphorus		
	MC7	MC8	LO	MC7	MC8	LO	MC7	MC8	LO
Jan.	0.73	0.71	0.61	0.65	0.73	0.56	0.28	0.29	0.29
Feb.	0.78	0.79	0.61	0.86	0.74	0.32	0.43	0.29	0.42
Mar.	0.60	0.61	0.75	0.86	0.78	0.34	0.60	0.60	0.58
Apr.	1.14	1.04	0.52	0.38	0.27	0.34	0.43	0.33	0.38
May	0.39	0.63	0.41	0.10	0.16	0.08	0.42	0.33	0.55
June	0.38	0.68	0.37	0.14	0.11	0.14	0.57	0.36	0.53
July	0.58	0.47	0.38	0.17	0.08	0.23	0.60	0.44	0.51
Aug.	0.37	0.25	0.31	0.15	0.14	0.14	1.00	0.67	0.50
Sept.	0.43	0.32	0.37	0.07	0.27	0.12	0.56	0.44	0.48
Oct.	0.58	0.45	0.53	0.16	0.12	0.10	0.62	0.48	0.48
Nov.	0.97	0.73	0.89	0.20	0.34	0.23	0.29	0.23	0.39
Dec.	0.67	0.71	0.76	0.20	0.23	0.22	0.20	0.25	0.29

Source: After Dawson et al. (1984).

Similar patterns of inorganic nitrogen and total phosphorus were observed by other researchers in the Upper Mississippi River. Presumably, this is the result of autotrophic uptake during the growing season and decomposition of macrophytes in autumn (Dawson et al., 1984). Nitrogen uptake by two Lake Onalaska macrophytes, *Nymphaea tuberosa* and *Ceratophyllum demersum*, was high and may have limited nitrogen availability for other organisms until autumn senescence (Smart, 1980). The importance of autotrophic uptake is also indicated by low summer concentrations of nitrate-nitrogen in vegetated habitats. In Pool 19, for example, mean nitrate-nitrogen during August 1983 was considerably lower in vegetated backwater habitats (0.04 mg L^{-1}) and somewhat lower in the vegetated main-channel border habitat (0.23 mg L^{-1}) than in either the main channel (0.28 mg L^{-1}) or unvegetated main-channel border (0.28 mg L^{-1}) habitats. On the other hand, mean August ammonia-nitrogen was somewhat higher in vegetated (0.22 to 0.23 mg L^{-1}) than in unvegetated (0.17 mg L^{-1}) habitats (Jahn and Anderson, 1986).

Changes in inorganic nitrogen are also associated with seasonal changes in temperature and flow. The reduction in ammonia-nitrogen in Pools 7 and 8 (Table 1.5) between March and April may be the result of increased nitrification, which would be enhanced by warming temperatures, since the decline in ammonia-nitrogen is accompanied by an increase in nitrate-nitrogen. Increased flow during April may have also reduced ammonia concentrations via dilution. However, nitrate-nitrogen concentrations in the main-channel sites are highest in April, despite any dilution by the high flow. In fact, approximately 28% of the annual nitrate transport occurs in April. Unlike the main-channel sites, nitrate-nitrogen concentrations in Lake Onalaska do not exhibit an April maximum, which suggests that hydrological influences affecting the mainstem are involved. Increased tributary inputs may contribute to the elevated nitrate concentrations, but Dawson et al. (1984) reported that the mean monthly concentrations of nitrate-nitrogen from nearby tributaries (i.e., Black River, La Crosse River, and Halfway Creek) were similar to or lower than their respective annual means. Instead, increases in nitrate during April may be the result of seasonal flooding. Spring flooding would flush accumulated organic matter and nitrogen from backwaters and wetlands (Fremling and Claflin, 1984). Floodplain forests may also be a significant source of nitrate. The inundation of forested islands in Pool 19 resulted in significant increases in dissolved organic carbon in the main channel (Grumbaugh and Anderson, 1987), and it would be reasonable to expect that inundation would also result in elevations of nitrate-nitrogen. Moreover, the floodplain habitat is more extensive in the northern pools that it is in Pool 19.

Reduced runoff and/or binding to sediments may account for low winter concentrations of total phosphorus, while temperature-mediated decomposition may account for summer maxima (Dawson et al., 1984). On the other hand, higher temperatures may reduce the bioavailability of phosphorus by increasing the formation of calcite-phosphate complexes (Huff, 1986). The March maxima for total phosphorus in the main-channel sites coincided with a more than twofold increase in monthly mean discharge, which suggests that resuspension of benthic accumulations and/or increased tributary inputs were involved.

Dissolved oxygen concentrations vary both seasonally and among habitats. Main channel and main-channel border habitats are usually well oxygenated, while backwater habitats are often poorly oxygenated (Dawson et al., 1984; Elstad, 1986). For example, the 10-year mean concentrations of dissolved oxygen in the main channels of Pools 7 and 8 were 11.6 and 11.8 mg L^{-1}, respectively; concentrations were never less than 6.0 mg L^{-1}. On the other hand, dissolved oxygen averaged only 7.4 mg L^{-1} in Lake Onalaska during the same period. Concentrations were reasonably high during autumn and spring, but monthly means during July and August were 3.2 and 4.0 mg L^{-1}, respectively. Concentrations as low as 1.7 mg L^{-1} were recorded during January and February, when ice covered the lake (Dawson et al., 1984). Summer dissolved-oxygen concentrations were also low (0.4 to 5.3 mg L^{-1}) in a number of smaller, more eutrophic backwaters in Pool 8 (Elstad, 1977).

Discharges of organic waste and toxics have affected parts of the Upper Mississippi River. Discharges from Minneapolis–St. Paul have resulted in anaerobic sediments in much of the 50-km reach downstream from the Twin Cities and in Lake Pepin, which serves as a giant settlement basin (Elstad, 1986). Cadmium, lead, and other heavy metals are also concentrated in the sediments of Lake Pepin (Baily and Rada, 1984). Contamination of commercial fish species in Lake Pepin with polychlorinated biphenyls (PCBs) has prompted the issuance of advisories on fish consumption and seizures of commercial catches (Fremling and Claflin, 1984). The reach below the confluence of the Illinois River is also significantly affected by organic and toxic waste, but contaminants in most other parts of the river are moderate (Jahn and Anderson, 1986). However, as with suspended sediments, contaminants tend to accumulate in the more productive backwaters (Luoma, 1984).

ECOSYSTEM DYNAMICS

Detritus and Dissolved Organic Carbon

Detritus and dissolved organic carbon (DOC) are important sources of organic matter in the Upper Mississippi River. These inputs originate from upstream reaches, tributaries within each pool, floodplains, macrophyte beds, and direct anthropogenic sources. Of these, direct anthropogenic input is probably significant to the overall carbon budget only in Pools 1 to 4 and Pool 26 (Jahn and Anderson, 1986). In contrast, anthropogenic inputs were estimated to account for only 0.04% of the total annual carbon input for Pool 19 (Fremling et al., 1989).

Inputs from reaches upstream of Lock and Dam 18 have been estimated to account for most (85.73%) of the total organic carbon input into Pool 19 (Fremling et al., 1989), which is somewhat lower than the upstream contribution to mean flow (95.2%) (Bhowmik and Adams, 1986). The organic carbon input from tributaries within Pool 19 has been estimated to be 6.76% of the total input (Fremling et al., 1989), which is somewhat higher than their contribution to the pool's mean flow (4.8%) (Bhowmik and Adams, 1986). These tributaries drain agricultural watersheds and have relatively high gradients (Jahn and Anderson, 1986). As such, they contribute disproportionately (22.7%) to the suspended sediment load of Pool 19 (Bhowmik and Adams, 1986) and would also be expected to contribute disproportionately to organic carbon inputs. Because suspended sediment loads from tributaries entering the northern pools are relatively low (Nielsen et al., 1984), tributary inputs of organic carbon into the northern pools may also be relatively low.

Floodplains and macrophyte beds have been estimated to contribute 6.09% and 1.20%, respectively, to the total organic carbon inputs to Pool 19. Although these inputs are smaller than those originating from upstream and tributary sources, they probably contribute higher-quality organic carbon (Fremling et al., 1989). However, floodplains and macrophyte beds may contribute more to the total organic matter input of other pools in the Upper Mississippi River.

Allochthonous inputs of detritus and DOC from floodplains represent one of the most important sources of organic matter inputs for large floodplain rivers such as the Upper Mississippi River (Junk et al., 1989). Potential inputs were reduced substantially when the floodplain forests and meadows in the lower reaches of each pool were permanently inundated following impoundment. Extensive levee construction along Pools 19 to 26 has also greatly reduced potential inputs from the floodplain (Peck and Smart, 1986). The loss of floodplain habitat is especially high along Pool 19. The four levee and drainage districts that operate within the Pool 19 region reclaimed approximately 16,000 ha of former floodplain following impoundment in 1913. By 1975, there was less than 5200 ha of active floodplain remaining. This loss of floodplain habitat can also be illustrated by the reduction in the lateral expansion of the river during the spring rise. At Burlington, Iowa, for example, the preimpoundment lateral extension would have been approximately 3400 m. Levees have reduced this lateral extension to 30 m (Grumbaugh and Anderson, 1987).

Floodplain inputs (81×10^6 kg C or 6.09% or total inputs) for Pool 19 were calculated by extrapolating measured floodplain inputs from Burlington Island to the entire active floodplain (Fremling et al., 1989). Further extrapolation to the 16,000 ha of leveed floodplain would yield a total floodplain input estimate of 330×10^6 kg C, which would amount to 20.89% of the (revised) total organic carbon input. Additions of the permanently inundated floodplain of the lower pool would increase potential floodplain inputs even more. Moreover, the raising of the river stage and the modification of the flooding cycle by the 2.7-m navigation channel has reduced the duration of inundation and may have otherwise significantly altered floodplain–river dynamics (Grumbaugh and Anderson, 1987).

Floodplain exports from Burlington Island were estimated by comparing upstream and downstream differences in total organic carbon (TOC) transport. This island, which is actually a complex of small islands laced with small chutes and side channels, constitutes the only significant floodplain habitat in this reach of Pool 19. The greatest longitudinal change in TOC transport occurred during autumnal leaf fall (early November) when downstream increases of 1.09×10^6 kg C day^{-1} and 0.93×10^6 kg C day^{-1} were recorded for DOC and FPOC (fine-particulate organic carbon), respectively. However, this autumnal pulse was short in duration. Samples collected during the peak of the spring flood (early March) yielded significant increases in DOC and a nonsignificant decrease in FPOC. The increase in DOC was attributed to the leaching of DOC from floodplain detritus and plants, which may have been combined with a net floodplain retention of FPOC. DOC enrichment continued in a decreasing spring flood sample (mid-March), but at about half the magnitude experienced earlier during the flood. A modest downstream increase in DOC was measured during a postflood, low-flow sample (mid-June), which if generated by the floodplain would probably have been the result of soil leaching. Finally, a late August sample indicated a slight decrease in downstream DOC transport; FPOC remained unchanged for the mid-March, June, and August samples. The August sample was taken shortly after an algal bloom was observed in the river. One possible explanation for the downstream decrease is that there was a net microbial uptake of the algal-generated DOC in the shaded chutes of the island (Grumbaugh and Anderson, 1989).

The type of vegetation probably substantially influences the organic matter export. The floodplains of Burlington Island are dominated by alluvial forest (Grumbaugh and Anderson, 1989). Undeveloped floodplains in other parts of the Upper Mississippi River are characterized by a mosaic of alluvial forest, brush, sedge meadows, and *Phalaris* meadows (Peck and Smart, 1986). The organic matter export dynamics of these meadows may be substantially different from those of the alluvial forest. For one thing, meadow biomass is compact and more prone to submergence than forest vegetation. Moreover, the growth tends to be less woody than forest vegetation, so it may be less refractory. Finally, meadows may serve as superior retention sites, which would increase the availability of particulate organic matter within the inundated floodplain for much of the spring rise. The stabilization of low flows by the navigation dams has contributed to the succession of meadows to alluvial forest in the middle reaches of several pools (Peck and Smart, 1986).

Aquatic macrophyte beds are the other major source of organic matter within the Upper Mississippi River. In contrast to floodplain inputs, the contribution of macrophyte beds to the organic carbon budget has apparently increased since impoundment (Jahn and Anderson, 1986). They provide an estimated 16×106 kg C to Pool 19, or 1.20% of the total annual carbon input. This estimate was based on the aboveground biomass accumulation of an emergent species, *Sagittaria latifolia,* and a floating-leafed species, *Nelumbo lutea,* rather than on the net above- and belowground production of the entire complex of submergent, emergent, and floating-leafed species and their epiphytes. Consequently, total inputs may be significantly different (Fremling et al., 1989).

Macrophyte beds contribute organic carbon to consumers primarily as DOC exudate, as sloughed leaves, and as detritus following autumnal senescence. DOC and sloughed leaves, which would not be included in estimates of production using biomass change, would occur in spring and summer, as well as with autumn senescence. In particular, *Sagittaria latifolia* experiences heavy leaf sloughing and regeneration during spring (Grumbaugh et al., 1986). Through much of the summer, dense growth of intact macrophytes would physically retain much of the sloughed material. In addition, currents tend to either be minimal or nonexistent. As a result, most sloughed leaves and exudates would probably remain within the beds. During the spring floods, however, currents in the backwaters approach those recorded in the main channel (Eckblad et al., 1984). In addition, lower spring macrophyte biomass would result in lower physical retention. Consequently, spring export of this material to the main channel would probably be high.

Decomposition following autumn senescence is rapid for both *Sagittaria latifolia* and *Nelumbo lutea.* Senescence for *S. latifolia* began in late October and there was no standing biomass left by November. Senescence for *N. lutea* was first observed in September and was complete by November. Some stalks and seedpods persisted through to January but were gone by March. Despite this dramatic decline in standing biomass, there were no significant increases in sediment organic matter. Mean concentrations of sediment organic matter were not significantly higher during September, October, and November than they were in July and August, but the highest concentrations for both species were recorded during June (Table 1.6). The absence of a pronounced pulse in

TABLE 1.6. *Mean Standing Stock (g AFDW m^{-2}) for Standing Organic Matter and Sediment Organic Matter from* Sagittaria latifolia *and* Nelumbo lutea *Macrophyte Beds in Nauvoo Flats Wildlife Refuge, Pool 19, Upper Mississippi River, June 1983 to January 1984[a]*

	Sagittaria latifolia				Nelumbo lutea			
	Standing		Sediment		Standing		Sediment	
June	14	(4)	1054	(362)	9	(9)	399	(204)
July	280	(55)	759	(524)	145	(41)	279	(62)
Aug.	635	(167)	741	(403)	311	(127)	206	(104)
Sept.	529	(161)	935	(63)	337	(67)	270	(66)
Oct.	550	(398)	854	(326)	115	(49)	282	(75)
Nov.	0		889	(261)	48	(30)	271	(86)
Jan.	0		695	(117)	45	(15)	240	(78)

Source: After Grumbaugh et al. (1986).
[a]Standard deviation in parentheses.

sediment organic matter following autumn senescence indicates that the detritus is rapidly utilized by decomposers or quickly exported out of the macrophyte beds (Grumbaugh et al., 1986).

There are substantial differences in the storage of organic matter among habitats. Accumulations of organic matter tend to be greater in depositional backwater and lower pool habitats than in the more erosional sites. For example, the concentration of organic matter in sediments from the upper reaches of Pool 13 was low in the main channel (0.6%), relatively low in the main-channel border (1.1%) and tailwaters (1.3%), intermediate in side channels (3.5%), and highest in sloughs (6.8%) and floodplain lakes (6.8%) (Herbert et al., 1984). In the lower reach of Pool 19, the sediment organic matter content from seven main-channel border stations ranged from 3.2 to 6.4% (Butts et al., 1982).

Studies concerning seasonal changes in benthic organic matter were not found in the literature, but accumulations in depositional sites would probably be greatest during low flow. This would be complicated, however, by the resuspension of sediments by barge and boat traffic, which is typically high during periods of low flow (Smart et al., 1986). Sedimentation results in the burial of a considerable amount of organic matter. In Pool 19, burial was estimated to account for 5.48% of the total annual organic carbon input. This estimate was based on a mean organic matter content of 2.1% in sediment cores from Pool 19 and on estimated rates of sedimentation (Fremling et al., 1989). Burial of organic matter may also be high in other parts of the Upper Mississippi River. The organic matter content from sediment cores collected in the lower reach of Pool 7 averaged 4.05% for sediments deposited from 1964 to 1977. Given that carbon averaged 66% of the total organic matter content, this would represent an organic carbon content of 2.7%. Corresponding concentrations of organic matter from the lower reaches of Pools 8 and 9 were 2.83% (1.9% C) and 2.79% (1.8% C), respectively (Richie, 1988).

The mean concentration of suspended POC for five sample periods during a 1984–1985 survey in Pool 19 was 6.5 mg L^{-1}. This mean is within the upper end of the range reported in the literature. Mean DOC concentration was 12.5 mg L^{-1}. On average, DOC accounted for 66% of TOC. POC concentrations were highest during peak spring flooding, presumably as a result of flushing of particulates from floodplains and emergent macrophyte beds, but were relatively low in the other samples. DOC concentrations were relatively low during peak flooding, probably because of dilution. DOC concentrations were highest during autumnal leaf fall and during summer low flow (Grumbaugh and Anderson, 1989).

In a 1984 study of water column TOC entering Pool 19, more than half of the annual organic carbon transport occurred during the spring rise, while most of the remaining occurred during the lesser autumn rise. POC dominated TOC transport during the rising limb of the spring hydrograph, while DOC dominated throughout the rest of the year. Significantly, DOC transport during the early and peak stages of the spring rise was about as low as during

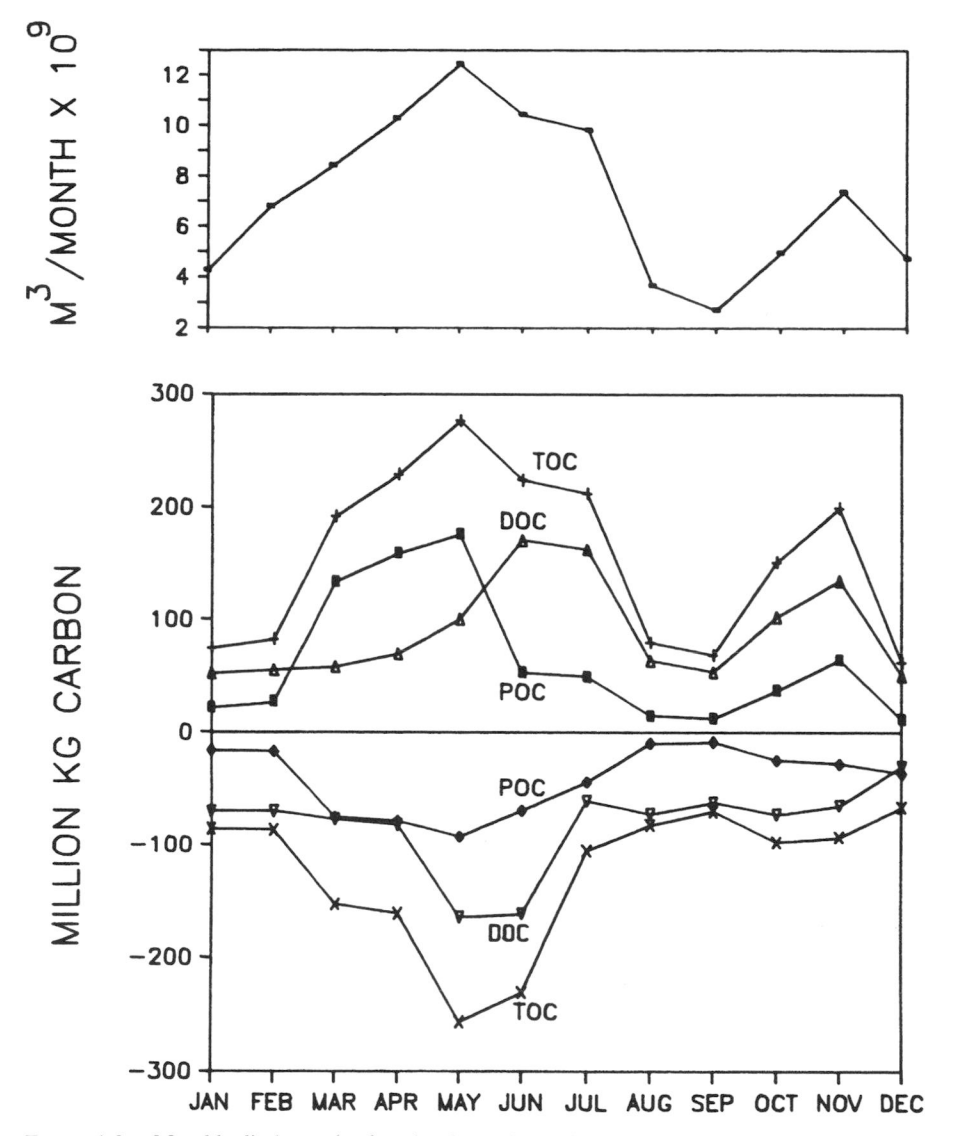

FIGURE 1.3.   Monthly discharge (top) and estimated monthly organic carbon inputs (bottom) for Pool 19, Upper Mississippi River. TOC, total organic carbon; DOC, dissolved organic carbon; POC, particulate organic carbon. (Modified from Fremling et al., 1989. Reproduced with permission of the Minister of Supply and Services, Canada 1996.)

summer and winter low flows. POC transport was high in the early phase of the spring rise, moderately high during the autumn rise, and low throughout the rest of the year (Fremling et al., 1989) (Figure 1.3). This seasonal pattern suggests that a considerable amount of POC is entrained from floodplains, senescent macrophyte beds, and/or backwater benthic accumulations during the earlier part of the spring rise, while leaching from floodplains, macro-phytes, and possibly algae contributes to DOC transport during the descending phase of the spring rise. Autochthonous sources (i.e., algae, macrophytes, and heterotrophs) probably account for most of the DOC being transported during low flow (Fremling et al., 1989; Jahn and Anderson, 1986).

The contribution of macrophyte beds to low-flow DOC is evident in an August 1983 study of DOC concentrations among selected habitats in Pool 19. DOC in the main channel averaged 7.6 mg L^{-1}, while DOC in side-channel and unvegetated main-channel border habitats averaged 8.1 and 8.3 mg L^{-1}, respectively. The vegetated main-channel border habitat averaged 9.5 mg L^{-1}, while the vegetated backwater habitat averaged 12.3 mg L^{-1} (Jahn and Anderson, 1986).

Periphyton Production

Production by benthic algae attached to substrates may be relatively modest in the Upper Mississippi River. For much of the year, turbidity restricts periphytic diatoms to depths of less than 0.5 or 1.0 m (Luttenton et al., 1986). Light penetration is not sufficient to support benthic algae in most of the main-channel border habitat of Pool 19 (Jahn and Anderson, 1986), and shading by emergent and floating-leafed macrophytes probably limits algal production in many shallow border and backwater habitats.

On the other hand, epiphytic algae are probably abundant on submerged macrophytes. For example, dense growths of epiphytes have been observed on one filamentous green alga, *Cladophora,* which can account for up to 40% of the summer macrophyte biomass colonizing shallow rock substrates (e.g., wing dams and riprap) adjacent to the main channel (Luttenton and Rada, 1986; Luttenton et al., 1986). The prevalence of epiphytic algae is also suggested in Pool 19. Habitat-specific phytoplankton cell densities tended to be higher in vegetated sites than in more open sites of the main-channel border. Moreover, characteristically periphytic taxa such as *Achnanthes* and *Cocconeis* were abundant in these planktonic samples (Jahn and Anderson, 1986). Epiphytic algae can be abundant on wing dams (Fremling and Claflin, 1984; Lewis, 1984), although sedimentation and dredge spoil disposal has reduced this habitat. Algae may have also been abundant on snags, but snagging operations, channel maintenance, and sedimentation have greatly reduced this habitat.

In addition to light limitation, periphytic and benthic algae in the Upper Mississippi River are affected by turbulence generated by commercial navigation. From July through October, when ship traffic is heaviest, glass-slide samples from the main-channel border habitats of Pools 5 and 9 yielded an assemblage dominated by two or three taxa, including *Cocconeis placentula* var. *euglypta, C. placentula* var. *lineata, Navicula tripunctata* var. *schizone-moides,* and/or *Stigeoclonium lubricum.* This summer–autumn assemblage was characterized by the predominance of adnate taxons and two-dimensional (i.e., flat) architecture. In contrast, samples collected when ship traffic was reduced (May and June, November and December) yielded a more diverse, three-dimensional assemblage characterized by *Melosira varians, Stephanodiscus* spp., *Diatoma vulgare, Meridion circulare, Synedra ulna, S. ulna* var. *oxyrhynchus, Gomphonema angustatum, G. olivaceum, Cymbella minuta,* and/or *N. tripunctata* var. *schizonemoides* (Luttenton et al., 1986).

The effect of navigation-generated turbulence was also observed with *Cladophora* epiphytes in Pool 5. Adnate *Cocconeis pediculus* occurred in almost monospecific stands on *Cladophora* filaments collected from a site exposed to turbulence generated by ship traffic. On the other hand, filaments collected from a more protected site yielded a more diverse, three-dimensional assemblage characterized by *Diatoma vulgare, Synedra ulna,* and *Rhoicosphenia curvata* (Luttenton and Rada, 1986). Similarly, glass-slide samples collected during August from a variety of habitats in Pool 8 exhibited patterns of community composition and architecture that corresponded to their exposure to ship traffic. Glass slides adjacent to the main channel were heavily dominated by *Cocconeis placentula* var. *euglypta; C. pediculus* and *Navicula tripunctata* var. *schizonemoides* were common. Glass slides collected from more protected, off-channel sites yielded a diverse, three-dimensional assemblage, including *Cyclotella meneghiniana, Melosira granulata, Stephanodiscus* spp., *Gomphonema* spp., *N. tripunctata* var. *schizonemoides, Nitzschia fonticola,* and *N. kuetzingiana* (Luttenton et al., 1986).

Discriminant function analysis indicated that the off-channel samples from Pool 8 collected during August were statistically indistinguishable from the spring and late autumn samples collected from the main-channel border of Pool 5, but both were significantly different from the summer–early autumn samples from Pool 5 and the August near-channel samples collected in Pool 8. This suggests that the effects of wave action in the main-channel border habitat exceed those of temperature in determining the community structure of attached diatoms (Luttenton and Rada, 1986). On the other hand, temperature appears to be important for green and blue-green algae. Diatoms dominated the cell densities from glass slides in Pool 5 from late August through early May, but green algae, especially *Stigeoclonium lubricum* and a palmaloid stage of *Chlamydomonas,* were abundant from late June through early August and common through early November. Blue-green algae were moderately common from July through September. However, green and blue-green algae were never common in the glass-slide samples from Pool 9 (Luttenton et al., 1986).

Cell densities, chlorophyll *a* concentrations, and ash-free dry weight (AFDW) biomass from the glass-slide samples from the main-channel borders of Pool 5 were usually much larger than those from Pool 9. These differences are unexplained, but a summer flood and/or greater exposure to the effects of navigation may have suppressed populations in the Pool 9 samples. In addition, seasonal patterns of algal abundance from one pool did not correspond to the patterns observed in the other pool (Figure 1.4). For instance, cell densities in

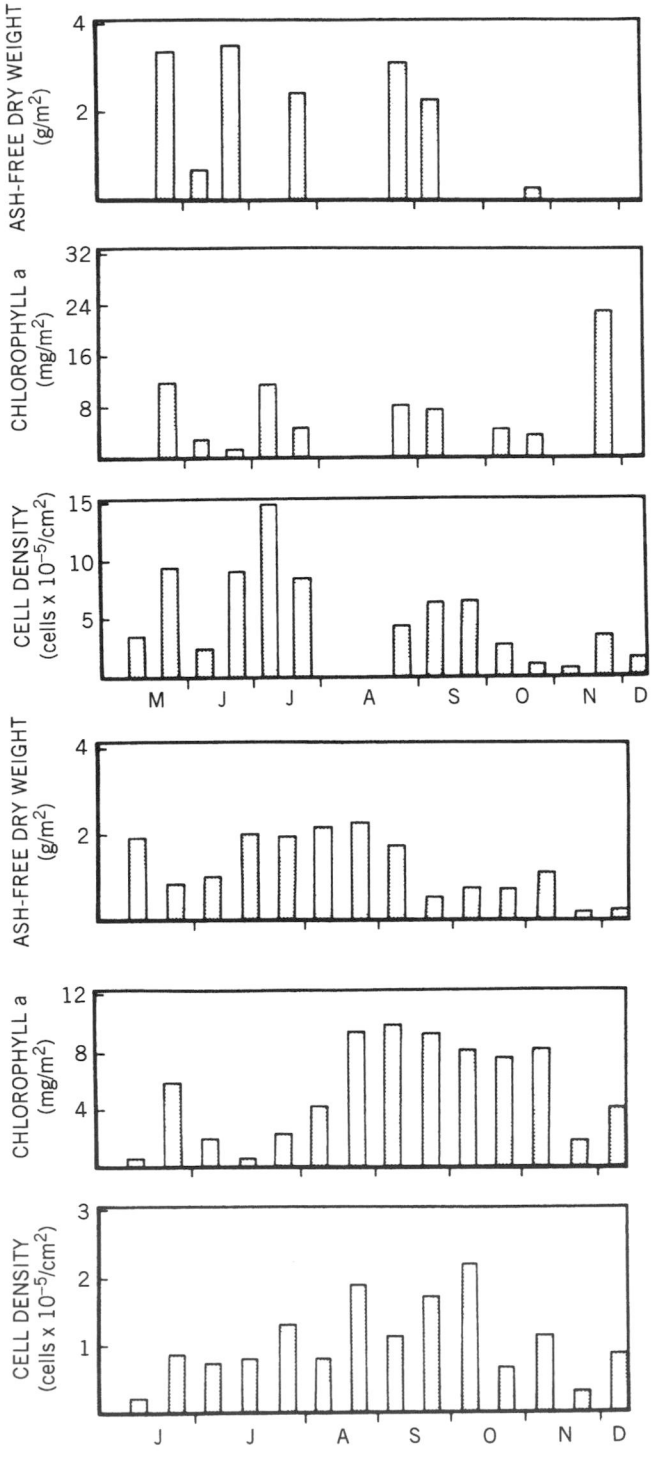

FIGURE 1.4. Seasonal cell densities, chlorophyll *a,* and ash-free dry weight of periphyton collected from glass slides located in the main channel borders of Navigation Pool 5 (top) and Navigation Pool 9 (bottom), Upper Mississippi River. (From Luttenton et al., 1986.)

Pool 5 were generally highest in late spring and early summer, whereas those in Pool 5 were generally higher from midsummer through midautumn. Seasonal patterns of biomass and chlorophyll *a* in Pool 8 were obscured by missing data, but chlorophyll *a* was significantly correlated with cell density in Pool 9. Biomass in Pool 9, which tended to be higher in early and midsummer, was not correlated with cell density or chlorophyll *a*, possibly because the summer biomass estimates included trichopteran and chironomid grazers (Luttenton and Rada, 1986; Luttenton et al., 1986).

The limiting effects of turbidity and turbulence would be expected to decrease from late autumn through early spring, when commercial navigation is less extensive. Consequently, the areal extent of periphyton in the Upper Mississippi River would be expected to increase during the cooler time of the year. In fact, Luttenton et al. (1986) reported that periphyton colonized substrates as deep as 5 m during autumn, winter, and early spring. In addition, they reported extensive accumulations of diatoms such as *Nitzschia subcapitellata* on sandy shoals at depths of 0.2 to 1.0 m during January and February.

Phytoplankton Production
In these studies phytoplankton are cells that were floating in the water. It is often largely composed of cells detached from substrates that may divide while in suspension. Early studies in the Upper Mississippi River reported that diatoms dominated phytoplankton populations (Galtsoff, 1924, as cited in Jahn and Anderson, 1986; Reinhard, 1931). For instance, diatoms accounted for 86.4% of the total phytoplankton biovolume in the unimpounded reach between Minneapolis and Winona, while green algae accounted for 4.3%, blue-green algae accounted for 7.6%, and green flagellates accounted for 1.6%. *Cyclotella meneghiniana, Melosira granulata,* and *Asterionella formosa* were the most abundant diatoms collected in the unpolluted stations located between the outlet of Lake Pepin and Winona. *C. meneghiniana* and *A. formosa* were most abundant during April and May, least abundant during summer, and relatively abundant during autumn and winter. *M. granulata* was most abundant in spring and summer but was also common through autumn. Some of the other diatoms, including *Melosira varians, Synedra* spp., and *Stephanodiscus niagarae,* were common throughout the year, while others, including *Diatoma vulgare,* were uncommon during summer. The most abundant blue-green alga, *Aphanizomenon flos-aquae,* was restricted to the warmer period between May and October. Two abundant green algae, *Actinastrum hantschii* and *Pediastrum* spp., were also restricted to late spring and summer, while two others, *Scenedesmus dimorphus* and *S. quadricaudus,* were also abundant in autumn (Reinhard, 1931).

During a 1968 study conducted in Pool 19, phytoplankton cell densities from a backwater site were highest in March, second highest in June, and lowest in July. Diatoms dominated the February, March, and April samples; *Stephanodiscus* accounted for 80 to 96% of the cell density in samples collected during February, March, and April; and other diatoms accounted for most of the remainder. Samples collected during June, July, and August were more diverse, with diatoms accounting for 32 to 46%, green algae accounting for 29 to 58%, and blue-green algae accounting for 12 to 30% of the total. *Cyclotella, Melosira, Nitzschia,* and *Stephanodiscus* were the most common diatoms. *Ankistrodesmus* and *Scenedesmus* were the most common green algae, and *Merismopedia* and *Microcystis* were the most common blue-green algae (Gale and Lowe, 1971).

Diatoms were more dominant in samples collected in an open main-channel border site during June, July, and August than they were in the backwater site. Diatoms accounted for 62 to 82%, while green algae accounted for 6 to 16%, and blue-greens accounted for 11 to 24%. *Cyclotella, Melosira,* and *Stephanodiscus* were the most abundant diatoms, *Scenedesmus* was the most abundant green alga, and *Chroococcus* and *Microcystis* were the most abundant blue-green algae (Gale and Lowe, 1971).

The most extensive study of phytoplankton in Pool 19 was conducted during 1982 and 1983. Cell densities and biomass in the main channel and main-channel border habitats exhibited maxima in March, April, May, and August, and minima during June, July, and winter. Diatoms accounted for most of the cell density from winter through spring, but green algae became abundant from late spring through early autumn, and blue-green algae became abundant in late summer. A bloom by a blue-green alga, *Microcystis,* was frequently noted in September (Engman, 1984, as cited in Jahn and Anderson, 1986).

During the summer, differences in the abundance and taxonomic composition of phytoplankton in Pool 19 were noted both longitudinally and among habitats. Cell densities were typically lowest in the main channel and in unvegetated main-channel border habitats, somewhat higher in side channels, relatively high in vegetated main-channel border habitats, and highest in a backwater from the upper pool. In addition, cell densities in the lower pool tended to be lower than they were in the middle and upper pools. Interestingly, the most abundant diatoms were pennate rather than centric taxa. Three commonly attached diatom genera: *Achnanthes, Cocconeis,* and *Navicula,* dominated all habitats sampled in the lower pool (river mile 378; km 608), while two others, *Nitzschia* and *Synedra,* were relatively abundant in the middle pool (mile 389; km 626) and upper pool (mile 396; km 637). Of the green algae, *Scenedesmus quadricauda* was relatively abundant in most habitats in the middle pool, while *Ankistrodesmus* was relatively abundant in the upper pool. Two other green algae, *Scenedesmus dimorphus* and *Micractinium pusillum,* were abundant in a vegetated main-channel border site in the middle reach. The high densities reported from a backwater site in the upper pool were due to high densities of *Nitzschia, Synedra, Ankistrodesmus,* and three flagellated protozoans, *Euglena, Phacus,* and *Trachelomonas* (Engman, 1984, as cited by Jahn and Anderson, 1986).

Phytoplankton production in Pool 19 has been estimated at 2×10^6 kg C yr^{-1}. This estimated production, which was based on seasonal cell counts by Engman (1984), accounts for only 0.15% of the total estimated annual input for the pool (Fremling et al., 1989). Phytoplankton production—and its importance to the carbon budget—may be higher in other pools, especially in the backwater-rich northern pools. Phytoplankton studies in Pools 3 and 6 were estimated with volume data but with an assumption of unity for specific gravity (i.e., 1 mm^3 = 1 mg), phytoplankton fresh weight biomass in Pool 3 ranged from 0.1 to 46.9 mg L^{-1} (Baker and Baker, 1981), while that for Pool 6 ranged from 0.36 to 10.4 mg L^{-1} (Huff, 1986). In contrast, the maximum ash-free dry weight biomass recorded in Pool 19 was only 0.2 mg L^{-1} (Engman, 1984, as cited in Fremling et al., 1989).

Differences in flow, resulting in differences in both retention time and dilution, strongly influence phytoplankton abundance. In Pool 19 this was evident with the lower populations recorded in the main channel and main-channel border compared to backwater and vegetated sites (Engman, 1984, as cited in Jahn and Anderson, 1986). Similarly, differences in flow strongly influence phytoplankton abundance in Pool 3. Reduced biomass (0.1 to 13.1 mg L^{-1}) during 1975 compared to biomass in 1976 (0.1 to 46.9 mg L^{-1}) is associated with greater mean discharge and base flow during 1975. Moreover, two discharge maxima (midspring and early summer) were recorded during 1975, whereas only one (early spring) was recorded in 1976 (Baker and Baker, 1979, 1981). Chlorophyll *a* concentrations and light-saturated primary production (i.e., primary production on clear days within 0.4 m of the surface) were also significantly and consistently higher in 1976 than in 1975. In addition, biomass and chlorophyll *a* concentrations in a large backwater lake (Sturgeon Lake) were generally greater than those recorded in the main channel, largely because of greater retention time (Baker and Baker, 1979).

Seasonally, mean chlorophyll *a* concentrations during 1975 increased from 20 mg m^{-3} to 47 mg m^{-3} between May and November, while the 1976 means increased from 20 mg m^{-3} to 190 mg m^{-3} between April and November. Light-saturated primary production reached a maximum of 0.37 mg O$_2$ L^{-1} h^{-1} during 1975, but no seasonal trend was evident. During 1976, primary production increased rapidly following early April flooding, reached a maximum of 1.60 mg O$_2$ L^{-1} h^{-1} during August, and declined through November (Baker and Baker, 1979).

Light-saturated specific rates of primary production (i.e., production per unit of chlorophyll *a*) in Pool 3 exhibited no significant differences between 1975 and 1976. In fact, the seasonal patterns for both years were nearly identical, with maxima recorded in spring and late summer and in early autumn. Regressions of the specific rates of primary production with temperature indicated that those samples collected during spring (April through June) exhibited a pronounced temperature optimum of 15°C, whereas those collected during summer and autumn (July through November) increased linearly with increasing temperature. The differences between the spring and summer–autumn regressions may be the result of taxonomically specific re-

sponses to temperature. The spring regression may be a result of the dominance of the spring assemblage by centric diatoms, whereas the summer–
autumn regression may have been heavily influenced by blue-green algae
(Baker and Baker, 1979).

Diatoms dominated phytoplankton biomass in Pool 3. While diatoms were
dominant or codominant throughout the study, their biomass was highest in
late spring, early summer, and midautumn. *Stephanodiscus niagarae, Cyclotella meneghiniana,* and *Melosira granulata* accounted for most of the late
spring and early summer maxima, while *C. meneghiniana, M. granulata,
Nitzschia acicularis,* and *N. palea* accounted for most of the autumn maxima.
Blue-green algae, dominated by *Oscillatoria agardhii* and *Aphanizomenon
flos-aquae,* were abundant during summer and common during autumn.
Green algae, dominated by *Ankistrodesmus falcatus* var. *spiriformis,* were
fairly common throughout the sample periods, whereas cryptomonads, dominated by *Chroomonas acuta,* were common only during summer (Baker and
Baker, 1981).

Diatoms also dominated the phytoplankton in four stations from Pool 7,
accounting for 72% of the total biovolume. Diatoms were dominated by five
centric species, *Melosira italica, M. granulata, M. varians, Stephanodiscus
niagarae,* and *S. hantzschii,* as well as one pennate species, *Synedra ulna.*
Blue-green algae accounted for 20.5% of the total biovolume and were
strongly dominated by *Aphanizomenon flos-aquae* and *Microcystis aruginosa.*
Green algae accounted for 6% of the total biovolume. *Cryptophyta, Eugleno-
phyta,* and *Pyrrophyta* were present but not abundant (Huff, 1986).

Cell biovolume for the four stations in Pool 7 ranged from 0.36 to 10.40
mm^3 L^{-1} and averaged 4.18 mm^3 L^{-1}. Among the four stations, mean biovolume was highest in the main-channel station adjacent to Lock and Dam 7
(6.14 mm^3 L^{-1}), intermediate in an upstream main-channel station (3.98 mm^3
L^{-1}) and one station in Lake Onalaska (4.12 mm^3 L^{-1}), and lowest in another
station in Lake Onalaska (2.49 mm^3 L^{-1}). Seasonal patterns of abundance
varied among the four stations, but diatoms were typically dominant, except
during the late summer blooms of blue-green algae (Huff, 1986) (Figure 1.5).

Some of the seasonal changes in Pool 7 phytoplankters can be attributed to
seasonal changes in physical characteristics. For instance, blue-green algae
were abundant, with one exception, only when temperatures were at least
25°C. Similarly, *Stephanodiscus* spp. were usually abundant during the cooler
months of the sample period (i.e., May and June). However, seasonality of
Melosira spp. often varied among stations. For example, *M. granulata* and *M.
italica* exhibited distinct late summer maxima in the main-channel station near
Lock and Dam 7, but both occurred irregularly at the other three stations. One
of these, *M. italica,* is known to sink during summer stratification in some
English lakes, but recurring summer turbulence may facilitate summer blooms
in the Upper Mississippi. Moreover, frequent and rapid resuspension of sediments by wind action and boat traffic obscures any relationship between phytoplankton abundance and turbidity (Huff, 1986).

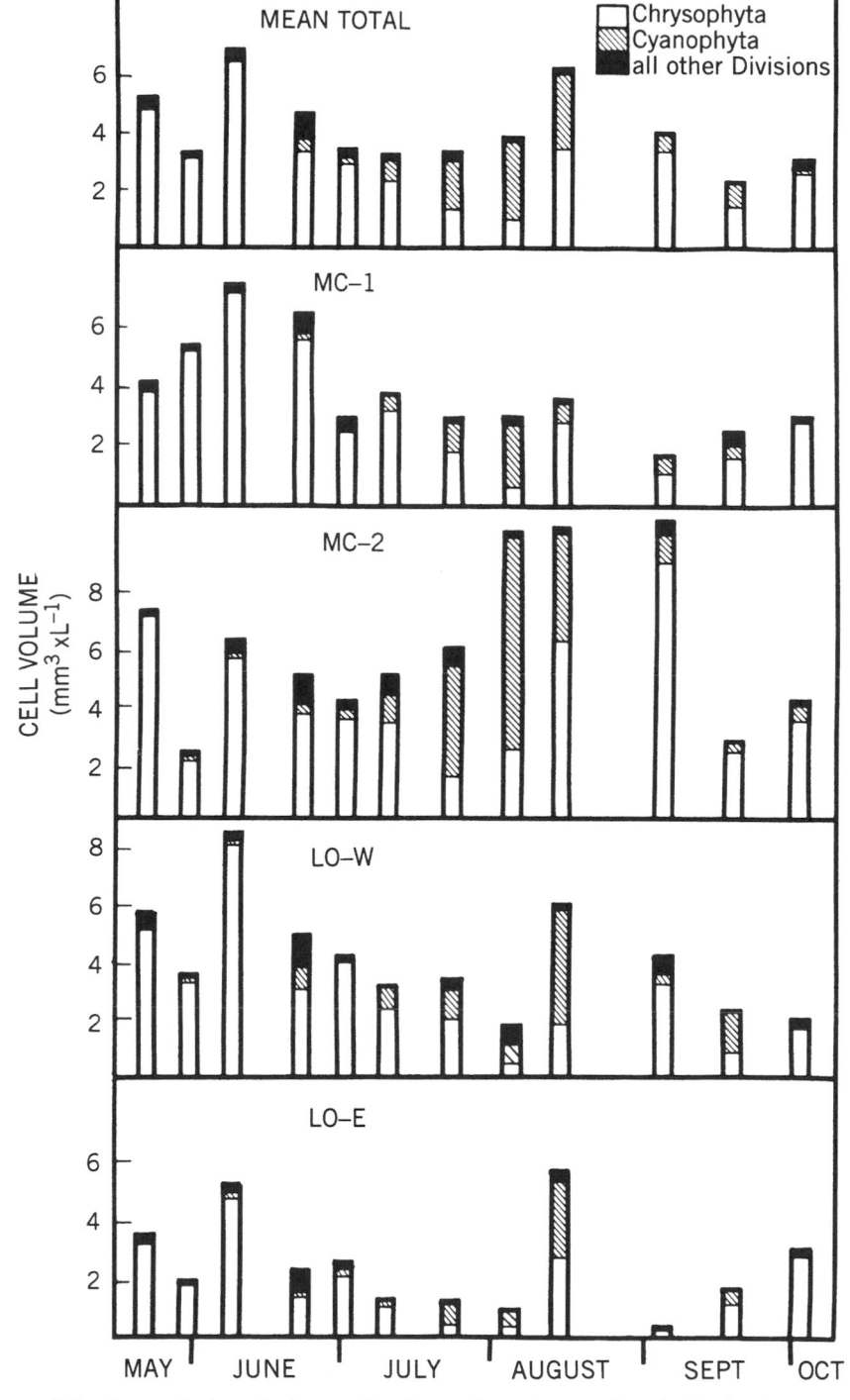

FIGURE 1.5. Seasonal phytoplankton cell volumes from four stations in Navigation Pool 7, Upper Mississippi River, 1984. MC-1, main-channel station located at river km 1136.8; MC-2, main-channel station located just upstream from Lock & Dam 7 (river km 1130.3); LO-W and LO-E are two stations located 1 km apart in Lake Onalaska, a large lake adjacent to the main-channel stations. (From Huff, 1986.)

Nutrient limitation is probably not an important factor in regulating phytoplankton abundance nor seasonal succession (Baker and Baker, 1981; Fremling
et al., 1989; Huff, 1986). However, seasonal patterns of nutrient uptake and
release by macrophytes may result in nutrient limitation in some backwaters.

Phytoplankton production in the Upper Mississippi River appears to have
increased since impoundment. For instance, phytoplankton biomass in Pool 3
during 1975 (0.01 to 13.1 mg L^{-1}) and 1976 (0.01 to 46.9 mg L^{-1}) was as much
as 10-fold (0.04 to 4.0 mg L^{-1}). The expansion and creation of backwater
habitat with impoundment combined with greater retention during summer
low flows would be expected to promote the development of planktonic assemblages. Nutrient enrichment also appears to have increased phytoplankton
production (Baker and Baker, 1979, 1981).

Zooplankton Production
One of the earliest studies on zooplankton in the Upper Mississippi was conducted in the reach between the Twin Cities and Winona, Minnesota (Pool 6)
during 1928. Rotifers accounted for 36.3% of the mean biovolume, while
entomostracans accounted for 46.1% and heterotrophic protozoans accounted
for 17.5%. Rotifers exhibited maxima in biovolume during May and early June,
while entomostracans exhibited maxima during May, early June, late July,
August, and September. *Keratella cochlearis* was the most abundant rotifer,
and was widely distributed, both seasonally and longitudinally. *Polyarthra
trigla, K. quadrata,* and *Brachionus* spp. were common to abundant. The export of lentic entomostracans from Lake Pepin increased downstream densities. Cladocera were generally infrequent, but because of their relatively large
body size, they accounted for a significant proportion of the biovolume.
Bosminia longirostris and *Daphnia longispina* were the most numerous
cladocerans. Nauplii were the most abundant copepod taxon, with *Cyclops* spp.
and *Diaptomus oregonensis* accounting for most of the mature copepods (Reinhard, 1931).

Zooplankton densities in Pool 19 varied among habitats and seasonally. In
general, densities are highest in sites with reduced currents. For instance,
entomostracan densities during a 1921 study in the lower pool ranged from 0.7
to 38 L^{-1}, whereas densities from the middle pool ranged from 0 to 0.4 L^{-1}
(Galtsoff, 1924, as cited in Jahn and Anderson, 1986). In a 1982 and 1983
study, densities were typically highest in a backwater and a shallow unvegetated main-channel border site with negligible current, while they were low in
the main channel, main-channel border, and the side-channel site with appre-
ciable currents. Seasonally, densities in the backwater site, which were low
during May, increased progressively from August to October to December. In
contrast, densities in main channel and main-channel border sites were highest in May and decreased from August to December. May maxima in the main
channel and main-channel border habitats were typically dominated by
rotifers, while entomostracans were usually most numerous during August.

Backwater entomostracans were most abundant during August and December, while backwater rotifers were most abundant during October and December. Side-channel rotifers were most abundant in December, while entomostracans were most abundant in August (Pillard, 1983, as cited in Jahn and Anderson, 1986).

Brachionius calycifrons was the most abundant rotifer during the 1982 and 1983 study in Pool 19, and *B. quadridentata, Euchlanis* spp., and *Keratella cochlearis* were common. *Bosminia longirostris* and *Daphnia retrocurva* were the most common cladocerans, and *Cyclops* spp. were the most common copepods (Pillard, 1983, as cited in Jahn and Anderson, 1986). In a 1921 study, copepods, dominated by *Diaptomus* and *Cyclops,* occurred at densities more than twofold greater than those recorded for cladocerans (Galtsoff, 1924, as cited in Jahn and Anderson, 1986).

Studies in Pool 9 (Eckblad et al., 1984) and Pool 13 (Shaeffer and Nickum, 1986a) indicate that backwaters are important sources for zooplankton in the main channel. This may also be the case for Pool 19. Seasonal maxima for the main channel and main-channel border habitats occurred during May (Pillard, 1983, as cited in Jahn and Anderson, 1986), which is consistent with the flushing of backwaters during the spring rise. However, density maxima in Pools 24, 25, and 26 generally occurred during late summer (Colbert et al., 1975, as cited in Jahn and Anderson, 1986).

Macrophyte Production
Extensive backwater habitat combined with the nearly lentic conditions in the lower pools facilitates the development of one of the most prominent features of the Upper Mississippi River, its extensive macrophyte beds. Estimates for biomass and growth rates are often within the upper range reported in the literature (Grumbaugh et al., 1986; Sefton, 1976). For instance, aboveground standing stocks greater than 300 g m^{-2} have been recorded by researchers from a number of navigation pools (Claflin, 1973; Grumbaugh et al., 1986; Peck and Smart, 1986; Sefton, 1976). In turn, these beds modify local physicochemical conditions, constitute a significant source of organic matter, and provide important habitat for other organisms (Fremling et al., 1989; Peck and Smart, 1986; Sefton, 1976).

There are three major growth forms of aquatic macrophytes: emergent, floating-leafed, and submergent. All three types are important contributors to macrophyte production in the Upper Mississippi River. Emergent assemblages occupy protected sites subject to water-level fluctuations from 0 to 1 m, typically in protected backwaters or the shallow margins of the main or side channels. Floating-leafed macrophytes generally occur in somewhat deeper but still protected water. Submergents occur at a variety of depths, but unlike emergents and floating-leafed taxa, can also occur in moderate currents (Peck and Smart, 1986; Swanson and Sohmer, 1978).

Sagittaria latifolia and *S. rigida* are the two most abundant emergent macrophytes in the Upper Mississippi. *S. latifolia* typically occurs in monotypic stands in protected backwaters and along channel margins where wave action is pronounced, but currents are reduced. *S. rigida* also occurs in monotypic stands, usually in deeper water adjacent to beds of *S. latifolia*. Other emergents, such as *Sparganium eurycarpum, Phalaris arudinaceae,* and *Typha latifolia,* may occur in the shallower and drier margins of *S. latifolia* beds (Blitgen, 1981; Eckblad et al., 1977; Grumbaugh et al., 1986; Peck and Smart, 1986; Sefton, 1976; Swanson and Sohmer, 1978). *Scirpus fluviatilis* can form dense stands but is usually much less frequent (Peck and Smart, 1986).

   Nelumbo lutea and *Nymphaea tuberosa* are the two most abundant floating-leafed species. *N. lutea* often forms monotypic stands in the deeper-water habitats bordering *Sagittaria* beds. *N. tuberosa* is most common in shallow backwaters and in the deeper water of the lower pools. Lemnaceae, including *Lemna minor, Spirodela polyrhiza,* and *Wolffia* spp., frequently form dense late summer populations among stands of emergent and floating-leafed species (Grumbaugh et al., 1986; Sefton, 1976; Swanson and Sohmer, 1978). *Potamogeton nodosus,* which has been classified by different authors as a floating-leafed and/or submergent species, is also abundant, especially in shallow sandy sites with moderately fast currents and among the deepwater assemblages of the lower pools (Sefton, 1976).

   Ceratophyllum demersum, Elodea canadensis, Vallisneria americana, Potamogeton spp., and *Heteranthera dubia* are the most abundant submergents in the Upper Mississippi River. *C. demersum, E. canadense,* and *V. americana* are widespread, but the first two are usually abundant only in shallow, quiet backwaters, while *V. americana* is most abundant in the swifter, deeper (0.9 to 1.5 m) waters of the lower pool and some side channels. *H. dubia, Potamogeton nodosus,* and *P. richardsonii* are usually associated with *V. americana* in the deepwater assemblages of the lower pools. *H. dubia, P. nodosus,* and *P. pectinatus* are also abundant in shallow sites with significant current (Sefton, 1976).

   The extent of macrophyte development varies considerably among pools. Based on remote sensing studies, macrophyte assemblages account for at least 20% and as much as 80% of the total water area from Pool 5 through Pool 13. Pools 5A to 10 have high relative coverage by emergent/floating-leafed beds, whereas Pools 7, 8, and 9 have the highest concentrations of floating-leafed/ submergent beds. Downstream from Pool 13, however, macrophyte coverage is considerably lower. Total relative coverage is low in Pools 15, 20, 21, and 22, and moderately low in Pools 14, 16 to 19, and 24 to 26. By virtue of their large water areas, macrophyte beds are extensive in Pools 19, 25, and 26, but not as extensive as they are in some of the northern pools (e.g., Pools 8 and 9) (Figure 1.6). These differences in macrophyte coverage are attributable to differences in habitat. Backwaters and side channels comprise a much greater percentage of the total water area in the northern pools, whereas main-channel border habitat accounts for most of the aquatic habitat in the southern pools (Peck and Smart, 1986).

   One of the most extensive studies of macrophytes in the Upper Mississippi

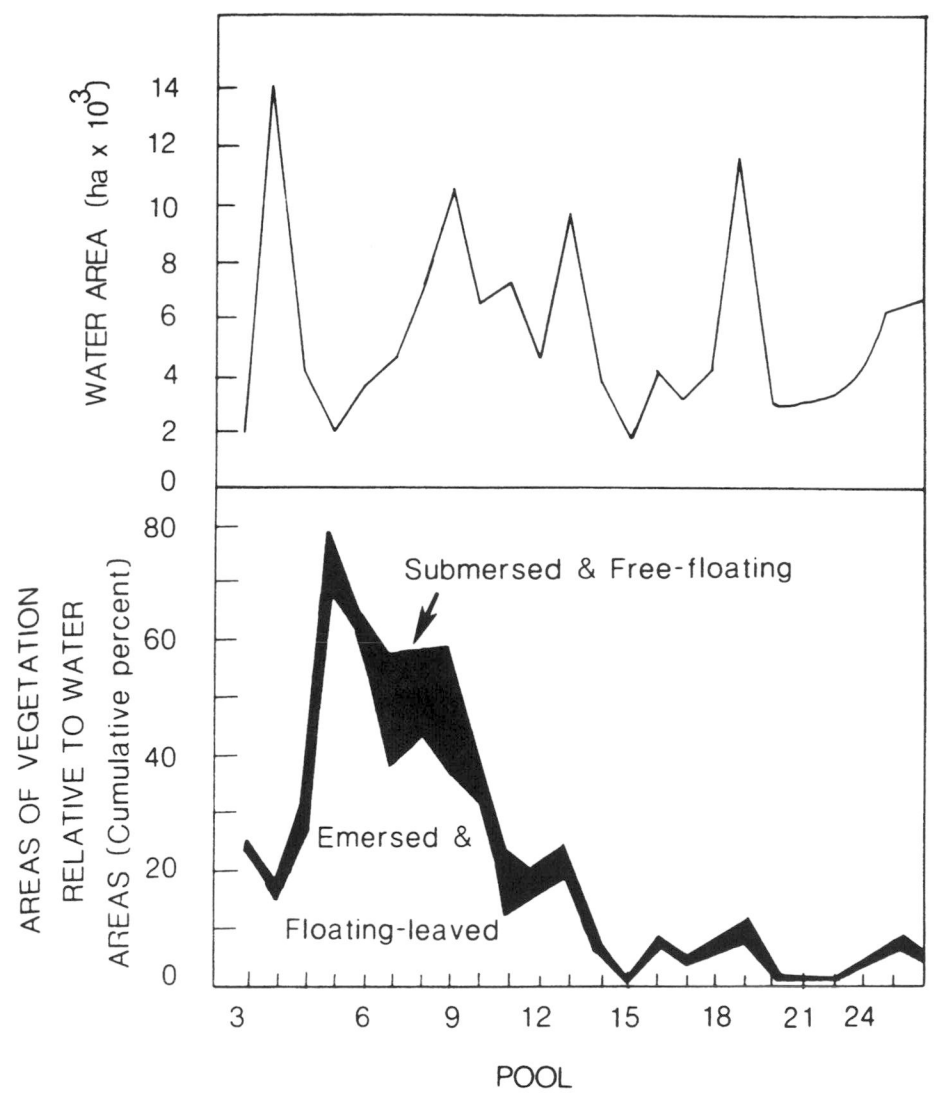

FIGURE 1.6.   Relative coverage of aquatic macrophyte life-forms in navigation pools based on remote sensing data (bottom) compared with the water area (top). (From Peck and Smart, 1986.)

involved 41 sites located in the middle and lower reaches of Pool 8. During 1975, mean total biomass of 132.8 g m^{-2} was recorded during an early summer (June–early July) sampling period, and 181.7 g m^{-2} was recorded during a later (July–August) sampling period; means include only those sites with vegetation (Sefton, 1976).

Ceratophyllum demersum was the most widely distributed species recorded in Pool 8, accounting for a relative frequency of 18.7%. *Sagittaria latifolia,*

TABLE 1.7. *Relative Frequency, Relative Biomass, Mean Biomass, and Maximum Biomass for Aquatic Macrophytes in Pool 8, Upper Mississippi River, Summer 1975*

	Relative Frequency (%)	Relative Biomass (%)	Mean Biomass[a] (g m^{-2})	Maximum Biomass (g m^{-2})
Emergent				
Phalaris arundinacea	0.7	0.1	3.1	8.5
Polygonum cocineum	0.2	0.3	38.9	122.2
Sagittaria latifolia	11.6	45.2	161.9	606.6
S. rigida	4.5	8.5	78.4	395.4
Scirpus validus	0.2	1.1	189.2	287.6
Sparganium eurycarpum	0.2	0.6	104.6	226.6
Floating-leafed				
Nelumbo lutea	3.6	4.3	50.1	229.8
Numphar varigatum	0.4	0.6	71.0	133.2
Nymphaea tuberosa	3.8	4.6	49.9	182.2
Lemnaceae	5.6	3.4	28.2	120.0
Submergent				
Ceratophyllum demersum	18.7	5.6	14.0	182.4
Elodea canadensis	7.4	0.8	4.9	146.4
Heteranthera dubia	5.0	1.4	12.1	126.0
Myriophyllum exalbescens	0.2	<0.1	0.1	0.9
Najas flexilis	0.3	<0.1	1.4	4.4
Potamogeton crispus	8.2	1.2	5.0	62.8
P. foliosus	3.3	0.3	2.3	40.1
P. nodosus	6.2	5.1	33.5	145.6
P. pectinatus	6.6	1.1	7.0	76.4
P. richardsonii	0.6	0.3	14.2	104.0
P. zosteriformis	1.4	0.1	4.2	42.4
Sagittaria rigida f. *fluvitans*	1.6	0.6	8.2	45.0
Vallisneria americana	9.2	14.3	62.5	331.6

Source: After Sefton (1976).
[a]Mean biomass only for those samples containing that taxon.

Vallisneria americana, Potamogeton crispus, Elodea canadensis, P. nodosus, P. pectinatus, Lemnaceae, and *Heteranthera dubia* were also widespread, accounting for 5% or more of the total relative frequency. Although widely distributed, *C. demersum* yielded a relatively modest mean biomass of 14.0 g m^{-2} and accounted for 5.6% of the total biomass. On the other hand, *S. latifolia,* which accounted for 18.7% of the relative frequency, yielded a much higher mean biomass (161.9 g m^{-2}) and accounted for 45.2% of the total biomass. *V. americana, Sagittaria rigida, P. nodosus, Nelumbo lutea,* and *Nymphaea tuberosa* were other important contributors to the total biomass (Sefton, 1976) (Table 1.7).

Submergent species in Pool 8 were widespread (i.e., frequent), but with the exceptions of *Vallisneria americana* and *Potamogeton nodosus,* they usually yielded low aboveground biomass. On the other hand, emergents and floating-leafed species, which are less frequent, yielded considerably higher mean biomass. However, maximum biomass for several submergent species was well within the range recorded for emergent and floating-leafed species (Sefton, 1976) (Table 1.7).

Macrophytes from a middle pool station and a lower pool station were investigated more intensively during 1976. The middle pool station was a shallow backwater site characterized by *Sagittaria* spp., *Nelumbo lutea*, and a number of submergents. Mean biomass increased from 36.6 g m^{-2} on May 18 to 331.7 g m^{-2} on August 25. The lower pool station was an open, deeper location characterized by *Vallisneria americana, Potamogeton nodosus, Heteranthera dubia, Nymphaea tuberosa,* and a macroalga, *Cladophora.* Mean biomass increased from 2.5 g m^{-2} on June 1 to 174.4 g m^{-2} on August 24 (Sefton, 1976, 1977). It is evident that the percentage of increase was much larger in the lower, deeper pool.

Seasonal patterns of growth differ between the middle pool and lower pool stations in Pool 8. For instance, substantial growth is evident in the middle pool station by June 15, but growth in the lower pool station is delayed by several weeks (Tables 1.8 and 1.9). Moreover, seasonal patterns of growth vary considerably among species, among growth forms, and with species between stations. In the middle pool station, emergent and floating-leafed species increased in biomass through summer, whereas most submergent species either exhibited little change or changed irregularly (Table 1.8). On the other hand, submergents in the lower pool station exhibited seasonal increases, although they were delayed relative to those of the middle pool station (Sefton, 1976, 1977) (Table 1.9).

TABLE 1.8. *Seasonal Mean Biomass (g m^{-2}) for Selected Aquatic Macrophytes in a Backwater Middle Pool Station in Pool 8, Upper Mississippi River, Summer 1977*[a]

	May 28	June 15	June 29	July 15	July 29	Aug. 25
Emergent						
Sagittaria latifolia	24.9	109.2	224.1	362.7	249.5	249.9
S. rigida	17.9	63.7	67.1	109.0	139.1	63.7
Floating-leafed						
Nelumbo lutea	1.0	26.5	53.1	112.7	174.0	221.9
Lemnaceae	0.0	2.6	8.3	52.3	60.0	39.5
Submergent						
Ceratophyllum demersum	20.8	17.6	18.7	28.9	11.5	27.9
Elodea canadensis	39.9	48.5	48.1	28.6	31.8	44.4
Heteranthera dubia	0.2	14.0	21.4	19.3	27.0	5.4
Potamogeton nodosus	4.2	10.7	17.7	19.6	11.3	16.1

Source: After Sefton (1976).
[a]There were 24 sites within this station. Of these, the sites were included for this table only when the taxon occurred on at least five of the six sample dates and the taxon had a mean biomass above 1 g m^{-2}. An exception was made for Lemnaceae, which typically develops late in the season. Sites for Lemnaceae were included when it occurred on three or more consecutive sampling dates.

TABLE 1.9.   *Seasonal Mean Biomass (g m^{-2}) for Selected Aquatic Macrophytes in a Lower Pool Station in Pool 8, Upper Mississippi River, Summer 1976[a]*

	June 1	June 16	July 1	July 21	Aug. 2	Aug. 24
Macroalgae						
Cladophora sp.	0.0	0.0	0.5	23.5	47.4	51.0
Floating-leafed						
Nymphaea tuberosa	2.0	1.6	9.4	13.7	29.1	5.6
Submergent						
Ceratophyllum demersum	0.2	0.4	0.9	17.9	16.8	19.5
Heteranthera dubia	<0.1	0.0	0.3	11.8	68.6	74.6
Potamogeton nodosus	1.4	11.9	42.5	55.0	65.6	20.3
P. pectinatus	0.6	5.7	9.9	10.8	9.2	8.5
Vallisneria americana	1.4	7.1	15.7	58.6	85.4	87.7

Source: After Sefton (1976).
[a]There were 15 sites within this station. Of these, the sites were included for this table only when the taxon occurred in at least four of the six sample dates and the taxon had a mean biomass above 1 g m^{-2}. An exception was made for *Cladophora,* which typically develops late in the season. Sites for *Cladophora* were included when it occurred on three or more consecutive sampling dates.

Estimates of growth rates (or productivity) for macrophytes in Pool 8 were calculated by evaluating seasonal changes in aboveground biomass during 1976. The growth rate of the two most abundant emergents from the middle pool station, *Sagittaria latifolia* and *S. rigida,* averaged 10.3 and 5.6 g m^{-2} day^{-1}, respectively. Maximum growth rates of 12.9 and 12.8 g m^{-2} day^{-1} were recorded for *S. latifolia* in early and late July, while a maximum rate of 10.2 g m^{-2} was recorded for *S. rigida* in late July. The mean growth rates for *Nelumbo lutea* (middle pool) and *Nymphaea tuberosa* (lower pool) were 2.7 and 1.4 g m^{-2} day^{-1}, respectively. Both species exhibited their greatest increase in biomass in late July, with *N. lutea* growing at a rate of 4.8 g m^{-2} day^{-1} and *N. tuberosa* growing at a rate of 2.6 g m^{-2} day^{-1}. The mean growth rates for submergent species were typically much lower than those for emergent species and sometimes lower than those of floating-leafed species. Three of the most abundant submergents, *Vallisneria americana, Potamogeton nodosus,* and *Heteranthera dubia,* exhibited mean growth rates of 1.4, 0.9, and 1.4 g m^{-2} day^{-1}, respectively, in the lower pool station. Growth rates for both *V. americana* and *H. dubia* were highest in early July (2.5 g m^{-2} day^{-1}) and late July (2.5 g m^{-2} day^{-1}), while growth for *P. nodosus* was highest (2.3 g m^{-2} day^{-1}) in late June. Other submergents, particularly in the middle pool site, exhibited little net growth or even a net loss of biomass during 1976. In part, this lack of net growth was the result of mid- and late summer encroachment of floating-leafed *N. lutea* into the shallow habitats previously occupied by submergent species (Sefton, 1976, 1977).

Macrophyte growth was also investigated in Pool 19, where *Sagittaria latifolia* and *Nelumbo lutea* occupied large monotypic beds in shallower portions of the main-channel border. As was the case with these two species in Pool 8, there was a progressive increase in biomass throughout the summer. *S. latifolia* increased from a mean aboveground biomass of 14 g m^{-2} in early June to a maximum of 635 g m^{-2} in August, while *N. lutea* increased from a mean of 9 g m^{-2} in June to 331 g m^{-2} in August. The growth rates of *S. latifolia* were similar to those recorded in Pool 8, but those of *N. lutea* were somewhat higher. The rate of biomass accumulation for *S. latifolia* averaged 7 g m^{-2} day^{-1} from June to July and 13 g m^{-2} day^{-1} from July to August. The mean biomass accumulation rate for *N. lutea* between June and July was 4 g m^{-2} day^{-1}, while the mean from July to August was 7 g m^{-2} day^{-1}. Changes between August and September were not significant for either species, but subsequent declines occurred following senescence (Grumbaugh et al., 1986).

In Big Lake, Pool 9, aboveground biomass of *Sagittaria* beds increased from 47.7 g m^{-2} to 266.0 g m^{-2} from July 3 to August 1. This resulted in a mean rate of biomass accumulation of 14.9 g m^{-2} day^{-1}. Belowground increases in biomass during this period averaged 4.4 g m^{-2} day^{-1} and the growth of new tubers apparently did not start until August (Eckblad et al., 1977).

Measuring changes in aboveground biomass may significantly underestimate growth rates and net production in aquatic macrophytes. For instance, *Sagittaria latifolia* experienced rapid leaf loss during the early growing season in a study from the Illinois River and may also lose considerable early season biomass in the Upper Mississippi River (Grumbaugh et al., 1986). Leaf loss may be even greater for submergent species, especially those that live in faster currents. Increased sloughing by some submergent species is suggested by some data from the 1976 study in Pool 8. Senescent material, which one would expect to be largely entrained in sites with strong currents, never accounted for more than 7% of the total aboveground biomass of *Ceratophyllum demersum, Elodea canadensis, Potamogeton nodosus,* and *P. zosteriformis* in the middle pool station, whereas senescent material accounted for 38 to 78% of the late summer aboveground biomass of *Nelumbo lutea* and *Sagittaria* spp. However, senescent material also accounted for as much as 56% of the late summer biomass for one submergent species, *Heteranthera dubia*. Similarly, most submergent macrophytes in the lower pool site contained little senescent material. The two major exceptions are *P. nodosus*, in which senescent material accounted for 46% of its late summer biomass, and *P. crispus*, which reaches maximum biomass in early summer, after which it forms overwintering burs, senesceces, and then becomes much less abundant (Sefton, 1976).

Fast currents prevent the development of macrophytes in the main channel and faster portions of many side channels (Jahn and Anderson, 1986; McConville et al., 1986; Sefton, 1976; Swanson and Sohmer, 1978). In Pool 8, for example, macrophytes were not collected in any site with summer currents faster than 30 cm s^{-1} (Peck and Smart, 1986). Fast currents apparently contribute to the paucity of macrophytes in the upper areas of most pools (McConville et al., 1986; Sefton, 1976), but fluctuating water levels are also signifi-

TABLE 1.10. *Patch Number, Areal Coverage, and Patch Size for Aquatic Macrophytes in the Main-Channel Border Habitats That Are "Exclusive" or Rock Structures in the Upper, Middle, and Lower Reaches of Pool 5A, Upper Mississippi River, 1980 and 1983*

	Upper Pool	Middle Pool	Lower Pool
Summer 1980			
Number of patches	13	36	30
Areal coverage (ha)	1.20	3.41	7.46
Mean patch size (m²)	900	900	2500
Range (m²)	<10–7400	<10–4700	<10–14,800
Summer 1983			
Number of patches	10	38	27
Areal coverage (ha)	0.32	2.66	6.98
Mean patch size (m²)	350	700	2600
Range (m²)	<10–1500	<10–7900	<10–22,500

Source: After McConville et al. (1986).

cant. In Pool 5A, for example, the upper areas experience fluctuations that are greater than 1.1 m, whereas fluctuations in the lower areas are less than 0.5 m (McConville et al., 1986).

Differences in current velocities and water-level fluctuations have contributed to the within-pool differences in the patch frequency, patch size, and areal coverage of submerged macrophytes in Pool 5A. Macrophyte beds are substantially more frequent in the middle and lower pools than in the upper pool. Despite the somewhat greater frequency of patches in the middle pool, total macrophyte coverage is approximately threefold greater in the lower pool because of larger mean patch sizes. Increased discharge and the resulting increase in turbidity during 1983 contributed to reduced macrophyte abundance. In terms of the total flora, this decline was evident only in the middle and upper areas (Table 1.10). However, two of the more abundant species of the lower pool, *Potamogeton crispus* and *P. pectinatus,* also declined during 1983 (McConville et al., 1986).

The extent of macrophyte growth is also limited by depth. A depth of 1.9 m appeared to be the lower limit for macrophytes in Pool 8 (Sefton, 1976). In Pool 19, macrophytes are generally absent from depths greater than 1.5 m (Jahn and Anderson, 1986). Depth affects macrophytes primarily because of reduced light penetration, but interannual differences in flow or other environmental conditions can complicate the effects of depth. This was evident with the 1976 and 1977 drought. Increased light penetration, via reduced flows and reduced suspended sediment inputs, contributed to a threefold increase in the coverage of macrophyte beds in the Montrose Flats area of Pool 19. This expansion was largely the result of macrophytes colonizing deeper portions of the main-channel border. However, this expanded community has persisted despite the return of normal flows and turbidities. This persistence is apparently dependent on the use of stored root reserves until the new growth reaches the euphotic zone; sprouts from seeds have not been observed (Sparks et al., 1990).

Impoundment of the Upper Mississippi River has dramatically altered the distribution and increased the production of macrophytes by stabilizing water levels and by increasing the total amount of nonchannel aquatic habitat (Peck and Smart, 1986). Changes have also occurred in the relative abundance of different species. *Nelumbo lutea,* which is currently one of the more abundant species, was previously restricted to minor backwater in the unimpounded river (Sohmer, 1977). Flow stabilization has eliminated the occasional dry periods required by some emergent species and greatly reduced their distribution. Some submergent assemblages were replaced with pondweeds (*Potamogeton*). In general, lotic species declined while lentic species were favored (Smart et al., 1986).

Sedimentation and navigation have affected and are continuing to affect the macrophyte flora of the Upper Mississippi in a variety of ways. Sedimentation has increased macrophyte production in the main-channel border habitat of Pool 19, by creating shallow-water habitat (Jahn and Anderson, 1986; Junk et al., 1989). On the other hand, sedimentation is filling in productive backwater habitats (Fremling and Claflin, 1984; Holland, 1986; Peck and Smart, 1986; Smart et al., 1986). Sedimentation has transformed many backwaters into broad expanses of uniform, shallow habitat, thereby reducing the diversity of habitats available to submergent species. Sedimentation in the southern pools has transformed some backwater lakes into silt flats vegetated by agricultural weeds. Barge traffic results in the resuspension and transport of sediments from the channel to backwaters. This, in turn, impairs submergents but favors emergents. Wave action from barge traffic also affects aquatic macrophytes. The predominance of *Sagittaria latifolia* along the margins of the main-channel border may in part be facilitated by its tolerance to wave action (Peck and Smart, 1986).

Strong winds are characteristic of the Upper Mississippi River Valley (Eckblad et al., 1977), and sedimentation has aggravated their destructive effects. By reducing depths and increasing the prevalence of silt and clay sediments, sedimentation augments wind action by increasing turbulence and substrate instability and by prolonging periods of elevated turbidity. The interaction of wind and sedimentation has been a major contributor to the decline in macrophyte production in the Illinois River and may also become important to the Upper Mississippi River (Sparks, 1984).

Invertebrate Production

Macroinvertebrates other than mussels in the Upper Mississippi River can be very productive and diverse, but abundance, taxonomic richness, and taxonomic composition vary considerably from site to site. This variability is indicative of the considerable habitat diversity that characterizes the Upper Mississippi. Studies from several pools have demonstrated that these differ-

TABLE 1.11. *Benthic Macroinvertebrate Density, Standing Stock, and Taxonomic Richness for Less Eutrophic and More Eutrophic Sites within the Middle and Lower Reaches of Pool 8, Upper Mississippi River, Summer 1975*

	Less Eutrophic	More Eutrophic
Density (number m^{-2})		
Mean	2504	7621
Range	237–11,744	2095–19,975
Standing stock (g m^{-2})		
Mean	13.6	42.5
Range	0.2–53.7	1.0–164.9
Taxonomic richness		
Mean	30	26
Range	14–54	2–44

Source: After Elstad (1986).

ences are attributable to a number of factors, of which current velocity, substrate, and aquatic macrophytes appear to be particularly important.

Differences in benthic macroinvertebrate abundance from site to site are exemplified by collections from 41 sites in the middle and lower reaches of Pool 8 during the summer of 1975. Densities ranged from 237 to 19,975 animals m^{-2} and standing stocks ranged from 0.25 to 198.36 g m^{-2}. The 41 sites span a continuum from less eutrophic (i.e., swifter currents, sandy substrates, low sediment organic matter, greater oxygen saturation, and little or no macrophyte growth) to more eutrophic (i.e., reduced current, silt–clay sediments, high organic matter, lower oxygen saturation, and extensive macrophyte growth). Although overlap was considerable, density and biomass tended to be higher in the more eutrophic sites than in the less eutrophic sites. On the other hand, taxonomic richness tended to be lower in the more eutrophic sites (Elstad, 1977, 1986) (Table 1.11).

Most of the 41 sites sampled by Elstad (1977) are classifiable as main channel, side channel (sandy substrates, fast current), main-channel border (fast to slow currents, broad, shallow bottoms of silt and clay), sloughs–lakes (slow currents, silty substrates, little current, isolated from main channel) and stagnant ponds (no currents, silty substrates). These habitats generally conform to the less eutrophic–more eutrophic continuum presented by Elstad (1977), except that the main-channel border sites, which were concentrated in the lower pool, span a range of currents. However, they are consistently dominated by silt and clay substrates, and usually contain high standing crops of aquatic macrophytes.

Comparisons of these habitats in Pool 8 indicate that the main and side channels had relatively low standing stocks and densities. Densities tended to be relatively high in the main-channel border, sloughs/lakes, and stagnant ponds, but standing stocks varied considerably. Standing stocks were highest

TABLE 1.12. *Habitat-Specific Density, Wet Weight Standing Crops, and Taxonomic Richness of Benthic Macroinvertebrates in Pool 8, Upper Mississippi River, Summer 1975*

Habitat:[a]	MC	SC	MCB	Sl/L	P
Sample Size:	3	26	16	20	10
Density (number m^{-2})					
Mean	1,808	1,709	8,162	6,881	7,526
Minimum	508	461	3,705	3,354	2,842
Maximum	6,586	4,291	19,975	13,436	18,740
Standing stock (g m^{-2})					
Mean	12.29	10.72	94.65	38.88	8.71
Minimum	0.26	0.21	8.45	12.14	0.97
Maximum	46.84	53.70	198.36	110.00	18.68
Taxonomic richness					
Mean	25	30	39	30	13
Minimum	15	14	27	18	2
Maximum	38	46	59	47	26

Source: After Elstad (1977).

[a]MC, main channel; SC, side channel; MCB, main-channel border; Sl/L, sloughs and lakes; P, stagnant ponds.

in the main-channel borders, intermediate in the sloughs/lakes, and low in the stagnant ponds. Taxonomic richness was highest in the main-channel border and lowest in the stagnant ponds (Table 1.12).

Habitat preferences of the more abundant taxons affected the patterns of abundance evident for these habitats. Oligochaetes were ubiquitous but were least numerous in the main and side channels and most numerous in the stagnant ponds. They, along with *Asellus militaris* (Isopoda) and several chironomids (e.g., *Chironomus* spp. and *Endochironomus* spp.), occurred at high densities, but because of their small size, total biomass was relatively low. Conversely, the sandy sediments of the main and side channels contained relatively few individuals but included several large-bodied taxons (e.g., *Cheumatopsyche* spp.) as well as small-bodied taxons (e.g., Ceratopogonidae). The main-channel border and slough–lake habitats contained high densities of a variety of small-bodied taxons, including Oligochaetes, amphipods, and Chironomidae, as well as large-bodied taxons, including burrowing mayflies (*Hexagenia* spp.) and fingernail clams (Sphaeriidae). Abundance was greatest in the main-channel border habitats, in large measure because of the abundance of Sphaeriidae (Table 1.13).

Substantial differences in benthic macroinvertebrate abundance were also evident along a transect in the middle reach of Pool 7 (Tables 1.14 to 1.16). Standing stocks in the main channel averaged only 0.38 g m^{-2} (Table 1.14). The Upper Black River, which is essentially a large side channel paralleling the main channel, had low standing stocks in the midchannel, but they increased considerably near the margins (sites 12, 16, and 17) (Table 1.16). Both

TABLE 1.13. *Habitat-Specific Mean Densities (number m^{-2}) for Macroinvertebrates in Pool 8, Upper Mississippi River, Summer 1975*

	Habitat[a]				
	MC	SC	MCB	Sl/L	P
Turbellaria					
Total	0	16	65	25	0
Nematoda					
Total	52	54	226	116	40
Hirudinea					
Total	25	14	194	188	146
Oligochaeta					
Total	1518	1250	3518	3970	5852
Gastropoda					
Amnicola	1	4	146	2	0
Physa	0	2	30	4	0
Bivalvia					
Sphaeriidae	2	59	1641	205	0
Isopoda					
Asellus militaris	1	12	195	64	12
Amphipoda					
Hyalella azteca	8	44	351	394	988
Ephemeroptera					
Brachycercus sp.	19	20	6	4	0
Hexagenia spp.	42	62	179	448	24
Megaloptera					
Sialis sp.	0	1	<1	8	1
Trichoptera					
Cheumatopsyche	13	102	6	4	0
Hydropsyche	1	11	<1	1	0
Oecetis	4	2	18	2	0
Chaoboridae					
Chaoborus	5	2	3	19	0
Ceratopogonidae					
Atrichopogon	48	23	0	<1	0
Palpomyia	58	39	4	24	2
Chironomidae					
Chironomus	1	1	76	290	66
Coleotanypus	4	7	20	12	2
Cryptochironomus	9	20	14	15	16
Endochironomus	1	24	12	261	100
Glyptotendipes	1	18	5	56	12
Pentaneura	7	12	36	19	46
Polypedilum	6	32	30	51	73
Tanytarsus	1	3	22	2	0
Xenochironomus	3	7	18	1	0

Source: After Elstad (1977).

[a]MC, main channel; SC, side channel; MCB, main-channel border; Sl/L, sloughs and floodplain lakes; P, stagnant ponds.

TABLE 1.14.   *Standing Stocks (g m^{-2}) of Benthic Macroinvertebrates and Aquatic Macrophytes Along Main-Channel Portion of a Transect (West to East) Through the Middle Reach of Pool 7, Upper Mississippi River, Summer 1973*

	Transect Site				
	1	2	3	4	5
Oligochaeta					
Total	0	0.03	0	0.04	0
Hirudinea					
Total	0	0	0	0	0
Mollusca					
Total	0.90	0	0	0	0
Isopoda					
Asellus sp.	0	0	0	0	0
Amphipoda					
Total	0	0.29	0	0.03	0
Ephemeroptera					
Burrowing	0	0	0	0	0
Other Ephemeroptera	0	0	0	0	0
Diptera					
Ceratopogonidae	0.10	0.20	0.05	0.01	0.11
Chironomidae	0.02	0	0	0.05	0.01
Other Diptera	0	0	0	0.03	0.01
Other Insecta					
Coleoptera	0	0	0	0	0
Trichoptera	0	0	0	0	<0.01
Total biomass	1.02	0.52	0.05	0.16	0.13
Macrophyte biomass	0	0	0	0	0

Source: After Claflin (1973).

the main channel and the Upper Black River portions of the transect were characterized by shifting sand, fast currents, and a paucity of macrophyte growth. In between the two channels, six vegetated sites (sites 6 to 11) located in slough and lake habitats yielded substantially higher standing stocks, averaging 10.09 g m^{-2} and ranging from 2.46 to 26.96 g m^{-2} (Claflin, 1973; Elstad, 1986) (Table 1.15).

The depauperate benthic assemblages of the main channel and midchannel side channel in Pool 7 are characterized by modest populations of Oligochaetes, Amphipoda, Ceratopogonidae, and/or Chironomidae. The more productive sites near the periphery of the side channel are characterized by high standing crops of Mollusca, which were probably dominated by Sphaeriidae. A productive and diverse assemblage of macroinvertebrates, including Oligochaeta, Mollusca, Isopoda, Amphipoda, burrowing mayflies (e.g., *Hexagenia*), and Diptera, characterized the benthos of the vegetated slough and lake habitats (Claflin, 1973) (Tables 1.14 to 1.16).

Of the 17 transect sites in Pool 7, the two with the highest standing stocks

TABLE 1.15. *Standing Stocks (g m⁻²) of Benthic Macroinvertebrates and Aquatic Macrophytes Along the Backwater (Sloughs and Lakes) Portion of a Transect (West to East) Through the Middle Reach of Pool 7, Upper Mississippi River, Summer 1973*

	Transect Site					
	6	7	8	9	10	11
Oligochaeta						
Total	0.23	1.51	0.90	0.30	0.26	0
Hirudinea						
Total	0.04	0	0.70	0	0.40	0.04
Mollusca						
Total	4.02	3.02	1.01	2.01	21.11	2.01
Isopoda						
Asellus sp.	0.41	0.40	1.40	0.04	0.62	0
Amphipoda						
Total	0.31	0	4.50	0.08	0.50	0
Ephemeroptera						
Burrowing	5.28	0.73	2.94	0	3.50	0
Other Ephemeroptera	0.30	0.02	0.10	<0.01	0.11	0
Diptera						
Ceratopogonidae	0.01	0	0.03	0	<0.01	0.02
Chironomidae	0.15	0.01	0.08	0.02	0.28	<0.01
Other Diptera	0.83	0.16	0.17	0	0.17	0
Other Insecta						
Coleoptera	0.09	0.01	0	0	0.01	0
Trichoptera	0	0	0.23	0	0	0
Total biomass	11.41	5.56	12.09	2.46	26.96	2.08
Macrophyte biomass	122.0	136.5	301.5	540.0	14.3	512.6

Source: After Claflin (1973).

(sites 10 and 17) contained either little macrophyte growth (site 10) or none (site 17). Moreover, both of these sites were heavily dominated by Mollusca (Claflin, 1973) (Tables 1.15 and 1.16). A similar pattern was observed in Big Lake, a large floodplain lake in the middle reach of Pool 9. Total benthic standing crop was more than fourfold higher in open sites in Big Lake than in *Sagittaria* beds. In addition, Sphaeriidae, especially *Musculum transversum* and *Hexagenia* spp., were strongly dominant in the open-water sites; *Hexagenia* spp. were also abundant in site 10 of Pool 7. Both the open-water sites and the *Sagittaria* beds contained a diverse assemblage of Sphaeriidae, Hirudinea, Oligochaeta, *Asellus* sp., *Hexagenia* spp., and Diptera, but Gastropoda and *Hyalella azteca* (Amphipoda) were abundant only in the vegetated sites (Eckblad et al., 1977) (Table 1.17).

Sampling for benthic macroinvertebrates in the Upper Mississippi River has occurred primarily during the summer months, but a study of benthic assemblages in the middle and upper reaches of Pool 13 was conducted in late winter. Total densities during this winter study were lowest in tailwater (777 m⁻²) and main channel (1566 m⁻²) habitats, intermediate (3822 m⁻²) in side

TABLE 1.16. *Standing Stocks (g m^{-2}) of Benthic Macroinvertebrates and Aquatic Macrophytes Along the Upper Black River Portion of a Transect (West to East) Through the Middle Reach of Pool 7, Upper Mississippi River, Summer 1973*

	Transect Site						
	12	13	14	15	16	17	18
Oligochaeta							
Total	0	0.02	0.01	0	0.07	0.47	—
Hirudinea							
Total	0	0	0	0	0.01	0.24	—
Mollusca							
Total	2.01	0	0	0	4.02	14.07	—
Isopoda							
Asellus sp.	0	0	0	0	0	0.01	—
Amphipoda							
Total	0.01	0.02	0.03	0	0	0.02	—
Ephemeroptera							
Burrowing	0	0	0	0	0	0.09	—
Other Ephemeroptera	0	<0.01	0.02	0	0	0.22	—
Diptera							
Ceratopogonidae	0.01	0.02	0	<0.01	<0.01	0.01	—
Chironomidae	<0.01	0.02	<0.01	<0.01	0.01	0.18	—
Other Diptera	0.01	0	0	0	0.01	0.07	—
Other Insecta							
Coleoptera	0	0	0	0	0	<0.01	—
Trichoptera	0	0.02	0	0.03	0	0	—
Total biomass	2.04	0.10	0.05	0.04	4.11	15.39	—
Macrophyte biomass	0	0	0	0	0	0	174.2

Source: After Claflin (1973).

channels, and highest in slough (9318 m^{-2}), lake (7169 m^{-2}), and sandy main-channel border (7264 m^{-2}) habitats. Nematoda, Oligochaeta, and Chironomidae were numerous in all habitats, but nematodes and oligochaetes were most numerous in sloughs, whereas chironomids were most numerous in the main-channel border. *Hexagenia* was numerous in main-channel border and backwater habitats, while Ostracoda and Ceratopogonidae were numerous only in the backwaters. Hydropsychidae (*Cheumatopsyche, Hydropsyche,* and *Potamyia*) were most numerous in the tailwaters and in the main channel (Herbert et al., 1984) (Table 1.18). In a late summer and early autumn study of the main-channel border habitat of Pool 13, densities were dominated by *Oligochaeta* (51%), *Ephemeroptera* (21%), and *Diptera* (18%); *Hexagenia* accounted for 64% of the standing stock (Hall, 1980, as cited in Herbert et al., 1984).

Main- and side-channel habitats in other southern pools exhibited patterns similar to those encountered in Pool 19, albeit at lower densities. The main-channel habitat in Pool 26 is composed primarily of sand and the benthos is characterized by low numbers (<500 m^{-2}) of oligochaetes and chironomids.

TABLE 1.17. *Numbers and Dry Weights of Macroinvertebrates from a Site within Emergent* Sagittaria *sp. and an Open-Water Site (means* ± *SE)[a]*

	Numbers/m^2			
	Sagittaria		Open Water	
**Sphaerium* sp.	83.3 ±	14.62	1419.8 ±	235.38
**Hexagenia* sp.	115.4 ±	36.15	602.5 ±	75.41
Chironomus sp.	439.1 ±	36.63	314.1 ±	55.44
Palpomyia sp.	35.3 ±	11.56	48.1 ±	19.07
Miscellaneous Diptera	237.2 ±	64.67	282.0 ±	40.84
Branchiura sowerbyi	19.2 ±	19.23	115.4 ±	96.53
Miscellaneous Oligochaeta	115.4 ±	41.84	185.9 ±	63.71
Asellus sp.	96.2 ±	37.16	57.7 ±	22.21
Helobdella sp.	60.9 ±	15.24	214.7 ±	89.57
***Hyalella azteca*	1173.0 ±	362.25	9.6 ±	6.57
**Physa integra*	137.8 ±	53.57	0 ±	0
Gyraulus parvus	32.1 ±	14.62	0 ±	0
Campeloma sp.	0 ±	0	3.2 ±	3.21

	Mg/m^2			
	Sagittaria		Open Water	
**Sphaerium* sp.	799.7 ±	276.24	17,665.6 ±	2231.16
**Hexagenia* sp.	857.3 ±	396.37	10,737.9 ±	2106.23
Chironomus sp.	1233.9 ±	99.96	923.7 ±	293.76
Palpomyia sp.	28.2 ±	9.49	41.3 ±	17.37
Miscellaneous Diptera	68.0 ±	16.71	103.2 ±	35.44
Branchiura sowerbyi	27.2 ±	27.24	248.7 ±	218.66
Miscellaneous Oligochaeta	51.0 ±	15.90	253.5 ±	89.92
Asellus sp.	55.8 ±	21.62	59.3 ±	37.12
Helobdella sp.	58.7 ±	21.81	167.3 ±	55.03
***Hyalella azteca*	440.7 ±	127.91	4.2 ±	3.16
**Physa integra*	1052.5 ±	532.08	0 ±	0
Gyraulus parvus	113.1 ±	54.77	0 ±	0
Campeloma sp.	2458.2 ±	2458.23	0 ±	0

[a]Means were based upon 6 Ponar grab samples along eastern edge of Big Lake on 9 July 1974. Significant differences were tested using the Wilcoxon Rank Sum statistic, and levels of significance (for both numbers and weights) are indicated to left of taxa; * = $P < 0.05$, ** = $P < 0.01$.

Much of the more erosional side-channel habitat in Pool 26 is also sandy and depauperate, but contained somewhat higher densities (<1000 m^{-2}). Those side channels containing coarse sand and cobble substrates supported a fauna dominated by hydropsychids, especially *Potamyia flava* (Anderson and Day, 1986; Seagle et al., 1982). In Pool 20, the main-channel habitat in the tailwaters of Lock and Dam 19 contained cobble and supported another hydropsychid-dominated assemblage (Teska, 1979, as cited in Jahn and Anderson, 1986).

Chironomidae and Oligochaeta dominated macroinvertebrate assemblages

TABLE 1.18. *Mean Density (number m^{-2}) of Late Winter Benthic Macroinvertebrates in Selected Habitats from the Middle and Upper Reaches of Pool 13, Upper Mississippi River, February 26 to March 6, 1983*

	Habitat[a]					
	TW	MC	MCB	SC	Sl	L
Nematoda						
Total	194	161	213	182	1913	456
Oligochaeta						
Total	105	1023	1797	1500	5234	2006
Mollusca						
Gastropoda	1	7	0	0	11	0
Sphaeriidae	23	54	0	43	52	295
Unionidae	3	1	1	0	0	0
Crustacea						
Amphipoda	40	2	0	4	2	17
Isopoda	2	0	0	0	0	0
Ostracoda	12	0	6	164	252	775
Ephemeroptera						
Hexagenia	2	1	142	231	402	66
Other Ephemeroptera	1	1	0	4	0	0
Trichoptera						
Cheumatopsyche	61	56	5	0	7	0
Hydropsyche	4	12	0	0	0	0
Potamyia	179	36	5	0	7	0
Other Trichoptera	1	0	1	0	0	39
Diptera						
Ceratopogonidae	14	8	90	591	644	841
Chironomidae	122	166	5000	1024	766	2639
Other Diptera	0	0	1	43	0	25
Other invertebrates						
Insects	8	6	2	2	33	10
Noninsects	5	32	1	38	11	0
Total density	777	1566	7264	3822	9318	7169

Source: After Herbert et al. (1984).

[a]TW, tailwaters; MC, main channel; MCB, main-channel border; SC, side channel; Sl, slough; L, floodplain lake.

in the sandy side- and main-channel border habitats in the upper reaches of Pool 26. In the lower reaches of Pool 26, increased silt deposition (some of it from the turbid Illinois River) results in an increased abundance, primarily through increases in oligochaetes and *Hexagenia* spp. (Anderson and Day, 1986; Seagle et al., 1982).

Comparison of two off-channel sites in Pools 20 and 21 suggests the importance of substrates and/or currents in macroinvertebrate abundance. Buzzard Slough is a side channel with relatively fast currents (32 cm s^{-1}) located in Pool 20. Substrates consist of fine to coarse sand in midchannel and mud mixed with fine sand and detritus along the margins. Cottonwood Slough is a sluggish slough located in Pool 21. It has a mean summer current velocity of only 7

TABLE 1.19. *Density (number m^{-2}) of Benthic Macroinvertebrates from the Swift (32 cm s^{-1}) Buzzard Slough (Pool 20) and the Sluggish (7 cm s^{-1}) Cottonwood Slough (Pool 21), Upper Mississippi River, 1978*

	Buzzard Slough			Cottonwood Slough		
	June	July	Aug.	June	July	Aug.
Oligochaeta	785	917	581	1248	569	457
Hexagenia	2	0	781	135[a]	17	670
Chironomidae	226	161	520	263	100	424
Other	331	535	179	63	12	119
Total density	1670	1344	1613	2061	1709	698

Source: After Neuswanger et al. (1982).
[a]Significant difference between sites.

cm s^{-1} and muddy substrates. Oligochaeta, Chironomidae, and *Hexagenia* were dominant taxons in both sites, but significantly greater density and/or biomass for all three taxons were recorded in Cottonwood Slough during at least one of the three sample periods. Moreover, there was a nonsignificant increase in the combined abundance of other taxons in Buzzard Slough. Perhaps most important, however, is that although August densities of *Hexagenia* were high for both sites, *Hexagenia* biomass was high only in Cottonwood Slough (Neuswanger et al., 1982) (Tables 1.19 and 1.20).

Several characteristics of the benthic macroinvertebrate fauna are common for all these pools. Abundance tends to be low in sandy sites, whether they are located in the main channel, side channel, or main-channel border. Low abundance in these sandy sites is probably a consequence of the shifting sand (Anderson and Day, 1986). Where coarser, and presumably more stable, substrates occur, macroinvertebrate abundance increases, largely through increases in Hydropsychidae. Abundance also increases substantially in the silt–clay substrates of sloughs, floodplain lakes, and macrophyte beds. However,

TABLE 1.20. *Standing Stocks (g m^{-2}) of Benthic Macroinvertebrates from the Swift (32 cm s^{-1}) Buzzard Slough (Pool 20) and the Sluggish (7 cm s^{-1}) Cottonwood Slough (Pool 21), Upper Mississippi River, 1978*

	Buzzard Slough			Cottonwood Slough		
	June	July	Aug.	June	July	Aug.
Oligochaeta	1.00	1.42	1.05	2.35[a]	1.58	1.82
Hexagenia	0.01	0.00	0.78	5.54[a]	0.11	2.78
Chrionomidae	0.07	0.03	0.19	0.28[a]	0.09[a]	0.43[a]
Other	0.36	0.72	0.26	0.05	0.00	0.10
Total biomass	1.44	2.17	2.28	8.22[a]	1.78	5.13[a]

Source: After Neuswanger et al. (1982).
[a]Significant difference between sites.

macroinvertebrate abundance is greatest in the silt–clay substrates of the main-channel border habitats located in the lower reaches of each pool. These highly productive main-channel border habitats were not present in the river prior to impoundment.

One of the more striking differences among pools in the Upper Mississippi River is the abundance of Sphaeriidae. It is extremely abundant in the downstream main-channel border habitats of Pools 8 and 19 and is also abundant in other channel border or backwater habitats in Pools 7, 8, and 9 (Anderson and Day, 1986; Claflin, 1973; Eckblad et al., 1977; Elstad, 1977; Gale, 1975; Jahn and Anderson, 1986). On the other hand, Sphaeriidae are not at all abundant in similar habitats from Pools 20, 21, and 26 (Anderson and Day, 1986; Jahn and Anderson, 1986; Neuswanger et al., 1982; Seagle et al., 1982). One possible explanation for the differences is the extent and proximity of macrophyte beds. Macrophyte stands are poorly developed in many of the lower pools, including Pools 20, 21, and 26, whereas, they are extensive in Pools 7, 8, 9, and 19 (Jahn and Anderson, 1986; Peck and Smart, 1986). The most abundant sphaerid, *Musculum transversum,* tends to be most abundant in those unvegetated main-channel border sites adjacent to macrophyte beds, which suggests that the beds supply an important source of trophic support (Grumbaugh et al., 1986).

Macroinvertebrate assemblages within macrophyte beds are considerably more diverse than those in other habitats. For instance, a total of 140 epiphytic taxons were collected from three submergent macrophyte species, *Ceratophyllum demersum, Vallisneria americana,* and *Myriophyllum spicatum,* sampled from Lake Onalaska, Pool 7. In another study in Lake Onalaska, a total of 131 taxons were collected on and underneath two emergent species, *Sparganium eurycarpum* and *Sagittaria latifolia,* and one floating-leafed species, *Nymphaea tuberosa* (Blitgen, 1981).

In Lake Onalaska, the mean standing stocks for epiphytic macroinvertebrates on *Sparganium eurycarpum, Sagittaria latifolia,* and *Nymphaea tuberosa* were 0.36, 0.32, and 0.26 g m^{-2}, respectively. Benthic standing stocks from within the macrophyte beds were consistently greater than those recorded on the plants. In addition, the mean standing crops within the beds exhibited a ranking that was the opposite of that recorded for the epiphytic samples. Benthic macroinvertebrates under *N. tuberosa* averaged 5.73 g m^{-2}, whereas those under *S. latifolia* and *S. eurycarpum* averaged 2.63 and 2.08 g m^{-2}, respectively. Benthic standing stocks for a nearby open-water (i.e., unvegetated) site averaged 6.06 g m^{-2}, but this mean includes winter and spring samples that were not included in the other benthic samples. Using only those samples collected concurrently with the benthic samples from the vegetated sites, the mean standing stock for the open-water site would be 4.83 g m^{-2}. Both epiphytic and benthic standing stocks were highly variable. Seasonal patterns are not evident with the epiphytic samples and with the benthic samples from the emergent beds, but benthic standing stocks underneath *N. tuberosa* tended to be lowest in spring and early summer, while those in the

TABLE 1.21.   *Standing Stock (g m^{-2}) for Epiphytic (P) and Benthic (B) Macroinvertebrates Taken from Aquatic Macrophyte Beds of* Sparganium eurycarpum, Sagittaria latifolia, *and* Nymphaea tuberosa, *and from a Nearby Open-Water Site in Lake Onalaska, Pool 7, Upper Mississippi River, 1976 and 1977*

	Sparganium		*Sagittaria*		*Nymphaea*		Open
	P	B	P	B	P	B	B
1976							
June 16	0.33	4.50	0.18	3.44	0.05	4.55	3.12
June 24	0.02	0.19	0.30	4.57	0.14	4.98	4.17
July 1	0.06	1.69	0.34	2.25	0.16	4.28	6.17
July 16	0.03	2.02	0.13	3.06	0.43	7.29	4.84
July 22	0.90	2.15	0.48	3.07	0.77	6.10	2.43
July 30	0.08	1.50	0.19	1.68	0.51	7.16	4.44
Aug. 5	0.07	1.41	0.08	1.51	0.24	6.40	2.74
Aug. 12	0.11	2.05	0.46	4.40	0.34	8.36	3.75
Aug. 19	0.09	2.46	0.21	1.58	0.12	6.82	3.70
Aug. 26	0.14	2.14	0.99	1.37	0.12	6.20	3.74
Sept. 3	0.10	1.17	0.25	1.36	0.09	4.88	3.22
Sept. 10	0.18	0.76	0.28	2.32	0.12	7.69	6.76
Sept. 17	0.87	1.56	0.51	2.42	0.26	5.19	5.93
Sept. 26	0.01	2.57	0.02	4.09	0.18	7.09	8.20
Oct. 1	—	2.74	—	1.01	—	4.48	6.45
Oct. 15	—	1.94	—	2.81	—	5.58	12.38
Oct. 29	—	2.74	—	2.68	—	10.99	8.96
Nov. 12	—	5.61	—	3.98	—	5.06	10.83
Nov. 26	—	—	—	—	—	—	8.96
Dec. 10	—	—	—	—	—	—	8.04
1977							
Jan. 7	—	—	—	—	—	—	4.92
Feb. 4	—	—	—	—	—	—	10.92
Mar. 4	—	—	—	—	—	—	5.94
Apr. 1	—	—	—	—	—	—	14.07
Apr. 29	—	—	—	—	—	—	7.79
May 27	—	—	—	—	—	—	6.48
June 11–12	0.07	1.93	0.32	1.48	0.09	4.02	9.22
June 18	0.19	2.04	0.41	3.37	0.11	3.69	2.94
June 25	0.71	0.50	0.13	1.83	0.66	3.37	2.14
July 2	0.86	3.02	0.34	2.72	0.26	3.38	2.21
July 9	0.31	1.27	0.44	6.56	0.31	4.33	2.31

Source: After Blitgen (1981).

open-water site were generally low during early and midsummer and high during autumn, winter, and spring (Blitgen, 1981) (Table 1.21).

Mean epiphytic macroinvertebrate densities on *Sparganium eurycarpum, Sagittaria latifolia,* and *Nymphaea tuberosa* were 137, 217, and 500 m^{-2}, respectively. The corresponding mean benthic densities were 1126, 1161, and 1516 m^{-2}, respectively. The mean benthic density for the open-water site was 1679 m^{-2}, but it would be 1588 m^{-2} if the winter-through-midspring samples

TABLE 1.22.   *Densities (number m^{-2}) for Epiphytic (P) and Benthic (B) Macroinvertebrates Taken from Aquatic Macrophyte Beds of* Sparganium eurycarpum, Sagittaria latifolia, *and* Nymphaea tuberosa, *and from a Nearby Open-Water Site in Lake Onalaska, Pool 7, Upper Mississippi River, 1976 and 1977*

	Sparganium		Sagittaria		Nymphaea		Open
	P	B	P	B	P	B	B
1976							
June 16	219	1951	246	1326	53	940	729
June 24	107	1531	83	2270	107	1280	1145
July 1	172	1037	98	713	184	711	999
July 16	133	1512	115	2158	527	2491	1176
July 22	176	2832	109	2124	954	2160	863
July 30	158	1593	272	1278	956	1729	1187
Aug. 5	96	944	117	908	517	1123	1226
Aug. 12	203	1044	412	1221	463	2146	1263
Aug. 19	193	677	257	1139	448	2451	1282
Aug. 26	160	782	656	828	499	1869	1095
Sept. 3	96	1796	238	575	518	1729	977
Sept. 10	222	517	219	1304	667	1275	1106
Sept. 17	217	711	463	1230	911	1128	1333
Sept. 26	38	1796	48	1962	811	2334	2596
Oct. 1	—	1238	—	722	—	1800	2117
Oct. 15	—	773	—	934	—	1707	3066
Oct. 29	—	799	—	949	—	2175	4095
Nov. 12	—	1464	—	1102	—	1562	5206
Nov. 26	—	—	—	—	—	—	2079
Dec. 10	—	—	—	—	—	—	2124
1977							
Jan. 7	—	—	—	—	—	—	704
Feb. 4	—	—	—	—	—	—	1935
Mar. 4	—	—	—	—	—	—	3229
Apr. 1	—	—	—	—	—	—	2386
Apr. 29	—	—	—	—	—	—	1555
May 27	—	—	—	—	—	—	1492
June 11–12	90	331	145	243	188	375	1964
June 18	48	458	174	739	183	346	932
June 25	50	184	131	744	226	558	503
July 2	107	1123	126	994	546	1121	728
July 9	109	808	210	1323	737	1848	946

Source: After Blitgen (1981).

were excluded. Densities were variable at all sites, but late spring and early summer densities tended to be relatively high in the benthic samples under *S. eurycarpum* and *S. latifolia,* while densities on and underneath *N. tuberosa* tended to be lower in late spring. Benthic densities in the open-water site tended to be higher from autumn through midspring than during the growing season (Blitgen, 1981) (Table 1.22).

The benthic and epiphytic samples were dominated numerically by Oligo-

TABLE 1.23.   *Total Number of Epiphytic (P) and Benthic (B) Macroinvertebrates Collected in Aquatic Macrophyte Beds of* Sparganium eurycarpum, Sagittaria latifolia, *and* Nymphaea tuberosa, *and in a Nearby Open-Water Site in Lake Onalaska, Pool 7, Upper Mississippi River, 1976 and 1977*

	Sparganium		*Sagittaria*		*Nymphaea*		Open
	P	B	P	B	P	B	B
Turbellaria							
Total	15	15	13	40	89	54	351
Nematoda							
Total	24	107	41	184	7	87	209
Oligochaeta							
Total	481	7,108	80	6,333	450	6,207	6,326
Hirudinea							
Helobdella elongata	21	531	59	624	2	1,275	81
H. stagnalis	358	1,761	873	2,634	195	0	580
Other Hirudinea	37	59	139	81	91	285	98
Gastropoda							
Amnicola spp.	2	23	4	35	189	856	4,080
Gyraulus spp.	30	86	23	119	40	23	90
Physa spp.	16	89	35	100	189	16	354
Valvata spp.	1	3	0	0	1	175	1,314
Other Gastropoda	11	15	16	10	6	163	162
Bivalvia							
Sphaeriidae	5	623	3	394	0	574	1,649
Unionidae	0	1	0	0	0	0	0
Hydracarina							
Total	4	5	8	4	150	20	93
Isopoda							
Asellus spp.	138	1,671	412	2,090	12	645	3,205
Amphipoda							
Gammarus spp.	0	5	0	9	0	0	0
Hyalella azteca	90	781	152	1,297	1,065	2,084	7,373
Odonata							
Total	0	6	2	2	28	32	164
Hemiptera							
Total	3	28	2	48	89	22	18
Coleoptera							
Total	31	60	24	76	28	91	41
Trichoptera							
Total	3	17	16	36	304	572	1,612
Lepidoptera							
Pyralidae	1	20	1	51	1,126	10	38
Diptera							
Palpomyia spp.	120	38	253	24	135	249	227
Chironomus spp.	3	104	4	246	6	3,873	852
Dicrotendipes spp.	21	125	62	200	36	182	2,649
Einfeldia spp.	0	1	0	6	0	618	732
Endochironomus spp.	17	61	12	43	77	103	355
Lauterborniella spp.	33	83	41	200	3	91	178
Polypedilum spp.	92	129	44	68	970	103	99
Procladius spp.	0	81	2	87	1	316	504

TABLE 1.23. *(Continued)*

	Sparganium		*Sagittaria*		*Nymphaea*		Open
	P	B	P	B	P	B	B
Diptera (cont.)							
Tanytarsus spp.	3	80	1	55	0	82	582
Other Chironomidae	6	86	67	210	151	1,629	910
Hexatoma spp.	0	307	0	215	0	12	0
Other Diptera	6	170	10	119	56	10	14
Other							
Total	3	22	3	14	7	18	38
Total macroinvertebrates	1,575	14,301	2,401	15,654	5,503	20,069	34,297

Source: After Blitgen (1981).

chaeta, Hirudinea, Gastropoda, Sphaeriidae, *Asellus* spp., *Hyalella azteca,* Ceratopogonidae, and Chironomidae. In general, those taxons that were dominant in the benthic samples were also dominant in the corresponding epiphytic samples. However, some abundant taxons, including Oligochaeta, Sphaeriidae, several Chironomidae, and *Hexatoma* spp. (Diptera: Tipulidae), were collected primarily in benthic samples. In fact, most taxons that were collected on the plants were also collected underneath them. Pyralidae (primarily *Nymphula* spp.) was the only abundant taxon that was collected primarily on plants; it occurred in high densities on *Nymphaea tuberosa* during autumn (Blitgen, 1981) (Table 1.23).

Total densities and the densities of many taxons increased from the shallow-water *Sparganium eurycarpum* bed to the deeper-water *Nymphaea tuberosa* bed and/or the open-water site. This increase was evident for *Amnicola* spp., *Valvata* spp., Sphaeriidae, *Hyalella azteca,* Odonata, Trichoptera, and a number of Chironomidae. A number of others, including Nematoda, *Oligochaeta,* and *Asellus* spp., exhibited patterns that appeared to be independent of depth or presence of macrophytes. Some, including *Helobdella elongata* and *H. stagnalis,* were most abundant within the macrophyte beds. *Hexatoma* spp. were collected primarily in benthic samples under *S. eurycarpum* and *Sagittaria latifolia* (Table 1.23).

Hyalella azteca was the most abundant taxon collected on three submergent macrophyte species (*Ceratophyllum demersum, Vallisneria americana,* and *Myriophyllum spicatum*) sampled from Lake Onalaska, Pool 7. Gastropoda, Odonata, Hemiptera, Trichoptera, and Chironomidae were common to abundant. Gastropoda were dominated by *Physa* spp., *Gyraulus* spp., and *Amnicola* spp. Odonata dominated by *Enallagma* sp., Corixidae, *Microvelia,* and *Plea striola* were the most common hemipterans. *Leptocerus americanus, Oecetis cinerascens, Nectopsyche* spp., *Hydroptila* spp., *Orthotrichia* spp., *Oxyethira* spp., and Hydropsychidae were the more common trichopterans. Chironomidae were dominated by *Rheotanytarsus exiguus* group, *Paratanytarsus* sp., *Endochironomus nigracans,* and *Cricotopus sylvestrus* group.

Macroinvertebrates associated with macrophyte beds have also been studied in other pools of the Upper Mississippi River. In the vegetated main-channel border habitat of Pool 19, biomass and diversity were relatively high in the submergent and floating macrophyte zones but tended to decline in the emergent zone, probably because of the increased organic matter and oxygen demand as well as the increasingly ephemeral quality of the habitat. Several taxons were associated with one or two of the three macrophyte zones. For example, *Asellus* was concentrated in the emergent zone (i.e., with *Sagittaria latifolia*), whereas others, such as *Sigara* (Hemiptera) and *Physa*, were most common in floating or submerged vegetation (Anderson and Day, 1986). Several nematode taxons also varied within the macrophyte beds of Pool 19. Of the three most abundant taxons, *Ironus* was concentrated in the emergent and floating zone, while *Plectus* was most abundant in the submergent zone; the other abundant taxon, *Tobrilus*, was ubiquitous (Jahn and Anderson, 1986). Elsewhere in Pool 19, *Hyalella azteca*, *Physa anatina*, *Amnicola lustrica*, *Helisoma trivolvis*, and *Valvata tricarinata* were associated with submergent macrophytes (Gale, 1975; Sparks, 1980).

Benthic samples from within *Sagittaria* beds in Big Lake, Pool 9, yielded relatively high densities and/or standing crops of *Hyalella azteca*, *Gyraulus parvus*, and *Physa integra* (Eckblad et al., 1977). In Pool 8, high densities of *Physa*, *Amnicola*, and *Asellus* were associated with submergent macrophytes, especially *Ceratophyllum demersum* and *Vallisneria americana*. Although much less common, *Siphlonurus* (Ephemeroptera) was also associated with submergent macrophytes, while both *Nymphula* and *Paraponyx* (Lepidoptera) were found underneath the leaves of floating-leafed Nymphaeaceae (Elstad, 1977).

The seasonal abundance of macroinvertebrates within and adjacent to macrophyte beds would be expected to vary with seasonal changes in the macrophyte beds. Such a relationship is suggested by the seasonality of benthic macroinvertebrates in Lake Onalaska. Although highly variable, benthic biomass and density for the open-water site tended to be higher following macrophyte senescence in September than during the height of the growing season (Tables 1.21 and 1.22). These autumn maxima were largely the result of autumn increases in Oligochaeta, *Hyalella azteca*, and Chironomidae. For another abundant taxon, *Asellus* spp., benthic populations within the macrophyte beds were highest during plant senescence, while populations in the open-water site were highest during winter and early spring (Blitgen, 1981). A similar pattern was observed in an unvegetated backwater site in Pool 19. Macroinvertebrate abundance at this site, which was adjacent to some submerged macrophyte beds, was relatively high in late spring, low throughout summer, and again relatively high in autumn following plant senescence. The autumn increases were largely the result of the movement of *Valvata tricarinata*, *Amnicola lustrica*, *H. azteca*, and Chironomidae from the macrophytes to the sediments (Gale, 1975).

The aufwuchs, or hard substrate habitat, supports a macroinvertebrate fauna considerably different from that encountered in most benthic and epiphytic habitats. It is also very productive. For example, next to *Musculum transversum* and *Hexagenia* spp., the most abundant large-bodied macroinvertebrate in Pool 19 is *Hydropsyche orris*. This species can be found in benthic sites, where cobble substrates are available, such as in the tailwaters of Lock and Dam 18. However, it will occur in dense mats of up to 10,000 m^{-2} on any solid substrate in flowing water. These mats may become so dense that they can cause fouling of mooring lines and fish nets (Jahn and Anderson, 1986). Relative to sand, silt, clay, and macrophytes, hard substrates are infrequent in the Upper Mississippi River and are largely limited to the more erosional channels, wing dams, and riprap. Prior to the navigation improvements, snags would have also added significantly to the availability of hard substrates.

High densities and standing crops have been reported for artificial substrates throughout the Upper Mississippi River. In Pool 26, mean densities for multiplate and basket samplers were 12,566 and 15,040 m^{-2}, respectively. *Potamyia flava* and *Hydropsyche orris* accounted for 80 to 90% of the density, while Chironomidae accounted for approximately 10% (Seagle et al., 1982). Mean densities for multiplate and basket samplers placed adjacent to wing dams in Pool 13 were 6739 and 20,029 m^{-2}, respectively. Mean standing crops were 39.8 and 77.5 g m^{-2}, respectively. Hydropsychidae accounted for 88 to 91% of the density and 86 to 91% of the biomass; *P. flava* and *Cheumatopsyche* sp. were the most abundant hydropsychids, and *Hydropsyche* was common. Other taxa included Oligochaeta, Gastropoda, Sphaeriidae, Unionidae, *Gomphus* (Odonata), Ceratopogonidae, and Chironomidae (Hall, 1982).

In Pool 5A, macroinvertebrates colonizing wing dams were generally more abundant than those colonizing riprap banks. Within the wing dam habitat, abundance was greater in the microhabitats with faster current than in those with reduced currents, but differences in abundance were not associated with depth or extent of periphyton growth (Lewis, 1984). The influence of current velocities is suggested in the comparison of artificial substrate samples collected in Buzzard Slough (Pool 20) and Cottonwood Slough (Pool 21). From June through August, mean densities from Buzzard Slough, which had a mean summer current velocity of 32 cm s^{-1}, ranged from 2014 to 5014 m^{-2}, whereas mean densities from Cottonwood Slough, which averaged 7 cm s^{-1}, ranged from 181 to 368 m^{-2}. The differences for mean standing stocks, which ranged from 6.94 to 8.99 g m^{-2} in Buzzard Slough and 0.35 to 0.83 g m^{-2} in Cottonwood Slough, were even greater. Trichoptera, Ephemeroptera, and Chironomidae were common to abundant on the artificial substrates; most of the mayfly taxons (i.e., *Stenonema, Ameletus, Caenis,* and *Isonychia*) were uncommon to absent in most benthic samples. Hydropsychidae accounted for 47 to 75% of the density and 74 to 84% of the biomass in the more productive Buzzard Slough. On the other hand, Hydropsychidae and Ephemeroptera were considerably less abundant in Cottonwood Slough, which was usually dominated by Chironomidae (Neuswanger et al., 1982) (Tables 1.24 and 1.25).

Macroinvertebrate drift in the Upper Mississippi River includes both

TABLE 1.24.   *Density (number m^{-2}) of Aufwuchs Macroinvertebrates from the Swift (32 cm s^{-1}) Buzzard Slough (Pool 20) and the Sluggish (7 cm s^{-1}) Cottonwood Slough (Pool 21), Upper Mississippi River, 1978[a]*

	Buzzard Slough			Cottonwood Slough		
	June	July	Aug.	June	July	Aug.
Odonata						
Argia	+	9[b]	26	0	4	24
Ephemeroptera						
Ameletus	0	102[b]	49[b]	0	2	0
Caenis	688[b]	295[b]	388[b]	2	35	7
Hexagenia	1	0	76	3	1	37
Isonychia	49[b]	172[b]	7[b]	0	3	0
Stenonema	104[b]	174[b]	177[b]	0	6	4
Trichoptera						
Hydropsychidae	2441[b]	3785[b]	944[b]	+	68	+
Cyrnellus	13[b]	84[b]	65	0	31	145[b]
Neureclypsis	10[b]	24[b]	10[b]	+	4	0
Pupae	105[b]	26[b]	58[b]	0	+	1
Diptera						
Chironomidae	134	325[b]	155	155	52	137
Other Diptera	26	47	59	21	8	13
Total density	3571[b]	5043[b]	2014[b]	181	214	368

Source: After Neuswanger et al. (1982).
[a]+ = present (density not determined).
[b]Significant difference between sites.

benthic and aufwuchs taxons and was shown to vary with habitat, time of day, and depth. Drift densities in the unvegetated main-channel border of Pool 19 generally ranged between 2.5 and 3.0 L^{-1} (2500 and 3000 m^{-3}), whereas those in the main channel ranged between 1.5 and 2.0 L^{-1} (1500 and 2000 m^{-3}); little to no drift was collected in the macrophyte beds. Higher drift densities in the main-channel border are believed to be the result of entrainment from the productive benthos (Jahn and Anderson, 1986). Differences in drift densities between main channel and main-channel border habitats were not as pronounced in Pool 26. This is surprising since the border samples were taken downstream from wing dams. Drift densities in the main channel and below the wing dam from a lower pool site averaged 4.1 and 4.4 m^{-3}, respectively, while those from a middle pool site ranged from 7.8 to 9.0 m^{-3}, respectively. However, there were taxonomic differences between the two habitats. Ephemeroptera (*Hexagenia limbata, Pentagenia vittigera, Baetis* sp., and *Caenis* sp.) accounted for 43% of the main-channel drift, while Diptera (primarily *Chaoborus* sp.) accounted for 35% and Trichoptera (*Hydropsyche orris* and *Potamyia flava*) accounted for only 5%. Diptera (57%) dominated wing dam samples, while Ephemeroptera accounted for 24% and Trichoptera accounted for 11% (Seagle et al., 1982).

Other studies report that backwater drift densities are substantially higher

TABLE 1.25. *Standing Stocks (g m^{-2}) of Aufwuchs Macroinvertebrates from the Swift (32 cm s^{-1}) Buzzard Slough (Pool 20) and the Sluggish (7 cm s^{-1}) Cottonwood Slough (Pool 21), Upper Mississippi River, 1978*

	Buzzard Slough			Cottonwood Slough		
	June	July	Aug.	June	July	Aug.
Odonata						
Argia	0.02	0.01	0.04	0.00	<0.01	0.13[a]
Ephemeroptera						
Ameletus	0.00	0.06[a]	0.09[a]	0.00	<0.01	0.00
Caenis	0.32[a]	0.08[a]	0.31[a]	<0.01	0.02	0.01
Hexagenia	<0.01	0.00	0.04	0.01	<0.01	0.09
Isonychia	0.45[a]	0.37[a]	0.09[a]	0.00	<0.01	0.00
Stenonema	0.05[a]	0.09[a]	0.22[a]	0.00	0.01	0.01
Trichoptera						
Cyrnellus	0.02[a]	0.07	0.19	0.00	0.05	0.25
Neureclypsis	0.04[a]	0.07[a]	0.06[a]	<0.01	0.01	0.00
Hydropsychidae	7.14[a]	5.83[a]	5.29[a]	<0.01	0.07	<0.01
Pupae	0.79[a]	0.20[a]	0.61[a]	0.00	<0.01	<0.01
Diptera						
Chironomidae	0.06	0.11[a]	0.10	0.18[a]	0.03	0.15
Other Diptera	0.11	0.06	0.08	0.64	0.16	0.08
Total biomass	8.99[a]	6.94[a]	7.11[a]	0.83	0.35	0.72

Source: After Neuswanger et al. (1982).
[a]Significant difference between sites.

than those in the main channel. The taxonomic composition is also different. Moreover, there is some indication that backwaters may provide an important source of drifters for the main channel. In Pool 9, the mean drift density for two backwater sites was 771.1 per 100 m^3, whereas drift densities in the main-channel sites upstream from these backwater inflows averaged 74.0 per 100 m^3 and those below the backwater inflows averaged 146.5 per 100 m^3. Increases in the drift densities of the downstream main-channel samples were primarily the result of increases in taxons that were most abundant in the backwaters (i.e., *Hydra, Hexagenia,* Chironomidae, and fish fry) (Eckblad et al., 1984) (Table 1.26). Similar results were obtained from a study of main-channel and backwater drift in Pool 13. The mean surface drift density from three backwater sites was 2087.8 per 100 m^3, while the mean drift densities were 849.4 and 900.0 per 100 m^3 for the upstream and downstream main-channel sites, respectively. However, the influence of backwater export on main-channel drift is less clear (Shaeffer and Nickum, 1986a) (Table 1.27).

Given the overriding influence of habitat type on macroinvertebrate assemblages in the Upper Mississippi River, differences in overall productivity would be expected to vary considerably among pools. This was the case in the comparisons of the benthos from Pool 19 with that of Pool 21 (Jahn and Anderson, 1986) and of Pool 19 with Pool 26 (Anderson and Day, 1986). The

TABLE 1.26.   *Mean Macroinvertebrate Drift Densities (number per 100 m³) for Two Backwater Sites and Their Respective Upstream and Downstream Main-Channel Sites in Pool 9, Upper Mississippi River, June and July 1983*

	Upstream Main Channel	Backwater	Downstream Main Channel
Cnideria			
Hydra sp.	9.0	326.0	35.5
Oligochaeta			
Total	0.7	10.6	1.1
Amphipoda			
Hyalella azteca	31.0	77.5	28.9
Ephemeroptera			
Hexagenia spp.	4.1	60.0	13.3
Other Ephemeroptera	1.7	8.1	1.6
Hemiptera			
Corixidae	0.9	63.4	2.4
Coleoptera			
Stenelmis sp.	1.8	6.8	6.7
Trichoptera			
Hydropsychidae	2.1	4.6	1.1
Nectopsyche sp.	0.1	0.7	0.1
Diptera			
Ceratopogonidae	0.2	5.2	0.5
Chaoborus sp.	2.2	9.9	1.1
Chironomidae	10.0	113.7	36.6
Other			
Fish fry	2.7	43.1	12.0
Other invertebrates	7.5	44.1	5.9
Total drift density	74.0	771.1	146.5

Source: After Eckblad et al. (1984).

presence of extensive macrophyte beds and the predominance of the extremely productive muddy and shallow main-channel border habitat contributed to substantially greater diversity and productivity of macroinvertebrates in Pool 19. In contrast, production and diversity in Pools 20 and 26 were largely limited by the prevalence of shifting sand in the main channel and main-channel border habitats (Anderson and Day, 1986; Jahn and Anderson, 1986). In fact, benthic abundance in Pool 26 was higher below the confluence of the silt-laden Illinois River, apparently because the imported silt helped stabilize the sandy substrates (Seagle et al., 1982).

Comparisons between Pool 19 and the pools flowing through the Driftless Area were not found in the literature, but the prevalence of productive backwater and main-channel border habitats as well as the expansive macrophyte beds suggest that these pools are also substantially more productive than many of the more southerly pools. Significantly, the most productive habitats of the Upper Mississippi River (i.e., main-channel borders, macrophyte beds, floodplain lakes, and sloughs) are those that were either created or greatly

TABLE 1.27. *Mean Surface Macroinvertebrate Drift Densities (number per 100 m³) from Three Backwater Sites and Their Respective Upstream and Downstream Main Channel Sites in Pool 13, Upper Mississippi River, April–August 1983*

	Upstream Main Channel	Backwater	Downstream Main Channel
Amphipoda			
Hyalella azteca	81.7	75.2	72.7
Ephemeroptera			
Baetis sp.	112.4	5.6	84.7
Ephoron sp.	12.1	7.4	13.1
Hexagenia spp.	120.2	75.2	273.5
Isonychia spp.	16.2	4.0	19.3
Stenonema spp.	9.1	4.1	9.5
Ephemerellidae	19.4	43.1	15.5
Other Ephemeroptera	5.9	3.7	4.4
Hemiptera			
Corixidae	23.9	85.6	20.8
Coleoptera			
Elmidae	6.9	3.6	8.5
Other Coleoptera	0.6	6.7	2.3
Trichoptera			
Cheumatopsyche spp.	13.5	4.4	13.8
Hydropsyche sp.	43.6	19.0	28.2
Potamyia flava	238.2	87.2	155.4
Other Hydropsychidae	9.5	4.0	33.3
Leptocerus sp.	2.7	20.0	8.0
Diptera			
Ceratopogonidae	3.3	28.1	6.7
Chaoboridae	72.7	1176.6	49.9
Chironomidae	12.3	65.1	19.0
Other Diptera	39.9	229.6	57.0
Other			
Total	4.4	8.8	2.1
Total drift density	849.4	2007.8	900.0

Source: After Shaeffer and Nickum (1986a).

enlarged by impoundment (Chen and Simmons, 1986; Fremling and Claflin, 1984; Peck and Smart, 1986).

Comparisons of postimpoundment and preimpoundment productivity are frustrated by the paucity of preimpoundment studies. Presumably, the upper third of a navigation pool is most representative of the preimpounded river (Fremling and Claflin, 1984; Rasmussen, 1979b). Given this, macroinvertebrate production would be concentrated in backwater sloughs, floodplain lakes, and along the vegetated margins of sandy main and side channels. These habitats would not be as extensive as those in the impounded river, but they would still have been relatively well developed. Minimum pool elevations may have enhanced summer productivity in many backwaters by reducing seasonal desiccation, but they have also promoted increased eutrophication (Fremling and Claflin, 1984). The loss of snag habitat and the construction of wing dams have certainly influenced the aufwuchs in important but poorly understood ways. Similarly, the effects of changes in the flooding regime and the extent of floodplain inundation are poorly understood but are probably significant. In general, however, it is believed that invertebrate diversity has increased following the completion of the navigation pools (Smart et al., 1986).

Changes in Habitats and Fauna. Changes in habitat composition and macroinvertebrate populations continued well after completion of the navigation pools. Pool 19 is 20 to 25 years older than the other pools and has been regarded as an example of what is in store for the other navigation pools (Grumbaugh and Anderson, 1989). Net sedimentation has resulted in the creation of an expansive, shallow main-channel border habitat dominated by silt–clay substrates. This new habitat supported huge increases in the populations of burrowing *Hexagenia* spp. (Fremling, 1970). By the late 1960s, sedimentation raised the nearshore portion of the main-channel border bottom to within the 1-m photic zone, thereby promoting significant macrophyte production. This autochthonous production has in turn supported the very high densities ($100,000$ m^{-2}) of *Musculum transversum* reported by Gale (1975) (Junk et al., 1989). Encroachment of the macrophyte beds into the unvegetated main-channel border habitat has facilitated the partial replacement of *M. transversum* with *Sphaerium striatinum* in the submerged macrophyte zone. A dramatic decline in *M. transversum* populations occurred during the 1976 and 1977 drought, possibly because of increased concentrations of an assortment of toxics. In some locations, populations remained depressed, albeit still productive, well after the end of the drought, as a result of accelerating encroachment by macrophytes. In one site, for example, *M. transversum* accounted for 90% of the predrought (summer) benthic biomass, but since 1978 it has accounted for approximately half, while *S. striatinum,* leeches, gastropods, and chironomids have increased (Sparks et al., 1990).

Successional changes in the northerly pools of the Driftless Area would be expected to differ somewhat from those that have occurred in Pool 19. Sedimentation is filling in many of the more productive backwaters and side channels. Marshes are displacing aquatic macrophyte beds and open habitats. In midpool reaches, marsh vegetation is being replaced by terrestrial vegetation (Smart et al., 1986). Recent investigations in Pool 8 indicate that macroinvertebrate diversity and productivity has declined (Claflin, personal communication).

Freshwater Mussel (Unionidae) Production

The Unionidae (freshwater mussels) are a commercially and historically important component of the invertebrate fauna of the Upper Mississippi River. In addition, the effects of anthropogenic influences on the unionid productivity and diversity are better understood than they are for other macroinvertebrates. In short, the unionids are substantially less productive and considerably less diverse than they were 100 years ago (Fuller, 1980a).

Large-scale commercial exploitation of this diverse and productive fauna started in 1891 at a pearl button factory in Muscatine, Iowa. The industry expanded rapidly and within 10 years the mussel beds near Muscatine were severely depleted. Consequently, harvesting expanded to other reaches of the Upper Mississippi River, but these areas also experienced severe overharvesting by 1920. By the mid-1920s, the majority of mussel shells supplied to the factories along the river were imported from outside the basin. The industry collapsed in the 1940s with the introduction of plastics (UMRCC, 1990).

In addition to the devastation inflicted by the pearl button fishery, the fauna has been decimated by navigation projects (i.e., snagging, rapids excavation, wing dams, impoundments, and dredging), pollution, siltation, gravel mining, and the introduction of the asiatic clam, *Corbicula fluminea*. Since the mid-1960s, the fauna has been subjected to another commercial fishery, in which the shell material is used for the Japanese cultured pearl industry. The effects of this second, regulated fishery are uncertain (Fuller, 1980a; Latendresse, 1980; UMRCC, 1990).

Historical surveys indicate that there has been a decline in the productivity and diversity of the unionid fauna in the Upper Mississippi River. Of the 50 species groups that have been recorded in the river, 48 had been recorded prior to the first extensive efforts at navigation improvements, and only 39 had been recorded since 1966 (Fuller, 1980a; Perry, 1979). An extensive preimpoundment survey (Ellis, 1931) yielded only 38 taxons (van der Schalie and van der Schalie, 1950, as cited in Fuller, 1980a), which indicates that much of the faunal loss had occurred since the turn of the century, while faunal loss since then has not been as drastic. However, substantial changes in geographic distributions and community composition have occurred since the 1930 and 1931 survey (Fuller, 1980a). This is evident when one compares the diversity of the 1930 and 1931 survey with that of later surveys.

In the 1930 and 1931 survey, two species, *Lampsilis teres* and *Leptodea fragilis,* accounted for 13.8% and 10.1%, respectively, of the total collection. Of the remaining taxons, 16 accounted for 1.1 to 6.9% each, while the other 16 accounted for less than 1% each. Although this distribution could be considered as skewed toward the dominance of relatively few taxons—partly through a collection bias for *L. teres* and *L. fragilis*—it is considerably more even (i.e., more diverse) in its distribution of relative abundances than are later surveys. During a 1977 survey, for example, *Ablema plicata* (34.7%), *Truncilla donaciformis* (14.2%), and *Quadrula pustulosa* (9.1%) accounted for more than half of the total. Of the remaining 28 taxons, 17 accounted for 1.1 to 6.3% each and 14 accounted for less than 1% each (Fuller, 1980a). Similarly, *A. plicata* and *Megalonaias gigantea* accounted for 54.5% of the total collection during a 1975 collection of Pools 8, 9, and 10 (Coon et al., 1977).

During the heyday of the pearl button industry, the most sought-after species were *Elliptio dilatata, Fusconaia ebena, Obovaria olivaria, Ellipsaria lineolata, Potamilus capax,* and *Quadrula metanerva* (Perry, 1979). Of these, *P. capax* is either greatly reduced or extinct, *E. lineolata* is greatly reduced, and *Q. meta-*

nerva, which was probably never really common, is rare. *E. dilatata* is somewhat less common but has been geographically constricted. *F. ebena,* once accounting for 80% of the population in the great mussel beds, is now seriously endangered. Only *O. olivaria* is still common and widely distributed (Fuller, 1980a). *Ablema plicata, Fusconaia flava, Lampsilis ovata ventricosa, Megalonaias gigantea, Obliquaria reflexa, Obovaria olivaria, Proptera alata, P. laevissima, Quadrula nodulata, Q. pustulosa, Q. quadrula,* and *Truncilla donaciformis* were common to abundant species in several recent surveys conducted in a number of sites throughout the Upper Mississippi River (Coon et al., 1977; Fuller, 1980a; Havlik, 1983; Jahn and Anderson, 1986; Miller, 1988; Perry, 1979).

A variety of factors have contributed to the changes in abundance and distribution of these species. Overharvesting probably contributed to the range reduction of *Elliptio dilatata,* which was once a major component of the great mussel beds. The once abundant *Fusconaia ebena* also probably suffered major mortality in the pearl button fishery, but it is the exclusion of its dominant glochidiate host, the anadromous skipjack herring (*Alosa chrysochloris*), which has rendered it functionally extinct. On the other hand, the wide host range for *F. flava, Lampsilis ovata ventricosa,* and *Ablema plicata* has probably contributed to their success. Degraded water quality appears to have hindered *Lampsilis teres,* restricted the northern distribution of a number of other species, and contributed to the demise of a number of less common species. On the other hand, two widespread and abundant species, *A. plicata* and *Obliquaria reflexa,* appear to be particularly tolerant of pollution. Impoundment has favored at least one important genus, *Quadrula* (Fuller, 1980a).

The influence of habitat and water quality are evident in the recent distribution of unionids in the Upper Mississippi River. In a 1977 to 1979 survey of Pools 1 to 10, unionids were either absent or severely limited in Pools 1 and 2, uncommon in Pool 3 and Lake Pepin, rare in lower Pools 4, 5, and 5A, and increasingly abundant and diverse from Pool 6 through Pool 10 (Fuller, 1980a, b). The paucity of unionids in Pools 1 through 4 is attributable to municipal, agricultural, and industrial pollution from the Twin Cities and the Minnesota River subbasin. The poorly developed fauna in lower Pool 4 and Pools 5 and 5A is attributable to the predominance of unstable sandy substrates originating from the Chippewa River and to the detrimental effects of wing dams (Fuller, 1980a). Another survey, conducted from 1975 to 1979, in Pools 9 to 26 and in the free-flowing but channelized Middle Mississippi River indicated that many unionids are frequent in Pools 9 to 19, less frequent in Pools 20 to 26, and infrequent in the Middle Mississippi River (Perry, 1979) (Table 1.28). Other sources (e.g., Fuller, 1980a; Jahn and Anderson, 1986) have also reported that unionids are uncommon below Pool 19.

Fish Production

The fish fauna in the Upper Mississippi River is diverse. At least 135 species have been recorded in the river since the late nineteenth century, of which 106

TABLE 1.28. *Frequency (%) of Collection for Selected Freshwater Mussels (Unionidae) in a 1975–1979 Survey of Pools 9 to 26 in the Upper Mississippi River and in the Middle Mississippi River (MMR)*

Pools: Number of Collections:	9–13 10	14–18 35	19 9	20–26 14	MMR 12
Actinonais carinata	20	26	11	0	0
Amblema plicata	90	91	78	93	50
Anodonta grandis corpulenta	70	14	33	21	50
Ellipsaria lineolata	50	60	22	29	25
Elliptio dilatus	20	3	0	0	0
Fusconaia ebena	0	9	0	29	0
F. flava	80	83	78	57	0
Lampsilis ventricosa	60	69	44	36	0
Leptodea fragilis	50	66	33	36	67
Ligumia recta	50	34	0	21	0
Megalonais nervosa	70	40	22	36	17
Obliquaria reflexa	70	54	55	71	8
Obovaria olivaria	70	69	44	71	25
Potamilus alatus	60	37	22	43	25
P. capax	0	0	0	8	0
P. laevissimus	0	43	44	7	75
Quadrula metanerva	20	29	0	29	0
Q. nodulata	80	31	77	43	0
Q. pustulosa	90	86	66	79	17
Q. quadrula	70	69	66	79	8
Truncilla donaciformis	30	34	11	36	25
T. truncata	60	63	22	43	25

Source: After Perry (1979).

are considered to be members of the current fauna; 29 species are considered strays and/or have not been recorded in recent surveys. Gizzard shad (*Dorosoma cepedianum*), carp (*Cyprinus carpio*), emerald shiner (*Notropis atherinoides*), river shiner (*N. blennius*), bullhead minnow (*Pimephales vigilax*), and bluegill (*Lepomis macrochirus*) are consistently abundant throughout the Upper Mississippi River. Gars (*Lepisosteus* spp.), bowfin (*Amia calva*), mooneye (*Hiodon tergisus*), carpsuckers (*Carpiodes* spp.), buffalos (*Ictiobus* spp.), shorthead redhorse (*Moxostoma macrolepidotum*), channel catfish (*Ictalurus punctatus*), flathead catfish (*Pylodictis olivaris*), largemouth bass (*Micropterus salmoides*), crappie (*Pomoxis* spp.), sauger (*Stizostedion canadense*), walleye (*S. vitreum*), white bass (*Morone chrysops*), freshwater drum (*Aplodinotus grunniens*), and several cyprinids are common and often abundant throughout the river. A number of other taxons, including shovelnose sturgeon (*Scaphirhynchus platorynchus*) and paddlefish (*Polydon spathula*), can be locally abundant (Fremling et al., 1989; Rasmussen, 1979c; Van Vooren, 1983) (Table 1.29).

A number of species exhibit substantial longitudinal changes in abundance (Table 1.29). The Upper Mississippi River is within the southern limits of the

TABLE 1.29. *Distribution and Relative Abundance of Common to Abundant Fishes in Five Reaches of the Upper Mississippi River[a]*

	Pools				
	1–4	5–10	11–15	16–19	20–26
Petromyzontidae					
Ichthyomyzon castaneus	+	+	+	+	O
I. unicuspis	O	O	O	O	+
Acipenseridae					
Scaphirhynchus platorynchus	O	O	O	O	O
Polydontidae					
Polydon spathula	+	+	O	O	O
Lepisosteidae					
Lepisosteus osseus	C	C	C	C	C
L. platostomus	C	C	C	C	C
Amiidae					
Amia clava	C	C	C	C	C
Anguillidae					
Anguilla rostrata	O	O	+	+	O
Hiodontidae					
Hiodon alosoides	+	+	+	+	O
H. tergisus	C	C	C	C	O
Clupeidae					
Alosa chrysochloris	+	+	+	H	O
Dorosoma cepedianum	A	A	A	A	A
Catostomidae					
Carpiodes carpio	O	C	C	C	C
C. cyprinus	C	C	C	C	C
C. velifer	O	O	O	+	O
Catostomus commersoni	C	C	S	S	S
Ictiobus bubalus	O	C	C	C	C
I. cyprinellus	C	C	C	C	C
Minytrema melanops	O	C	O	+	−
Moxostoma anisurum	O	O	+	+	+
M. erythrurum	+	O	+	+	+
M. macrolepidotum	C	C	C	O	O
Cyprinidae					
Cyprinus carpio	A	A	A	A	A
Hybognanthus hankinsoni	+	O	−	−	−
Hybopsis aestivalis	C	C	C	C	C
H. gracilis	−	−	+	−	O
H. storeriana	C	C	C	C	C
Nocomis biguttatus	C	−	−	−	−
Notemigonus chrysoleucas	O	O	O	O	O
Notropis atherinoides	A	A	A	A	A
N. blennius	A	A	A	A	A
N. buchanani	H	H	+	C	C
N. cornutus	O	O	+	+	+
N. dorsalis	O	O	O	O	O
N. heterodon	O	−	−	−	−
N. hudsonius	C	C	C	C	C
N. lutrensis	−	−	+	C	C
N. nubilus	O	−	−	−	−
N. spilopterus	C	C	C	C	O
N. umbratilis	O	O	S	S	−
N. volucellus	O	O	−	−	−

TABLE 1.29. *(Continued)*

	Pools				
	1–4	5–10	11–15	16–19	20–26
Cyprinidae *(cont.)*					
Pimephales notatus	O	O	O	O	O
P. vigilax	A	A	A	A	A
Ictaluridae					
Ictalurus furcatus	H	–	H	H	O
I. melas	O	O	O	O	O
I. natalis	O	O	O	O	O
I. nebulosus	O	O	+	+	+
I. punctatus	C	C	C	C	C
Noturus flavus	H	+	+	+	O
N. gyrinus	O	O	O	+	+
Pylodictis olivaris	C	C	O	O	C
Esocidae					
Esox lucius	C	C	C	O	O
Percopsidae					
Percopsis omiscomaycus	O	O	+	+	+
Gadidae					
Lota lota	O	+	+	+	+
Cyprinodontidae					
Fundulus notatus	–	–	–	O	O
Poeciliidae					
Gambusia affinis	–	–	+	+	O
Atherinidae					
Labidesthes sicculus	C	C	C	O	O
Centrarchidae					
Ambloplites rupestris	C	C	+	+	+
Lepomis cyanellus	O	O	O	O	O
L. gibbosus	O	C	C	+	–
L. gulosus	H	+	+	O	O
L. humilis	O	O	C	C	C
L. macrochirus	A	A	A	A	A
Micropterus dolomieui	O	O	+	+	+
M. salmoides	C	C	C	C	C
Pomoxis annularis	C	C	C	C	C
P. nigromaculatus	C	C	C	C	C
Percidae					
Ammocrypta clara	O	O	O	O	O
Perca flavescens	C	C	O	O	H
Percina caprodes	C	C	C	O	O
P. shumardi	C	C	C	C	C
Stizostedion canadense	C	C	C	C	C
S. vitreum	C	C	C	C	O
Percithyidae					
Morone chrysops	C	C	C	C	C
M. mississippiensis	H	O	+	+	O
Sciaenidae					
Aplodinotus grunniens	C	C	C	C	A

Source: After Fremling et al. (1989), reproduced with permission of the Minister of Supply and Services, Canada 1996.

[a]A, abundant in all surveys; C, common to abundant in most surveys; O, may be locally abundant; +, uncommon or rare; S, probable strays; H, historical records (not recorded in the last 10 years); –, not found.

geographic ranges of several species, such as northern pike (*Esox lucius*), burbot (*Lota*), trout-perch (*Percopsis omiscomaycus*), and yellow perch (*Perca flavescens*), all of which are more abundant in the northern pools. Other, more widely distributed species, such as white sucker (*Catostomus commersoni*), rockbass (*Ambloplites rupestris*), and brook silverside (*Labidesthes sicculus*), are also more abundant in the northern pools, probably because of habitat availability, cooler temperatures, and/or reduced turbidity. Several species with more southerly distributions, such as warmouth (*Lepomis gulosus*) and orange-spotted sunfish (*L. humilis*), are more common in the southern pools (Fremling et al., 1989; Lee et al., 1980).

For some southern fishes, such as ghost shiner (*Notropis buchanani*), there has apparently been a range reduction (i.e., they have not been recorded in the northern pools within the last 10 years). In such cases, the locks and dams may have hindered recolonization following local extinctions. The series of locks and dams of the Upper Mississippi River have minimized spawning runs by the widely distributed and highly migratory skipjack herring (*Alosa chrysochloris*). Impoundment has also affected populations of three other species, *Scaphirhynchus platorynchus,* blue sucker (*Cycleptus elongatus*), and blue catfish (*Ictalurus furcatus*). All three have declined in the Upper Mississippi but are currently abundant in the swift currents of the free-flowing Middle and Lower Mississippi. On the other hand, impoundment has favored other species, including *Dorosoma cepedianum,* brook silverside (*Labidesthes sicculus*), *Pomoxis annularis, P. nigromaculatus,* and *Morone chrysops* (Farabee, 1979; Fremling et al., 1989; Lee et al., 1980).

In addition to being highly diverse, the fishes of the Upper Mississippi River are also highly productive, especially in the backwaters. Rotenone standing stock estimates from 20 backwater sites in Pools 5A, 8, 13, 14, and 18 averaged 357.7 lb/acre (401.0 kg ha^{-1}) and ranged from 39.1 to 831.1 lb/acre (43.8 to 931.7 kg ha^{-1}) (Pitlo, 1987). Many floodplain lakes may provide important sites for sports fisheries for centrarchids and *Esox lucius* (Fremling et al., 1989). Sloughs provide important sport and commercial fisheries sites for *Ictiobus* spp., *Cyprinus carpio, E. lucius,* centrarchids, and *Aplodinotus grunniens.* Both sloughs and floodplain lakes provide critical spawning and nursery habitat for a number of species (Fremling et al., 1989; Holland and Huston, 1985; Sylvester and Broughton, 1983).

The main-channel border habitat can also be productive. In Pool 13, primacord standing stocks from six main-channel border samples averaged 667.6 lb/acre (748.4 kg ha^{-1}) and ranged from 7.8 to 2691.7 lb/acre (8.7 to 3017.4 kg ha^{-1}). The unusually high maximum (2691.7 lb/acre) was made during low stage, when schools of *Scaphirhynchus platorynchus, Ictiobus bubalus, Ictalurus punctatus,* and *Aplodinotus grunniens* had retreated to a deep trough from other habitats. Excluding this maximum, the primacord samples would have averaged 262.7 lb/acre (294.5 kg ha^{-1}) and ranged from 7.8 to 594.5 lb/acre (8.7 to 666.4 kg ha^{-1}) (Pitlo, 1987). Submerged wing dams and riprap, which are found throughout the main-channel border, probably

enhance fish production by increasing habitat heterogeneity and benthic production (Fremling et al., 1989).

Tailwaters provide the river's richest sports fishery for *Ictalurus punctatus,
Stizostedion canadense, S. vitreum, Morone chrysops,* and *Aplodinotus grunniens; Dorosoma cepedianum* are also abundant. On the other hand, the sport
and commercial fishery of the main channel is limited. Surveys in the main
channel usually yield fewer fish than do other habitats, partly because of sampling difficulties. Nonetheless, main-channel fish production is probably low as
a result of repeated disturbance by barge traffic, unproductive benthos, and
lack of habitat structure (Fremling et al., 1989). However, the main channel
provides an important nursery habitat for *Ictalurus punctatus* (Holland-Bartels
and Duval, 1988). In addition, *I. punctatus* and flathead catfish (*Pylodictis
olivaris*) overwinter in the main channel, achieving concentrations as high as
49,834 and 2491 fish ha^{-1}, respectively (Talbot, 1984, as cited in Fremling and
Claflin, 1984). Side channels have the swift currents and sandy substrates that
characterize the less productive main channels, but they also provide greater
habitat structure, and the banks are vegetated by macrophytes that are affected
less by barge traffic. The standing stocks from two side-channel sites were 79
and 152 kg ha^{-1}. Fish production in the lower, lentic reach of each navigation
pool is limited by the lack of cover and hard substrates. However, the pelagic
larvae of *Dorosoma cepedianum* and *A. grunniens* are often very abundant
(Fremling et al., 1989).

High variability within pools makes difficult a comparison of fish production among the pools of the Upper Mississippi River. For example, rotenone
standing stocks from seven backwater lake collections in Pool 5A (44 to 932 kg
ha^{-1}) encompassed the entire range for 20 rotenone collections from five
different pools (Table 1.30). The standing stocks from eight backwater
rotenone collections in Pool 14 (92 to 727 kg ha^{-1}) were also wide (Table 1.31).
The variability was even greater for the primacord samples from the main-
channel border of Pool 13 (Pitlo, 1987) (Table 1.32).

Another way of comparing fish production among pools in the Upper Mississippi River is the comparison of commercial and sports fisheries catches.
Not surprisingly, the catch from each pool is largely a function of its total
surface area. For instance, Pools 4, 8, 9, 10, 13, and 19 are the largest pools in
the Upper Mississippi, while total commercial harvest from 1953 to 1977 was
highest in Pools 4, 8, 9, 13, 18, and 19 (Kline and Golden, 1979b). However,
when commercial catches are expressed on a per unit area basis, it becomes
evident that other factors are involved. For instance, catch per unit area was
especially high in Pools 18 and 8 (Fremling et al., 1989). In general, catches
per unit area were higher in the northern and central pools than they were in
the southern pools. With three exceptions (Pools 5, 6, and 16), catches per
unit area were greater than or equal to 30 kg ha^{-1} in Pools 3 to 18, while they
were less than or equal to 30 kg ha^{-1} in Pools 19 to 26 (Figure 1.7). A
longitudinal change is also suggested in sport catches from seven pools (Kline
and Golden, 1979a) (Table 1.33).

TABLE 1.30.   *Rotenone Standing Stocks (kg ha^{-1}) for Fish Collected in a Backwater Lake in Pool 5A, Upper Mississippi River, 1948 to 1952 and 1983*

Year:	1948	1949	1951	1952	1948	1983	1983
Site of the Backwater Lakes (river km):	1183	1183	1183	1183	1182	1183	1182
Polydontidae							
Polydon spathula	0	0	0	6	0	0	0
Lepisosteidae							
Lepisosteus osseus	<1	7	<1	<1	<1	<1	0
L. platostomus	2	30	0	0	5	1	0
Amiidae							
Amia calva	37	95	72	102	14	6	0
Clupeidae							
Dorosoma cepedianum	2	176	1	1	1	398	70
Catostomidae							
Carpiodes carpio	1	0	4	1	<1	60	17
Ictiobus bubalus	0	3	0	0	0	9	<1
I. cyprinellus	6	9	0	0	<1	21	0
Minytrema melanops	7	33	40	20	0	88	4
Other Catostomidae	1	1	1	0	<1	4	1
Cyprinidae							
Cyprinus carpio	110	185	2	33	2	105	4
Other Cyprinidae	2	1	1	0	1	3	4
Ictaluridae							
Ictalurus punctatus	21	42	22	40	5	14	3
Pylodictis olivaris	3	0	0	4	0	1	0
Other Ictaluridae	<1	<1	<1	<1	<1	1	0
Esocidae							
Esox lucius	24	15	27	1	<1	5	1
Centrarchidae							
Lepomis macrochirus	4	13	8	1	2	20	1
Micropterus salmoides	1	10	11	1	1	5	1
Pomoxis annularis	7	10	16	20	4	8	1
P. nigromaculatus	4	25	14	24	3	19	2
Other Centrarchidae	1	<1	1	0	1	4	2
Percidae							
Stizostedion canadense	2	2	1	2	1	2	4
S. vitreum	1	7	4	6	0	1	1
Other Percidae	<1	1	1	<1	0	1	<1
Percithyidae							
Morone chrysops	1	2	0	3	<1	<1	1
Sciaenidae							
Aplodinotus grunniens	5	11	2	23	3	155	1
Other							
Total	<1	<1	<1	<1	<1	<1	<1
Total standing stock	243	678	227	306	44	932	119

Source: After Pitlo (1987).

TABLE 1.31. *Rotenone Standing Crops (kg ha^{-1}) for Fishes in Seven Slough Collections and One Backwater Lake Collection from Pool 14, Upper Mississippi River, Late Summer Through Early Autumn 1977 to 1984*

Year:	1977	1979	1981	1984	1981	1984	1981	1984
Site of Backwaters (river km):	824	823	823	823	817	817	814	814
Lepisosteidae								
Lepisosteus osseus	0	<1	3	8	<1	<1	0	0
L. platostomus	0	0	1	2	<1	7	0	0
Amiidae								
Amia calva	8	1	<1	4	25	8	5	7
Clupeidae								
Dorosoma cepedianum	62	366	472	15	164	109	20	3
Catostomidae								
Carpiodes carpio	70	7	2	8	34	125	5	1
Ictiobus bubalus	7	1	2	0	16	7	<1	0
I. cyprinellus	<1	5	1	26	24	8	0	0
Minytrema melanops	0	7	0	<1	<1	5	0	0
Other Catostomidae	4	0	0	0	1	3	0	0
Cyprinidae								
Cyprinus carpio	297	231	42	53	37	97	9	1
Other Cyprinidae	3	0	<1	1	<1	1	<1	2
Ictaluridae								
Ictalurus punctatus	15	4	9	22	3	11	2	0
Other Ictaluridae	<1	<1	<1	<1	4	8	<1	<1
Esocidae								
Esox lucius	16	58	42	21	6	7	0	<1
Centrarchidae								
Lepomis macrochirus	18	4	5	5	96	82	27	54
Micropterus salmoides	4	3	2	5	15	13	5	12
Pomoxis annularis	94	21	10	11	41	14	10	<1
P. nigromaculatus	5	6	7	4	17	18	11	9
Other Centrarchidae	1	1	1	6	1	1	<1	2
Percidae								
Stizostedion canadense	16	<1	4	1	0	1	<1	0
Other Percidae	1	0	<1	<1	<1	<1	<1	<1
Percithyidae								
Morone chrysops	3	6	1	<1	<1	1	1	<1
Sciaenidae								
Aplodinotus grunniens	7	5	6	22	15	4	1	1
Other								
Total	0	<1	8	<1	0	<1	0	<1
Total standing stock	631	727	619	216	501	533	96	92

Source: After Pitlo (1987).

TABLE 1.32. *Primacord Standing Stocks (kg ha⁻¹) for Fish Collected from Three Main-Channel Border Sites in Pool 13, Upper Mississippi River, 1983 and 1984*

Sample Date: Site:	May 1983 b	Oct. 1983 a	Oct. 1983 b	Oct. 1984 a	Oct. 1984 b	Oct. 1984 c
Acipenseridae						
Scaphirhynchus	53	0	545	0	0	0
platorynchus						
Lepisosteidae						
Lepisosteus platostomus	0	0	0	0	6	0
Hiodontidae						
Hiodon tergisus	9	<1	<1	2	0	3
Clupeidae						
Dorosoma cepedianum	0	49	123	<1	2	9
Catostomidae						
Ictiobus bubalus	28	77	1166	0	83	19
I. cyprinellus	0	0	0	0	0	5
Moxostoma	495	0	176	0	0	0
macrolepidotum						
Cyprinidae						
Cyprinus carpio	0	99	13	0	0	54
Hybopsis storeriana	0	1	0	1	0	<1
Minnows	0	<1	0	0	0	0
Ictaluridae						
Ictalurus punctatus	43	0	427	4	0	200
Pylodictis olivaris	6	2	20	0	0	17
Centrarchidae						
Lepomis macrochirus	0	0	<1	0	0	0
Pomoxis annularis	0	0	<1	0	0	0
P. nigromaculatus	0	0	0	0	2	0
Percidae						
Stizostedion canadense	0	1	0	0	0	0
Darters	0	<1	0	0	0	0
Percithyidae						
Morone chrysops	0	0	2	0	0	6
Sciaenidae						
Aplodinotus grunniens	3	7	544	2	52	91
Total standing stock	666	236	3017	9	156	405

Source: After Pitlo (1987).

While commercial and sport fisheries are also dependent on factors other than fish production (e.g., angler access and proximity to markets), the longitudinal differences in catch per unit area probably correspond to differences in fish production. This apparent longitudinal pattern in productivity has been attributed to the more extensive backwater habitats, macrophyte beds, and forested floodplains in the northern pools and the prevalence of open main-channel border habitat and agriculturally developed floodplains in the southern pools (Fremling et al., 1989; Kline and Golden, 1979a; Peck and Smart, 1986).

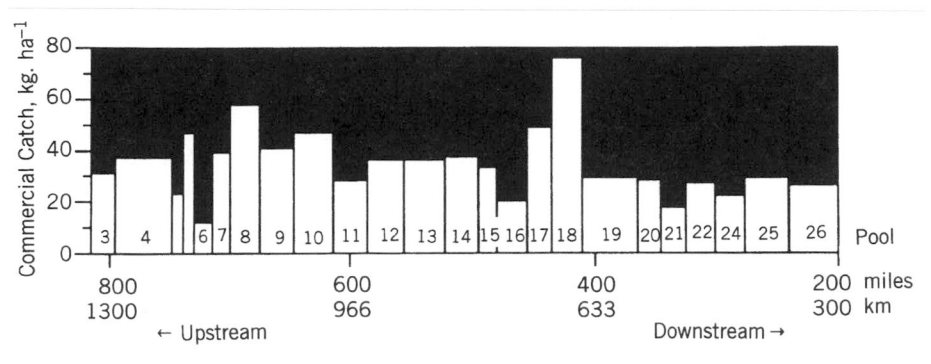

FIGURE 1.7. Commercial fisheries catches per unit area for the navigation pools of the Upper Mississippi River. The widths of the bars denote the length of the pools. (From Lubinski et al., 1981, as used in Fremling et al., 1989. Reproduced with permission of the Minister of Supply and Services, Canada 1996.)

The importance of floodplains, macrophyte beds, and backwater habitats to fish production is suggested by the changes in commercial catches in the Illinois River. This river, with its low gradient, extensive backwaters, and oversized floodplains exhibited many of the hydrological and geomorphological characteristics typical of large floodplain rivers such as the Mississippi. Catch per unit area was especially high during 1908 (77.7 to 200.0 kg ha^{-1}), when the backwaters and floodplains were still largely intact. In fact, the Illinois River fishery was the most productive fishery in the United States at the turn of the century. Catch per unit area declined substantially by the 1950s (45.6 kg ha^{-1}) following the extensive development of floodplains and reclamation of backwaters. Catch per unit area declined even more by the 1970s (8.4 kg ha^{-1}) as large-scale conversion of farmlands from field crops (e.g., cereals) to row crops (e.g., soybeans) accelerated soil erosion, which in turn seriously degraded most of the remaining backwaters (Fremling et al., 1989; Sparks, 1984). In the Upper Mississippi River, the continuing loss of backwater habitat to sedimentation, especially in the northern pools, currently poses a seri-

TABLE 1.33. *Catch per Unit Area (kg ha^{-1}) of Sport Fishes from Seven Pools in the Upper Mississippi River*

Pool	1962–1963	1967–1968	1972–1973	Mean
4	14.4	18.6	14.6	15.9
5	11.8	12.6	16.4	13.6
7	15.0	12.0	12.0	13.0
11	6.7	8.1	14.0	9.6
13	1.8	4.7	3.7	3.4
18	8.6	8.0	0.8	5.8
26	2.2	2.5	3.9	2.9

Source: After Kline and Golden (1979a).

ous threat to fish populations (Holland, 1986; Holland and Huston, 1985; Lubinski et al., 1986; Shaeffer and Nickum, 1986b; Sylvester and Broughton, 1983).

Most fish in the Upper Mississippi either frequent or are concentrated in backwaters. This habitat-specific distribution is exemplified by a 1981 study in the middle reach of Pool 7. A total of 902 fishes belonging to 36 species were collected with hoop and gill nets located in the main channel, backwaters, and connecting side channels. Most species were found in all three habitats, but the frequency of capture and species richness was greater away from the main channel (Table 1.34). Only three species, *Scaphirhynchus platorynchus,* white sucker (*Catostomus commersoni*), and blue sucker (*Cycleptus elongatus*), were collected exclusively in the main channel, and each of these were represented by only a single specimen. To some extent, the greater frequency of capture in the backwaters and their connecting side channels is probably the result of greater capture efficiency. Nonetheless, capture in the backwaters demonstrates backwater habitat use (Sylvester and Broughton, 1983).

The importance of backwaters, macrophytes, and floodplains to the fishes of the Upper Mississippi River is also evident in their natural histories. *Lepisosteus platostomus, Amia calva, Ictiobus bubalus, I. cyprinellus, I. niger, Cyprinus carpio, Esox lucius, Pomoxis annularis,* and *Perca flavescens* use aquatic macrophytes for spawning sites or nest construction (Holland and Huston, 1984; Lubinski et al., 1986; Sparks, 1984), and *Micropterus salmoides* will often spawn within emergent macrophyte beds (Becker, 1983). Others, including *Dorosoma cepedianum, Ictiobus* spp., *Labidesthes sicculus,* most centrarchids, and *Aplodinotus grunniens,* spawn in open backwaters. At least six species, *D. cepedianum, I. bubalus, I. cyprinellus, I. niger, C. carpio,* and *Stizostedion vitreum,* spawn on floodplain vegetation (Becker, 1983; Lubinski et al., 1986).

Backwaters and inundated floodplains are also important nursery sites for many species (Fremling et al., 1989; Grumbaugh and Anderson, 1987; Holland, 1986; Junk et al., 1989). Within the river itself, concentrations of larval fish are generally highest in the backwaters. Catostomidae, *Pomoxis* spp., and *Perca flavescens* are typical of spring backwater larval assemblages, while *Lepomis* spp. and *Dorosoma cepedianum* are abundant in late spring and summer (Holland, 1986; Shaeffer and Nickum, 1986b). Young-of-the-year (YOY) of several species are also concentrated in the backwaters (Holland and Huston, 1985; Shaeffer and Nickum, 1986b). Catch per unit efforts (CPUEs) for late spring samples collected in a backwater from Pool 7 were dominated by *Esox lucius.* By early summer, total YOY CPUEs increased because of increased numbers of other taxons, including unidentified Catostomidae and Cyprinidae, pirate perch (*Aphredoderus sayanus*), *Micropterus salmoides,* and *Pomoxis nigromaculatus.* Midsummer samples were dominated by *Lepomis macrochirus, M. salmoides,* and *P. nigromaculatus,* while *L. macrochirus* dominated late summer samples (Table 1.35). Differences in dissolved oxygen saturation and currents appeared to be the major factors

TABLE 1.34. *Habitat-Specific Distribution of Selected Fishes Based on the Number of Captures with 26 Sets of Hoop and Gill Nets Located in the Middle and Lower Reaches of Pool 7, Upper Mississippi River, February–August 1981*

	Main Channel	Side Channel	Backwater
Lepisosteidae			
Lepisosteus spp.	0	7	5
Amiidae			
Amia calva	0	7	7
Hiodontidae			
Hiodon tergisus	2	5	7
Catostomidae			
Carpiodes cyprinus	1	2	6
Cycleptus elongatus	1	0	0
Ictiobus bubalus	7	4	2
Minytrema melanops	1	7	8
Moxostoma spp.	17	22	32
Other Catostomidae	1	3	1
Cyprinidae			
Cyprinus carpio	4	9	15
Notemigonus chrysoleucas	0	0	1
Ictaluridae			
Ictalurus punctatus	4	3	8
Other Ictaluridae	0	8	6
Esocidae			
Esox lucius	2	8	13
Centrarchidae			
Ambloplites rupestris	8	9	9
Micropterus salmoides	1	6	5
Pomoxis nigromaculatus	4	7	13
Other Centrarchidae	2	7	7
Percidae			
Perca flavescens	5	4	9
Stizostedion canadense	5	6	5
Stizostedion vitreum	2	0	5
Percithyidae			
Morone chrysops	2	5	8
Scianidae			
Aplodinotus grunniens	9	10	11
Other			
Total	2	2	4
Total number of species	24	30	28
Total number of fish	128	297	477

Source: After Sylvester and Broughton (1983).

TABLE 1.35. *Seining Catch per Unit Effort (CPUE) of Young-of-the-Year Fish in a Backwater Lake in Pool 7, Upper Mississippi River, May–September 1982*

	Late Spring	Early Summer	Midsummer	Late Summer
Lepisosteidae				
Lepisosteus osseus	0	0.1	0.1	<0.1
Clupeidae				
Dorosoma cepedianum	0	0	0.4	0.4
Catostomidae				
Unidentified	0	4.8	4.5	3.2
Cyprinidae				
Unidentified	0	7.2	1.9	0.5
Esocidae				
Esox lucius	3.4	4.1	1.5	1.4
Aphredoderidae				
Aphredoderus sayanus	0	4.4	0.4	1.0
Atherinidae				
Labidesthes sicculus	0	0.3	2.5	3.1
Centrarchidae				
Ambloplites rupestris	<0.1	0.1	0.4	1.0
Lepomis macrochirus	0	0.8	6.2	32.5
Micropterus salmoides	0.4	28.4	8.2	4.6
Pomoxis nigromaculatus	0.2	9.4	6.6	4.0
Percidae				
Ammocrypta clara	0	0.8	0.9	1.2
Perca flavescens	0.4	0.7	0.8	0.6
Stizostedion vitreum	0	0.1	<0.1	0
Percithyidae				
Morone chrysops	0.3	<0.1	1.4	1.5
Sciaenidae				
Aplodinotus grunniens	0.1	0	0	<0.1
Total CPUE	4.8	60.8	35.9	55.1

Source: After Holland and Huston (1985).

contributing to differences among sites within the backwater (Holland and Huston, 1985).

Tolerance to low levels of dissolved oxygen saturation characterizes the backwater fish fauna (Junk et al., 1989). *Lepisosteus* spp., *Amia calva, Cyprinus carpio, Ictiobus cyprinellus,* bullheads (*Ictalurus* spp.), and *Lepomis* spp. are tolerant of hypoxic conditions during the summer. *Esox lucius, Ictalurus* spp., and *Perca flavescens* are tolerant of winter hypoxia. Air breathing, which is employed by *Lepisosteus* spp. and *A. calva,* is one adaptation to low levels of dissolved oxygen (Becker, 1983). Another adaptation, which is employed by *E. lucius,* is the adhesion of eggs and larvae onto macrophytes. In this way, these vulnerable early life stages are removed from oxygen demanding sediments (Holland and Huston, 1984).

Most fish in the Upper Mississippi River typically spawn some time from

April through June. Many of those preferring cooler summer temperatures, such as *Moxostoma* spp., *Perca flavescens,* and *Stizostedion* spp., tend to spawn in April and May, while many of those characteristic of the backwaters during summer, including *Lepisosteus* spp., *Dorosoma cepedianum, Ictalurus* spp., and *Pomoxis* spp., tend to spawn later in the spring. Spawning for a number of other fishes, including carpsuckers (*Carpiodes* spp.), *Cyprinus carpio, Hybopsis storeriana, Notropis atherinoides, N. blennius, N. spilopterus, Pimephales vigilax, Lepomis* spp., and *Micropterus salmoides,* also occurs in late spring but may extend well into summer. Some of these later breeders, including *C. carpio* and *M. salmoides,* may spawn more than once a season (Becker, 1983). In fact, the extended spawning season and potential for multiple broods is one factor credited for the success of *C. carpio* in the Upper Mississippi (Lubinski et al., 1986).

Spring spawning would facilitate the use of the inundated floodplains for spawning and nursery sites. It would also facilitate the colonization of seasonally isolated floodplain lakes and ponds. The timing of the seasonal floods with warming temperatures is probably one major factor influencing the year-class strength for these spring spawners. For instance, an early receding of the seasonal flood or a delay in warming may result in poor reproduction or larval survivorship. On the other hand, those species capable of protracted or multiple spawning may gain during nonoptimal flood years (Junk et al., 1989; Risotto and Turner, 1985). One major concern in the Upper Mississippi River is that the attenuation of the spring floods and isolation of the floodplain from the river with levees has reduced the availability of the floodplain for important commercial and sport fishes. Returning reclaimed floodplains to the river–floodplain system is seen as one way to both improve fisheries and reduce the potential for destructive flooding (Grumbaugh and Anderson, 1987).

Variations in discharge can have significant effects on spawning and recruitment of Upper Mississippi River fishes. The timing and duration of the spring floods could have a significant effect on species that use the inundated floodplain. For instance, if the flood comes early and is of relatively short duration, the floodplain habitat may not become available for fishes requiring warmer spawning conditions (Junk et al., 1989). Fish with spawning or early life stages occurring in backwaters are also subject to changes in water levels. Relatively low spring water levels are known to enhance populations of *Cyprinus carpio* by reducing turbidity and increasing macrophyte growth. This in turn improves their egg adherence and increases the production of epiphytic diet items. High flows increase the availability of floodplain habitat, but they may also increase the chances of stranding (Lubinski et al., 1986). Stranding can also occur in low-flow years, when the backwaters themselves are desiccated. Mass strandings during low summer flows were common before the construction of the navigation pools and prompted major fish rescue efforts, which were initiated in 1876 and reached their maximum in the 1920s (Carlander et al., 1963; Fremling et al., 1989).

TABLE 1.36. *Mean Larval Fish Densities (number per 100 m³) from Three Backwater Sites and Their Respective Upstream and Downstream Main-Channel Sites in Pool 13, Upper Mississippi River, April–August 1983*

	Upstream Main Channel	Backwater	Downstream Main Channel
Hiodontidae			
Hiodon tergisus	0.2	1.1	1.1
Clupeidae			
Dorosoma cepedianum	1.9	74.1	5.1
Catostomidae			
Carpiodes spp.	0.7	0.6	1.1
Ictiobus spp.	0.9	0.4	1.6
Minytrema melanops	0.3	0.2	0.2
Cyprinidae			
Cyprinus carpio	8.5	3.3	5.0
Hybopsis storeriana	1.1	3.3	1.5
Notropis atherinoides	12.0	54.7	85.2
Cyprinid type 1	2.0	0.2	1.8
Cyprinid type 2	1.9	1.9	2.7
Cyprinid type 3	0.4	0.2	0.9
Cyprinid type 4	0.4	0.1	0.5
Unidentified	1.3	0.7	1.1
Centrarchidae			
Lepomis spp.	0.3	15.2	1.7
Pomoxis spp.	0.2	4.1	1.2
Percidae			
Percina spp.	1.2	1.8	2.7
Stizostedion spp.	0.2	0.8	0.8
Unidentified	0.4	2.4	2.1
Percithyidae			
Morone chrysops	0.1	0.7	0.4
Sciaenidae			
Aplodinotus grunniens	26.5	13.9	55.1
Total drift density	60.4	179.7	170.9

Source: After Shaeffer and Nickum (1986b).

Variations in discharge can also affect populations in the main channel and the main-channel border. The flushing of backwaters may increase larval densities in the main channel (Holland, 1986). The export of larval fish from backwaters into the main channel was suggested by a study conducted in Pool 13. Larval densities were higher in backwater sites and main-channel sites receiving flow from those backwaters than they were in upstream main-channel sites (Shaeffer and Nickum, 1986b) (Table 1.36). Variations in discharge also influence the recruitment of a main-channel species, *Ictalurus punctatus.* Young-of-the-year densities in Pool 7 were higher in a year receiving normal flow (1985) than in a year with higher-than-normal early summer flow (1984) or a year with higher-than-normal flows from midsummer through early October (1986). In addition, back-calculations from length frequencies indicated that spawning was protracted in the two high-flow years, whereas spawning was concentrated in June during the more normal year. *I. punctatus* builds nests in undercut banks, around drift brush and logs, all of which would offer less protection under high-flow conditions (Holland-Bartels and Duval, 1988). On the other hand, interannual variations in discharge were not associated with differences in the recruitment of *Aplodinotus grunniens* (Butler, 1965).

A number of fish species have been introduced into the Upper Mississippi River. Unsuccessful efforts to introduce American shad (*Alosa sapidissima*) and Atlantic salmon (*Salma salar*) were attempted as early as 1872. Controversial introductions of striped bass (*Morone saxatilis*) and wipers (hybrids of *M. chrysops* and *M. saxatilis*) have been attempted in recent years (Fremling et al., 1989).

Cyprinus carpio is the most successful and most important introduced species in the Upper Mississippi River. It was introduced into the river accidentally sometime before 1883, and by 1889 it accounted for a proportion of the commercial harvest equal to that of buffalos (*Ictiobus* spp.). Since the turn of the century, *C. carpio* has become the dominant commercial species, accounting for approximately half of the total catch. However, its contribution to the fishery has declined in recent years, primarily because of concerns for PCB contamination. Competition for space and food from this particularly adaptable species is believed to have contributed to early declines in catches of native *Ictiobus* spp. In addition, space competition with nest builders (e.g., *Micropterus salmoides*) may be severe in a number of backwaters. Indeed, continuing sedimentation and eutrophication in the northern pools may enable *C. carpio* to displace a variety of sport fishes (Lubinski et al., 1986).

Another introduced cyprinid, grass carp (*Ctenopharyngdon idella*), first appeared in commercial catches from Pool 25 in 1975. Since then it has been collected as far north as Pool 5A, but natural reproduction has not been reported (Fremling et al., 1989). There is concern that *C. idella,* which was introduced into the United States for the control of aquatic weeds, may achieve pest status in the Upper Mississippi River by destroying productive macrophyte beds (Becker, 1983).

In general, the productivity of the fish in the Upper Mississippi River has been enhanced by the construction of the navigation pools. This enhancement is primarily the result of the stabilization of summer flow, which reduces the dewatering of backwaters and the creation of rich slough and pool habitat in the middle pool reaches (Fremling and Claflin, 1984). Impoundment has reduced habitat quality for certain species (e.g., *Acipenser fluvescens, Scaphirhynchus platorynchus, Cycleptus elongatus,* and *Ictalurus furcatus*) but enhanced it for others (e.g., *Dorosoma cepedianum, Cyprinus carpio, Esox lucius, Micropterus salmoides, Pomoxis* spp., and *Morone chrysops*) (Claflin, 1973; Farabee, 1979; Fremling et al., 1989). Diversity and productivity in backwater lakes and sloughs are highest in the deeper, less eutrophic backwaters (Fremling et al., 1989). Unfortunately, the increased sedimentation and eutrophication that has accompanied impoundment now threatens these productive habitats (Fremling and Claflin, 1984).

COMMUNITIES OF AQUATIC LIFE

Functional Relationships

Allochthonous floodplain inputs, upstream and tributary inputs, and autochthonous inputs from macrophyte beds are three important sources of organic matter for the Upper Mississippi River. Attached algae and phytoplankton may or may not be important. In Pool 19, upstream inputs have been estimated to contribute 85.73% of the total organic carbon input, while tributary inputs are estimated to contribute an additional 6.76%. The greatly reduced floodplains contributed an estimated 6.09%, while aquatic macrophytes contribute an additional 1.20%. Phytoplankton, on the other hand, are estimated to contribute only 0.15%. No estimate is available for attached algae (Fremling et al., 1989). However, the importance of these organic carbon sources in other reaches of the Upper Mississippi may differ considerably.

For one thing, floodplains upstream from Pool 19 have not been leveed as extensively as those within and downstream of Pool 19 (Peck and Smart, 1986). The more accessible floodplains of the middle and northern pools may provide substantially greater amounts of organic carbon than they do in Pool 19. Moreover, inputs from floodplains appear to be of higher quality than upstream inputs and more likely to enhance secondary production (Junk et al., 1989).

The importance of macrophytes as a source of organic matter also probably differs substantially among reaches. Macrophytes are much more extensively developed in the pools of the Driftless Area than they are in Pool 19. In addition, macrophytes are even more limited in other southern pools (e.g., Pool 20) (Jahn and Anderson, 1986; Peck and Smart, 1986). Presumably, macrophyte organic carbon, whether it is in the form of dissolved organic carbon, particulate sloughed matter, or particulate detritus, is higher in quality than organic carbon imported from upstream reaches.

The nature and timing of these contributions may differ significantly with the growth form. For example, emergents and floating-leafed species, which typically accumulate biomass throughout the growing season (Grumbaugh et al., 1986; Sefton, 1976), probably contribute organic matter primarily as postsenescent detritus. On the other hand, many submergent species do not exhibit accumulations of biomass through the growing season or exhibit autumnal maxima in the percent of their biomass that is senescent (Sefton, 1976), which suggests that sloughing during the growing season may be considerable. Moreover, submerged species are, by definition, totally immersed, and may as a result leach greater amounts of dissolved organic matter than emergent and floating-leafed species. If these speculations hold true, submergent species would provide a considerable amount of their organic matter contribution during the growing season, whereas emergent and floating-leafed species will contribute most of their organic matter following autumnal senescence.

The insignificant contribution of phytoplankton to the organic carbon inputs for Pool 19 appears not to be representative for other parts of the Upper Mississippi River. Phytoplankton have been reported to be considerably more abundant in Pool 3 (Baker and Baker, 1979, 1981) and Pool 7 (Huff, 1986) than in Pool 19 (Fremling et al., 1989). On the other hand, phytoplankton populations in some other pools (e.g., Pool 20) are less productive than those in Pool 19 (Jahn and Anderson, 1986). These differences in phytoplankton production are largely attributable to differences in the extent of backwater habitat.

The importance of algae to the trophic dynamics of the Upper Mississippi River are poorly understood. Attached algae are believed to be unimportant in Pool 19 because of turbidity and the paucity of substrates (Jahn and Anderson, 1986). However, epiphytic diatoms were abundant on one macroalga, *Cladophora* (Luttenton and Rada, 1986) and are probably also abundant on a number of macrophytes. Presumably, epiphytic algae would vary in abundance with the abundance of macrophytes, especially submergent taxa. Moreover, attached algae appear to be abundant in some backwaters during winter (Baker and Baker, 1979) and may be abundant in the sediments of macrophyte beds in early spring. In addition, attached algae can be abundant on channelization structures.

The importance of these sources of organic matter has changed as a result of anthropogenic modifications to the river. For instance, impoundment has resulted in increased macrophyte production (Peck and Smart, 1986) and reduced seasonal floodplain inundation. In addition, floodplain reclamation has reduced the availability of existing floodplains (Grumbaugh and Anderson, 1987). Consequently, floodplain inputs have probably become less important, whereas macrophyte inputs have become more important. Moreover, minimum pool elevations have resulted in the permanent inundation of many backwaters, which in turn has altered decompositional processes characterized by periodic desiccation. Hence backwaters have become increasingly eutrophic (Fremling and Claflin, 1984). Sedimentation and boat traffic have also probably contributed to changes in the quality and availability of organic matter within the river, especially that originating from macrophytes and algae.

Differences in the utilization of these sources of organic matter are indicated by differences in the functional organization of macroinvertebrate assemblages. The diverse macroinvertebrate assemblages that occur within macrophyte beds contain a variety of feeding types. These beds contain food resources in the form of living macrophytes, macrophyte detritus, high-bacterial standing crops, epiphytic algae, and a host of invertebrate prey.

Herbivorous shredders in the macrophyte beds are represented primarily by Pyralidae (Lepidoptera), Curculionidae (Coleoptera), and Leptoceridae

(Trichoptera). Piercing herbivores are represented by *Sigara* spp. (Hemiptera), *Haliplus* spp. (Coleoptera), and Hydroptilidae (Trichoptera). There are also stylet-bearing herbivorous nematodes, such as *Ironus* sp. Four gastropod scrapers, *Amnicola* spp., *Physa* spp., *Valvata* spp., and *Gyraulus* spp., are often very abundant in macrophyte beds. *Asellus,* a scraper-gatherer, is also commonly abundant. They, along with the abundant *Hyalella azteca,* which is omnivorous, probably feed extensively on epiphytic and benthic bacteria, epiphytic algae, and macrophyte detritus. Deposit-feeding nematodes (e.g., *Plectus* and *Tobrilus*), oligochaetes, and chironomids (e.g., *Chironomus, Dicrotendipes,* and *Lauterborniella*) are abundant feeders on bacteria and detritus. Other chironomids, including *Cricotopus, Endochironomus, Glyptotendipes,* and *Polypedilum,* may feed on algae and/or macrophytes as well. Microfilter feeders, including *Rheotanytarsus* (Chironomidae) and *Sphaerium striatinum,* are often abundant among submerged macrophytes.

There is also a diverse assemblage of macroinvertebrate carnivores in the macrophyte beds. Hirudinea and Chironomidae are the two most abundant carnivore taxons. *Helobdella elongata, H. stagnalis,* and *Erpobdella punctata* are three of the more abundant leeches collected in macrophyte beds. Carnivorous chironomids include *Pentaneura, Procladius,* and *Cryptochironomus.* Other carnivores, including *Bezzia* and *Palpomyia* (Ceratopogonidae), *Hexatoma* (Tipulidae), *Enallagma* (Odonata), *Plea striola* (Hemiptera), and *Sialis* (Megaloptera), are also common to abundant in macrophyte beds.

The array of feeding types changes in the open water, depositional benthos (i.e., unvegetated slough, lake, and silty main-channel border habitats). Macroinvertebrates in these habitats are characterized primarily as deposit feeders and microfilter feeders. Biomass is dominated by the deposit-feeding *Hexagenia* spp. and the microfilter-feeding *Musculum transversum.* Deposit-feeding oligochaetes, nematodes (e.g., *Tobrilus*), and chironomids (e.g., *Einfeldia* and *Dicrotendipes*) are still abundant, as are a number of gastropod grazers (e.g., *Fontigens, Somatogyrus,* and *Physa*).

Trophic support for primary macroinvertebrate consumers in the open water depositional habitats generally originates from other areas. Algae may provide some trophic support, but a study on feeding by *Musculum transversum* suggests that ingested algae are largely undigested (Gale and Lowe, 1971). Instead, most of the trophic support is probably supplied by fine detritus. In fact, macrophyte beds appear to be especially important sources of high-quality fine detritus (Grumbaugh et al., 1986; Junk et al., 1989).

Meiofauna. Seasonally, organic carbon inputs in the unvegetated main-channel border habitat would be expected to be highest during the spring rise, when organic matter is flushed from floodplains and backwaters, and in autumn, following macrophyte senescence and leaf fall. The coupling of these inputs with benthic production is suggested by the spring and autumn maxima in macroinvertebrate biomass in the unvegetated main channel border habitat of Pool 19 (Jahn and Anderson, 1986). The importance of these pulses is also suggested by the life histories of *Hexagenia* and *Musculum transversum.*

Benthic biomass for *Hexagenia* spp. is greatest during spring but is greatly reduced during summer because of mass emergences that occur in late spring and early summer (Fremling, 1970). Benthic populations of *Hexagenia* recover in autumn. Reproduction in *Musculum transversum* appears to be bimodal, with new clams appearing in midautumn and late spring. Following reproduction, the adults die, while the young may burrow as deep as 20 cm, possibly to avoid any number of unfavorable conditions (Jahn and Anderson, 1986). Despite intense predation, biomass and the number of reproductive adults (i.e., >5 mm) increase rapidly during autumn (Sparks, 1980).

Hirudinea may be the most abundant macroinvertebrate carnivores in unvegetated depositional habitats. Three leeches, *Erpobdella punctata, Glossiphonia complanata,* and *Helobdella stagnalis,* dominated the macroinvertebrate carnivores in the main-channel border of Pool 19. Leeches increased rapidly in September and continued to be abundant through at least December. Glossiphoniidae, especially *G. complanata,* are important predators on Sphaeriidae, and the autumn increase may have been a functional response to increases in *Musculum transversum* (Gale, 1975). Macroinvertebrate carnivores may move onto unvegetated sediments following the autumn senescence in macrophytes. Such increases in abundance were observed for Odonata in Lake Onalaska but not for Hirudinea and Turbellaria (Blitgen, 1981).

The prevalence of unstable sand substrates is a major factor limiting benthic macroinvertebrates in erosional side channels and main-channel habitats. Densities are typically dominated by deposit-feeding oligochaetes and chironomids and by detritivorous and carnivorous Ceratopogonidae (Anderson and Day, 1986; Claflin, 1973; Elstad, 1977).

However, macroinvertebrates become extremely abundant in erosional sites when hard substrates are available. Aufwuchs assemblages in the unmodified river were limited primarily to snags and a few rapids, while those in the present river are most abundant in the tailwaters and on submerged dikes and revetments. The feeding types in aufwuchs assemblages differ considerably from those encountered in other benthic habitats. While deposit feeders comprise an important part of the aufwuchs, they are often as abundant as filter feeders and scrapers (Anderson and Day, 1986; Jahn and Anderson, 1986; Herbert et al., 1984; Neuswanger et al., 1982).

Macrofilter-feeding Hydropsychidae, represented primarily by *Hydropsyche orris, Potamyia flava,* and *Cheumatopsyche* spp., are often overwhelmingly dominant on hard substrates located in the current (Neuswanger et al., 1982; Seagle et al., 1982). Hydropsychids appear to be habitat-limited rather than food-limited. In Pool 19, for instance, *H. orris* will occur in dense mats on virtually any appropriate substrate (Jahn and Anderson, 1986). *H. orris* has a larger capture net mesh size than *P. flava* and *Cheumatopsyche* spp. and is generally more abundant in faster water. It also appears to be strongly carnivorous, whereas the other two taxons feed predominantly on detritus and algae (Fremling, 1960). Nonetheless, *H. orris* may experience a longitudinal diet shift within Pool 19. Those individuals inhabiting the tailwaters and the lower pool probably depend heavily on zooplankton, whereas most entrained detritus may be too small for capture. On the other hand, coarser particles of detritus are more available in the middle and upper pools, but zooplankters are probably too infrequent to provide significant trophic support (Jahn and Anderson, 1986).

Microfilter feeders are also common to abundant in aufwuchs assemblages. As with the macrofilter feeders, the presence of firm substrates in current provides microfilter feeders with access to organic matter in the water column. *Cyrnellus, Neureclypsis* (Trichoptera), and *Isonychia* (Ephemeroptera) were three abundant microfilter feeders in an aufwuchs study in Pool 20 (Neuswanger et al., 1982). Microfilter-feeding Chironomidae (e.g., *Rheotanytarsus*) may also be numerous. Fine detritus and algae are probably the primary food items for *Neureclypsis* and *Isonychia,* but *Cyrnellus* is probably carnivorous.

Mayfly scraper-gatherers constitute another significant component of the aufwuchs macroinvertebrate assemblage. These taxons, including *Stenonema, Ameletus,* and *Caenis,* were typically uncommon in benthic samples (Anderson and Day, 1986; Elstad, 1977) but have been reported to be abundant in aufwuchs samples from other rivers, such as the Missouri River (Carter et al., 1982). These taxons may feed heavily on attached algae as well as on detritus.

Microfilter-feeding Unionidae can be found in a wide variety of benthic habitats, including some that are largely depauperate of other taxons (i.e., sandy main and side channels). They may have been especially influential in the trophic dynamics of the river before their diverse and productive populations were decimated by the pearl button industry.

The diversity of habitats present in the Upper Mississippi River provides a variety of food resources for its diverse fish fauna. There are a number of fish feeding types, ranging from opportunistic omnivores to planktivores to bottom feeders to piscivores.

Planktivory features prominently in the diets of several fish. *Polydon spathula* feeds primarily on backwater zooplankton (Farabee, 1979). *Dorosoma cepedianum* initially feeds on zooplankton but will include phytoplankton as they mature; larger individuals become benthic feeders. *Ictiobus cyprinellus,* pugnose shiner (*Notropis emiliae*), spottail shiner (*N. hudsonius*), and *Labidesthes sicculus* commonly feed on zooplankton and/or phytoplankton (Becker, 1983; Smith, 1979). Planktivory also features prominently in the early life stages for a number of species for which the backwaters provide nursery habitats. For example, young *Amia calva, Esox lucius, Lepomis macrochirus, Micropterus salmoides, Pomoxis nigromaculatus, Perca flavescens, Stizostedion vitreum,* and *Morone chrysops* feed primarily on zooplankton, while older individuals feed on invertebrates and/or fish (Becker, 1983; Farabee, 1979; Pflieger, 1975; Smith, 1979). Young *Cyprinus carpio* shift from being planktivores to opportunistic omnivores (Lubinski et al., 1986). Immature *Notropis atherinoides* also feed primarily on plankton (Becker, 1983).

Benthic algae contribute to the diets of several omnivores, including

Carpiodes spp., *Notropis hudsonius, N. volucellus,* and *Pimephales vigilax.* Macrophyte tissue has been ingested by two other omnivores, *Cyprinus carpio* and *Ictalurus punctatus.* Detritus, which accumulates in backwaters, is a common diet item for several large species, including several catostomids (*Catostomus commersoni, Carpiodes carpio, C. cyprinus,* and *C. velifer*) (Becker, 1983; Smith, 1979), and *Cyprinus carpio. C. carpio* is also known to feed on terrestrial plant material during floodplain inundation (Lubinski et al., 1986).

Macroinvertebrates are eaten by the majority of Upper Mississippi fishes. Benthic macroinvertebrates contribute much if not most of the diet for several omnivorous species, including *Cyprinus carpio, Catostomus commersoni, Notropis hudsonius, Pimephales vigilax,* and *Ictalurus punctatus.* Benthic prey are the primary food item for several other species, including *Scaphirhynchus platorynchus, Hiodon tergisus, Ictiobus bubalus, I. niger, Minytrema melanops, Moxostoma* spp., *Hybopsis* spp., bullheads (*Ictalurus* spp.), *Percopsis omiscomaycus,* darters (*Etheostoma* and *Percina*), and *Aplodinotus grunniens* (Becker, 1983; Farabee, 1979; Smith, 1979). Epiphytic invertebrates are important food items for *Ambloplites rupestris, Lepomis macrochirus,* and *Perca flavescens* (Holland and Huston, 1985).

The large populations of *Hexagenia* spp. and *Musculum transversum* in Pool 19 serve as important prey items for a number of species. *Aplodinotus grunniens* and *Cyprinus carpio* have been reported to feed heavily on *Hexagenia* nymphs (Jahn and Anderson, 1986; Lubinski et al., 1986). *M. transversum* is an important diet item for several species, including older *Dorosoma cepedianum, Ictiobus bubalus, Cyprinus carpio, Ictalurus melas, I. punctatus,* and *A. grunniens* (Gale and Lowe, 1971; Jahn and Anderson, 1986; Jude, 1973). Elsewhere, *Hiodon tergisus* and *Ictiobus niger* are reported to feed on molluscs (Becker, 1983).

Drifting macroinvertebrates provide an important food for some of the more abundant fish. Adult Hydropsychidae contributed significantly to the gut contents of *Ictalurus punctatus, Hiodon tergisus, Morone chrysops,* and *Aplodinotus grunniens* in the vicinity of Lock and Dam 19. Adult *Hexagenia* were eaten by *I. punctatus, H. tergisus,* and *M. chrysops* (Jahn and Anderson, 1986). Drifting macroinvertebrates also contribute significantly to a number of other surface and midwater feeders, including *Notropis atherinoides, N. blennius, N. hudsonius, N. spilopterus,* and *Labidesthes sicculus* (Becker, 1983; Smith, 1979).

Fish are important prey items for the adults of several species; immatures usually feed on zooplankton, epiphytic invertebrates, or benthic invertebrates. Adult *Lepisosteus* spp., *Esox lucius, Pomoxis nigromaculatus, Stizostedion canadense, S. vitreum,* and *Morone chrysops* are primarily piscivores. Adult *Amia calva, Hiodon tergisus, Ictalurus punctatus, Pylodictis olivaris, Ambloplites rupestris, Micropterus salmoides, Pomoxis annularis, Perca flavescens,* and *Aplodinotus grunniens* also feed on fishes (Becker, 1983; Farabee, 1979; Smith, 1979).

The Upper Mississippi River lies along one of the major flyways for migratory waterfowl. In particular, Pool 19 may be the most important inland area for migrating diving ducks in North America. Lesser scaup, canvasbacks, ringnecks, goldeneyes, ruddy ducks, common merganser, and red-breasted mergansers are important species of diving ducks that stop over along the Upper Mississippi during their spring and/or autumn migrations. Of these, canvasbacks and lesser scaups are the most numerous (Jahn and Anderson, 1986).

Diving ducks feed in the shallow, mud-bottomed areas, and their stopovers result in extremely intense episodes of feeding. For example, it has been estimated that diving ducks consumed approximately 24% of the September 1967 standing stock of *Musculum transversum* and *Sphaerium transversum* in Pool 19 (Gale and Lowe, 1971). Studies in Pool 19 have revealed that lesser scaup and canvasback feed on a variety of items, including Sphaeriidae, Gastropoda, *Hexagenia,* Trichoptera, and macrophytes (Jahn and Anderson, 1986; Sparks, 1980).

The plasticity of the diving duck's diet was demonstrated with a series of feeding studies conducted in Pool 19. During a study conducted during the late 1940s, the diets for both lesser scaups and canvasbacks were dominated by Gastropoda and Ephemeroptera (presumably, *Hexagenia*); Sphaeriidae were moderately important in lesser scaup diets (Korschgen, 1948, as cited in Jahn and Anderson, 1986). A 1966–1968 study reported a shift in the diets of these two species, which may reflect a response to change in benthic production. Gastropoda and Ephemeroptera continued to be important components of the diets of both ducks, but there were substantial increases in the consumption of macrophytes (especially *Potamogeton*) and Sphaeriidae by canvasbacks, while there was a dramatic increase in the consumption by lesser scaups of Sphaeriidae and "unidentified clams" (Thompson, 1969, as cited in Jahn and Anderson, 1986; Sparks, 1980). The 1976 and 1977 drought, which resulted in an increase in macrophyte coverage and a decrease in *Musculum transversum* populations, also resulted in another diet shift. Consumption of Sphaeriidae during a 1977 and 1978 study declined sharply, while the consumption of phytophilic gastropods increased. In addition, canvasbacks fed intensively on overwintering buds of *Vallisneria americana* during the spring of 1978. Earlier studies did not report any intake of *V. americana* by canvasbacks (Paveglio and Steffeck, 1978, as cited in Sparks, 1980).

The Upper Mississippi River is also an important habitat for dabbling ducks, including mallard and wood ducks. Dabbling ducks are generally less dependent on the river than diving ducks, but the extensive wetlands, backwaters, and vegetated main-channel borders of the river do provide significant nesting and feeding habitat (Jahn and Anderson, 1986).

Structure of Aquatic Communities

General Characteristics.   The Upper Mississippi River was originally a free-flowing island-braided river, with substantial changes in river stage. In the 1930s a series of locks and dams were constructed that transformed the free-flowing river into a series of shallow rivers and lakes. However, the various habitats of lotic and lentic conditions and of vegetation still exist. Figure 1.1 shows the structure of the Upper Mississippi River. Pool 19 has been chosen to illustrate the various communities of aquatic life that are present in the Upper Mississippi River.

The structure of the river consists of a main channel, side channels that often connect with the main channel, lakes, and pools that are typically lentic but may at times connect with the main channel or side channels and have a fair amount of flow or lotic conditions. The main channel is characterized by currents of variable flow. Sand, hard clay, and gravel form the substrates of this channel. This channel is bordered by a shallower zone that lies between the main channel and the shoreline. Whereas the currents in the main channel are moderate to swift, those near the shoreline are reduced. Sand and rocks may dominate the main channel, whereas the sides of the channel often contain hard clay, soft clay, and silt. Sometimes, sand is present.

The side channels are subsidiary channels that carry flow for most of the year and have relatively swift currents. Their substrates are predominantly sandy. These subsidiary channels are in contact with the river throughout the year but increased in flow during high-flow periods. In addition to sand are gravel, hard clay, and silt, and in some places a soft muck is present.

The floodplain lakes and ponds are isolated during low flow but may connect to the main river during high flow. Through much of the year they are isolated. The substrates of these lakes are mainly silt, clay, and muck, which is similar to the substrates present in sloughs. The various habitats described above present a great many different types of flow and substrate conditions for aquatic life.

The bedrock of Pool 19, which is evident only in the main channel, consists of Keokuk and Burlington limestone of the Mississippian age (Jahn and Anderson, 1986). Sedimentation has been very high in Pool 19, as it has the oldest of the locks, being constructed some 50 years earlier than those authorized later. The lock and dam of Pool 19 was designed with surface lift gates which are more efficient in trapping sediments than the rolling gates employed in most of the other dams. Pool 19 has silted up considerably and has lost about 50% of its original impoundment capacity. Seasonally, the river flow is characterized by a spring rise, which occurs somewhere between February and late spring and lasts for a mean of 209 days.

Turbidity tends to be highest during the spring rise and lowest during the winter. In the spring, the rise is due to faster currents and greater tributary inputs. The turbidity is lower in winter as the result of low flows and ice cover.

The chemical characteristics of the Upper Mississippi River range from hard to very hard in calcium carbonate hardness. The pH is circumneutral to slightly alkaline and the specific conductance is relatively high.

The waters of the Upper Mississippi River are eutrophic, and concentrations of nitrogen, phosphorus, and silica are generally not limiting to primary production. Anthropogenic enrichment comes from both point and nonpoint sources. Water quality usually deteriorates during low flow and consequent dry periods. For example, during the drought of 1976, the concentration of nonionized ammonia reached a maximum of 0.198 mg L^{-1}. It is believed that such high concentrations may have contributed to the sudden decline in the fingernail clam, *Musculium transversum*. Over time the discharge of both toxic and nontoxic waste has influenced the quality of water of the Upper Mississippi and hence the structure of the aquatic communities.

Detritus and Dissolved Organic Carbon. Detritus and dissolved organic carbon are important sources of organic matter in the Upper Mississippi. Macrophytes contribute a large proportion of the total organic carbon in Pool 19. Besides organic matter contributed by the swamps and wetlands, the beds within the pool contribute organic carbon. This organic carbon is primarily in the form of dissolved organic carbon exudates and particulates from sloughed leaves and autumnal senescence. The DOC and the sloughed leaves, which would not be included in the estimated production using biomass change, would occur in the spring and summer as well as in autumn senescence.

In particular, *Sagittaria latifolia* experiences heavy leaf sloughing and degeneration in the spring. During spring floods, when the currents in the backwaters and the main stream increase, the organic load from these sources increases. Following frost in the fall, *Sagittaria latifolia* and *Nelumbo lutea* die and produce an organic load. However, the mean concentrations of sediment organic matter were not significantly higher during September, October, and November than they were in July and August. The highest concentration from both of the foregoing species was recorded in June.

Organic matter tends to accumulate to a greater extent in depositional backwaters and lower pool habitats than in the erosional sites. In the lower reaches of Pool 19, the sediment organic content from seven main-channel border stations ranges from 3.2 to 6.4%. It is evident that macrophytes contribute large amounts to the nutrient levels in the river.

Patterns of benthic macroinvertebrate abundance and taxonomic composition among habitats in the lower reaches of Pool 19 generally conform to those observed in the more northern pools. The shifting sand of the main channel contained low densities of macroinvertebrates, many of which apparently originated from elsewhere. The shallow, silt–clay substrates of the unvegetated main channel border contained very high densities of large-bodied *Musculum transversum* (100 to 10,000 m^{-2}) and *Hexagenia* spp. (500 to 3000 m^{-2}) as well as high densities of small-bodied Chironomidae (100 m^{-2}) and Oligochaeta ($>500\ m^{-2}$). *M. transversum* and *Hexagenia* spp. declined precipitously where the unvegetated main-channel border graded into the nearshore macrophyte beds. Another sphaeriid, *Sphaerium striatinum,* replaces *M. transversum* in the submerged macrophyte zone, but it too becomes rare in the shallower floating-leafed macrophyte zone. A diverse and productive assemblage of gastropods, oligochaetes, isopods, amphipods, chironomids, and other insects occurred in the macrophyte zone (Anderson and Day, 1986).

Benthic macroinvertebrates in the upper reaches of Pool 19 differed somewhat from those encountered in the lower pool. The biggest difference between the upper and lower reaches of Pool 19 occurred within the erosional habitats of the main channel and side channels. The coarse sand and cobble substrates of the upper main channel supported a distinctive assemblage dominated by Hydropsychidae (Trichoptera), especially *Hydropsyche orris.* Hydropsychid-dominated assemblages also occupied the coarser substrates of side channels, but *Cheumatopsyche* were often more abundant then *H. orris.* On the other hand, the assemblages encountered in macrophyte zones from backwaters and along channel margins in the upper pool were similar to those encountered in the macrophyte beds of the lower pool. *Musculum transversum* and *Hexagenia* spp. dominated the unvegetated main-channel borders of the upper pool but occurred at lower densities than in corresponding habitats from the lower pool (Anderson and Day, 1986).

Phytoplankton. The phytoplankton from April to July was composed of about 40% diatoms, 33% green algae, and about 11% blue-green algae. A centric diatom, *Stephanodiscus astraea* var. *minutula,* was abundant in the spring and *Melosira ambigua* was abundant in the fall. The fall and spring were the times of greatest peaks of diatoms. The blue-green alga, *Microcystis,* was noted frequently in September.

Zooplankton. The zooplankton consisted mainly of rotifers and Crustacea, the rotifers far outnumbering all other small planktonic invertebrates. *Keratella,* a rotifer, was the most abundant genus, with an average density of 47 organisms per liter. Other abundant genera were *Brachionus, Polyarthra, Synchaeta,* and *Trichocera.* The highest density usually occurred in late summer or fall (Jahn and Anderson, 1986).

Throughout the pool a total of 36 taxons were identified. Both rotifers and Cladocera were common. Of the 36 taxons, 20 were rotifers; 12 taxons of Cladocera were also found. The maximum density of rotifer species ranged from very low for Trichoptera to very common for *Brachionus calyciflorus.* The greatest species peaks were in August and May. The biggest peaks for Crustacea were in August. The most common species were *Daphnia retrocurva* and *D. cyclops.* Generally, high densities and diversity of rotifers and Crustacea came from the channel and channel borders in May and June samples. Galstoff (1924) indicated higher crustacean densities in the lower lacustrinelike reaches of Pool 19. Aquatic macrophytes seemed to limit zooplankton production, but the macrophyte growing season, June through August, is short and these shallow areas have abundant zooplankton populations in the fall after plant senescence.

Vegetation Habitats. Vegetation communities were common in Pool 19. These communities fall into three general groups: emerged vegetation, which usually consists of monocotyledons and dicotyledons; floating vegetation; and submerged vegetation. The first group consisted of the American lotus, *Nelumbo lutea;* water dock, *Rumex orbiculatus;* and duck potato, *Sagittaria latifolia.* Also present along the banks with their roots in the water were *Hybiscus militaris, Asclepias incarnata,* and *Bidens cernua.*

Associated with the emerged vegetation was an abundant meiofauna where nematodes with a density ranging from 128,000 m^{-2} to about 1,100,000 m^{-2} were present. These were in the vegetation in the main channel. Also present in the floating vegetation were a great many of the meiofauna. A common genus was *Tobrilus* sp., a bacterial-feeding nematode. Other abundant genera were the bacterial feeder *Plectus* sp. and the plant feeder *Ironus* sp. In general, the benthic rotifers were about half as abundant as the nematodes in all but the main channel.

The three major types of aquatic macrophytes were emergent, floating leaves, and submergent. The first group consisted of the American lotus, *Nelumbo lutea;* water dock, *Rumex orbiculatus;* and duck potato, *Sagittaria latifolia.* Also present along the banks with their roots in water were *Hybiscus militaris, Asclepias incarnata,* and *Bidens cernua.*

The second group consisted of a floating mass of vegetation containing big duckweed, *Spirodela polyrhiza;* duckweed, *Lemna minor;* Columbus water meal, *Wolffia columbiana;* papilary water weed, *W. papulifera;* and dotted water meal, *W. punctata.* Other leafy vegetation that was probably floating included *Ceratophyllum demersum, Nelumbo lutea, Elodea canadensis, E. nuttalli, Vallisneria americana,* and *Najas flexilis,* together with three other species of *Najas* (Table 1.37) and *Zannichellia palustris.*

The third group, submerged vegetation, was composed of *Ceratophyllum demersum* (coontail); *Elodea canadensis,* and *E. nuttalli,* commonly known as water weeds; *Najas gracillima* (slender naiad); and *N. flexilis* (brittle naiad). Also submerged were the curly pond weed, *Potamogeton crispus,* and the small spiny naiad, *Najas minor.* Other species found here and there submerged were *P. foliosus, P. nodosus, P. pectinatus,* and *P. pusillus.* Also submerged was wild celery, *Vallisneria americana;* the horned pond weed, *Zannichellia palustris;* and water star grass, *Heteranthera dubia.* Other species, such as *Echinochloa walteri* and *Leersia oryzoides,* had their roots and parts of their stems in shallow water.

Submerged macrophytes support a rather large population of epiphytic algae. They are part of the lentic habitat. For example, dense growths of epiphytic diatoms have been observed on the filamentous green alga *Cladophora,* which accounts for up to 40% of the summer biomass, colonizing shallow rock substrates and adjacent to the main channel.

The greatest density of algae occurred in April. About 40% of these species were diatoms and 33% were green algae, about 11% were blue-green algae. However, algal blooms of the blue-green alga, *Microcystis,* were frequently noted in September. Blue-greens were usually abundant in the late summer and early fall. In vegetative areas, pennate diatom densities and diversity were the highest, and the community was dominated by species of *Achnanthes.* However, the macrophyte beds were dominated by *Cocconeis* sp. The highest diversity of plankton was in the backwaters.

Macrophyte beds are extensive in Pool 19, but not as extensive as they are in some northern pools such as Pools 8 and 9. However, many species were

(text continues on page 127)

TABLE 1.37. *Species List: Upper Mississippi River*

Taxon	Substrate[a]			Site[b]	Source[c]	Comment[d]
		Lentic	Lotic			
	V	M,S	G,R			
SUPERKINGDOM PROKARYOTAE						
KINGDOM MONERA						
Division Cyanophycota						
Class Cyanophyceae						
Order Chroococcales						
Family Chroococcaceae						
*Anacystis incerta		X		19	j	
*A. marina		X		19	j	
*A. montana		X		19	j	
*A. thermalis		X		19	j	
*Anacystis sp.		X		19	j	
Aphanocapsa sp.		X		7	d	
*Coleosphaerium collinsii		X		19	j	
Coleosphaerium sp.		X		7	d	
Gleocapsa sp.				19	j	
*Gleothece rupestris		X		19	j	
Gleothece sp.		X		7,19	j,d	
*Gomphosphaeria lacustris		X	X	19	j	
Gomphosphaeria sp.		X	X	7	j	
*Marssoniella elegans		X	X	7,19	j,d	
*Merismopedia glauca			X	7,19	j,d	
M. guadruplicata			X	19	j	
Microcystis aeruginosa		X	X	7	h	
*Microcystis sp.		X	X	7,19	j,d	
Synechocystis aquatilis				19	j	
Order Nostocales						
Family Nostocaceae						
*Anabaena circinalis			X	19	j	
*A. spiroides			X	19	j	
*Anabaena sp.			X	7,19	j,d	
*Aphanizomenon flos-aquae		X		7,19	h,j,d	
Family Oscillatoriaceae						
*Oscillatoria curviceps		X		19	j	
*O. ornata		X		19	j	
Oscillatoria sp.		X		7	d	
*Schizothrix calcicola		X		19	j	
*Schizothrix sp.		X		19	j	
Spirulina laxa				7	d	
S. subsale				19	j	
Family Rivulariaceae						
Rivularia haematites			X	7	d	

Continued

TABLE 1.37.   (Continued)

Taxon	Substrate[a]			Site[b]	Source[c]	Comment[d]
	V	Lentic M,S	Lotic G,R			
SUPERKINGDOM EUKARYOTAE						
KINGDOM PLANTAE						
Subkingdom Thallobionta						
Division Chlorophycota						
Class Chlorophyceae						
Order Tetrasporales						
Family Coccomyxaceae						
Elakatothrix gelatinosa				7	d	
Family Palmellaceae						
*Dispora crucigenioides		X		19	j	
*Gloeocystis gigas		X		19	j	
*G. planctonica		X		19	j	
*Gloeocystis sp.		X		19	j	
*Sphaerocystis schroeteri		X		7,19	j,d	
Order Chlorococcales						
Family Characiaceae						
Characium ambiguum				7	d	
Family Chlorococcaceae						
Acanthosphaera zachariasi				7	d	
Ankyra judayi				19	j	
Golenkinia radiata				7	d	
Family Coelastraceae						
Coelastrum microsporum				7	d	
Family Dictosphaeriaceae						
*Dictyosphaerium ehrenbergianum	X	X		19	j	
D. pulchellum				7,19	j,d	
Family Hydrodictyaceae						
Hydrodictyon reticulatum				7	d	
Pediastrum boryanum				7,19	j,d	
*P. boryanum var. longicorne	X	X		19	j	
*P. boryanum var. undulatum	X	X		7,19	d	
P. duplex				7,19	j,d	
P. simplex				7,19	j,d	
P. simplex var. duodenarium				19	j	
*P. tetras	X	X		19	j	
P. tetras var. tetraodon	X			19	j	
Family Oocystaceae						
*Ankistrodesmus braunii		X		19	j	
*A. convolutus		X		19	j	
*A. falcatus		X		7,19	j,d	
*A. spiralis		X		19	j	
Cerasteruas staryastroides				7	d	
Chlorella vulgaris				7	d	
Chlorella sp.				7	d	

TABLE 1.37.   (Continued)

Taxon	V	Lentic M,S	Lotic G,R	Site[b]	Source[c]	Comment[d]
Family Oocystaceae (cont.)						
*Chodatella ciliata		X		19	j	
*C. quadriseta		X		19	j	
Echinosphaerella limnetica		X		7	d	
*Kirchneriella elongata		X		19	j	
K. lunaris		X		19	j	
Kirchneriella sp.		X		19	j	
Nephrocytium agardhianum				19	j	
Nephrocytium sp.				19	j	
Oocystis borgei				19	j	
O. parva				19	j	
Polyedriopsis spinulosa				19	j,d	
Quadrigula chodatii				7,19	d	
Quadrigula sp.				7	j	
Selenastrum gracile				19	d	
*S. westii		X		7	j	
*Selenastrum sp.		X		19	j	
*Tetraedon caudatum				19	j	
*T. minimum		X		19	j	
*T. muticum		X		19	j	
*T. pentaedricum		X		19	j	
*T. regulare		X		19	j	
T. setigerum				7	d	
*T. trigonum		X		19	j	
*T. trigonum var. gracile		X		19	j	
Family Scenedesmaceae						
*Actinastrum hantzschii		X		7,19	j,d	
*A. hantzschii var. fluviatile		X		7,19	j,d	
Crucigenia quadrata				19	j	
C. tetrapedia				7,19	j,d	
*Micractinium pusillum		X		19	j	
M. pusillum var. elegans		X		7	d	
*M. quadrisetum		X		19	j	
*Scenedesmus arcuatus	X	X		19	j	
*S. armatus	X	X		19	j	
*S. bijuga	X	X		19	j	
*S. brasiliensis	X	X		19	j	
*S. denticulatus	X	X		19	j	
*S. dimorphus	X	X		19	j	
*S. opoliensis	X	X		19	j	
*S. quadricauda	X	X		7,19	j,d	
S. quadricauda var. maximus	X	X		7	d	
S. quadricauda var. westii	X	X		7	d	
Tetradesmus sp.	X			19	j	
*Tetrastrum staurogeniaforme	X	X		19	j	

Continued

TABLE 1.37.   (Continued)

Taxon	V	Lentic M,S	Lotic G,R	Site[b]	Source[c]	Comment[d]
Family Treubariaceae						
Treubaria crassipina				19	j	
T. setigerum				19	j	
Order Ulotrichales						
Family Ulotrichaceae						
Ulothrix cylindricum			X	7	d	
U. zonata			X	7	d	
Order Chaetophorales						
Family Chaetophoraceae						
Draparnaldia sp.			X	7	d	
Stigeoclonium lubricum			X	5	l	
Order Siphonocladales						
Family Cladophoraceae						
Cladophora fracta			X	7	d	
Cladophora sp.	X		X	5,8,9	l,s	
Order Zygnematales						
Family Desmidiaceae						
Closteriopsis longissima		X	X	19	j	
Closterium dianae	X	X	X	19	j	
C. ehrenbergii		X	X	19	j	
C. gracile		X	X	19	j	
C. intermedium		X	X	19	j	
Closterium sp.		X	X	7,19	j,d	
Cosmarium formulosum		X	X	19	j	
C. subcrenatum		X	X	19	j	
Cosmarium sp.		X	X	19	j	
Pleurotaenium coronatum			X	19	j	
Staurastrum cuspidatum		X	X	19	j	
S. gracile			X	19	j	
S. leptocladum			X	19	j	
S. oxcycanthum			X	19	j	
Staurastrum sp.			X	7,19	j,d	
Family Zygnemataceae						
Mougeotia sp.			X	7	d	
Spirogyra sp.			X	7	d	
Division Chromophycota						
Class Xanthophyceae						
Order Mischoccoccales						
Family Ophiocytaceae						
Ophiocytium capitatum		X		19	j	
O. capitatum var. *longispinum*		X		19	j	
Order Tribonematales						
Family Tribonemataceae						
Tribonema sp.		X		19	j	

TABLE 1.37. (*Continued*)

Taxon	V	M,S	G,R	Site[b]	Source[c]	Comment[d]
		Lentic	Lotic			
Class Bacillariophyceae						
Order Eupodiscales						
Family Coscinodiscaceae						
Coscinodiscus sp.			X	5,7,9	v,d	
Cyclotella atomus			X	5,9	v	
*C. chaetoceros		X		19	j	
C. comensis				5	v	
C. comta			X	5,9	v	
*C. glomerata			X	5,19	j,v	
*C. kuetzingiana			X	9,19	j,v	
*C. melosiroides			X	19	j	
*C. meneghiniana			X	5,7,9,19	v,j	
C. michiganiana			X	9	v	
C. pseudostelligera			X	5,9	v	
C. stelligera			X	5,9	v	
C. stelligera var. *tenuis*			X	5	v	
C. striata				5,9	v	
C. striata var. *ambigua*			X	5	v	
*Cyclotella spp.		X	X	7,19	j,d,h	
*Melosira ambigua			X	5,7	h,v	
M. distans				5,9	v	
*M. granulata			X	5,7,9,19	j,h,v	
M. granulata var. *angustissima*			X	5	v	
*M. italica			X	5,7,9,19	j,v,h	
M. italica var. *tenuissima*			X	5	v	
*M. varians	X		X	5,7,9,19	j,v,h	
*Melosira sp.			X	19	j	
*Stephanodiscus astraea		X		7,19	h,j	
*S. astraea var. minutula		X		19	j	
S. dubius		X		5,7	v	
*S. hantzschii		X	X	5,7,9,19	j,v,h	
S. invistatus			X	5,9	v	
S. minutus			X	5	v	
*S. niagarae		X	X	5,7,9,19	j,v,h	
S. niagarae var. *magnifica*			X	5	v	
S. rotula				5,9	v	
S. tenuis				5,9	v	
*Stephanodiscus sp.		X		7,19	j,d	
Family Thalassiosiracea						
Thalassiosira fluviatilis			X	5	v	
Order Biddulphiales						
Family Biddulphiaceae						
Biddulphia laevis			X	5	v	

Continued

TABLE 1.37.   (Continued)

Taxon	Substrate[a]			Site[b]	Source[c]	Comment[d]
	V	Lentic M,S	Lotic G,R			
Order Rhizosoleniales						
Family Rhizosoleniaceae						
Rhizosolenia sp.				7	d	
Order Fragilariales						
Family Fragilariaceae						
Asterionella formosa		X		5,9,19	j,v	
A. formosa var. *gracillima*		X		19	j	
Asterionella sp.				7	d	
Diatoma anceps			X	9	v	
D. tenue			X	5,9	v	
D. tenue var. *elongatum*			X	5,9	v	
*D. vulgare			X	5,9,19	j,v	
Diatoma sp.				19	j	
Fragilaria brevistriata			X	5	v	
*F. capucina		X	X	5,9,19	j,v	
F. capucina var. *mesolepta*			X	5,9	v	
F. construens			X	5,9	v	
F. construens var. *binodus*			X	5	v	
F. construens var. *pumila*			X	5,9	v	
F. construens var. *venter*			X	5,9	v	
*F. crotonensis		X	X	5,9,19	j,v	
F. crotonensis var. *oregona*			X	9	v	
F. lapponica				5	v	
F. leptostauron		X	X	5,9	v	
F. leptostauron var. *dubia*			X	5	v	
F. leptostauron var. *rhomboides*			X	5	v	
F. pinnata				5,9	v	
F. pinnata var. *intercedens*			X	9	v	
F. pinnata var. *lancettula*			X	5	v	
F. vaucheriae			X	5,9	v	
Fragilaria sp.				7,19	j,d	
*Meridion circulare		X	X	5,9,19	j,v	
M. circulare var. *constrictum*			X	5	v	
Opephora martyi		X	X	5,9	v	
*Synedra acus			X	5,9,19	v	
S. cyclopum var. *robustum*			X	9	v	
*S. delicatissima		X	X	5,9,19	j,v	
S. delicatissima var. *angustissima*			X	5,9	v	
S. filiformis var. *exilis*			X	5	v	
S. goulardi				5	v	
S. incisa		X	X	5	v	
S. minuscula			X	9	v	
S. parasitica			X	5,9	v	
S. parasitica var. *subconstricta*			X	5,9	v	

TABLE 1.37. *(Continued)*

Taxon	V	M,S (Lentic)	G,R (Lotic)	Site[b]	Source[c]	Comment[d]
Family Fragilariaceae *(cont.)*						
*S. pulchella		X		5,9,19	j,v	
*S. radians		X		5,9,19	j,v	
S. rumpens			X	5,9,19	j,v	
S. rumpens var. *familaris*			X	5,9	v	
S. rumpens var. *fragilarioides*			X	5,9	v	
S. rumpens var. *meneghiniana*			X	5,9	v	
S. socia			X	5,9	v	
*S. tenera	X	X	X	19	j	
S. ulna	X			5,7,9,19	j,v,h	
S. ulna var. *amphirhynchus*	X			9	v	
S. ulna var. *contracta*	X			9	v	
S. ulna var. *danica*	X			5	v	
S. ulna var. *oxyrhynchus*	X			5,9	v	
*Tabellaria fenestrata	X	X	X	5,9,19	j,v	
T. flocculosa	X		X	5,9	v	
*Tabellaria sp.			X	7,19	j,d	
Order Eunotiales						
Family Eunotiaceae						
*Amphicampa mirabilis	X	X		19	j	
Eunotia arcus			X	9	v	
E. arcus var. *bidens*			X	9	v	
E. curvata			X	5,9	v	
E. exigua			X	9	v	
E. hexagluphis				5	v	
E. lunaris				5	v	
E. monodon			X	5,9	v	
E. pectinalis		X		5,9	v	
*E. pectinalis var. *minor*		X		19	j	
*E. rostellata		X		19	j	
E. vanheurckii var. *intermedia*	X		X	5	v	
Eunotia sp.				19	j	
Order Achnanthales						
Family Achnanthaceae						
*Achnanthes affinis		X	X	19	j	
A. clevei			X	5	v	
A. clevei var. *rostrata*			X	5	v	
A. exigua				5,9	v	
A. exigua var. *constricta*			X	9	v	
*A. exilis		X		19	j	
A. hauckiana var. *rostrata*			X	5,9	v	
A. hungarica			X	5,9	v	
*A. lanceolata		X	X	5,9,19	j,v	
A. lanceolata var. *apiculata*			X	5,9	v	
A. lanceolata var. *dubia*			X	5,9	v	

Continued

TABLE 1.37.   (Continued)

Taxon	V	M,S	G,R	Site[b]	Source[c]	Comment[d]
Family Achnanthaceae (cont.)						
A. lanceolata var. {c.f. ommisa}			X	5,9	v	
A. lapponica var. ninckei			X	5	v	
A. lewisiana				5	v	
*A. linearis	X		X	5,9,19	v,j	
*A. minutissima	X		X	5,19	v,j	
*Achnanthes sp.				19	j	
*Cocconeis pediculus	X		X	5,9,19	j,v	
*C. placentula	X		X	19	j	
C. placentula var. euglypta	X		X	5,9	v	
C. placentula var. lineata	X		X	5,9	v	
*Cocconeis sp.	X		X	19	j	
*Rhoicosphenia curvata		X	X	5,9,19	j,v	
Order Naviculales						
Family Cymbellaceae						
Amphora ovalis				5,9	v	
A. ovalis var. affinis				5	v	
A. ovalis var. pediculus		X		5,9	v	
A. perpusilla				5,9	v	
A. venta				5,9	v	
Amphora sp.				19	j	
Cymbella affinis	X			19	j	
C. angustata	X			19	j	
C. aspera			X	5	v	
C. cistula			X	5	v	
C. lanceolata			X	5	v	
C. mexicana				5	v	
C. minuta				5,9	v	
C. minuta var. pseudogracilis			X	9	v	
C. minuta var. silesiaca			X	5,9	v	
C. naviculiformis			X	5,9	v	
*C. parva	X	X		19	j	
C. prostrata			X	5,9	v	
C. sinuata			X	5	v	
C. triangulum			X	5,9	v	
*C. tumida			X	5,9,19	j,v	
Family Entomoneidaceae						
Entomoneis ornata			X	5,9	v	
Family Gomphonemaceae						
*Gomphonema accuminatum	X		X	5,19	j,v	
G. affine			X	9	v	
G. angustatum			X	5,9	v	
G. angustatum var. obtusatum			X	5,9	v	
G. angustatum var. sarcophagus				5,9	v	
*G. constrictum	X		X	19	j	

TABLE 1.37. *(Continued)*

Taxon	Substrate[a] Lentic V	M,S	Lotic G,R	Site[b]	Source[c]	Comment[d]
Family Gomphonemaceae *(cont.)*						
G. constrictum var. capitatum			X	9	v	
G. dichotomum			X	5,9	v	
G. germinatum	X			19	j	
G. gracile				5,9	v	
G. grovei			X	5	v	
G. intricatum			X	5,9	v	
G. intricatum var. pulvinatum			X	5,9	v	
*G. olivaceum	X		X	5,9,19	j,v	
G. olivaceum var. calcarea			X	9	v	
*G. parvulum	X		X	5,9,19	j,v	
G. simus			X	9	v	
G. subclavatum var. commutatum			X	5,9	v	
G. subclavatum var. mexicanum			X	5,9	v	
G. tenellum			X	5,9	v	
*G. truncatum		X	X	5,19	j,v	
G. ventricosum		X	X	9	v	
Family Naviculaceae						
Anomoeoneis follis				19	j	
A. serians				19	j	
Anomoeoneis sp.				19	j	
*Caloneis bacillaris		X	X	5,9,19	j,v	
C. hyalina			X	5	v	
C. lewisii			X	9	v	
C. limosa			X	5	v	
C. silicula				5	v	
*Caloneis sp.		X		19	j	
Capartogramma crucicula			X	5,9	v	
Diploneis finnica			X	5	v	
D. oculata			X	9	v	
D. puella			X	5	v	
D. smithii			X	5	v	
*Frustulia rhomboides	X	X	X	19	j	
F. rhomboides var. amphipleuroides				5,9	v	
*Gyrosigma acuminatum		X		5,19	j,v	
G. obtusatum				5,9	v	
*G. scalproides		X		5,9,19	j,v	
G. sciotense				5,9	v	
*G. spencerii		X		9,19	j,v	
G. wormleyi				19	j	
Navicula c.f. accomoda				9	v	

Continued

TABLE 1.37.   (Continued)

Taxon	V	M,S	G,R	Site[b]	Source[c]	Comment[d]
Family Naviculaceae (*cont.*)						
N. americana				5	v	
*N. anglica	X	X		5,9,19	j,v	
N. angusta				5	v	
N. arvensis				5,9	v	
N. bacillum		X		5	v	
N. capitata		X	X	5	v	
N. capitata var. *hungarica*				5,9	v	
N. cincta	X			9	v	
N. confervaceae	X			5	v	
N. cryptocephala	X			5,9,19	v	
N. cryptocephala f. *minuta*				5	v	
N. cryptocephala var. *veneta*	X				v	
*N. cuspidata		X		5,9,19	j,v	
*N. cuspidata var. *major*		X		9	v	
N. decussis				5,9	v	
N. dicephala				5,9	v	
*N. elginensis		X		5,9,19	j,v	
N. elginensis var. *rostrata*				5,9	v	
*N. exigua		X		5,19	j,v	
N. exigua var. *capitata*				5,9	v	
N. festiva				9	v	
N. gastrum				5,9	v	
N. hambergii				5	v	
N. ingrata				9	v	
N. integra				5,9	v	
N. c.f lacustris			X	5	v	
N. lanceolata			X	5,9	v	
N. luzonensis			X	5	v	
N. menisculus			X	5,9	v	
N. menisculus var. *upsaliensis*			X	5,9	v	
*N. minima		X		5,9	v	
N. mutica				5,9	v	
N. mutica var. *stigma*			X	5,9	v	
N. palaearctica				5	v	
N. paucivisitata				5	v	
N. pelliculosa				9	v	
N. placentula				5	v	
N. placentula var. *rostrata*				5	v	
*N. protracta		X		5,9,19	j,v	
N. pseudoreinhardtii				5,9	v	
N. pupula				5,9,19	j,v	
N. pupula var. *capitata*				9	v	
N. pupula var. *elliptica*				5	v	
N. pupula var. *rectangularis*				5,9	v	
N. radiosa				5,9	v	

TABLE 1.37. *(Continued)*

Taxon	V	M,S	G,R	Site[b]	Source[c]	Comment[d]
		Lentic	Lotic			
				Substrate[a]		
Family Gomphonemaceae *(cont.)*						
N. radiosa var. parva				5	v	
N. radiosa var. tenella				5,9	v	
N. reinhardtii				5,9	v	
N. reinhardtii var. elliptica				9	v	
N. rhynchocephala				5,9,19	j,v	
N. rhynchocephala var. amphiceros				9	v	
N. rhynchocephala var. germainii			X	5,9	v	
N. salinarum var. intermedia			X	5,9	v	
N. schroeteri var. escambia			X	5,9	v	
N. scutelloides			X	5	v	
N. secreta var. apiculata			X	5	v	
N. secura			X	9	v	
*N. seminulum		X	X	5,9,19	j,v	
N. symmetrica			X	5,9	v	
N. tantula			X	5	v	
N. tenera				5,9	v	
N. terminata				5,9	v	
*N. tripunctata		X		5,9,19	j,v	
N. tripunctata var. schizonemoides				5,9	v	
N. vaucheriae				9	v	
N. viridula				5,9	v	
N. viridula var. avenacea				5,9	v	
N. viridula var. linearis				5,9	v	
N. viridula var. rostellata				5,9	v	
N. vulpina				5	v	
*Navicula spp.	X	X		7,19	j,d	
Neidium affine			X	9	v	
N. iridis			X	5	v	
Pinnularia acrosphaeria			X	5	v	
P. appendiculata				19	j	
P. biceps		X		5,9	v	
*P. brevissonii		X		19	v	
P. dactylus				9	v	
P. nodosus				5	v	
P. subcapitata				9	v	
P. viridis				5	v	
Pleurosigma delicatulum				5,9	v	
*Stauroneis anceps		X		9,19	j,v	
S. ignorata				5	v	
S. phoenicenteron			X	5	v	
*S. smithii		X	X	19	j	

Continued

TABLE 1.37.   (Continued)

Taxon	V	M,S	G,R	Site[b]	Source[c]	Comment[d]
Family Gomphonemaceae (cont.)						
S. thermicola			X	5	v	
*Stauroneis sp.		X		19	j	
Order Epithemiales						
Family Epithemiaceae						
Epithemia adnata			X	5,9	v	
E. argus			X	9	v	
E. sorex			X	5	v	
E. turgica var. westermannii			X	5,9	v	
Rhopalodia gibba			X	5,9	v	
Order Bacillariales						
Family Nitzschiaceae						
Bacillaria paradoxa			X	9	v	
Cymbellonitzschia diluviana			X	5	v	
*Hantzschia amphioxys		X		19	j	
*H. amphioxys var. capitata		X		19	j	
Nitzschia acicularis				5,9,19	v,j	
N. acicularis var. closterioides				9	v	
N. acuta				5,9	v	
N. adamata				9	v	
N. affinis				9	v	
N. amphibia				5,9	v	
N. amphibia var. abbreviata				9	v	
N. brevissima				9	v	
N. capitellata				5,9	v	
N. clausii				5	v	
N. {c.f. communis var. abbreviata}				5	v	
*N. denticula		X		19	j	
N. dissipata				5,9	v	
N. filiformis				5,9	v	
N. fonticola				5,9	v	
N. frustulum				5,9	v	
N. gracilis				5,9	v	
N. holsatica				9	v	
N. hungarica				9	v	
N. lacunarum				9	v	
N. laevissima				9	v	
*N. linearis		X		5,9,19	j,v	
*N. longissima		X		19	j	
N. obtusa var. scalpelliformis				9	v	
*N. palea		X		5,9,19	j,v	
N. paleacea				5	v	
N. recta		X		5,9	v	
N. sigmoidea				5,9,19	j,v	

TABLE 1.37. *(Continued)*

Taxon	V	Lentic M,S	Lotic G,R	Site[b]	Source[c]	Comment[d]
Family Nitzschiaceae (*cont.*)						
N. subcapitalleta				5,9	v	
N. triblionella				5,9	v	
N. triblionella var. *levidensis*				5	v	
N. triblionella var. *victoriae*				5	v	
N. vermicularis		X		5,19	j,v	
Nitzschia spp.		X		19	j	
Order Surirellales						
Family Surirellaceae						
Camplodiscus noricus		X		19	j	
Camplodiscus sp.		X	X	5,19	j,v	
Cymatopleura elliptica		X		19	j	
C. *solea*		X	X	5,9,19	j,v	
Surirella angusta		X	X	5,9,19	j,v	
S. *didyma*				19	j	
S. *gracilis*				5	v	
S. *iowensis*				5	v	
S. linearis		X		19	j	
S. minuta		X		19	j	
S. *multiplicata*			X	9	v	
S. ovata		X	X	5,9,19	j,v	
S. *robusta*				5,9	v	
Surirella sp.		X		19	j	
Class Dinophyceae						
Order Gymnodiniales						
Family Gymnodiniaceae						
Gymnodinium sp.		X		19	j	
Order Peridinales						
Family Ceratiaceae						
Ceratium hirudinella			X	7,19	j,d	
Family Glenodiniaceae						
Glenodinium quadridens			X	19	j	
Glenodinium sp.			X	19	j	
Family Peridiniaceae						
Peridinium cinctum			X	19	j	
Peridinium sp.			X	19	j	
Order Phytodiniacaea						
Family Dinococcaceae						
Cystodinium cornifax				7	d	

Continued

TABLE 1.37.   (*Continued*)

Taxon	V	Lentic M,S	Lotic G,R	Site[b]	Source[c]	Comment[d]
Subkingdom						
Embryobionta						
Division Filicophyta						
Class Filicopsida						
Order Salviniales						
Family Azollaceae						
Azolla mexicana		X		19	j	
Division Magnoliophyta						
Class Dicotyledoneae						
Order Nymphaeales						
Family Ceratophyllaceae						
Ceratophyllum demersum		X	X	5,5a,7–9,19	d,p,m,j,o	
Family Nelumbonaceae						
Nelumbo lutea		X		5a,7–9,19	p,m,j	
Family Nymphaeaceae						
Numphar variegatum		X		8	p	
Nymphaea tuberosa		X		5,7,8	p	
Order Caryophyllales						
Family Amaranthaceae						
Amaranthus tumerculatus				19	j	
Order Polygonales						
Family Polygonaceae						
Polygonum amphibium	X			19	j	
P. cocineum		X	X	8	p	
P. hydropiperoides	X			19	j	
P. orientale	X			19	j	
P. punctatum	X			19	j	
Rumex orbiculatus	X			19	j	
R. verticallatus	X			19	j	
Order Malvales						
Family Malvaceae						
Hybiscus militaris	X			19	j	
Order Haloragales						
Family Haloragaceae						
Myriophyllum exalbescens		X	X	7,8	p,d	
M. spicatum (= *M. exalbescens?*)		X	X	7	o	
Order Myrtales						
Family Onagraceae						
Ludwigia palustris var. *americana*	X		X	8	s	
Order Geraniales						
Family Asclepiadaceae						
Asclepias incarnata	X			19	j	

TABLE 1.37. *(Continued)*

Taxon	V	Lentic M,S	Lotic G,R	Site[b]	Source[c]	Comment[d]
Order Scrophulariales						
Family Scrophulariaceae						
Lindernia dubia	X		X	8	s	
Order Asterales						
Family Asteraceae						
Bidens beckii	X		X	7	j	
*B. cernua	X		X	19	j	
Class Monocotyledoneae						
Order Alismales						
Family Alismaceae						
Sagittaria graminea	X		X	7	d	
*S. latifolia	X		X	5,7–9,19	p,j,d	
S. rigida		X	X	7,8	p	
S. rigida f. *fluvitans*		X	X	8	p	
Order Hydrocharitales						
Family Hydrocharitaceae						
*Elodea canadensis	X	X	X	5a,7–9,19	p,m,j,d	
*E. nuttalli		X	X	5a,19	m,j	
*Vallisneria americana	X	X	X	5a,7–9,19	p,m,d,j,o	
Order Najadales						
Family Najadaceae						
*Najas flexilis	X	X	X	7,8,19	p,j,d	
*N. gracillima	X	X	X	19	j	
*N. guadalupensis		X	X	19	j	
*N. minor	X	X	X	19	j	
*Zannichellia palustris	X	X	X	19	j	
Family Potamogetonaceae						
Potamogeton americanus		X	X	5a	m	
P. amplifolius		X		7	d	
*P. crispus	X	X	X	5a,7–9,19	j,p,m	
*P. foliosus		X	X	5a,7,8,19	p,m,j,d	
P. friesii		X		7	d	
P. gramineus			X	7	d	
P. illinoensis		X		7	d	
P. natans		X		7	d	
*P. nodosus	X	X	X	5,8,19	p,j	
*P. pectinatus	X	X	X	5a,7,8,19	p,m,j,d	
*P. pusillus	X		X	19	j	
P. richardsonii		X	X	5a,8	p,m	
P. zosteriformis		X	X	7,8	p,d	
Order Arales						
Family Lemnaceae						
*Lemna minor	X	X		8,19	j	
*Spirodela polyrhiza	X	X		8,19	j	
*Wolffia columbiana	X	X		8,19	j	

Continued

TABLE 1.37. (Continued)

Taxon	V	Lentic M,S	Lotic G,R	Site[b]	Source[c]	Comment[d]
Family Lemnaceae (cont.)						
*W. papulifera	X	X		19	j	
*W. punctata	X	X		19	j	
unident. spp.		X		8	p	
Order Cyperales						
Family Cyperaceae						
Eleocharis acicularis	X			7	d	
Scirpus acutus	X			7	d	
S. americanus	X			7	d	
S. fluviatilis	X			19	j	
S. tabernaemontanii	X			19	j	
S. validus	X		X	5,7,8	p,d	
Family Poaceae						
*Echinochloa walteri	X			19	j	
*Leersia oryzoides	X		X	19	j	
Phalaris arundinacea	X		X	7,8	p,d	
Phragmites communis	X		X	7	d	
Order Typhales						
Family Sparganiaceae						
*Sparganium eurycarpum		X	X	5,7,8,19	p,j,d	
Family Typhaceae						
Typha latifolia	X		X	7	d	
Typha spp.		X	X	19	j	
Order Iliales						
Family Pontederiaceae						
*Heteranthera dubia	X	X	X	5a,8,19	p,m	
Pontederia cordata	X		X	7	d	
KINGDOM ANIMALIA						
Subkingdom Protozoa						
Class Mastigophora						
Order Chrysomonadida						
Family Chromulinidae						
Chrysophaerella longispina				7	d	
Mallomonas alpina	X	X			7	d
Family Ochromonadidae						
*Dinobryon divergens	X	X			19	j
*D. sertularia	X	X		19	j	
*D. sociale	X	X		19	j	
Dinobryon sp.		X		7	d	
Family Syncryptidae						
Synura ulvella				7	d	
Synura sp.				19	j	

TABLE 1.37. *(Continued)*

Taxon	V	Lentic M,S	Lotic G,R	Site[b]	Source[c]	Comment[d]
Order Cryptomonadida						
Family Cryptomonadidae						
Cryptomonas erosa	X	X		19	j	
Cryptomonas sp.	X	X		19	j	
Rhodomonas sp.	X	X		19	j	
Order Phytomonadida						
Family Carteriidae						
Carteria mulitiflilis	X	X		19	j	
Carteria sp.	X	X		19	j	
Family Chlamydomonadidae						
Chlamydomonas spp.	X	X		7,19	h,j	
Pteromonas aculeata				19	j	
Family Phacotidae						
Phacotus lenticularis	X	X		19	j	
Family Volvocidae						
Endorina elegans		X		7	d	
Gonium formosum		X		19	j	
G. pectorale		X		7,19	j,d	
G. sociale		X		19	j	
Pandorina morum				7,19	j,d	
Volvox aureus				7	d	
Order Euglenoidida						
Family Euglenidae						
Euglena acus	X	X		19	j	
E. acutissima	X	X		19	j	
E. elastica	X	X		19	j	
Euglena sp.	X	X		7,19	j,d	
Phacus acuminata	X	X		19	j	
P. angustatum	X	X		19	j	
P. longicauda	X	X		19	j	
P. pleuronectes	X	X		19	j	
P. pyrum	X	X		19	j	
P. tortus	X	X		19	j	
Phacus sp.	X	X		7,19	j,d	
Trachelomonas creba	X	X		19	j	
T. hispida		X		19	j	
T. pulcherrima		X		19	j	
T. schaunislandii		X		19	j	
T. similis		X		19	j	
Trachelomonas spp.		X		19	j	
Subkingdom Parazoa						
Phylum Porifera						
Class Demospongiae						
Order Haplosclerida						
Family Spongillidae						
unident. spp.	X			7	o	

Continued

TABLE 1.37.　(Continued)

Taxon	Substrate[a]			Site[b]	Source[c]	Comment[d]
	V	Lentic M,S	Lotic G,R			
Subkingdom Eumetazoa						
Phylum Cnideria						
Class Hydrozoa						
Order Hydroida						
Family Hydridae						
*Hydra americana	X	X	X	19	j	
Hydra sp.		X	X	7,9	o,g	
unident. spp.			X	13	r	
Phylum Platyhelminthes						
Class Turbellaria						
Order Tricladida						
unident. spp.	X		X	7,8,13	e,r	
Family Planariidae						
Dugesia spp.			X	7	o	
Phylum Rotifera						
Class Digonota						
Order Bdelloidea						
Family Philodonidae						
*Minobia spp.	X	X		19	j	
Class Monogononta						
Order Ploima						
Family Asplanchnidae						
*Asplanchna spp.	X	X		19	j	
Family Brachionidae						
*Brachionus angularis	X	X		19	j	
*B. calyciflorus	X	X		19	j	
*B. caudatus	X	X		19	j	
*B. quadridentata	X	X		19	j	
*Keratella cochlearis	X	X		19	j	
*K. quadrata	X	X		19	j	
*Notholca striata	X	X		19	j	
*Platyais patulus	X	X		19	j	
*P. quadricornis	X	X		19	j	
Family Euchlanidae						
*Euchlanis spp.	X	X		19	j	
Family Lecanidae						
*Lecane spp.	X	X		19	j	
Family Synchaetidae						
*Polyarthra spp.	X	X		19	j	
*Synchaeta spp.	X	X		19	j	
Family Trichoceridae						
*Trichocera sp.	X	X		19	j	
Family Trichotriidae						
*Trichotria spp.	X	X		19	j	
Order Flosculariacea						
Family Conochilidae						
*Conochiliodes sp.		X		19	j	

TABLE 1.37. (Continued)

Taxon	Substrate[a]			Site[b]	Source[c]	Comment[d]
		Lentic	Lotic			
	V	M,S	G,R			
Family Filiniidae						
Filinia longiseta	X	X		19	j	
Testudinella spp.	X	X		19	j	
Phylum Nemata						
Class Adenophora						
unident. spp.	X	X		7,8,13	r,o,e,b	
Order Enoplida						
Cryptonchus sp.	X			19	j	
Ironus sp.		X		19	j	
Tobrilus sp.	X	X		19	j	
Tripyla sp.		X		19	j	
Order Dorylaimida						
Alaimus sp.		X		19	j	
Dorylaimus sp.	X	X		19	j	
Mesodorylaimus sp.	X	X		19	j	
Order Araeolaimida						
Anochus sp.		X		19	j	
Aphanolaimus sp.	X	X		19	j	
Chronogaster sp.	X	X		19	j	
Plectus sp.		X		19	j	
Rhabdolaimus sp.	X	X		19	j	
Order Chromadorida						
Achromadora sp.	X	X		19	j	
Chromatorita sp.	X	X		19	j	
Ethmolaimus sp.	X	X		19	j	
Order Monohysterida						
Monohystrella sp.		X		19	j	
Class Secernetea						
Order Rhabditida						
Acrobeloides sp.	X	X		19	j	
Butlerius sp.		X		19	j	
Rhabditis sp.	X	X		19	j	
Order Diplogaterida						
Diplogaster sp.	X	X		19	j	
Order Tylenchida						
Ditylenchus sp.	X	X		19	j	
Paratylenchus sp.	X	X		19	j	
Order Aphelenchida						
Aphelenchus sp.	X	X		19	j	
Phylum Nematomorpha						
Class Gordioida						
Order Gordea						
Family Gordiidae						
Gordius sp.				19	j	

Continued

TABLE 1.37.   *(Continued)*

Taxon	V	M,S	G,R	Site[b]	Source[c]	Comment[d]
Phylum Mollusca						
Class Gastropoda						
Order Mesogastropoda						
Family Hydrobiidae						
Amnicola binneyana				19	j	
A. lustrica		X	X	19	j	
A. sayana	X	X		19	j	
Amnicola spp.	X	X		7,8,13	e,o,b	
Fontigens nickliniana	X	X		19	j	
Somatogyrus depressus		X		19	j	
S. isogonus		X	X	19	j	
S. subglobosus		X		19	j	
Family Pleuroceridae						
Pleurocera acuta	X	X	X	7,19	o,j	
Pleurocera spp.	X	X	X	7,8	e.o	
Family Valvatidae						
Valvata sincera	X			8	e	
V. tricarinata	X			7,8	o,e	
Valvata sp.	X			7,8,19	e,j,b	
Family Viviparidae						
Campeloma crassula		X		19	j	
C. decisum		X	X	19	j	
Campeloma sp.	X	X		7–9	e,i,b	
Lioplax subcarinata		X		19	j	
L. subculosa		X		19	j	
Lioplax spp.		X		7,8,13	e,r,b	
Viviparus georgianus	X	X		19	j	
V. intertextus	X	X		19	j	
Viviparus sp.		X	X	7,8,13	e,r,b	
Order Basommatophora						
Family Ancylidae						
Ferrissia sp.	X			7	o,e	
Laevapex fuscus	X			19	j	
Laevapex sp.				19	j	
Family Lymnaeidae						
Stagnicola emarginata				8	e	
Family Physidae						
Physa antina	X			19	j	
P. gyrina	X	X		19	j	
P. integra	X	X		19	f	
Physa sp.		X	X	7,8	e,o,b	
Family Planorbidae						
Aplexa sp.				8	e	
Gyraulus parvus	X	X		9	f	
Gyraulus spp.	X	X		7,8,13	o,e,r	
Helisoma trivolis	X	X		19	j	

TABLE 1.37. *(Continued)*

Taxon	V	M,S	G,R	Site[b]	Source[c]	Comment[d]
		Lentic	Lotic			
Family Planorbidae *(cont.)*						
Helisoma spp.	X	X		7,8	e,o,b	
Menetus spp.		X	X	7	b	
Class Bivalvia						
Order Unionoida						
Family Margaritiferidae						
Cumberlandia (=			X	19	j	
Margaritifera?) monodonta						
Family Unionidae						
*Actinonais carinata	X	X	X	8,9,19	j,c	
A. ligamentina				7	t	
A. ligamentina carinata (= A.				7,8,13	k,a	
carinata?)						
Alasmidonta marginata				7,8	a	
Amblema peruviana		X			c	
*A. plicata	X	X	X	7–9,13,19	j,k,a	
A. rariplicata		X		8	e	
Anodonta grandis		X		7–9	k,a	
A. grandis corpulenta				7–9,13,19	j,k,a	
*A. imbecilis	X	X		7,8,19	j,k,a	
A. suborbiculata		X		8	a	
Anodonta sp.	X			8,9	c	
*Arcidens confragosus		X		7–9,13,19	j,a,k,c	
*Carunculina parvus	X	X		8,19	j,e	
Cyclonaias tuberculata			X	7,8	a	
*Ellipsaria lineolata	X	X	X	7,8,19	j,a	
Elliptio crassidens crassidens				7,8	a	
E. dilatus				7–9	c,a	
Fusconaia ebena				7,8,19	j,a	
F. flava				7–9,13,19	j,k,a	
F. undata				8,9	c,e	
Lampsilis anodontoides		X	X	8	c,e	
L. anodontoides falliciosa (=		X	X	8,9	c	
L. falliciosa?)						
*L. falliciosa	X	X		19	j	
L. higginsi			X	7,8	a	
*L. ovata ventricosa	X	X	X	9,13,19	j,k	
L. radiata luteola		X		7,8	a	
L. teres				7,8,19	j,a	
L. teres f. anodontoides				7,8	a	
L. ventricosa (= L.o.		X		7–9	c,a	
ventricosa?)						
*Lasmigona complanata	X	X		7,8,19	j,a	
L. costata			X	7,8	a	
*Leptodea fragilis	X	X	X	7–9,13,19	k,r,c,a,t	

Continued

TABLE 1.37.   *(Continued)*

Taxon	V	M,S	G,R	Site[b]	Source[c]	Comment[d]
		Substrate[a]				
		Lentic	Lotic			
Family Unionidae *(cont.)*						
L. laevissima		X		9	c	
Ligumia recta	X		X	7,8,19	j,a	
Magnonais nervosa				7,8	a	
Megalonais gigantea				8,9,19	j,c	
M. nervosa (= gigantea?)				9,13,19	k	
Obliquaria reflexa	X	X	X	7–9,13,19	a,j,k,c,e	
Obovaria olivaria	X	X	X	7–9,13,19	a,j,k,r,c	
Plagiola (= Ellipsaria?) lineolata	X	X	X	13,19	k	
Pleurobasus cyphyus		X	X	7,8	a,t	
Pleurobema sintoxia				7,8	a	
P. rubrum				8	a	
Potamilus (= Proptera?) alatus				7–9,13,19	k,a	
P. (= Proptera?) laevissimus	X	X		7,19	k,t	
P. ohiensis				7,8	a	
Proptera alata	X	X	X	8,9,19	j,c	
P. laevissima	X	X		19	j	
Proptera sp.			X	7	t	
Quadrula metanerva			X	7,8,19	j,a,e	
Q. nodulata	X	X	X	7–9,13,19	j,k,r,c,a	
Q. pustulosa	X	X	X	7–9,13,19	j,k,c,a,e	
Q. quadrula	X	X	X	7–9,13,19	j,k,c,a,e	
Strophitus rugosus		X	X	8	c	
S. undulatus		X	X	7,8,13,19	j,k,a,t	
Tritogonia verrucosa		X	X	7,8	a	
Truncilla donaciformis	X	X	X	7,8,13,19	j,k,r,c,a	
T. truncata	X	X	X	7–9,13,19	j,k,r,a,e	
Order Veneroida						
Family Corbiculidae						
Corbicula fluminea		X	X	8,9,19	j,c	
Family Sphaeriidae						
Musculium transversum		X		9,19	j,i	
Musculium spp.		X		7,8	e,b	
Pisidium compressum				19	j	
P. nitidum				19	j	
P. variabile				19	j	
Pisidium spp.		X		7,8,19	e,j,b	
Sphaerium lacustre				19	j	
S. simile		X		19	j	
S. striatinum		X		9,19	j,i	
Sphaerium spp.		X		8,13	e,r,b	

TABLE 1.37. *(Continued)*

Taxon	Substrate[a] Lentic V	Substrate[a] Lentic M,S	Substrate[a] Lotic G,R	Site[b]	Source[c]	Comment[d]
Phylum Annelida						
Class Hirudinoidia						
Order Rhynchobdellida						
Family Glossiphoniidae						
Abloglossiphonia heteroclita		X		7	o	
Batracobdella phalera	X	X		7	b	
Glossiphonia camplanata	X	X		7,19	j,b	
G. (= Abloglossiphonia?) heteroclita	X	X		7	b	
Helobdella elongata	X	X		7	o,b	
H. fusca		X	X	7,19	j,o,b	
H. lineata	X	X		7	b	
H. nepheloidea		X		19	j	
H. stagnalis	X	X		7,19	j,o,b	
H. transversa	X			7	o	
H. triserialis	X			7	o	
Helobdella sp.				9	f	
Placobdella montifera	X	X		7,19	j,o,b	
P. ornata	X			7	b	
P. parasitica		X		7,19	j,b	
P. translucens	X			7	o	
Placobdella spp.	X			7	o	
Family Piscicolidae						
Illinobdella sp.		X		19	j	
Order Arhynchobdellida						
Family Erpobdellidae						
Erpobdella punctata	X	X	X	7,19	j,b	
Nephelopsis obscura				19	j	
unident. spp.	X			7	o	
Family Hirudinidae						
Haemopis marmorata				19	j	
Class Oligochaeta						
unident. spp.	X	X	X	7–9,13	e,i,r,b	
Order Haplotaxida						
Family Naididae						
Chaetogaster limnaei				19	j	
Chaetogaster sp.				19	j	
Dero sp.				19	j	
Nais spp.				19	j	
Pristina sp.				19	j	
Stylaria lacustris	X			7	o	
Family Tubificidae						
Brachiura sowerbyi		X		9,19	j,i	
Limnodrilus hoffmeisteri		X		19	j	
Limnodrilus sp.		X		19	j	
Tubifex tubifex		X		19	j	

Continued

TABLE 1.37.   (Continued)

Taxon	V	M,S	G,R	Site[b]	Source[c]	Comment[d]
Order Aelosossomatida						
Family Aeolosomatidae						
*Aeolosoma spp.	X			7,19	j,o	
Phylum Arthropoda						
Class Arachnida						
Order Acariformes						
unident. spp.	X			7,8	o,e	
Family Arrenuridae						
Arrenurus sp.		X		7,8	e,b	
Family Hydrachnidae						
Hydrachna spp.		X		7	b	
Family Hydraphantidae						
Hydraphantes spp.		X		7	b	
Family Hygrobatidae						
Hygrobates spp.				7	b	
Family Lebertiidae						
Lebertia spp.		X		7	b	
Family Limnesiidae						
Limnesia sp.		X		7,13	r,b	
Family Pionidae						
Forelia spp.		X		7	b	
Family Thyasidae						
Thyas sp.		X		7	b	
Family Unionicolidae						
Neumania spp.		X		7	b	
Unionicola spp.				7	b	
Class Crustacea						
Subclass Cephalocarida						
(= Branchiopoda)						
Order Cladocera						
Family Bosminidae						
*Bosmina longirostris		X		19	j	
Family Chydoridae						
*Alona costata		X		19	j	
*A. rectangularis		X		19	j	
*Ceriodaphnia reticulata		X		19	j	
*Eurycercus lamellatus		X		19	j	
Family Daphinidae						
*Daphnia parvula		X		19	j	
D. pulex		X		19	j	
*D. retrocurva		X		19	j	
Family Leptodoridae						
*Leptodora kindtii			X	19	j	
Family Macrothricidae						
*Macrothrix spp.			X	19	j	

TABLE 1.37. (Continued)

Taxon	V	M,S	G,R	Site[b]	Source[c]	Comment[d]
		Lentic	Lotic			
Family Polyphemidae						
Polyphemus pediculus				19	j	
Family Sididae						
*Diaphasoma brachyurum			X	19	j	
Subclass Ostracoda						
unident. spp.	X	X		7,13	r,o	
Subclass Copepoda						
unident. nauplii				19	j	
Order Calanoida						
Family Diaptomidae						
Diaptomus spp.				19	j	
Order Cyclopoida						
Family Argulidae						
Argulus sp.				13	s	
Family Cyclopodae						
Cyclops spp.				19	j	
Subclass Malacostraca						
Order Isopoda						
Family Asellidae						
*Asellus brevicaudus	X			19	j	
A. communis		X		7	o	
*A. intermedius	X	X		19	j	
A. militaris		X		8	e	
Asellus spp.	X	X	X	7,9,13	i,r,o,b	
Order Amphipoda						
Family Gammaridae						
Gammarus fasciatus	X	X		8	e	
Gammarus spp.	X	X		7,13	r,b	
Family Talitridae						
*Hyalella azteca	X		X	7–9,19	e,j,i,o,b	
Hyalella sp.	X		X	13	r	
Order Decapoda						
Family Cambaridae						
Cambarus diogenes				19	j	
Orconectes virilis				19	j	
Family Palaemonidae						
*Palaemonetes kadiakensis	X			19	j	
Palaemonetes spp.	X			7	o	
Class Insecta						
Order Collembola						
Family Hypogasturidae						
*Hypogastura sp.	X	X		19	j	
Family Isotomidae						
*Isotomurus palustris			X	19	j	

Continued

TABLE 1.37.   (Continued)

Taxon	V	M,S	G,R	Site[b]	Source[c]	Comment[d]
		Lentic	Lotic			
Family Poduridae						
unident. spp.	X			7	o	
Order Odonata						
Suborder Zygoptera						
Family Calopterygidae						
*Agrion (= Calopteryx?) sp.			X	19	j	
Family Coenagrionidae						
*Argia spp.		X	X	19	j	
Chromagrion sp.	X	X		13	r	
*Enallagma spp.	X		X	7,8,19	j,o,e	
*Ischnura spp.	X			7,19	j,o	
Nehalennia spp.	X			7	o	
unident. spp.				13	s	
Family Lestidae						
*Lestes sp.	X	X		8,19	j,e	
Suborder Anisoptera						
Family Aeshnidae						
*Aeshna sp.	X	X		19	j	
*Anax junius	X	X		7,19	j	
Anax sp.	X			8	e	
Family Corduliidae						
*Somatochlora spp.		X	X	19	j	
Tetragoneuria spp.	X	X		7	b	
Family Gomphidae						
Dromogomphus sp.		X		8	e	
*Gomphus spp.		X		7,8,19	j,e,b	
Ophiogomphus sp.		X		8	e	
unident. spp.		X		13	r	
Family Libelludidae						
*Libellula spp.	X	X		7,19	j,b	
*Pachydiplax sp.		X		19	j	
Perithemis spp.		X		7	b	
*Sympterum sp.	X			19	j	
Family Macromiidae						
*Macromia sp.		X		19	j	
Order Ephemeroptera						
Suborder Schistonota						
Family Baetidae						
*Baetis spp.	X		X	7,13,19	o,j,s	
Callibaetis spp.	X			7	b	
Family Ephemeridae						
Ephemera sp.		X	X	13	s	
*Hexagenia bilineata		X		8,9,13,19	e,i,j,r	
*H. limbata		X		7–9,13,19	e,j,i,r,b	

TABLE 1.37. *(Continued)*

Taxon	Substrate[a]			Site[b]	Source[c]	Comment[d]
	Lentic		Lotic			
	V	M,S	G,R			
Family Heptageniidae						
Anepeorus simplex		X	X		j	
Anepeorus sp.		X	X	13	s	
Heptagenia inconspicua			X	19	j	
H. maculipennis			X	19	j	
Heptagenia sp.			X	13	s	
Pseudiron centralis			X	19	j	
Pseudiron sp.			X	13	s	
Stenacron interpunctatum	X		X	19	j	
Stenonema bipunctatum	X		X	19	j	
S. integrum	X		X	19	j	
Stenonema sp.	X		X	8,9,13,19	j,e,r,s,g	
unident. spp.	X			7	o	
Family Palingeniidae						
Pentagenia vittigera		X	X	8,19	e,j	
Family Polymitarcydae						
Ephoron sp.		X		8,13,19	e,j,s	
Family Potamanthidae						
Potamanthus verticis			X	19	j	
Family Siphlonuridae						
Isonychia sicca	X		X	19	j	
Isonychia sp.			X	8,9,13	e,s,g	
Siphlonurus sp.	X	X		8	e	
Suborder Pannota						
Family Caenidae						
Brachycercus sp.	X	X		7,8	e,o	
Caenis hilaris	X		X	19	j	
C. simulans		X	X	19	j	
Caenis spp.		X	X	7,8,13,19	o,e,j,i	
Family Ephemerellidae						
Ephemerella stenuata	X			7	o	
Ephemerella spp.	X			7,13	o,b,s	
Family Tricorythidae						
Tricorythodes atratus	X	X		19	j	
Tricorythodes spp.	X	X		7–9	e,o,g	
Order Plecoptera						
Family Perlidae						
Perlesta placida		X	X	7,8	o,e	
Perlesta sp.		X	X	13	r	
Family Perlodidae						
Isoperla bilineata			X	19	j	
Isoperla sp.			X	13	r,s	

Continued

TABLE 1.37.   (Continued)

Taxon	Substrate[a] Lentic V	Substrate[a] Lentic M,S	Substrate[a] Lotic G,R	Site[b]	Source[c]	Comment[d]
Order Hemiptera						
Family Belostomatidae						
Belostoma fluminea	X			19	j	
Belostoma spp.	X			7	o,b	
Lethocerus spp.		X	X	7	o	
Family Corixidae						
Hesperocorixa sp.			X	19	j	
Palmacorixa sp.	X			19	j	
Sigara spp.		X	X	19	j	
Trichocorixa spp.	X			7,8,19	e,j,b	
unident. spp.	X			7–9,13	o,e,r,s,g	
Family Gerridae						
Gerris spp.		X		7,19	o,j	
Family Heloridae						
Hebrus sp.	X			19	j	
Family Mesoveliidae						
Mesovelia sp.				7,19	j,o	
Family Nepidae						
Ranatra sp.	X			7,19	j,o	
Family Notonectidae						
Buenoa sp.		X	X	7,8,19	e,j,b	
Notonecta sp.				7,8,19	j,e,b	
Family Pleidae						
Neoplea sp.		X	X	19	j	
Plea striola		X		7	o,b	
Family Veliidae						
Microvelia sp.		X		7,19	j,o	
Order Megaloptera						
Family Corydalidae						
Chauliodes sp.	X			7,8	o,e,b	
Nigronia sp.		X		7	o	
Protochauliodes sp.		X		7	o	
Family Sialidae						
Sialis sp.	X	X		7,8,13,19	o,e,j,r,b	
Order Coleoptera						
Suborder Adephaga						
Family Dytiscidae						
Agabus sp.	X	X		7,19	j,b	
Bidessonotus sp.		X	X	7	o	
Coptotomus spp.	X		X	7	b	
Cybister sp.	X			19	j	
Dytiscus sp.	X			19	j	
Hydroporus sp.	X			19	j,b	
Hydrovatus spp.			X	7	b	
Hygrotus spp.	X			7	b	
Laccophilus proximus	X			7	o	

TABLE 1.37. *(Continued)*

Taxon	V	M,S	G,R	Site[b]	Source[c]	Comment[d]
Family Dytiscidae *(cont.)*						
Laccophilus sp.	X	X		7,19	j,o,b	
Liodessus spp.	X			7	o	
unident. spp.				13	s	
Family Gyrinidae						
Dineutus sp.		X		8,19	e,j	
Gyrinus sp.				8,19	e,j	
unident. spp.				13	s	
Family Haliplidae						
Brychius spp.	X		X	7	b	
Haliplus sp.	X			7,19	j,o,b	
Peltodytes sp.	X			7,19	j,b	
Suborder Polyphaga						
Family Chrysomelidae						
Donacia sp.		X		7,8	e,b	
Family Curculionidae						
Listronotus spp.	X			7	b	
Notaris sp.	X	X		7	b	
unident. spp.	X			7	o	
Family Elmidae						
Dubiraphia sp.	X	X	X	7,8,13	e,r,o,b	
Macronychus glabratus	X			7	o	
Stenelmis sp.		X	X	7–9,13,19	e,o,j,r,g,b	
unident. spp.				13	s	
Family Helodidae						
Cyphon spp.	X	X		7	b	
Scirtes sp.	X	X		7	b	
Family Hydrophilidae						
Berosus spp.		X		7,19	j,b	
Enochrus spp.	X	X		7	b	
Helophorus sp.	X	X	X	8,19	e,j	
Laccobius sp.	X			19	j	
Tropisternus spp.	X	X		7,19	j,b	
Family Lampyridae						
unident. spp.				7	b	
Order Trichoptera						
Family Brachycentridae						
Brachycentrus americanus	X			7	o	
Family Hydropsychidae						
Cheumatopsyche campyla			X	19	j	
Cheumatopsyche spp.			X	7–9,13	j,e,r,s,g,o	
Hydropsyche bidens			X	19	j	
H. orris			X	9,19	j,g	
H. phalerata			X	19	j	
Hydropsyche spp.	X	X	X	7,8,13	o,e,r,s,b	

Continued

TABLE 1.37.   (Continued)

Taxon	V	Lentic M,S	Lotic G,R	Site[b]	Source[c]	Comment[d]
Family Hydropsychidae (cont.)						
*Potamyia flava			X	19	j	
Potamyia sp.			X	9,13	h,s,g	
Family Hydroptilidae						
Agraylea multipunctata	X	X	X	7	o	
Agraylea spp.	X	X	X	7	o,b	
Dibusa spp.	X		X	7	b	
*Hydroptila ajax	X			19	j	
H. albicorni		X	X	7	o	
*H. waubesiana	X			7,19	j,o	
Hydroptila spp.	X			7,8	o,e	
Mayatrichia ayama				19	j	
*Orthotrichia tarsalis	X			19	j	
*Orthotrichia spp.	X			7,13,19	j,o,r,b	
Oxyethira spp.	X			7	o,b	
Stactobiella sp.			X	8	e	
Family Leptoceridae						
*Athripsodes (= Ceraclea?) flavus			X	19	j	
*A. (= Ceraclea?) transversus			X	19	j	
Ceraclea spp.		X		7	o	
Leptocella (= Nectopsyche?) sp.	X			9	g	
Leptocerus americana	X			7	o	
Leptocerus spp.	X			7,8,13	s,e,b	
Nectopsyche candida	X			7	o	
N. diarina	X			7	o	
N. pavida	X			7	o	
Nectopsyche spp.	X			7,8	o,e	
Oecetis cinerascens	X	X		7	o	
*O. inconspicua	X	X		7,19	j,o	
Oecetis spp.	X	X		7,8,13	e,o,r,b	
Triaenodes spp.	X		X	7,8	o,e,b	
Family Phryganeidae						
Phryganea sp.	X	X		7	b	
Family Polycentropodidae						
*Cyrnellus marginalis	X			19	j	
Cyrnellus sp.	X			8	e	
*Neureclypsis crepuscularis	X			19	j	
Neureclypsis sp.	X			7,8	e,o,b	
Phylocentropus sp.				8	e	
Polycentropus centralis		X		7	o	
P. cinerus		X		7	o	
P. gracilis		X		7	o	
Polycentropus spp.		X		7,8,13	r,e,o	

TABLE 1.37.   (Continued)

Taxon	Substrate[a]			Site[b]	Source[c]	Comment[d]
		Lentic	Lotic			
	V	M,S	G,R			
Order Lepidoptera						
Family Pyralidae						
*Acentropus sp.	X		X	19	j	
*Neocataclysta sp.	X			7,19	j,o	
Nymphula sp.	X			7,8	e,o,b	
Paragyractis sp.	X			7	o,b	
Paraponyx sp.	X			7,8	e,o,b	
unident. spp.				13	r	
Order Diptera						
Suborder Nematocera						
Family Ceratopogonidae						
Atrichopogon sp.	X	X		8	e	
*Bezzia sp.	X	X		7,8,19	j,o,e,b	
Dasyhelea sp.	X	X	X	8	e	
*Palpomyia sp.	X	X	X	8,9,19	e,j,i,b	
unident. spp.				9,13	r,s,g,e	
Family Chaoboridae						
*Chaoborus sp.		X		8,9,19	j,g,e	
unident. sp.		X		13	i,s	
Family Chironomidae						
*Ablabesmyia sp.	X		X	7,19	j,o	
Anatopynia sp.				19	j	
Cardiocladius sp.			X	8	e	
*Chironomus sp.	X	X		7–9,19	e,j,i,b	
*Clinotanypus spp.		X	X	7,8,19	j,e,b	
*Coelotanypus spp.		X		7,8,19	e,j,b	
Corynoneura sp.	X	X			j,b	
Cricotopus bicintus	X			7	o	
C. intersectus	X			7	o	
C. sylvestris gr.	X			7	o	
*Cricotopus sp.	X	X	X	7,8,19	e,j,b	
*Cryptochironomus sp.		X	X	7,8,19	e,j,b	
Cryptocladopelma sp.	X	X		8	e,b	
Demicryptochironomus sp.		X		8	e	
Dicrotendipes neomodestus		X		7	o	
D. nervosus		X		7	o	
*Dicrotendipes sp.		X		7,8,19	j,e,b	
Einfeldia sp.		X		7,8	e,b	
Endochironomus nigricans	X	X		7	o	
E. subtendeus	X	X		7	o	
*Endochironomus spp.	X	X		7,8,19	e,o,j,b	
Epoicocladius sp.			X	8	e	
*Eukiefferiella sp.		X	X	7,8,19	j,e,b	
Glyptotendipes lobiferus		X		7	o	
Glyptotendipes spp.		X		7,8	e,o	

Continued

TABLE 1.37.   (Continued)

Taxon	V	M,S	G,R	Site[b]	Source[c]	Comment[d]
		Lentic	Lotic			
Family Chironomidae (*cont.*)						
Harnischia sp.	X			8	e	
Lauterborniella sp.				7	b	
Microtendipes spp.	X	X	X	7,8,19	j,e,b	
Nanocladius distinctus		X	X	7	o	
N. spiniplenus		X	X	7	o	
Nanocladius spp.		X	X	7	o	
Nilothauma babiyi			X	7	o	
Orthocladius sp.		X	X	7	o,b	
Parachironomus abortivus		X		7	o	
P. frequens		X		7	o	
Parachironomus spp.	X	X		7,8,19	j,o,e,b	
Paracladopelma sp.				8,19	j,e	
Paralauterborniella sp.	X			8	e	
Paratanytarsus spp.		X	X	7,8	e,b	
Paratendipes sp.		X	X	8,19	j,e	
Pentaneura sp.	X	X		7,8,19	e,j,b	
Phaenopsectra sp.	X	X	X	7,19	j,o,b	
Polypedilum convictum	X	X		7	o	
P. illinoense	X	X		7	o	
Polypedilum spp.	X	X		7,8,19	o,e,j,b	
Procladius sp.	X	X		7,8,19	j,e,b	
Psectrocladius sp.	X	X		7,8	e,b	
Psectrotanypus sp.			X	8	e	
Pseudochironomus sp.	X	X	X	7,8	e,b	
Rheocricotopus robacki	X		X	7	o	
Rheotanytarsus exiguus gr.			X	7	o	
Rheotanytarsus sp.	X		X	8,19	j,e	
Smittia sp.		X		8	e	
Stempellina sp.				8	e	
Stenochironomus sp.	X			8,19	j,e	
Stictochironomus sp.		X	X	8	e	
Sympotthastia sp.			X	8	e	
Tanypus sp.		X		7,8,19	b,j,e	
Tanytarsus spp.	X	X		7,8	e,b	
Thienemaniella fusca		X	X	7	o	
Thienemaniella spp.		X	X	7	o	
Xenochironomus sp.		X	X	8	e	
unident. spp.				9,13	r,s,g	
Family Culicidae						
Anopheles spp.		X	X	7	b	
Culex spp.				7	b	
unident. pupae				19	j	
Family Psychodidae						
Psychoda sp.		X	X	7,8	o,e	

TABLE 1.37. *(Continued)*

Taxon	Substrate[a] V	Lentic M,S	Lotic G,R	Site[b]	Source[c]	Comment[d]
Family Simuliidae						
Eusimulium sp.	X		X	8	e	
Prosimulium sp.			X	19	j	
Simulium sp.			X	8	e	
Unident. spp.	X	X	X	7,13	r,o	
Family Tipulidae						
Erioptera sp.		X	X	7	b	
Helius sp.		X			j	
Hexatoma spp.		X	X	7	b	
Limnophila spp.		X	X	7	b	
Tipula sp.		X	X		j	
Suborder Brachycera						
Family Ephydridae						
Ephydra spp.	X	X		7	b	
Hyrellia spp.	X			7	o,b	
Lemnaphila spp.	X			7	b	
Notiphila spp.	X	X		7	o,b	
Family Muscidae						
Limnophora sp.		X		19	j	
Family Sciomyzidae						
Renocera sp.		X		7	b	
Sepedon sp.				7	b	
Family Stratiomyidae						
Euparyphus sp.		X		8	e	
Odontomyia sp.	X	X		7,19	j,o,b	O
Family Syrphidae						
Eristalis spp.		X		7	b	
Family Tabanidae						
Chrysops spp.		X		7,8,19	e,j,b	O
Tabanus spp.	X	X		7,19	j,b	C
Phylum Bryozoa						
Class Ectoprocta						
Order Phylactolaemata						
Family Pectinatellidae						
Pectinatella magnifica		X		7	o	
Family Plumatellidae						
Plumatella spp.		X		19	j	
Phylum Chordata						
Subphylum Vertebrata						
Class Cephalaspidomorphi						
Order Petromyzontiformes						
Family Petromyzontidae						
Ichthyomyzon castaneus		X	X	M1–M5	f	U
I. unicuspis		X	X	M1–M5	f	O

Continued

TABLE 1.37.   *(Continued)*

Taxon	V	M,S	G,R	Site[b]	Source[c]	Comment[d]
		Substrate[a]				
		Lentic	Lotic			
Class Osteichthyes						
Order Acipenseriformes						
Family Acipenseridae						
*Acipenser fulvescens		X	X	M1–M5	f	R
*Scaphirhynchus albus		X	X	M5	f	
*S. platorynchus		X	X	M1–M5	f	O
Family Polydontidae						
*Polydon spathula	X	X	X	M1–M5	f	O
Order Lepisosteiformes						
Family Lepisosteidae						
Lepisosteus oculatus	X	X	X	M5	f	C
*L. osseus	X	X	X	M1–M5	f	C
*L. platostomus	X	X	X	M1–M5	f	
L. spathula	X	X	X	M5	f	C
Order Amiiformes						
Family Amiidae						
*Amia calva	X	X		M1–M5	f	
Order Anguilliformes						
Family Anguillidae						
*Anguilla rostrata	X	X	X	M1–M5	f	U
Order Osteoglossiformes						
Family Hiodontidae						
*Hiodon alosoides		X	X	M1–M5	f	U
*H. tergisus		X	X	M1–M5	f	C
Order Clupeiformes						
Family Clupeidae						
*Alosa chrysochloris		X	X	M1–M5	f	H
*Dorosoma cepedianum	X	X	X	M1–M5	f	A
*D. petenense		X	X	M5	f	
Order Cypriniformes						
Family Catostomidae						
*Carpiodes carpio	X	X		M1–M5	f	C
*C. cyprinus		X	X	M1–M5	f	C
*C. velifer		X	X	M1–M5	f	U
Catostomus commersoni	X		X	M1,M2	f	
*Cycleptus elongatus		X	X	M1–M5	f	U
Hypentelium nigricans			X	M1–M3	f	
*Ictiobus bubalus		X	X	M1–M5	f	C
*I. cyprinellus	X	X		M1–M5	f	C
*I. niger		X	X	M2–M5	f	U
*Minytrema melanops	X	X		M1–M4	f	U
*Moxostoma anisurum		X	X	M1–M5	f	R
M. carinatum		X	X	M1–M3	f	R
*M. erythrurum		X	X	M1–M5	f	O
*M. macrolepidotum		X	X	M1–M5	f	
M. valeciennesi		X	X	M2,M3	f	

TABLE 1.37. (Continued)

Taxon	Substrate[a] Lentic V	Substrate[a] Lentic M,S	Substrate[a] Lotic G,R	Site[b]	Source[c]	Comment[d]
Family Cyprinidae						
Ctenopharyngodon idella	X	X		M2	f	
*Cyprinus carpio		X	X	M1–M5	f	A
Hybognathus hankinsoni		X		M1,M2	f	
H. nuchalis		X		M1–M3,M5	f	
*Hybopsis aestivalis		X	X	M1–M5	f	C
H. gelida		X	X	M5	f	
H. gracilis		X	X	M3,M5	f	
*H. storeriana	X	X	X	M1–M5	f	C
Nocomis biguttatus	X	X	X	M1	f	
*Notemigonus chrysoleucas	X	X		M1–M5	f	O
*Notropis amnis	X	X		M2,M3	f	
*N. atherinoides		X		M1–M5	f	A
*N. blennius		X	X	M1–M5	f	A
*N. buchanani	X	X	X	M3–M5	f	C
*N. cornutus			X	M1–M5	f	R
*N. dorsalis		X		M1–M5	f	O
*N. emiliae	X	X		M1–M4	f	U
*N. heterodon	X	X		M1	f	
*N. heterolepis	X	X	X	M1	f	
*N. hudsonius		X	X	M1–M5	f	C
*N. lutrensis		X	X	M3–M5	f	C
N. nubilis			X	M1	f	
N. rubellus			X	M1–M3	f	
N. shumardi			X	M3,M5	f	
*N. spilopterus			X	M1–M5	f	C
*N. stramineus			X	M1–M5	f	O
*N. texanus	X	X		M1–M3	f	
*N. umbratilis	X	X	X	M1,M2	f	
*N. volucellus	X	X	X	M1,M2	f	
*Phenacobius mirabilis		X	X	M3–M5	f	U
*Pimephales notatus	X	X		M1–M5	f	O
*P. promelas	X	X		M1–M5	f	U
*P. vigilax	X	X		M1–M5	f	A
Order Siluriformes						
Family Ictaluridae						
*Ictalurus furcatus		X	X	M5	f	
*I. melas	X	X		M1–M5	f	O
*I. natalis	X	X	X	M1–M5	f	O
*I. nebulosus	X			M1–M5	f	R
*I. punctatus		X	X	M1–M5	f	C
*Noturus flavus		X	X	M2–M5	f	U
*N. gyrinus	X	X		M1–M5	f	U
N. nocturnus		X	X	M5	f	
*Pylodictis olivaris	X	X		M1–M5	f	O

Continued

TABLE 1.37.   (Continued)

Taxon	V	M,S	G,R	Site[b]	Source[c]	Comment[d]
Order Salmoniformes						
Family Esocidae						
Esox americanus	X	X		M3	f	
E. lucius	X	X		M1–M5	f	O
Order Percopsiformes						
Family Aphredoderidae						
Aphredoderus sayanus	X	X		M2	f	
Family Percopsidae						
Percopsis omiscomaycus	X	X	X	M1–M5	f	U
Order Gadiformes						
Family Gadidae						
Lota lota	X	X	X	M1–M5	f	R
Order Cyprinodontiformes						
Family Cypridontidae						
Fundulus notatus	X	X		M4,M5	f	O
Family Poeciliidae						
Gambusia affinis	X	X		M3–M5	f	R
Order Atheriniformes						
Family Atherinidae						
Labidesthes sicculus		X	X	M1–M5	f	O
Order Perciformes						
Family Centrarchidae						
Ambloplites rupestris	X		X	M1–M5	f	R
Lepomis cyanellus	X	X		M1–M5	f	O
L. gibbosus	X	X		M1–M4	f	U
L. gulosus	X	X		M2–M5	f	O
L. humilis	X	X		M1–M5	f	C
L. macrochirus	X	X		M1–M5	f	A
Micropterus dolomieui			X	M1–M5	f	U
M. salmoides	X	X	X	M1–M5	f	C
Pomoxis annularis	X	X		M1–M5	f	C
P. nigromaculatus	X	X		M1–M5	f	C
Family Percidae						
Ammocrypta asprella		X	X	M2	f	
A. clara	X	X	X	M1–M5	f	O
Etheostoma asprigene	X	X		M2,M3	f	
E. caeruleum			X	M2	f	
E. nigrum		X	X	M1–M5	f	U
Perca flavescens	X	X	X	M1–M4	f	O
Percina caprodes		X	X	M1–M5	f	O
P. phoxocephala			X	M2–M5	f	R
P. shumardi			X	M1–M5	f	C
Stizostedion canadense	X	X	X	M1–M5	f	C
S. vitreum	X	X	X	M1–M5	f	C

TABLE 1.37. *(Continued)*

Taxon	Substrate[a]			Site[b]	Source[c]	Comment[d]
		Lentic	Lotic			
	V	M,S	G,R			
Family Percithyidae						
*Morone chrysops		X	X	M1–M5	f	C
*M. mississippiensis		X	X	M2–M5	f	U
Family Sciaenidae						
*Aplodinotus grunniens		X		M1–M5	f	C

*Species discussed in the section "Structure of Aquatic Communities" based on the knowledge of R. Patrick.

[a]V, vegetation; M, mud; S, sand; G, gravel; R, rocks.

[b]Sites for algae, vascular plants, and invertebrates refer to the Navigation Pool. Sites for fishes refers to the following reaches: M1, Pools 1–4; M2, Pools 5–10; M3, Pools 11–15; M4, Pools 16–19; M5, Pools 20–26.

[c]*Phytoplankton:* h, Huff (1986) (Pool 7); j, Jahn and Anderson (1986) (Pool 19); d, Claflin (1973) (Pool 7). *Periphyton:* v, Vansteenburg et al. (1984) (Pools 5 and 9); l, Luttenton et al. (1986) (Pools 5 and 9); j, Jahn and Anderson (1986) (Pool 19). *Macrophytes:* s, Sefton (1977) (Pool 8); k, Peck and Smart (1986) (Pools 8, 7, 5); m, McConville et al. (1986) (Pool 5a); j, Jahn and Anderson (1986) (Pool 19); d, Claflin (1973) (Pool 7). *Invertebrates:* e, Elstad (1977); i, Eckblad et al. (1977) (Pool 9); g, Eckblad et al. (1984) (Pool 9); r, Hubert et al. (1984) (Pool 13); j, Jahn and Anderson (1986) (Pool 19); p, Perry (1979) (Pools 9, 13, 19) (Unionidae); c, Coon et al. (1977) (Pools 8 and 9); a, Havlik (1983) (unionids in 7 and 8); b, Miller (1988) (unionids in 7); o, Chilton (1990) (Pool 7); t, Blitgen (1981) (Pool 7). *Fish:* i, Fremling et al. (1989).

[d]UMR-4, Pools 16–19 (SE Iowa–NE Missouri, Illinois): U, uncommon, does not usually appear in sample collections; populations are small, but species in this category do not appear to be on the verge of extirpation; O, occasionally collected, not generally distributed, but local concentrations may occur; R, considered to be rare; some species in this category may be on the verge of extirpation; C, commonly taken in most sample collections; makes up a large portion of some samples; A, abundantly taken in all river surveys; H, records of occurrence are available, but no collections have been documented in the last 10 years.

found in the lentic habitats associated with the vegetation. A number of protozoans were found in the lentic habitats. They were particularly common in the shallow waters where mud and silt had accumulated but also in and among the vegetation. They were the primary producers such as *Dinobryon divergens, D. sociale,* and *D. sertularia.* Two species of *Cryptomonas* that are also primary producers were in this habitat, as was an unidentified species of *Rhodomonas.* Other phytoflagellates that were quite common in this pool but which are not definitely identified with a habitat were two species of the genus *Carteria,* unidentified species of *Chlamydomonas,* and *Phacotus lenticularis.*

Common in these lentic habitats associated with vegetation where the water was shallow and there was very little if any current were four species of *Euglena,* all of which are autotrophs, and seven species of *Phacus* (Table 1.37). Other Euglenidae found in this habitat were *Trachelomonas creba* and some unidentified species of this genus. Associated with the vegetation were *Hydra americana,* an omnivore, and some unidentified species of sponge.

Several rotifers were found in this habitat. Most of these were found in the plankton, but they probably are associated primarily with the vegetation and the pools or other lentic habitats. They are unidentified species of the genera *Minobia* and *Asplanchna,* which are probably carnivores, four species of the omnivorous genus *Brachionus,* unidentified species of the genus *Euchlanis,* two species of the genus *Keratella,* and one species of the genus *Notholca.* The last three genera are omnivores. Other rotifers associated with the vegetation and the lentic habitats were two species of the omnivorous genus *Platyais* and unidentified species of the genus *Trichotria.* These genera as well as the genus *Lecane* are omnivores.

Found in and among the vegetation in the lentic habitat were unidentified species of the genera *Polyarthra* and *Synchaeta.* They were also found in the lentic habitats. It is often difficult to distinguish between lentic and vegetation habitats, as the vegetation often produces a lentic habitat. Another rotifer found in these habitats was *Trichocera.* Another species associated with the vegetation was *Filinia longiseta.* It was also found associated with the shallow lentic habitats, as were species of the genus *Testudinella,* all of which are omnivores.

Quite a few taxons belonging to the phylum Nemata were associated with the vegetation. They were an unidentified species each of *Cryptonchus, Tobrilus, Dorylaimus, Mesodorylaimus, Aphanolaimus, Chronogaster* sp., *Rhabdolaimus, Achromadora, Chromatorita,* and *Ethmolaimus.* Other Nemata belonging to the order Rhabditida were *Acrobeloides* sp. and *Rhabditis* sp. *Diplogaster* sp., *Ditylenchus* sp., *Paratylenchus* sp., and *Aphelenchus* sp. were all in and among the vegetation.

Dictyosphaerium ehrenbergianum was also present in this habitat. *Pediastrum boryanum* var. *longicorne, P. boryanum* var. *undulatum,* and *P. tetras,* which are colonial algae, were found floating in the water in these sloughs and backwaters. Eight species belonging to the genus *Scenedesmus* were found in these lentic vegetative habitats, particularly in the sloughs and backwaters, as was *Tetrastrum staurogeniaforme.*

These lentic vegetative conditions were favorite habitats for several other species of algae. They were desmids belonging to the genera *Closterium, Cosmarium, Closteriopsis,* and *Staurastrum.*

The genus *Laevapex* was present, as were two species of the genus *Physa,* which are detritivore-omnivores. *Helisoma trivolis,* a detritivore-omnivore, was also found crawling in and among the vegetation.

Several unionids were found in and among the vegetation. They were *Actinonais carinata,* one species of the genus *Amblema, Anodonta imbecilis, Arcidens confragosus, Carunculina parvus, Ellipsaria lineolata, Lampsilis fallaciosa, L. ovata ventricosa, Lasmigona complanata, Leptodea fragilis, Ligumia racta, Obliquaria reflexa, Obovaria olivaria, Plagiola lineolata, Potamilus laevissimus, Proptera alata, P. laevissima, Quadrula nodulata, Q. pustulosa, Q. quadrula, Truncilla donaciformis,* and *T. truncata.* All of these are herbivore-detritivores; that is, they eat protozoans, bacteria, various algae, and so on, that are found floating in the water, as they are filter feeders.

Worms were commonly found in and among the vegetation, particularly in the debris and around the crown of the plants. They were *Glossiphonia camplanata, Helobdella stagnalis, Placobdella montifera,* and *Erpobdella punctata.* All of these are leeches and therefore are carnivores. They feed on snails, oligochaetes, insects, and other invertebrates. These leeches were undoubtedly feeding on the invertebrates that were associated with the plants.

A few Crustacea were found associated with the vegetation. They were the isopod *Asellus brevicaudus,* a detritivore-omnivore, as is *A. intermedius.* An amphipod, *Hyalella azteca,* which is a detritivore, was also found in this habitat, as was a species of the genus *Palaemonetes, P. kadiakensis,* a herbivore-omnivore.

Insects were fairly common in and among the vegetation. Species of the carnivorous genera *Enallagma, Ischnura,* and *Lestes* were found here. Also present were the carnivorous *Aeshna,* the omnivorous species *Anax junius,* carnivorous species belonging to the genus *Libellula,* and unidentified species of the genus *Sympterum.* A few mayflies were found in this habitat. They were species belonging to the genus *Baetis,* which are herbivore-detritivores, one species belonging to the genus *Stenacron,* and three species belonging to the genus *Stenonema,* all of which are omnivores, as was *Isonychia sicca.* Another mayfly found in and among the vegetation was *Caenis hilaris,* an omnivore. *Tricorythodes atratus* was crawling over the vegetation. This species is an omnivore. No stoneflies were found in this habitat.

Of the true bugs that were present, *Belostoma fluminea,* which is a carnivore, was probably found in and among the vegetation. Other species in this habitat were the herbivore-detritivore, *Palmacorixa,* and species of the omnivorous genus *Trichocorixa.* An unidentified species of the genus *Ranatra* was present. This genus is typically carnivorous. The order Megaloptera was represented by one species belonging to the genus *Sialis,* which is probably an omnivore. This was a favorite habitat for several beetles. They were mostly unidentified species belonging to the genera *Agabus, Cybister, Dytiscus, Hydroporus,* and *Laccophilus.* All of these are carnivores. Other bugs were unidentified species of the herbivore genera *Haliplus, Peltodytes, Helophorus, Laccobius,* as well as species of the genus *Tropisternus,* which are known to be herbivorous.

A few Trichoptera, otherwise known as caddisflies, were found in and among the vegetation. They were *Hydroptila ajax,* a herbivore; *H. waubesiana,* also a herbivore; as were two species of the genus *Orthotrichia.* Other caddisflies found in this area were *Oecetis inconspicua,* a herbivore-omnivore; *Cyrnellus marginalis,* an omnivore; and *Neureclypsis crepuscularis,* an omnivore. The order Lepidoptera was represented by an unidentified species of *Neocataclysta,* a herbivore.

The true flies were represented by a few species of the ceratopogonids. They were an unidentified species of *Bezzia,* which is omnivorous, and *Palpomyia,* also an omnivore. Several species of chironomids were found in and among the detritus associated with the vegetation. They were a species of the omnivorous genus *Ablabesmyia,* the herbivorous genus *Chironomus,* and a detritivore-herbivore, *Cricotopus* sp. Also present were unidentified species of the herbivorous genus *Endochironomus* and unidentified species of the omnivorous genera *Microtendipes* and *Parachironomus*. Other omnivorous genera that were represented in this habitat were unidentified species of *Pentaneura, Phaenopsectra,* and *Polypedilum*. Other chironomids present were an unidentified species of the carnivorous genus *Procladius,* and an unidentified species each of the omnivorous genera *Rheotanytarsus* and *Stenochironomus*. Other flies found in this habitat were an unidentified species of the genus *Odontomyia,* which is probably an omnivore, and unidentified species of the genus *Tabanus,* which is carnivorous.

Several fish were found associated with the vegetation. They were an omnivore-carnivore, *Polydon spathula;* a carnivore, *Lipisosteus osseus;* and *L. platostomus,* also a carnivore. *Amia calva* and *Anguilla rostrata,* which are carnivores, were also in and among the vegetation, along with the eel, *Dorosoma cepedianum,* an omnivore. Present were various cyprinids, such as *Carpiodes carpio,* an omnivore-carnivore; *Ictiobus cyprinellus,* an omnivore-carnivore; *Minytrema melanops,* a carnivore; *Notemigonus chrysoleucas,* a carnivore; *Notropis buchanani,* a carnivore; *N. emiliae,* a carnivore; *Pimephales notatus,* an omnivore; *P. promelas,* an omnivore; and *P. vigilax,* an omnivore. Ictalurids found here were *Ictalurus melas,* an omnivore; *I. natalis,* an omnivore; *I. nebulosus,* an omnivore; *Noturus gyrinus,* a carnivore; and *Pylodictis olivaris,* a carnivore. Other fish found here were *Esox lucius,* a carnivore; *Percopsis omiscomaycus,* a carnivore; *Lota lota,* a carnivore; *Fundulus notatus,* an omnivore; *Gambusia affinis,* an omnivore; *Ambloplites rupestris,* a carnivore; four carnivorous species of *Lepomis; Lepomis macrochirus,* an omnivore; *Micropterus salmoides,* an omnivore; two species of *Pomoxis,* both carnivores; *Ammocrypta clara,* a carnivore; *Perca flavescens,* a carnivore; *Stizostedion canadense,* a carnivore; and *S. vitreum,* a carnivore.

Lentic Habitats. Lentic habitats in which mud and silt are deposited are common habitats in Pool 19. They are sloughs and small lakes. Also, side channels where the current is very slow are present. Main-channel border habitats are also present. In Pool 19 there are small islands and side channels, which tend to be more extensive in the middle and upper reaches of this pool. However, in the channel proper, lotic habitats are common where the current is quite swift and sand and gravel are the substrates.

In the lentic habitats there were a number of blue-green algae. Five species of *Anacystis* were found in these habitats growing on the surface of this mud and silt. Sometimes they were found on the detritus in these lentic habitats. Also present were *Coleosphaerium collinsii, Gleothece rupestris,* and *Gomphosphaeria lacustris*. Other blue-green algae in this habitat were *Marssoniella elegans,* an unidentified species of *Microcystis,* and as one might expect, *Aphanizomenon flos-aquae*. The genus *Oscillatoria* was represented by two species in this habitat and the genus *Schizothrix* by at least two species. These are filamentous algae, often found on the surface of detritus. Five species belonging to the Tetrasporales, which are green algae, were found here.

There were one species of *Dispora,* three species belonging to the genus *Gleocystis,* as well as *Sphaerocystis schroeteri.*

Many other green colonial and single-cell green algae were present. There were three taxons belonging to the genus *Pediastrum.* This is a colonial alga, as is the genus *Ankistrodesmus.* Four species of this genus were found in this habitat. Other green algae were *Chodatella ciliata* and *C. quadriseta.* Also present was *Kirchneriella elongata.* The genus *Selenastrum* was represented by two taxons and the genus *Tetraedon* by six taxons. This was a favorite habitat for species belonging to the family Scenedesmaceae. Two taxons belonging to the genus *Actinastrum* were present, two belonging to the genus *Micractinum,* and eight belonging to the genus *Scenedesmus.* This is a genus that is often found in somewhat polluted water that is enriched with nitrogen and phosphorus. *Tetrastrum staurogeniaforme* was also present.

As one might expect, there were several taxons of desmids in this habitat. There were five taxons belonging to the genus *Closterium,* one to the genus *Closteriopsis,* and three to the genus *Cosmarium.* Also present was one taxon belonging to the genus *Staurastrum.* Other green algae were two taxons belonging to the genus *Ophiocytium* and one belonging to the family Tribonemataceae, an unidentified species of *Tribonema.*

Numerous diatoms were found in this habitat living on the surface or in the surface of the mud and the silt and also attached to the debris that accumulated in these lentic habitats, such as in the sloughs and backwaters. They were two species of the genus *Cyclotella.* Also present were five taxons belonging to the genus *Stephanodiscus* (Table 1.37). Two taxons belonging to the genus *Asterionella* were found here. They probably were floating in the shallow water, perhaps in and among the vegetation in these pools. The diatom flora was fairly well developed in this habitat. There were two taxons belonging to the genus *Fragilaria* and one taxon belonging to the genus *Meridion.* The genus *Synedra* was represented by four taxons. The family Eunotiaceae was found on the surface of the silt and in among the debris. Two genera were present, one taxon belonged to the genus *Amphicampa* and two taxons belonged to the genus *Eunotia.* Attached to the debris were *Achnanthes affinis* and *A. exilis* as well as *A. lanceolata.* On the surface of the muddy silt was *Rhoicosphenia curvata.* Attached to debris, probably wood and leaves, was one taxon belonging to the genus *Cymbella.* Also attached to the debris were a species of *Gomphonema, Caloneis bacillaris,* as well as an unknown species of this genus.

This was a favorite habitat for several species of *Gyrosigma* that were found in the surface mud. Three taxons were present. Also present was one taxon belonging to the genus *Frustulia.* Eight taxons of *Navicula* were found in these lentic habitats of the pools. One taxon belonging to the genus *Pinnularia* was also present in the surface of the mud. The genus *Stauroneis* was represented by three taxons in this habitat. *Hantzschia amphioxys* and its variety *capitata* were also found on the surface of the mud. Various species of *Nitzschia* were found in these lentic habitats, which were backwaters, pools, and marginal areas where the current was greatly reduced. Here one found *Nitzschia denticula, N. linearis, N. longissima, N. palea, N. vermicularis,* and some unidentified taxons of the genus *Nitzschia.* Some of the species of the family Surirellaceae found this habitat optimum for their development. They were two taxons belonging to the genus *Camplodiscus,* one taxon belonging to the genus *Cymatopleura,* and five taxons belonging to the genus *Surirella.* Dinophyceae were represented by a species belonging to the genus *Gymnodinium.* It was found swimming in the shallow waters of these lentic habitats.

In these lentic habitats, particularly in sloughs and backwaters, were found several aquatic plants, which formed excellent habitats for many of the invertebrates. These are listed in Table 1.37. Many protozoans were found in these lentic habitats. Living over and above the substrates was a *Chlamydomonas* sp. The family Volvocaceae was represented by three species of the genus *Gonium* (Table 1.37). There were present four taxons belonging to the genus *Euglena,* all autotrophs, and seven taxons of the genus *Phacus,* all autotrophs. These genera all belong to the family Euglenidae.

Attached to the detritus in the beds of these pools and to the stems of aquatic plants growing in these lentic habitats was *Hydra americana,* an oligotroph. These lentic habitats were optimum for certain species of rotifers. Here were found unidentified species of *Minobia* and unidentified species of the genus *Asplanchna,* which are carnivores; four species of the genus *Brachionus,* which are omnivores; unidentified species of the genus *Euchlanis;* two species belonging to the genus *Keratella;* one species belonging to the genus *Notholca;* two species of *Platyais;* and unidentified species of *Trichotria.* All of these are omnivores. Other omnivorous genera that were present were unidentified species of *Lecane, Polyarthra,* and *Synchaeta.* Also present was an unidentified species of the genus *Trichocera.* Belonging to the family Conochilidae were other omnivores belonging to the genus *Conochiliodes,* and to the family Testudinellidae two taxons, one belonging to the genus *Filinia* and the other to the genus *Testudinella.*

A number of nematodes were found among the detritus in this habitat. They were unidentified species of the genera *Ironus, Tobrilus,* and *Tripyla.* Also present were unidentified species of the genera *Alaimus, Dorylaimus,* and *Mesodorylaimus.* This was also a favorite habitat for five species belonging to the order Araeolaimida. This is an order of nematodes and they were found in and among the detritus and soft silt. The order Chromadorida was represented by three species: *Achromadora* sp., *Chromatorita* sp., and *Ethmolaimus* sp. Other nematodes that were present were unidentified species of the genera *Monohystrella, Acrobeloides, Butlerius,* and *Rhabditis.* The nematodes seemed to be best developed in this pool; at least this is the pool for which we have the most numerous records. Other genera that were present were unidentified species of the genera *Diplogaster, Ditylenchus, Paratylenchus,* and *Aphelenchus.*

Many gastropods were found in these lentic habitats. They were often associated with submerged vegetation or with the detritus that accumulated in the beds of sloughs, pools, and in and among the vegetation. The gastropods were represented by two species of *Amnicola, Fontigens nickliniana, Somatogyrus depressus, S. isogonus,* and *S. subglobosus.* Also present was *Pleurocera acuta.* All of these taxons are believed to be detritivore-omnivores. Other gastropods found in these habitats in Pool 19 were *Campeloma crassula, C. decisum, Lioplax subcarinata, L. subculosa, Viviparus georgianus, V. intertextus, Physa gyrina,* and *Helisoma trivolis.*

Where there was a moderate amount of current, particularly in these backwaters but also along the margins of the main river, there were various bivalves. Present were one taxon belonging to the genus *Actinonais; Amblema plicata; Anodonta imbecilis;* and *Arcidens confragosus.* Other species present were *Carunculina parvus, Ellipsaria lineolata,* and one taxon belonging to the genus *Lampsilis.* As stated above, all of these are filter feeders and are probably detritivore-herbivores. Another species was *Lampsilis ovata ventricosa. Lasmigona complanata* was also found in this habitat, as was *Leptodea fragilis.* One taxon belonging to the genus *Obliquaria,* one to the genus *Obovaria,* and *Plagiola lineolata* were also present. A species belonging to the genus designated as *Potamilus* was found. This is probably the same as the genus *Proptera.* Three taxons belonging to this genus were found in this habitat, as were three species belonging to the genus *Quadrula.* All of these filter feeders are detritivore-herbivores. *Strophitus undulatus, Truncilla donaciformis,* and *T. truncata* were three other species found in this habitat.

This was a favorite habitat for certain of the sphaerid clams. They are often found in water that is enriched with organic pollution. Here were species belonging to the genera *Musculium* and *Pisidium.* All of these are detritivore-herbivores. In other words, they are filter feeders. Also present in this habitat were three species belonging to the genus *Sphaerium* and *Corbicula fluminea,* all detritivore-omnivores. These species are particularly successful in water that receives some organic enrichment, as does the Upper Mississippi.

Various leeches were found in this habitat, probably living on fish or invertebrates. They were *Glossiphonia camplanata, Helobdella nepheloidea, Helobdella stagnalis, Placobdella montifera,* and *P. parasitica.* Another taxon belonging to the leeches, *Illinobdella* sp., was also collected in this habitat. It is a carnivore, as is *Erpobdella punctata.*

Several tubificids were found in this habitat. They tend to be detritivores but will eat almost anything and therefore are probably detritivore-omnivores or detritivore-herbivores. They were *Brachiura sowerbyi,* two taxons belonging to the genus *Limnodrilus,* and *Tubifex tubifex.*

In the lentic habitats, in among the vegetation and also in the shallow water of pools, were found a number of Cladocera. They were *Bosmina longirostris,* an omnivore, and *Alona costata,* a herbivore-detritivore, as is *A. rectangularis.* Other herbivore-detritivores belong to the genera *Ceriodaphnia, Eurycercus,* and *Daphnia.*

Several isopods that are detritivore-omnivores were also in these lentic habitats. This was a favorite habitat for the isopod, *Asellus.* One taxon belonging to this genus was found in this pool. A Collembola belonging to the genus *Hypogastura* was found in and among the vegetation in these lentic habitats. It is a detritivore-omnivore.

The odonates were represented by several species. Present were unidentified species of the genus *Argia*, which are omnivorous and of the genus *Lestes* sp., which is a carnivore. Also present were *Aeshna* sp., an omnivore, and *Anax junius*, an omnivore, as are species of the genus *Somatochlora*. Also present in this habitat were unidentified species of the carnivorous genera *Gomphus*, *Libellula*, and *Pachydiplax* and the omnivorous genus *Macromia*. A few mayflies were found in this area, particularly species belonging to the genus *Hexagenia*, which are omnivorous; *Pentagenia vittigera*, which is an omnivore; and *Ephoron* sp., also an omnivore. Of the family Caenidae, several species were found in this habitat. They were the omnivorous genus *Caenis*, represented by two or more species, some of them unidentified. Belonging to the Tricorythidae, a family of mayflies, was the species *Tricorythodes atratus*, an omnivore. The Hemiptera were represented by species belonging to the family Corixidae. These were unidentified species of the genus *Sigara*, which are probably herbivore-detritivores. Also present were unidentified species of the genus *Gerris*, which are probably omnivores. The family Notonectidae was represented by a single taxon in this habitat, an unidentified species of *Buenoa*, which is probably a carnivore. Also present was a carnivorous species of the genus *Neoplea*, which belongs to the family Pleidae. Other bugs that were present belong to the genus *Microvelia*, which is believed to be carnivorous.

The Megaloptera were represented by the genus *Sialis* sp., which is an omnivore, and beetles were represented by a few species. They were the carnivorous *Agabus* sp., *Laccophilus* sp., and an omnivorous species of the genus *Dineutus*. Other bugs that were present belonged to the genera *Stenelmis*, an omnivore; *Berosus*, a herbivore; *Helophorus*, a herbivore; and *Tropisternus*, a herbivore. Probably more than one species was present, but they were not identified as to species. Caddisflies present belonged to the genus *Oecetis*. One species was present, which is a herbivore-omnivore.

The true flies, that is the Diptera, were represented by several species. Belonging to the family Ceratopogonidae were unidentified species of the genus *Bezzia*, which are omnivores, and *Palpomyia* sp., also an omnivore. Another omnivore that was present was an unidentified species of the genus *Chaoborus*. The chironomids were represented by several species in these lentic habitats. They were *Chironomus* sp., which is probably a herbivore; *Clinotanypus* spp., carnivores; and *Coelotanypus* spp., also carnivores. *Cricotopus*, a detritivore-herbivore, was found in and among the detritus, as were the carnivorous *Cryptochironomus* and an unidentified species of the genus *Dicrotendipes*, which is an omnivore. Other chironomids in this habitat were unidentified species of *Endochironomus*, herbivores; an unidentified species of the genus *Eukiefferiella*, which is carnivorous; and several taxons belonging to the genus *Microtendipes*, which are omnivores, as are *Parachironomus* sp.,

Paratendipes sp., *Pentaneura* sp., and *Phaenopsectra* sp. Several unidentified taxons of *Polypedilum* are all probably omnivores. A single species of the genus *Procladius* was collected, which is probably a carnivore. A single species of the genus *Tanypus* was found, which is a detritivore-omnivore. Other Diptera found in this habitat were an unidentified species of the genus *Odontomyia*, which is probably an omnivore, and one or more species each of the genera *Chrysops* and *Tabanus,* which are omnivorous. These are horseflies. The debris in these habitats, particularly sticks and small pieces of stone and so on, were favorite habitats for species of the omnivorous genus *Plumatella.*

In these lentic habitats were found several species of fish. Many of them were grazing on the insects, worms, and other organisms in the habitat or feeding on the vegetation. Some of them certainly did not spend all their life history in these habitats, but used them mainly as feeding grounds. The species collected were *Ichthyomyzon castaneus,* a carnivore, and *I. unicuspis,* a carnivore. Other fish found in these lentic habitats were *Acipenser fulvescens,* a carnivore; *Scaphirhynchus platorynchus,* a carnivore; and *Polydon spathula,* which is an omnivore, perhaps a carnivore. The family Lepisosteidae was represented by *Lepisosteus osseus* and *L. platostomus,* carnivores. *Amia calva,* which is a carnivore, and *Anguilla rostrata, Hiodon alosoides,* and *H. tergisus,* which are carnivores, were found here. The family Clupeidae was represented by *Alosa chrysochloris,* a carnivore, and *Dorosoma cepedianum,* an omnivore. The cyprinids were represented by *Carpiodes carpio* and *Carpiodes cyprinus,* which are omnivores; *Carpiodes velifer* and *Cycleptus elongatus,* omnivores; the catfish *Ictiobus bubalus* and *I. cyprinellus,* omnivores; and *I. niger,* an omnivore. Other species were *Minytrema melanops,* which is a carnivore. *Moxostoma anisurum,* a carnivore; *M. erythrurum,* an omnivore; *M. macrolepidotum,* a carnivore; *Cyprinus carpio,* an omnivore; *Hybopsis aestivalis,* an omnivore; *H. storeriana,* a carnivore; *Notemigonus chrysoleucas,* a carnivore; seven species of *Notropis* (four carnivores, three omnivores); *Phenacobius mirabilis,* an omnivore; three species of *Pimephales,* omnivores; four species of *Ictalurus,* all omnivores; two species of *Noturus,* carnivores; *Pylodictis olivaris,* a carnivore; *Esox lucius,* a carnivore; *Percopsis omiscomaycus,* a carnivore; *Lota lota,* a carnivore; *Fundulus notatus,* an omnivore; and *Gambusia affinis,* an omnivore. Other fish found here were *Labidesthes sicculus,* an omnivore; four carnivorous species of *Lepomis; Lepomis macrochirus,* an omnivore; *Micropterus salmoides,* an omnivore; two carnivorous species of *Pomoxis; Ammocrypta clara,* a carnivore; *Etheostoma nigrum,* a carnivore; *Perca flavescens,* a carnivore; *Percina caprodes,* a carnivore; two species of *Stizostedion,* carnivores; two species of *Morone,* carnivores; and *Aplodinotus grunniens,* a carnivore.

Lotic Habitats. The currents of the lotic habitats were confined primarily to the main course of flow of the river. This flow at times was quite variable, and therefore many different habitats existed in what would be classed as lotic habitats. The bed of the river was mainly gravel and rocks or hard pieces of wood or similar substances that were embedded or snagged into the fast-flowing water. In this habitat several algae were found in Pool 19. They were the blue-green algae, *Marssoniella elegans* and *Merismopedia glauca,* which were in and among the gravel associated with these lotic habitats. Other blue-green algae attached to the rocks and rubble or to the larger gravel were three species of *Anabaena.*

The diatoms *Cyclotella glomerata, C. kuetzingiana, C. melosiroides,* and *C. meneghiniana* were found in gravel associated with the rocks in the area where the current was not as rapid. Also in this habitat were some unidentified species of the genus *Cyclotella. Melosira granulata* was found attached to some of the rocks, as were *M. italica* and *M. varians.* An unidentified species of *Melosira* was also found in this habitat. *Stephanodiscus hantzschii* and *S. niagarae* were found in the gravel where the current was less rapid. Another species found lodged in crevices or in and among the gravel was *Diatoma vulgare.* Also in and among the gravel, sometimes apparently attached to the rocks, was *Fragilaria capucina.* In and among the gravel was found *Fragilaria crotonensis.* This is often found in plankton and may have been lodged there rather than actually growing in this habitat. Attached to the gravel was *Meridion circulare. Synedra acus* was also found in and among the gravel, as was *S. delicatissima. Tabellaria fenestrata* and an unidentified species of *Tabellaria* were found attached to the larger gravel in these lotic habitats. *Achnanthes affinis, A. lanceolata, A. linearis,* and *A. minutissima* were found attached to the gravel and in some cases to the surfaces of rocks where the current was less rapid. *Cocconeis pediculus* was found attached to the rocks, as was *C. placentula.* They are typically found in moderate current. Also in this habitat were an unidentified species of *Cocconeis* and *Rhoicosphenia curvata.* A few *Cymbellas,* all *Cymbella tumida,* were found attached to the rocks.

The family Gomphonemaceae was represented by several species in these lotic habitats, where the current was variable: *Gomphonema acuminatum, G. constrictum, G. olivaceum, G. parvulum,* and *G. truncatum.* A few specimens of *Frustulia rhomboides* were found in and among the gravel where the current was less rapid. Only one *Navicula* was found in and among the gravel and rocks in these lotic habitats in Pool 19, *N. seminulum. Stauroneis smithii* was also found here. Several species of *Epithemia* were found attached to the rocks or gravel or other hard substrates in these lotic habitats. However, no species of *Epithemia* or *Rhopalodia* were found in these habitats in Pool 19. In and among the gravel in these lotic habitats were *Surirella angusta* and *S. ovata.* Several species belonging to the order Peridinales were also found in and among the gravel. They were *Ceratium hirudinella, Glenodinium quadridens, Glenodinium* sp., *Peridinium cinctum,* and *Peridinium* sp.

In the moderate current in these lotic habitats were *Elodea canadensis* and *E. nuttalli.* Also present were *Vallisneria americana* and *Najas flexilis.* All of these monocotyledons occurred in the moderate-current areas. Other species belonging to the genus *Najas* found in this habitat were *N. gracillima, N. quadralupensis,* and *N. minor,* as well as *Zannichellia palustris.* The *Potamo-*

geton species *P. crispus, P. foliosus, P. nodosus, P. pectinatus,* and *P. pusillus* occurred here. Found in moderate current were *Sparganium eurycarpum* and unidentified species of *Typha.*

Although various protozoans undoubtedly occurred in this habitat, none were definitely recorded from it. Attached to the rocks were several *Hydra* belonging to the species *H. americana.* Since this is a filter feeder, it is probably an omnivore. A few molluscs were also recorded from these lotic habitats. They were *Amnicola lustrica,* which might be found in and among the gravel, as might be *Somatogyrus isogonus.* Another gastropod found in this lotic habitat was *Pleurocera acuta.* In and among the gravel might be *Campeloma decisum* and certain of the Unionidae. They would be in and among the gravel: for example, *Cumberlandia (= Margaritifera?) monodonta, Actinonais carinata,* and *Amblema plicata,* herbivore-detritivores; and *Ellipsaria lineolata,* a herbivore-detritivore. *Lampsilis ovata ventricosa* was in and among the gravel. This is also a detritivore-omnivore, as are *Leptodea fragilis* and *Ligumia recta.* Other unionids found where the current was moderate were *Obliquaria reflexa* and *Obovaria olivaria* as well as *Plagiola lineolata* and *Proptera alata.* Four species belonging to the genus *Quadrula* might also be found in the gravel in these lotic habitats, as well as *Strophitus undulatus, Truncilla donaciformis,* and *T. truncata.* A few *Corbicula fluminea* were also found in and among the gravel. These are detritivore-omnivores.

The leech, *Helobdella fusca,* which is a carnivore, was also found in this habitat, as was the leech, *Erpobdella punctata.* They were undoubtedly feeding on the fish and other species in this habitat. Several Crustacea were also found in and among the gravel: *Leptodora kindtii, Macrothrix,* and *Diaphasoma brachyurum,* all detritivore-omnivores. Belonging to the order Collembola was *Isotomurus palustris,* an omnivore, which was found in and among the gravel.

A few odonates were found crawling over the rocks. They were an unidentified species of *Agrion,* an omnivore, and unidentified species of *Argia,* also omnivores. Also found in this habitat were unidentified species of *Enallagma,* which are carnivores, and *Somatochlora,* unidentified species that are probably omnivores.

A number of mayflies were found crawling over the rocks or in and among the gravel. They were unidentified species of *Baetis,* herbivore-detritivores; *Heptagenia inconspicua,* an omnivore; *H. maculipennis,* an omnivore; *Pseudiron centralis,* an omnivore; *Stenacron interpunctatum,* an omnivore; *Stenonema bipunctatum,* an omnivore; *S. integrum,* an omnivore; as well as an unidentified species of the genus *Stenonema.* Other mayflies found in this habitat were *Isonychia sicca,* an omnivore; *Pentagenia vittigera,* an omnivore; and *Potamanthus verticis,* an omnivore; as well as several omnivores belonging to the Caenidae: *Caenis hilaris, C. simulans,* and unidentified species of *Caenis.* A few stoneflies were found on the rocks: *Isoperla bilineata,* a carnivore; *Hesperocorixa* sp., a carnivore; unidentified species of *Sigara,* herbivore-omnivores; *Buenoa* sp., a carnivore; and *Neoplea* sp., a carnivore.

The elmid, *Stenelmis* sp., which is an omnivore, was also found in this habitat, as was *Helophorus* sp., a herbivore. Various caddisflies were found attached to the rocks in this habitat. They were *Cheumatopsyche campyla*, an omnivore; *Hydropsyche bidens*, an omnivore; *H. orris*, an omnivore; *H. phalerata*, an omnivore; and *Potamyia flava*, a herbivore-omnivore. Other Trichoptera or caddisflies in these lotic habitats were *Athripsodes* (= *Ceraclea?*) *flavus* and *A. transversus*, both carnivores with a preference for herbivory. One Lepidoptera was present in these lotic habitats, the herbivore, *Acentropus* sp.

The Diptera were represented by several species. Those that were present in this lotic habitat were the omnivorous *Ablabesmyia* sp.; the carnivorous *Clinotanypus* spp.; the detritivore-herbivore, *Cricotopus* sp.; and an unidentified species of the carnivorous *Cryptochironomus* sp. Other Diptera present were an unidentified species of the carnivorous *Eukiefferiella* sp. and unidentified species of the omnivorous *Microtendipes*. Other chironomids present were the omnivorous *Paratendipes* sp.; *Phaenopsectra* sp., an omnivore; and *Rheotanytarsus* sp., which is also an omnivore. Also present was the simulid, *Prosimulium* sp., which is an omnivore. Another fly species present was the carnivorous *Limnophora* sp.

Several fish were found in and among the rocks and gravel. They were the carnivorous *Ichthyomyzon castaneus* and *I. unicuspis*. Other fish present in this habitat were species in areas where the current was not very strong and which occupied habitats associated with sand and gravel. They were *Acipenser fulvescens*, which is a carnivore; *Scaphirhynchus platorynchus*, which is a carnivore; and *Polydon spathula*, which is a carnivore-omnivore. Other species in these lotic areas where the current was moderate were the carnivorous *Lepisosteus osseus* and *L. platostomus*, both carnivores. Other carnivorous species identified with the habitat were *Anguilla rostrata*, *Hiodon alosoides*, and *H. tergisus*. Several species of the family Clupeidae were present: *Alosa chrysochloris*, which is an omnivore but mainly a carnivore; *Dorosoma cepedianum*, which is an omnivore; and *D. pentenense*, which is a carnivore. Several cyprinids were found in this habitat. They were *Carpiodes cyprinus*, an omnivore-carnivore; *C. velifer*, an omnivore; *Cycleptus elongatus*, also an omnivore; *Ictiobus bubalus*, which is an omnivore but sometimes behaves as a carnivore; and *I. niger*, an omnivore. Other species found in the gravel and rocks were *Moxostoma anisurum*, a carnivore; *M. erythrurum*, an omnivore; and *M. macrolepidotum*, a carnivore, which in some cases seems to be omnivorous. Also present were the omnivorous *Cyprinus carpio*, which often feeds on detritus; the omnivore, *Hybopsis aestivalis;* and the carnivore, *H. storeriana*. Other fish encountered in Pool 19 were *Notropis blennius*, which is an omnivore; *N. buchanani*, a carnivore; *N. cornutus*, an omnivore; *N. hudsonius*, which is omnivorous sometimes acting as a carnivore; and *N. lutrensis*, an omnivore. In the lesser current areas were *Notropis spilopterus*, which is typically an omnivore but may be carnivorous at times, and *N. stramineus*, an omnivore. Other fish in the sand and gravel where the flow was less fast were

Phenacobius mirabilis, Ictalurus natalis, and *I. punctatus,* all omnivorous. Other species found in the sand and gravel were the carnivorous *Noturus flavus, Percopsis omiscomaycus, Lota lota,* and *Labidesthes sicculus.* A great many species of the Perciformes, which belong to the family Centrarchidae, were found in Pool 19. They were *Ambloplites rupestris,* a carnivore; *Micropterus dolomieui,* a carnivore; *M. salmoides,* an omnivore; and the carnivorous *Ammocrypta clara, Etheostoma nigrum, Perca flavescens, Percina caprodes, P. phoxocephala, P. shumardi, Stizostedion canadense,* and *S. vitreum.* Other species found in this lotic habitat were the carnivorous *Morone chrysops* and *M. mississippiensis.*

Conclusions. The importance of various species in the functioning of the ecosystems varied from season to season in Pool 19. It is interesting to note that the blue-green algae were very common in the spring and late summer. They were found in areas of macrophyte development, backwaters, and where there was a confluence of tributaries. In the vegetative areas, pennate diatom densities and diversity were highest and the community was dominated by various species of *Achnanthes.* In the channel and channel borders adjacent to macrophyte beds, the diversity was dominated by the genus *Cocconeis.* In the backwaters in a unique assemblage of phytoplankton were found *Ankistrodesmus, Euglena,* and *Nitzschia,* occurring at high densities. Also present in relatively high densities in backwaters were species of the genus *Trachelomonas.* Below the confluence of the tributaries with the main channel were high densities of *Nitzschia.* It is interesting to note that the diversity of algal species is usually highest near the upper reaches of the pool.

In the zooplankton, the rotifers far outnumbered other small planktonic invertebrates. Species of the genus *Keratella* were most abundant. Other abundant genera were *Brachionus, Polyarthra, Synchaeta,* and *Trichocera.* The Cladocera were very common and the copepods were about twice as abundant as the Cladocera. They were dominated by the genera *Diaptomus* and *Cyclops.* The rotifers were found to be the dominant zooplankton, followed by copepods and Cladocera. Of the rotifers, *Brachionus calyciflorus* was dominant.

The meiofauna, which consists mainly of rotifers, tardigrads, nematodes, and gastrotrichs, was important in maintaining the dynamics of the decomposer-based nutrient cycle. Nematodes were the most abundant species in the meiofauna in Pool 19. In most habitats, benthic rotifers were about half as abundant as nematodes.

Of the macroinvertebrates in Pool 19, three insect orders contributed substantially to this diversity. They included the midges, the mayflies, and the caddisflies. The diversity of mussels and snails was also high. However, the greatest density and biomass was due to the fingernail clam, caddis larvae, and burrowing mayfly. In many of the channel-bordered habitats, the codominants were the fingernail clam and burrowing mayfly.

In Pool 19 the fish fauna was very diverse, due largely to the great diversity of habitats and food supplies. The fingernail clam and the insects, particularly mayflies and caddisflies, were the most important food items for many of the fish.

SUMMARY

The Upper Mississippi River extends from the Minneapolis–St. Paul metropolitan area to the confluence with the Missouri River near St. Louis. It covers much of north-central United States. Formerly, it was an island-braided river with substantial seasonal changes in river stage. However, it has been greatly modified for navigational purposes and now consists of a series of locks and dams. This has transformed the free-flowing river into a series of shallow river-lakes. These changes have greatly altered the natural association of organisms that live in the river. Not only have these changes altered the natural riverine communities of organisms but they also have altered sedimentation dynamics and increased eutrophication. The Upper Mississippi River drains portions of the Superior Upland and Central Lowland Physiographic Provinces. Much of northern Wisconsin as well as part of northeastern Minnesota lie within the Superior Upland. Four subdivisions of the Central Lowland Province are present within the basin.

The most dramatic changes by man to the Upper Mississippi River came with the authorization of a 9-ft navigation channel in 1930, which maintained a minimum pool elevation at or near the sites of the dam. A depth of at least 2.75 m was maintained throughout the main channel. Supplemental dredging also helped to maintain the channels. This series of locks and dams has transformed the Upper Mississippi River from an island-braided free-flowing river into a series of shallow river lakes, that is, navigation pools.

Although the Mississippi is a large river, transportation is impeded during the winter due to the sediment load associated with the ice brought down from the tributaries. Today, the Mississippi River is a series of dams and backwaters. The Upper Mississippi is a very artificial river. Nevertheless, it offers a variety of aquatic habitats, varying from side channels, sloughs, and floodplain lakes or ponds to tailwaters characterized by fast currents and coarse sediments. The main channel is characterized by swift currents, sand and gravels, and borders on a shallow zone, which is between the channel and the shoreline. Floodplain lakes and ponds are lentic habitats that are connected to the main river during high flow, but remain isolated from it during most of the year. Backwater habitats are sloughs and floodplain lakes. They account for about half or more of the total aquatic habitats. Many of these backwater habitats are being threatened by increased sedimentation, which will destroy them.

Turbidity is a problem in the Mississippi. It seems to be lowest in the areas that have negligible current. Turbidity tends to be highest in the spring rise and lowest during the winter. Chemically, the Mississippi River is a hard to very hard calcium–magnesium–bicarbonate stream. pH ranges from neutral to a considerable amount above neutral. Alkalinity and total conductivity are high. The tributaries of the river introduce a considerable amount of hardness (384 mg L^{-1}), sulfates (120 mg L^{-1}), and chlorides (41 mg L^{-1}). The mean total hardness at St. Paul is 205 mg L^{-1}. At Minneapolis and St. Paul, the river receives medium-hard and soft waters from tributaries draining the relatively inert deposits in the Superior Uplands Province. The river then flows through the Driftless Area and the hardness increases, reaching a total hardness of 195 mg L^{-1} by the time the river reaches Keokuk in Pool 19. Nitrates, ammonia, and phosphates are high. However, the river is well oxygenated.

The vegetation in the backwaters consumes a considerable amount of nitrate-nitrogen. For example, in Pool 19 the mean nitrate-nitrogen during August 1983 was considerably lower in vegetative backwater habitats (0.04 mg L^{-1}) and somewhat lower in the vegetative main-channel habitats (0.23 mg L^{-1}) than in either of the main channels or the unvegetated main-channel border, where it was approximately 0.28 mg L^{-1}. In contrast, ammonia-nitrogen was highest among the vegetation. Such change is also important in the nitrogen concentration.

Dissolved oxygen is very variable, often being extremely low. Considerable pollution enters the Mississippi River, particularly from its tributaries such as the Illinois River. The tributaries and the vegetation within the pool, such as in the backwaters, contribute a considerable amount of total organic carbon. Aquatic macrophyte beds are extensive in the Upper Mississippi and are a major source of organic matter. The macrophyte beds also contribute organic carbon, primarily as DOC exudates. Organic matter was greater in the depositional backwaters and lower pool habitats than in the more erosional sites. It was relatively low in the main-channel border and tailwaters, intermediate in the side channels, and highest in the sloughs and floodplain lakes. In Pool 19 the mean concentration of suspended POC was 6.5 mg L^{-1}. This is within the upper end of the range reported in the literature. Mean DOC concentration was 12.5 mg L^{-1}. DOC concentrations were highest during peak spring flooding.

Phytoplankton production is relatively low in the Upper Mississippi, whereas epiphytic algae growing on the macrophytes are relatively abundant. However, the green algae, *Cladophora,* which grows on various substrates, accounted for 40% of the summer macrophyte biomass. It mainly colonized shallow rock substrates adjacent to the main channel. Epiphytic algae such as species of *Achnanthes* and *Cocconeis* can be abundant at times in these reservoirs. Navigation greatly affected the type of diatom flora on the *Cladophora,* limiting the species that were present where the influence was great, whereas in protected areas the diatom flora was more diverse. Phytoplankton, which is mainly scuffed-up benthic forms, was variable in these reservoirs. In the Upper Mississippi, diatoms accounted for 86.4% of the total phytoplankton by volume in the impounded reach between Minneapolis and Winnona; green algae, 4.3%; blue-green algae, 7.6%; and green flagellates, 1.6%. Algae in the phytoplankton varies greatly with location and time of year. In many of the pools, diatoms dominated the phytoplankton.

Zooplankton in the reach between the twin cities (Minneapolis and St.

Paul) and Winnona, Minnesota, during 1928 was composed of rotifers, 16.3% by volume; entomostracans, 46.1%; and heterotrophic protozoans, 17.5%. Rotifers exhibited a maximum in biovolume during May and June, while entomostracans exhibited maximums during May, early June, late July, August, and September. The most abundant rotifer was *Keratella cochlearis*. In Pool 19, zooplankton varied with habitats. In general, densities were highest in sites with reduced currents. The dominant species of rotifer varies with the pool and with the time of year. In 1982–1983 studies in Pool 19, *Brachionus calycifloris* was the most abundant rotifer.

Macrophytes are very abundant in these pools. There are three major growth forms of aquatic macrophytes: emergent, floating leaf, and submergent. All of these are important in the Mississippi River. *Sagittaria latifolia* and *S. rigida* are the two most important emergent macrophytes in the Upper Mississippi. *Nelumbo lutea* and *Nymphaea tuberosa* are the most abundant floating-leaf species. The most abundant submergent species are *Ceratophyllum demersum, Elodea canadensis, Vallisneria americana, Potamogeton* spp., and *Heteranthera dubia*. The extent of macrophyte development varies greatly with pools.

Invertebrate production other than mussels in the Upper Mississippi can be very productive and diverse. However, abundance, taxonomic richness, and taxonomic composition vary considerably from site to site. Comparison of various habitats in Pool 8 indicated that the main and side channels had relatively low standing crops and densities.

The differences in benthic macroinvertebrate abundance from site to site were exemplified by collections from 41 sites in the middle and lower reaches of Pool 8 during the summer of 1975. Densities ranged from 237 to 19,975 animals m^{-2} and standing stocks ranged from 0.25 to 198.36 g m^{-2}. These 41 sites span a continuum from less eutrophic—that is, swifter current, sandy substrates, low-sediment organic matter, greater oxygen saturation, and little or no macrophyte growth—to more eutrophic conditions with reduced current, silt–clay sediment, high organic matter, low oxygen saturations, and extensive macrophyte growth. Although overlap was considerable, density in biomass tended to be higher in the more eutrophic sites than in the less eutrophic sites. On the other hand, taxonomic richness tended to be lower in the more eutrophic sites. Forty-one sites were collected by Elstad (1977) and would be classified as main channel, side channel with sandy substrates and fast currents, main-channel border with fast to slow currents and broad shallow bottoms of silt and clay, sloughs and lakes with little current and silty substrates, and stagnant pools. These habitats generally conform to the gradation from less autotrophic to more eutrophic presented by Elstad (1977), except that the main-channel borders, which are concentrated in the lowest pools, span a range of currents. Comparison of these habitats in Pool 8 indicated that the side channels had relatively low standing crops and densities.

Densities tended to be relatively high in the main-channel borders, sloughs/lakes, and stagnant ponds, but standing stock varied considerably. Standing stocks were highest in the main-channel borders, intermediate in the sloughs and lakes, and low in the stagnant pools. Taxonomic richness was highest in the main-channel borders and lowest in the stagnant pools.

Substantial differences in benthic macroinvertebrate abundance were evident along a transect in the middle reach of Pool 7. Standing stocks in the main channel averaged only 0.38 g m^{-2}. Standing stocks from the midchannel in the upper Black River, which is essentially a large side channel paralleling the main channel, were also low, but the standing stocks increased considerably near the margins of Sites 12 and 17. Both the main channel and the Upper Black River portions of the transect were characterized by shifting sand and fast currents and a paucity of macrophyte growth. In between the channels, six vegetative sites located in slough and lake habitats yielded substantially higher standing stocks, averaging 10.09 g m^{-2} and ranging from 2.46 to 26.96 g m^{-2}.

The benthic assemblages of the main channel, midchannel, and side channel in Pool 7 were characterized by modest populations of oligochaetes, amphipods, Ceratopogonidae, and/or Chironomidae. The more productive sites were near the periphery of the side channels and are characterized by high standing crops of molluscs, probably dominated by the Sphaeriidae. A productive and diverse assemblage of macroinvertebrates included oligochaetes, molluscs, isopods, amphipods, burrowing mayflies, and Diptera. These were found in the benthos of the vegetative sloughs and lake water. Winter sampling of the macroinvertebrate benthos indicated that total densities were lowest in the tailwater and main-channel habitats, intermediate in the side channels, and highest in the sloughs, lakes, and sandy main-channel borders. Nematodes, oligochaetes, and chironomids were numerous in all habitats, but nematodes and oligochaetes were most numerous in the sloughs, whereas chironomids were most numerous in the main-channel border. This was in the winter.

The abundance of macroinvertebrates is greatly influenced by substrates and currents in off-channel sites. There are several characteristics of benthic macroinvertebrate faunas that are common for all these pools. Abundance tends to be low in sandy sites whether they are located in the main channel, side channel, or main-channel borders. Low abundance in these sandy sites is probably a consequence of the shifting sand, whereas in coarser and presumably more stable substrates, macroinvertebrate abundance increases largely through the increase in Hydropsychidae. Abundance also increases substantially in the silt–clay substrates of sloughs, floodplain lakes, and macrophyte beds. Macroinvertebrate abundance is greatest in the silt–clay substrates of the main-channel border habitats located in the lower reaches of each pool. These highly productive main-channel border habitats were not present in the river prior to impoundment.

One of the more striking differences among pools in the Upper Mississippi River is the abundance of Sphaeriidae. The most abundant sphaerid, *Musculum transversum,* tends to be most abundant in those unvegetated main-channel border sites adjacent to macrophyte beds, which suggests that the beds supply an important source of trophic support. The macroinvertebrate habitats within macrophyte beds are considerably more diverse than those at other habitats. These habitats were dominated numerically by Oligochaeta, Hirudinea, Gastropoda, Sphaeriidae, *Asellus* spp., *Hyalella azteca,* Ceratopogonidae, and Chironomidae.

The density of many taxa increase from the shallow water to the deeper water where vegetation was present. The aufwuchs or hard substrate habitats supported a macroinvertebrate fauna considerably different from that encountered in most benthic and epiphytic habitats, which is also very productive. For example, next to *Musculum transversum* and *Hexagenia* spp., the most abundant large-body invertebrate in Pool 19 is *Hydropsyche orris.*

Artificial substrates throughout the Mississippi River support high densities and standing crops of invertebrates. In Pool 5A macroinvertebrates colonizing wing dams were generally more abundant than those colonizing riprap banks. Within the wing dam habitat, abundance was greater in microhabitats with faster current than in those with reduced currents, but differences in abundance were not associated with depth or extent or periphyton growth.

Macroinvertebrate drift in the Upper Mississippi River included both benthic and aufwuchs taxa and has been shown to vary with habitat, time of day, and depth. Macroinvertebrate assemblages differed in overall productivity among the pools. The amount of habitat is important. For example, the presence of extensive beds and predominance of the extremely productive muddy and shallow main-channel border habitats contributed to substantially greater diversity and productivity of macroinvertebrates in Pool 19. In contrast, production and diversity in Pools 20 and 26 were largely limited by the presence of shifting sand in the main channel and main-channel border habitats. Changes in habitat composition and macroinvertebrate populations have occurred and continued to occur well after the completion of the navigation pools.

Pool 19 is 20 to 25 years older than other pools and may show what will probably happen in other pools. Net sedimentation has resulted in the creation of an expansive shallow main-channel border habitat dominated by silt and clay substrates. This new habitat supports huge increases in populations of the burrowing mayfly, *Hexagenia* spp.

By the late 1960s the sedimentation raised the nearshore portion of the main-channel border bottom to within the photosynthetic zone, thereby promoting significant macrophyte production. This autochthonous production has, in turn, supported the very high densities of *Musculum transversum.* Encroachment of the macrophyte beds into the unvegetated main-channel border habitat has facilitated partial replacement of *M. transversum* with *Sphaerium striatinum* in the submerged macrophyte zone. The presence of pollution causes a reduction in the macrophytes and hence the supported fauna and flora.

Unionidae (freshwater mussels) have been an important component of the invertebrate fauna of the Upper Mississippi. Large-scale commercial exploitation of this diverse, productive fauna started in 1891 at a pearl button factory in Muscatine, Iowa. However, within 10 years the mussel fauna was depleted and harvesting expanded to other reaches in the Upper Mississippi. Historically, surveys indicate that there has been a decline in the productivity and diversity of the unionid fauna in the Upper Mississippi. Of the 50 species groups that have been recorded in the river, 48 had been recorded prior to the first extensive efforts of navigation impoundment and only 39 have been recorded since then. Studies indicate that much of the faunal loss occurred since the turn of the century; the faunal loss since then has not been as drastic. In the 1930–1931 survey, two species, *Lampsilis teres* and *Leptodea fragilis,* accounted for 13.8% and 10.1% respectively, of the total collection. Of the remaining taxons, 16 accounted for 1.1 to 6.9% each, while the other 16 accounted for less than 1%. In the heyday of the pearl industry, the most sought-after species were *Elliptio dilata, Fusconaia ebena, Obovaria olivaria, Ellipsaria lineolata, Potamilus capax,* and *Quadrula metanerva.* Of these, *P. capax* is either greatly reduced or extinct. The extinction that has occurred is due to a variety of factors, one of the most important being overharvesting. The zebra mussel and pollution also may be important.

Fish Fauna. The fish fauna in the Upper Mississippi River is diverse. At least 135 species have been recorded in the river since the late nineteenth century, of which 106 are considered to be members of the current fauna. Thirty-nine species are considered strays. A number of species exhibit substantial longitudinal changes in abundance. The Upper Mississippi is within the southern limits of the geographic range of several species, all of which are more abundant in the northern pools. Others are widely distributed species. Several species that have southerly distribution are more abundant in the more southern pools. The fish fauna in the Upper Mississippi is not only highly diverse but also highly productive especially in the backwaters. The main-channel border habitats may also be quite productive in some of the pools.

Tailwaters provide the river's richest sport fisheries. High variability within pools makes comparison of fish production among the pools of the Upper Mississippi River difficult. The importance of floodplains, macrophyte beds, and backwater habitats for fish production is suggested by the changes in commercial catches in the Illinois River. This river, with its low gradient, extensive backwaters, and oversized floodplains, exhibits many of the hydrological and geomorphological characteristics typical of large floodplain rivers such as the Mississippi. Catches were largest when the backwaters and floodplains were still intact in the Illinois River.

A decline in the fisheries occurred when the farmland was shifted from field crops to row crops, which accelerated soil erosion and seriously degraded most of the remaining backwaters in the Upper Mississippi River. This loss of backwater habitat severely threatens some of the fish populations. These backwaters, macrophyte beds, and floodplain ponds are very important to the fisheries. When they are eliminated or degraded, it greatly affects the fish population.

Variation in discharge can have significant effects on the spawning and recruitment of Upper Mississippi River fishes, because much of the spring spawning occurs in inundated floodplains. These are also nursery grounds, and elimination of these sites affects the fisheries. Variation in discharge can also affect populations in the main channel and the main-channel border. Flushing backwaters may increase larval densities in the main channel. The export of larval fish from backwaters into the main channel has been suggested by a study conducted in Pool 13. Larval densities were higher in backwater and main-channel sites receiving flow from the backwaters than they were in upstream main-channel sites. Several fish have been introduced into the Upper Mississippi River, and these affect the success of some of the native fish.

In general, the productivity of the fish in the Upper Mississippi River has been enhanced by construction of the navigation pool. This enhancement is primarily the result of stabilization of summer flow, which reduces the dewatering of the backwaters and the creation of rich sloughs and pool habitats in the middle pool reaches. Impoundment has reduced habitat quality for certain species but enhanced it for others. Diversity and productivity in backwaters and sloughs are highest in deeper, less eutrophic backwaters. Unfortunately, the increases in sedimentation and eutrophication that have accompanied impoundments now threaten the productivity of these habitats.

The Structure of Communities. From April to July the phytoplankton was composed about 40% of diatoms, 33% of green algae, and about 11% of blue-green algae. The zooplankton consisted primarily of rotifers and Crustacea. The rotifers far outnumbered all other planktonic invertebrates. *Keratella,* a rotifer, was the most abundant genus, with an average density of 47 organisms per liter. Other abundant genera were *Brachionus, Polyarthra, Synchaeta,* and *Trichocera.* Cladocera were also common. There were 21 taxa of rotifers and 13 taxa of Cladocera. Vegetative communities were common in Pool 19. Many emergent and submergent plants occurred, which were important habitats. Associated with the emerged vegetation was an abundant meiofauna where nematodes were most important. This meiofauna was also present on the floating vegetation. The macrophyte beds in the lentic habitats are extensive in Pool 19 and they are rich in aquatic life.

The three major types of vegetative habitats were emergent, floating leaves, and submergent. Emergent vegetation supported a rather large population of epiphytic algae. For example, dense growths of epiphytic diatoms were observed on the filamentous green algae, *Cladophora,* which accounts for up to 40% of the summer biomass. It colonizes shallow rock substrates adjacent to the main channel. The greatest density of algae occurred in April. Blue-green algae were usually abundant in late summer or early fall.

Worms were commonly found in and among the vegetation. A few crustaceans were associated with the vegetation. Insects were fairly common among the vegetation. They consisted of carnivorous, omnivorous, and herbivorous genera as well as those that feed primarily on detritus. True bugs were also present, and a few Trichoptera were in and among the vegetation. Several fish were found in and among the vegetation. Thus one finds that there are in these vegetative habitats, species representing all stages of the nutrient and energy transfer: that is, detritivore-herbivores, omnivores, and carnivores.

The lentic habitats supported a great variety of aquatic life. Detritus was common in the pools and supported various invertebrates. These lentic habitats were also favorable for several species of algae, particularly unicellular algae. A number of protozoans were found in these lentic habitats. They were particularly common in shallow water. Protozoans were common in these lentic habitats. Rotifers were also common. Found in and among the vegetation were various species of the genera *Polyarthra* and *Synchaeta.* A number of nematodes were also found in and among the detritus. Gastropods were quite common in these lentic habitats. Two species of snails were common in this habitat, *Physa* sp. and *Helisoma trivolis.* This was a favorite habitat for several species of sphaerid clams. Various leeches were also found. Several tubificids were found in these lentic habitats. In the vegetation in these lentic habitats were found a number of species of Cladocera. Isopods were present, as were several species of odonates, mayflies, Hemiptera, Megaloptera, beetles, and true flies in these lentic habitats. A number of fish were also found in these lentic habitats with various food habits, from those of omnivores to those of carnivores.

The lotic habitats were found primarily in the main channel of the river. Diatoms were quite prevalent in these habitats. Also present were some of the blue-green algae. In moderate currents were found a number of plants, such as *Elodea canadensis* and other floating or rooted aquatics. Protozoans were quite common in and among the gravel and associated with plants in these habitats. Leeches were also found in these habitats. Crustaceans were found in and among the gravel. Odonates were crawling over the rocks and vegetation. A number of mayflies were also found crawling over the rocks and in and among the gravel. Elmid beetles, which are omnivores, were also found in this habitat, as well as *Helophorus* sp., a herbivore. Caddisflies were found attached to several of the rocks. Most of these are filter feeders and therefore are omnivorous, feeding on very small protozoans, algae, and so on. Diptera were represented by several species, particularly chironomids. Some of these are omnivores, others carnivores. Several fish were found in among the rocks and gravel, representing a variety of food habits.

From these studies it is evident that the Upper Mississippi, with its present locks and dams, is very productive; that changing the natural shape and flow of the river has altered the fauna and flora but that a highly diverse fauna and flora now exist in the river in the upper reaches above St. Louis. All stages of the foodweb seem to be present, and diversity is high in the various locks.

BIBLIOGRAPHY

Anderson, R. V., and D. M. Day. 1986. Predictive quality of macroinvertebrates–habitat associations in lower navigation pools of the Mississippi River. Hydrobiologia 136: 101–112.

Baily, P. A., and R. G. Rada. 1984. Distribution and enrichment of trace metals (Cd, Cr, Cu, Ni, Pb, and Se) in bottom sediments of Navigation Pools 4 (Lake Pepin), 5, and 9 of the Upper Mississippi River. pp. 119–138. *In* J. G. Wiener, R. V. Anderson, and D. R. McConville, eds., Contaminants in the Upper Mississippi River: proceedings of the 15th annual meeting of the Mississippi River Research Consortium. Ann Arbor Science, Ann Arbor, Mich.

Baker, A. L., and K. K. Baker. 1979. Effects of temperature and current discharge on the concentration and photosynthetic activity of the phytoplankton in the Upper Mississippi River. Freshwater Biol. 9: 191–198.

Baker, K. K., and A. L. Baker. 1981. Seasonal succession of the phytoplankton of the Upper Mississippi River. Hydrobiologia 83: 295–301.

Becker, G. C. 1983. The fishes of Wisconsin. Univ. Wisconsin Press, Madison, Wis. 1052 pp.

Bhowmik, N. G., and J. R. Adams. 1986. The hydrologic environment of Pool 19 of the Mississippi River. Hydrobiologia 136: 21–30.

Blitgen, B. A. 1981. Aufwuchs and benthic macroinvertebrate community structure associated with three species of rooted aquatic macrophytes in Lake Onalaska, 1976–1977. Master's thesis. Univ. Wisconsin—La Crosse, La Crosse, Wis. 136 pp.

Butler, R. L. 1965. Freshwater drum, *Aplodinotus grunniens,* in the navigation impoundments of the Upper Mississippi River. Trans. Am. Fish. Soc. 94: 339–349.

Butts, R. A., R. L. Evans, and R. E. Sparks. 1982. Sediment oxygen demand–fingernail clam relationship in the Mississippi River Keokuk Pool. Trans. Ill. Acad. Sci. 75(1–2): 29–40.

Carlander, K. D., R. S. Campbell, and W. H. Irwin. 1963. Mid-continent states. pp. 317–348. *In* D. G. Frey, ed., Limnology in North America. Univ. Wisconsin Press, Madison, Wis.

Carlander, K. D., C. A. Carlson, V. Gooch, and T. L. Wenke. 1967. Populations of *Hexagenia* mayfly naiads in Pool 19, Mississippi River, Keokuk Pool. Trans. Ill. Acad. Sci. 75: 19–39.

Carlson, C. A., Jr. 1968. Summer bottom fauna of the Mississippi River, above Dam 19, Keokuk, Iowa. Ecology 49: 162–169.

Carter, S. R., K. R. Bazata, and D. L. Andersen. 1982. Macroinvertebrate communities of the channelized Missouri River near two nuclear power stations. pp. 147–182. *In* L. W. Hesse, G. L. Hergenrader, H. S. Lewis, S. D. Reetz, and A. B. Schlesinger, eds., The Middle Missouri River: a collection of papers on the biology with special reference to power station effects. Missouri River Study Group, Norfolk, NE.

Chen, Y. H., and D. B. Simmons. 1986. Hydrology, hydraulics, and geomorphology of the Upper Mississippi River System. Hydrobiologia 136: 5–20.

Chilton, E. W. 1990. Macroinvertebrate communities associated with three aquatic macroinvertebrates (*Ceratophyllum demersum, Myriophyllum spicatum,* and *Vallisneria americana*) in Lake Onalaska, Wisconsin. U.S. Fish and Wildlife Service, National Fisheries Research Center, La Crosse, Wis. J. Freshwater Ecol. 5(4): 455–465.

Claflin, T. O. 1973. Final report. Environmental impact assessment of the northern section of the Upper Mississippi River, Pool 8. Report to the St. Paul District Corps of Engineers. River Studies Center, Univ. Wisconsin–La Crosse, La Crosse, Wis. 229 pp.

Claflin, T.O. Personal communication. Univ. Wisconsin–La Crosse, La Crosse, Wis.

Colbert, B. K., J. E. Scott, J. H. Johnson, and R. C. Soloman. 1975. Environmental inventory and assessment of navigation pools 24, 25, and 26. Upper Mississippi and Lower Illinois Rivers. An aquatic analysis. U.S. Army Corps of Engineers, St. Louis, Mo. 527 pp.

Coon, T. G., J. W. Eckblad, and P. M. Trygstad. 1977. Relative abundance and growth of mussels (Mollusca: Eulamellibranchia) in Pools, 8, 9, and 10 of the Upper Mississippi River. Freshwater Biol. 7(3): 279–285.

Dawson, V. K., G. A. Jackson, and C. E. Korschgen. 1984. Water chemistry at selected sites on Pools 7 and 8 of the Upper Mississippi River: a ten-year survey. pp. 279–298. *In* J. G. Wiener,

R. V. Anderson, and D. R. McConville, eds., Contaminants in the Upper Mississippi River: proceedings of the 15th annual meeting of the Mississippi River Research Consortium. Butterworth, Newton, Mass.

Eckblad, J. W., N. L. Peterson, K. Ostle, and A. Temte. 1977. The morphometry, benthos and sedimentation rates of a floodplain lake in Pool 9 of the Upper Mississippi River. Am. Midl. Nat. 97: 433–443.

Eckblad, J. W., C. S. Volden, and L. S. Weilgart. 1984. Allochthonous drift from backwaters to the main channel of the Mississippi River. Am. Midl. Nat. 111: 16–22.

Ellis, M. M. 1931. A survey of conditions affecting fisheries in the Upper Mississippi River. U.S. Govt. Printing Office, Washington, D.C.

Elstad, C. E. 1977. Macrobenthic survey of Navigation Pool No. 8 of the Upper Mississippi River with special reference to ecological relationships. Master's thesis. Univ. Wisconsin—La Crosse, La Crosse, Wis. 231 pp.

Elstad, C. E. 1986. Macrobenthic distribution and community structure in the upper navigation pools of the Upper Mississippi River. Hydrobiologia 136: 85–100 (pools 7 and 8)

Engman, J. A. 1984. Phytoplankton distribution in Pool 19, Mississippi River. Master's thesis. Western Illinois Univ., Macomb, Ill. 184 pp.

Farabee, G. B. 1979. Life histories of important sport and commercial fishes of the Upper Mississippi River. pp. 41–68. *In* J. L. Rasmussen, ed., Compendium of fisheries information on the Upper Mississippi River. Upper Mississippi River Conservation Committee, Rock Island, Ill.

Fenneman, N. M. 1938. Physiography of eastern United States. McGraw-Hill, New York. 714 pp.

Fremling, C. R. 1960. Biology and possible control of nuisance caddisflies of the Upper Mississippi River. Iowa State Univ. Agric. Home Exp. Stn. Res. Bull. 483: 856–879.

Fremling, C. R. 1970. Mayfly distribution as a water quality index. Water Pollut. Control Res. Ser. 16030 DQH 11/70. Water Quality Office, U.S. Environmental Protection Agency, Washington, D.C.

Fremling, C. R., and T. O. Claflin. 1984. Ecological history of the Upper Mississippi River. pp. 5–24. *In* J. G. Weiner, R. V. Anderson, and D. R. McConville, eds., Contaminants in the Upper Mississippi River. Butterworth, Newton, Mass.

Fremling, C. R., J. L. Rasmussen, R. E. Sparks, S. P. Cobbs, C. F. Bryan, and T. O. Claflin. 1989. Mississippi River fisheries: a case history. pp. 309–351. *In* D. P. Dodge, ed., Proceedings of the international large river symposium. Can. Spec. Publ. Fish. Aquat. Sci. 106. Canadian Government Publications Centre, Ottawa, Canada.

Fuller, S. L. H. 1980a. Historical and current distributions of fresh-water mussels (Mollusca: Bivalvia: Unionidae) in the Upper Mississippi River. pp. 72–119. *In* J. L. Rasmussen, ed., Proceedings of the UMRCC symposium on Upper Mississippi River bivalve mollusks. Upper Mississippi River Conservation Committee, Rock Island, Ill.

Fuller, S. L. H. 1980b. Final report: freshwater mussels (Mollusca: Bivalvia: Unionidae) of the Upper Mississippi River: observations at selected sites within the 9-foot channel navigation project on behalf of the Army Corps of Engineers. Academy of Natural Sciences of Philadelphia, Philadelphia, Pa.

Gale, W. F. 1975. Bottom fauna of a segment of Pool 19, Mississippi River, near Fort Madison, Iowa, 1967–1968. Iowa State J. Res. 49: 353–372.

Gale, W. F., and R. L. Lowe. 1971. Phytoplankton ingestion by fingernail clam, *Sphaerium transversum* (Say), in Pool 19, Mississippi River. Ecology 52(3): 507–513.

Galtsoff, P. S. 1924. Limnological observations of the Upper Mississippi, 1921. Bull. Bur. Fish., Wash. 39: 374–438.

Grumbaugh, J. W., and R. V. Anderson. 1987. Spatial and temporal availability of floodplain habitat: long-term changes at Pool 19, Mississippi River. Am. Midl. Nat. 119(2): 402–411.

Grumbaugh, J. W., and R. V. Anderson. 1989. Upper Mississippi River: seasonal and floodplain influences on organic matter transport. Hydrobiologia 174(3): 235–244.

Grumbaugh, J. W., R. V. Anderson, D. M. Day, K. S. Lubinski, and R. E. Sparks. 1986.

Production and fate of organic matter from *Sagittaria latifolia* and *Nelumbo lutea* on Pool 19, Mississippi River. J. Freshwater Ecol. 3(4): 477–484.

Hall, T. J. 1980. Influences of wing dam notching on aquatic macroinvertebrates in Pool 13, Upper Mississippi River: the prenotching study. Master's thesis. Univ. Wisconsin—Stevens Point, Stevens Point, Wis. 168 pp.

Hall, T. J. 1982. Colonizing macroinvertebrates in the Upper Mississippi River with comparison of basket and multiplate samplers. Freshwater Biol. 12(3): 211–215.

Havlik, M. E. 1983. Naiad mollusk populations (Bivalvia: Unionidae) in Pools 7 and 8 of the Mississippi River near La Crosse, Wisconsin. Am. Malacol. Bull. 1: 51–60.

Holland, L. E. 1986. Distribution of early life history stages of fishes in selected pools of the Upper Mississippi River. Hydrobiologia 136: 121–130 (Pools 5, 7).

Holland, L. E., and M. L. Huston. 1984. Relationship of young-of-the-year northern pike to aquatic vegetation types in backwaters of the Upper Mississippi River. North Am. J. Fish. Manage. 112: 293–301.

Holland, L. E., and M. L. Huston. 1985. Distribution and food habits of young-of-the-year fishes in a backwater lake of the Upper Mississippi River. J. Freshwater Ecol. 3(1): 81–91.

Holland, L. E., and J. R. Sylvester. 1983. Distribution of larval fishes related to potential navigation impacts on the Upper Mississippi River, Pool 7. Trans. Am. Fish. Soc. 112: 293–301.

Holland-Bartels, L. E., and M. C. Duval. 1988. Variations in abundance of young-of-the-year channel catfish in a navigation pool of the Upper Mississippi River. Trans. Am. Fish. Soc. 117(2): 202–208.

Hoopes, D. T. 1960. Utilization of mayflies and caddisflies by some Mississippi River fishes. Trans. Am. Fish. Soc. 89(1): 32–34.

Hubert, W. A., G. E. Darnell, and D. E. Darnell. 1984. Late-winter abundance and substrate associations of benthos in Pool 13, Upper Mississippi River. Proc. Iowa Acad. Sci. 91(4): 147–152.

Huff, D. R. 1986. Phytoplankton communities in Navigation Pool No. 7 of the Upper Mississippi River. Hydrobiologia 136: 47–56.

Jahn, L. A., and R. V. Anderson. 1986. The ecology of Pools 19 and 20, Upper Mississippi River: a community profile. U.S. Fish Wildl. Serv. Biol. Rep. 85(7.6). U.S. Department of the Interior, Washington, D.C. 142 pp.

Jude, D. J. 1973. Food and feeding habits of gizzard shad in Pool 19, Mississippi River. Trans. Am. Fish. Soc. 102: 378–383.

Junk, W. J., P. B. Bayley, and R. E. Sparks. 1989. The flood pulse concept in river–floodplain systems. pp. 110–127. *In* D. P. Dodge, ed., Proceedings of the international large river symposium. Can. Spec. Publ. Fish. Aquat. Sci. 106. Canadian Government Publications Centre, Ottawa, Canada.

Kline, D. R., and J. L. Golden. 1979a. Analysis of Upper Mississippi River sport fishery between 1962 and 1973. pp. 69–81. *In* J. L. Rasmussen, ed., Compendium of fisheries information on the Upper Mississippi River. Upper Mississippi River Conservation Committee, Rock Island, Ill.

Kline, D. R., and J. L. Golden. 1979b. Analysis of the Upper Mississippi River commercial fishery. pp. 82–117. *In* J. L. Rasmussen, ed., Compendium of fisheries information on the Upper Mississippi River. Upper Mississippi River Conservation Committee, Rock Island, Ill.

Korschgen, L. G. 1948. Unpublished data.

Latendresse, J. 1980. A look at the Upper Mississippi River mussel shell industry and the Japanese cultured pearl industry. pp. 170–178. *In* J. L. Rasmussen, ed., Proceedings of the UMRCC symposium on Upper Mississippi River bivalve mollusks. Upper Mississippi River Conservation Committee, Rock Island, Ill.

Lee, D. S., C. R. Gilbert, C. H. Hocutt, R. E. Jenkins, D. E. McAllister, and J. R. Stauffer, Jr. 1980. Atlas of North American fishes. A publication of the North Carolina Biological Survey. North Carolina State Museum of Nat. Hist. Raleigh, N.C. 854 pp.

Lewis, R. B. 1984. Pool 5A main channel border macroinvertebrates. pp. 148–149. *In* Proceedings of the 40th annual meeting of the Upper Mississippi River Conservation Committee. Upper Mississippi River Conservation Committee, Rock Island, Ill.

Lubinski, K. S., M. J. Wallendorf, and M. C. Reese. 1981. Analysis of the Upper Mississippi River system—correlations between physical, biological, and navigation variables. Upper Miss. River Basin Assoc., St. Paul, Minn. 50 pp.

Lubinski, K. S., A. Van Vooren, G. Farabee, J. Janecek, and S. D. Jackson. 1986. Common carp in the Upper Mississippi River. Hydrobiologia 136: 141–154.

Luoma, S. N. 1984. Contaminants in the Upper Mississippi River: summary and conclusion. pp. 345–356. *In* J. G. Wiener, R. V. Anderson, and D. R. McConville, eds., Contaminants in the Upper Mississippi River: proceedings of the 15th annual meeting of the Mississippi River Research Consortium. Butterworth, Newton, Mass.

Luttenton, M. L., and R. G. Rada. 1986. Effects of disturbance on epiphytic community structure. J. Phycol. 22(3): 320–326.

Luttenton, M. L., J. B. Vansteenburg, and R. G. Rada. 1986. Phycoperiphyton in selected reaches of the Upper Mississippi River: community composition, architecture, and productivity. Hydrobiologia 136: 31–46.

McConville, D. R., and J. D. Fossum. 1981. Movement patterns of walleye (*Stizostedium* v. *vitreum*) in Pool 3 of the Upper Mississippi River as determined by ultrasonic telemetry. J. Freshwater Ecol. 1(3): 287–293.

McConville, D. R., D. D. Anderson, R. N. Vose, and D. B. Wilcox. 1986. The species composition, occurrence and temporal stability of submerged aquatic macrophyte patches along the main channel of Pool 5A, Upper Mississippi River. Hydrobiologia 136: 77–84.

McHenry, J. R., J. C. Ritchie, C. M. Cooper, and J. Verdon. 1984. Recent rates of sedimentation in the Mississippi River. pp. 99–118. *In* J. G. Wiener, R. V. Anderson, and D. R. McConville, eds., Contaminants in the Upper Mississippi River: proceedings of the 15th annual meeting of the Mississippi River Research Consortium. Butterworth, Newton, Mass.

Miller, A. C. 1988. Mussel fauna associated with wing dams in Pool 7 of the Mississippi River. J. Freshwater Ecol. 4(3): 299–302.

MPCA. 1978. Water quality sampling program, Minnesota lakes and streams: a compilation of analytical data, Minnesota monitoring stations, Vol. 8, 1970–1975. Minnesota Pollution Control Agency, Division of Water Quality, Surface Groundwater Section, St. Paul, Minn.

Neuswanger, D. J., W. W. Taylor, and J. B. Reynolds. 1982. Comparison of macroinvertebrate herpobenthos and haptobenthos in side channel and slough in the Upper Mississippi River. Freshwater Invertebr. Biol. 1:13–24.

Nielsen, D. N., R. G. Rada, and M. M. Smart. 1984. Sediments of the Upper Mississippi River: their sources, distribution, and characteristics. pp. 67–98. *In* J. G. Wiener, R. V. Anderson, and D. R. McConville, eds., Contaminants in the Upper Mississippi River: proceedings of the 15th annual meeting of the Mississippi River Research Consortium. Butterworth, Newton, Mass.

Paveglio, F. L., and D. W. Steffeck. 1978. The relationship of aquatic plants and Mollusca to the food habits and populations of diving ducks on the Keokuk Pool (Pool 19), Mississippi River, 1977. Cont. Rep. U.S. Fish and Wildlife Service, North Prairie Wildlife Research Station, Jamestown, N. Dak.

Peck, J. H., and M. M. Smart. 1986. An assessment of aquatic and wetland vegetation of the Upper Mississippi River. Hydrobiologia 136: 57–76.

Perry, E. W. 1979. A survey of Upper Mississippi River mussels. pp. 118–139. *In* J. L. Rasmussen, ed., Compendium of fisheries information on the Upper Mississippi River. Upper Mississippi River Conservation Committee, Rock Island, Ill.

Pflieger, W. L. 1975. The fishes of Missouri. Missouri Department of Conservation, Jefferson City, Mo. 343 pp.

Pillard, D. A. 1983. An examination of the zooplankton of Pool 19, Mississippi River, and the effects of filtering collectors. Master's thesis. Western Illinois Univ., Macomb, Ill. 137 pp.

Pitlo, J. 1987. Standing stock of fishes in the Upper Mississippi River. Upper Mississippi River Conservation Committee, Fisheries Section, Rock Island, Ill.

Rasmussen, J. L. 1979a. Description of the Upper Mississippi River. pp. 3–20. *In* J. L. Rasmussen, ed., Compendium of fisheries information on the Upper Mississippi River. Upper Mississippi River Conservation Committee, Rock Island, Ill.

Rasmussen, J. L. 1979b. Distribution and relative abundance of Upper Mississippi River fishes. pp. 30–40. *In* J. L. Rasmussen, ed., Compendium of fisheries information on the Upper Mississippi River. Upper Mississippi River Conservation Committee, Rock Island, Ill.

Rasmussen, J. L., ed. 1979c. A compendium of fishery information on the Upper Mississippi River, 2nd ed., Spec. Publ. Upper Mississippi River Conservation Committee, Rock Island, Ill. 259 pp.

Reinhard, E. G. 1931. The plankton ecology of the Upper Mississippi, Minneapolis to Winnona. Ecol. Monogr. 1(4): 395–464.

Richie, J. C. 1988. Organic matter content in sediments of three navigation pools along the Upper Mississippi River. J. Freshwater Ecol. 4(3): 343–349.

Risotto, S. P., and R. E. Turner. 1985. Annual fluctuations in abundance of the commercial fisheries of the Mississippi River and its tributaries. North Am. J. Fish. Manage. 5: 557–574.

Seagle, H. H., Jr., J. C. Hutton, and K. S. Lubinski. 1982. A comparison of benthic invertebrate community composition in the Mississippi and Illinois Rivers, Pool 26. J. Freshwater Ecol. 1(6): 637–650.

Sefton, D. F. 1976. The biomass and productivity of aquatic macrophytes in Navigation Pool 8 of the Upper Mississippi River. Master's thesis. Univ. Wisconsin–La Crosse, La Crosse, Wis. 175 pp.

Sefton, D. F. 1977. Productivity and biomass of vascular macrophytes in the Upper Mississippi River. pp. 53–61. *In* B. DeWitt and E. Soloway, eds., Wetlands ecology, values and impacts. Proceedings of the Waubesa conference on wetlands, June 2–5, 1977. Institute of Environment Study, Univ. Wisconsin, Madison, Wis.

Shaeffer, W. A., and J. G. Nickum. 1986a. Relative abundance of macroinvertebrates found in habitats associated with backwater area confluences in Pool 13 of the Upper Mississippi River. Hydrobiologia 136: 113–120.

Shaeffer, W. A., and J. G. Nickum. 1986b. Backwater areas as nursery habitats for fishes in Pool 13 of the Upper Mississippi River. Hydrobiologia 136: 131–140.

Smart, M. M. 1980. Annual changes of nitrogen and phosphorus in two aquatic macrophytes (*Nymphaea tuberosa* and *Ceratophyllum demersum*). Hydrobiologia 70(1–2): 31–35.

Smart, M. M., K. S. Lubinski, and R. A. Schnick. 1986. Introduction to the ecological perspectives of the Upper Mississippi River. Hydrobiologia 136: 1–4.

Smith, P. W. 1979. The fishes of Illinois. Univ. Illinois Press, Urbana, Ill. 314 pp.

Sohmer, S. H. 1977. Aspects of the biology of *Nelumbo pentapetala* (Walter) Fernald, the American lotus, on the Upper Mississippi River. Trans Wis. Acad. Sci. Arts Lett. 65: 258–273.

Sparks, R. E. 1980. Response of the fingernail clam populations in the Keokuk Pool (Pool 19) to the 1976–77 drought. pp. 43–71. *In* J. L. Rasmussen, ed., Proceedings of the UMRCC symposium on Upper Mississippi River bivalve mollusks. Upper Mississippi River Conservation Committee, Rock Island, Ill.

Sparks, R. E. 1984. The role of contaminants in the decline of the Illinois River: implications for the Upper Mississippi. pp. 25–66. *In* J. G. Wiener, R. V. Anderson, and D. R. McConville, eds. Contaminants in the Upper Mississippi River: proceedings of the 15th annual meeting of the Mississippi River Research Consortium. Butterworth, Newton, Mass.

Sparks, R. E., P. B. Bayley, S. L. Kohler, and L. L. Osborne. 1980. Disturbance and recovery of large floodplains rivers. Environ. Manage. 14(5): 699–709.

Swanson, S. D., and S. H. Sohmer, 1978. The vascular flora of Navigation Pool 8 of the Upper Mississippi River. Proc. Iowa Acad. Sci. 85: 45–61.

Sylvester, J. R., and J. D. Broughton. 1983. Distribution and relative abundance of fish in Pool 7 of the Upper Mississippi River. North Am. J. Fish. Manage. 3(1): 67–71.

Talbot, M. J. 1984. Evaluation of flathead catfish habitat selection. *In* Miss. River Work Unit Annu. Report 1982–83. Wis. Dept. Nat. Resources, La Crosse, Wis., pp. 87–103.

Teska, S. R. 1979. A survey of the macroinvertebrate bottom fauna of the upper portion of Pool 20, Mississippi River. Master's thesis. Western Illinois Univ., Macomb, Ill. 56 pp.

Thompson, J. D. 1969. Feeding behavior of diving ducks on Keokuk Pool, Mississippi River. Master's thesis. Iowa State Univ., Ames, Iowa. 79 pp.

Upper Mississippi River Conservation Committee. 1990. A strategic plan for the management of the freshwater mussel resources of the Upper Mississippi River. UMRCC, Rock Island, Ill.

U.S. Geological Survey. 1970. Atlas of the United States. USGS, Washington, D.C.

U.S. Geological Survey. 1975. Quality of surface waters of the United States, 1970. Parts 4 and 5. St. Lawrence River Basin, and Hudson Bay and Upper Mississippi River Basins. Water-Supply Pap. 2154. USGS, Washington, D.C.

van der Schalie, H., and A. van der Schalie. 1950. The mussels of the Mississippi River. Am. Midl. Nat. 44: 448–466.

Vansteenburg, J. B., M. R. Luttenton, and R. G. Rada. 1984. A floristic analysis of the attached diatoms in selected areas of the Upper Mississippi River. Proc. Iowa Acad. Sci. 91: 52–56.

Van Vooren, A. 1983. Distribution and relative abundance of Upper Mississippi River fishes. Bulletin. Upper Mississippi River Conservation Committee, Fish Technical Section, Rock Island, Ill. 20 pp.

Wisconsin Department of Natural Resources. 1973. State of Wisconsin: surface water quality monitoring data: 1969–72. Division of Environmental Protection, Wisconsin Department of Natural Resources, Madison, Wis.

CHAPTER 2

Lower Mississippi—Atchafalaya River

INTRODUCTION

In terms of flow, the Atchafalaya River is one of the largest rivers in the United States. It is also one of the shortest and youngest. Geological evidence indicates that the river did not exist 500 years ago. Moreover, for much of its existence, the Atchafalaya was only a minor stream. The transformation of this modest stream to a major river occurred within the last 160 years as a result of both natural and anthropogenic modifications. Ironically, although the Atchafalaya owes its present character to these modifications, it is, in many respects, exemplary of the natural conditions prevalent in the pre-settlement Lower Mississippi River.

PHYSICAL CHARACTERISTICS

The Atchafalaya River Basin covers 8345 km^2 of low-lying ($<$10 m above mean sea level) topography located in south-central Louisiana (Lambou and Hern, 1983). The basin is located entirely within the Mississippi Deltaic Plain, a broad alluvial deposit formed since the stabilization of sea levels at the beginning of the Holocene. The formation of the deltaic plain occurred in a nonuniform fashion with a series of at least six overlapping deltaic lobes; new lobes are formed when former meander channels are abandoned by the Mississippi River. Of these lobes, only the Atchafalaya and the present-day Mississippi are currently active (Day et al., 1988; van Heerden and Roberts, 1980).

The Atchafalaya Basin is bounded by alluvial ridges (i.e., natural levees) formed by two former meander channels. The Teche Diversion, which was abandoned in approximately the year 400, bounds the western and southern basin. The Laforche Diversion, which was abandoned in approximately the year 1200, borders the basin to the north and east (Holland, 1977; USACE, 1952). The age of these two diversions combined with geological evidence of former river meander patterns north of the Atchafalaya Basin indicate that the Atchafalaya River was captured in approximately the year 1500 by the meander loop of the Lower Mississippi, which also receives the Red River. In any case, a map that resulted from the 1542 DeSoto expedition depicts it as an active distributary of the Mississippi (USACE, 1952).

For the first 300 years of its existence as a distributary, the Atchafalaya trapped floating debris from the Lower Mississippi and Red Rivers. As a result, a logjam extending for perhaps 30 km choked the upper reach and restricted flow for the rest of the drainage. Human settlements during this period were concentrated in the slightly higher elevations of the northern basin, while extensive swamps and shallow lakes deterred settlement in the central and southern basins (USACE, 1952).

In 1831, the Shreve's cutoff isolated the river meander that connected the Red River and the Atchafalaya River to the main flow of the Lower Mississippi. The lower arm of the meander, which has since been renamed the Old River, quickly filled up with sediment, while the upper arm continued to convey water from the Red River to the main trunk. Another result of this cutoff was the cessation of growth in the logjam of the Upper Atchafalaya. In response, local inhabitants began to remove the debris, and by 1855 the channel of the upper Atchafalaya was cleared (USACE, 1952).

Removal of the debris resulted in the progressive diversion of the Red River's flow into the Atchafalaya River. This increased flow deepened and widened the channel, which in turn diverted even more of the Red River's flow. It also resulted in both the loss of riverside properties via bank erosion and the progressive isolation of the Old River from the Mississippi. To prevent loss of riverside properties, a levee system was constructed along the Upper Atchafalaya, and by 1910 extended past Krotz Springs, some 68 km downstream from the head of the river. In 1891, a sill and dam were constructed across the Atchafalaya in the hopes of forcing low flow discharge from the Red River through the upper arm of the former meander loop. However, this approach was abandoned by 1896 and the upper arm silted up entirely (USACE, 1952).

Meanwhile, a navigation channel was maintained through the silted lower arm of the meander loop (i.e., the Old River). Without this continually dredged channel, stream capture of the Red River by the Atchafalaya probably would have completely isolated both rivers from the Lower Mississippi. But the maintenance of this channel, combined with a number of other water projects, eventually resulted in a situation in which flow from both the Red and Mississippi Rivers would be captured by the Atchafalaya (USACE, 1952).

The gradient of the Atchafalaya is approximately threefold that of the Lower Mississippi, and thus the Atchafalaya would have been a likely candidate for the capture of the Lower Mississippi's flow. However, a number of factors inhibited this diversion. One of the most important was the hydraulic inefficiency of the Atchafalaya Basin. Another was the inability of the Atchafalaya to convey water out of its basin, past the natural levees that formed its southern borders and into the Gulf of Mexico (USACE, 1952).

In the interest of improving discharge capacity within the Atchafalaya Basin, extensive dredging in the lower, unleveed basin was conducted during the 1930s, and a second outlet to the gulf, Wax Lake Outlet, was completed in 1941. Modifications were also made to the upper, leveed river. The resulting improvements in hydraulic efficiency of the Atchafalaya reduced flooding from the Red River but also facilitated the conveyance of low-flow water from the Lower Mississippi River via the Old River. Consequently, the channel through the previously silted Old River became self-maintaining, and diversion of the Lower Mississippi accelerated. This diversion was further aggravated after 1945 with the completion of the Carr Point Cutoff, which effectively shortened the distance of the Old River and created a more favorable angle of entry for the Mississippi's flow (USACE, 1952).

Conditions for the capture of the Mississippi by the Atchafalaya had become critical, and it was predicted that stream capture would be complete by the 1970s (USACE, 1952). To prevent the dewatering of downstream Mississippi reaches, the Old River Control Structure, which became operational in 1963, was constructed to regulate flow in the Atchafalaya (Fremling et al., 1989). This structure is part of the Mississippi River and Tributaries Project (MR&T), which was formed to regulate discharge in the Lower Mississippi System. During normal years, the Atchafalaya is intended to convey 30% of the combined flow from the Mississippi and Red Rivers. During unusually high flood years, the Atchafalaya Basin is intended to convey half of the floodwaters from the Lower Mississippi (Wells and Demas, 1977).

Implementation of the MR&T, combined with previous modifications, has partitioned the 8345-km^2 basin into three major areas. The upper basin, which occupies 18% (1497 km^2) of the basin, consists of the leveed Atchafalaya River, the Morganza Floodway, the West Atchafalaya Floodway, and a number of smaller subbasins isolated by an extensive network of levees. With the exception of infrequent overflow from the Mississippi via the Morganza Floodway, the upper basin is hydrologically isolated from the leveed river and the flow from the Red and Mississippi Rivers. An additional 57% (4719 km^2) is isolated from the Atchafalaya River by a series of guide levees transecting the western, eastern, and southernmost portions of the original basin. The remaining 25% (2129 km^2) of the basin is referred to as the Atchafalaya Basin Floodway. This area is regularly subjected to prolonged seasonal overbank flooding from the Atchafalaya River. In fact, 67% of the floodway is typically

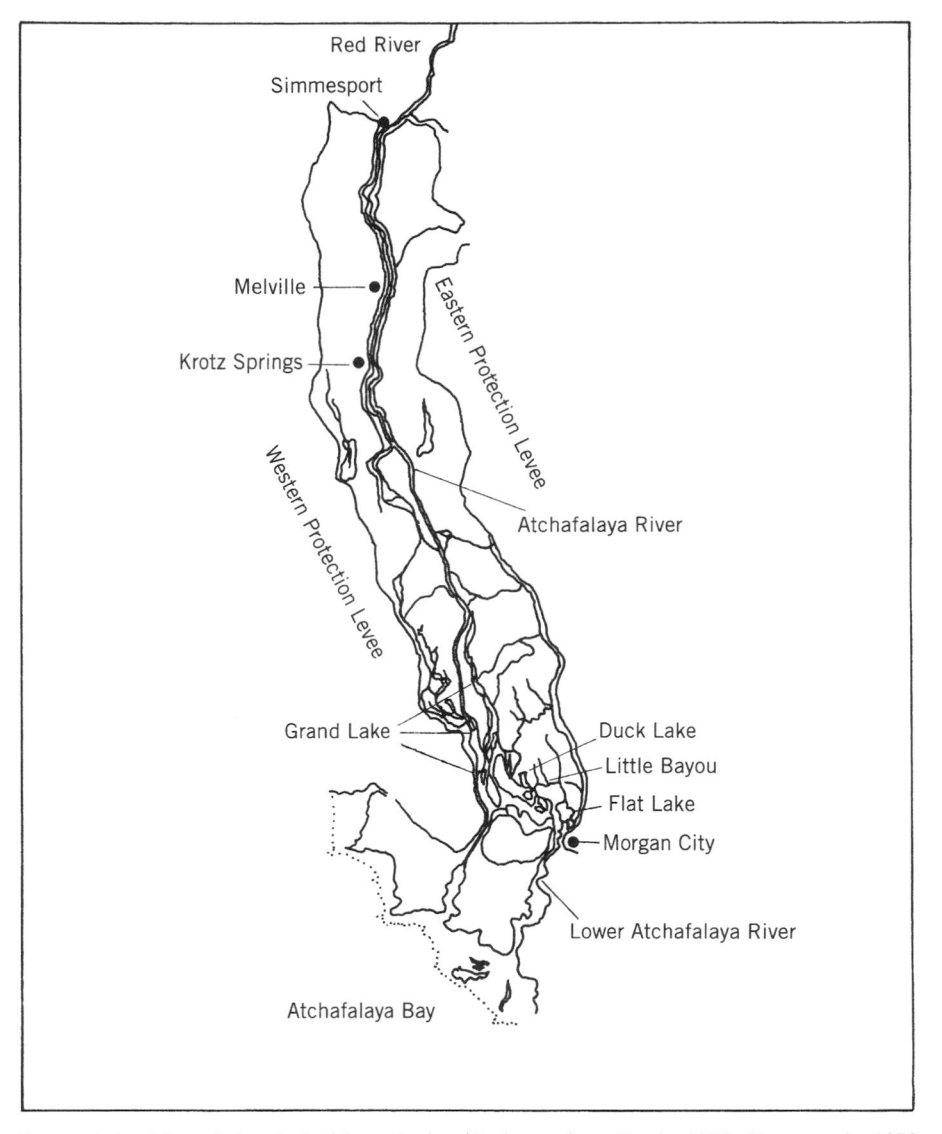

FIGURE 2.1. Map of the Atchafalaya Basin. (Redrawn from Beck, 1977; Hern et al., 1978; Lambou and Hern, 1983).

inundated each year (Beck, 1977; Lambou and Hern, 1983; Levine, 1977; Wells and Demas, 1977). A map of the basin and significant study areas is presented in Figure 2.1.

Isolation from the river has facilitated deforestation and agricultural development throughout much of the upper, western, and eastern portions of the original basin (Hern et al., 1978; Holland et al., 1983). On the other hand, the watershed within the Atchafalaya Basin Floodway is covered by the largest bottomland hardwood swamp in North America, extensive cypress–tupelo gum swamps, and a series of shallow river-lakes. Extensive freshwater and brackish marshes cover much of the semi-isolated basin south of the Atchafalaya Basin Floodway (Fremling et al., 1989; Stone et al., 1978).

The Atchafalaya River is approximately 217 km long. For the first 84 km, the river flows in a straight, single channel confined by artificial levees. The channel is deep (24 to 55 m) and currents are swift. Variations in river stage are considerable, but overbank flooding is rare (Hern et al., 1978; USACE, 1952).

Downstream from the leveed reach, the river enters the Atchafalaya Basin Floodway, the river widens, becomes shallower, and velocities drop. Under natural conditions the channel would have become braided, but dredging during the 1930s resulted in a relatively well defined main channel (Bryan et al., 1974; USACE, 1952). Nonetheless, the floodway contains a maze of distributaries, bayous, lakes, and cypress–tupelo gum swamps. Exchanges among these diverse habitats vary with seasonal flooding. During periods of high flow, most of the Atchafalaya Basin Floodway is inundated, and at the peak of flooding, the system essentially becomes a 24- to 32-km-wide sheet of water flowing toward the gulf. During low-flow periods, the waters retreat into lentic habitats (i.e., cypress–tupelo gum swamps, bayous, and lakes) and lotic habitats (i.e., distributaries and the main channel) (Beck, 1977; Bryan et al., 1975; Hern et al., 1978; Holland et al., 1983; Wells and Demas, 1977).

A large proportion of the southern Atchafalaya Basin Floodway is covered with three large shallow lakes (Grand Lake, Six Mile Lake, and Flat Lake). In addition to collecting flow from the maze of channels within the basin, they also receive flow from portions of the upper, western, and eastern basins, which are otherwise isolated from the system. Except for the openings of the Lower Atchafalaya River and the Wax Lake Outlet, these lakes are separated from the coastal wetlands by levees. Combined, these two outlets account for almost all the flow exported from the greater basin to Atchafalaya Bay and, eventually, the Gulf of Mexico (Denes and Bayley, 1983; USACE, 1952; Wells and Demas, 1977).

Diversion of flow from the Lower Mississippi and Red Rivers has also resulted in the diversion of much of their sediment loads. One consequence of diverting sediment away from the Lower Mississippi is the aggravation of ongoing degradation in the Mississippi Delta. Another consequence is the dramatic increase in sediment loads in the Atchafalaya Basin Floodway. The effect of this sediment load has been profound. Formerly, the lower basin was covered by a large shallow lake, but alluviation has created a lacustrine delta. This has transformed the lower floodway into a maze of lakes, distributaries, and swamps (Fremling et al., 1989; USACE, 1952). This process has been especially evident since the accelerated capture of the Lower Mississippi in the late 1940s (Bryan et al., 1974).

There is some indication that sedimentation within the basin may be approaching some sort of dynamic equilibrium. Since the early 1970s, sediment has been transported out of the basin and has formed a new delta in Atchafalaya Bay. Significantly, the Atchafalaya Bay Delta is the only post-grading delta in the Mississippi Deltaic Plain; other estuaries, including the Mississippi, are currently degrading. However, substantial delta formation in the Atchafalaya appears to be limited to high-flow years (i.e., 1973, 1974, 1975, and 1978) when the basin experiences a net loss of sediments via scour (van Heerden and Roberts, 1980; Wells and Demas, 1977).

Modifications to the Atchafalaya have been substantial. However, the flooding regime, extensive swamp forests, and diversity of habitats of the unleveed Atchafalaya Basin Floodway may be more representative of the predevelopment Lower Mississippi than is the current, extensively leveed and heavily polluted Mississippi. For this reason, in the rest of this chapter we focus on the habitats and biota of the unleveed Atchafalaya Basin Floodway.

The main channel and distributaries are the primary lotic habitats within the Atchafalaya Basin Floodway. Both contain swiftly flowing water throughout the year. Velocities as high as 2.65 ms^{-1} have been recorded in the main channel (Holland et al., 1983). Depths in the main channel typically range from 14 to 24 m, but maximum depths of only 6 m occur where the main channel flows through an arm of Grand Lake (Bryan et al., 1974; USACE, 1952). Depths in the distributaries are shallower (e.g., 6 to 8 m) (Beck, 1977; Holland et al., 1983). Substrates in the main channel typically range from shifting sands to vertical walls of hard clay, but clay–sand mixtures occur in some areas of reduced current, while a midchannel mixture of sand–gravel–cobble was recorded in one downstream reach (Bryan et al., 1974). Substrates in the distributaries are similar to those in the main channel but tend to be somewhat finer (Holland et al., 1983). A third class of lotic habitat, open-end canals, have been constructed throughout the floodway, primarily to provide access for petroleum extraction (Beck, 1977; Bryan et al., 1974).

A number of lentic and quasilentic habitats have been identified in the Atchafalaya Basin Floodway: headwater lake, dead-end canal, bayou, backwater lake (swamp-lake), and cypress–tupelo gum swamp (Bryan et al., 1975; Fremling et al., 1989). As a general rule, currents are slight to negligible during periods of low flow but moderate to swift during high flow (Beck, 1977; Hern et al., 1978; Holland et al., 1983).

Lentic and quasilentic habitats are distinguished largely by the influence of lotic waters and the openness of their habitats. Cypress–tupelo gum swamps are typically canopied with an overstory of cypress (*Taxodium distinctum*) and gum tupelo (*Nyssa aquatica*) and are affected by lotic waters only during the height of overbank flooding. Substrates are typically dominated by fine and coarse detritus. Bayous are creeklike bodies of water which are also typically canopied and largely unaffected by lotic waters for much of the year. However, lotic influences during high water result in the concentration of coarse detritus along the shore and a mixture of fine detritus and silt at midchannel. Depths are generally less than 4 m. Backwater lakes (or swamp-lakes) are open, relatively shallow (<6 m) bodies of waters that are strongly influenced by adjacent swamps during most of the year but are flushed by lotic waters during higher flows. Substrates range from detritus to silt or sand. Headwater lakes are quasilentic bodies of water which are similar to swamp-lakes in that they are open and relatively shallow. They differ, however, in that lotic influences are greater than swamp influences. Substrates range from silt to sand. Dead-end canals are simply dead-end artificial canals with predominantly sand substrates (Beck, 1977; Bryan et al., 1974; Holland, 1977).

Distinctions among these habitats are often obscure. For instance, backwater lakes (or swamp-lakes) are, by definition, strongly influenced by adjacent swamps, but the relative influences of swamp and distributary waters can vary greatly even between nearby sites (Holland, 1977). Habitat characteristics can also vary greatly within a given lake. For example, Flat Lake, which is more than 2 km wide, receives inputs of sediment-rich waters from both the east and west, but also receives clear, darkly stained water from the north. Consequently, water quality and substrate composition for a site within the lake depend on its proximity to one or more of these sources (Bryan et al., 1974).

Location within the Atchafalaya Basin Floodway is another factor that affects the characteristics of lentic and quasilentic habitats. The Fordoche area, located in the northwestern part of the floodway, is partially isolated from the river via a southwest-extending levee. Consequently, overbank flooding enters the area via backflow from the south and inundation is typically shorter in duration and extent than in other parts of the floodway. The extent and duration of inundation is greater for the Buffalo Cove area, which is located in the midwestern part of the floodway (Hern et al., 1978; Lambou and Hern, 1983).

Location is also a factor because alluviation has been more extensive in the western half of the basin than in the east. For example, the Buffalo Cove area is part of the lacustrine delta that has formed over the northwestern corner of the once-extensive Grand Lake. Sedimentation is still conspicuous in several of the area's lakes. In contrast, the Duck Lake and Flat Lake areas of the southeastern floodway retain much of their original physiography (Bryan et al., 1974). One consequence is that the lakes from the western floodway tend to be shallower (# 4 m) than those in the eastern floodway (# 6m) (Holland et al., 1983; Wells and Demas, 1977). Alluvation also results in different overstory vegetation. Cypress–tupelo gum swamps predominate in swamps and undisturbed lentic shores, but willows will colonize the more recently created riparian zones. Consequently, willows are prevalent in many parts of the Buffalo Cove area but are generally limited to the western portion of the eastern floodway, where the Atchafalaya River and some of its distributaries have deposited silt. Willows are also prevalent along the main channel and distributaries (Beck, 1977; Bryan et al., 1974).

With respect to its length and watershed area, the Atchafalaya River is only a medium-sized river, but inflows from the Red and Mississippi Rivers give it the hydrology of a large river. In fact, it is the sixth-largest river in North

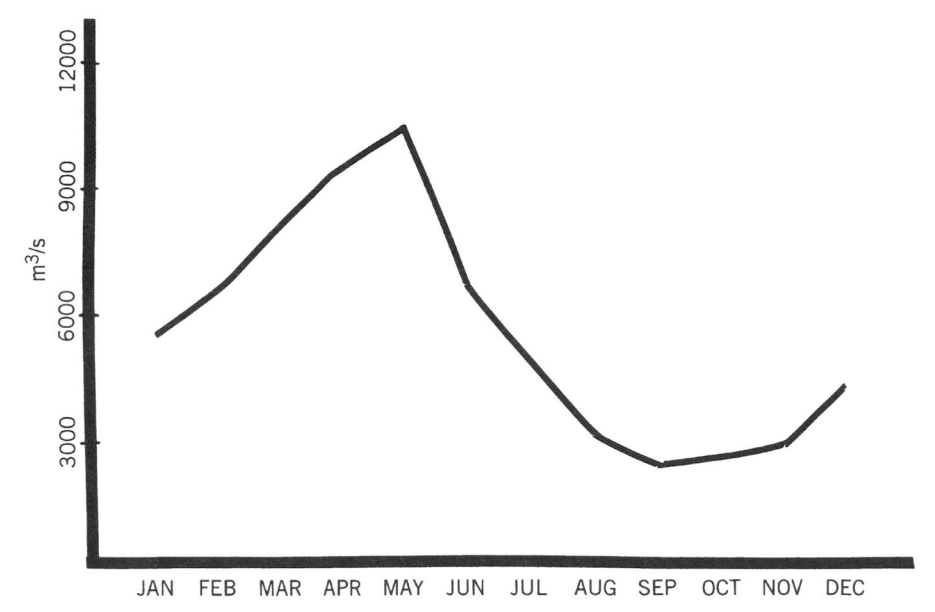

FIGURE 2.2.   Mean monthly discharge for the Atchafalaya River at Simmesport, Louisiana, 1940 to 1981. (From Denes and Bayley, 1983. Used with permission of the Louisiana Academy of Sciences.)

America in terms of discharge (Fremling et al., 1989). It is estimated that 98% of the Atchafalaya's flow originates from the Red and Mississippi Rivers (Denes and Bayley, 1983). Although the Atchafalaya receives virtually all of the Red River's flow, discharge is dominated by inflow from the much larger Mississippi River. The Lower Mississippi accounts for 50% or more of the Atchafalaya's total flow for 90% of the time, and more than 75% of the flow for 50% of the time. During all but extremely high flood years, virtually all of the discharge entering the Atchafalaya Basin Floodway enters via the leveed river past Simmesport, which is located 8 km downstream from the head of the Atchafalaya River (Levine, 1977; Wells and Demas, 1977). However, flows from isolated parts of the basin can enter the lowermost portion of the basin via the Intercoastal Waterway (Bryan et al., 1975). Of the water that leaves the watershed and enters Atchafalaya Bay, approximately 70% exits via the Lower Atchafalaya River and 30% exits via the Wax Lake Outlet (Wells and Demas, 1977).

Since the completion of the Old River Control Structure in 1963, median flow past Simmesport has been 5380 m^3 s^{-1} (Wells and Demas, 1977). As indicated in Figure 2.2, mean monthly discharges past Simmesport (1963–1971) generally increased in early winter and peaked from mid to late spring. They then dropped sharply to seasonal lows in late summer and autumn (Lambou and Hern, 1983). The magnitudes and details of flow may vary from year to year, but day-to-day changes in river stages are minimized by the huge watersheds contributing to the river's flow. High flows are primarily the result of the cumulative effects of snowmelt and high rainfall within the Mississippi Basin. Low autumn flows are the result of low rainfall, while low late summer flows are the result of the combination of high evapotranspiration and moderate rainfall (Denes and Bayley, 1983).

The combination of high discharge and low elevations result in dramatic seasonal transformations in the floodway. During high winter and spring discharges, overbank flooding commonly results in inundation of as much as 67% of the floodway. One of the major effects of this seasonal flooding is the inundation of overflow habitats which are covered primarily by bottomland hardwood forests. Overbank flooding also results in the active exchange among virtually all of the permanent aquatic habitats. During low-flow periods, however, the overflow habitats are dewatered and aquatic habitats are confined to the main channel distributaries, lakes, bayous, canals, and cypress–tupelo gum swamps (Bryan et al., 1974, 1975; Hern et al., 1978; Wells and Demas, 1977). The 91-km^2 Buffalo Cove Subunit is exemplary of the transformation that results from overbank flooding. Approximately 16% of the area could be regarded as permanent water (i.e., bayous, cypress–gum tupelo swamps, distributaries, and lakes), but 87% of the subunit's area is inundated for 4 to 8 months (Lambou and Hern, 1983).

High sediment loads from the Red and Mississippi Rivers result in high sediment loads and suspended sediment concentrations within the Atchafalaya. From 1964 to 1974, for instance, a mean of 260,000 tons/day of suspended sediments were transported past Simmesport to the Atchafalaya Basin and/or Atchafalaya Bay. The mean suspended sediment concentration at Simmesport for the same period is 460 mg L^{-1}. Concentrations generally increase with increases in discharge, but they are highest in the ascending limb of the hydrograph (Wells and Demas, 1977).

The large lakes in the southern Atchafalaya Basin Floodway had been the site for significant accumulation of sediments, but since about 1950, an increasing proportion of the load has been transported through the Lower Atchafalaya River and Wax Lake Outlet into the Atchafalaya Bay. From 1965 to 1971, records from these two outlets indicate that approximately 75% of the load passing Simmesport is transported out of the basin. This proportion is even greater during major flood years, when the basin experiences a net loss of sediments (Wells and Demas, 1977).

Turbidity is high for the main channel and distributary habitats of the Atchafalaya Basin Floodway. Turbidity within two main-channel stations ranged from 70 to 200 mg L^{-1} and 70 to 240 mg L^{-1}, respectively (Bryan et al., 1974). Turbidities from a number of distributaries in the western floodway averaged 85 mg L^{-1} and ranged from 5 to 220 mg L^{-1}. Monthly means for the distributaries were consistently greater than 40 mg L^{-1} throughout the year, while they were greater than 80 mg L^{-1} during October through March, June, and July (Bryan et al., 1975).

Turbidities in lentic and quasilentic habitats were largely dependent on their proximity to turbid lotic channels. Cypress–tupelo gum swamp stations in the Buffalo Cove area recorded turbidities averaging 38 mg L^{-1} and ranging from 0 to 80 mg L^{-1}. Concentrations greater than 40 mg L^{-1} were recorded during winter and spring high flows, but low-flow swamps were typically clear and darkly stained. Turbidities from two eastern floodway bayous averaged only 14 mg L^{-1} and ranged from 1 to 50 mg L^{-1}. (This mean and range excludes an unusually high recording of 400 mg L^{-1} in November 1974; none of the other 46 samples, including others on the same date, exceeded 50 mg L^{-1}) (Bryan et al., 1974, 1975).

Turbidities in lakes were highly variable. A composite of two eastern and two western lakes yielded a mean turbidity of 49 mg L^{-1} and a range of 7 to 200 mg L^{-1} (Bryan et al., 1975). Turbidities were highest during flooding and often very low during low flow, but a lake's turbidity is greatly influenced by its proximity to turbid lotic channels. For example, one lake site (WB) in the Buffalo Cove area, which was relatively isolated from distributaries during low flow, yielded a mean of 49 mg L^{-1} and a range of 7 to 80 mg L^{-1}. In contrast, a nearby lake (WF), which is strongly influenced by distributary flows, yielded a mean of 97 mg L^{-1} and a range of 60 to 140 mg L^{-1}. In the eastern floodway, Duck Lake and Flat Lake both experience substantial spatial variation in turbidity. Waters along their western margins are turbid as a result of inputs of sediment-rich waters from the main channel, but other portions of both lakes are typically clear and darkly stained (Bryan et al., 1974).

Investigations in the Fordoche area indicated that turbidities in overflow habitats were dependent on a site's proximity to the ascending or receding edge of floodwaters. Essentially, those sites that had been inundated for a couple of weeks tended to yield lower fixed nonfilterable residues (i.e., suspended inorganic particulates) than do sites located adjacent to the floodwaters' edge or sites located in permanent habitats (Pollard et al., 1981). Whether this relationship occurs in the overflow habitats in other parts of the floodway is unclear, since riverine inputs of suspended sediments to the Fordoche area are apparently lower than those in more strongly influenced areas (e.g., Buffalo Cove).

Climate in the Atchafalaya Basin is subtropical and typical of the Gulf coast region. Summers are uniformly hot and humid. Although winters are milder but humid, they are more variable because of alternating influences from cold continental air and warm tropical air. Mean annual rainfall is 147 to 157 cm yr^{-1}, with rainfall being highest in June and August and lowest in September and October (Beck, 1977).

The Atchafalaya River and its associated waters are warm-water habitats. Temperatures in the leveed river near Krotz Springs ranged from 3 to 31.0°C. Temperatures exceeding 20°C were recorded from April through October, while temperatures exceeding 30°C were recorded from June through September; temperatures were consistently greater than 24°C throughout this same period (Wells and Demas, 1977).

In general, temperatures within cypress–tupelo gum swamps were some-what less variable than those recorded from other habitats. For example, temperatures recorded from swamp habitat samples in the Buffalo Cove area ranged from 8.9 to 29.0°C, while samples from bayous, lakes, and dis-tributaries ranged from 3.0 to 32.0°C, 6.5 to 31.2°C, and 1.8 to 31.5°C, respec-tively. However, diurnal and surface to bottom differences in lentic habitats were greater than those in the distributaries or the main channel. Moreover, stratification probably occurred in any lentic habitat (>1 m in depth) during periods of calm weather (Bryan et al., 1975).

CHEMICAL CHARACTERISTICS

Water in the Atchafalaya River is medium-hard to very hard. Total hardness at Melville, which lies within the leveed upper basin, averaged 144 mg L^{-1} and ranged from 60 to 190 mg L^{-1}. Alkalinity averaged 105 mg L^{-1} and ranged from 48 to 142 mg L^{-1}. pH averaged 7.4 and ranged from 6.6 to 8.1. Specific conductance averaged 385 μS cm^{-1} and ranged from 176 to 699 μS cm^{-1} (Fremling et al., 1989).

Because flow in the Atchafalaya originates primarily from the Red and Mississippi Rivers, its chemical characteristics are determined primarily by the chemical characteristics of these two rivers. Water from both the Missis-sippi and Red Rivers ranges from medium-hard to very hard, but sulfate and chloride concentration maxima are higher in the Red River. During high spring flow, the overriding influence of the Mississippi's flow results in chemi-cal characteristics in the Atchafalaya that are most similar to those of the Mississippi. During other times, the Atchafalaya may also resemble either the Red River or one of is major downstream tributaries, the Black River (Wells and Demas, 1977).

Changes in the inorganic constituents of water passing through the Atchafa-laya Basin are modest. For instance, specific conductance within the main channel generally changes less than 30 μS cm^{-1} between Simmesport and Morgan City. In fact, most of this change is restricted to the lower reaches of the Atchafalaya Basin Floodway. Moreover, the change is evident primarily during low flows (Wells and Demas, 1977).

Habitat-specific chemical characteristics within the Atchafalaya Basin Flood-way exhibit pronounced changes in accordance with flood stage. Differences among habitats are minimal during high flow as large volumes of floodwaters spread throughout much of the floodway. However, habitat differences are pronounced during periods of low flow as cypress–tupelo gum swamps and other backwaters become isolated from distributaries and the main channel (Bryan et al., 1975; Holland et al., 1983; Wells and Demas, 1977). This pattern is evident in Table 2.1. Low-flow conditions resulted in increase for most of the water chemistry parameters, with increases generally being greatest in the swamps and least in the distributaries. The major exceptions to this pattern are the low-flow decreases in sulfate and noncarbonate hardness in swamps and

TABLE 2.1. *Representative High Flow (Mean of March–May 1974) and Low Flow (Mean of August–October 1975) Chemical Characteristics Among Habitats[a] in the Atchafalaya Basin Floodway, Louisiana*

	High Flow				Low Flow			
	S	B	L	D	S	B	L	D
Alkalinity (mg L^{-1})	104	100	100	103	170	131	130	122
Calcium hardness (mg L^{-1})	109	110	111	110	158	125	128	125
Noncarbonate hardness (mg L^{-1})	27	28	30	28	17	18	19	25
Calcium (mg L^{-1})	30	29	30	31	40	33	33	34
Magnesium (mg L^{-1})	8	9	8	8	15	11	11	10
Sulfate (mg L^{-1})	34	31	31	31	20	17	27	36
Chloride (mg L^{-1})	14	15	16	15	50	34	28	22
Specific conductance (μS cm^{-1})	252	236	247	258	357	375	336	372

Source: After Bryan et al. (1975).
[a]S, cypress–tupelo gum swamp; B, bayou; L, lake; D, distributaries.

bayous. This decrease was apparently caused by sulfate-reducing bacteria (Wells and Demas, 1977).

pH within the Atchafalaya Basin Floodway varied from moderately acidic to alkaline. Swamp habitats (6.2 to 8.4) exhibited a greater range and lower minima than bayou (6.7 to 8.3), lake (6.6 to 8.4), and distributary (6.9 to 8.2) habitats, but variation within a habitat during any given month was nearly as great as the variation recorded for that habitat throughout the year (Bryan et al., 1975) (Table 2.2).

Macronutrient concentrations in the Atchafalaya Basin are moderately low. Total nitrogen is generally less than 1.5 mg L^{-1}, with more than 90% typically being in the form of nitrate-nitrogen or organic nitrogen. Total phosphorus is generally less than 0.15 mg L^{-1}. These moderate levels of macronutrients for a river that receives water containing residues of many types of effluent are primarily a result of the moderate concentrations entering the basin and a large amount of flow. For instance, nitrate-nitrogen concentrations at Simmesport ranged from 0.28 to 1.30 mg L^{-1}, while total phosphorus ranged from 0.11 to 0.40 mg L^{-1}. Moreover, the within-basin processing appears to have little net influence on macronutrient export to the estuary, since concentrations of nitrate-nitrogen (0.24 to 1.10 mg L^{-1}) and total phosphorus (0.09 to 0.53 mg L^{-1}) in the Lower Atchafalaya River and Wax Lake Outlet were similar to those recorded at Simmesport (Wells and Demas, 1977).

While within-basin processes may not significantly alter overall macronutrient export to Atchafalaya Bay, differences among floodway habitats can be pronounced, especially during low flow. For example, Wells and Demas (1977) reported that during an August 1975 survey, nitrate-nitrogen from riverine (i.e., distributary and main-channel) samples ranged from 0.29 to

TABLE 2.2.   *Seasonal Changes in Monthly pH Among*
Habitats[a] in the Atchafalaya Basin Floodway, Louisiana

	Swamp	Bayou	Lake	Distributary
1973				
Aug.	—	—	7.3	7.6
Sept.	6.9–7.8	—	7.1–8.1	7.6–8.0
Oct.	7.8–8.4	7.4–8.0	7.3–8.4	7.8–8.1
Nov.	6.3–8.1	7.0–8.2	6.9–8.2	7.4–8.1
Dec.	6.9–7.9	6.9–7.2	7.1–8.1	7.5–8.0
1974				
Jan.	—	6.6–7.9	6.8–7.9	8.0
Feb.	7.0–7.4	7.1–7.3	7.0–7.7	7.3–7.6
Mar.	6.9–7.2	6.7–7.2	6.9–7.7	7.3–7.6
Apr.	7.0–7.9	6.8–7.2	6.7–8.0	7.3–8.1
May	6.8–7.2	6.9–7.1	7.1–7.8	6.9–7.8
June	6.9–7.5	6.9–7.4	7.0–7.9	7.2–7.6
July	6.4–7.6	6.9–7.6	6.6–7.7	7.1–7.7
Aug.	6.2–7.8	7.6–8.3	—	7.4–8.2
Sept.	7.1–7.7	6.9–7.0	6.6–8.1	7.4–8.0
Oct.	6.7–7.1	6.7–7.8	6.6–8.0	7.1–7.7
Nov.	7.7–7.9	7.0–7.8	7.1–8.1	7.7–7.9
Dec.	6.6–7.9	6.7–7.4	6.8–8.1	7.1–8.2
1975				
Jan.	—	8.2–8.3	7.6–8.4	7.6–8.1
Feb.	—	6.8–7.2	6.7–7.7	7.6–8.0
Mar.	—	7.1–7.2	7.8–7.9	7.3–7.7

Source: After Bryan et al. (1975).

[a]Cypress–tupelo gum swamp habitats, collected primarily from
the Buffalo Cove area; bayou habitats, collected primarily from the
Little Bayou Sorrel; lake habitats, collected from Buffalo Cove
Lake, Shaw Island Lake (western floodway), Duck Lake, and Flat
Lake (eastern floodway); distributary habitat, collected in the west-
ern floodway.

0.52 mg L^{-1}, while 90% of the lentic samples from the east floodway were less
than 0.10 mg L^{-1}, and concentrations from the west floodway lentic samples
were consistently less than the detection limit (0.01 mg L^{-1}).

Seasonal and habitat differences in nitrogen were apparent in another study
of floodway habitats. Nitrate-nitrogen was relatively high throughout the year
in distributary waters, but lakes apparently experienced a moderate decrease
during late summer and early autumn. Nitrate-nitrogen was typically low in
bayou samples and variable in cypress–tupelo gum swamp samples. Ammonia-
nitrogen was typically below detection limit for all habitats except during late
summer and early autumn; concentrations were also substantially higher in
lentic habitats than in distributaries. Concentrations of organic nitrogen were
typically low or undetectable during winter and spring, and high in summer and
autumn; high concentrations of organic nitrogen appeared first in the distributaries (Bryan et al., 1975) (Table 2.3).

TABLE 2.3. *Seasonal Changes in Monthly Mean Concentrations ($\mu g \, L^{-1}$) for Nitrate-Nitrogen (NO_3), Ammonia-Nitrogen (NH_3), and Organic Nitrogen (ON) Among Habitats[a] in the Atchafalaya Basin Floodway, Louisiana*

	Swamp			Bayou			Lake			Distributary		
	NO_3	NH_3	ON	NO_3	NH_3	ON	NO_3	NH_3	ON	NO_3	NH_3	ON
1973												
Sept.	<10	10	20	—	—	10	130	20	40	420	40	40
Oct.	—	—	—	110	<10	30	500	110	40	740	<10	10
Nov.	70	<10	<10	440	<10	40	300	<10	10	620	<10	30
Dec.	50	<10	10	70	—	—	320	<10	20	300	50	30
1974												
Jan.	—	—	—	100	<10	<10	330	<10	—	500	<10	20
Feb.	520	<10	10	340	<10	<10	500	<10	<10	530	<10	<10
Mar.	320	<10	<10	100	<10	<10	240	90	20	480	<10	10
Apr.	450	<10	<10	30	<10	120	400	<10	<10	580	<10	—
May	90	<10	<10	40	<10	<10	510	<10	20	260	<10	30
June	500	<10	<10	40	<10	<10	620	<10	90	1000	<10	300
July	500	<10	<10	40	<10	—	400	<10	30	850	<10	—
Aug.	<10	<10	540	160	60	590	140	40	440	760	10	630
Sept.	444	111	850	—	—	—	210	90	390	650	10	600
Oct.	10	120	430	50	60	430	130	80	420	470	10	600
Nov.	450	30	370	150	30	310	340	20	440	470	20	790
Dec.	120	40	280	10	10	230	370	30	300	490	40	550
Mean	230	40	270	140	10	150	340	30	150	470	10	180

Source: After Bryan et al. (1975).

[a]Cypress–tupelo gum swamp habitats, collected primarily from the Buffalo Cove area; bayou habitats, collected primarily from the Little Bayou Sorrel; lake habitats, collected from Buffalo Cove Lake, Shaw Island Lake (western floodway), Duck Lake, and Flat Lake (eastern floodway); distributary habitat, collected in the western floodway.

Seasonal and habitat differences were also evident for phosphorus. Total phosphorus and orthophosphate-phosphorus concentrations were typically greater in distributary habitats than in the lakes, bayous, and swamps. However, total phosphorus concentrations in the distributaries were comparable to those in the other habitats during late summer, while distributary orthophosphate was similar to corresponding lentic samples during late summer and autumn. Seasonality was not evident within the lentic habitats (Bryan et al., 1975) (Table 2.4).

The main channel of the Atchafalaya River is consistently well oxygenated. Water entering the basin past Simmesport ranged from 70 to 97% saturation, and water exiting the basin through the Lower Atchafalaya River and Wax Lake Outlet ranged from 60 to 97% saturation. Main-channel water within the Atchafalaya Basin Floodway ranged from 57 to 82% saturation. The distributaries are somewhat less well oxygenated, with percent saturations ranging from 36 to 94%. Seasonally, percent saturations are highest during

TABLE 2.4. *Seasonal Changes in Monthly Mean Concentrations (mg L⁻¹) of Total Phosphorus and Orthophosphate Phosphorus Among Habitats[a] in the Atchafalaya Basin, Louisiana, September 1973 to December 1974*

	Total Phosphorus				Orthophosphate-Phosphorous			
	S	B	L	D	S	B	L	D
1973								
Sept.	0.01	—	0.07	0.06	0.01	—	0.04	0.02
Oct.	—	0.16	0.25	0.44	—	0.05	0.09	0.13
Nov.	0.06	0.10	0.17	0.32	0.03	0.07	0.10	0.18
Dec.	0.05	1.10	0.21	0.51	0.05	0.38	0.12	0.28
1974								
Jan.	—	0.06	0.16	0.28	—	<0.01	0.08	0.14
Feb.	0.14	0.11	0.12	0.18	0.14	0.05	0.08	0.10
Mar.	0.15	0.11	0.15	0.23	0.06	0.04	0.05	0.13
Apr.	0.13	0.08	0.12	0.27	0.05	0.02	0.06	0.17
May	0.07	0.10	0.14	0.14	0.06	0.02	0.06	0.14
June	0.10	0.04	0.10	0.38	0.04	0.01	0.06	0.22
July	0.12	0.03	0.09	0.28	0.04	0.01	0.05	0.22
Aug.	0.07	0.06	0.10	0.12	0.06	0.04	0.03	0.06
Sept.	0.19	—	0.31	0.12	0.06	—	0.13	0.07
Oct.	0.20	0.11	0.13	0.25	0.09	0.06	0.06	0.05
Nov.	0.13	0.08	0.14	0.36	0.07	0.02	0.06	0.06
Dec.	0.08	0.03	0.11	0.30	0.05	0.03	0.06	0.09

Source: After Bryan et al. (1975).

[a]S, cypress–tupelo gum swamp habitats, collected primarily from the Buffalo Cove area; B, bayou habitats, collected primarily from the Little Bayou Sorrel; L, lake habitats, collected from Buffalo Cove Lake, Shaw Island Lake (western floodway), Duck Lake, and Flat Lake (eastern floodway); D, distributary habitat, collected in the western floodway.

periods of high winter flows and lowest during low late summer flows (Wells and Demas, 1977).

Seasonal differences in dissolved oxygen in cypress–tupelo gum swamps, bayous, and lakes can be pronounced (Table 2.5). While somewhat lower than those recorded in distributary habitats, the levels of dissolved oxygen recorded in cypress–tupelo gum swamps and bayous during periods of high flow indicate they are relatively well oxygenated. On the other hand, low flow typically results in low levels of dissolved oxygen, particularly in summer, when elevated temperatures promote high oxygen demand (Bryan et al., 1975; Holland et al., 1983; Wells and Demas, 1977).

Oxygen dynamics in lakes vary with their degree of isolation from both swamp and riverine influences. Lakes that are strongly influenced by adjacent swamps and are relatively isolated from distributaries during low flow (e.g., Buffalo Cove Lake) will typically exhibit very low oxygen levels during summer and autumn. On the other hand, some lakes (e.g., Flat Lake and Grand Lake) experience high levels of dissolved oxygen (including supersaturation) during this same period because of phytoplankton blooms (Bryan et al., 1975; Wells and Demas, 1977).

TABLE 2.5. *Seasonal Changes in Dissolved Oxygen (DO, mg L^{-1}) and Percent Saturation[a] (S) Among Habitats in the Atchafalaya Basin Floodway, Louisiana, August 1973 to March 1975*

	Swamp[b]		Bayou		Lake		Distributary	
	DO	S	DO	S	DO	S	DO	S
1973								
Aug.	—	—	—	—	3.4	43	4.6	59
Sept.	3.0	63	3.9	49	5.2	66	6.3	78
Oct.	4.6	54	3.8	43	6.1	70	6.8	82
Nov.	2.9	29	4.4	45	5.7	59	—	—
Dec.	4.5	43	4.6	40	6.2	59	7.6	68
1974								
Jan.	—	—	5.1	50	9.0	80	—	—
Feb.	6.3	58	5.9	56	6.6	61	7.2	66
Mar.	5.0	51	3.8	42	7.1	75	8.3	85
Apr.	4.5	47	2.8	31	5.6	60	6.5	67
May	2.8	33	1.8	20	4.1	47	4.8	57
June	1.2	14	1.2	15	2.9	36	4.5	54
July	0.6	7	0.9	11	2.2	27	4.2	53
Aug.	0.0	0	3.8	49	3.8	49	4.7	60
Sept.	5.7	69	2.1	26	5.3	65	7.6	94
Oct.	0.8	9	3.9	43	4.2	47	6.0	67
Nov.	6.8	69	4.6	45	6.4	65	6.7	69
Dec.	5.4	48	4.7	42	7.6	68	9.1	80
1975								
Jan.	—	—	4.1	37	7.8	70	8.0	72
Feb.	—	—	4.4	44	7.8	74	9.4	84
Mar.	—	—	2.8	27	8.8	89	8.4	78

Source: Modified from Bryan et al. (1975).

[a]Percent saturation was determined from mean temperatures and mean dissolved oxygen concentrations.

[b]Cypress–tupelo gum swamp.

Measurements of redox potentials indicated that reducing conditions were recorded either in cypress–tupelo gum swamps, bayous, or lakes. These events were associated with pH values below 7.0 and dissolved oxygen concentrations of less than 0.5 mg L^{-1}. Such events were also associated with high levels of reduced sulfur and detectable levels of reduced nitrogen. Interestingly, two sites that yielded low redox potentials (Buffalo Cove Swamp and Buffalo Cove Lake) also yielded some of the highest redox potentials either with the onset of winter and higher water, or immediately after vigorous mixing caused by local storms (Bryan et al., 1975).

Anoxic conditions commonly resulted in fish kills within the floodway. Although one may expect them during low-flow conditions, they also occur during periods of relatively high flow. For example, a significant fish kill occurred in Buffalo Cove Lake during May 1974 following inputs of oxygen-depleted swamp water. A particularly extensive die-off followed the passage of Hurricane Carmen during September 1974. The storm apparently caused oxygen depletion by dumping substantial quantities of terrestrial vegetation into aquatic habitats, which in turn greatly increased oxygen demand. The storm may have also resuspended substantial quantities of reduced organic sediments. In any case, approximately 440 km^2 of the eastern floodway was rendered unsuitable for fish for at least two weeks (Bryan et al., 1975; Wells and Demas, 1977).

A more detailed study of the effects of swamp passage on water quality was conducted in the Buffalo Cove area during 1975. In general, changes in oxygen saturation, macronutrients, and suspended solids with swamp passage were minimal during high April flows (19,600 m^3 s^{-1} at Simmesport). On the other hand, swamp passage resulted in some changes during lower March flows (15,800 m^3 s^{-1}) and resulted in dramatic changes during even low June flows (12,300 m^3 s^{-1}). Swamp passage during the relatively high March flows resulted in moderate declines in oxygen saturation, significant declines in total phosphorus, and an approximately two-thirds decline in suspended solids; changes in nitrate-nitrogen and organic nitrogen were minimal. During June, dissolved oxygen declined from approximately 85% saturation to less than 30% saturation within the first mile of swamp. Substantial decreases in total phosphorus, nitrate-nitrogen, and suspended solids occurred with swamp passage during June, especially within the first mile of swamp passage. Changes in organic nitrogen with swamp passage during June were erratic (Wells and Demas, 1977).

Unlike much of the Lower Mississippi River, the Atchafalaya Basin Floodway is relatively free of nutrient enrichment, municipal waste, heavy metals, and insecticides (Bernard and Renner, 1980; Wells and Demas, 1977). Applications of chloroxyphenoxy herbicides for the management of aquatic weeds have resulted in some elevated concentrations of this pesticide, but these were still lower than the recommended limits for drinking water (Wells and Demas, 1977).

Aside from contributing to the diversion of flow from the Red and Mississippi Rivers, the most significant anthropogenic modifications of water quality in the Atchafalaya Basin Floodway may be those associated with petroleum extraction. Oil and natural gas fields are scattered throughout Louisiana and the Atchafalaya Basin. Those most likely to affect the localities covered in this chapter are located in the vicinity of Little Bayou Sorrel (Station EB) and Duck Lake (Station EA), which are located in the southeastern floodway (Bryan et al., 1974; Fremling et al., 1989; Wells and Demas, 1977). Pumping platforms, storage tanks, and related structures crowd the southern portion of Duck Lake. However, detrimental effects of this activity on the biota within the lake were not obvious. Moreover, the lake supported an active sport fishery (Bryan et al., 1974).

Evidence of the impact of petroleum extraction activities on water chemistry is inconclusive. Contamination with brine effluents was indicated during an August 1975 water quality survey by Wells and Demas (1977) in which there were excessively high specific conductance values (761 to 862 μS cm^{-1}) in Little Bayou Sorrel (862 μS cm^{-1}) and a nearby site. However, specific conductance from 114 Little Bayou Sorrel samples collected from September 1974 through March 1975 ranged from 150 to 550 μS cm^{-1}, which is within the range reported for other, presumably unaffected sites (Bryan et al., 1975). Similarly, conductivity values from Duck Lake measured from August 1973 to May 1974 ranged from 106 to 529 μS cm^{-1} (Bryan et al., 1974). The only chemical anomaly associated with Duck Lake was one excessively high pH reading of 11.1; all other pH readings from Duck Lake ranged between 6.6 and 8.4 (Bryan et al., 1975). References to the levels of toxic organics resulting from petroleum extraction were not found in the literature.

ECOSYSTEM DYNAMICS

Detritus and Dissolved Organic Carbon

One of the major factors influencing organic matter dynamics in the Atchafalaya Basin Floodway is the annual cycle of overbank flooding and dewatering. Seasonal flooding determines the structure and productivity of the terrestrial plant communities that dominate organic matter inputs originating from within the basin. It also facilitates the transfer of this terrestrial production to the aquatic environment.

Most of the Atchafalaya Basin Floodway is covered by cypress–tupelo gum and bottomland hardwood swamp forests. Both of these communities are tolerant to extensive flooding, but the bottomland hardwood forest is concentrated on slightly higher and less extensively flooded ground, while the cypress–tupelo gum forest is concentrated in or alongside permanent and semipermanent bodies of water (Bryan et al., 1974; Conner and Day, 1976; Hern et al., 1978). A third, less extensive community, dominated by willows, occupies the riparian zones along the main channel, distributaries, canals, and recently alluviated shores of lakes.

Estimates of productivity in the swamp forests of the Atchafalaya Basin were not found in the literature, but estimates from other localities suggest that productivity is high. For instance, annual biomass production in a cypress–tupelo gum forest and a bottomland hardwood forest in the nearby Barataria Basin (Louisiana) averaged 1120 and 1374 g m^{-2} yr^{-1}, respectively (Conner and Day, 1976). Seasonal flooding was found to contribute significantly to the biomass production of cypress swamp forests in Florida, primarily through phosphorus enrichment (Brown, 1981). Similar enhancement of biomass production probably occurs in the Atchafalaya Basin (Conner and Day, 1976).

Organic matter inputs from the swamp forests of the Atchafalaya Basin Floodway are also probably very high. For instance, nonwoody litterfall for cypress–tupelo gum and bottomland hardwood forests in the Barataria Basin averaged 620 and 574 g m^{-2} yr^{-1}, respectively. Litterfall in both types of forest peaks in November (Conner and Day, 1976). In addition to litterfall, significant inputs of allochthonous organic matter probably originate from herbaceous vegetation, which rapidly colonizes the forest floor following the receding of floodwaters (Beck, 1977). However, the importance of this herbaceous input probably varies considerably with the extent of flooding. In the Barataria Basin, for instance, herbaceous vegetation in the bottomland hardwood forest averaged 200 g DW m^{-2} yr^{-1}, while herbaceous vegetation in the cypress–tupelo gum swamps averaged only 20 g DW m^{-2} yr^{-1} (Conner and Day, 1976).

Lowland topography and slow currents probably result in a high degree of particulate organic matter (POM) retention in permanent lentic habitats. Quantitative estimates of detrital standing stocks were not found in the literature, but the substrate classification scheme presented by Beck (1977) suggests that POM retention is very high. For instance, substrates from cypress–tupelo gum swamps, bayous, and lakes were typically classified as pulpy peat (fine detritus mixed with mud) and/or detritus rather than sand or mud. High retention is also suggested by an inflow–outflow study of organic matter in the Buffalo Cove and Fordoche areas. This study demonstrated that at least during years with below-average discharge, these two areas were POM sinks (Lambou and Hern, 1983). In contrast, POM accumulation in overflow habitats may be relatively low. For instance, Conner and Day (1976) reported that the litter layer in bottomland hardwood forests in the Barataria Basin was relatively thin, which suggests that the litter was either effectively processed or was transported to permanent aquatic habitats during flooding.

The accumulations of detritus in permanent aquatic habitats suggest that litter processing is relatively inefficient. Minimal mechanical processing in these typically sluggish habitats is probably one factor contributing to inefficient processing, but low levels of dissolved oxygen may be more important. Water temperatures in the subtropical Atchafalaya Basin remain relatively high even during winter and spring. This in turn fosters high microbial respiration, which depresses benthic dissolved oxygen concentrations. For instance, benthic dissolved oxygen from permanent and overflow habitats in the Fordoche area was usually less than 2.0 mg L^{-1} throughout the year and commonly less than 0.5 mg L^{-1} even during high spring flows. Significantly, concentrations are somewhat higher at the edge of ascending floodwaters (Pollard et al., 1981), presumably because microbial populations were still underdeveloped.

Leaching of dissolved organic carbon (DOC) accounts for most leaf litter decomposition in blackwater Coastal Plain swamp–stream systems in North Carolina (Mulholland, 1981) and Georgia (Cuffney and Wallace, 1987). Leaching is probably similarly important in the Atchafalaya (Lambou and Hern, 1983). Leached DOC provides trophic support for a productive microbial community, which in turn could support a sizable detritivore population. However, microbial populations may compete with detritivores both by depressing dissolved oxygen concentrations and converting labile POC and DOC constituents into refractory constituents.

Microbial oxygen depression and conversion of labile organic carbon to refractory compounds may account for the distribution of macroinvertebrate detritivores. Deposit-feeding (e.g., Tubificidae), scraping (e.g., Isopoda), and shredding (e.g., crayfish) detritivores located within cypress–tupelo gum swamps and bayous are concentrated on the roots of water hyacinth (*Eichhornia crassipes*) throughout the year. But they are abundant in the benthos only during high flow (Beck, 1977; Hunner and Barr, 1981). High benthic abundance during high flow is probably the result of a combination of conditions. One is the seasonal pulse of allochthonous detritus from overflow habitats. However, the inflow of well-oxygenated riverine water and seasonally cooler temperatures may enhance the detritivores' ability to use this organic matter pulse by minimizing competition from microbes. As temperatures increase and floodwaters recede, microbial metabolism depletes both labile carbon and dissolved oxygen.

The roots of *Eichhornia crassipes* and other floating macrophytes provide a refuge from the anoxic benthos during much of the year. They may also produce pockets of photosynthentically evolved oxygen. Moreover, they provide trophic support for epiphytic production by exuding autochthonous DOC and by providing both senescent and living plant tissue (Beck, 1977; Bryan et al., 1974). Freezes can cause significant diebacks of *E. crassipes,* which in turn forces epiphytic taxa to descend to the benthos. This in turn will increase benthic populations (Beck, 1977) but may affect their production adversely. For instance, freeze-induced diebacks of *E. crassipes* often result in significant reductions in commercial crayfish landings (Fremling et al., 1989).

Crayfish, especially *Procambarus clarkii,* are probably the most important detritivore in overflow habitats (Hunner and Barr, 1981), but their distribution is also probably largely influenced by competition from microbes. *P. clarkii* populations in inundated bottomland hardwood forests were concentrated along the rising or receding edge of floodwaters. The edge sites are probably favored because they have higher concentrations of dissolved oxygen and, presumably, they contain the least processed and most labile detritus (Pollard et al., 1981).

Although microbial metabolism may spatially and temporally restrict many detritivores, they may enhance the production of filter-feeding zooplankton and macroinvertebrates. For instance, free-living bacteria imported from the inundated floodplain constituted one of the most important fractions of allochthonous inputs of suspended particulate organic carbon (POC) in the Ogeechee River, which is a subtropical blackwater river located in Georgia (Edwards, 1987).

The concentrations of water column organic carbon within the Atchafalaya Basin Floodway are relatively high. Lambou and Hern (1983) reported that total organic carbon (TOC) ranged from 7.9 to 12.1 mg L^{-1}, DOC ranged from 4.0 to 8.3 mg L^{-1}, and particulate organic carbon (POC) ranged from 3.2

to 5.3 mg L^{-1}. Similarly, Bryan et al. (1975) reported that concentrations of organic carbon in swamp, bayou, lake, and distributary habitats averaged 7.2, 5.2, 6.7, and 8.0 mg L^{-1}, respectively. Much of this organic carbon probably originated from outside the basin. For instance, the weighted mean concentrations of TOC, DOC, and POC from water entering the basin were 9.7, 3.8, and 5.9 mg L^{-1}, respectively (Lambou and Hern, 1983). In comparison, mean concentrations recorded in the Mississippi River near St. Francisville were 7.9, 3.5, and 4.4 mg L^{-1}, respectively (Malcolm and Durum, 1976). The concentrations suggest that the Mississippi River contributed proportionately more DOC to the Atchafalaya, while the Red River contributed proportionately more POC.

Although the Atchafalaya receives considerable amounts of organic carbon from outside the basin, within-basin processes are clearly significant. The weighted mean TOC concentration entering the basin during 1976 was 9.7 mg L^{-1}, of which 39% was DOC and 61% was POC. Upon leaving the basin via the Lower Atchafalaya River and the Wax Lake Outlet, the weighted mean concentration of TOC was 7.8 mg L^{-1}, of which 51% was DOC and 49% was POC. In terms of organic carbon transport, the Atchafalaya Basin Floodway acted as a net sink for TOC, retaining 2.2×10^8 kg C yr^{-1}. Significantly, all of this net retention was for POC; the floodway exported 0.2×10^8 kg C yr^{-1} of DOC more than it imported (Lambou and Hern, 1983).

Much of the net POC retention in the Atchafalaya Basin Floodway is probably the result of burial (Lambou and Hern, 1983). These estimates of carbon fluxes were made with data collected during 1976, when total discharge through the Atchafalaya was well below average. Consequently, the alluviation that would result in the burial of POC was probably considerably higher than "normal." In fact, the floodway may actually experience net exports of POC during other years, especially very wet years (e.g., 1973 and 1974), when within-basin scour results in the net exports of sediments.

The other process that could result in the net retention of POC and net export of DOC is passage through backwater habitats and inundated floodplains. Vegetation, debris, and reduced currents would result in physical retention of POC, while filter feeding would result in biological retention. Enhanced biological retention of POC is supported by Beck's (1977) observation that filter-feeding fingernail clams (Sphaeriidae) were more numerous in swamps and bayous than in other habitats. Net exports of DOC would result from the leaching of allochthonous inputs. In fact, the darkly stained waters draining swamps and bayous indicated that considerable amounts of DOC are being generated within the swamps.

Inferences on the relative contributions of burial and backwater passage on the retention of POC and export of DOC can be made by comparing the net areal exports from total floodway and two of its subunits presented in Table 2.6. The total floodway exhibited a net areal POC retention of 11.4×10^4 kg km^{-2} and a net aerial DOC export of 1.1×10^4 kg km^{-2}. Net DOC exports for the Fordoche (northwest floodway) and Buffalo Cove (west-central floodway)

TABLE 2.6. *Flooding Duration, Water Flux, and Organic Carbon Flux for the Atchafalaya Basin Floodway, Two Subunits Subject to Overbank Flooding (Buffalo Cove and Fordoche), and a Subunit of the Basin Isolated from Overbank Flooding (Pat Bay), Atchafalaya River Basin, Louisiana*

	Atchafalaya Basin Floodway			Isolated Subunit
Area (km²):	Total Floodway 2129	Buffalo Cove 91	Fordoche 270	Pat Bay 45
Percent inundated				
<1 month	—	3	36	54
1–4 months	—	10	7	12
4–8 months	—	52	21	19
8–11 months	—	19	7	8
>11 months	—	16	29	7
Annual water flux (10^6 m³)				
Inflow	115,060	28	1179	5
Outflow	115,060	29	1348	7
Gross import				
TOC (kg)	11.2×10^8	2.2×10^6	13.5×10^6	0.7×10^6
TOC concentration (mg L^{-1})	9.7	8.6	11.5	12.1
% DOC	39	30	53	63
% POC	61	70	47	37
Gross export				
TOC (kg)	9.0×10^8	2.9×10^6	15.7×10^6	1.1×10^6
TOC concentration (mg L^{-1})	7.8	10.8	11.7	14.2
% DOC	51	56	65	43
% POC	49	44	35	57
Net export (kg)				
TOC	-2.2×10^8	0.7×10^6	2.2×10^6	0.4×10^6
DOC	0.2×10^8	1.0×10^6	3.1×10^6	$<0.1 \times 10^6$
POC	-2.4×10^8	-0.3×10^6	-0.9×10^6	0.4×10^6
Net areal export (kg km^{-2})				
TOC	-10.3×10^4	0.8×10^4	0.8×10^4	0.9×10^4
DOC	1.1×10^4	1.1×10^4	1.2×10^4	0.1×10^4
POC	-11.4×10^4	-0.3×10^4	-0.4×10^4	0.8×10^4

Source: Modified from Lambou and Hern (1983).

subunits was nearly identical with that estimated for the floodway as a whole. Net areal retention of POC in the two subunits was also nearly identical. However, both were less than 1% of the net areal retention of POC for the total floodway. Apparently, most of the net POC retention is occurring elsewhere. This retention is probably the result of burial in the remnant lakes and backwaters of the lower floodway (e.g., Grand Lake).

The similarity of net areal DOC exports and net POC retention for the Fordoche and Buffalo Cove areas is remarkable. The Buffalo Cove area is subject to considerably more overbank flooding and alluviation than the

Fordoche area, while the Fordoche area receives a greater amount of surface runoff than does the Buffalo Cove area (Bryan et al., 1974; Lambou and Hern, 1983) (Table 2.6). One interesting possibility for these similarities is suggested by the observation by Wells and Demas (1977) that most of the drops in macronutrient and dissolved oxygen concentrations occurring during swamp passage occurred within the first kilometer of passage. It may be that processes affecting DOC export (and POC retention) are largely localized at the interface of swamp and open waters.

Phytoplankton Production
Despite the availability of lentic habitats within the Atchafalaya Basin Floodway, phytoplankton production from these habitats is typically modest for most of the year. For instance, of 47 late autumn through late spring samples collected during 1974 and 1975, densities averaged only 1368 units L^{-1} and never exceeded 9624 units mL^{-1}. In contrast, mean densities from three lakes located within leveed eastern portions of the basin were 8000 units mL^{-1} (Pat Bay), 28,000 units mL^{-1} (Penchant), and 90,000 units mL^{-1} (Lake Verret) (Hern et al., 1978).

Nutrient limitation probably is not a major factor limiting phytoplankton in the Atchafalaya Basin Floodway. Instead, production is limited primarily by low light levels resulting from high suspended sediment concentrations (Hern et al., 1978) and the abrasive effects of the sediment loads. Phytoplankton production may be relatively high in some lakes during periods of low turbidity. Late summer and early autumn phytoplankton maxima are commonplace in Flat and Six Mile Lakes, which are two of the larger lakes located within the southern floodway (Bryan et al., 1975; Wells and Demas, 1977).

Late summer blooms have also been recorded in canal habitats in the Fordoche area (Pollard et al., 1981). Occasional blooms have been recorded in at least one headwater lake located in the Buffalo Cove area, but again, only during periods of low turbidity (Holland et al., 1983).

Chlorophyll *a* concentrations were significantly higher and more variable during periods of low flow (when light extinction by suspended sediments is likely to be lowest) than during periods of high flow. Mean low-flow concentrations were higher in headwater lake (15.1 mg L^{-1}) and distributary (12.7 mg L^{-1}) habitats than in cypress–tupelo gum swamp (5.3 mg L^{-1}) and swamp–lake (8.4 mg L^{-1}) habitats. During high flow, the differences among habitats were reduced. High flow concentrations in distributaries and headwater lakes averaged 2.5 and 2.0 mg L^{-1}, respectively, while swamp–lakes and swamps averaged 1.7 and 1.4 mg L^{-1}, respectively (Holland et al., 1983).

Differences in the taxonomic composition among habitats and seasons suggest the contrasting influences of river and swamp on phytoplankton assemblages. Although many of the algae were collected as phytoplankton, they are actually benthic species and live among the mud and debris or attached to the debris or vegetation. In general, habitat differences were more pronounced during periods of low flow and most uniform during periods of high flow (Bryan et al., 1975). Overall, river and distributary habitats were dominated by centric diatoms, including *Melosira distans, M. granulata, M. italica, Stephanodiscus* spp., and *Skeletonema potamos. Scenedesmus* spp., *Crucigenia* spp. (green algae), and *Anacystis* sp. (blue-green algae) were common. All of these typically occur attached to or among the substrate. In contrast, samples collected in cypress–tupelo gum swamps and swamp-influenced lakes and bayous contained a greater variety of taxa. In particular, swamp-influenced waters contained relatively high densities of autotrophic flagellates, including *Euglena* spp., *Trachelomonas* spp., *Cryptomonas* spp., *Chroomonas* spp., and *Chlamydomonas* spp. In addition, a number of green algae, including *Ankistrodesmus* spp. and *Dactylococcopsis irregularis,* and blue-green algae, including *Microcystis* spp. and *Oscillatoria* spp., were common in lentic, swamp-influenced waters but uncommon in lotic habitats (Bryan et al., 1975; Hern et al., 1978).

Differences among localities also influence phytoplankton assemblages. For instance, cypress–tupelo gum swamps, swamp–lakes, and bayous are present in both the Fordoche area and the Buffalo Cove area, but the extent and duration of overbank flooding in the former is substantially lower than in the latter (Lambou and Hern, 1983). The biological consequence of this difference in flooding is suggested by the differences in their phytoplankton assemblages. Autotrophic flagellates accounted for a greater percentage of the total density in the Fordoche samples (40%) than they did in the Buffalo Cove samples (24%). Conversely, diatoms accounted for 51% of the total density in the Buffalo Cove area, but accounted for only 30% of the density in the Fordoche area (Hern et al., 1978).

Similar inferences can be made with assemblages entering and leaving the Atchafalaya Basin Floodway. Inflow samples from the leveed Atchafalaya, Red River, and Old River Control Stations were dominated by diatoms, which accounted for 75% of the total mean density. In contrast, outlet samples located near the southern margin of the floodway contained a more diverse assemblage, in which flagellates, blue-green algae, and green algae accounted for 29%, 14%, and 8%, respectively, of the total density. Although diatoms accounted for 51% of the outlet assemblage, the taxonomic composition differed from that recorded in the inlet samples. Inlet samples were strongly dominated by centric diatoms (*Melosira* spp., *Stephanodiscus* spp., and *Skeletonema potamos*), while the outlet samples also yielded relatively high numbers of pennate taxa, including *Nitzschia* spp., *Gomphonema* spp., and *Navicula* spp. (Hern et al., 1978).

Overall, densities for diatoms, euglenoid flagellates, and green algae were highest during late summer and early autumn and low for the remainder of the year. However, several diatoms, including *Melosira, Cocconeis,* and *Navicula,* were also moderately common during spring, while *Cyclotella* was common throughout the year. Of the green algae, *Crucigenia* was moderately common from midspring through early autumn, while the euglenoid *Trachelomonas* was moderately common during spring and summer. Two blue-green algae, *Anacystis* and *Anabaena,* were relatively common throughout the year (Bryan et al., 1975). Seasonality was not evident in the samples collected by Hern et al. (1978), but these samples, which extended from November through June, did not include low-flow dates.

Periphyton Production
Information concerning periphytic algae in the Atchafalaya Basin is meager. However, most of the species recorded typically live in association with the benthos and/or debris and vegetation. The only explicit reference to benthic or attached algae comes from a study by Levine (1977) on juvenile and adult fathead minnows (*Pimephales vigilax*). Gut analysis on 446 of these nonselective bottom-feeders indicated that planktonic and predominantly benthic diatoms and an unidentified filamentous blue-green alga were frequently ingested. Of the diatoms, *Nitzschia* spp., *Navicula* spp., *Cyclotella* spp., *Melosira* spp., *Gyrosigma* spp., *Synedra* spp., and *Gomphonema* spp. were the most commonly ingested taxa.

Predominantly benthic algae were also collected in phytoplankton samples. Bryan et al. (1975) reported that two pennate diatoms, *Navicula* and *Cocconeis,* were common in a wide variety of habitats. Hern et al. (1978) also reported a number of predominantly benthic taxa. Most of these were infrequent and uncommon even when they were present. However, *Gomphonema* spp. and *Navicula* spp. were common in a number of samples from the lower floodway, while the primarily epiphytic *Cocconeis placentula* was relatively frequent and widespread throughout the basin.

Presumably, the high concentrations of suspended sediments that limit phytoplankton production also limit periphytic production. Scour and the paucity of hard substrates may also limit production within the main channel. The extent of periphytic production within lentic habitats is unknown. Canopy coverage and staining by swamp waters may limit light penetration in some sites, even when sediment levels are low. However, submerged macrophytes may provide suitable substrates for localized production and may help explain the prevalence of *Cocconeis placentula* in some phytoplankton samples.

Macrophyte Production
Aquatic macrophytes are typically absent from the main channel and distributaries of the Atchafalaya Basin Floodway, but they can be very abundant in cypress–tupelo gum swamps, bayous, lakes, and overflow habitats. For instance, the cypress–tupelo gum swamps and bayous adjacent to Buffalo Cove Lake contain dense growths of water hyacinths (*Eichhornia crassipes*), alligator weed (*Alternanthera philoxeroides*), *Cambomba caroliana,* and *Ceratophyllum demersum* (Holland, 1977; Holland et al., 1983). Duck and Flat Lakes supported dense stands of *E. crassipes, C. demersum, Vallisneria americana, Numphar* sp., and *Potamogeton* spp. (Bryan et al., 1974; Holland et al.,

1983). Little Bayou Sorrel supports dense stands of *E. crassipes, Ranunculus* sp., *Myriophyllum* sp., and occasional patches of *Potamogeton* sp. (Beck, 1977; Bryan et al., 1974). Dense growths of *C. demersum* and duckweed (Lemnaceae) were reported from a canal in the Lake Sorrel area (east-central floodway) (Beck, 1977). Dense growths of *E. crassipes* and Lemnaceae as well as patches of *Ceratophyllum demersum* were reported in canal and over-flow habitats in the Fordoche area (Pollard et al., 1981).

Eichhornia crassipes is probably the most important aquatic macrophyte in the Atchafalaya system. Its success may in part be due to its floating life-form, which would enable it to thrive in turbid waters. This introduced species is an aquatic weed that clogs lentic waterbodies throughout the Gulf region. Within the Atchafalaya Basin Floodway, *E. crassipes* commonly develops dense growths which can cover some swamps and smaller bayous during periods of low flow. However, flushing during periods of high flow generally limits their populations and clears occluded habitats (Beck, 1977). Nonetheless, *E. crassipes* has achieved pest status in some Atchafalaya localities and has been controlled with the application of herbicides (Bryan et al., 1974).

A number of other introduced species can also become aquatic weeds. One of these, *Alternanthera philoxeroides,* has been reported as being abundant in some portions of the Atchafalaya Basin Floodway, while parish records suggest that others, including hydrilla (*Hydrilla verticillata*) and eurasian watermilfoil (*Myriophyllum spicatum*), have the potential to achieve pest status (Montz, 1980). Parish records also suggest that several previously unmentioned native species may be abundant in backwater habitats within the Atchafalaya Basin Floodway. These include *Limnobium spongia, Pistia stratiotes, Heteranthera limosa, Myriophyllum brasiliense, Sagittaria platyphylla,* and *S. latifolia* (Curry and Allen, 1973; Montz, 1980).

No estimates of macrophyte production in the Atchafalaya System were found in the literature, but a number of observations indicate that production can be substantial. For instance, *Eichhornia crassipes* and Lemnaceae located in overflow habitats in the Fordoche area commonly reach 85% coverage or greater within a month or two of inundation. Dense growths (90 to 95% coverage) of Lemnaceae were also evident in two nearby canal sites during November, even though the sites were essentially clear from winter through summer (Pollard et al., 1981). Beck (1977) reported that *E. crassipes* commonly occludes the channel of Little Bayou Sorrel during periods of low flow but is flushed out during high flow.

Zooplankton Production
Taxonomic richness was high for rotifer and crustacean zooplankton from the Atchafalaya Basin Floodway. Holland (1977) identified a total of 69 rotifer taxa, and Bryan et al. (1975) identified a total of 112 planktonic crustaceans in the Buffalo Cove and Duck Lake/Flat Lake/Little Bayou Sorrel areas. Pollard et al. (1981) identified 101 planktonic taxa (38 entomostracans, 51 rotifers, and

TABLE 2.7. *Seasonal and Habitat-Specific Densities (D, number m^{-3}) and Taxonomic Richness (T) of Planktonic Rotifers in the Atchafalaya Basin Floodway, Louisiana, 1973–1974*

	River		Distributary		Lake		Swamp[a]	
	D	T	D	T	D	T	D	T
Jan.	—	—	678	3	1,978	38	1,691	29
Feb.	1,323	7	3,435	25	2,559	41	1,327	32
Mar.	5,476	11	9,872	17	3,857	39	4,059	26
Apr.	17,664	15	3,708	16	5,027	43	1,863	32
May	6,129	3	2,921	17	2,753	39	329	20
June	1,002	9	890	16	621	36	408	17
July	362	12	428	20	641	39	668	28
Aug.	3,651	7	777	25	1,669	39	1,739	16
Sept.	3,179	21	3,774	13	1,594	4	1,806	29
Oct.	1,374	8	1,204	25	1,698	44	3,718	35
Nov.	3,341	7	2,059	10	4,471	47	4,111	39
Dec.	4,316	10	3,568	8	2,092	18	3,674	28
Mean	4,347	9	2,776	16	2,413	36	2,116	28

Source: After Holland (1977).
[a]Cypress–tupelo gum swamp.

12 protozoans) from distributary, canal, and overflow (bottomland hardwood forest) habitats in the Fordoche area. Rotifer densities averaged 3149 m^{-3} and ranged from 362 to 17,664 m^{-3} (Holland, 1977). Densities for copepod nauplii averaged 4365 m^{-3} and ranged from 200 to 38,000 m^{-3}. Densities per sample were not presented for identifiable crustaceans, but combined seasonal mean densities ranged from approximately 360 to 5500 m^{-3}, and overall station means ranged from approximately 700 to 3100 m^{-3} (Bryan et al., 1975).

Zooplankton densities in the Buffalo Cove and Duck Lake/Flat Lake/Little Bayou Sorrel areas differed among permanent aquatic habitats. Among rotifers, mean densities were higher in the main channel (4347 m^{-3}) than in the distributaries (2776 m^{-3}), lakes (2413 m^{-3}), and cypress–tupelo gum swamps (2116 m^{-3}), primarily because of substantially higher densities during peak spring flows (Holland, 1977) (Table 2.7).

Mean densities for copepod nauplii were greater in the lentic habitats than in lotic habitats during most of the year, but the reverse was true during spring. Mean densities for identifiable crustaceans were greater in main channel and distributary habitats (approximately 2400 m^{-3}) than in lake, bayou, and cypress–gum tupelo swamp habitats (approximately 1400 m^{-3}). However, lentic/lotic differences are considerably less pronounced if one considers only those lentic samples originating from the Buffalo Cove area, where the mean density was approximately 2000 m^{-3}; mean densities were substantially lower in the Duck Lake/Flat Lake/Little Bayou Sorrel area (approx. 700 m^{-3}) (Bryan et al., 1975).

Habitat-specific patterns for taxonomic richness contrast with those for mean densities. Taxonomic richness for rotifers in the main channel and distributaries averaged 9 and 16 taxa, respectively, while those for lakes and swamps averaged 36 and 28, respectively (Holland, 1977). Habitat-specific measures of taxonomic richness were not presented for crustaceans, but both Holland (1977) and Bryan et al. (1975) commented that plankton samples from lentic habitats generally contained a variety of benthic and littoral taxa as well as euplanktonic taxa, whereas lotic samples were strongly dominated by euplanktonic taxa. In general, lotic stations can be characterized as having relatively few taxa occurring at relatively high densities, while lentic habitats contain a greater variety of taxa, often at lower densities.

Estimates of zooplankton densities are not available for samples from the Fordoche area, but there were habitat-specific differences in the total number collected. In general, numbers were higher in the inundated bottomland hardwood forest than in permanent sites. Habitat-specific differences in relative abundance were not evident for Protozoa, Rotifera, and Copepoda, but Cladocera accounted for a somewhat greater proportion of zooplankton in overflow sites than they did in distributary and canal sites (Pollard et al., 1981).

In order of decreasing density, *Keratella cochlearis, Brachionus calyciflorus, Kellicottia bostoniensis, B. patulus, B. angularis,* and *Testudinella patina* were the most numerous planktonic rotifers in the Buffalo Cove and Duck Lake/ Flat Lake/Little Bayou Sorrel areas. *B. calyciflorus* is a euplanktonic form that was rare in lake and cypress–tupelo gum swamp samples but was particularly abundant in the main channel and distributaries. In fact, this species recorded the highest density of any taxa, yielding 12,741 m^{-3} in a main-channel station during April. *K. bostoniensis* was found in all habitats from late autumn through winter but persisted in lake and cypress–tupelo gum swamp habitats through May. *K. cochlearis* was also found in habitats. *B. patulus* and *T. patina* were concentrated in lake and cypress–tupelo gum swamp samples, while *B. calyciflorus* was common to abundant in main-channel, distributary, and lake habitats (Holland, 1977).

Cluster analysis on these rotifer assemblages indicated that similarities among stations generally corresponded to their habitat classification. Cypress–tupelo gum swamps associated with swamp–lakes and bayous, while the main channel clustered with distributaries. The quasilentic headwater lake clustered with swampy waters during low flow and with distributaries during high water. Interestingly, the clustering among lentic habitats was more pronounced during low flow than during high flow, which is contrary to expectations based on flow-dependent patterns of water quality (Holland et al., 1983).

Crustacean densities in the Buffalo Cove and Duck Lake/Flat Lake/Little Bayou Sorrel areas were dominated by copepod nauplii (4356 m^{-3}), cyclopoid copepodites (795 m^{-3}), calanoid copepodites (404 m^{-3}), and the cladoceran *Bosmina longirostris* (368 m^{-3}). *Ceriodaphnia quadrangula, Moina micrura, Diaphasoma leutenbergianum, Daphnia parvula, Chydorus sphaericus, Holo-*

pedium amazonicum, and *Diaphanosoma brachyurum* were other abundant cladocerans. *Eurytrema affinis, Diaptomus pallidus, D. reinhardii*, and *D. siciloides* were the most abundant identifiable calanoid copepods, while *Cyclops thomasi, C. vernalis*, and *Tropocyclops prasinus* were the most abundant identifiable cyclopoid copepods. Unidentified Cypridae (Ostracoda) were abundant, and harpactacoids were fairly common (Bryan et al., 1975).

Rotifers and copepods numerically dominated zooplankton collections in the Fordoche area. *Brachionus havanensis, Kellicottia bostoniensis*, and *Conochilus/Collotheca* spp. were the most numerous rotifers. A number of other rotifers, including *B. caudatus, B. calyciflorus*, and *Keratella cochlearis*, were common. Copepods were typically numerically dominated by nauplii and cyclopoid copepodites. *Mesocyclops edax* was the most abundant identifiable copepod. *Bosmina longirostris*, unidentified Sididae, and *Daphnia parvula* were the most abundant cladocerans. Unidentified *Sarcodina* and *Centrophyxis* spp. were the most numerous protozoans. Maxima for Copepoda and Protozoa occurred in June, while maxima for Cladocera and Rotifera occurred in April (Pollard et al., 1981).

Spring samples of crustacean zooplankton during another study of bayou and distributary habitats located in the Grand River area (east-central floodway) yielded many of the same dominant taxons. *Bosmina longirostris* was the most numerous taxon. *Ceriodaphnia quadrangula, Diaphanosoma brachyurum, Daphnia ambigua, D. parvula, D. pulex, Acanthocyclops vernalis*, copepod nauplii, cyclopoid copepodites, and calanoid copepodites were also common to abundant (Clary, 1985).

The effects of swamp and lotic influences on the distribution of selected crustaceans can be seen in Table 2.8, which presents the ranking of the 10 most numerous taxons per station sampled by Bryan et al. (1975). For instance, *Bosminia longirostris, Chydorus sphaericus*, and unidentified Cypridae were abundant in nearly every station, whereas *Holopedium amazonicum* was abundant only in main-channel and distributary stations, and *Canthocamptus* spp. was abundant only in cypress–tupelo gum swamp and swamp-like sites. Closer inspection, however, reveals that although *Bosmina longirostris* is ranked among the top 10 taxons in all 11 stations, it is generally most abundant in lotic habitats. *B. longirostris* is also ranked first in two other stations. One of these (station WF) has been classified as a headwater lake by Holland et al. (1983) and is more strongly influenced by lotic waters than by swamp waters, while the total mean density of the other station (station EA) is low (approximately 500 m^{-3}). Similarly, unidentified Cypridae tended to be most abundant in cypress–tupelo gum swamp and swamp-influenced waters.

Some patterns in the habitat distribution of higher groups of crustacean zooplankton are also evident. Calanoid copepods were abundant in all habitats, but typically accounted for more than 20% of the total mean density in cypress–tupelo gum swamps and lakes and only 10 to 20% of the mean density

TABLE 2.8. *Mean Planktonic Entomostracan Ranking of the 10 Most Numerous Mature Taxons from 11 Stations[a] in the Atchafalaya Basin Floodway, Louisiana, September 1973 to September 1974*

	Swamp		Swamp-Lake				Lake	Distributary		River	
	WA	EB	EA	EC	WB	WD	WF	WC	WG	RA	RB
Cladocera											
Alona rectangula	—	—	7	1	—	—	—	—	—	—	—
Alona spp.	—	4	5	—	—	—	—	—	—	—	—
Bosmina longirostris	2	5	1	3	3	5	1	1	1	1	1
Ceriodaphnia lacustris	—	—	—	—	—	—	—	—	—	—	7
C. quadrangula	9	—	—	—	2	7	2	2	9	5	3
C. rigaudi	—	—	—	—	—	—	10	—	—	—	—
Ceriodaphnia spp.	—	—	—	7	—	—	—	—	—	—	—
Chydorus sphaericus	3	3	2	2	4	6	7	3	5	—	—
Daphnia parvula	—	—	—	—	—	—	—	—	—	7	—
Daphnia pulex	8	—	—	6	—	—	9	6	4	—	2
Diaphanosoma brachyrum	—	—	—	—	8	4	—	—	—	—	—
D. leuchtenbergianum	—	—	6	9	7	2	5	9	—	9	6
Holopedium amozonicum	—	—	—	—	—	—	—	7	7	4	4
Ilyocryptus spinifer	—	9	—	—	—	—	—	—	—	—	—
Kurzia latissima	5	7	—	8	—	—	—	—	—	—	—
Leydigia quadrangularis	4	—	—	—	—	—	—	—	—	—	—
Moina brachiata	—	—	—	—	—	8	—	—	—	3	—
M. micrura	—	6	4	—	—	1	6	—	—	10	—
Moina spp.	—	2	5	—	—	—	—	—	—	—	—
Simocephalus vetulus	6	—	—	10	—	—	—	—	—	—	—
Ostracoda											
Unidentified Cypridae	1	1	4	6	1	3	4	4	6	—	10
Calanoida											
Diaptomus pallidus	—	—	—	—	10	—	—	—	—	—	—
D. reinhardi	—	—	—	—	—	—	—	—	10	—	—
Eurytemora affinis	10	10	—	—	—	10	3	5	3	8	9
Cylopoida											
Cyclops thomasi	7	—	—	—	5	—	8	8	2	6	8
C. vernalis	—	—	—	—	—	—	—	—	8	2	5
Ergasilus spp.	—	—	—	—	—	9	—	—	—	—	—
Macrocyclops albidus	—	—	8	—	—	—	—	—	—	—	—
Harpactacoida											
Canthocamptus spp.	—	8	3	—	9	—	—	—	—	—	—

Source: Modified from Bryan et al. (1975).

[a]Stations beginning with a "W" (e.g., WA) are located in the Buffalo Cove area. Stations EA, EB, and EC are located in Duck Lake, Little Bayou Sorrel, and Flat Lake, respectively. Station EB is regarded here as a swamp station. Station WF receives more distributary influence than do the swamp-lakes. A dash denotes that a taxon was not among the 10 most numerous at that station.

in main-channel stations. Cyclopoid copepods were more numerous in the more lotic habitats, where they accounted for 5 to 20% of the mean density. In contrast, they accounted for less than 5% of the total in swamp-influenced waters. Cladocera were relatively abundant in all habitats, and as already mentioned, cyprid ostracods were more abundant in swamp-influenced waters (Bryan et al., 1975).

Seasonal mean densities of identifiable crustacean zooplankters ranged from less than 600 m^{-3} in June, July, and September (1974) to more than 5400 m^{-3} in the high-flow month of March. Mean densities were also relatively high (1500 to 3000 m^{-3}) during the high-flow months of December through February, and April (1974). Two secondary maxima (approximately 1800 m^{-3} each) occurred during discharge minima in September (1973) and August (1974). *Bosmina longirostris,* which reaches a maximum in March, was abundant for most of the year but was rare in June and July. Most of the other abundant or frequent cladocerans experienced density maxima sometime between December and March. Cyclopoid copepods were abundant in September 1973, December through April, and in August 1974. Calanoid copepods were common in most months and abundant in March and April. Cyprid ostracods were common year round but were especially numerous from January through April (Bryan et al., 1975).

Seasonal values of habitat-specific density and taxonomic richness of rotifers are presented in Table 2.7. Seasonal patterns for densities are generally similar among stations, with minima in late spring and early summer and maxima occurring from late summer or early autumn through mid- to late spring. However, there is a lag among habitats in density minima that suggests an association with flooding dynamics. Minima in cypress–tupelo gum swamp habitats (May to July) preceded those in the other habitats, whereas the main-channel minimum is limited to one month (July). Cypress–tupelo gum swamps are among the first to experience changing water quality with declining river stage, and this may be reflected in the rotifer populations (Holland, 1977; Holland et al., 1983).

One conspicuous feature of the populations of both rotifer and crustacean zooplankton is that their seasonal trends differ significantly from that of the phytoplankton. Phytoplankton populations are generally greatest during late summer or early autumn. In contrast, zooplankton are generally more abundant during winter and spring, although low flow maxima (especially for rotifers) do occur. This suggests that zooplankton populations are influenced less by phytoplankton abundance than by factors associated with seasonal flooding. One possibility is that elevated zooplankton densities during periods of high flow result from the flushing of benthic, epiphytic, and littoral taxons into the plankton. However, while flushing may explain the appearance of tychoplankters, most of the abundant euplankters (e.g., *Brachionus calyciflorus* and *Bosminia longirostris*) also experience density maxima during high flow (Bryan et al., 1975; Holland, 1977; Holland et al., 1983).

Invertebrate Production

Benthic collections from main-channel, distributary, lake, bayou, cypress–gum tupelo swamp, and canal habitats yielded a total of 254 taxa during one study of invertebrates in the Atchafalaya Basin Floodway. Despite greater sampling intensity in riverine stations (i.e., distributaries and the main channel), the most numerous and most frequent taxons were collected primarily from swamp and bayou sites. Densities in swamp and bayou habitats averaged 3768 m^{-2} and 3292 m^{-2}, respectively, while mean densities were intermediate in lake (1840 m^{-2}) and canal (1593 m^{-2}) habitats, and low in riverine (327 m^{-2}) habitats (Beck, 1977).

Benthic macroinvertebrate assemblages from main-channel and distributary samples differed substantially from those collected in other habitats (Table 2.9). Samples of hard clay substrates were dominated by *Tortopus* sp., a burrowing mayfly, which was rare or absent in other habitats. Another burrowing mayfly, *Pentagenia vittigera*, was moderately common in hard clay and was also rare elsewhere. Tubificidae (Oligochaeta), *Coelotanypus* sp. (Chironomidae), and *Sphaerium* were moderately common in sandy riverine substrates. Two amphipods, *Gammarus fasciatus* and *Corophium lacustre*, were often associated with the burrowing mayflies. Although a total of 102 taxons were collected from sand and hard clay substrates in the main channel and distributaries, most of these were very infrequent and may have been imported via the drift (Beck, 1977).

Strong currents and persistently high concentrations of suspended sediments probably account for the low densities recorded in main-channel and distributary sites. However, sampling difficulties may have also contributed to low densities. *Pentagenia vittigera* and *Tortopus* sp., which often occur in extremely high densities on vertical hard clay surfaces, are probably seriously underrepresented. In addition, snag habitats were not sampled. Elsewhere, snag-dwelling assemblages were found to be productive, diverse, and characterized by large populations of Heptageniidae, Hydropsychidae, and Simuliidae (Benke et al., 1984; Cudney and Wallace, 1980). These taxons were typically uncommon and infrequent in benthic samples from the Atchafalaya Basin Floodway (Beck, 1977). However, Heptageniidae and Hydropsychidae were numerous in drift samples from the Lower Mississippi River near St. Francisville (Obi and Conner, 1986).

In a study of main-channel benthic macroinvertebrates, Bryan et al. (1974) reported that densities were higher along the banks than in midchannel. Tubificidae predominated in soft clay and clay–sand substrates located near the shore, but midchannel sand was virtually empty. *Tortopus, Pentagenia, Lirceus* sp., and *Gammarus fasciatus* were common in hard clay along the banks but not in midchannel. The only midchannel site that yielded significant densities contained a mixture of clay and gravel. In it, *Lirceus* and *Hydropsyche* were abundant, and *Tortopus* and *G. fasciatus* were common. Although they were infrequent in benthic samples, Beck (1977) reported that

TABLE 2.9.   *Mean Habitat-Specific Densities* (number m^{-2}) *of Selected Benthic Macroinvertebrates in the Atchafalaya Basin Floodway, Louisiana, 1973–1976*

	Riverine	Lake	Canal	Bayou	Swamp
Oligochaeta					
Brachiura sowerbyi	—	14	31	—	—
Dero digitata	—	—	—	—	135
Ilyodrilus templetoni	—	—	17	323	—
Limnodrilus cervix	16	26	38	36	84
Peloscolex multisetosus	—	54	—	261	364
Unidentified Tubificidae	78	304	51	722	513
Gastropoda					
Gyraulus sp.	—	32	—	—	—
Littoridina sp.	—	31	—	—	—
Physa sp.	—	—	—	—	114
Vioscalba louisianae	4	422	—	—	—
Bivalvia					
Corbicula fluminea	7	19	179	—	—
Pisidium sp.	—	—	20	11	—
Sphaerium sp.	11	185	100	591	524
Isopoda					
Asellus laticaudatus	—	—	—	—	286
Lirceus lineatus	3	60	41	—	411
Amphipoda					
Corophium lacustre	11	18	—	0	—
Gammarus spp.	8	26	23	82	—
Hyalella azteca	—	—	0	—	63
Ephemeroptera					
Caenis sp.	—	—	—	36	6
Pentagenia vittigera	3	0	0	0	0
Tortopus sp.	98	—	0	0	0
Diptera: Chaoboridae					
Chaoborus punctipennis	7	4	373	39	535
Diptera: Ceratopogonidae					
Unidentified Ceratopogoninae	6	14	15	99	76
Diptera: Chironomidae					
Chironomus sp.	—	—	—	62	75
Cladotanytarsus sp.	—	15	0	53	7
Coleotanypus sp.	28	239	—	190	—
Dicrotendipes sp.	—	41	—	51	—
Polypedilum sp.	11	91	—	46	—
Procladius sp.	3	—	—	191	113
Mean total density	327	1840	1593	3292	3768

Source: Modified after Beck (1977).

Quadrula quadrula, Anodonta sp., and other freshwater mussels (Unionidae) were numerous on exposed beaches following the receding of floodwaters.

Lake samples were characterized by relatively high densities (1849 m^{-2}) and high taxonomic richness (140 taxons). To some extent, high sampling intensity may have contributed to the large number of taxa, but the relative diversity of microhabitats is probably more significant. In general, the detritus-rich littoral zones supported a more diverse assemblage than did the more open zones. Tubificids, *Vioscalba louisianae, Sphaerium* spp. (Bivalvia), *Lirceus lineatus* (Isopoda), *Coleotanypus* sp., and *Polypedilum* spp. (Chironomidae) were the more abundant taxons (Table 2.9). *Gyraulus* sp., *L. lineatus,* and *Dicrotendipes* sp. were probably associated with macrophytes. The gastropod, leech, and sponge fauna were developed more extensively in lake habitats than elsewhere (Beck, 1977).

Canals, which were constructed to facilitate petroleum extraction, present relatively recent habitats laden with black willow (*Salix niger*) detritus. The introduced asiatic clam *Corbicula fluminea, Sphaerium* spp., and *Chaoborus punctipennis* were the most numerous taxons, while tubificids were less abundant than in most other habitats (Beck, 1977).

Bayous supported high densities of Tubificidae, *Sphaerium* spp., *Gammarus tigrinus* gp., Ceratopogonidae (Diptera), and Chironomidae. *Ilyodrilus templetoni* and *Peloscolex multisetosus* were especially abundant identifiable tubificids, while *Coleotanypus* and *Procladius* were the most abundant chironomids (Table 2.9). Bayous supported the largest number of rarely occurring chironomids; three chironomids, *Lauterborniella, Phaenopsectra,* and *Psectrotanypus,* were restricted to bayou habitats. Phytophillic taxons were common along the shores. Epineustonic Coleoptera and Hemiptera (e.g., Gyrinidae and Gerridae) were abundant but generally avoided the sampling gear (Beck, 1977).

Despite low levels of dissolved oxygen and occasional reducing conditions, cypress–gum tupelo swamps yielded the highest mean density of benthic macroinvertebrates. The annual flushing of these detritus-rich habitats during high water is probably an important contributing factor since swamps in the leveed upper basin were not nearly as productive. Dense mats of water hyacinth (*Eichhornia crassipes*) probably contributed to the benthic abundance of phytophillic taxons such as *Dero digitata* (Naididae), *Lirceus lineatus, Asellus laticaudatus* (Isopoda), *Hyalella azteca* (Amphipoda), and *Physa* sp. (Gastropoda). Characteristically benthic organisms such as Tubificidae (including *Limnodrilus cervix* and *Peloscolex multisetosus*), *Sphaerium* spp., *Chaoborus punctipennis, Chironomus* sp., and *Procladius* sp., were also abundant (Beck, 1977) (Table 2.9).

The epiphytic assemblages from *Eichhornia crassipes* were very productive. For instance, densities from a swamp-lake in the Buffalo Cove area ranged from 4610 to 83,640 m^{-2}, while those from mats in an eastern floodway canal ranged from 3122 to 27,252 m^{-2} (Beck, 1977).

A total of 158 taxons were collected on *Eichhornia crassipes* from the

Buffalo Cove and eastern floodway sites. Isopoda (including *Asellus lati-caudatus, Lirceus lineatus,* and unidentified immatures), Amphipoda (including *Hyalella azteca, Gammarus tigrinus* gp., *Crangonyx pseudogracilis* gp., and unidentified amphipods), a mayfly (*Caenis* sp.), and an odonate (*Ischnura* sp.) accounted for more than 70% of the total number collected. These and a number of other abundant taxons including an oligochaete (*Dero digitata*), several gastropods (*Pseudosuccinea, Physa,* and *Helosoma*), a freshwater shrimp (*Palaemonetes kadiakensis*), and a chironomid (*Polypedilum*), preferred water hyacinth mats, although they were commonly encountered in benthic samples. A number of other taxons were recorded exclusively on the mats, three of which, a lepidopteran (*Nymphula*) and two chironomids (*Labrundinia neopilosella* and *Conchapelopia*), were abundant (Beck, 1977).

A total of 170 taxons were collected on *Eichhornia crassipes* collected from distributary, bayou, and bottomland hardwood swamp habitats in the Fordoche area. These phytophilic assemblages included nine protozoans, 13 rotifers, 36 entomostracans, 87 insects, and 25 other invertebrates. Most of the insects belonged to the Hemiptera (11 taxons), Coleoptera (31 taxons), and Diptera (26 taxons). *Simocephalus* spp. (Cladocera), Cyclopoid copepodites, and copepod nauplii were the most numerous entomostracans. Naididae, *Asellus* sp., *Hyalella azteca, Crangonyx* sp., *Palaemonetes kadiakensis, Enallagma/Ischnura* spp. (Odonata), *Glyptotendipes/Parachironomus* spp., *Labrundinia* sp., and *Polypedilum* spp. were the most numerous macroinvertebrates (Pollard et al., 1981).

With the exception of crayfish (see the following section, "Macrocrustacean Production"), no explicit information on benthic invertebrates from the seasonally inundated bottomland hardwood forest was found in the literature. The ephemeral nature of such habitats may make colonization difficult for many aquatic invertebrates. With epiphytic assemblages, for instance, some aquatic insects (e.g., chironomids and odonates) were less numerous in inundated bottomland hardwood forests than they were in the more permanent distributary and canal habitats. On the other hand, epiphytic amphipods and entomostracans were abundant in both permanent and seasonal habitats (Pollard et al., 1981). Amphipods and entomostracans were typically major diet items for juvenile fishes occupying overflow habitats (Clary, 1985; Levine, 1977; Pollard et al., 1981). While many of these crustaceans were probably planktonic and/or epiphytic, some may have been consumed in the benthos or on terrestrial plants.

The seasonal interaction of epiphytic (water hyacinth) and benthic assemblages (underneath the macrophytes) was investigated in Sorrel Lake, a swamp-lake located in the east-central floodway. This study indicated that abundance and taxonomic richness underneath the mats are generally complementary to those in the epiphytic assemblage. Epiphytic taxonomic richness generally increased from early spring through midsummer and remained high for the rest of the year in a fashion consistent with seasonal increases in macrophyte biomass. Epiphytic density was highly variable, possibly because distribution on the roots was highly aggregated. Benthic taxonomic richness was high in winter and early spring but low in summer and autumn (Beck, 1977).

Benthic densities under water hyacinth mats were influenced by macrophyte development, river stage, and dissolved oxygen levels. Winter and spring benthic assemblages yield high densities and were characterized by a relatively diverse assemblage of Tubificidae, Chironomidae, Sphaeriidae, phytophilic naidids, gastropods, isopods, and amphipods. Well-oxygenated water and an abundance of organic matter facilitated the abundance of several normally benthic taxa (e.g., Tubificidae), while cold air temperatures and the dieback of aerial macrophyte tissue probably contributed to the movement of phytophilic taxons to the benthos. Benthic densities and the proportion accounted for by phytophilic taxons were especially high in January ($>11,500$ m^{-2}) and February (24,000 m^{-2}) 1976 following a December freeze, which killed most of the hyacinths; this dieback was followed by the dropping of the dead macrophyte tissue to the benthos (Beck, 1977).

Benthic densities declined sharply in June following a sharp decline in dissolved oxygen. Relatively high densities returned in July and persisted through autumn, but they were primarily the result of abundant *Chaoborus punctipennis* and *Sphaerium* spp.; oligochaetes were less numerous than in winter and spring, while gastropods, isopods, and amphipods were rare (Beck, 1977). *Sphaerium* spp. and *C. punctipennis* probably came to dominate summer and autumn benthic assemblages because of their tolerance to low oxygen levels; Hart and Fuller (1974) reported that several species of Sphaeriidae were very tolerant of organic pollution, and Brigham et al. (1982) reported that *C. punctipennis* undergoes diurnal vertical migrations to replenish its oxygen supply.

The effect of water hyacinths on the benthos may become pronounced in summer and autumn. Shading results in a moderation of diel fluctuations and vertical differences in water temperatures. Moreover, declining water levels result in increasing contact between the roots and the benthos. These roots may provide a refuge from the oxygen-poor benthos, and in situ oxygen production may provide pockets of oxygen-rich microhabitat among the roots. In any case, benthic assemblages underneath hyacinth mats in Lake Sorrel were still dominated by *C. punctipennis* and Sphaeriidae well into autumn, although Tubificidae and Chironomidae were common (Beck, 1977).

Seasonal patterns in density and structure in benthic assemblages from cypress–tupelo swamp samples in the Buffalo Cove area were similar to those reported for the Lake Sorrel benthos. Total densities were approximately twofold higher during January and February than they were during the other months; a secondary maximum occurred in August. Taxonomic richness was also highest during winter, while it was lowest in August and September, apparently because of the inability of most taxons to tolerate low levels of dissolved oxygen. Winter maxima were characterized by an abundance of phytophilic taxons, including gastropods, isopods, and amphipods. The secondary maxima reported in August was primarily the result of high densities of *Chaoborus punctipennis* and *Sphaerium* spp. (Beck, 1977).

Seasonal patterns in bayou assemblages differed from swamp assemblages. Total densities were highly variable, with maxima and minima often occurring in consecutive samples. The major maxima occurred in March and June, while minima occurred in February, April, May, July, and August. Taxonomic richness generally varied with density, although only moderate increases in taxonomic richness accompanied the June density maxima. Oligochaeta, Chironomidae, and Sphaeriidae accounted for much of the June maxima, while Oligochaeta were important for the February maxima. Oligochaeta, Sphaeriidae, and Chironomidae were also moderately abundant during autumn (Beck, 1977).

Lakes exhibited little seasonal difference in mean densities, but taxonomic richness was relatively high in late summer, autumn, and March. Oligochaetes and Tanypodinae (Chironomidae) were less numerous during summer, while Sphaeriidae were most numerous during July, and gastropods were most numerous during autumn (Beck, 1977).

Densities in the riverine stations exhibited sharp maxima in March and June and minima from August through February and in April. The June maximum was the result of high densities of *Tortopus* sp. on hard clay substrates, whereas the March maximum was the result of increases in Oligochaeta and Chironomidae. Samples from canal habitats were insufficient for the determination of seasonality (Beck, 1977).

Macrocrustacean Production

Three groups of macrocrustaceans, crayfishes (Cambaridae), freshwater shrimps (*Macrobrachium ohione* and *Palaemonetes kadiakensis*), and blue crabs (*Callinectes sapidus*) are abundant in the Atchafalaya Basin Floodway but are not usually collected in standard benthic samples. Crayfish, *M. ohione,* and *C. sapidus* provided important commercial shellfish fisheries, while crayfish, *M. ohione,* and *P. kadiakensis* are important prey items for commercial and sport finfish fisheries (Bryan et al., 1975; Fremling et al., 1989; Pollard et al., 1981).

Crayfish.   Louisiana is the largest supplier of commercial crayfish in North America. The Atchafalaya Basin Floodway provides 40 to 60% of the state's total production and virtually all of its wild fishery (i.e., not aquaculture) (Bryan et al., 1974; Hunner and Barr, 1981). The red swamp crawfish (*Procambarus clarkii*) is the most important species in the fishery. The white river crawfish (*P. acutus*) is also commercially important (Fremling et al., 1989; Hunner and Barr, 1981; Pollard et al., 1981).

Both species use seasonally inundated habitats, but as its common name suggests, *Procambarus clarkii* is more common in lentic habitats, whereas *P. acutus* is more prevalent in lotic habitats (R. Bouchard, personal communication). This distribution with respect to habitats is at least partially explained by the fact that *P. clarkii* is more tolerant than *P. acutus* to both lower levels of dissolved oxygen and higher temperatures (Hunner and Barr, 1981).

Procambarus clarkii and *P. acutus* were once extremely abundant in overflow habitats throughout Louisiana and the Mississippi Alluvial Valley. However, extensive levee construction, swamp draining, and other modifications have greatly reduced their abundance. The Mississippi, Red, and Ouachita Rivers occasionally support major populations but only during years in which extremely high flood stages overtop their levees. Otherwise, major populations are confined to the Atchafalaya Basin Floodway (Hunner and Barr, 1981).

Procambarus clarkii and *P. acutus* accounted for 90.7% (204) and 8.9% (20) of the total catch in a 1974–1975 trap survey of permanent aquatic habitats in the Atchafalaya Basin Floodway; a single specimen of *Cambarus diogenes diogenes* was also captured. Trap catches were higher for swamp, bayou, and swamp-lake samples than for distributary, levee, and main-channel samples. The genus *Procambarus* was most numerous in swamp-influenced habitats, whereas *P. acutus* was most abundant along the protection levee and a canal (Bryan et al., 1975; O'Brien, 1977).

A seining survey was conducted from 1973 to 1975. Because of sampling difficulties caused by fluctuating water levels and dense vegetation, sampling was concentrated near the eastern and western protection levees, which afforded year-round access. A total of seven species were collected, which, in order of decreasing abundance, were *Procambarus clarkii, P. acutus, Orconectes lancifer, Cambarellus puer, C. shufeldtii, O. palmeri longimanus,* and *Cambarus diogenes diogenes.* The two most abundant species, *P. clarkii* and *P. acutus,* accounted for 60.5% and 36.6%, respectively, of the total. Total catch, catch per unit effort, and frequency of occurrence were substantially greater along the western protection levee. *P. acutus* also accounted for a greater proportion of the total along the western protection levee (41.2%) than along the eastern protection levee (16.6%) (Bryan et al., 1975; O'Brien, 1977).

Trap catches in a subsequent (1980) study conducted in bottomland hardwood overflow habitats in the Fordoche area indicated that *Procambarus clarkii* populations are strongly associated with the rising and falling of floodwaters. Trap catches from February through May were substantially higher at edge sites (i.e., at the edge of ascending or descending floodwaters) than in overflow habitats that had been inundated for longer periods; trap catches from permanent habitats (i.e., distributary and canal) were low. The concentration of *P. clarkii* along the edge of rising floodwaters suggests that they are feeding on recently immersed leaf litter. Presumably, these sites contain the richest detritus, which has not been subjected to prolonged submersion and prior decomposition (Pollard et al., 1981).

Trap catches in the Fordoche area study were highest in February (963), intermediate in March (427), April (601), May (613), and June (573), and almost nil in July (1). A mark and recapture study of trapped crayfish conducted in May resulted in an estimated density of 16.5 crayfish m^{-2} along one edge site. When extrapolated to other trap catches, this suggests that February edge densities would amount to almost 47 crayfish m^{-2}. The relatively low March catch (427) indicates one of the hazards of following the edge of ascending floodwaters. During 1980, flood stages in March were lower than those in December through February and April through early June. Apparently, this transient drop in flood stage resulted in the stranding of a large number of juveniles, which tend to be more concentrated than older individuals along the edge. Significantly, adults accounted for a greater percentage of total trap counts during March than during either February or April (Pollard et al., 1981).

The life cycle of *Procambarus clarkii* reflects its dependence on overflow habitats. Adults in the Atchafalaya Basin Floodway burrow in dewatered overflow habitats during periods of low flow (usually June through November) (Bryan et al., 1975; Pollard et al., 1981). Significantly, *P. clarkii* tends to burrow at sites that are among the first to be inundated (Pollard et al., 1981). Spawning in the Atchafalaya Basin Floodway is protracted but apparently peaks in autumn (Bryan et al., 1975). Protracted spawning was also reported in a 1938–1941 study of *P. clarkii* in eastern Louisiana (Penn, 1943).

The recruitment of juvenile *Procambarus clarkii* in eastern Louisiana extended from August through November (Penn, 1943). Juvenile *P. clarkii* in the Atchafalaya Basin Floodway were first recorded along protection levees in November and were most numerous from December through February (Bryan et al., 1975). Recruitment of juveniles in the Fordoche area was already well under way by the beginning of the study in February (Pollard et al., 1981). Growth during winter and early spring is typically rapid, and by April, most of the individuals developing from the autumn spawning are mature by the time the floodwaters recede (Bryan et al., 1975; O'Brien, 1977; Pollard et al., 1981).

The second most abundant crayfish, *Procambarus acutus,* tends to be less common than *P. clarkii* in swamp and overflow habitats and more common in lotic habitats (R. Bouchard, personal communication; Bryan et al., 1975; O'Brien, 1977). However, its life cycle also corresponds to the seasonal inundation of overflow habitats. It was typically burrowed in dewatered sites during periods of low flow (late summer and autumn). Spawning probably extends from May through November but probably peaks in October or November (O'Brien, 1977). Recruitment is also probably protracted but is apparently greatest during high flow. Juveniles collected along the western protection levee were first recorded in December and were most common from January through March (Bryan et al., 1975; O'Brien, 1977).

The commercial crayfish season typically extends from late December through June or July, with peak landings occurring in April and May (Bryan et al., 1975). Landings increase during wet years (e.g., 1973, 1974, and 1975), when extensive inundation promotes the generation of terrestrial detritus and the production of water hyacinths. Modest spring catches may result from reduced or delayed inundation. Catches may also be reduced by an extensive winter freezing of water hyacinths, which serve as important nursery habitat (Fremling et al., 1989; Hunner and Barr, 1981; O'Brien, 1977).

The five noncommercial species of crayfish were infrequent and rare in trap and seining collections from the Atchafalaya Basin Floodway (Bryan et al., 1975). One of these, *Orconectes lancifer,* is rarely collected throughout its range. One possible reason for its apparent scarcity is that it may inhabit the muddy bottoms of deeper waters (R. Bouchard, personal communication; Penn, 1959). If so, it would be less susceptible to sampling by traps and seines. Spawning for this species probably extends from October through January. Juveniles probably grow slowly during low summer flows and reach maturity by autumn (O'Brien, 1977).

Cambarellus puer and *C. shufeldtii* may be relatively abundant, but habitat preferences render them less susceptible to sampling by seines and traps. *Cambarellus* spp. are small-bodied crayfish that commonly occupy waters too shallow for the larger *Procambarus* spp. As such, they would probably be susceptible only to dip-net and hand collections (R. Bouchard, personal communication). In fact, more *C. shufeldtii* were collected by dip-netting in the vicinity of water hyacinths than by seining and trapping combined. Spawning by *C. shufeldtii* probably occurs year-round, with peaks occurring in late winter and early summer. The closely related *C. puer* probably also spawns in late winter and early summer (O'Brien, 1977).

Inefficient sampling probably accounts for the reported scarcity of *Cambarus diogenes diogenes.* This species tends to live in higher, drier habitats than most other crayfish and is confined largely to its burrows (R. Bouchard, personal communication; Penn, 1959; Rogers and Hunner, 1985). Scarcity or inefficient sampling may also account for the low numbers of *O. palmeri longimanus,* which is more commonly found in the small, swift-flowing upland stream in northwestern Louisiana (Penn, 1959).

River Shrimp. The Atchafalaya Basin Floodway supports large populations of two freshwater shrimps, *Macrobrachium ohione* (river shrimp) and *Palaemonetes* spp. (primarily *P. kadiakensis*). Both taxons appear to be important food items for several species of commercial and sport fishes, and *M. ohione* supports a sizable bait fishery (Bryan et al., 1975; Truesdale and Mermilliod, 1979).

Gunter (1937) reported that commercial shrimping for *Macrobrachium ohione* was limited to the warmer months, when the shrimp are either more abundant or more likely to be captured by traps placed in shallow water. A 1974–1975 trap survey in the Atchafalaya Basin Floodway conducted by Bryan et al. (1975) also revealed generally greater catches during the warmer months, but other factors were involved. Habitat is probably one such factor, since trap catches were low to nil in swamp and bayou habitats, higher in lake habitats, and highest in distributary and main-channel habitats (Table 2.10). Another probable factor is the effect of river stage on water quality. Trap captures in the swamp and bayou habitats were limited to spring high flows,

TABLE 2.10.   *Discharge and Trap Catches of River Shrimp*
(Macrobrachium ohione) from Selected Habitats[a] in the Buffalo Cove
and Flat Lake Areas of the Atchafalaya Basin Floodway,
Louisiana, 1974–1975

		Buffalo Cove			Flat Lake		
	Discharge (m^3 s^{-1})[b]	D	L	S	MC	L	B
1974							
Apr.	10,600–12,700	—	—	—	2	7	1
May	8,500–11,300	4	13	8	2	4	1
June	9,200–14,200	13	12	0	0	0	0
July	5,000–12,700	7	1	0	9	8	0
Aug.	2,800–4,200	1	0	0	43	0	0
Sept.	4,200–7,100	38	48	0	16	7	0
Oct.	2,800–5,700	40	4	0	23	7	0
Nov.	2,800–8,500	5	7	0	0	5	0
Dec.	7,000–8,500	1	0	0	0	1	0
1975							
Jan.	8,500–11,300	3	0	0	0	2	0
Feb.	10,600–12,700	2	0	0	2	7	0
Mar.	13,000–15,600	0	0	0	2	12	0

Source: Modified from Bryan et al. (1975).
[a]D, distributary; L, lake; S, cypress–tupelo gum swamp; MC, main channel; B, bayou.
[b]Discharge ranges (at Simmesport), which were estimated from Figure 2 in Bryan et al. (1975), are approximate.

while lake and distributary catches were nil during the August flow minimum. Conversely, main-channel catches were generally low during periods of high flow and high during periods of low flow. Finally, Station WD, which in Table 2.10 represents the lake habitat for the Buffalo Cove area, exhibits late spring and September maxima comparable to those recorded in a nearby distributary; Holland (1977) reported that this station resembled distributary stations during high flows and swamp-lake stations during low flows.

The results of seine hauls made on bars and current-swept shores of the main channel near Flat Lake and a distributary in the Buffalo Cove area are presented in Table 2.12. One immediate conclusion is that seasonal patterns in seine hauls differ substantially from those in trap catches. For instance, catches from seine hauls during late autumn were high, while those from traps were low. Catches from seine hauls in the distributary were very low from January through May and relatively high for the remaining months. Main-channel catches were more erratic, with high catches occurring in January, October, and November and very low catches occurring in March, May, and August. Overall, gender ratios were biased toward females, with the distributary averaging six males for every 10 females and the main channel averaging eight males for every 10 females. However, the gender ratio varied considerably over time.

TABLE 2.11. *Seine Catches, Gender Ratios, and Size Distributions*[a] *of River Shrimp* (Macrobrachium ohione) *from a Distributary Station (Station WC) and a Main-Channel Station (Station RB) in the Atchafalaya Basin Floodway, Louisiana, 1974*

	Total Catch	Gender Ratio (m:f)	Male Size		Female Size	
			<40 mm	>40 mm	<50 mm	>50 mm
Distributary						
Jan.	2	0:2	0	0	1	1
Feb.	5	0:5	0	0	0	5
Mar.	0	0:0	0	0	0	0
Apr.	0	0:0	0	0	0	0
May	4	1:3	1	0	0	3
June	37	13:24	5	8	5	19
July	27	7:20	5	2	20	0
Aug.	16	4:12	2	2	12	0
Sept.	24	4:20	3	1	18	2
Oct.	32	18:15	9	9	6	9
Nov.	31	13:19	6	7	9	10
Dec.	35	20:15	12	8	10	5
Main channel						
Jan.	90	61:29	19	42	19	10
Feb.	12	2:10	0	2	0	10
Mar.	2	1:1	0	1	0	1
Apr.	21	10:11	5	5	6	5
May	1	0:1	0	0	1	0
June	14	5:9	0	5	1	8
July	9	5:4	1	4	2	2
Aug.	3	1:2	1	0	2	0
Sept.	15	6:9	4	2	8	1
Oct.	52	24:28	19	5	27	1
Nov.	61	15:46	1	14	4	43
Dec.	30	8:22	4	4	10	12

Source: Modified from Bryan et al. (1975).
[a]Bryan et al. (1975) reported that the mean sizes of male and female shrimp were 40 and 50 mm, respectively. These values denote the number of shrimp below and above those means.

The mean size of male *Macrobrachium ohione* from seine hauls was 40 mm, while the mean size for females was 50 mm (Bryan et al., 1975). The generally low catches from distributary hauls from January through June were dominated by larger shrimp (i.e., greater than their respective means), whereas smaller (i.e., younger) individuals were more numerous during summer; autumn catches were made up of roughly equal numbers of younger and older individuals. Main-channel size distributions were less seasonally consistent. This is exemplified by the predominance of younger individuals in the October sample and the predominance of older individuals in the November sample (Table 2.11). Part of the variability encountered in the main channel may be a result of the difficulty of adequately sampling large river habitats. In his 1934 study of *M. ohione* in the Lower Mississippi, Gunter (1937) reported that age classes were often spatially segregated. Younger shrimp were generally restricted to shallow areas with reduced current, while older individuals were more commonly found in deeper (>10 ft) and faster water.

Spawning by *Macrobrachium ohione* in the Atchafalaya Basin is protracted, with berried females occurring from March through late September. Juveniles (i.e., less than 20 mm long) were recorded in April and from late summer through December (Bryan et al., 1975; Truesdale and Mermilliod, 1979). *M. ohione* also exhibited protracted spawning in the 1934 study in the Lower Mississippi (Gunter, 1937). This species is probably univoltine (Bryan et al., 1975).

Macrobrachium ohione, which is a strong swimmer (Pennak, 1989), may travel extensively within the Atchafalaya Basin. Trap catches in swamp and bayou habitats suggest that the shrimp may move into these habitats during peak flows and return to distributaries and the main channel during lower flows. If so, these movements may be responses to changes in food availability or physicochemical characteristics. Bryan et al. (1975) reported that *M. ohione* apparently preferred well-oxygenated waters and this presumed movement into and out of lentic habitats is consistent with changing levels of oxygenation. This movement is also consistent with the avoidance of extremely high concentrations of suspended sediments in riverine habitats. Gunter (1937) reported that episodes of high turbidity generally resulted in low trap catches and high mortality among those shrimp that were captured.

Movements by *Macrobrachium ohione* may also be associated with reproduction. For instance, a 1934 survey of *Macrobrachium ohione* in the Lower Mississippi revealed that males accounted for 37% of the total catch in samples collected prior to the appearance of berried females, and only 9% afterward. Moreover, incidental catches of *M. ohione* during a marine shrimp survey in Barataria Bay suggest that berried females may move into the upper reaches of estuaries during peak spring discharges. A total of 93 *M. ohione* were collected, of which more than 80% were berried females. In contrast, only 13% of the catch in the Lower Mississippi were berried females (Gunter, 1937). Movements associated with reproduction are also suggested from results obtained within the Atchafalaya Basin Floodway. Truesdale and Mermilliod (1979) reported that the paucity of preovigerous females (40 to 50 mm long) in seining and trap samples from May through July suggests that late summer ovigerous females were recruited from outside the sampling area.

Sampling for *Palaemonetes kadiakensis* was less extensive than it was for *Macrobrachium ohione*. Large numbers were collected incidentally in seine hauls from the distributary station during February (233 shrimp), March (198 shrimp), and April (34 shrimp). *M. ohione* was either absent or rare in these hauls, which suggests some kind of complementarity between the two taxons (Bryan et al., 1975). *P. kadiakensis* was abundant in net collections of macroinvertebrates associated with water hyacinth (*Eichhornia crassipes*), especially during midsummer (Beck, 1977; Pollard et al., 1981). Elsewhere in Louisiana, berried females of *P. kadiakensis* have been recorded from early

February through late October (Geagan, 1962). Like *M. ohione, P. kadia-kensis* is probably univoltine.

Blue Crab. Atchafalaya Bay and the Atchafalaya Basin Floodway support an extensive fishery for blue crab (*Callinectes sapidus*). Most of the commercial fishery within the floodway occurs in Grand Lake, Six-Mile Lake, and Duck Lake, but incidental catches have been reported throughout the basin. The commercial season extends from June to November. Cooler temperatures appear to be responsible for their scarcity during the remaining months. Either the crabs move out of the basin (into the coastal marshes or the bay), or they move to inaccessible localities within the basin (Bryan et al., 1974, 1975).

Crabs collected within the floodway were large (>75 mm) and predominantly male. Apparently, abundance within the basin is dependent on recruitment from Atchafalaya Basin or adjacent coastal marshes. This pattern of gender and age segregation is consistent with findings from estuaries within Louisiana and other Gulf states. Spawning usually occurs in warm, shallow intertidal flats with middle to low salinities. Following mating, the females move to more saline habitats while the males move to less saline or freshwater habitats (Bryan et al., 1974, 1975).

Fish Production
Despite its relatively small size, the Atchafalaya Basin hosts a rich fish fauna. Fremling et al. (1989) reported a total of 125 species characteristic of the basin and an additional 56 species that were probably either strays from tributaries outside the basin or strays from nearby marine zones. Connections to the Lower Mississippi and Red Rivers, as well as Atchafalaya Bay and the Gulf of Mexico, are certainly major contributors to the richness of the fauna. The variety of habitats in the Atchafalaya Basin Floodway also contribute to this diversity. Moreover, overbank flooding generates additional habitat each year (Bryan et al., 1975; Fremling et al., 1989).

In addition to being diverse, fish in the Atchafalaya Basin Floodway are extremely productive. The floodway has been estimated to contribute 60% of the freshwater commercial landings in Louisiana (Lambou, 1965). The floodway also supports a significant sport fishery (Fremling et al., 1989). Shad (Clupeiidae), buffalo (*Ictiobus* spp.), carp (*Cyprinus carpio*), catfish (Ictaluridae), and freshwater drum (*Aplodinotus grunniens*) are the major commercial species (Bryan et al., 1974; Fremling et al., 1989). Catfish, sunfish (*Lepomis* spp.), bass (*Micropterus* spp. and *Morone* spp.), and crappie (*Pomoxis* spp.) are the major sport fishes (Fremling et al., 1989; Lambou, 1965).

A series of rotenone samples from Grand Lake (southern floodway), Little Bayou Pigeon, and Bayou Postillion (east-central floodway) were conducted during autumn of 1975, 1976, and 1977. The overall mean standing stock was 860 kg ha $^{-1}$, which is at the upper limit of rotenone standing stock estimates made in the United States (Bryan and Sabins, 1979).

Difference in flow is probably the most important single factor influencing fish production. For instance, standing stocks in the floodway averaged 904 kg ha^{-1} during 1975 and 1976, whereas the mean for 1977 was 795 kg ha^{-1}. The populations sampled in 1975 and 1976 were largely affected by conditions present from 1974 through 1975, when flows were considerably higher than average. The populations sampled in 1977 were largely affected by 1976 flows, which were considerably lower than average. Flows in 1977 were slightly below average (Bryan and Sabins, 1979).

Interannual variations in flow are also associated with differences in community structure. Fish assemblages from the rotenone samples were classified into four major categories. Sport fishes are predominantly Centrarchidae and yellow bass (*Morone mississipiensis*). Predators include spotted gar (*Lepisosteus oculatus*) and bowfin (*Amia calva*). Commercial fishes include *Cyprinus carpio,* catfish, suckers (Catostomidae), and *Aplodinotus grunniens.* Forage species include gizzard shad (*Dorosoma cepedianum*) and striped mullet (*Mugil cephalus*). Standing stocks for commercial fishes declined by more than half between 1975 and 1976 (398 kg ha^{-1}) and 1977 (167 kg ha^{-1}). Less drastic declines were noted for sport fishes (from 145 kg ha^{-1} to 113 kg ha^{-1}), and predators (from 280 kg ha^{-1} to 208 kg ha^{-1}). On the other hand, forage fishes increased dramatically, from 72 kg ha^{-1} to 310 kg ha^{-1} (Bryan and Sabins, 1979).

Comparisons of standing stocks and community structure in the leveed upper basin suggest that differences in the floodway's standing stocks and community structure are probably attributable to differences in allochthonous and autochthonous inputs. The upper basin sites do not experience high turbidity and overbank flooding, but instead, exhibit high phytoplankton productivity. Total standing stocks averaged 555 kg ha^{-1}, which is 61% of the floodway standing stocks during 1975 and 1976 and 70% of that during 1977. More significantly, forage species (primarily *Dorosoma cepedianum*) accounted for 53% of the upper basin standing; sport, commercial, and predator fishes accounted for 4%, 16%, and 28%, respectively. In absolute terms, forage species standing stocks in the leveed upper basin (294 kg ha^{-1}) were similar to those in the lower basin during 1977 (310 kg ha^{-1}). *D. cepedianum* is planktivorous for most of its life cycle, and its abundance in the upper basin and in the floodway during 1977 is probably the result of elevated phytoplankton production (Bryan and Sabins, 1979). However, reduced predation pressures from piscivorous species may have also been important.

Lower populations of sport, commercial, and predator fishes during low-flow years (and in the upper basin) appear to be the result of reduced allochthonous inputs and/or reduced overflow habitat. The importance of allochthonous inputs into permanent aquatic habitats is difficult to gage. On the other hand, most of the common to abundant fishes in the Atchafalaya Basin Floodway use overflow habitats for spawning, nurseries, and/or foraging (Bryan et al., 1974, 1975; Clary, 1985; Fremling et al., 1989; Levine, 1977; Pollard et al., 1981) (Table 2.12).

TABLE 2.12. *Abundance and Habitat-Specific Distribution of Selected Fishes in the Atchafalaya Basin Floodway, Louisiana*

	Abundance		Distribution[c]				
	A1[a]	A2[b]	R	L	B/S	F	E/M
Acipenseridae							
Scaphirhynchus platorynchus	C	*	X				
Polydontidae							
Polydon spathula	O	*	X	x			
Lepisosteidae							
Lepisosteus oculatus	C	A		X	X		
L. osseus	R	U	X	X			
L. platostomus	R	U	X		X		
L. spathula	C	C	X	X	X	X	
Amiidae							
Amia calva	C	A	X	X	X	X	
Anguiliidae							
Anguilla rostrata	U	U	X				X
Hiodontidae							
Hiodon alosoides	C	R	X	x	x		
Clupeidae							
Alosa chrysochloris	C	U	X				
Brevoortia patronus	A	–	X			X	
Dorosoma cepedianum	A	A	X	X	X	X	
D. petenense	A	A	X	X	X	X	
Engraulidae							
Anchoa mitchilli	A	A	X				X
Catostomidae							
Carpiodes carpio	A	U		x	x	x	
Ictiobus bubalus	C	A	X	X	X	X	
I. cyprinellus	O	U		x	X		
Cyprinidae							
Cyprinus carpio	A	C	X	X	X	X	
Hybognathus nuchalis	C	U	X	x	x	x	
Hybopsis aestivalis	C	C	X				
H. storeriana	C	C	X	x			
Notemigonus crysoleucas	C	C	X	X	X	X	
Notropis atherinoides	A	A	X			X	
N. atrocaudalis	C	–	x				
N. blennius	A	C	X			X	
N. buchanani	U	U	X				
N. emiliae	U	A	X	X	X		
N. longirostris	O	–	x				
N. lutrensis	O	U	X				
N. potteri	S	C	X				
N. shumardi	A	A	X	X	X	X	
N. texanus	U	U				X	
N. venustus	C	U	x		X		
N. volucellus	C	A	X	X	X	X	
Pimephales notatus	C	–		x	x	x	
P. vigilax	U	A	X	X	X	X	

TABLE 2.12.   (Continued)

	Abundance		Distribution[c]				
	A1[a]	A2[b]	R	L	B/S	F	E/M
Ictaluridae							
Ictalurus furcatus	A	C	X	X	X	X	
I. melas	C	U		x	x	X	
I. natalis	R	A		X	X	X	
I. punctatus	A	A	X	X	X	X	
Noturus gyrinus	R	A	x	X	X	X	
Pylodictis olivaris	A	U	X	X			
Esocidae							
Esox americanus vermiculatus	C	U		x	x	X	
Aphredoderidae							
Aphredoderus sayanus	U	C		x	x	X	
Belonidae							
Strongylura marina	O	U	X	X	X	X	X
Cyprinodontidae							
Fundulus chrysotus	C	U		X	x		
F. olivaceus	U	U		X		X	
Lucania parva	U	C					X
Poeciliidae							
Gambusia affinis	A	A	X	X	X	X	
Heterandria formosa	O	U		X	X		
Poecilia latipinna	U	U		X		X	
Atherinidae							
Labidesthes sicculus	U	A		X	X	X	
Menidia beryllina	A	A	X	X	X	X	
Syngnathidae							
Syngnathus scovelli	U	C					X
Centrarchidae							
Centrarchus macropterus	O	U		x	x	X	
Elassoma zonatum	O	U			x	X	
Lepomis cyanellus	U	U			X		
L. gulosus	A	A	X	X	X	X	
L. humilus	C	U		x	X	X	
L. macrochirus	A	A	X	X	X	X	
L. marginatus	O	C		X	X	X	
L. megalotis	U	U		X			
L. microlophus	C	A	X	X	X	X	
L. punctatus	O	C		X	X	X	
L. symmetricus	O	U		x	x	X	
Micropterus punctulatus	O	R		x	x		
M. salmoides	A	C	X	X	X	X	
Pomoxis annularis	C	C	X	X	X	X	
P. nigromaculatus	A	A	X	X	X	X	
Mugilidae							
Mugil cephalus	A	C	X	X	X	X	X

TABLE 2.12. *(Continued)*

	Abundance		Distribution[c]				
	A1[a]	A2[b]	R	L	B/S	F	E/M
Percidae							
Etheostoma asprigene	O	U	X			X	
E. chlorosomum	U	C	X	X		X	
E. fusiforme	O	u			x	X	
E. gracile	O	U	X			X	
E. parvipinne	O	–			x		
E. proeliare	O	U	X		x	X	
E. zonale	O	–	x				
Stizostedion canadense	?	*	X				
Percithyidae							
Morone chrysops	A	C	X	x		X	
M. mississipiensis	C	C	X	X		X	
M. saxatilis	O	U	X				X
Sciaenidae							
Aplodinotus grunniens	A	C	X	X	X	X	
Cynoscion arenarius	C	–					x
C. nebulosus	C	–					x
Leiostomus xanthurus	C	–					x
Menticirrhus littoralis	C	–					x
Micropogonias undulatus	C	–					x
Pogonias cromis	C	–					x
Sciaenops ocellatus	C	–					x
Bothidae							
Paralichthys lethostigma	C	U	X				X
Soleidae							
Trinectes maculatus	C	U			x	x	X

Source: Bennett and McFarlane (1983), Boyer (1982), Bryan et al. (1975), Deegan and Thompson (1985), Fremling et al. (1989), and Lee et al. (1980).

[a]Abundance as presented by Fremling et al. (1989): A, abundant; C, common; O, occasionally or locally abundant or common; U, uncommon; R, rare; S, probable stray; —, not found.

[b]Abundance as presented in Bryan et al. (1975): A, abundant (>500 fishes seined, >60 in trammel net); C, common (>90 seined, >20 trammel net); U, uncommon (>10 seined, <20 trammel net); R, (<10 seined); *, not recorded but regarded as probably abundant in the undersampled main channel; —, not recorded; ?, uncertain.

[c]R, main channel and distributaries; L, lakes; B/S, bayous and swamps; F, overflow habitat; E/M, estuarine or marine affinities. "X" (uppercase) denotes habitat affinities reported by Bryan et al. (1975), while "x" (lowercase) denotes habitat affinities reported in other literature.

The use of overflow habitats by fishes is particularly evident in a study of permanent (distributary and canal) and overflow sites in the Fordoche area. Catches from trammel nets and electrofishing in permanent sites were relatively high during February, March, June, July, and August, but low during April and May. Catches within the inundated bottomland hardwood forest were relatively high from February through June, especially at the ascending or receding edge of the floodwaters. *Lepisosteus oculatus, Amia calva, Dorosoma cepedianum,* black bullhead (*Ictalurus melas*), yellow bullhead

TABLE 2.13. *Seasonal Distribution of Fishes (mean catch/site) Among Permanent (Canal and Distributary Habitats), Overflow (Bottomland Hardwoods), and Edge (Edge of Ascending or Receding Floodwaters) Sites in the Fordoche Area, Atchafalaya Basin Floodway, Louisiana, 1980*[a]

	Feb.	Mar.	Apr.	May	June	July	Aug.
Lepisosteus spp.							
Permanent	<1	1	0	1	1	23	9
Overflow	0	1	3	8	10	nf	nf
Edge	0	1	9	2	16	4	2
Amia calva							
Permanent	<1	2	1	2	1	7	7
Overflow	<1	2	3	3	2	nf	nf
Edge	0	2	15	2	1	2	1
Dorosoma spp.							
Permanent	27	12	<1	<1	1	4	35
Overflow	3	1	2	0	0	nf	nf
Edge	1	11	1	1	0	12	5
Ictalurus spp.							
Permanent	0	5	0	0	1	7	5
Overflow	<1	1	1	1	1	nf	nf
Edge	0	4	5	2	2	2	0
Centrarchidae							
Permanent	2	16	1	3	19	75	19
Overflow	6	3	3	11	10	nf	nf
Edge	12	16	9	34	34	86	28
Other fishes							
Permanent	6	4	0	1	7	3	2
Overflow	1	<1	<1	1	0	nf	nf
Edge	2	1	1	1	9	2	1
Total mean catch/site							
Permanent	34	39	1	6	36	133	86
Overflow	9	8	12	24	19	nf	nf
Edge	14	34	40	45	56	62	37
Number of sites							
Permanent	6	6	6	6	6	6	6
Overflow	5	4	9	10	6	0	0
Edge	2	2	3	4	3	2[a]	1[a]

Source: After Pollard et al. (1981).

[a]nf, Not flooded. Edge sites from February through June were located within the inundated bottomland hardwood forest. Edge sites during July and August were located adjacent to or in the canal, and as such they probably have more in common with the permanent sites than do the other edge sites. "Overflow" denotes overflow sites located away from the ascending or descending edge of floodwaters.

(*I. natalis*), flier (*Centrarchus macropterus*), warmouth (*Lepomis gulosus*), bluegill (*L. macrochirus*), largemouth bass (*Micropterus salmoides*), and black crappie (*Pomoxis nigromaculatus*) were the more abundant species (Pollard et al., 1981) (Table 2.13).

Overflow habitats are important spawning and/or nursery habitats for a variety of species. Reports of spawning in overflow habitats in the Atchafalaya Basin Floodway were rather limited; spawning was observed only by several species of darters (*Etheostoma* spp.). In contrast, spawning by several species of centrarchids has been observed in swamp and bayou habitats. Moreover, ripe females of *Lepisosteus oculatus, Amia calva,* and *Ictalurus natalis* were concentrated in swamps and bayous (Bryan et al., 1974).

However, the paucity of observed spawning in overflow habitats may be the result of sampling bias, since the overflow habitats sampled by Bryan et al. (1974, 1975) were limited primarily to grassy sites adjacent to protection levees. Studies of fish populations in the Fordoche area suggest that spawning may be more prevalent in inundated bottomland hardwood swamps, where large numbers of *A. calva, Ictalurus* spp., and Centrarchidae were recorded. These three taxons are shallow nest builders, and during high water, suitable nesting habitat was concentrated in the overflow habitats (Pollard et al., 1981). Spawning in overflow habitats is common in other localities. In one of the last remaining active floodplains of the Lower Mississippi River (near St. Francisville, Louisiana), Boyer (1982) collected the adhesive eggs of shad (*Dorosoma* spp.), carp (*Cyprinus carpio*), and buffalo (*Ictiobus* spp.).

Many species use overflow habitats for nurseries. Large numbers of immature *Dorosoma cepedianum,* threadfin shad (*D. petenense*), *Ictalurus natalis, Lepomis gulosus, L. macrochirus, Micropterus salmoides,* and *Pomoxis nigromaculatus* were recorded in overflow habitat within the Atchafalaya Basin Floodway (Bryan et al., 1974, 1975; Clary, 1985; Levine, 1977; Pollard et al., 1981). Mixed populations of mosquitofish (*Gambusia affinis*), silversides (*Menidia*), and bullhead minnow (*Pimephales vigilax*) were also recorded in overflow habitat (Bryan et al., 1975). The use of overflow habitat as nursery habitat is perhaps best studied in the unleveed Lower Mississippi near St. Francisville, where Boyer (1982) recorded 35 larvae and early juvenile taxons, of which *Dorosoma* spp., *Ictiobus* spp., silvery minnow (*Hybognathus nuchalis*), temperate bass (*Morone* spp.), *Pomoxis* spp., and *Etheostoma* spp. were most numerous.

Several species exhibit ontogenic habitat partitioning. For example, the young of *Lepomis gulosus, L. macrochirus,* and *Micropterus salmoides* are concentrated in overflow habitats and the shallow waters of permanent lentic habitats, while the adults are concentrated in deeper waters (Bryan et al., 1975). The early life-history stages of several other ubiquitous species, including channel catfish (*Ictalurus punctatus*) and *Aplodinotus grunniens,* are concentrated in shallow habitats, whereas the adults are more widely distributed. On the other hand, the young of *Dorosoma cepedianum* and threadfin shad (*D. petenense*) are widely dispersed, while the adults are concentrated in riverine and lake habitats (Bryan et al., 1974). Even among early life-history stages there appear to be ontogenic shifts in habitat use. For instance, Boyer (1982) reported that recently hatched larvae tended to be more abundant in the pelagic areas of inundated floodplains, whereas older larvae and early juveniles dominated shallower zones.

Many of the larger species exhibit seasonal patterns of habitat use that correspond to seasonal changes in water quality. In the Buffalo Cove area, for instance, smallmouth buffalo (*Ictiobus bubalus*), *Lepomis gulosus, Micropterus salmoides,* white crappie (*Pomoxis annularis*), and *P. nigromaculatus* were confined to distributary and lake habitats during low flow when bayou and swamp dissolved oxygen levels were low. With increased flows and improved oxygen concentrations, however, these species move into bayou, cypress–tupelo gum swamp, and overflow habitats. Seasonal movements into and out of swamp and overflow habitats were not as pronounced for two other large species, *Lepisosteus oculatus* and *Amia calva,* both of which are facultative air breathers. A number of smaller species, including *Gambusia affinis, Menidia beryllina,* and *Pimephales vigilax,* also persisted in oxygen-depleted swamp and bayou habitats. On the other hand, other small fishes, such as darters (*Etheostoma* spp.), madtom (*Noturus gyrinus*), and gulf pipefish (*Syngnathus scovelli*), exhibited seasonal movements (Bryan et al., 1975).

Most of the more abundant species associated with swamps, bayous, and overflow habitats are also common in lakes (Table 2.12). Centrachidae (e.g., *Lepomis gulosus* and *L. macrochirus*) were especially common. Spawning centrarchids were frequent, as were young-of-the-year. Juvenile *Dorosoma* spp., pugnose shiner (*Notropis emiliae*), (*N. shumardi*), *Pimephales vigilax, Noturus gyrinus,* golden topminnow (*Fundulus chrysotus*), *Gambusia affinis,* and the killifish (*Heterandria formosa*) were common along the shores. *Ictalurus natalis* was the most common catfish, while *I. furcatus, I. punctatus,* and flathead catfish (*Pylodictis olivaris*) were common primarily during high water (Bryan et al., 1974).

A number of fishes are commonly associated with macrophytes, which can be abundant in swamp, bayou, and lake habitats. *Gambusia affinis, Elassoma zonatum, Fundulus chrysotus,* blackspotted topminnow (*F. olivaceous*), pirate perch (*Aphredoderus sayanus*), and grass pickerel (*Esox americanus*) were the most numerous fishes associated with water hyacinths; 12 other species were also collected (Beck, 1977). Elsewhere, preference for vegetated habitats has been reported for a number of common to abundant taxons, including *Lepisosteus oculatus, Cyprinus carpio,* golden shiner (*Notemigonus chrysoleucas*), and several Centrarchidae (Lee et al., 1980).

The main channel and the larger distributaries are characterized by significant populations of skipjack herring (*Alosa chrysochloris*), *Dorosoma cepedianum, D. petenense, Ictalurus furcatus, I. punctatus, Pylodictis olivaris, Mugil cephalus, Morone chrysops,* and *Aplodinotus grunniens.* Several other species, including shovelnose sturgeon (*Scaphirhynchus platorynchus*), paddlefish (*Polydon spathula*), *M. mississipiensis,* striped bass (*Morone saxatilis*), and sauger (*Stizostedion canadense*), may also be numerous in the main channel. These habitats support the major concentration of adult *Dorosoma* within the floodway, while the shallow waters along the banks are an important nursery habitat for *I. furcatus, I. punctatus,* and *A. grunniens* (Bryan et al., 1975). Shore zones also support populations of several cyprinids, including speckled chub (*Hybopsis aestivalis*), emerald shiner (*Notropis atheri-noides*), river shiner (*N. blennius*), and *N. shumardi* (Bryan et al., 1974).

The Atchafalaya Basin supports a number of primarily marine or estuarine fishes. Some of these, including bay anchovy (*Antocha mitchilli*), *Syngnathus scovelli,* and *Mugil cephalus,* occurred in relatively high numbers in the surveys of Bryan et al. (1974, 1975). Several others, including gulf menhaden (*Brevoortia patronus*), several drums (Scianidae), southern flounder (*Paralichthys lethostigma*), and hogchoker (*Trinectes maculatus*), were reported as common to abundant by Fremling et al. (1989) (Table 2.12).

With the exception of some of the Scianidae, the above-mentioned marine and estuarine taxons commonly extend upstream from estuarine reaches of rivers in the Gulf states (Deegan and Thompson, 1985; Lee et al., 1980). In the largely freshwater Atchafalaya Delta, fish populations contained a combination of freshwater, estuarine, and marine species. Typically, freshwater fishes (e.g., *Lepisosteus oculatus, Dorosoma cepedianum, D. petenense, Ictalurus furcatus, I. punctatus,* and *Aplodinotus grunniens*) resided in the delta from late autumn through late spring or early summer, whereas several estuarine/marine species (e.g., *Brevoortia patronus, Anchoa mitchilli, Micropoganias undulatus,* and *Paralichthys lethostigma*) moved into the delta from more saline habitats during late winter or early spring and left during late summer or early autumn (Deegan and Thompson, 1985).

Interannual variations of flow may have considerable effect on the spawning success and recruitment of many fishes in the Atchafalaya Basin Floodway. Many species, especially some of those common in backwater habitats, spawn during or just prior to maximum flows. For instance, ripe females of *Amia calva* were recorded from January through April, while ripe females of *Lepomis gulosus, Micropterus salmoides,* white crappie (*Pomoxis annularis*), and *P. nigromaculatus* were recorded from March through May or June (Bryan et al., 1975). Elsewhere in the Gulf states, river carpsucker (*Carpiodes carpio*), *Ictiobus* spp., *Esox americanus vermiculatus*), and banded pygmy sunfish (*Elassoma zonatum*) spawn from March through April or May (Cook, 1959; Lee et al., 1980).

Fishes that reproduce in distributaries and main-channel habitats may extend spawning into early or midsummer. *Ictalurus furcatus* and *I. punctatus* probably begin spawning in early spring and peak in June or July. Both *Morone chrysops* and *Aplodinotus grunniens* appear to begin spawning in March and continue into summer (Bryan et al., 1975). In Mississippi, goldeye (*Hiodon alosoides*) spawns in early spring (Cook, 1959). *Dorosoma cepedianum,* from the Savannah River, spawns in April and early May (Bennett and McFarlane, 1983).

Protracted and/or multiple spawning occurs in a number of the more abundant species. Protracted spawning within the Atchafalaya Basin Floodway has been reported for *Lepisosteus oculatus, Cyprinus carpio, Lepomis macrochirus,* and *L. microlophus.* Elsewhere in the Gulf states, *Hybognathus nuchalis, Notemigonus chrysoleucas, Notropis atherinoides, N. blennius,* red shiner (*N. lutrensis*), bluntnose minnow (*Pimephales notatus*), *Gambusia affinis,* and inland silverside (*Menidia beryllina*) probably spawn from spring through summer and even into autumn (Cook, 1959; Lee et al., 1980).

Delayed or protracted spawning may favor some species during years in which overbank flooding is reduced. For instance, Bryan and Sabins (1979) reported that *Micropterus salmoides* and *Pomoxis nigromaculatus,* which were abundant during 1975 to 1976, declined substantially during the reduced flow conditions of 1977. Both of these species make extensive use of swamps, bayous, and overflow habitats, and both are spring spawners (Bryan et al., 1975). In contrast, *Lepomis macrochirus,* which is a protracted spawner, increased in abundance during 1977 (Bryan and Sabins, 1979).

COMMUNITIES OF AQUATIC LIFE

Functional Relationships
Trophic support for aquatic production in the Atchafalaya Basin Floodway comes primarily from allochthonous organic matter. Input of this allochthonous organic matter occurs primarily during overbank flooding and is achieved by consumption within the seasonally inundated habitats and transport of detritus and DOC to permanent aquatic habitats. The magnitude and timing of this input varies with variations in the extent, duration, and timing of overbank flooding. In years with less extensive flooding, inputs from the bottomland hardwood swamps (including the herbaceous vegetation) will be sharply reduced. Moreover, seasonal flooding enhances the production of terrestrial vegetation, which in turn enhances potential inputs in following years. In years with shorter flooding duration, floodplain colonizers (e.g., zooplankton, crayfish, and juvenile fishes) may either have insufficient time to mature or become stranded. The timing of overbank flooding also influences organic matter inputs and consumer production. Spawning and development in fish and invertebrates are typically temperature mediated. As such, many taxons may be unable to capitalize on floodplain inundation if it occurs too early or too late.

Allochthonous inputs originating from overflow habitats are available in the form of detritus and leached DOC. Allochthonous, free-living bacteria may also be important, as they are in the Ogeechee River in Georgia. In any case, overflow habitats host substantial zooplankton, crayfish, and fish populations. Crayfish, especially *Procambarus clarkii* and *Cambarellus* spp., are probably the most important consumers of larger detritus. Zooplankton, including Ostracoda, Cladocera, Rotifera, and Copepoda, probably feed on fine detritus, free-living bacteria, and bacteriophagous protozoans.

Zooplankton in overflow habitats provide significant trophic support for fish nurseries. Copepods and cladocerans were important prey items for larval *Lepomis gulosus* and *Pomoxis nigromaculatus,* larval and juvenile *Micropterus salmoides,* and juvenile *Ictalurus punctatus* (Clary, 1985; Levine, 1977;

Pollard et al., 1981). Ontogenic diet shifts have been reported for the three centrarchids. To a large measure this shift is an increase in prey size corresponding to an increase in fish size. For instance, larval *Lepomis gulosus* and *Pomoxis nigromaculatus* first fed on small copepod nauplii and copepodites, then shifted to larger prey (i.e., Cladocera) as they matured (Clary, 1985). Juvenile *Micropterus salmoides* 20 to 40 mm in length fed primarily on planktonic crustaceans (copepods and cladocerans) and small pelagic insects (e.g., Diptera). As they matured, they shifted away from entomostracans and toward Hemiptera and small fish, especially *Gambusia affinis* (Levine, 1977).

Studies of young-of-the-year (YOY) *Micropterus salmoides* in the Fordoche area demonstrate the interaction of fish growth, habitat availability, and ontogenic diet shifts. Copepoda and Cladocera were the predominant prey items for YOY during April, May, and June, but there was a sudden shift to *Palaemonetes kadiakensis* and small fishes during July and August. Significantly, YOY were concentrated in overflow habitats (especially edge sites) from April through June, but receding waters forced them into a nearby canal during July and August. Growth certainly facilitated the shift from entomostracans to larger prey, but the suddenness of the diet shift suggests other factors. Indeed, entomostracans virtually disappeared from their diet once the overflow habitats were vacated (Pollard et al., 1981). Several studies (e.g., Bryan et al., 1975; Clary, 1985; Pollard et al., 1981) have indicated that zooplankton are plentiful in other habitats (i.e., canals and distributaries) as well, but they are probably more easily taken in the reduced currents and shallower depths of overflow habitats (Clary, 1985).

Feeding or probable feeding on zooplankton by a number of other fishes, which frequent overflow habitats, have been reported from other localities. These include immature *Lepisosteus oculatus,* and *Dorosoma* spp., as well as immature and/or mature *Cyprinus carpio, Notemigonus chrysoleucas, Notropis atherinoides, N. blennius,* mimic shiner (*N. volucellus*), *Fundulus olivaceus, Gambusia affinis, Labidesthes sicculus, Menidia beryllina,* flier (*Centrarchus macropterus*), *Elassoma zonatum, Mugil cephalus,* and *Etheostoma* spp. (Bennett and McFarlane, 1983; Lee et al., 1980; Pfleiger, 1975).

Other items are important diet components for fish frequenting overflow habitats. One of the most important inhabitants of overflow habitats, *Procambarus clarkii,* has been recorded in the diet of several of the larger fishes, including *Lepisosteus oculatus, Amia calva, Ictalurus furcatus, I. natalis, Lepomis gulosus, Micropterus salmoides,* and *Pomoxis nigromaculatus* (Bryan et al., 1975).

Amphipods, dipterans, and hemipterans were important prey for immature *I. punctatus* and *M. salmoides* (Levine, 1977). Insects, amphipods, and isopods are also probably important prey items for other fishes, including *Ictiobus bubalus, Gambusia affinis, Menidia beryllina, Centrarchus macropterus,* and *Etheostoma* spp. In addition, detritus in overflow habitats may be eaten by a number of other fishes, including river carpsucker (*Carpiodes cyprinus*), *I. bubalus,* and *Cyprinus carpio* (Lee et al., 1980).

Aquatic macrophytes, which are concentrated in cypress–tupelo gum swamps, bayous, littoral zones of lakes, and some overflow habitats, provide the second major source of trophic support for primary consumers in the Atchafalaya Basin Floodway. Macrophytes such as water hyacinths support diverse and abundant invertebrate faunas, ranging from protozoans, rotifers, and entomostracans to isopods, amphipods, insects, shrimp, and crayfish. Many of these taxons feed directly on live tissue and/or macrophyte detritus. They may also feed on epiphytic microbial communities which are dependent on DOC exudates.

The benthic accumulations of autochthonous and allochthonous detritus that accumulate in cypress–tupelo gum swamps, bayous, and the littoral zones of lakes support a variety of deposit-feeding invertebrates (e.g., oligochaetes, isopods, amphipods, and chironomids), at least during high flow. These benthic invertebrates, together with epiphytic taxons, are important prey items for a variety of fishes. *Ictiobus* spp., *Cyprinus carpio, Pimephales notatus, P. vigilax, Ictalurus melas, I. natalis, I. punctatus,* spotted sunfish (*Lepomis punctatus*), and *Etheostoma* spp. are among the more abundant bottom feeders. Immature grass pickerel (*Esox americanus*), pirate perch (*Aphredoderus sayanus*), *Elassoma zonatum,* and *Lepomis macrochirus* are among the more abundant consumers of epiphytic invertebrates. A variety of surface-feeding fishes, including *Notemigonus chrysoleucas, Notropis atherinoides, N. emiliae, Labidesthes sicculus,* and *Gambusia affinis,* are also associated with macrophytes (Beck, 1977; Lee et al., 1980).

The macrophytes themselves probably provide either living or detrital food for some fishes, including *Ictiobus* spp., *Cyprinus carpio,* and *Pimephales notatus* (Lee et al., 1980; Pfleiger, 1975). Phytophagy is certainly exhibited by the grass carp (*Ctenopharyngodon idella*), which has been introduced into a number of North American localities to control aquatic weeds. A small but apparently viable population exists in the Atchafalaya Basin (Fremling et al., 1989). Algae may also be important for some fishes. For instance, *P. vigilax* was found to feed on benthic diatoms and filamentous blue-green algae, as well as benthic invertebrates (Levine, 1977).

Suspended POM originating from overflow habitats and macrophyte beds provides a potentially very important source of trophic support for filter feeders. The Atchafalaya does not exhibit the productive assemblage of net-spinning caddisflies (e.g., Hydropsychidae) that characterizes many other rivers, including the Lower Mississippi. This may, to some extent, be the result of sampling bias, since snags and drift samples were not taken. In any case, filter-feeding fingernail clams (Sphaeriidae) were extremely abundant in cypress–tupelo gum swamps, bayous, and lakes. Other filter-feeding bivalves were also recorded. *Corbicula fluminea* were abundant in the sandy sediments of at least one canal site. Freshwater mussels (Unionidae) were noted in riverine sites, although their abundance is uncertain (Beck, 1977). Sphaeriidae were important prey for *Lepomis microlophus* (Bryan et al., 1974, 1975) and may have also been important for *Aplodinotus grunniens.*

Filter feeding is probably important for zooplankton, which are found in a variety of permanent habitats. Entomostracans were most abundant during high flows (Bryan et al., 1975), which suggests that they were strongly dependent on allochthonous detritus. On the other hand, seasonality was not pronounced for rotifers (Holland, 1977). Increases in zooplankton may also follow low-flow phytoplankton blooms in some lentic habitats. In any case, open-water zooplankton and/or phytoplankton are consumed by a number of fishes, including *Brevoortia patronus,* immature *Dorosoma cepedianum, D. petenense, Anchoa mitchilli, Menidia beryllina,* and *Mugil cephalus* (Deegan and Thompson, 1985; Lee et al., 1980). Planktivorous *Polydon spathula* may be abundant in the main channel (Bryan et al., 1975).

Drifting and terrestrial invertebrates (e.g., amphipods and insects) are important prey items for a variety of midwater or surface-swimming fishes common to main-channel and distributary habitats. Skipjack herring (*Alosa chrysochloris*), goldeye (*Hiodon alosoides*), and *Notropis blennius* are three surface and midwater feeders that are largely restricted to riverine habitats. Several of the planktivores (e.g., *Anchoa mitchilli, Menidia beryllina,* and *Mugil cephalus*) as well as some of those commonly associated with macrophytes (e.g., *Notropis atherinoides*) may also feed on insects and amphipods (Bryan et al., 1975; Lee et al., 1980; Pfleiger, 1975).

Investigations of the main channel and distributaries indicated that these habitats contain modest populations of benthic invertebrates. Some deposit-feeding oligochaetes and chironomids were concentrated in shallow areas, while relatively high densities of two mayflies, *Tortopus* sp. and *Pentagenia vittigera,* burrowed into hard clay (Beck, 1977; Bryan et al., 1974).

Nonetheless, these riverine habitats support an abundant assemblage of bottom feeders. *Scaphyrhynchus platorynchus,* adult *Dorosoma cepedianum, Ictalurus furcatus, I. punctatus, Pylodictis olivaris, Aplodinotus grunniens,* and *Paralichthys lethostigma* are some of the more common large bottom feeders. *Hybopsis aestivalis* and *H. storeriana* are two common cyprinid bottom feeders. In addition, the main channel and distributaries host significant populations of several other shiners, including blackspot shiner (*Notropis atrocaudalis*), ghost shiner (*N. buchanani*), chub shiner (*N. potteri*), *N. shumardi,* and blacktail shiner (*N. venustus*). Diet information for these shiners is very limited, but some may also be bottom feeders.

Riverine habitats also support large populations of river shrimp (*Macrobrachium ohione*). Diet studies on these highly mobile shrimps are limited, but they apparently feed on both plant and animal material (Truesdale and Mermilliod, 1979). It may be that they, as well as some of the fishes, compensate for the unproductive benthos by foraging over large areas. In any case, *M. ohione* is an important prey for several fishes, including *Pylodictis olivaris, Pomoxis annularis, Morone chrysops,* and *Paralichthys lethostigma* (Bryan et al., 1974, 1975). *Callinectes sapidus* also feeds on *M. ohione* (Truesdale and Mermilliod, 1979).

Piscivory features prominently in most of the larger fishes. In some cases (e.g., *Morone chrysops* and *Paralichthys lethostigma*), the piscivores appear to depend primarily on prey located in riverine and lake habitats. Several piscivores (i.e., *Ictalurus furcatus, I. natalis, I. punctatus, L. gulosus,* and *Pomoxis nigromaculatus*), however, move into the more productive swamp, bayou, and/or overflow habitats during high water to feed on crayfish (especially, *Procambarus clarkii*). Declining water quality forces them to vacate these habitats during low water. They then move into lake and riverine habitats and feed on fish and/or *Macrobrachium ohione.* Two large air-breathing carnivores, *Lepisosteus oculatus* and *Amia calva,* are able to forage for crayfish in swamp and bayou habitats during low water (Bryan et al., 1974, 1975).

Structure of Aquatic Communities
The Atchafalaya River receives its flow from the Mississippi River and the Red River. As a result, the fauna and flora of this river are largely determined by the species in these two rivers and the connected swamps and waterways. Also, the species that are adapted to the special conditions existing in the Atchafalaya River may have invaded through the air or by animals such as birds or by other means. A few species may have come into the fresh waters from the Gulf. These would be species with a wide tolerance level to salinity and might be able to survive in certain parts of the Atchafalaya River.

In describing the structure of the various types of aquatic communities in the Atchafalaya River, I have considered the structure of those communities that might be in the river channel proper. In the lower reaches, the Atchafalaya River becomes a complex system of rivers, bayous, lakes, and human-made canals. Therefore, it would be very difficult in these areas to separate out the various types of communities of aquatic life without intensive study. It is for this reason that I have confined my studies to associations that one might find in the channel proper particularly associated with vegetation or in lentic or lotic habitats.

The Mississippi River is sometimes referred to as the Old River. Waters from sources other than the Mississippi River and Red River, such as the swamps and the Black River, may also enter the Atchafalaya River. Much of the aquatic life has been obtained by collecting plankton. However, it is very evident that these species are not truly planktonic forms, but rather, they are characteristic of lotic or lentic habitats or from vegetation. We have searched the literature to find the true habitat of these species and have constructed the communities of aquatic life with this knowledge.

The banks of the Atchafalaya channel may be covered with vegetation, and in the shallow waters a considerable number of species of aquatic plants may be found (Table 2.14). These plants form the vegetative habitats which support their own ecosystem, as will be described. Behind the immediate banks are swamplike areas with varying amounts of water. Their conductivity and oxygen content values are often much lower than those of the channel proper. The fauna and flora in these areas are typically what one would find in a swamp.

(text continues on page 244)

TABLE 2.14. *Species List: Atchafalaya River*

| | | Substrate[a] | | |
| | | Lentic | Lotic | |
Taxon	V	M,S	G,R	Source[b]
SUPERKINGDOM PROKARYOTAE				
KINGDOM MONERA				
Division Cyanophycota				
Class Cyanophyceae				
Order Chroococcales				
Family Chroococcaceae				
Agmenellum sp.		X		s
Anacystis sp.		X		s
Aphanocapsa elachista		X		p
Aphanocapsa sp.	X	X		p
Coccochloris sp.				s
Gomphosphaeria sp.	X	X		s
Merismopedia punctata		X		p
M. tenuissima		X		p
Microcystis incerta		X		p
Microcystis sp.		X		p
Order Nostocales				
Family Nostocaceae				
Anabaena sp.	X	X	X	p
Anabaenopsis raciborskii				p
Aphanizomenon flos-aquae	X			p
Nostoc sp.	X	X		s
Family Oscillatoriaceae				
Lyngbya sp.		X	X	s,p
Oscillatoria amphibia		X	X	p
O. limnetica		X	X	p
O. splendida		X		p
Oscillatoria sp.		X	X	s,p
Phormidium sp.			X	s,p
Raphidiopsis curvata				p
Spirulina sp.	X	X		s
Family Rivulariaceae				
Rivularia sp.	X		X	p
SUPERKINGDOM EUKARYOTAE				
KINGDOM PLANTAE				
Subkingdom Thallobionta				
Division Chlorophycota				
Class Chlorophyceae				
Order Tetrasporales				
Family Palmellaceae				
Elakatothrix gelatinosa				p
Gloeocystis planctonica				p
Sphaerocystis? shroeteri				p

Continued

TABLE 2.14.   (Continued)

Taxon	Substrate[a]			Source[b]
		Lentic	Lotic	
	V	M,S	G,R	
Family Tetrasporaceae				
Schizochlamys delicatula				p
Order Chlorococcales				
Family Characiaceae				
Schroeteria sp.				s
Family Coelastraceae				
Coelastrum cambricum var. intermedium	X	X		p
C. microsporum	X	X		p
C. sphaericum	X	X		p
Family Hydrodictyaceae				
*Pediastrum biradiatum	X	X		p
*P. boryanum	X	X		p
*P. duplex	X	X		p
*P. duplex var. clathratum	X	X		p
*P. tetras	X	X		p
*Pediastrum spp.			X	s,p
Family Micratiniaceae				
Golenkinia sp.				s
Family Oocystaceae				
*Ankistrodesmus convolutus?	X	X		p
*A. falcatus	X	X		p
*A. falcatus var. mirabilis	X	X		p
Ankistrodesmus spp.		X		s,p
Botryococcus sp.				s
Chlorella sp.				s,p
Closteridium sp.				s
Dactylococcopsis irregularis				p
Dictosphaerium pulchellum		X		p
Dictosphaerium sp.		X		s
Franceia droescheri				p
*Kirchneriella linearis	X	X		p
Kirchneriella sp.	X	X		s
Lagerheimia sp.				s
Oocystis borgei				p
O. cirtiformis				p
O. pusilla				p
Oocystis spp.				s,p
Schroederia setigera				p
*Selenastrum sp.			X	s
Tetraedon minimum				p
T. regulare var. granulata				p
T. trigonum				p
T. trigonum var. gracile				p
T. tumidulum				p
Tetraedon sp.				s
Trochiscia sp.				s

TABLE 2.14. *(Continued)*

Taxon	V	Lentic M,S	Lotic G,R	Source[b]
Family Scenedesmaceae				
Actinastrum hantzschii	X	X		p
A. hantzschii var. *fluviatile*	X	X		p
Actinastrum sp.	X	X		s,p
Crucigenia apiculata	X	X		p
C. crucifera	X	X		p
C. fenestrata	X	X		p
C. quadrata	X	X		p
C. tetrapedia	X	X		p
Crucigenia spp.	X	X		s,p
Micractinium pusillum				p
Scenedesmus abundans	X	X		p
S. acuminatus	X	X		p
S. acutus	X	X		p
S. bicaudatus	X			p
S. bijuga	X	X		p
S. bijuga var. *flexuosa*	X	X		p
S. bijuga f. *irregularis*	X	X		p
S. denticulatus	X	X		p
S. dimorphus	X	X		p
S. intermedius	X	X		p
S. intermedius var. *bicaudatus*	X	X		p
S. ovalternus	X	X		p
S. protuberans	X	X		p
S. quadricaudata	X	X		p
S. raciborskii f. *granulatus*	X	X		p
Scenedesmus spp.	X	X		s,p
Tetrastrum elegans				p
T. staurogeniaeforme				p
Tetrastrum sp.				s
Order Oedogoniales				
Family Oedogoniaceae				
Bulbochaete sp.	X		X	s
Order Zygnematales				
Family Desmidiaceae				
Closterium kutzingii	X	X		p
Closterium sp.	X	X		s,p
Cosmarium sp.	X	X		s
Euastrum sp.	X	X		s
Hyalotheca sp.	X	X		s
Micrasterias sp.	X	X		s
Phymatodocis sp.	X	X		s
Pleurataenium sp.	X	X		s
Staurastrum sp.	X	X		s

Continued

TABLE 2.14.   (*Continued*)

Taxon	V	Lentic M,S	Lotic G,R	Source[b]
Family Mesotaeniaceae				
Mesotaenium sp.	X	X		s
Netrium sp.	X			s
Spirotaenia sp.	X	X		s
Family Zygnemataceae				
Mougeotia sp.	X	X	X	p
Spirogyra sp.	X	X	X	s
Division Chromophycota				
Class Bacillariophyceae				
Order Eupodiscales				
Family Coscinodiscaceae				
Centritractus sp.		X		s
Coscinodiscus lacustris		X		p
C. rothii var. subsalsa		X		p
Coscinodiscus sp.		X		s
Cyclotella bodanica		X		p
C. glomerata		X		p
C. menenghiniana	X	X	X	p
C. michiganiana			X	p
Cyclotella sp.			X	s,p
Melosira distans	X	X	X	p
M. granulata	X	X	X	p
M. granulata var. angustissima			X	p
M. granulata var. angustissima f. spiralis			X	p
M. islandica	X			p
M. italica			X	p
M. varians	X	X	X	p
Melosira spp.	X	X		p,s
Ophiocytium sp.				s
Skeletonema potamos				p
Stephanodiscus astraea	X	X	X	p
S. niagarae	X	X	X	p
Stephanodiscus spp.	X	X		s,p
Order Biddulphiales				
Family Chaetoceraceae				
Atteya sp.				s
Order Fragilariales				
Family Fragilariaceae				
Asterionella formosa	X	X		p
A. formosa var. gracillima	X	X		p
Diatoma vulgare	X	X	X	p
Fragilaria crotonensis	X		X	p
Fragilaria sp.	X		X	s
Meridion sp.	X	X	X	s
Synedra acus	X		X	p
S. ulna	X	X	X	p
Synedra spp.	X	X		s,p
Tabellaria fenestrata	X	X	X	p

TABLE 2.14. *(Continued)*

Taxon	V	Lentic M,S	Lotic G,R	Source[b]
Order Eunotiales				
Family Eunotiaceae				
Eunotia curvata	X		X	p
Eunotia sp.	X			p
Order Achnanthales				
Family Achnanthaceae				
Achnanthes lanceolata var. *dubia*	X	X	X	p
Achnanthes sp.	X		X	s,p
Cocconeis placentula	X	X	X	p
C. placentula var. *euglypta*	X	X	X	p
*Cocconeis spp.	X		X	s,p
Order Naviculales				
Family Cymbellaceae				
*Amphora sp.	X	X		s
Cymbella turgida	X	X	X	p
Cymbella spp.	X			s,p
Family Gomphonemaceae				
Gomphonema angustatum	X	X	X	p
G. angustatum var. producta	X			p
G. olivaceum	X	X	X	p
G. parvulum	X	X	X	p
*Gomphonema spp.	X	X		s,p
Family Naviculaceae				
Anemoeoneis sp.				
Gyrosigma kutzingii	X	X	X	p
G. scalproides		X	X	p
Gyrosigma spp.				s,p
Mastogloia braunii	X	X		p
Navicula exigua	X	X	X	p
N. radiosa	X		X	p
N. vulpina	X		X	p
Navicula spp.				s,p
*Pinnularia sp.		X	X	s
Pleurosigma delicatulum	X	X		p
Stauroneis sp.				p
Order Epithemialea				
Family Epithemiaceae				
Epithemia turgida	X		X	p
Order Bacillariales				
Family Nitzschiaceae				
Hantzschia amphioxys	X	X	X	p
Nitzschia acicularis	X	X		p
N. actinastroides	X	X		p
N. angustata	X	X		p

Continued

TABLE 2.14.   (*Continued*)

Taxon	V	Lentic M,S	Lotic G,R	Source[b]
		Substrate[a]		
Family Nitzschiaceae (*cont.*)				
N. filiformis	X	X		p
N. holsatica			X	p
N. palea	X	X	X	p
N. paradoxa	X	X		p
N. reversa?	X	X		p
N. sigmoidea	X	X	X	p
N. tryblionella var. levidensis	X	X	X	p
Nitzschia spp.				s,p
Order Surirellales				
Family Surirellaceae				
Surirella linearis	X	X		p
S. ovata	X	X		p
Surirella spp.	X	X		s,p
Class Dinophyceae				
Order Gymnodiniales				
Family Gymnodiniaceae				
Gymnodinium albulum			X	p
G. ordinatum			X	p
Gymnodinium sp.			X	s
Order Peridinales				
Family Ceratiaceae				
Ceratium hirundinella			X	p
f. brachyceras				
Family Glenodiniaceae				
Glenodinium oculatum			X	p
Glenodinium sp.			X	s
Subkingdom Embryobionta				
Division Filicophyta				
Class Filicopsida				
Order Salviniales				
Family Azollaceae				
Azolla carolinia	X			H
Division Magnoliophyta				
Class Dicotyledoneae				
Order Nymphaeales				
Family Cambombaceae				
Brasenia schreberi	X	X		M
Cabomba caroliniana	X	X		M,b,s
Family Ceratophyllaceae				
Ceratophyllum demersum		X		M,b,H,s
Family Nelumbonaceae				
Nelumbo lutea	X	X		M
Family Nymphaeaceae				
Nymphaea mexicana	X	X		M
Nymphaea sp.	X	X		H,s

TABLE 2.14.   (Continued)

Taxon	V	Substrate[a] Lentic M,S	Lotic G,R	Source[b]
Order Ranunculales				
Family Ranunculaceae				
*Ranunculus sp.	X	X		b
Order Caryophyllales				
Family Amarnathaceae				
*Alternanthera philoxeroides	X	X		M,H
Order Polygonales				
Family Polygonaceae				
*Polygonum spp.	X	X		H
Order Salicales				
Family Salicaceae				
Salix nigra	X	X		b,s
Order Primulales				
Family Primulaceae				
*Hottonia inflata	X	X		M
Order Haloragales				
Family Haloragaceae				
*Myriophyllum brasiliense	X	X		M
(= M. aquaticum?)				
*M. exalbescens	X	X		M
M. heterophylum	X	X		M
*M. pinnatum	X	X		M
M. spicatum	X	X		M
Myriophyllum sp.	X	X		
*Prosperpinaca palustris		X		M
Order Myrtales				
Family Onagraceae				
*Ludwigia spp.		X		
Order Apiales				
Family Apiaceae				
(= Umbelliferaceae)				
Hydrocotyl spp.	X	X		
Order Scrophulariales				
Family Lentibulariaceae				
*Utricularia biflora	X	X		M
*U. foliosa	X	X		M
*U. gibba	X	X		M
*U. vulgaris	X	X		M
Family Scrophulariaceae				
Bacopa sp.		X		H
Class Monocotyledoneae				
Order Alismales				
Family Alismaceae				
*Sagittaria calycina	X	X		M
*S. falcata	X	X		M

Continued

TABLE 2.14. (*Continued*)

Taxon	V	Lentic M,S	Lotic G,R	Source[b]
Family Alismaceae (*cont.*)				
*S. latifolia	X	X		M
S. platyphylla	X	X		M
Sagittaria spp.	X	X		H
Order Hydrocharitales				
Family Hydrocharitaceae				
Egeria densa	X	X		M
*Hydrilla verticillata	X	X		M
Limnobium spongia	X	X		M,C
Vallisneria americana	X	X		M,h,s
Order Najadales				
Family Najadaceae				
*Najas guadalupensis	X	X		M
*Najas sp.	X	X		
Family Potamogetonaceae				
Potamogeton spp.	X	X		
Order Arales				
Family Araceae				
*Pistia stratiotes	X	X		M
Family Lemnaceae				
*Lemna minor	X	X	X	C
Lemna spp.			X	
Spirodela polyrrhiza			X	C
unident. spp.				
Order Juncales				
Family Juncaceae				
Juncus spp.	X	X		
Order Cyperales				
Family Cyperaceae				
*Eleocharis spp.	X	X		
Scirpus spp.	X	X		
Order Typhales				
Family Typhaceae				
*Typha spp.	X	X		
Order Iliales				
Family Pontederiaceae				
*Eichhornia crassipes	X	X		M,b,s,h
*Heterantheria dubia	X	X		M
*H. limosa	X	X		M
*H. reniformis	X	X		M
*Pontederia cordata	X	X		M
*Pontederia sp.	X	X		H

TABLE 2.14. *(Continued)*

Taxon	V	Lentic M,S	Lotic G,R	Source[b]
KINGDOM ANIMALIA				
Subkingdom Protozoa				
Class Mastigophora				
Order Chrysomonadida				
Family Chromulinidae				
Chrysococcus? rufescens				p
Mallomonas alpina				p
Mallomonas sp.				p
Family Ochromonadidae				
Dinobryon bavaricum	X			p
D. divergens	X			p
Dinobryon sp.	X			p
Family Syncryptidae				
Synura ulvella		X		p
Order Cryptomonadida				
Family Cryptomonadidae				
Chroomonas acuta		X		p
C. nordstedtii		X		p
Cryptomonas erosa	X			p
C. marssonii	X			p
C. reflexa	X			p
Order Phytomonadida				
Family Carteriidae				
Carteria cordiformis	X			p
Spermatozoopsis exultans	X			p
Family Chlamydomonadidae				
Chlamydomonas globosa	X	X		p
Chlamydomonas sp.	X	X		s,p
Family Phacotidae				
Pteromonas angulosa				p
P. cruciata				p
Family Volvocidae				
Pandorina morum		X		p
Volvox sp.		X		s,p
Order Euglenoidida				
Family Astasiidae				
Uroceolus sp.				s
Family Euglenidae				
Cryptoglena sp.				s
Euglena acus?	X	X		p
E. gracilis	X	X		p
E. oxyuris	X	X		p
E. oxyuris var. *minor*	X	X		p
E. tripteris	X	X		p
Euglena spp.	X	X	X	s,p

Continued

TABLE 2.14. (*Continued*)

Taxon	V	Lentic M,S	Lotic G,R	Source[b]
Family Euglenidae (*cont.*)				
Leplocinclis acuta		X		p
L. fusiformis		X		p
Leplocinclis spp.		X		s,p
Phacus acuminatus		X		p
P. anomalus		X		p
P. caudatus		X		p
P. curvicauda		X		p
P. helikoides		X		p
P. longicauda		X		p
P. megalopsis		X		p
P. nordstedtii		X		p
P. orbicularis		X		p
P. pleuronectes		X		p
P. pyrum		X		p
P. suecicus		X		p
P. tortus		X		p
P. trimarginatus		X		p
Phacus spp.		X		s,p
*Trachelomonas caudata?	X			p
*T. creba	X			p
*T. fluviatilis	X			p
*T. hispida	X			p
*T. intermedia	X			p
*T. lacustris	X			p
*T. planctonica	X			p
*T. pulcherrima	X			p
*T. rotundata	X			p
*T. schaunislandii	X			p
*T. sparse-setulosa?	X			p
*T. urceolata	X			p
*T. verrucosa	X			p
*T. volvocina	X			p
*Trachelomonas spp.	X			s,p
Class Sarcodina				
Order Amoebida				
Family Amoebidae				
*Astramoeba sp.	X			
Order Testacida				
Family Arcellidae				
*Arcella dentata	X	X		
*Arcella sp.	X	X		
Family Difflugiidae				
*Centrophyxis sp.	X	X		
unident. spp.	X	X		

TABLE 2.14. (*Continued*)

Taxon	V	Lentic M,S	Lotic G,R	Source[b]
Class Ciliata				
Order Hymenostomatida				
Family Parameciidae				
Paramecium sp.		X	X	s
Order Peritrichida				
Family Epistylidae				
Epistylis sp.	X	X	X	s,a
Opercularis sp.		X	X	s
Family Ophrydiidae				
Ophrydium sp.			X	s
Family Scyphiidae				
Scyphidia sp.	X			b
Family Vaginicollidae				
Platycola sp.		X	X	s
Pyxicola sp.		X	X	s
Vaginicola sp.		X	X	s
Family Vorticellidae				
Charchesium sp.			X	s
Vorticella sp.	X		X	s,a
Zoothamnium sp.			X	s
unident. spp.		X		b
Class Suctoria				
Order Suctorida				
Family Acinetidae				
Tokophyra sp.	X			
Subkingdom Parazoa				
Phylum Porifera				
Class Demospongiae				
Order Haplosclerida				
Family Spongillidae				
Corvospongilla sp.		X	X	b
Eunapius fragilis	X	X	X	b,s
Spongilla ingloviformis		X	X	b,s
Spongilla spp.		X	X	s
Trochospongilla horrida			X	b
T. leidyi	X	X	X	b
unident. spp.				b
Subkingdom Eumetazoa				
Phylum Cnidaria				
Class Hydrozoa				
Order Hydroida				
Family Clavidae				
Cordylophora lacustris		X		b,s

Continued

TABLE 2.14. *(Continued)*

Taxon	V	Lentic M,S	Lotic G,R	Source[b]
Family Hydridae				
*Chlorohydra viridis		X	X	s
*Hydra americana	X	X	X	b,s
*Hydra sp.	X		X	
Phylum Platyhelminthes				
Class Turbellaria				
Order Tricladida				
Family Planariidae				
*Dugesia tigrina	X	X	X	b,s
*Phagocita vellata	X	X	X	s
Order Catenulida				
Family Catenulidae				
*Catenula sp.		X	X	s
Order Neorhabdocoela				
Family Typhloplanidae				
*unident. spp.			X	s
Order Rhabdocela				
Family Macrostomidae				
*Macrostomum sp.	X	X		b
Phylum Nemertea				
Class Enopla				
Order Hoplonemertea				
*Prostoma rubrum	X			b
Phylum Gastrochricha				
unident. spp.	X		X	s,a
Phylum Rotifera				
Class Digonota				
Order Bdelloidea				
Family Philodonidae				
Philodina spp.	X	X	X	h
Class Monogononta				
Order Ploima				
Family Asplanchnidae				
Asplanchina sp.	X	X		h,a
Family Brachionidae				
*Brachionus angularis	X	X		h,a
*B. bidentata	X	X		h
*B. budapestinensis	X	X		h,a
*B. calyciflorus	X	X		h
*B. caudatus	X	X		h,a
*B. c. perdonatus	X	X		a
*B. c. vulatus	X	X		a
*B. falcatus	X	X		h
*B. havanaensis	X	X		h,a
*B. patulus	X	X		h,a
*B. patulus f. macrocanthus	X	X		h,a

TABLE 2.14. *(Continued)*

Taxon	V	Lentic M,S	Lotic G,R	Source[b]
Family Brachionidae *(cont.)*				
B. quadridentata	X	X		h,a
B. rubens	X	X		h
B. urceolaris	X			h,a
B. zahniseri	X			h,a
Kellicottia bostoniensis	X			h,a
K. longispina	X			h
Keratella cochlearis	X	X		h,a
K. c. f. tecta	X	X		h
K. crassa	X	X		h
K. earlinae	X	X		h
K. mixta	X	X		h
K. quadrata	X	X		h,a
K. reticulata	X	X		
K. serratula	X	X		h
K. valga	X	X		h,a
Notholca acuminata	X	X		h,a
Notholca sp.	X	X		h
Platyais quadridentata	X	X		h,a
Family Colurellidae				
Colurella spp.	X	X		h
Lepadella ovalis	X	X		h
Family Euchlanidae				
Beauchampiella eudactylotum	X	X		H
Dipleuchlanis propatula	X	X		h
Euchlanis spp.	X	X		h,a
Family Gastropodidae				
Ascomorpha sp.	X	X		H
Gastropus hyptopus	X	X		h
G. minor	X	X		h
G. stylifer	X	X		h
Gastropus sp.	X	X		h
Family Lecanidae				
Lecane curvicornis	X	X		h
L. hastata	X	X		h
L. leontina	X	X		h
L. ludwigi	X	X		h
L. luna	X	X		h
L. ohionensis	X			a
Lecane spp.	X	X		H,a
Monostyla (= Lecane?) bulba	X	X		h,a
M. (= Lecane?) cornuta	X			h
M. (= Lecane?) quadridentata	X	X		h
M. (= Lecane?) spp.	X	X		h,a

Continued

TABLE 2.14.   (*Continued*)

Taxon	V	M,S	G,R	Source[b]
Substrate[a]		*Lentic*	*Lotic*	
Family Mytilinidae				
Mytilina sp	X	X		h,a
Family Notommatidae				
*Cephalodella spp.	X	X		h,a
*Scaridium longicaudatum	X	X		h
Family Synchaetidae				
*Pleosoma sp.	X	X		h
*Polyarthra euryptera	X			h
P. major		X		
*P. vulgaris	X			h
Polyarthra spp.		X		h,a
Synchaeta pectinata		X		h
S. stylata		X		h
Synchaeta spp.		X	X	h
Family Tricocercidae				
*Tricocerca cylindrica	X	X	X	h
*T. longiseta	X	X	X	h
*T. multicrinis	X	X	X	h
*T. porcellus		X	X	h
*T. similis		X	X	h
*Tricocerca spp.		X	X	
Family Tricotridae				
*Tricotria tetracitis	X	X		h,a
Order Collotheceae				
Family Collothecidae				
*Collotheca baltonica	X			
*Collotheca sp.	X			h,a
Order Flosculariacea				
Family Conochilidae				
*Conochiloides spp.	X	X		h
*Conochilus spp.	X	X		H,a
Family Hexarthridae				
Hexarthra mira	X			h
Hexarthra sp.	X			
Family Testudinellidae				
Filinia brachiata	X			h
F. longiseta	X			h,a
F. opoliensis	X			h
Pompholyx sp.	X			h
Testudinella mucronata	X			
T. patina	X			h,a
Trochosphaera solstitialis	X	X		
Phylum Nemata				
Class Adenophorea				
**unident. spp.	X	X	X	b,s

TABLE 2.14. *(Continued)*

Taxon	V	Lentic M,S	Lotic G,R	Source[b]
Phylum Mollusca				
Class Gastropoda				
Order Mesogastropoda				
Family Hydrobiidae				
*Amnicola sp.		X		s
*Clappia sp.	X	X	X	b,s
*Littoridina sp.	X	X	X	b,s
*Lyogyrus sp.		X		b,s
*Paludestrina sp.		X		b,s
*Somatogyrus sp.	X	X		b,s
*Vioscalba louisianae	X	X	X	b
*unident. spp.	X			
Family Pleuroceridae				
*Goniobasis sp.	X	X		s
Family Viviparidae				
Viviparus sp.	X			b,s
Order Basommatophora				
Family Ancylidae				
*Ferrissia sp.	X	X		b,s,a
*Laevipex sp.	X			b,s
Family Lymnaeidae				
*Lymnaea sp.	X	X	X	b,s
*Pseudosuccinea sp.	X	X		b,s
Family Physidae				
*Physa sp.	X	X	X	b,s,a
Family Planorbidae				
*Gyraulus sp.	X	X	X	b,a
*Helisoma sp.	X	X		b,a
Planorbella sp.	X			
*Promenetus sp.		X		b
Promenetus × Micromenentes sp.	X			a
Class Bivalvia				
Order Unionoida				
Family Unionidae				
*Anodonta sp.		X	X	b,s
*Leptodea sp.		X	X	b,s
*Quadrula quadrula		X	X	b,s
unident. spp.		X		b
Order Veneroida				
Family Corbiculidae				
*Corbicula manilensis	X	X	X	b,s
(= C. fluminea?)				
Family Sphaeriidae				
*Eupera cubensis	X	X		b,s
*Pisidium casternatum		X		s

Continued

TABLE 2.14.   (Continued)

Taxon	V	Lentic M,S	Lotic G,R	Source[b]
Family Sphaeriidae (*cont.*)				
Pisidium sp.		X		b
Sphaerium corneum		X		b,s
S. partumeum		X		b,s
S. securis		X		b,s
S. (= Musculum?) transversum		X		b,s
Sphaerium sp.	X	X	X	b,s
Phylum Annelida				
Class Hirudinoidea				
Order Rhynchobdellida				
Family Glossiphoniidae				
Batracobdella sp.		X		b
Glossiphonia heteroclita	X	X		b
Helobdella elongata		X	X	b
H. fusca	X	X		b
H. lineata	X	X		b
H. stagnalis		X		b,s
Helobdella sp.				s
Oculobdella lucida		X		s
Placobdella multilineata	X			b
P. papillifera		X	X	b
P. parasitica	X	X		b,s
Placobdella sp.				s
Family Piscicolidae				
*unident. spp.	X	X		b,s
Order Pharyngobdellida				
Family Erpobdellidae				
Mooreobdella microstoma	X	X		b
unident. spp.				s
Family Hirudinidae				
Macrobdella ditetra	X	X	X	b
Philobdella sp.		X	X	b,s
Class Oligochaeta				
Order Lumbriculida				
Family Lumbriculidae				
*unident. spp.		X		b,s
Order Haplotaxida				
Family Glossoscolecidae				
*unident. spp.		X		b,s
Family Naididae				
Aulophorus furcatus	X			b
A. vagus	X			b
Dero digitata	X			b
D. limnosa	X			b,s
Dero sp.	X			b
Haemonais waldvogeli	X	X		b
Nais pseudotobtusa	X			b

TABLE 2.14. *(Continued)*

Taxon	V	Lentic M,S	Lotic G,R	Source[b]
Family Naididae (*cont.*)				
Pristina plumaseta	X			b
unident. spp.	X			
Family Tubificidae				
Aulodrilus americanus		X		b,s
A. pigueti	X	X		b,s
A. pluriseta		X		b,s
Branchiura sowerbyi		X		b,s
Ilyodrilus templetoni		X	X	b,s
Limnodrilus augustipennis		X	X	b,s
L. cervix		X	X	b,s
L. claparedeianus		X	X	
L. hoffmeisteri		X	X	b,s
L. profundicola		X	X	s
L. psammophilus		X	X	
Peloscolex ferox		X		s
P. freyi		X		
P. multisetosus		X	X	s
Potamothrix vedjovskyi		X		s
Tubifex newaensis		X	X	s
unident. spp.		X	X	b,s
Phylum Arthropoda				
Class Arachnida				
Order Acariformes				
Family Arrenuridae				
Arrenurus sp.	X	X	X	b,s,a
Family Diplodontidae				
Diplodontus despiciens	X	X	X	
Family Hydraphantidae				
Hydraphantes sp.	X			
Family Lebertidae				
Lebertia sp.	X			
Family Limnesiidae				
unident. spp.				s
Family Limnocharidae				s
unident. spp.				s
Family Mideidae × Mideopsidae				
unident. spp.	X		X	s,b
Family Unionicolidae				
Unionicola sp.	X			

Continued

TABLE 2.14. *(Continued)*

Taxon	V	Lentic M,S	Lotic G,R	Source[b]
Class Crustacea				
Subclass Cephalocarida				
(= Branchiopoda)				
Order Cladocera				
Family Bosminidae				
Bosmina longirostris	X			s,c,a
Eubosmina tubicen	X		X	s
Family Chydoridae				
Alona affinis	X			s
A. barbulata	X			s
A. circumfimbriata	X			s
*A. costata	X			s,a
A. eximia	X			s
A. globulosa	X			s
*A. guttata	X			s,a
*A. quadrangularis	X		X	s
*A. rectangularis	X			s,a
A. setulosa	X			s
Alona spp.	X			s
Alonella acutirostris	X			s
*A. diaphana	X			s,a
A. excisa	X			s,a
A. hamulata	X			s
Alonella spp.	X			s
Camptocercus c. f. rectirostris		X		s,a
Camptocercus spp.		X		
*Chydorus sphaericus	X	X	X	s,a
Chydorus spp.	X	X		
Dunhevedia serrata		X		s
Eurylona c. f. lammelatus		X		s
E. orientalis		X		s
*Kurzia latissima	X			s,a
*Leydigia acanthocercoides	X	X		s
*L. leydigia	X	X		s
*L. quadrangularis	X			
Oxyrella tenuicaudis		X		s
Pleuroxus denticulatus	X			s,a
P. hamulatus	X			s
*Pleuroxus sp.	X			a
Pseudochydorus globosus		X		s
Family Daphinidae				
Ceriodaphnia lacustris	X			s
C. laticaudata	X			s
C. megalops	X			s
C. pulchella	X			s
C. quadrangula	X			s

TABLE 2.14. *(Continued)*

Taxon	V	M,S	G,R	Source[b]
		Substrate[a]		
		Lentic	Lotic	
Family Daphinidae *(cont.)*				
C. reticulata	X			s
C. rigaudi	X			s
*Ceriodaphnia sp.	X			b,s
*Daphnia ambigua	X			s,c,a
D. catawba	X			s,c
D. laevis	X			s,c
D. longiremis	X			s
*D. parvula	X			s,c,a
D. pulex	X			s,c,a
D. retrocurva	X			s
D. schodleri	X			s
D. similis	X			s
*Daphnia sp.	X			b,s
Moina affinis	X			s
*M. brachiata gp.	X			s,a
M. macrocopa	X			s
M. micrura	X			s,a
*Scaphloleberis kingi	X			s,a
*Simocephalus expinosus	X			s,a
S. serrulatus	X			s,c,a
*S. vetulus	X	X		s,c
*Simocephalus spp.	X	X		
unident. spp.	X	X		
Family Holopedium				
Holopedium amazonicum				s
*unident. spp.	X			
Family Leptodoridae				
Leptodora kindtii		X		s
Family Macrothricidae				
Grimaldina brazzai		X		s
*Ilyocryptus sordidus	X	X		s
*I. spinifer	X	X		s,a
Macrothrix laticornis		X		s
Family Sididae				
Diaphanosoma brachyurum		X		s,c
D. leuchtenbergianum		X		s
Latona setifera		X		s
Latonopis occidentalis		X		s
*Pseudosida bidentata	X			s,a
*Sida crystallina	X			s,a
Sida sp.	X			
unident. spp.	X			

Continued

TABLE 2.14.　*(Continued)*

Taxon	V	Lentic M,S	Lotic G,R	Source[b]
Order Anastraca				
Family Artemiidae				
*Artemia salina	X			
Subclass Ostracoda				
Order Podocopina				
Family Cypridae				
*Cadona sp.		X	X	b,s
*Cypria sp.		X		b,s
Cypridopsis sp.		X		s
*Herpetocypris sp.	X	X	X	b,s
Ilyocypris sp.				
unident. spp.	X	X		
Family Cytheridae				
unident. spp.				s
Subclass Copepoda				
Order Calanoida				
Family Centropagidae				
*Osphranticum labronectum	X			s,a
Family Diaptomidae				
Diaptomus birgei	X			s
D. bougalusensis	X			
D. calvipes	X			s
D. clavipoides	X			s
D. dorsalis	X			s
D. louisianensis	X			s
D. mississippiensis	X			s
D. morrei	X			s
D. pallidus	X			s
D. pygmaeus	X			s
D. reighardi	X			s
D. sanguienus	X			s
D. saskatchewanensis	X			s
D. siciloides	X			s
D. sinuatus	X			s
D. virginiensis	X			s
*Diaptomus spp.	X			s,a
Leptodiaptomus sicilis		X		
Skiskodiaptomus reighardi		X		
Family Temoridae				
*Eurytemora affinis	X			
Order Harpacticoida				
Family Canthocamptidae				
Attheyella spp.		X		s
Canthocamptus rovertockeri		X		s
Canthocamptus spp.		X		s

TABLE 2.14. *(Continued)*

Taxon	V	Lentic M,S	Lotic G,R	Source[b]
Order Cyclopodia				
Family Cyclopodae				
*Acanthocyclops vernalis	X	X		
Cyclops bicuspidatus	X	X		s
C. b. lubbocki	X	X		s
C. b. thomasi	X	X		a
C. exilis	X	X		s
C. scutifer	X	X		s
C. thomasi	X	X		s
C. variacans ruebellas	X	X		s
*C. (= Acanthocyclops?) vernalis	X	X		s,a
*Ectocyclops phaleratus	X			
Eucyclops agilis		X		s,a
E. prionophorus		X		s
*E. speratus		X		s
Halicyclops spp.		X		s
*Macrocyclops albidus	X	X	X	
*M. ater	X			
M. distinctus	X			s
*Mesocyclops edax	X		X	
*M. fuscus	X			s
M. inversus	X			s
M. leuckarti	X			s,a
Orthocyclops modestus	X	X		s,a
Paracyclops fimbriatus	X	X		s
Tropocyclops prasinus	X	X		s,a
T. p. mexicanus	X	X		s
Family Ergasilidae				
Ergasilus chantauquaensis	X	X		s
Ergasilus spp.	X	X		s
Subclass Branchiura				
Order Arguloida				
Family Argulidae				
*Argulus spp.	X	X		b,s
Subclass Malacostraca				
Order Mysidacea				
Family Mysidae				
*Taphromysis louisianae	X	X		b,s
Order Isopoda				
Family Anthuridae				
*Cyanthura polita	X	X	X	b,s
Family Asellidae				
*Asellus laticaudatus	X	X		b,s
*A. obtusa	X	X		b,s

Continued

TABLE 2.14.   (*Continued*)

Taxon	V	Lentic M,S	Lotic G,R	Source[b]
Family Asellidae (*cont.*)				
Asellus sp.	X	X	X	b,s,a
Lirceus lineatus	X	X		
Lirceus sp.	X	X	X	b,s,a
unident. spp.		X		
Order Amphipoda				
Family Corophiidae				
Corophium lacustre	X	X	X	
Family Gammaridae				
Crangonyx pseudogracilis gr.	X	X		
Crangonyx sp.	X	X	X	
Gammarus fasciatus	X	X		s
G. tigrinus gr.	X	X	X	
Gammarus sp.	X	X		b,s,a
Synurella bifurca		X		s
unident. spp.		X		b
Family Talitridae				
Hyalella azteca	X	X	X	b,s,a
Order Decapoda				
Family Cambaridae				
Cambarellus puer		X		s
C. shufeldtii		X		s
Cambarellus sp.	X			a
Cambarus diogenes diogenes		X	X	s
Orconectes lancifer	X	X		b,s
O. palmeri longimanus	X	X		s
Procambarus acutus acutus		X	X	f,s
P. clarkii	X	X		f,b,s,a
Family Palaemonidae				
Macrobrachium ohione	X	X	X	b,s
Palaemonetes kadiakensis	X			b,s,a
Family Portunidae				
Callinectes sapidus		X	X	s
Class Insecta				
Order Collembola				
Family Entomobryidae				
unident. spp.		X	X	s
Family Hypogasturidae				
unident. spp.		X	X	s
Family Poduridae				
Podura aquatica			X	b
Family Smithuridae				
Smithurus sp.			X	b

TABLE 2.14.   *(Continued)*

Taxon	V	Lentic M,S	Lotic G,R	Source[b]
Order Odonata				
Suborder Zygoptera				
Family Coenagrionidae				
*Agrion (= Coenagrion?) sp.	X			b
*Amphiagrion saucium	X	X	X	b
*Anomalagrion hastatus	X	X		b,s
*Enallagma sp.	X			b,s,a
*Ischnura sp.	X			b,s,a
*Nehallennia sp.	X			a
*unident. spp.				b
Family Lestidae				
*Lestes sp.	X			b,s
Suborder Anisoptera				
Family Aeschnidae				
*Boyeria grafiana	X	X		a
*Coryphaeschna ingens	X			b
*Gomphaeschna sp.	X			a
Family Corduliidae				
*Somatochlora sp.		X		b,s
Family Gomphidae				
*Aphylla sp.		X		b,s
*Dromogomphus sp.		X	X	b,s
*Erpetogomphus sp.		X	X	b,s
Gomphoides williamsoni				b,s
*Gomphus sp.		X	X	b,s
Ophiogomphus sp.		X	X	b,s
*Progomphus obscuris		X	X	b,s
unident. spp.				b
Family Libellulidae				
Dythemis sp.		X	X	b,s
*Erythemis sp.		X		b,s,a
*Erythrodiplax sp.	X			b,s
*Lepthemis vesiculosa		X		a
*Libellula sp.	X	X		b,s
*Macrothemis sp.	X			s
*Nannothemis bella	X			b
*Orthemis ferruginae		X		a
*Pachydiplex longipennis		X		a
*Perithemis domita		X	X	b,s
*Tramea sp.	X	X		b
*unident. spp.	X			b
Family Macromiidae				
Didymops sp.		X		b,s
*Macromia sp.		X	X	b,s

Continued

TABLE 2.14. *(Continued)*

| | | Lentic | Lotic | |
Taxon	V	M,S	G,R	Source[b]
Order Ephemeroptera				
Suborder Schistonota				
Family Baetidae				
Callibaetis sp.	X			a
Cloeon sp.			X	b
Family Ephemeridae				
Hexagenia bilineata		X	X	b
*Hexagenia sp.		X	X	s
Family Heptageniidae				
Heptagenia sp.			X	b,s
Stenacron sp.			X	a
Stenonema sp.			X	b
Family Leptophlebiidae				
Paraleptophlebia sp.		X		b,s
Family Palingeniidae				
Pentagenia vittigera		X		b
*Pentagenia sp.		X		b
Family Polymitarcydae				
*Tortopus sp.				
Family Siphlonuridae				
*Siphlonurus sp.	X	X		s
Suborder Pannota				
Family Caenidae				
Brachycercus sp.		X		b,s
*Caenis sp.		X		b,s,a
Family Neoephemeridae				
*Orieanthus sp.		X		
(= Neoephemera?) sp.		X		b,s
Order Hemiptera				
Family Belostomatidae				
Belostoma flumineum	X	X		b,a
*Belostoma sp.	X	X		s
Lethocerus americanus	X	X		b
Family Corixidae				
Trichocorixa naias	X	X		a
*unident. spp.	X			b,s
Family Gerridae				
*Gerris sp.	X	X		b,s,a
*Trepobates sp.	X	X		b,a
Family Hebridae				
Hebrus sp.	X			a
*Naeogeus sp.		X		b,s
Family Hydrometridae				
Hydrometra australis	X	X		b
*Hydrometra sp.	X	X		s,a

TABLE 2.14. (*Continued*)

Taxon	V	Lentic M,S	Lotic G,R	Source[b]
Family Macroveliidae				
Macrovelia horni	X	X	X	b
Family Mesovelidae				
Mesovelia sp.	X			a
Family Naucoridae				
Pelocoris femoratus	X			b,a
Pelocoris sp.	X			b
Family Nepidae				
Ranatra beunoi	X	X		a
R. fusca		X		b
Ranatra sp.		X		b
Family Notonectidae				
Notonecta sp.	X	X	X	b,s
Family Pleidae				
Plea striola	X			b
Plea sp.	X			a
Family Velidae				
Velia sp.	X	X		a
Order Neuroptera				
Family Sisyridae				
Climacia sp.	X	X		b,s
Sisyra sp.	X			a
Order Megaloptera				
Family Corydalidae				
Chauliodes sp.		X		b,s,a
Family Sialidae				
Sialis sp.		X	X	b,s
Order Coleoptera				
Suborder Adephaga				
Family Dytiscidae				
Bidessus sp.	X	X	X	a
Copelatus sp.	X	X		a
Cybister sp.	X			b,a
Derovatellus sp.		X		a
Dytiscus sp.	X	X		b
Graphoderus sp.	X			b
Hydroporus sp.	X	X		b,a
Hydrovatus sp.		X	X	a
Hygrotus sp.	X	X	X	b,s
Laccophilus sp.	X	X		b,a
Matus sp.	X	X	X	a
Oreodytes sp.	X	X	X	a
unident. spp.				b

Continued

TABLE 2.14.   *(Continued)*

Taxon	V	Lentic M,S	Lotic G,R	Source[b]
Family Gyrinidae				
Dineutes sp.	X			b,s,a
Gyrinus sp.	X			b,a
Family Haliplidae				
Haliplus sp.	X	X		b
Peltodytes sp.	X		X	b,s,a
Family Hydraenidae				
Hydraena sp.			X	a
Family Noteridae				
Colipus inflatus		X		a
Hydrocanthus sp.	X			a
Notomicrus sp.		X	X	a
Suphisellus sp.	X	X	X	a
Suborder Polyphaga				
Family Chrysomelidae				
Donacia sp.	X			b,s,a
Family Curculionidae				
Lissorhoptrus sp.	X			a
Onychylis spp.	X			a
Tanysphyrus sp.	X			a
unident. spp.	X			b
Family Dryopidae				
Dryops sp.	X			b
Family Elmidae				
Lara sp.			X	b
Microcylloepus sp.	X	X	X	b
unident. spp.	X			b
Family Helodidae				
Cyphon sp.	X			a
Microcara sp.	X			a
Family Hydrophilidae				
Berosus sp.	X	X		b,a
Cymbiodyta sp.	X	X	X	a
Derallus altus	X	X		a
Enochrus sp.	X	X		a
Hydrochus sp.			X	a
Hydrophilus triangularis	X	X		b
Paracymus sp.		X	X	b
Tropisternus sp.		X		b
Family Scirtidae				
unident. spp.	X			b
Order Trichoptera				
Family Hydropsychidae				
Cheumatopsyche sp.			X	b
Hydropsyche sp.			X	b,s
unident. spp.				b

TABLE 2.14. *(Continued)*

Taxon	V	Lentic M,S	Lotic G,R	Source[b]
Family Hydroptilidae				
Orthotrichia sp.	X			b,s
Stactobiella sp.	X	X	X	a
Family Leptoceridae				
Oecetis spp.	X	X	X	b,s,a
Family Limnephilidae				
*unident. spp.	X			a
Family Polycentropodidae				
Cyrenellus sp.		X		b,s
Polycentropus sp.		X	X	b,s
Order Lepidoptera				
Family Pyralidae				
Acentropus sp.	X			a
Nymphula sp.	X			b
Paragyractis sp.			X	a
Order Diptera				
Suborder Nematocera				
Family Ceratopogonidae				
Alluaudomyia splendida		X		a
Dasynelea sp.		X		a
Palpomyia sp.		X	X	s,a
Stilobezzia sp.	X	X		b,s
unident. Ceratopogoninae	X	X	X	b,a
Family Chaoboridae				
Chaoborus punctipennis	X	X	X	b,s,a
Family Chironomidae				
Ablabesmyia sp.	X	X	X	b,s,a
Anatopynia sp.				b,s
Brillia spp.	X	X	X	b
Chironomus sp.	X	X		b,s,a
Cladotanytarsus sp.	X	X	X	b
Clinotanypus sp.	X	X	X	b,s
Coelotanypus sp.	X	X	X	b,s
Conchapelopia sp.	X	X	X	b
Corynoneura scutellata	X	X		b,s
Corynoneura sp.	X	X		b
Cryptochironomus sp.	X	X	X	b
Demicryptochironomus sp.		X	X	b
Dicrotendipes sp.	X	X		b,s,a
Einfeldia sp.	X	X	X	b,s
Endochironomus sp.		X		b,s
Glyptotendipes sp.	X	X		b,a
Harnischia sp.	X	X		b,s
Kiefferulus sp.	X	X		b,s
Labrundinia neopilosella	X		X	b

Continued

TABLE 2.14.   (*Continued*)

Taxon	V	Lentic M,S	Lotic G,R	Source[b]
Family Chironomidae (*cont.*)				
Labrundinia sp.	X		X	a
Larsia sp.	X	X	X	a
Lauterborniella sp.		X		b,s
Micropsectra sp.	X	X		b,s
Microtendipes sp.	X	X		b,s
Nanocladius sp.	X		X	a
Omisus pica	X	X	X	b,s
Orthocladius sp.	X	X	X	b,s
Parachironomus sp.	X	X	X	b,s,a
Paracladopelma sp.	X	X	X	b,s
Paralauterborniella sp.	X		X	b,s
Paratanytarsus sp.	X	X		a
Paratendipes sp.	X	X		b,s
Pentaneura sp.	X	X	X	b,s
Phaenopsectra sp.	X	X		b,s
Polypedilum spp.	X		X	b,s,a
Procladius sp.	X	X		b,s
Psectrocladius sp.	X	X		b,s
Psectrotanypus sp.		X		b
Rheotanytarsus sp.			X	s
Stempellina sp.		X	X	b,s
Stenochironomus sp.	X		X	b,s
Stictochironomus sp.		X		b
Tanypus sp.	X	X	X	b,s
Tanytarsus spp.	X		X	b,s,a
Thienemanniella sp.	X	X	X	b
Tribelos sp.	X	X		b,s
Trichocladius sp.				b,s
Trissocladius sp.		X	X	b,s
Xenochironomus sp.			X	b,s
Zavrelimyia sp.	X	X	X	b
unident. spp.				b
Family Culicidae				
Aedes sp.	X	X		b
Anopheles sp.	X	X		b,a
Culex sp.	X	X		b,a
Culiseta sp.	X	X		b
Uranotaenia sp.	X	X		a
unident. spp.				b
Family Psychodidae				
Psychoda sp.	X	X		a

TABLE 2.14. *(Continued)*

Taxon	V	Substrate[a] Lentic M,S	Lotic G,R	Source[b]
Family Tipulidae				
Erioptera sp.	X	X	X	b,s
Geranomyia (=*Limonia?*) sp.		X	X	b,s
Helius sp.		X		b,a
Limonia sp.		X	X	s
Prionocera sp.	X	X		s
Suborder Brachycera				
Family Ephydridae				
Hydrellia sp.	X			b
Lemnaphila scotlandea	X			a
Family Muscidae				
Limnophora sp.			X	b
Lispe sp.	X	X		b,s
Family Sciomyzidae				
Antichaeta sp.	X	X		a
Dictya sp.	X			a
Renocera sp.	X			a
Family Stratiomyidae				
Eulalia sp.	X	X		a
Odontomyia sp.	X			b,s
Stratiomyia sp.	X	X	X	b
Family Tabanidae				
Tabanus sp.	X	X		b,s,a
Phylum Bryozoa				
Class Ectoprocta				
Order Phylactolaemata				
Family Lophopodidae				
Pectinatella magnifica			X	b,s
Family Plumatellidae				
Plumatella repens	X			b
Phylum Chordata				
Subphylum Vertebrata				
Class Osteichthyes				
Order Acipenseriformes				
Family Acipenseridae				
Acipenser oxyrhynchus		X		f
Scaphirhynchus albus		X	X	f
S. *platorynchus*		X	X	f
Family Polydontidae				
Polydon spathula		X		f

Continued

TABLE 2.14.   (Continued)

Taxon	V	Lentic M,S	Lotic G,R	Source[b]
Order Lepisosteiformes				
Family Lepisosteidae				
*Lepisosteus oculatus	X	X	X	f,a
*L. osseus	X	X		f,b,a
*L. platostomus	X			f
*L. spathula	X	X		f,a
Order Amiiformes				
Family Amiidae				
*Amia calva	X			f,a
Order Osteoglossiformes				
Family Hiodontidae				
*Hiodon alosoides		X	X	f
Order Anguilliformes				
Family Anguillidae				
*Anguilla rostrata			X	f
Order Clupeiformes				
Family Clupeidae				
*Alosa alabamae			X	f
*A. chrysochloris			X	f
*Brevoortia patronus		X	X	f
*Dorosoma cepedianum	X	X		f,a
*D. petenense		X	X	f,a
Family Engraulidae				
*Anchoa mitchelli		X	X	f
Order Cypriniformes				
Family Catostomidae				
*Carpiodes carpio		X	X	f
*C. cyprinus	X	X	X	f
*Cycleptus elongatus	X	X	X	f
*Erimyzon oblongus	X	X		f
*E. succetta	X	X		f
*Ictiobus bubalus	X	X	X	f
*I. cyprinellus	X	X		f,a
*I. niger	X	X	X	f,a
*Minytrema melanops	X	X		f
Family Cyprinidae				
*Crassius auritus	X	X		f
*Cyprinus carpio	X	X		f,a
*Ctenopharyngodon idella	X	X		f
*Hybognathus hayi	X	X		f
*H. nuchalis	X	X		f
*H. placitus		X	X	f
Hybopsis aestivalis		X	X	f
*H. storeriana	X	X		f
*Notemigonus crysoleucas	X	X		f,a

TABLE 2.14.   *(Continued)*

| | | Substrate[a] | | |
| | | Lentic | Lotic | |
Taxon	V	M,S	G,R	Source[b]
Family Cyprinidae *(cont.)*				
*Notropis amnis		X	X	f
*N. atherinoides	X	X	X	f
*N. atrocaudalis		X	X	f
*N. bairdi		X	X	f
*N. blennius		X	X	f
*N. boops		X	X	f
*N. buchanani		X	X	f
*N. emiliae	X	X	X	f,b
*N. longirostris		X	X	f
*N. lutrensis		X	X	f
*N. maculatus		X	X	a
*N. potteri		X	X	f
*N. shumardi		X	X	f
*N. texanus	X	X		f
*N. umbratilis	X	X		f
*N. venustus		X		f
*N. volucellus		X		f
*N. whipplei		X	X	f
*Phenacobius mirabilis		X	X	f
*Phoxinus erythrogaster		X	X	f
*Pimephales notatus	X	X	X	f
*P. promelas	X	X		f
P. tenellus		X	X	f
P. vigilax		X		f,b
Order Siluriformes				
Family Ariidae				
*Arius felix		X		f
Family Ictaluridae				
*Ictalurus furcatus		X	X	f,a
*I. melas	X	X		f,a
*I. natalis	X	X		f,a
*I. nebulosus	X	X	X	f
*I. punctatus		X	X	f,a
*Noturus gyrinus	X	X		f,b
*N. nocturnus		X	X	f
*Pylodictis olivaris		X		f
Order Salmoniformes				
Family Esocidae				
*Esox americanus vermiculatus	X	X		f,b,a
*E. niger	X	X		f,a
Order Percopsiformes				
Family Aphredoderidae				
*Aphredoderus sayanus	X	X		f,b,a

Continued

TABLE 2.14.   (Continued)

Taxon	V	Lentic M,S	Lotic G,R	Source[b]
Order Cyprinodontiformes				
Family Belonidae				
Strongylura marina		X		f
Family Cyprinodontidae				
Cyprinodon variegatus		X	X	f
*Fundulus chrysotus	X	X		f,b,a
*F. grandis	X	X	X	f
F. notatus			X	f
*F. olivaceus	X	X		f,b
*Lucania parva	X	X		f
Family Poeciliidae				
*Gambusia affinis	X	X		f,b,a
*Heterandria formosa	X	X		f,b
*Poecilia latipinna	X	X		f,b
Order Atheriniformes				
Family Atherinidae				
*Labidesthes sicculus		X	X	f,b,a
*Membras martinica	X	X	X	
*Menidia beryllina		X	X	f
*Menidia sp.	X	X	X	
Order Syngnathiformes				
Family Syngnathidae				
*Syngnathus scovelli	X	X		f
Order Perciformes				
Family Centrarchidae				
*Ambloplites ariommus	X	X	X	f
*Centrarchus macropterus	X	X		f,a
*Elassoma zonatum	X	X		f,b,a
*Lepomis cyanellus	X	X		f,a
*L. gulosus	X	X		f,a
*L. humilus	X	X		f,a
*L. macrochirus	X	X		f,b,a
*L. marginatus	X	X		f
*L. megalotis	X	X	X	f,b,a
*L. microlophus	X	X		f,a
*L. punctatus	X	X		f,a
*L. symmetricus	X	X		f,a
*Micropterus punctulatus		X	X	f
*M. salmoides	X	X	X	f,a
*Pomoxis annularis	X	X		f,a
*P. nigromaculatus	X	X		f,b,a
Family Mugilidae				
*Mugil cephalus		X		f,a
*M. curema		X		

TABLE 2.14. *(Continued)*

| | | Lentic | Lotic | |
Taxon	V	M,S	G,R	Source[b]
Family Percidae				
*Ammocrypta asprella		X	X	f
*A. clara		X	X	f
*A. vivax		X	X	f
*Etheostoma asprigene		X		f
*E. chlorosomum		X		f
*E. fusiforme	X	X		f
*E. gracile		X		f
*E. parvipinne	X	X		f
*E. proeliare	X	X		f,b
*E. zonale	X	X		f
*Percina caprodes	X	X		f
*P. copelandi		X	X	f
*P. shumardi		X	X	f
*P. uranidae		X	X	f
Family Percithyidae				
*Morone chrysops		X	X	f
*M. mississipiensis	X	X	X	f,a
*M. saxatilis		X	X	f
Family Sciaenidae				
*Aplodinotus grunniens	X	X		f,a
*Bairdiella chrysoura	X	X	X	f
*Cynoscion arenarius		X	X	f
*C. nebulosus	X	X	X	f
*Leiostomus xanthurus		X	X	f
*Menticirrhus littoralis		X	X	f
*Micropogonias undulatus		X	X	f
*Pogonias cromis		X	X	f
*Sciaenops ocellatus		X	X	f
Order Pleuronectiformes				
Family Bothidae				
*Paralichthys lethostigma		X		f
Family Soleidae				
*Trinectes maculatus		X	X	f

*Species discussed in the section "Structure of Aquatic Communities" based on knowledge of R. Patrick.

[a]V, vegetation; M, mud; S, sand; G, gravel; R, rock.

[b]*Phytoplankton:* p, Hern et al. (1978); s, Fremling et al. (1989). *Zooplankton:* h, Holland (1977) (rotifers); s, Fremling et al. (1989); c, Clary (1985); a, Pollard et al. (1981). *Macroinvertebrates:* b, Beck (1977); s, Fremling et al. (1989); a, Pollard et al. (1981). *Macrophytes:* M, Montz (1980); C, Conner and Day (1976) (Barataria swamp forest macrophytes); H, Hunner and Barr (1981) (probable swamp habitat macrophytes). *Fish:* f, Fremling et al. (1989); a, Pollard et al. (1981).

Vegetative Habitats.   Flow in the Atchafalaya River is variable. There are many lentic areas in among the vegetated areas and shallows along the banks and in backwaters. Table 2.14 lists the species that have been found in the Atchafalaya ecosystems. Many of the plants are rooted in the soft sediment. Others typically float in the water surface. Most of the plants will have both types of habitat; that is, they may be rooted in the surface muds, but their leaves will extend to the surface and float on the surface, as is the case of the order Nymphaeales (Table 2.14). Other species present belonged to the orders Nymphaeales, Ranunculales, Caryophyllales, Polygonales, Haloragales, and Myrtales. This aquatic vegetation provides a variety of flow conditions as well as food and shelter for many species. In and among the vegetation were several species of blue-green algae. They were *Aphanocapsa* sp., *Gomphosphaeria* sp., *Anabaena* sp., and *Nostoc* sp. Other blue-green algae were *Spirulina* sp. and *Rivularia* sp. The order Chlorococcales was represented by five taxons belonging to the genus *Pediastrum,* three taxons belonging to the genus *Ankistrodesmus* and *Kirchneriella* sp. A few filamentous green algae belonging to the Oedogoniales were present. Desmids were fairly common in the detritus in the vegetative habitats. They were two species belonging to the genus *Closterium,* one species belonging to the genus *Cosmarium,* one species belonging to the genus *Hyalotheca* sp., and one species belonging to the genus *Micrasterias.* Other desmids in this habitat were *Phyamatodocis* sp., *Staurastrum* sp., *Mesotaenium* sp., and *Spirotaenia* sp. The filamentous green algae present were *Mougeotia* sp. and *Spirogyra* sp. They were found among the vegetation associated with the stems and detritus, whereas the desmids were mainly on the surface of the detritus.

Diatoms were fairly common in this habitat. On the surface of the mud was *Cyclotella meneghiniana.* Five taxons belonging to the genus *Melosira* were found attached to debris or to the leaves and stems in the vegetative habitat. Lying on the debris were three taxons belonging to the genus *Stephanodiscus* (Table 2.14). Certain species of the family Fragillariaceae were also present. Attached to the leaves of the vegetation were *Asterionella formosa* and *Diatoma vulgare.* Also present in and among the vegetation were an unidentified species of *Meridion* and three taxons belonging to the genus *Synedra* and *Tabellaria fenestrata.* The species of *Synedra* and *Tabellaria* were found attached to leaves in the vegetative habitat. Lying on the surface of the debris in this habitat were *Eunotia curvata* and *Achnanthes lanceolata.* Three taxons belonging to the genus *Cocconeis* were also present as were *Amphora* sp. and *Cymbella turgida.* They were attached to the debris as were four taxons belonging to the genus *Gomphonema.* Lying on the surface of the debris in the vegetative habitat were *Gyrosigma kutzingii, Mastogloia braunii,* and three taxons belonging to the genus *Navicula.* Also in the debris was found *Pleurosigma delicatulum,* and on the surface of leaves, particularly at the base of the vegetation, was *Epithemia turgida.* The family Nitzschiaceae had many taxons common in the debris in these vegetative habitats. They were *Hantz-*

schia amphioxys and nine taxons belonging to the genus *Nitzschia.* Lying on the surface of the mud were *Surirella linearis* and *S. ovata.*

Partially submerged but also with leaves on the surface of the water were an unidentified species of the genera *Ranunculus, Alteranthera philoxeroides,* and *Polygonum.* Trailing in the water were the leaves of *Salix nigra.* Rooted along the edges of the stream in the riverine portion which is described here was *Hottonia inflata.* Floating on the surface, partially submerged and partially emerged, were *Myriophyllum* prob. *aquaticum?, M. exalbescens,* and *M. pinnatum.* Several *Utricularia* were found in and among the other plants. There were four taxons belonging to the genus *Utricularia.* Partially emergent and partially submerged were three taxons belonging to the genus *Sagittaria.* Other species present were *Hydrilla verticillata* and two species of the pondweed *Najas.* Also present were *Pistia stratiotes* and floating on the surface of the water was *Lemna minor.*

Along the margins of the stream in lentic habitats was part of the vegetative habitat. This consisted of species of *Eleocharis,* several species of *Typha.* Other species floating on the surface of the water were *Eichornia crassipes,* three taxons belonging to the genus *Heterantheria,* and two taxons belonging to the genus *Pontederia.* This aquatic vegetation provided a variety of flow conditions as well as food and shelter for many species.

Protozoan species that have been found in and among the vegetation are starred in Table 2.14. Most of the protozoans, such as the Mastigophora, derive much of their energy from the sun and fix carbon dioxide by photosynthesis. They are the food of many species. The protozoans (i.e., those that belong to the Chrysomonodida, the Cryptomonadida, the Phytomonadida, and the Euglenoidida) are photosynthetic and furnish the base of the food chain for many other species. The class Sarcodina is represented by relatively few species. Two species of the genus *Arcella* were found which are omnivores and live in and among the vegetation, as probably do unknown species of *Astramoeba* and *Centrophyxis* (Table 2.14).

The ciliates (class Ciliata) that were found in and among this vegetation were species of *Epistylis, Scyphidia,* and *Vorticella,* which were attached to the leaves of the vegetation in many cases. A single suctorian, *Tokophyra* sp., was found in this habitat.

Attached to the vegetation were two taxons of sponge, *Eunapius fragilis* and *Trochospongilla leidyi,* which are both detritivore-omnivores. Other species attached to the vegetation were two species of *Hydra,* which are known to be omnivores. Crawling over the vegetation were the omnivores *Dugesia tigrina* and *Phagocita vellata.* Also present in this habitat were unidentified species of the genera *Catenula* and *Macrostomum,* which are detritivore-omnivores. The Nemertea was represented by one taxon, *Prostoma rubrum,* a detritivore-omnivore.

Rotifers were very commonly associated with the vegetation. Fifteen taxons belonging to the genus *Brachionus* were present in and among the vegetation.

As far as we know, all of these are omnivores. Other species of rotifers present in this habitat were two species of *Kellicottia*, nine taxons belonging to the genus *Keratella*, two taxons belonging to the genus *Notholca*, and one taxon belonging to the genus *Platyais*. As far as we know, all of these are omnivores (Table 2.14).

This was indeed a favorite habitat for rotifers. Here were also found two taxons belonging to the family Colurellidae, both of which are omnivores, and three taxons belonging to the family Euchlanidae, which are omnivores. The family Gastropodidae was represented by five taxons, all of which are omnivores. Species belonging to the family Lecanidae were also present in and among the vegetation. Seven taxons of *Lecane* were identified, all of which are believed to be omnivores, and four taxons belonging to the genus *Monostyla*, all omnivores, were also present. These various omnivorous species feed on a variety of organisms, such as protozoans, bacteria, and algae, as well as bits of detritus. Other omnivores that were present were *Cephalodella* spp. *Scaridium longicaudatum* was present, which is thought to be mainly a herbivore. Other rotifers that were present in and among the vegetation were the omnivores *Pleosoma* sp., *Polyarthra euryptera*, and *P. vulgaris*. The family Tricocercidae was represented by three taxons belonging to the genus *Tricocerca*, all of which are omnivores; one taxon belonging to the family Tricotridae; and two taxons belonging to the genus *Collotheca* were also present. Also present were species belonging to the genera *Conochilus* and *Conochiloides*. Thus it is evident that this is a very favorable habitat for rotifers.

A number of molluscs were found in this area. The gastropods were represented by species belonging to the genera *Clappia* and *Littoridina*, *Somatogyrus* sp., *Vioscalba lovisianae*, *Goniobasis* sp., and unidentified species of the genera *Ferrissia* sp., *Laevipex* sp., *Lymnaea* sp., *Pseudosuccinea* sp., and *Physa* sp., which are detritivore-omnivores. Other detritivore-omnivores that were present were *Gyraulus* sp. and *Helisoma* sp.

Three bivalves were found in this habitat. They were *Corbicula manilensis*, *Eupera cubensis*, and an unidentified species of the genus *Sphaerium*. All of these are probably detritivore-omnivores. Crawling in and among the vegetation and the detritus at the base of the vegetation were several annelids. Those belonging to the class Hirudinoidea were *Glossiphonia heteroclita*, *Helobdella lineata* and *H. fusca*, carnivores, and *Placobdella multilineata*, *P. parasitica*, and *Mooreobdella microstoma*, and the leech *Macrobdella ditetra*.

The oligochaetes associated with the vegetation were several. These were all detritivore-omnivores. Belonging to the family Naididae were two species of *Aulophorus*, three of *Dero*, one of *Haemonais*, one of *Nais*, and one of *Pristina*. One tubificid might be found in this habitat. It was *Aulodrilus pigueti*, a detritivore-omnivore. Several Arachnida were found in and among the vegetation; they belonged to the genera *Arrenurus*, *Diplodontus*, *Hydraphantes*, and *Lebertia*. Also present were unidentified species of the family Mideidae/ Mideopsidae and an unidentified species of the family Unionicolidae.

Several Crustacea were found in this habitat: one species, an omnivore, *Bosminia longirostris,* belonging to the family Bosminidae; four taxons belonging to the genus *Alona,* which are probably herbivore-detritivores; one species belonging to the genus *Alonella;* one species belonging to the genus *Chydorus;* one to the genus *Kurzia;* three to the genus *Leydigia;* and one to the genus *Pleuroxus.* The family Daphinidae was represented by ten taxons. All of these are believed to be detritivore-herbivores (Table 2.14). The family Holopedium was represented by one taxon (unidentified species), and the family Macrothricidae by two taxons. The family Sididae was represented by two taxons and the family Artemiidae by one species, *Artemia salina.*

The subclass Ostracoda was represented by two unidentified species belonging to the family Cypridae and by an unidentified species of the genus *Herpetocypris* (Table 2.14). The subclass Copepoda was represented by a few species in this habitat: *Osphranticum labronectum, Diaptomus* spp., and *Eurytemora affinis.* The order Cyclopodia, family Cyclopidae was represented by *Acanthocyclops vernalis, Cyclops vernalis,* and *Ectocyclops phaleratus.* Other species belonging to the subclass Copepoda were *Macrocyclops albidus, M. ater, Mesocyclops edax,* and *M. fuscus.*

The subclass Branchiura was represented by unidentified species of the genus *Argulus,* whereas the subclass Malacostraca was represented by *Taphromysis louisianae; Cyanthura polita;* three taxons belonging to the genus *Asellus,* and two taxons belonging to the genus *Lirceus.* The order Amphipoda was represented by *Corophium lacustre; Crangonyx pseudogracilis* (this group) a detritivore-omnivore; and one unknown species of the same genus. The genus *Gammarus,* which are also detritivore-omnivores, was represented by three taxons. *Hyalella azteca,* a detritivore, was also present. The order Decapoda was represented by one species of *Cambarellus,* an omnivore; *Orconectes lancifer,* and *Procambarus clarkii.* Other decapods that were present, *Macrobrachium ohione* and *Palaemonetes kadiakensis,* belonged to the family Palaemonidae.

Aquatic insects were fairly common in and among the vegetation. Several odonates were found in this habitat. They belong to the genera *Agrion, Amphiagrion, Anomalagrion, Enallagma, Ischnura,* and *Nehallennia.* These are all carnivores. Other carnivorous species were a taxon belonging to the genus *Lestes* and one taxon each belonging to the genera *Boyeria, Coryphaeschna,* and *Gomphaeschna.* All of the dragonflies are carnivores. Other carnivores were an unidentified species of the genus *Erythrodiplax,* which is found in and among the vegetation, along with the carnivorous *Libellula* sp., *Macrothemis* sp., and *Nannothemis bella.* Other carnivores probably were an unidentified species of the genus *Tramea* and unidentified species of the family Libellulidae.

Mayflies were represented by two species: *Callibaetis* sp., and omnivore, and *Siphlonurus* sp., a carnivore-omnivore. The true bugs were fairly well represented in and among the vegetation. They were two species of the genus *Belostoma,* both of which are carnivores, and the species *Lethocerus ameri-*

canus, a carnivore. Unidentified species probably of the family Corixidae, probably belonging to the genus *Trichocorixa,* which is carnivorous, were found, as was *T. naias.* Gerrids were represented by two species: an unidentified species of the genus *Gerris,* probably a carnivore, and an unidentified species of the genus *Trepobates,* probably a carnivore. Most of the true bugs are carnivorous. Other species in and among the vegetation were two species of the genus *Hydrometra,* all carnivores; the species *Macrovelia horni,* a carnivore; an unidentified species of the genus *Mesovelia;* and two species of the genus *Pelocoris.* One species of *Ranatra, Ranatra beunoi,* which is a carnivore, was present, as was an unidentified species of the genus *Notonecta,* which is probably a carnivore. Two species of the genus *Plea* were found in and among the detritus. They are both carnivores, as are an unidentified species of the genus *Velia* and an unidentified species of the genus *Climacia,* a carnivore. This species belongs to the family Sisyridae.

Beetles seemed to prefer this vegetative habitat. Present were the following carnivorous species: *Bidessus* sp., *Copelatus* sp., *Cybister* sp., *Dytiscus* sp., *Graphoderus* sp., *Hydroporus* sp., *Hygrotus* sp., *Laccophilus* sp., *Matus* sp., and *Oreodytes* sp. The gyrinid beetles were represented by a single genus, an unidentified species of the genus *Gyrinus,* which is an omnivore. The family Haliplidae was represented by *Haliplus* sp. and *Peltodytes* sp., herbivores. Other species that were present were two species belonging to the family Noteridae: *Hydrocanthus* sp. and *Suphisellus* sp., both omnivores. The family Chrysomelidae was represented by a single species, *Donacia* sp., which is a herbivore. Other unidentified species present belonged to the following genera: *Lissorhoptrus* sp., *Onychylis* spp., and *Tanysphyrus* sp. The family Dryopidae was present and represented by the genus *Dryops* sp. The elmids were represented by a species of *Microcylloepus,* an omnivore. Also present were unidentified taxons of the genera *Cyphon* sp. and *Microcara* sp. The hydrophilids were represented by five species, all of which are probably herbivores. Only two of them, *Hydrophilus triangularis* and *Derallus altus,* were positively identified.

Caddisflies were also present attached to the vegetation. They were the omnivorous *Stactobiella* and unidentified species of the family Limnephilidae, which were probably carnivores. Another carnivorous species that was present belonged to the genus *Oecetis.* Other species present belonged to the genera *Acentropus* and *Nymphula,* which may be omnivores. The ceratopogonids present were a species belonging to the genus *Stilobezzia,* an omnivore; a species of *Chaoborus.* Belonging to the family Chironomidae were a species of *Ablabesmyia,* which is an omnivore, and *Brillia* sp. The genera *Cladotanytarsus* sp. and *Chironomus* sp. were represented by single species and are probably herbivores, whereas *Clinotanypus* and *Coelotanypus* sp. are carnivores, as is *Conchapelopia* sp. Two species belonging to the omnivorous genus *Corynoneura* and *Cryptochironomus* sp. were also present, as were the omnivorous species *Dicrotendipes, Einfeldia,* and *Glyptotendipes.* Other omnivores that were in and among the vegetation were *Keifferulus* sp.; *Labrundinia,* which was represented by two species; and an unidentified species of *Larsia.* An unidentified species of *Micropsectra* was also present, as well as *Microtendipes* sp., *Nanocladius* sp., *Omisus pica,* and *Orthocladius* sp. Other omnivorous species were *Parachironomus* sp., *Paracladopelma* sp., *Paralauterborniella* sp., and *Paratanytarsus* sp. Three other omnivorous chironomids were present: unidentified species of the genera *Paratendipes, Pentaneura, Phaenopsectra, Polypedilum,* and *Procladius.* The species *Psectrocladius* and a species of *Stenochironomus* are also probably omnivores, as are unidentified species belonging to the genera *Tanypus* and *Tanytarsus.* Other chironomids that were present were unidentified species of the genera *Thienemanniella, Tribelos,* and *Trissocladius* which are omnivorous, as are species belonging to the mosquito family, *Aedes* sp. and *Anopheles* sp. Other unidentified species belonging to this family were a species of *Culex,* a species of *Culiseta,* and an unidentified species of *Uranotaenia.* Also present was *Psychoda* sp. The family Tipulidae was represented by two species, *Erioptera* sp. and *Prionocera* sp. The family Ephydridae was represented by two species, *Hydrellia* sp. and *Lemnaphila scotlandea.* Also present was one species belonging to the genus *Lispe* of the family Muscidae. Other species that were present were an unidentified species of the genus *Antichaeta,* one species of the genus *Dictya,* and a species of the genus *Renocera.* These three genera belong to the family Sciomyzidae. The family Stratiomyidae was represented by three species of the genera *Eulalia, Odontomyia,* and *Stratiomyia.* The Tabanidae were represented by a single species, *Tabanus* sp. Attached to the vegetation was one bryozoan, *Plumatella repens,* which is probably an omnivore.

Several species of fish were found in and among the vegetation. Among these were four species of the genus *Lepisosteus,* all carnivores (Table 2.14). One species belonging to the family Amiidae was present, the carnivorous *Amia calva.* One species of *Dorosoma, D. cepedianum,* an omnivore, was present. Other omnivorous species in and among the vegetation were *Carpiodes cyprinus, Cycleptus elongatus, Erimyzon oblongus, E. succetta,* and *Ictiobus bubalus.* All of these are omnivorous species and belong to the family Catostomidae. Other species belonging to this family were the herbivorous *Ictiobus cyprinellus,* the omnivorous *I. niger,* and *Minytrema melanops,* which is a carnivore. Cyprinids present in and among the vegetation included *Crassius auritus,* an omnivore; *Cyprinus carpio,* an omnivore; *Ctenopharyngodon idella,* a herbivore; and two herbivorous species belonging to the genus *Hybognathus* (Table 2.14). Also present was one carnivorous species, *Hybopsis storeriana.* Other cyprinids in and among the vegetation were *Notemigonus crysoleucas,* an omnivore; a carnivore, *Notropis atherinoides; N. emiliae,* also a carnivore; *N. texanus,* and *N. umbratilis* which are omnivores. Other omnivorous species in this habitat belonging to this family were *Pimephales notatus* and *P. promelas.* Several catfish were found in and among the vegetation. They were the carnivorous *Ictalurus melas* and the omnivorous *I. natalis* and *I. nebulosus.* Other species were the carnivorous *Noturus gyrinus.* Two species of salmonid fishes found here were *Esox americanus vermiculatus* and

E. niger, both carnivores. Another carnivorous species found in the vegetation was *Aphredoderus sayanus.* Several species belonging to the genus *Fundulus* were found in and among the vegetation. They were the carnivorous *Fundulus chrysotus,* the omnivorous *F. grandis,* and the carnivorous *F. olivaceus.* Another carnivore present was *Lucania parva.* Several species belonging to the family Poeciliidae were present: the omnivorous *Gambusia affinis,* the omnivorous *Heterandria formosa,* and the omnivorous *Poecilia latipinna.* Other species that might be found in and among the vegetation were the omnivorous *Membras martinica* and an unidentified species of *Menidia.* Both of these are believed to be omnivorous. The carnivorous species *Syngnathus scovelli* was also present.

The centrarchids were represented by a very large number of species in these vegetation habitats. Of course, all of them would not be present in any one habitat. Many of them fed in and among the vegetation, whereas some of them bred in this location. They were *Ambloplites ariommus,* a carnivore; *Centrarchus macropterus,* an omnivore; *Elassoma zonatum,* a carnivore; and nine species of *Lepomis, L. cyanellus, L. gulosus, L. humilis, L. marginatus, L. megalotis, L. microlophus,* and *L. symmetricus,* which are carnivores. The omnivorous species *L. macrochirus* and *L. punctatus* were also present. One species belonging to the omnivorous genus *Micropterus, M. salmoides,* was present. Other species present in and among the vegetation were the carnivorous *Pomoxis annularis* and *P. nigromaculatus.* The family Percidae was represented by five species in that habitat: the carnivorous *Etheostoma fusiforme, E. parvipinne, E. proeliare,* and *E. zonale.* One species of the genus *Percina, P. caprodes,* which is a carnivore, was found here. Other carnivorous species were *Aplodinotus grunniens, Bairdiella chrysoura,* and *Cynoscion nebulosus.*

Lentic Habitats.   The lentic habitats were the most common habitats for species occupancy in the Atchafalaya River. They occurred along the edges of the river where the current was slow, in pools, or in backwaters. They supported a large fauna and flora. On the detritus and soft mud were found several species of blue-green algae: *Agmenellum* sp., *Anacystis* sp., *Aphanocapsa elachista,* and an unidentified species of *Aphanocapsa.* Also present were an unidentified species of *Gomphosphaeria,* two species of *Merismopedia,* and two species of *Microcystis* (Table 2.14). Also present in and among the detritus were *Anabaena* sp. and *Nostoc* sp. *Lyngbia* sp. and four species belonging to the genus *Oscillatoria* were present. These filaments were found in and among the detritus. A few specimens of *Spirulina* might occur in this habitat.

Certain species of desmids were also fairly common in these lentic habitats. They were two species of *Closterium,* one species of *Cosmarium,* and one species of each of the following genera: *Hyalotheca* sp., *Micrasterias* sp., *Phymatodocis* sp., and *Staurastrum* sp. Other desmids found in this habitat were an unidentified species of *Mesotaenium* and an unidentified species of *Spirotaenia.* The filamentous green algae *Mougeotia* and *Spirogyra* were also present.

In these lentic habitats were a few dicotyledons: *Utricularia biflora, U.*

foliosa, U. gibba, and *U. vulgaris.* These were submerged and floating in the habitat. Also present were two taxons belonging to the order Arales: *Pistia stratiotes* and *Lemna minor.*

Diatoms were fairly common in this habitat: one species belonging to the genus *Centritractus,* three taxons belonging to the genus *Coscinodiscus,* and three taxons belonging to the genus *Cyclotella.* A few filaments of *Melosira* were found attached to the detritus and to twigs in these slow-flowing areas. They were *Melosira varians* and *Melosira* spp. Other *Melosira* found were *M. varians* and unidentified species. Living on the surface of the mud were three species of the genus *Stephanodiscus.* One species of *Asterionella, Asterionella formosa,* was found in this habitat. The genus *Diatoma* was represented by a single species, as was the genus *Meridion,* the genus *Synedra* by two species. They were found on the surface of the mud. Also present in this habitat was *Tabellaria fenestrata.* Living also probably attached to detritus were *Achnanthes lanceolata* var. *dubia, Cocconeis placentula,* and *C. placentula* var. *euglypta.* An unidentified species of *Amphora* was also present. Growing attached to debris were *Gomphonema angustatum* and *G. parvulum,* along with some unidentified species of *Gomphonema.* On the surface of the mud were *Gyrosigma kutzingii* and *Mastogloia braunii.* Probably moving in and among the surface sediments were *Pleurosigma delicatulum.* The genus *Hantzschia* is often found in this type of habitat. There were one species of *Hantzschia* and eight species of the closely related genus *Nitzschia.* This was a favorite habitat for *Surirella linearis* and *S. ovata.*

The genus *Pediastrum* was quite common in this habitat. It was represented by five species. The colonial green algae *Ankistrodesmus* was represented by three taxons and the genus *Kirchneriella* by one taxon.

In these slow-water habitats various species of protozoa were present: two species of the genus *Chlamydomonas,* one species of *Pandorina,* and one species of *Volvox.* This was also a favorite habitat of a few species of the shelled amoebas. They were *Arcella dentata,* an omnivore; an unidentified species of *Arcella;* and an unidentified species of *Centrophyxis.* Several protozoans that are peritrichs were found in these lentic habitats: *Epistylis* sp. and *Opercularis* sp. Also present were *Platycola* sp., *Pyxicola* sp., and *Vaginicola* sp. All these peritrichs are bacterial feeders.

Several sponges were found attached to the detritus and wood deposited in these lentic habitats. They were *Corvospongilla* sp., *Eunapius fragilis, Spongilla ingloviformis,* and unidentified species of *Spongilla.* Another sponge found in this habitat was *Trochospongilla leidyi.* All of these are detritivore-omnivores. Attached to the wood and other debris in these lentic habitats were a few hydroids, for example *Corydylophora lacustris, Chlorohydra viridis,* and *Hydra americana.* These are omnivores.

This was a favorite habitat for some flatworms, including *Dugesia tigrina* and *Phagocita vellata,* both of which are detritivore-omnivores, as probably was an unknown species of the genus *Catenula.* A rhabdocelan was found in this habitat which was a detritivore-omnivore. It was a species of *Macrostomum.*

Rotifers were very common in this habitat. Thirteen species of *Brachionus,* which are omnivores, were encountered (Table 2.14), as well as nine species of *Keratella,* which are omnivores (Table 2.14). Other omnivorous rotifers found in this habitat were *Notholca acuminata,* an unidentified species of *Notholca,* and *Platyais quadridentata.* Other rotifers were *Colurella* spp., which are omnivores; *Lepadella ovalis,* an omnivore; and *Beauchampiella eudactylotum, Dipleuchlanis propatula,* and *Euchlanis* spp., all of which are omnivores. Five species belonging to the family Gastropodidae were present, all omnivores. The genus *Lecane,* which is omnivorous, was represented by six species (Table 2.14). Also present were *Monostyla bulba,* an omnivore; *M. quadridentata,* an omnivore; and unidentified species of this genus. Other species present included the genus *Cephalodella,* which are omnivores, and the herbivorous *Scaridium longicaudatum.* In these lentic habitats, particularly in pools and backwaters, were several species belonging to the family Synchaetidae. They belong to the genera *Pleosoma, Polyarthra,* and *Synchaeta,* all omnivorous (Table 2.14). There were five species belonging to the genus *Tricocerca,* all omnivores. Also present was *Tricotria tetracitis,* an omnivore. Present were unidentified species of the genera *Conochilus* and *Conochiloides,* which are omnivores.

Organisms belonging to the family Nemata were present. They were unidentified species of Adenophorea. Gastropods were fairly common in these lentic habitats, including *Amnicola* sp., *Clappia* sp., *Littoridina* sp., *Lyogyrus* sp., and *Paludestrina* sp. Other species were *Somatogyrus* sp. and *Vioscalba louisianae,* both of which are probably omnivore-detritivores. *Goniobasis* sp. was found crawling over the detritus and is probably a detritivore-omnivore. Attached to wood or to the surface of other types of debris was *Ferrissia* sp., a detritivore-omnivore. Also present were *Lymnaea,* a detritivore-omnivore, and *Pseudosuccinea* sp., probably a detritivore-omnivore.

Several snails were quite common in this habitat: a detritivore-omnivore, probably an unidentified species of *Physa;* an unidentified species of *Gyraulus;* and an unidentified species of *Helisoma.* All of these genera are probably detritivore-omnivores, as probably is *Promenetus* sp. Several bivalves were found in this habitat: the detritivore-omnivores *Anodonta, Leptodea,* and *Quadrula.* Another detritivore-omnivore in this habitat was *Corbicula* prob. *fluminea.* Several sphaerid clams were also found here: *Eupera cubensis, Pisidium casternatum, Pisidium* sp., *Sphaerium corneum,* and *S. partumeum,* as well as *S. securis* and *S. transversum* and one unidentified species of this genus. All of these are detritivore-omnivores.

These lentic areas were favorable habitats for several species of leeches, all of which are carnivorous. They were *Batracobdella* sp., *Glossiphonia heteroclita, Helobdella fusca, H. lineata,* and *H. stagnalis.* Also present were the leeches *Placobdella parasitica* and *P. papillifera.* All of these leeches should be classified as carnivores. Other species belonging to the class Hirudinoidea were an unidentified species of the family Piscicolidae and *Mooreobdella microstoma. Macrobdella ditetra* was also present. Several oligochaete worms were found in this habitat. They were unidentified species belonging to the family Lumbriculidae, unidentified species belonging to the family Glosso-scolecidae, and a detritivore-omnivore, *Haemonais waldvogeli.* Tubificid worms were quite common in this habitat, especially in the loose mud of pools and backwaters. They were *Aulodrilus americanus, A. piqueti, A. pluriseta, Branchiura sowerbyi, Ilyodrilus templetoni,* and the genus *Limnodrilus,* which was represented by six species (Table 2.14). Other tubificids found were three species belonging to the genus *Peloscolex* and unidentified species belonging to the genus *Tubifex.* All of these are probably detritivore-herbivores, often feeding on bacteria.

The arachnids were represented by a single species belonging to the genus *Arrenurus* and *Diplodontus despiciens.* Crustacea found were a species of *Alona* and a species of *Chydorus, Chydorus sphaericus.* Also present were two species belonging to the genus *Leydigia.* Other crustaceans found in this habitat were *Simocephalus vetulus* and unidentified species of this genus. Two species belonging to the family Macrothricidae, *Ilyocryptus sordidus* and *I. spinifer* were present. Ostracods were represented by four species: unidentified species of *Cadona, Cypria, Herpetocypris,* and *Ilyocypris.*

In the pools were also found five species belonging to the order Cyclopodia: *Acanthocyclops vernalis, Cyclops vernalis, Eucyclops speratus,* and *Macrocyclops albidus.* Belonging to the subclass Branchiura, unidentified species of *Argulus* were found, as was one species of the family Mysidae, *Taphromysis louisianae.* Quite a few isopods were identified in this habitat. They were one species belonging to the genus *Cyanthura,* three species belonging to the genus *Asellus,* and two species belonging to the genus *Lirceus.* The amphipod *Corophium lacustre,* which is a detritivore-omnivore, was also in this habitat, as were *Crangonyx pseudogracilis,* an unidentified species of *Crangonyx, Gammarus fasciatus, G. tigrinus,* and another unidentified species of this genus. *Hyalella azteca* was fairly common in this habitat.

Several crayfish were found in these lentic habitats: the omnivorous *Cambarus diogenes diogenes, Cambarellus puer, C. shufeldtii, Orconectes lancifer, Procambarus acutus acutus,* and *P. clarkii.* They were often found associated with debris. Other decapods found in this habitat were *Macrobrachium ohione* and *Callinectes sapidus.*

These lentic habitats (i.e., the margins of the river where the flow was slow and sediments had been deposited, the pools, and the backwaters) were favorable habitats for many species of insects. Here one found the odonates, *Anomalagrion hastatus, Amphiagrion saucium* which are carnivores, as well as unidentified species of the carnivorous genera *Somatochlora* and *Boyeria.* The Gomphidae were represented by one species that was found in and among the vegetation in these lentic habitats, an unidentified species of the carnivorous *Aphylla, Dromogomphus* sp., *Erpetogomphus* sp., and *Gomphus* sp. Other species that were found were an unidentified species of the genus *Erythemis, Lepthemis vesiculosa,* and *Libellula* sp. which are also carnivores. *Orthemis ferruginae, Pachydiplex longipennis,* and *Perithemis domita* as well as an unidentified species of *Tramea,* are all carnivores and might be found in these lentic habitats.

The mayflies were not as numerous as the odonates. Here was *Hexagenia bilineata* and an unidentified species of *Hexagenia,* both of which are omnivores. Other mayflies found in this habitat were two species of *Pentagenia* and an unidentified species of *Tortopus.* The omnivorous genus *Caenis* was represented by an unidentified species; also there was *Orienathus* sp. Hemiptera or bugs were represented by species of *Belostoma, Trichocorixa, Gerris, Trepobates, Naeogeus;* two species of *Hydrometra;* one species of *Macrovelia, M. horni;* three species of the genus *Ranatra,* all of which are carnivores. Also present were *Notonecta* sp. and *Velia* sp. This seemed to be a favorable habitat for the omnivorous craneflies, *Chauliodes* sp. and *Sialis.* The neuropteran *Climacia* sp. was also present.

Beetles were quite common in this habitat. They were unidentified species of the genera *Bidessus, Copelatus, Derovatellus, Dytiscus, Hydroporus, Hydrovatus, Hygrotus, Laccophilus, Matus,* and *Oreodytes,* all of which are carnivores. The gyrinids were not present in this habitat. However, belonging to the family Haliplidae was the herbivorous *Haliplus* sp. The family Noteridae was represented by *Colipus inflatus,* an omnivore, and the omnivorous *Notomicrus* sp. and *Suphisellus* sp. Also present was *Microcylloepus* sp. The family Hydrophilidae were represented by species, all herbivores.

Caddisflies were not as numerous in this habitat. Present was *Stactobiella* sp., an omnivore; unidentified species of the genus *Oecetis,* which are carnivores; as well as an unidentified species of *Cyrnellus,* an omnivore. The ceratopogonids (Diptera) were represented by unidentified species of the omnivorous genera *Palpomyia* and *Stilobezzia.* One chaoborid was present, *Chaoborus punctipennis.*

The chironomids were represented by many species. Present were unidentified species of *Ablabesmyia* sp. and *Brillia* spp., all of which are probably omnivores; *Chironomus* sp., which is a herbivore; and several carnivorous species: *Clinotanypus* sp., *Coelotanypus* sp., and *Cryptochironomus* sp. Omnivorous chironomids were *Demicryptochironomus, Endochironomus,* and *Harnischia* sp. Also present were unidentified species of the omnivorous genera *Lauterborniella* and *Microtendipes.* Other species that were present belonged to the genera *Orthocladius* and *Parachironomus.* Also present were *Paratendipes* sp. and *Pentaneura* sp., both of which are omnivorous, as is the genus *Phaenopsectra* sp. An unidentified species of the carnivorous genus *Procladius* was also present. Other chironomids that might occur in this habitat were *Stempellina* sp., *Stictochironomus* sp., and *Tanypus* sp. Most of these are omnivorous. Other chironomids found in this habitat were *Tribellos* sp. and *Trissocladius* sp. One taxon belonging to the suborder Brachycera, family Muscidae, was an unidentified species of *Lispe.*

Numerous fish were found in this habitat. They probably had come into the pools to feed or were feeding along the margins of the stream. However, they were found occurring in these lentic areas. They were the carnivorous

Acipenser oxyrhynchus and *Scaphirhynchus albus.* The omnivorous *Polydon spathula* was also present. Three species were present belonging to the genus *Lepisosteus: L. oculatus, L. osseus,* and *L. spathula,* all of which are carnivores. Another carnivorous species found in these pool areas was *Hiodon alosoides.* The family Clupeidae was represented by *Brevoortia patronus, Dorosoma cepedianum,* and *D. petenense.* All of these are omnivores. The omnivorous *Anchoa mitchelli* was also found along the margins of the streams, often in and among vegetation where the current was relatively slow. Two species of carp, *Carpiodes carpio* and *C. cyprinus,* were also found in this habitat. Both of these are omnivores, as is *Cycleptus elongatus,* which was found in these lentic habitats. Other species sometimes found in these habitats were *Erimyzon oblongus* and *E. succetta. Ictiobus bubalus,* which is a carnivore, and *I. cyprinellus,* which is a herbivore, occurred in backwaters. Here also was *I. niger,* an omnivore. In some of these lentic habitats was the carnivore, *Minytrema melanops,* the omnivores *Crassius auritus* and *Cyprinus carpio,* and three herbivorous species belonging to the genus *Hybognathus* (Table 2.14). *Ctenopharyngodon idella,* a herbivore, was present, as were *Hybopsis aestivalis,* an omnivore, and *Notemigonus crysoleucas.* The genus *Notropis* was represented by 10 species that are carnivores and five species that are omnivores. Other cyprinids that were present were the carnivorous *Phenacobius mirabilis,* the omnivorous *Phoxinus erythrogaster,* and four omnivorous species belonging to the genus *Pimephales.*

The order Siluriformes was prevalent in this habitat. One species, *Arius felix,* a carnivore, belongs to the *Ariidae.* The genus *Ictalurus* was represented by five species, two carnivores and three omnivores. The genus *Noturus* was represented by two species, both carnivores. *Pylodictis olivaris,* an omnivore, was also present in these lentic habitats. The salmonid fishes were represented by two species belonging to the genus *Esox,* both of which are carnivores (Table 2.14). The carnivorous *Aphredoderus sayanus* was also present. The family Cyprinodontidae was fairly common in these lentic habitats. The carnivore *Fundulus chrysotus* was often found. *F. grandis,* an omnivore, was present. Another carnivore found here was *Lucania parva.* Other omnivorous fish that were present were *Gambusia affinis, Heterandria formosa,* and *Poecilia latipinna.* One might also find in and among the detritus in these lentic habitats the carnivorous *Labidesthes sicculus;* one species of the genus *Membras,* an omnivore; and two species of *Menidia,* also omnivores. The carnivore *Syngnathus scovelli* has been recorded from these lentic habitats in the river. The centrarchids were well represented in these habitats. Present were *Centrarchus macropterus;* the carnivore *Elassoma zonatum;* seven species of the genus *Lepomis* that were carnivores; and two species, *L. macrochirus* and *L. punctatus,* which are omnivores. Other species present were two omnivorous species belonging to the genus *Micropterus* and two species belonging to the carnivorous genus *Pomoxis.* The family Mugilidae was represented by two herbivorous species belonging to the genus *Mugil.* The family Percidae was represented by a fairly large number of species in this habitat. Seven of them belong to the carnivorous genus *Etheostoma.* Other species present from this family were the carnivorous *Percina capriodes* and *P. copelandi.* Other carnivores present were *Aplodinotus grunniens, Bairdiella chrysoura,* and *Cynoscion arenarius.* The omnivorous *Leiostomus xanthurus* and the carnivorous *Menticirrhus littoralis, Micropogonias undulatus, Pogonias cromis,* and *Sciaenops ocellatus* were also present. The order Pleuronectiformes was represented by two species, *Paralichthys lethostigma,* a carnivore, and *Trinectes maculatus,* an omnivore.

Lotic Habitats.   The lotic habitats in the Atchafalaya River were usually found in association with debris that had been deposited in the river: for example, logs or other wood debris or even refuse of various types lodged in the bed, creating an obstruction to the flow and more rapid currents. In these areas the habitat is usually sand and hard material: wood, rocks, or cement. Here we find lotic associations. Growing attached to the substrate were filaments of the blue-green algae, *Phormidium* and *Rivularia,* along with filaments of the blue-green algae, *Anabaena* sp., *Lyngbya* sp., and three taxons belonging to the genus *Oscillatoria.* Also found were species of *Pediastrum* and *Selenastrum,* and the filamentous green algae *Mougeotia* sp. and *Spirogyra* sp. This was a favorite habitat for numerous diatom species, such as one species of *Cyclotella* and five taxons belonging to the genus *Melosira.* Also present in this habitat were two taxons belonging to the genus *Stephanodiscus.* Other species found in this habitat were *Diatoma vulgare,* an unidentified species of *Meridion, Synedra acus, S. ulna,* and *Tabellaria fenestrata.* Forming filaments attached to these hard substrates or to the sand were a species of *Eunotia curvata, Achnanthes lanceolata* var. *dubia,* and three taxons belonging to the genus *Cocconeis.* Other attached species in this habitat were one species of *Cymbella* and three taxons belonging to the genus *Gomphonema.* Lying in the crevices were *Gyrosigma kutzingii* and *G. scalproides* and three taxons belonging to the genus *Navicula.* Also present was an unidentified species of *Pinnularia* (Table 2.14).

Attached to the wood was *Epithemia turgida.* Present was *Hantzschia amphioxys.* Four taxons belonging to the genus *Nitzschia* were also found. It was interesting to note that unidentified species of the genus *Pediastrum* were present. Other colonial green algae that were found were an unidentified species of *Selenastrum.* Many species of this genus are often found in waters enriched with nitrogen and phosphorus, in other words, where some sewage drainage may be present. An unidentified species of *Bulbochaete* was also present, as were filamentous species of green algae belonging to the genera *Mougeotia* and *Spirogyra.*

Many species of diatoms and several species of protozoans, as well as miscellaneous species in other groups, were found floating in the river. However, one cannot designate a certain habitat for these species, and therefore in developing the structure of the communities, they cannot be utilized.

As one might expect, in and among the crevices of the hard habitat were some species of protozoans, particularly a species of *Paramecium*, which is a dentritivore-omnivore. Two taxons belonging to the family Epistylidae were present. They are known to be bacterial feeders but may also eat other things. This was also true of unidentified species of the genera *Platycola, Pyxicola*, and *Vaginicola*. They are known to be bacterial feeders but may engulf other organisms. Detritivore-omnivores found in this habitat were *Charchesium* sp., *Vorticella* spp., and *Zoothamnium* sp.

This was a favorable habitat for several species of sponges: *Corvospongilla* sp., *Eunapius fragilis, Spongilla ingloviformis,* an unidentified species of *Spongilla, Trochospongilla horrida,* and *T. leidya,* all detritivore-omnivores. Two hydroids were found here, *Chlorohydra viridis* and *Hydra americana*. Crawling over the hard substrate were two triclads, *Dugesia tigrina* and *Phagocita vellata*, which are detritivore-herbivores, as is *Catenula* sp. and unidentified species belonging to the family Typhloplanidae. Several rotifers were found in the lotic habitats (Table 2.14).

Several snails were found in and among the debris: an unidentified species of *Clappia, Littoridina* sp., *Vioscalba louisianae,* unidentified species of *Physa*, an unidentified species of *Lymnaea*, and an unidentified species of *Gyraulus,* all detritivore-omnivores. Several unionids were found in and among the debris in fairly fast water. They were detritivore-omnivores belonging to the genera *Anodonta* sp., *Leptodea* sp., and *Quadrula*. Also present was *Corbicula manilensis,* a widespread species that in many rivers is making unavailable habitats formerly occupied by native species, thus altering significantly the unionid fauna of our rivers.

In the sand often associated with these lotic habitats was a detritivore-herbivore, *Sphaerium* sp. A few leaches were found here: *Helobdella elongata,* a carnivore, and *Placobdella papillifera,* an omnivore. *Macrobdella ditetra* was also present. Several taxons belonging to the family Tubificidae were crawling over the debris in areas where the current was moderately fast. They included one taxon belonging to the genus *Ilyodrilus* and six taxons belonging to the genus *Limnodrilus*, which is a detritivore-herbivore. Other species that were present in this habitat belonging to the family Tubificidae were *Peloscolex multisetosus* and the detritivore-herbivore *Tubifex newaensis*.

Three species belonging to the class Arachnida were present: an unidentified species of *Arrenurus, Diplodontus despiciens,* and an unidentified species (perhaps more than one) belonging to the family Mideidae. The family Chydoridae was represented by two species, *Alona quadrangularis* and *Chydorus sphaericus*. The subclass Ostracoda was represented by unidentified species of the genus *Cadona* and of the genera *Herpetocypris* and *Ilyocypris*.

The copepods were not well represented in this habitat. However, two species, *Macrocyclops albidus* and *Mesocyclops edax,* were present. The isopods were represented by two species, *Cyanthura polita, Asellus* sp., and amphipods, *Corophium lacustre,* which are detritivore-omnivores, were found in the crevices of the wood. One species of *Gammarus* was also found here, the

Gammarus tigrinus group. *Hyalella azteca,* which is a detritivore, was common. Two decapods were found, *Procambarus acutus* and *Macrobrachium ohione.* Also present was *Callinectes sapidus,* an omnivore.

Species of odonates found here were the carnivorous *Amphiagrion saucium, Dromogomphus* sp., *Erpetogomphus* sp., *Gomphus* sp., and *Progomphus obscuris.* Other odonates present were the carnivorous *Perithemis domita* and an unidentified species of *Macromia,* probably an omnivore.

Several species of mayflies were also found in this habitat: two species of the omnivorous genus *Hexagenia.* The hemipterans, *Macrovelia horni* and *Notonecta* sp., were present. The *Megaloptera, Sialis* sp. was present. Also present in the sand associated with the debris in these lotic habitats were unidentified species of *Bidessus* and *Hydrovatus,* the carnivorous *Hygrotus* sp., the carnivorous *Matus* sp., and the carnivorous *Oreodytes* sp. Other beetles found in this habitat were the omnivorous *Notomicrus* sp., *Peltodytes* sp., and *Suphisellus* sp. A few elmid beetles were found in this habitat: an unidentified species of *Lara,* which is a detritivore; *Microcylloepus* sp.; *Cymbiodyta* sp., a herbivore; *Hydrochus* sp.; and *Paracymus* sp., a herbivore.

The dipteran *Palpomyia* sp., which is an omnivore, was also found in and among the gravel in slower-flowing water. *Chaoborus punctipennis* was also present, as was an unidentified species of *Ablabesmyia,* a carnivore. Other chironomids present were *Brillia* sp., an unidentified species of *Cladotanytarsus; Clinotanypus* sp., probably a carnivore; and *Coelotanypus* sp., a carnivore. *Cryptochironomus,* which is a carnivore, was present, as was the omnivorous *Demicryptochironomus* and the omnivorous *Einfeldia, Labrundinia neopilosella, Labrundinia* sp. and *Larsia* sp. Crawling in and among the debris were *Omisus pica; Orthocladius* sp.; *Parachironomus* sp., which is known to be an omnivore; as is *Paracladopelma* sp. *Paralauterborniella* sp. is also probably an omnivore. *Polypedilum* spp., omnivores, were present. Other omnivores in this habitat were *Stempellina* sp., *Stenochironomus* sp., *Tanypus* sp., *Tanytarsus* sp., *Thienemanniella* sp., and *Trissocladius* sp. are probably omnivores. Attached to the wood was a bryozoan, *Pectinatella magnifica,* and *Erioptera* sp. was also present on the wood.

The lotic habitats provided a more unsheltered, more open environment for many species of fish, and as a result the currents in these habitats were affected by the forces of the wind, and most of these habitats favored the stronger currents. Belonging to the order Acipenseriformes were two taxons of the genus *Scaphirhynchus,* both carnivores. Also present were the carnivorous *Lepisosteus oculatus* and *Hiodon alosoides.* A single leach was found in these rapidly flowing habitats, the carnivorous *Anguilla rostrata.* Various culpeids were found here: the carnivorous *Alosa alabamae* and *A. chrysochloris.* The threadfin, *Brevoortia patronus,* was present in these exposed habitats. It is generally regarded as an omnivore. Other omnivores present were *Dorosoma petenense,* which lives in a relatively exposed habitat. It too is an omnivore. Other omnivores present in these lotic habitats were *Anchoa mitchelli, Carpiodes carpio,* and *C. cyprinus.* Another omnivore was *Cy-*

cleptus elongatus. Present are the smallmouth buffalo, *Ictiobus bubalus,* which is a carnivore, and *I. niger,* which is an omnivore. The minnow, *Hybognathus placitus,* which is mainly a herbivore, was found in and among the debris along with the omnivorous *Hybopsis aestivalis.* Several species belonging to the genus *Notropis,* often referred to as shiners, were found in and among the debris. They were *Notropis amnis,* often referred to as the pallid shiner. Other shiners found in this habitat were the carnivorous *Notropis atherinoides* and *N. atrocaudalis,* as well as *N. bairdi, N. blennius, N. boops, N. buchanani, N. emiliae, N. longirostris, N. lutrensis, N. maculatus, N. potteri,* and *N. shu-mardi.* These species are mostly carnivores; however, *N. lutrensis* and *N. maculatus* are omnivorous, as are *N. texanus, N. venustus,* and *N. volucellus. N. whipplei* is believed to be a carnivore.

Many of these species were found in areas where there was a considerable amount of sand and some vegetation and slow-flowing water in among the debris mounds. They may also have occasionally been found in the pools and slow-flowing habitats, as previously mentioned. Other species present were the carnivorous *Phenacobius mirabilis* and the omnivorous *Phoxinus erythro-gaster.* Two taxons belonging to the genus *Pimephales* were present, both omnivores. The carnivorous *Arius felix* was found in among the sand habitats, which were in slowly flowing water. The family Ictaluridae was well represented in both the slower and more rapidly flowing habitats. They were *Ictalurus furcatus,* a carnivore. Also present were two species of this genus which are omnivores, *I. nebulosus* and *I. punctatus.* Also present was the shiner, *Noturus nocturnus,* a carnivore. Several cyprinids were found in among the sand in areas where the current is slower: *Cyprinodon variegatus,* an omnivore; *Fundulus grandis* and *F. notatus,* omnivores; and *F. olivaceus,* a carnivore.

Other species present in this habitat, particularly in areas where the current was less rapid, were *Labidesthes sicculus,* a carnivore; *Membras martinica,* an omnivore; and two species of *Menidia,* both omnivores. The centrarchid family was represented in this habitat by several species: the carnivorous *Amblo-plites ariommus* and *Lepomis megalotus; Micropterus punctulatus,* an omni-vore; and *M. salmoides,* an omnivore. The Percidae, which are carnivores, were represented by six taxons: three species belonging to the genus *Ammo-crypta* and three species belonging to the genus *Percina.* All of these are darters commonly known to hide in and among the debris. Several eels were found in these lotic habitats where the current was less strong: *Morone chrysops, M. mississippiensis,* and *M. saxatilis,* all carnivores.

Other species encountered in this habitat were genera belonging to the family Sciaenidae: *Bairdiella chrysoura,* a carnivore; *Cynoscion arenarius,* a carnivore; *C. nebulosus,* a carnivore; *Leiostomus xanthurus,* an omnivore; *Menticirrhus littoralis,* a carnivore; *Micropogonias undulatus,* a carnivore; *Pogonias cromis,* a carnivore; and *Sciaenops ocellatus,* a carnivore. The hogchoker, *Trinectes maculatus,* an omnivore, was also found in the areas where the current was less strong. Thus we see that these lotic habitats, consisting primarily of debris of various types, particularly wood, supported a well-diversified fauna and flora. All stages of the food web were well represented by many species belonging to different phylogenetic groups.

SUMMARY

The Atchafalaya River is a complex system that is artificial river made by the confluence of the Red River and the Mississippi River and various interlocking lakes, swamps, streams. Originally, the channel was in natural condition, but the diversion of flows has made it rather artificial. The great diversity of habitats resulting from this complex waterway has produced a very large species pool which can potentially occupy the main channel. I have postulated the types of ecosystems one might find functioning in the main channel. The habitats in the main channel are primarily those associated with vegetation, lentic habitats, and lotic habitats formed mainly by the deposition of debris.

The chemical characteristics of the water make the Atchafalaya a medium to very hard river, but typically it is medium hard and often stained by swamp vegetation. Under such conditions the conductivity of the water may be decreased. The rate of flow and season of the year greatly affect whether a habitat is lentic or lotic. Cypress–tupelo gum swamps are typically lentic habitats but may become lotic at certain seasons of the year. The Atchafalaya River is a medium-sized river, but inflows from the Red and Mississippi Rivers give it the hydrology of a large river. In fact, it is the sixth-largest river in North America in terms of discharge. High sediment loads from the Red and Mississippi Rivers result in high sediment loads and suspended sediment concentrations within the Atchafalaya River. Turbidity is often high in the main channel and distributary habitats of the Atchafalaya basin and floodway. Turbidity in lentic and quasilentic habitats is largely dependent on their nearness to the turbid lotic channel.

Alkalinity averages 105 mg L^{-1} and ranges from 48 to 142 mg L^{-1} and the pH ranges from 6.6 to 8.2. Macronutrient concentrations are moderately low. Total nitrogen is usually less than 1.5 mg L^{-1}, with more than 90% typically being in the form of nitrate-nitrogen or organic nitrogen. Total phosphorus is generally less than 0.15 mg L^{-1}. Although the within-basin processes may not significantly alter the overall macronutrient export to Atchafalaya Bay, differences among floodway habitats can be pronounced, especially during low flow. For example, in an August 1975 survey, nitrate-nitrogen from riverine samples ranged from 0.29 to 0.52 mg L^{-1}, while 90% of the lentic samples from the eastern floodway were less than 0.1 mg L^{-1}, and concentrations from the western floodway lentic samples were consistently less than the detection limit (0.1 mg L^{-1}). The channel of the Atchafalaya River is consistently well oxygenated. However, oxygen can be very much reduced in some of the cypress–tupelo gum swamps in the bayous or lakes.

Estimates of the organic productivity in the swamp forest are relatively high. There is a high degree of particulate organic matter retention in permanent lentic habitats, which is probably caused by the lowland topography and slow current. The accumulation of detritus in permanent aquatic habitats suggests that litter processing is relatively inefficient. Leaching of dissolved organic carbon (DOC) accounts for mostly leaf-litter decomposition in backwater, coastal plains, swamp-stream systems in North Carolina and is probably similarly important in the Atchafalaya system. Leaching of DOC provides trophic support for a productive microbial community, which in turn could support a sizable detritivore population. Microbial populations may compete with detritivores by both depressing dissolved oxygen concentration and by converting labile POC and DOC constituents into refractory constituents.

The roots of the water hyacinth, *Eichhornia crassipes,* are a favorite habitat for Tubificidae, Isopoda, and crayfish. Roots of *E. crassipes* and other floating macrophytes provide a refuge from the anoxic habitats during much of the year. They may also be a source of food. Organic carbon is a very important source of food for organisms within the Atchafalaya system. Considerable amounts of organic carbon come from outside the basin. However, the within-basin production is clearly significant. Whereas a considerable amount of DOC is exported, large amounts of POC are retained in the system by burial and by biological activity.

Phytoplankton production is typically modest throughout the year, although many lentic habitats are available. Primary production is limited primarily by low light levels resulting from high suspended sediment concentrations and the abrasive effects of sediment loads. However in the lakes of the system, primary productivity may be fairly high when turbidity is low. During periods when suspended solids were lowest, the chlorophyl *a* concentrations were significantly higher.

Varying amounts of algae appear as phytoplankton, although they are truly scuffed-up benthic forms. Phytoplankton is generally more pronounced during periods of low flow. Distributary habitats, which were particularly common in the swamps, were dominated by centric diatoms and some bluegreens. Swamp waters also contained many of the photosynthetic flagelates and colonial green algae. The kinds of algae found were greatly influenced by the pattern of flooding in the various parts of the Atchafalaya Basin system. Most of the algae production was of species that are characteristic of lentic habitats, which may become phytoplankton during periods of changing and high flow.

Aquatic macrophytes are typically absent from the main channel and distributaries of the Atchafalaya Basin floodplain, but they are very abundant in the swamps, bayous, lakes, and overflow habitats. *Eichhornia crassipes* is probably the most important aquatic macrophyte in the Atchafalaya system. Its success is in part due to its floating life-form, which would enable it to thrive in turbid waters and be easily transported. In the Atchafalaya floodway, this species commonly develops dense growth which can cover some swamps and smaller bayous during periods of low flow. It can be transported into the more actively flowing areas. The production of these aquatic macrophytes is substantial in the system and furnishes desirable habitats for many species. Thus the vegetation habitat is an important one and supports a well-developed ecosystem.

Various zooplankton were characteristic of the various habitats in the system. For example, the taxonomic richness of rotifers was less in the main channel and distributaries than in the swamps and lakes. However, the lentic habitats did contain a large variety of these planktonic invertebrates. Copepods and cladocerans dominated the crustacean populations in the Buffalo Cove and Duck Lake/Flat Lake/Little Bayou Sorrel areas. It is interesting to note that one of the conspicuous features of the populations of rotifers and crustacean zooplankton is that their seasonal trends differ significantly from those of the phytoplankton. The phytoplankton populations are generally greatest during late summer or early autumn. In contrast, zooplankton are generally most abundant during winter and spring, although low flow maxima, especially of rotifers, do occur. This suggests that the size of the zooplankton population is influenced more by seasonal flooding than by phtoplankton abundance.

The benthic invertebrate population was best developed in the swamp and bayou sites, although there were well-established communities in the riverine stations. The benthic and macroinvertebrates from the main channel and distributary samples differed substantially from those collected in other habitats. The hard clay, strong currents, and persistently high concentrations of suspended sediments probably accounted for the low-density records in the main-channel and distributary sites. However, difficulty in collecting may also be a factor. The population seemed to be more dense along the banks than in midchannel. Tubificids predominated in the soft clays located near the shore. The clay was also a favorite habitat for some of the invertebrates. In general, the detritus-rich littoral zone supported more diverse assemblages than did the more open zones.

Despite low levels of dissolved oxygen and occasional reducing conditions, the cypress–gum tupelo swamps yielded the highest mean density of benthic macroinvertebrates. Habitats in these areas were often more favorable than those in the open channel for the development of the fauna.

In the bayous the densities of benthic macroinvertebrates varied considerably. The major maximum occurred in March and June, while minimums occurred in February, April, May, July, and August. Taxonomic richness generally varied with density, although only moderate increases in taxonomic richness accompanied the June density maximum. The benthic macroinvertebrates exhibited relatively high taxonomic richness in the late summer, autumn, and March.

In the riverine stations, the densities exhibited short maximums in March and June and minima from August through February and in April. The June maximum was the result of high densities of *Tortopus* sp. on hard clay substrates, whereas the March maximum was the result of increases in Oligochaeta and Chirinomidae.

Crayfish, freshwater shrimp, and blue crabs are abundant in the basin floodways but are not usually collected by standard benthic samples. Crayfish are abundant and have considerable economic value in this system. The Atchafalaya Basin floodway supports large populations of two freshwater shrimp, *Macrobrachium ohione* and *Palaemonetes* spp. Commercial shrimping is carried out on these species, particularly on *Macrobrachium ohione.* The collection of *Palaemonetes kadiakensis* occurred in large numbers in the distributary channels during February, March, and April. It is interesting to note that *M. ohione* was either absent or rare in these hauls, which suggests some kind of complementarity between the two taxa. The Atchafalaya Basin floodway supports an extensive fishery of the blue crab, *Callinectes sapidus.* Most of the crabs were collected in the floodways.

Fish fauna of the system is rich, as the basin supports 125 species and an additional 56 species that were probably strays from tributaries outside the basin or strays from nearby marine zones. Not only is the fish fauna very diverse, but it is very productive. The standing stock and community structure of fish in the upper basin differ significantly from the floodway standing stock and community structure. This was attributed to differences in the allochthonous and autochthonous inputs. The upper basin sites do not experience high turbidity and overbank flooding, and thus have a high phytoplankton productivity. Forage fish such as *Dorosoma cepedianum* are very common, whereas sport, commercial, and predatory fish are less numerous. Poor populations of sport, commercial, and predatory fishes appear to be the result of reduced allochthonous inputs and/or reduced overflow habitat. The importance of overflow habitats to the fish was particularly evident in a study of permanent distributary and canal waterways and overflow sites in the Fordoche area. The overflow sites are important spawning and/or nursery habitats for a variety of species. However, several species, such as the centrarchids, have been observed to prefer the swamps and bayou habitats. This is also true for *Lepisoteus oculatus, Amia calva,* and *Ictalurus natalis.* Many species use overflow habitats.

Several species exhibit ontogenic habitat partitioning. For example, the young of *Lepomis gulosus, L. macrochirus,* and *Macropterus salmoides* are concentrated in overflow habitats and the shallow waters of permanent lentic habitats, while the adults are concentrated in deeper water.

Many of the larger species of fish exhibit seasonal patterns of habitat use that correspond to seasonal changes in water quality. Most of the more abundant species associated with swamps, bayous, and overflow habitats are also common in lakes. Some species are commonly associated with macrophytes, which can be abundant in swamps, bayous, and lake habitats.

The main channel and the larger distributaries are characterized by significant populations of certain species. Parts of the Atchafalaya Basin support a number of primarily marine and estuarine fishes. This is because of the connection of these areas with the surrounding bays. A considerable amount of spawning takes place within the system, and species seem to select various types of waters for this activity.

The functioning of the communities in this basin is primarily dependent on allochthonous organic material. This input is produced within the system and is brought in from external areas. However, most of the allochthonous input originates from overflow habitats and is in the form of detritus and leached DOC.

As explained in the section "Structure of Aquatic Communities," the foodwebs that exist within the system involve a great many species. Each of the major habitats, such as those found in association with vegetation and those that are typical lentic or lotic habitats, is very diverse and robust, in that many species belonging to different phylogenetic groups are carrying out each major function.

BIBLIOGRAPHY

Beck, L. T., 1977. Temporal and spatial distribution of benthic macroinvertebrates in the Lower Atchafalaya Basin, Louisiana. Master's thesis. School of Forestry and Wildlife Management, Louisiana State Univ., Baton Rouge, La.

Benke, A. C., T. C. Van Arsdall, Jr., D. M. Gillespie, and F. K. Parrish. 1984. Invertebrate productivity in a subtropical blackwater river: the importance of habitat and life history. Ecol. Monogr. 54(1): 25–63.

Bennett, D. H., and R. W. McFarlane. 1983. The fishes of the Savannah River Plant: National Environmental Research Park. SRO-NERP-12. Savannah River Ecological Laboratory, Savannah River Site. 152 pp.

Bernard, D. L., and J. R. Renner. 1980. Modeling the Atchafalaya River. Proc. La. Acad. Sci. 43: 69–78.

Bouchard, R. Personal communication. Academy of Natural Sciences of Philadelphia, Philadelphia, Pa.

Boyer, B. E. 1982. Distribution and relative abundance of fish eggs, larvae and early juveniles in the inundated Mississippi River floodplain near Saint Francisville, Louisiana. Master's thesis. School of Forestry and Wildlife Management, Louisiana State Univ., Baton Rouge, La.

Brigham, A. R., W. V. Brigham, and A. Gnilka. 1982. Aquatic insects and oligochaetes of North and South Carolina. Midwest Aquatic Enterprises. Mahomet, Ill.

Brown, S. 1981. A comparison of the structure, primary productivity, and transpiration of cypress ecosystems in Florida. Ecol. Mongr. 51(4): 403–427.

Bryan, C. F., and D. S. Sabins. 1979. Management implications in water quality and fish standing stock information in the Atchafalaya River Basin, Louisiana. pp. 293–316. *In* J. W. Day, Jr., D. D. Culley, Jr., R. E. Turner, and A. J. Mumphrey, Jr., eds., Proceedings of the 3rd coastal marsh and estuary management symposium. Division of Continuing Education, Louisiana State Univ., Baton Rouge, La.

Bryan, C. F., F. M. Truesdale, D. S. Sabins, and C. R. Demas. 1974. A limnological survey of the Atchafalaya Basin. A progress report. U.S. Department of the Interior, Washington, D.C.

Bryan, C. F., F. M. Truesdale, and D. S. Sabins. 1975. Limnological studies of the Atchafalaya River Basin. U.S. Department of the Interior, Washington, D.C.

Clary, P. 1985. Habitat characteristics and food of larval black crappie (*Pomoxis nigromaculatus*) and warmouth (*Lepomis gulosus*) in selected overflow habitats of the Atchafalaya River Basin, Louisiana. Master's thesis, Louisiana State Univ., Baton Rouge, La. 56 pp.

Conner, W. H. and J. W. Day, Jr. 1976. Productivity and composition of a baldcypress–water tupelo site and a bottomland hardwood site in a Louisiana swamp. Am. J. Bot. 63(10): 1354–1364.

Cook, F. A. 1959. Freshwater fishes in Mississippi. Mississippi Game and Fish Commission, Jackson, Miss. 239 pp.

Cudney, M. D., and J. B. Wallace. 1980. Life cycles, microdistribution and production dynamics of six species of net-spinning caddisflies in a large southeastern (U.S.A.) river. Holarct. Ecol. 3(3): 169–182.

Cuffney, T. F., and J. B. Wallace. 1987. Leaf litter processing in Coastal Plains streams and floodplains of southeastern Georgia, U.S.A. Hydrobiol. Suppl. 76(1–2): 1–24.

Curry, M. G., and C. M. Allen. 1973. *Alismataceae* of Louisiana: taxonomy, distribution, and field key. Proc. La. Acad. Sci. 36: 88–95.

Day, J. W., Jr., W. B. Johnson, C. J. Madden, B. A. Thompson, L. A. Deegan, W. B. Sikora, and J. P. Sikora. 1988. The development of an estuarine ecosystem in a coastal freshwater deltaic environment. pp. 209–219. *In* J. W. Day, Jr., and W. H. Conner eds., Physical processes, ecological dynamics and management implications: results of research in the Atchafalaya Bay Delta. Louisiana Sea Grant College Program, Baton Rouge, La.

Deegan, L. A., and B. A. Thompson. 1985. The ecology of fish communities in the Mississippi River Deltaic Plain. pp. 35–56. *In* A. Yanez, ed., Fish community ecology in estuaries and lagoons: towards an ecosystem integration. Universidad Nacional Autónoma de Mexico Cuidad Universitaria, Mexico City, Mexico. (Reprinted in J. W. Day, Jr., and W. H. Conner, eds., Physical processes, ecological dynamics and management implications: results of research in the Atchafalaya Bay Delta. Louisiana Sea Grant College Program, Baton Rouge, La.)

Denes, T. A., and S. E. Bayley. 1983. Long-term rainfall, runoff, and discharge in the Atchafalaya River Basin, Louisiana. La. Acad. Sci. 46: 114–121.

Edwards, R. T. 1987. Sestonic bacteria as a food source for filtering invertebrates in two southeastern blackwater rivers. Limnol. Oceanogr. 32(1): 221–234.

Fremling, C. R., J. L. Rasmussen, R. E. Sparks, S. P. Cobb, C. F. Bryan, and T. O. Claflin. 1989. Mississippi River fisheries: a case history. pp. 309–351. *In* D. P. Dodge, ed., Proceedings of the international large river symposium. Can. Spec. Publ. Fish. Aquat. Sci. 106. Canadian Government Publications Centre, Ottawa, Canada.

Geagan, D. W. 1962. Notes on the distribution of the fresh water shrimp *Palaemonetes* (Heller) in Louisiana. Proc. La. Acad. Sci. 25: 58–62.

Gunter, G. 1937. Observations on the river shrimp, *Macrobrachium ohione*. Am. Mid. Nat. 18(6): 1038–1042.

Hart, C. W., Jr., and S. L. H. Fuller. 1974. Pollution ecology of freshwater invertebrates. Academic Press, San Diego, Calif. 389 pp.

Hern, S. C., W. D. Taylor, L. R. Williams, V. W. Lambou, M. K. Morris, F. A. Morris, and J. W. Hilgert. 1978. Distribution and importance of phytoplankton in the Atchafalaya Basin. Ecol. Res. Ser. 600/3–78/001. U.S. Environmental Protection Agency, Washington, D.C. (Univ. of Nevada at Las Vegas, Biological Sciences Department).

Holland, L. E. 1977. Distribution and ecology of plankton Rotifera in the Atchafalaya River Basin, Louisiana. Master's thesis. Louisiana State Univ., Baton Rouge, La. 90 pp.

Holland, L. E., C. F. Bryan, and J. P. Newman, Jr. 1983. Water quality and the rotifer populations in the Atchafalaya River Basin. Hydrobiologia 98(1): 55–69.

Hunner, J. V., and J. E. Barr. 1981. Red swamp crawfish: biology and exploitation. Center for Wetlands Research, Louisiana State Univ., Baton Rouge, La. 148 pp.

Lambou, V. W. 1965. The commercial and sport fisheries of the Atchafalaya Basin Floodway. Proc. 17th Ann. Conf. S.E. Assoc. Game Fish Comm. 1963: 256–281.

Lambou, V. W., and S. C. Hern. 1983. Transport of organic carbon in the Atchafalaya Basin, Louisiana. Hydrobiologia 98(1): 25–34.

Lee, D. C., C. R. Gilbert, C. H. Hocutt, R. E. Jenkins, D. E. McAllister, and J. R. Stauffer, Jr. 1980. Atlas of North American fishes. North Carolina State Museum of Natural History, Raleigh, N.C. 854 pp.

Levine, S. J. 1977. Food and feeding habits of juveniles and adults of selected forage, commercial, and sport fishes in the Atchafalaya Basin, Louisiana. Master's thesis. Louisiana State Univ., Baton Rouge, La. 63 pp.

Malcolm, R. I., and W. H. Durum. 1976. Organic carbon and nitrogen concentrations and annual organic load of six selected rivers of the United States. Water-Supply Pap. 1817-F. U. S. Geological Survey, Washington, D.C. 21 pp.

Montz, G. N. 1980. Distribution of selected aquatic plant species in Louisiana. Proc. La. Acad. Sci. 43: 119–138.

Mulholland, P. J. 1981. Organic carbon flow in a swamp-stream ecosystem. Ecol. Monogr. 51(3): 307–322.

Obi, A., and J. V. Conner. 1986. Spring and summer macroinvertebrate drift in the Lower Mississippi River, Louisiana, U.S.A. Hydrobiologia 139(2): 167–176.

O'Brien, T. P. 1977. Crawfishes of the Atchafalaya Basin, Louisiana, with emphasis on those species of commercial importance. Master's thesis. Agricultural and Mechanical College, Louisiana State Univ., Baton Rouge, La. 79 pp.

Penn G. H., Jr. 1943. A study of the life history of the Louisiana red crawfish, *Procambarus clarkii* (Girard). Ecology 24(1): 1–18.

Penn, G. H., Jr. 1959. An illustrated key to the crawfishes of Louisiana, with a summary of their distribution within the state. Tulane Stud. Zool. 7(1): 3–20.

Pennak, R. W. 1989. Fresh-water invertebrates of the United States, 3rd ed., Wiley, New York.

Pfleiger, W. L. 1975. The fishes of Missouri. Missouri Department of Conservation, Jefferson City, Mo. 343 pp.

Pollard, J. E., S. N. Melancon, and L. S. Blakey. 1981. Importance of bottomland hardwoods to an aquatic ecosystem: a study of the Henderson Lake area, Atchafalaya Basin, Louisiana. Environmental Monitoring Systems Laboratory, Office of Research and Development, U.S. Environmental Protection Agency, Las Vegas, Nev. 111 pp. plus appendixes.

Rogers, R., and J. V. Hunner. 1985. Comparison of burrows and burrowing behavior of five species of cambarid crawfish (Crustacea, Decapoda) from the Southern University campus, Baton Rouge, Louisiana. Proc. La. Acad. Sci. 48: 23–29.

Stone, J. H., L. M. Bahr, Jr., and J. W. Day, Jr. 1978. Effects of canals on freshwater marshes in coastal Louisiana and implications for management. pp. 299–320. *In* R. E. Good, D. F. Whigham, and R. L. Simpson, eds. Freshwater wetlands: ecological processes and management potential. Academic Press, San Diego, Calif. 378 pp.

Truesdale, F. M., and W. J. Mermilliod. 1979. The river shrimp *Macrobrachium ohione* (Smith) (Decapoda, Palaemonidae): its abundance, reproduction and growth in the Atchafalaya River Basin of Louisiana, U.S.A. Crustaceana 36(1): 61–73.

U.S. Army Corps of Engineers. 1952. Geological investigation of the Atchafalaya Basin and the problems of Mississippi River diversion. Report for Mississippi River Commission by the U.S. Army Corps of Engineers Waterways Experiment Station, Vicksburg, Miss. 145 pp.

van Heerden, I. L., and H. H. Roberts. 1980. The Atchafalaya Delta—Louisiana's new prograding coast. Trans. Gulf Assoc. Geol. Soc. 30: 497–506. (Reprinted in J. W. Day, Jr., and W. H. Conner, eds. Physical processes, ecological dynamics and management implications: results of research in the Atchafalaya Bay Delta. Louisiana Sea Grant College Program, Baton Rouge, La.)

Webb, D. W., and W. U. Brigham. 1982. Aquatic Diptera. pp. 11.1–11.111. *In* A. R. Brigham, W. U. Brigham, and A. Gnilka, eds. Aquatic insects and oligochaetes of North and South Carolina. Midwest Aquatic Enterprises, Mahomet, Ill.

Wells, F. C., and C. R. Demas. 1977. Hydrology and water quality of the Atchafalaya River Basin. Tech. Rep. 14. U.S. Fish and Wildlife Service, Louisiana Department of Public Works and U.S. Geological Survey, Baton Rouge, La. 53 pp.

CHAPTER 3

Main Stem—Missouri River

INTRODUCTION

The longest river in North America, the Missouri River, traverses much of the north-central United States. This naturally turbid river, also known as the Big Muddy, has often been described as being too thick to drink and too thin to plow. Turbid Great Plains rivers such as the Missouri have generally been regarded as being harsh and relatively unproductive aquatic environments. However, a variety of data suggest that the Missouri was and is in some reaches highly productive.

The Missouri River today is very different from the wild river seen by Lewis and Clark. A series of six main-stem impoundments in the upper part of the river have substantially reduced turbidity, regulated flow, and degraded the formerly alluvial channel. In addition, the lower part of the river has been channelized for navigation. Throughout its length the extensive floodplain has been, in many areas, either inundated behind dams or developed extensively for agricultural, industrial, or urban use. The river itself has been subjected to severe pollution, although recent pollution control measures have improved water quality considerably.

Reconstructing the characteristics of the natural river is difficult because natural or precontrol studies are almost nonexistent. However, a number of historical records and more recent studies give some indication of the biota and environmental conditions characteristic of the precontrol river. These include studies from the 1960s and 1970s of the biota and environment of two unchannelized reaches below the two lowermost dams, Fort Randall Dam and

Gavins Point Dam. Impoundment and flow regulation had been affected for at least 15 years by the time some of these studies were conducted, thus these sites must be regarded as representing a transitional environment. However, they offer information on certain habitats now largely absent from the river. Studies from the channelized river are also considered.

PHYSICAL CHARACTERISTICS

The Missouri River originates in southwestern Montana with the confluence of the Gallatin, Madison, and Jefferson Rivers and flows 3678 km to the east and southeast, to where it joins the Mississippi near St. Louis, Missouri. It drains an area of 1,354,564 km^2, which is approximately one-sixth of the contiguous United States and encompasses four major physiographic regions. The westernmost 10.5% of the basin, which includes parts of Saskatchewan (Canada), Montana, Wyoming, and Colorado, lies within the Rocky Mountains. Most of the basin (68.8%) lies within the semiarid Great Plains and encompasses portions of Montana, North and South Dakota, Nebraska, Colorado, and Kansas. An additional 16.8% of the basin lies within the more mesic Central Lowlands (including the Osage Plains) and includes the eastern parts of the Dakotas, Nebraska, and Kansas, as well as portions of Missouri, Iowa, and Minnesota. Most of the remaining basin drains portions of the Ozark Uplands in Missouri (Hesse et al., 1989c; Slizeski et al., 1982).

Once the river leaves the Rocky Mountains, it passes through watershed vegetation grading from semiarid shortgrass prairies and shrubland in the western Great Plains to mosaics of tallgrass prairies and oak–hickory woodlands in the east. Northern floodplain forests ascend the valleys of the Missouri and several of its major tributaries (USGS, 1970). Much of the upper river floodplain forest has been inundated by six main-stem impoundments, and approximately 95% of the floodplain forest in the lower river has been converted to agricultural, industrial, or urban land use (Bragg and Tatschi, 1977; Hesse et al., 1989c). Approximately half of the land use within the entire basin in pasture and rangeland, while another third is cropland. Most of the remaining is either forest or woodland (Slizeski et al., 1982).

Prior to Pleistocene glaciation the Missouri River flowed north into Hudson Bay. With the advancing ice sheets, however, the river was diverted southward and numerous east-flowing rivers were captured. This resulted in a substantial increase in drainage area. It also resulted in an anomalous drainage pattern in which the river lies significantly closer to the northern and eastern margin of the basin, and most of the major tributaries enter from the west or south. The Yellowstone, Milk, Little Missouri, Cheyenne, White, Niobrara, Platte, and Kansas Rivers are major east- or north-flowing tributaries. All of these tributaries drain large areas of the Great Plains, and some, including the Yellowstone and the Platte, also drain portions of the Rocky

Mountains. Downstream from where the river passes between Nebraska and South Dakota, however, an increasing number of tributaries enter from the north. The James, Big Sioux, Little Sioux, and Grand Rivers are major south-flowing tributaries draining predominantly Central Lowland subbasins. The eastern reaches of the Platte and Kansas Rivers also drain Central Lowlands subbasins (Hesse et al., 1989c).

In its upper reaches the Missouri is a cool, clearwater river flowing through canyons and rugged mountains. Silt loads increase dramatically with the entry of tributaries carrying the highly erosible alluvial deposits of the Great Plains (Hesse et al., 1989c). This sediment input has contributed to the aggrading nature of the Missouri River. Characteristically, the river is situated in a rock trough ranging up to 30 m in depth and 3 to 27 km in width. This trough had first been filled with glacial drift and then with alluvial deposits. The river itself and its floodplain lie atop these deep alluvial deposits (Hesse, 1990; Slizeski et al., 1982).

In its natural state the Missouri River and its floodplain were in a state of dynamic equilibrium of aggrading and degrading processes dependent on variations in discharge and sediment load. This dynamic equilibrium generated a diverse and dynamic array of aquatic habitats. The meandering and often braided main channel(s) wandered over the lower floodplain and contained numerous sandbars and pools. Shallow chutes (i.e., side channels), backups (i.e., chutes with their upstream ends sealed by sediments), and cattail (*Typha*) marshes were frequent. Cutoffs and oxbow lakes were also frequent (Hesse, 1990; Kallemeyn and Novotny, 1977; Schmulbach, 1974). This variety of aquatic habitats was augmented with tributaries. As they flow through the wide floodplain the currents of many smaller tributaries become sluggish and the channels become deeper and wider. In addition, the mouths of some tributaries are sealed by sediments and isolated from the river during low water (Dames et al., 1989).

An extensive floodplain forest up to 27 km wide developed in the alluvium-filled rock troughs of the Missouri and its major tributaries. The lower floodplain consisted of a broad area of terrestrial vegetation in varying states of succession caused by the river's wandering and seasonal flooding. Vegetational assemblages in the lower floodplain usually ranged from sedges and herbs to sandbar willow (*Salix exigua* spp. *interior*), cottonwood (*Populus deltoides*), and peachleaf willow (*S. amygdaloides*). Bank erosion, channel migration, and seasonal flooding resulted in the substantial input of snags into the river from this lower floodplain vegetation. A more mature forest containing *P. deltoides,* dogwood (*Cornus stolonifera*), elm (*Ulmus americana*), ash (*Fraxinus americana*), and maple (*Acer negundo*) developed beyond the reach of channel wandering and seasonal flooding but was subjected periodically to major floods (Hesse, 1990; Williams, 1970).

This natural river–floodplain system has been altered dramatically by human activity. The two most important agents of change are the series of

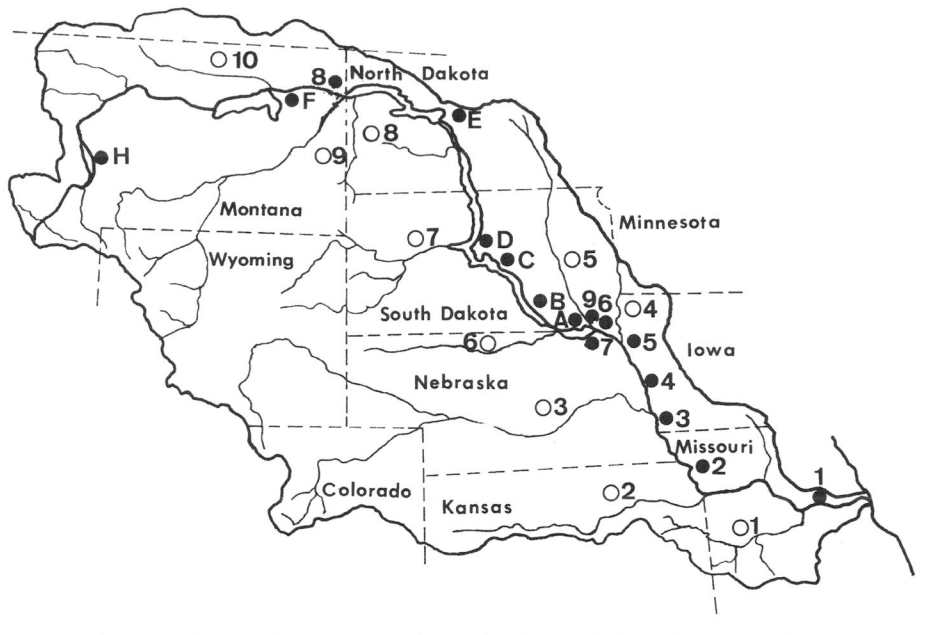

FIGURE 3.1   Map of the main-stem reservoirs, study sites, and tributaries of the Missouri River. (●) Numbers represent study sites: 1, Herman, Missouri; 2, St. Joseph, Missouri; 3, Nebraska City, Nebraska; 4, Omaha, Nebraska; 5, Sioux City, Iowa; 6, Vermillion, South Dakota; 7, Fort Calhoun Station, Nebraska; 8, Culbertson, Montana; 9, Yankton, South Dakota. (●) Letters represent mainstem reservoirs: A, Lewis and Clark Lake; B, Lake Francis Case; C, Big Bend Dam; D, Oahe Dam; E, Garrison Dam; F, Fort Peck Dam; H, Canyon Ferry Reservoir. (○) Numbers represent tributaries: 1, Osage; 2, Kansas; 3, Platte; 4, Big Sioux; 5, James; 6, Niobrara; 7, Cheyenne; 8, Little Missouri; 9, Yellowstone; 10, Milk.

mainstem impoundments in the upper river and the channelization of the lower river (Figure 3.1). Between 1938 and 1963 six main-stem impoundments were constructed in the upper river for flood control, irrigation, hydroelectric generation, water supply, and navigation control. Extending from Fort Peck Lake in north-central Montana (impounded by Fort Peck Dam at river km 2851) to Lewis and Clark Lake along the eastern border between South Dakota and Nebraska (impounded by Gavins Point Dam at km 1305), they impound 1233 km of the river. The lower 1202 km of the river have been channelized. Channelization between St. Louis and Kansas City (km 590) was authorized in 1912. A mandated 2.7-m-deep and 91-m-wide navigation channel extending from the mouth to Sioux City, Iowa (km 1178), was authorized in 1945 and was essentially completed in 1972. Bank stabilization has also been completed for a reach extending 44 km upstream from Sioux City (Hesse et al., 1989c; Pflieger and Grace, 1987; Schmulbach et al., 1975).

Channel maintenance structures such as wing dikes, spur dikes, and revetments (trail dikes) use the force of the river to scour a narrower and deeper channel that facilitates navigation. Instead of the 610- to 1829-m widths that characterized the unchannelized river, stabilized widths range from 180 m at Sioux City to 330 m at the mouth. This scouring action transformed the river profile from a widely offset "V" to a deeper and narrower trapazoid. This has resulted in the lowering of the river stage, which in turn has resulted in the draining of chutes, backups, and marshes. Oxbow lakes, once sporadically connected to the river, are now perched several meters above it. In addition, sedimentation of depositional areas created by wing dikes has eliminated many of the larger chutes (Hesse, 1990; Pflieger and Grace, 1987; Slizeski et al., 1982).

Consequently, channelization has eliminated nearly all of the backwater habitat in the lower river, and an estimated 50% of the total aquatic habitat area has been lost. Some habitat mitigation has been affected since 1974, but the lower reaches of tributaries are the primary remaining backwater habitat in the lower Missouri River (Dames et al., 1989; Hesse et al., 1989c; Pflieger and Grace, 1987; Whitley and Campbell, 1974).

In addition to the loss of backwater habitats, channelization has greatly altered important habitat characteristics in the main channel. Current velocities, which previously ranged from 0.5 to 1.5 m s^{-1} now range from 1.2 to 2.1 m s^{-1} throughout most of the channel. Except for the deep pools (up to 9 m) that develop downstream from pile dikes, the depth of the channelized river is relatively uniform and usually exceeds 3 m. By contrast, the depths of the alternating shoals and pools of the unchannelized river ranged up to 8 m but averaged less than 2 m (Kallemeyn and Novotny, 1977; Morris et al., 1968; Pflieger and Grace, 1987).

Sediments in both the channelized and unchannelized river are dominated by sand. Silt, clay, and organic matter accumulate in the backwater and marsh habitats and in the depositional zones at the downstream ends of dikes. Fine gravel can be found in some fast-water sites. Hard substrates provided by stone and wood channelization structures partially offset the loss of the extensive snag habitat of the natural river (Hesse et al., 1982c; Kallemeyn and Novotny, 1977; Morris et al., 1968; Pflieger and Grace, 1987).

One of the major effects of the main-stem impoundments on the Missouri River is flow regulation. During the navigation season (April through November) releases from Gavins Point Dam to the lower river range from 700 to 990 m^3 s^{-1}. Releases during the nonnavigation season (December through March) and water released for hydroelectric generation, water quality, and flood control purposes average 170 to 650 m^3 s^{-1}. Releases vary in response to annual and seasonal differences in upper basin water supply and inputs from downstream tributaries, but flows during the navigation season are relatively constant (Hesse et al., 1989c; Pflieger and Grace, 1987).

This regulated pattern of sustained high flow during the navigation season and reduced and more erratic flow during the rest of the year contrasts with that of the natural or precontrol river. Discharge patterns in the precontrol river were formed in large part by climatic differences within the basin. Most of the semiarid Great Plains and lowland portions of the Rocky Mountains receive less than 41 cm of precipitation annually, but precipitation as high as 127 cm yr^{-1} occurs in the higher elevations of the Rocky Mountains, much of it as snow (Slizeski et al., 1982). This resulted in characteristic seasonal flooding from March to April and in June. The early spring floods were caused by snowmelt within the plains and the breakup of riverine ice. The "June rise" was caused by the combination of mountain snowmelt and seasonally high rainfall throughout the basin. Because the crests of the flood stages in the larger rivers tend to flatten, both of these rises were typically gradual, although river ice often increased the destructiveness of the early spring floods. Flows were typically stable during the rest of the year (L. W. Hesse, personal communication; Hesse et al., 1989c; Slizeski et al., 1982). Climate within the Missouri River basin varies considerably and droughts extending for several years are commonplace (Slizeski et al., 1982).

Flooding from heavy runoff and ice jams, particularly in late spring, is still a major problem in the lower river. In part, this is a consequence of the greater precipitation that falls in the subhumid Central Lowlands, much of which occurs as intense thunderstorms. There is some indication that flooding in the lower river has become more intense (i.e., the river stage increases more quickly) since channelization and construction of the dams (L. W. Hesse, personal communications). Several possibilities, including increased surface runoff from agricultural watersheds, would lead to an increase in flooding intensity. However, channel alteration is probably the most significant cause. Instead of dispersing through backwaters and over low-lying floodplains, the floodwaters are now confined to a narrow channel.

In addition to the regulation of flow, the main-stem impoundments, by serving as sediment traps, have greatly reduced turbidity in the Big Muddy. From 1940 to 1952 the mean annual loading of suspended sediment at Omaha, Nebraska, was 148,930,000 metric tons (t). Following the closing of Gavins Point Dam in 1954, mean suspended sediment loading at Omaha declined by 81% to 29,487,000 t (Slizeski et al., 1982). From 1918 to 1952, mean annual turbidities at Kansas City ranged from 1300 to 3200 ppm but dropped an average of 65% (470 to 800 ppm) (Whitley and Campbell, 1974). Turbidities increase downstream from the impoundments as a result of bank erosion and tributary input. For example, turbidities in the tailwaters of Gavins Point Dam averaged 50 ppm, while the average increases to 568 ppm near Nebraska City, Nebraska (Morris et al., 1968).

The substantial decline in sediment loads and the loss of seasonal flooding have resulted in the nearly total destruction of the river–floodplain system in the unchannelized reaches of the Middle Missouri River. Discharges of sediment-poor waters from the reservoirs degrade the alluvial channels, thereby lowering the river level. For example, between 1929 and 1980 the river 8.3 km below Gavins Point Dam has dropped 2.26 m. Channel degradation continues until the entry of the Platte River, some 346 km downstream and well within the channelized reach. This lowering of the river level has resulted in the draining of chute, backup, and marsh habitats (Hesse et al., 1989c). The loss of sediment load and seasonal flooding has also altered the natural aggradation/degradation processes that resulted in channel migration and riverine–floodplain interactions (Hesse, 1990; Hesse et al., 1989a). Isolation of the floodplain from the river has resulted in the succession of more mature hardwood forest (Williams, 1970) and loss of snag habitat (Hesse, 1990).

During the 1960s and 1970s, a number of studies were conducted on two unchannelized reaches of the Middle Missouri River. One of the reaches extended from the tailwaters of Gavins Point Dam to the bank-stabilized region upstream from Sioux City. The other extended from the headwaters of Lewis and Clark Lake (formed by Gavins Point Dam) to the tailwaters of Fort Randall Dam, which is the next dam upstream. Study sites within these two reaches contained the chute, backup, marsh, pool, sandbar, and snag habitats that characterized the precontrol river (e.g., Kallemeyn and Novotny, 1977; Morris et al., 1968; Schmulbach, 1974; Volesky, 1969). However, the extent and characteristic of these habitats may have been somewhat different from that of the natural river because varying degrees of flow regulation and channel degradation had been in effect since the mid-1950s. Since then there has been almost total elimination of backwater habitat from the unchannelized reach below Gavins Point Dam. In addition, much of the sandbar habitat has also been lost. Some of the backwater and sandbar habitat still remains in the unchannelized reach below Fort Randall Dam (Hesse, 1990; Hesse et al., 1989b). However, hydroelectric power generation at Fort Randall Dam results in substantial diurnal fluctuations in flow. Discharge from the dam can vary from 0 to 45.3 $m^3 s^{-1}$ during the nonnavigation season, and there are times when much of the channel is desiccated. Mean discharges are much higher during the navigation season, but even then daily change can be as great as 1.5 m, thereby draining backwater habitats (L. W. Hesse, personal communication). Gavins Point Dam is a re-regulatory dam that evens out the erratic upstream releases and provides uniform flows for the downstream navigation channel (Hesse et al., 1989c; Kallemeyn and Novotny, 1977).

The Missouri River is a warm-water river. In the unchannelized reach below Gavins Point Dam, main-channel temperatures ranged from 3.0 to 29.5°C during an April through October study period, while chute temperatures ranged from 4.5 to 30.5°C (Morris et al., 1968). In a study of the unchannelized river below Fort Randall Dam, mean backup temperatures (20°C) were greater than those from both chutes (16°C) and main channel (17°C) habitats (Hesse et al., 1989b). Temperatures in the channelized river near Blair, Nebraska, ranged from 0.0 to 27°C (Todd and Bender, 1982). Freezing during the winter is extensive, and backwater habitats may totally freeze over. Winter freeze-up usually occurs in early December, while ice breakup occurs sometime in February or March. However, the river does not freeze over completely during mild winters (Vanden Berge and Vohs, 1977).

CHEMICAL CHARACTERISTICS

Throughout its length the streamwater of the Missouri is hard water to very hard water, alkaline, high in conductivity, and high in total dissolved solids (Table 3.1). By the time it leaves the Rocky Mountains in western Montana, its hardness is dominated by calcium, magnesium, and bicarbonate. For example, total hardness below Canyon Ferry Dam (western Montana) averaged 141 mg L^{-1} as $CaCO_3$ during water year 1970, while noncarbonate hardness averaged only 4 mg L^{-1}. Total hardness increases with passage through the semiarid Great Plains region of central and eastern Montana, so that by the time the river reaches the Montana–North Dakota border near Culbertson, Montana, total hardness averages 241 mg L^{-1}. Much of this increase in hardness is attributable to increases in the concentrations of alkaline sulfates; noncarbonate hardness increases to an average of 68 mg L^{-1}, and sulfates increase from 38 mg L^{-1} at Canyon Ferry Dam to 171 mg L^{-1} at Culbertson. Aside from moderate increases in sulfate and chloride, the concentrations of major inorganic constituents remain stable as the river passes Yankton, South Dakota (immediately below Gavins Point Dam), and Nebraska City, Nebraska (in the channelized river). Below Nebraska City,

TABLE 3.1. *Mean Values for Selected Chemical Characteristics at Six Stations on the Missouri River, Water Year 1970*

	Canyon Ferry Dam (Mont.)	Culbertson (Mont.)	Yankton (S. Dak.)	Nebraska City (Nebr.)	Hermann (Mo.)
River km	3609	2608	1297	905	158
Total hardness (mg L^{-1})	141	241	237	246	208
Noncarbonate hardness (mg L^{-1})	4	68	72	74	49
Calcium (mg L^{-1})	39	69	72	74	49
Magnesium (mg L^{-1})	12	22	21	21	17
Sulfate (mg L^{-1})	38	171	201	190	98
Chloride (mg L^{-1})	9	8	14	21	14
Bicarbonate (mg L^{-1})	169	197	199	204	187
Carbonate (mg L^{-1})	0	0	—	0	0
Alkalinity (mg L^{-1})	—	—	—	170	153
Conductivity (μs cm L^{-1})	367	654	740	727	533
Total dissolved solids (mg L^{-1})	227	438	492	489	353
pH	7.9	7.9	8.1	8.0	7.8

Source: After USGS (1975).

tributary inputs from the more mesic watersheds of the Central Lowlands (Iowa, eastern Nebraska, eastern Kansas, and Missouri) result in some dilution of the mineral-rich Missouri River. By the time the river reaches Hermann, Missouri (river km 158), mean total hardness averages 208 mg L^{-1} (USGS, 1975).

The concentrations of most dissolved inorganic constituents are high during low winter flows, but the normal pattern of reduced concentrations with increased flow is complicated by the regulated storage and discharge of large quantities of water by the mainstem dams. The concentrations of dissolved constituents in water stored behind the reservoirs are relatively uniform. Consequently, discharge maxima originating from reservoir releases result in only modest changes for dissolved constituents in downstream reaches. On the other hand, discharge maxima originating from runoff events (e.g., snowmelt) characteristically result in concentration minima. As a result, the concentrations of dissolved constituents are generally lowest during spring, when runoff events are more frequent, but are relatively stable during summer and autumn (Ford, 1982; Todd and Bender, 1982; USGS, 1975).

Macronutrient concentrations in the upper Missouri River are moderately low, indicating natural conditions while higher concentrations probably indicate the effects of fertilization by grazing herds and agriculture. For example, nitrate and dissolved phosphorus concentrations near Culbertson, Montana, ranged from 0.1 to 0.4 mg L^{-1} and 0.00 to 0.04 mg L^{-1}, respectively, during water year 1970 (USGS, 1975). Concentrations increase somewhat farther downstream, but macronutrient concentrations are still moderately low in the unchannelized reaches upstream from Sioux City. For example, the mean concentration for nitrates sampled at seven unchannelized stations averaged 0.1 mg L^{-1}, while total phosphorus averaged less than 0.1 mg L^{-1} (Hesse et al., 1989b). Enrichment experiments indicated that phytoplankton from both Lake Francis Case and Lewis and Clark Lake were phosphorus-limited (Martin and Novotny, 1975).

Macronutrient concentrations increase substantially in the channelized river because of the greater concentration of municipal and industrial (i.e., meatpacking plants) dischargers, as well as increased nonpoint pollution from agricultural sources (Ford, 1982). Serious enrichment is localized below point sources (e.g., Sioux City and Omaha) (Hesse et al., 1989c), but concentrations from other areas still supply adequate nutrients to support primary production. For example, from 1971 to 1973, monthly mean concentrations of nitrate-nitrogen ranged from 0.19 to 1.30 mg L^{-1} for samples collected near the Cooper Nuclear Station (river km 848 to 857), while soluble reactive orthophosphate-phosphorus ranged from 0.03 to 0.10 mg L^{-1} (Todd and Bender, 1982). Seasonally, both nitrogen and phosphorus were lowest in summer and highest in spring. Spring maxima are associated with high surface runoff, while summer minima are associated with higher autotrophic uptake, reduced surface runoff, and increased reservoir discharge (Ford, 1982; Todd and Bender, 1982).

Variations in dissolved oxygen concentrations and percent saturation occur in response to point-source pollution, nonpoint-source pollution, and
the releases from mainstem impoundments. In general, dissolved oxygen is
at or near saturation in the unchannelized reaches upstream from Sioux
City, whereas the greater concentrations of agricultural, urban, and industrial land use in downstream reaches often result in reduced levels of dissolved oxygen.

Public health problems related to point-source pollution became evident as
early as 1910, and by the 1950s and 1960s discharges from municipalities and
meatpackers had resulted in severely depressed levels of dissolved oxygen and
massive fish kills. For example, summer dissolved oxygen minima during 1950
were less than 5.0 mg L^{-1} at numerous sites between Nebraska City, Nebraska,
and Hermann, Missouri. With the implementation of primary and secondary
wastewater treatment facilities beginning in the mid-1960s, however, the impacts from these point sources have been greatly reduced (Ford, 1982;
Whitley and Campbell, 1974). Nonpoint-source pollution is currently the most
important cause of dissolved oxygen depression in the Missouri River.
Nonpoint-source impacts occur during periods of high surface runoff, when
inputs of macronutrients and organic matter are elevated and riverine sediments are resuspended (Ford, 1982; Todd and Bender, 1982).

Despite the problems caused by point and nonpoint pollution, water in the
channelized middle Missouri River is relatively well oxygenated. From 1971
to 1975, dissolved oxygen concentrations at ambient temperature stations
near Fort Calhoun Nuclear Station (river km 1039) ranged from 6.5 to 14.5 mg
L^{-1} and percent saturation ranged from 76 to 139%. The river is less well
oxygenated near Cooper Nuclear Station (km 857), which lies approximately
150 km downstream from Omaha; ambient temperature dissolved oxygen
ranged from 5.4 to 16.8 mg L^{-1} and percent saturation ranged from 56 to 134%
(Todd and Bender, 1982).

Supersaturation generated by lake phytoplankton and abiotic oxygenation
during dam releases are the two major mechanisms by which the main-stem
impoundments are believed to have contributed to high dissolved oxygen levels recorded in the unchannelized river (Ford, 1982; Morris et al., 1968). In
addition, these impoundments might reduce biological oxygen demand (BOD)
by trapping organic matter and enhancing photosynthesis by trapping suspended sediments. However, inputs of anthropogenic nutrients and BOD in
the unchannelized river upstream from Sioux City are substantially lower than
those for downstream reaches, which suggests that the unchannelized river
may have always been reasonably well oxygenated.

The water chemistry of the precontrol river is largely a matter of conjec-
ture. Given the basin's geochemistry, the concentrations of dissolved minerals
were probably high, but macronutrient and oxygen dynamics may have been
substantially different. Seasonal flooding in March and June may have increased inputs of dissolved and particulate organic nitrogen and carbon via
the inundation of floodplains and the flushing of wetlands. This in turn would

increase biochemical oxygen demand (BOD) by heterotrophic microbes. However, extrapolation of nutrient and oxygen dynamics from runoff events in the controlled river to seasonal flooding in the precontrol river is problematic because the precontrol floodplain and wetlands inputs were probably more refractory than inputs from livestock and domestic wastes. This suggests that the mineralization of precontrol inputs would have occurred over a substantially longer period than that which occurs with runoff events in the modified river.

The heterogeneity of habitats in the precontrol river may have contributed to significant between-habitat differences in water chemistry. For example, backwater habitats would probably have experienced greater evaporation and less flushing than those in the main channel. Inorganic and organic inputs from terrestrial and wetlands sources may have been more concentrated in backwaters. Unfortunately, no studies comparing the water chemistry of precontrol riverine habitats were found in the literature, and comparisons conducted in the impounded unchannelized river were contradictory. In a study of the unchannelized river below Gavins Point Dam, Morris et al. (1968) reported that there was little difference between chute and main-channel habitats with respect to pH and dissolved oxygen but that mean alkalinity and total dissolved solids were greater in the chutes during one of two study periods. During 1976, Kallemeyn and Novotny (1977) reported that measures of specific conductance were similar among samples collected at main channel, chute, and backup sites from three unchannelized stations. On the other hand, Hesse et al. (1989b) reported differences in specific conductance, total dissolved solids, hardness, and dissolved oxygen among main channel, chute, and backup habitats at an unchannelized station downstream from Fort Randall Dam (Table 3.2).

TABLE 3.2. *Comparisons of Selected Mean Chemical Characteristics Among Habitats in the Unchannelized Missouri River Below Fort Randall Dam, Nebraska[a]*

	Channel		Chute Inflow		Chute Outflow		Backup	
Total hardness (mg L^{-1})	276	(36)	226	(95)	225	(59)	260	(35)
Calcium hardness (mg L^{-1})	86	(66)	151	(47)	121	(24)	111	(94)
Specific conductance (μS cm L^{-1})	742	(108)	662	(94)	658	(96)	658	(102)
Total dissolved solids (mg L^{-1})	565	(33)	530	(44)	529	(30)	469	(61)
pH	7.6	(0.7)	7.3	(0.7)	7.1	(0.7)	7.7	(0.4)
Dissolved oxygen (mg L^{-1})	9.5	(1.3)	9.5	(2.0)	9.8	(1.7)	7.6	(2.2)

Source: After Hesse et al. (1989b).
[a]Standard deviation in parentheses.

ECOSYSTEM DYNAMICS

Detritus and Dissolved Organic Carbon
Prior to channelization and impoundment, the Missouri River may have received considerable inputs of detritus and dissolved organic carbon (DOC) from a number of sources. Sediment-laden Great Plains tributaries may have contained large quantities of suspended fine-particulate organic matter (FPOM), especially during periods of high flow. Bank erosion clearly resulted in the direct input of riparian vegetation, as was indicated by accumulations of snags and other woody debris. In addition, the extensive floodplain forest represented a potentially substantial source of allochthonous organic matter, which could be transported into the river via channel meandering and seasonal flooding (Hesse, 1987; Hesse et al., 1988).

Bank erosion, channel meandering, and floodplain inundation would have resulted in a complex interaction between the deposition, processing, and entrainment of organic matter within the river and its floodplain. Channel meandering would directly import some terrestrial vegetation and detritus but would also deposit sediments and associated FPOM elsewhere. The effects of spring floodplain inundation are not well understood. In the Ogeechee River, a sediment-poor river in the Georgia Coastal Plain, seasonal floodplain inundation results in the substantial input of floodplain detritus, DOC, and free-living bacteria (Benke and Meyer, 1988). However, high sediment loads in the Missouri may result in the burial of a considerable fraction of the organic matter lying on the floodplain floor. In this case the floodplain may actually have been a net organic matter sink rather than net source. Another possibility is that floodplain sedimentation could have selectively removed certain size fractions of detritus; ultrafine particulates and DOC could have remained in the water column, while larger particulates sank with the sediments.

Freshwater marshes bordering backups and chutes would probably have provided a predictably available source of detritus and DOC. With autumnal dieback, a significant proportion of the aboveground marsh vegetation would enter the detrital pool, but cold winter temperatures would probably have retarded microbial and invertebrate processing until the spring thaw. With spring surface runoff and flooding, some of the accumulated organic matter would then be exported into the river.

Channelization and impoundment have changed the processes affecting organic matter inputs in the river. Channelization has largely isolated the river from its floodplain by minimizing meandering, bank erosion, and floodplain inundation. Impoundments have affected detrital and DOC dynamics by trapping sediment and organic matter, greatly reducing spring flooding, and otherwise altering seasonal flow. In addition, degradation of the alluvial channels by sediment-poor dam discharges has lowered the river stage and isolated the river from marshy backwaters (Hesse, 1987).

Information on benthic particulate organic matter (POM) in the Missouri

River is limited. Accumulations of fine detritus were noted for the slow-water sites behind wing dikes in the channelized river (Hesse et al., 1982b; Morris et al., 1968). Detrital accumulations were also noted for some chute habitats but only in the channelized river (Morris et al., 1968). Presumably, benthic accumulations of detritus would be greatest in depositional sites such as behind wing dikes, in chutes, in backups, and in the marshes, while they would be low in the open, sandy channels. Studies in other Great Plains rivers indicated that main channel sediments are indeed poor in organic matter. For example, Jewell (1927) reported that when compared to Illinois rivers, the sandy sediments from the Kansas River near Manhattan, Kansas, contained very little organic matter. Williams et al. (1985) reported that the predominantly sandy sediments of the Big Blue River, Nebraska, also contained only traces of organic matter.

The influence of main-stem impoundments on concentrations of suspended POM (>0.074 mm) was investigated at one channelized and three unchannelized stations during April to October 1976. The trapping of organic matter behind Gavins Point Dam was illustrated by the longitudinal increase in POM concentrations below the dam. Main-channel concentrations increased from 0.111 mg AFDW (ash-free dry weight) L^{-1} at an unchannelized station 10 km below Gavins Point Dam to 0.505 mg AFDW L^{-1} at another unchannelized station approximately 45 km below the dam, to 2.331 mg AFDW L^{-1} in a channelized station approximately 160 km below the dam, while main-channel POM concentration in an unchannelized station upstream from Gavins Point Dam (0.245 mg AFDW L^{-1}) was more than double that from the downstream station closest to Gavins Point Dam. It is much reduced by organic matter trapping behind Fort Randall Dam, which lies approximately 34 km upstream (Kallemeyn and Novotny, 1977) (Table 3.3). In another comparison conducted during 1987 to 1988, Hesse et al. (1989b) reported that mean sestonic

TABLE 3.3. *Mean Habitat-Specific Concentrations (mg DWL^{-1}) of Organic Seston (>0.074 mm) for Four Stations in the Missouri River, April to October 1976*

	Unchannelized			Channelized
Station:[a]	1	2	3	4
River km:[b]	1382	1286	1253	1137
Main channel	0.245	0.111	0.505	2.331
Main-channel border	0.064	0.111	0.095	0.783
Chute	0.018	0.135	0.097	—
Backup	0.026	0.045	0.042	—

Source: After Kallemeyn and Novotny (1977).

[a]Station 1 is located below Fort Randall Dam; stations 2 and 3 are located in the unchannelized reach below Gavins Point Dam; and station 4 is located in the channelized reach 32 km downstream from Sioux City, Iowa.

[b]River km is the midpoint of the range presented by the authors.

FPOM and CPOM (coarse POM) concentrations from channelized stations were nearly double those from unchannelized stations.

There were considerable differences in concentrations of organic seston among habitats (Table 3.3). With the exception of the station immediately downstream from Gavins Point Dam, POM concentrations were highest in the main channel. POM concentrations were also high in the main-channel border habitat of the channelized station, but they were much lower in the main-channel border, chute, and backup habitats of the unchannelized river. Habitat-specific mean POM concentrations at all three unchannelized stations were consistently lowest in the backups. In addition, main-channel border, chute, and backup concentrations in the unchannelized station upstream from Gavins Point Dam were lower than in corresponding habitats below Gavins Point Dam (Kallemeyn and Novotny, 1977).

Water column organic matter was also studied at a channelized station near Nebraska City (river km 905) during 1969 to 1970. Suspended particulate organic carbon (POC) averaged 20.0 mg L^{-1} (>0.45 μm) and ranged from 0.5 to 190.0 mg L^{-1}. DOC concentrations for the same samples averaged 4.6 mg L^{-1} and ranged from 1.9 to 9.0 mg L^{-1}. Seasonally, DOC concentrations tended to be highest in winter and lowest in summer, while POC was lowest in winter (Malcolm and Durum, 1976) (Table 3.4).

Correlation analysis indicated that DOC concentrations were not significantly related to discharge. High seasonal flows may have diluted summer and autumn DOC concentrations and low winter flows, and freezing may have concentrated winter DOC. On the other hand, spring DOC was characterized by both high concentrations and high flows (Table 3.4). Increased surface runoff during spring thaw, especially from nearby feedlots, may be one reason for the elevated spring concentrations (Malcolm and Durum, 1976).

Unlike DOC, concentrations of POC were significantly and positively correlated with discharge (Malcolm and Durum, 1976) and suspended sediments (Table 3.4). However, this association may be complicated by seasonal effects or sources of discharge. The percentage of POC in suspended sediments varied seasonally, with higher mean percentages occurring in winter (4.9%) and spring (2.7%) than in summer (1.6%) and autumn (1.1%). The percentage of Kjeldahl nitrogen (KN) in sediments also varied seasonally, with mean percentages being highest in winter (0.6%) and lower (0.1 to 0.2%) in spring, summer, and autumn. One possible reason for the greater percentage of organic matter in winter and spring suspended sediments is that low winter temperatures may result in reduced biological uptake. The source of suspended sediments may also influence its organic content. Winter sediment loads in the channelized river are derived primarily from riverine sediments, whereas spring, summer, and autumn loads are heavily influenced by surface runoff (Slizeski et al., 1982).

In contrast to most lotic systems, especially main-stem rivers, concentrations of DOC in the Missouri River were substantially lower than those for POC. Even excluding the unusually high maximum (190.0 mg L^{-1}) recorded in

TABLE 3.4. *Dissolved Organic Carbon (DOC), Suspended Particulate Carbon (POC), Discharge, and Suspended Sediments in the Channelized Missouri River near Nebraska City, Nebraska*

	Discharge $(m^3 s^{-1})$	DOC $(mg L^{-1})$	POC $(mg L^{-1})$	Suspended Sediments		
				$(mg L^{-1})$	%POC	%KN[a]
Winter						
Jan. 20, 1969	651.3	4.5	0.7	8	8.2	1.2
Feb. 20, 1969	679.6	7.4	0.5	4	10.9	1.1
Dec. 12, 1969	566.3	1.9	2.8	66	4.3	0.3
Jan. 30, 1970	538.8	6.0	2.6	73	3.5	0.5
Feb. 24, 1970	1042.0	6.3	14.0	913	1.5	0.6
Mar. 12, 1970	951.4	8.4	7.3	718	1.0	0.2
Spring						
Mar. 19, 1969	1987.8	9.0	190.0	3068	6.2	0.2
Apr. 11, 1969	2803.3	3.5	27.0	1076	2.5	0.2
May 19, 1969	1523.4	3.6	2.6	3068	6.2	0.2
Apr. 8, 1970	1234.6	4.1	7.0	980	0.7	0.2
May 22, 1970	1090.2	3.6	4.0	370	1.1	0.4
June 6, 1970	1166.6	4.8	6.1	484	1.3	0.3
Summer						
June 20, 1969	1192.1	3.2	5.1	215	2.4	0.3
July 31, 1969	1376.2	1.9	21.0	1152	1.8	0.2
Autumn						
Sept. 30, 1969	1512.1	2.7	11.0	884	1.3	0.1
Oct. 21, 1969	1404.5	2.4	13.0	904	1.4	0.1
Nov. 28, 1969	1107.2	4.9	22.0	3986	0.6	0.1

Source: After Malcolm and Durum (1976).

[a]KN, Kjeldahl nitrogen.

March 1969, the mean concentration of POC (8.5 mg C L^{-1}) would still be nearly double that for DOC (4.3 mg L^{-1}). Using the same methodology, DOC was roughly equal to POC in the Brazos River (southeastern Texas) and Lower Mississippi (southern Louisiana) and exceeded POC in the Neuse River (eastern North Carolina), Ohio River (western Kentucky), and Sopchoppy River (Florida). The unusually low DOC/POC ratio for the Missouri River is the result of high POC concentrations, since mean DOC in the Missouri lies well within the DOC range of the other five rivers; only the blackwater Sopchoppy (27.0 mg L^{-1}) and the Neuse (7.1 mg L^{-1}) have higher DOC means (Malcolm and Durum, 1976).

Based on the concentrations and discharges measured at Nebraska City, the annual load of organic carbon exported from the Missouri River was estimated to be 7.4×10^8 kg yr^{-1}. Of this total, 79% was particulate and 21% was dissolved. The magnitude of the Missouri's organic matter content becomes evident when total export is compared to total discharge. For example, the Missouri accounts for less than 10% of the Lower Mississippi's flow, but it accounts for 27% of the Lower Mississippi's organic carbon export. Similarly, the Missouri accounts for 32% of the Lower Mississippi's export of POC, while the Ohio River, which accounts for 47% of the Lower Mississippi's flow, accounts for only 22% of its organic carbon (Malcolm and Durum, 1976).

While the organic carbon export estimate of Malcolm and Durum (1976) is impressive, it is based on concentrations found in a highly modified river in which impoundments trap organic material and channelization limits exchange between the river and the floodplain. One estimate of organic matter export from the precontrol river was based on the observed correlation between suspended sediments with organic matter and the documented decline in sediment loads following main-stem impoundment during the 1950s and 1960s. Given the correlation between sediment loads and organic carbon and the more than 80% decline in sediment loads, it follows that the export estimate by Malcolm and Durum represents less than 20% of the precontrol export (Hesse et al., 1988).

Refinement of this crude estimate for precontrol organic matter export is confounded by our lack of knowledge concerning a variety of factors affecting the export and storage of organic matter. For example, the modified Missouri receives point-source inputs from municipalities and nonpoint-source inputs from agriculture. How do these inputs compare to those from natural floodplains and prairie watersheds? Prior to the conversion of most of the Missouri's basin to agriculture, sediment inputs were probably derived primarily from bank erosion, flooding, and channel meandering. Since agricultural development, however, a considerable amount of the sediment inputs have been derived from surface erosion. How does this change in sediment inputs affect the relationship between sediment inputs and organic matter inputs? Even the propensity of the river to export or retain organic matter has changed. On the one hand, main-stem impoundments trap considerable amounts of particulate organic matter. On the other hand, the narrower, deeper, and swifter channel of the modified river is probably less retentive than the precontrol channel, which was wider and shallower and contained numerous backwaters.

Regardless of the uncertainties involved with estimating the organic matter loading of the precontrol river, it seems likely that it was primarily dependent on allochthonous inputs from the floodplains and/or tributaries. One line of reasoning supporting this is that the naturally high turbidity and unstable benthos would have greatly limited autotrophic production. The other is that substantial inputs of organic matter would accompany the high inputs of sediments (Hesse et al., 1988). The modified Missouri River is also heterotrophic (Berner, 1951; Hesse et al., 1982c; Whitley and Campbell, 1974), although reduced turbidity may have increased the importance of primary producers (Hesse et al., 1982c).

Periphyton Primary Production
Studies of predimpoundment periphyton were not found in the literature, but the high sediment loads probably limited production via lower light penetra-

tion, sedimentation, and scouring. Even with reduced sediment loads that characterize the present river, however, light penetration is greatly reduced. For example, Nelson (1974) found that an average of only 54.5% of surface illumination penetrates to a depth of 35 cm and that less than 25% penetrates to a depth of 65 cm. Periphyton was probably also greatly reduced by shifting sand substrates. Epipeltic algal assemblages may have been a common feature of the shallower backwater habitats, but periods of very high turbidity and sedimentation may have limited these assemblages and kept them in early successional stages. Snags provided the primary hard substrates in the precontrol river, but this substrate is now greatly reduced. The importance of snags is suggested by a study in Lewis and Clark Lake in which periphyton algae were concentrated on submersed trees (Benson and Cowell, 1968, as cited in Hesse et al., 1989c).

Snags were still relatively plentiful in the unchannelized study reach below Gavins Point Dam during the early 1970s, although sediment loads had already been greatly reduced. Using cottonwood stakes as artificial substrates, it was found that chlorophyll *a* concentrations, ash-free dry weight (AFDW) biomass, and diatom cell densities were greater and more variable in the fast-water (>0.75 m s^{-1}) main-channel site (station 1) located 10 m from shore than in two slow-water (<0.1 m s^{-1}) sites located at the downstream ends of chutes (stations 2 and 3). All three measures of algal abundance decreased with depth (5 cm, 35 cm, and 65 cm) in the main-channel site, but such trends were either weaker or not evident in the chutes. In fact, mean biomass in the two chute sites increased with depth (Nelson, 1974) (Tables 3.5 to 3.7). Turbidity-induced light extinction may have accounted for the reduction in

TABLE 3.5. *Periphytic Diatom Cell Densities (cells mm^{-2}) from Artificial Substrates Collected in the Unchannelized Missouri River near Vermillion, South Dakota, 1973*

	Station 1 Main Channel (Fast Water)			Station 2 Chute (Slow Water)			Station 3 Chute (Slow Water)		
Depth (cm):	5	35	65	5	35	65	5	35	65
July 6	360	121	44	205	214	136	423	335	229
July 13	917	254	1030	258	530	485	493	864	794
July 30	4870	263	1735	674	846	746	300	364	402
Aug. 10	4891	659	48	452	272	222	508	451	412
Aug. 17	2302	2042	—	296	349	159	679	259	319
Sept. 5	462	—	—	775	963	704	1649	424	569
Sept. 13	156	184	—	511	258	739	85	94	234
Oct. 10	117	—	—	575	575	618	535	475	223
Oct. 24	113	168	337	108	60	37	40	54	26
Oct. 31	2981	2539	419	174	111	142	76	57	41
Nov. 14	3016	2475	1914	346	197	305	136	157	133
Mean	1835	976	790	398	398	390	448	321	307

Source: After Nelson (1974).

TABLE 3.6.   *Periphytic Algae Biomass (g AFDW m^{-2}) from Artificial Substrates Located in the Unchannelized Missouri River near Vermillion, South Dakota, 1973*

	Main Channel (Fast Water)			Chute (Slow Water)			Chute (Slow Water)		
Depth (cm):	5	35	65	5	35	65	5	35	65
July 6	4.2	2.4	0.5	2.3	0.8	0.5	1.7	0.7	0.4
July 13	19.5	19.9	18.0	7.7	9.7	14.1	7.6	7.1	21.1
July 30	40.6	28.6	12.4	10.6	10.9	9.2	8.8	9.7	11.8
Aug. 10	6.8	26.0	0.1	2.6	1.6	2.8	2.1	2.6	0.9
Aug. 17	44.9	20.9	—	3.3	4.3	21.6	5.5	4.5	5.6
Sept. 5	3.0	—	—	10.3	3.1	3.7	4.4	16.3	5.8
Sept. 13	28.5	24.0	—	3.9	1.3	1.3	0.1	11.4	6.7
Oct. 10	11.7	—	—	7.8	16.1	13.6	6.7	8.7	13.1
Oct. 24	1.6	1.3	0.8	3.6	1.6	0.3	14.7	2.2	13.9
Oct. 31	18.9	10.5	2.4	7.0	7.5	11.0	6.6	3.1	7.6
Nov. 14	13.1	11.3	1.8	4.7	4.4	3.6	5.9	6.4	5.8
Mean	17.5	13.2	6.4	5.8	5.6	7.4	5.8	6.6	7.5

Source: After Nelson (1974).

algal abundance with depth at the main-channel site, but Nelson (1974) reported that differences in turbidity and light penetration between sites were minor and as such probably did not account for the substantially greater abundance recorded in the main channel. On the other hand, stronger currents may have reduced sedimentation in the main channel. Conversely, reduced currents may have resulted in an increased deposition of nonalgal (i.e., detrital) AFDW biomass in some of the 35- and 65-cm samples from the two chute sites.

Except for the low abundances of the first samples (July 6), seasonality in algal abundance was obscured by interactions among depths and sites; abundance rankings within sites varied between depths and rankings within depths varied between sites. In general, maxima in the chutes occurred from mid-July through early October, whereas maxima in the fast-water site occurred from mid-July through mid-November. Interestingly, chlorophyll *a* concentrations were also relatively high for the 65-cm samples from the two chute sites (Table 3.6). Diatoms and filamentous green algae dominated the samples. Diatom cell densities were usually dominated by *Cymbella, Diatoma, Fragilaria, Synedra,* and *Navicula* (Nelson, 1974).

Rock and wood channelization structures have replaced snags as the dominant hard substrate in the channelized Missouri River. At the ambient temperature station (river km 1000) near the Fort Calhoun Nuclear Power Station (Nebraska), these substrates supported dense growths of two filamentous green algae, *Cladophora* and *Stigeoclonium,* and their epiphytic diatoms (Farrell and Tesar, 1982).

TABLE 3.7. *Periphytic Chlorophyll* a *Concentrations (mg m^{-2}) from Artificial Substrates Located in the Unchannelized Missouri River near Vermillion, South Dakota, 1973*

	Main Channel (Fast Water)			Chute (Slow Water)			Chute (Slow Water)		
Depth (cm):	5	35	65	5	35	65	5	35	65
July 6	1.2	0.5	0.5	0.2	0.2	0.2	1.0	0.5	0.2
July 13	17.1	8.1	7.0	1.0	0.3	0.5	1.7	1.5	1.3
July 30	5.8	6.2	4.7	2.6	2.4	1.2	1.4	1.3	0.9
Aug. 10	5.4	3.8	0.3	0.5	0.2	0.3	0.5	0.2	0.2
Aug. 17	1.2	1.1	—	0.5	0.3	0.3	0.5	0.2	0.2
Sept. 5	8.3	—	—	2.0	1.7	1.2	1.3	1.0	0.3
Sept. 13	0.5	0.5	—	0.8	0.2	0.2	0.5	0.2	0.2
Oct. 10	2.1	—	—	2.2	2.5	1.4	2.9	0.2	0.2
Oct. 24	1.3	1.2	1.1	0.3	0.5	0.3	0.5	0.5	0.2
Oct. 31	3.7	2.1	1.5	0.3	0.5	0.3	0.5	0.5	0.0
Nov. 14	11.9	11.4	2.5	0.8	1.5	2.1	0.5	0.5	1.2
Mean	5.3	3.9	2.5	1.0	0.9	0.7	1.0	0.6	0.5

Source: After Nelson (1974).

Periphyton cell densities and biovolumes collected from glass slides located in the ambient temperature station near the Fort Calhoun plant averaged 10,490 cells mm^{-2} and 34.14 μL dm^{-2}, respectively. On average, cell densities were higher in July and August than they were from early September through early December. On the other hand, average algal biovolume was higher from early October through early December. Diatoms and green algae were codominant during July and August, but diatoms became progressively more dominant from September through early December (Table 3.8). During 1974, chlorophyll *a* and total pigment (chlorophylls and carotenoids) averaged 30.08 and 60.24 mg m^{-2}, respectively. Pigment concentrations were higher during 1975, averaging 47.27 and 86.42 mg m^{-2}, respectively. Both years exhibited minima in August and maxima in October (Farrell and Tesar, 1982) (Table 3.9).

Navicula tripunctata var. *schizonemoides* was the dominant diatom on the glass slide samples in mid-July. *Gomphonema intricatum* was dominant in August and September, while *Cocconeis placentula* var. *euglypta* was abundant in late September. *N. tripunctata* var. *schizonemoides, Gomphonema olivaceum,* and *Diatoma vulgare* were dominant diatoms from late September through November. A soil or subaerial green alga, *Chlorococcum* sp., almost completely dominated August samples but was not found in late samples. The two other important green algae, *Chaetophora* sp. and *Characium* sp., were most abundant in August and September. *Lyngbya* sp., which was abundant in August and early September, was the only important blue-green alga. Short incubation times precluded significant growth by *Cladophora* and *Stigeoclonium* on the glass slides (Farrell and Tesar, 1982).

TABLE 3.8.   *Cell Density, Biovolume, and Relative Abundance of Diatoms, Green Algae, and Blue-Green Algae for Reference Station Periphyton Collected on Artificial Substrates in the Channelized Missouri River (river km 1000) near the Fort Calhoun Nuclear Station, Nebraska, 1975*

	Density (cells mm^{-2})	Relative Abundance (%)		
		Diatom	Green	Blue-green
July 14–Sept. 2	13,344	48.2	32.7	19.0
Sept. 8–Sept. 29	8,617	70.1	21.1	8.8
Oct. 6–Dec. 2	8,930	98.5	0.0	1.5
Mean	10,490	74.0	16.5	9.5
	Biovolume (μL dm^{-2})	Relative Abundance (%)		
		Diatom	Green	Blue-green
July 14–Sept. 2	32.38	41.9	56.0	2.1
Sept. 8–Sept. 29	30.43	52.5	46.6	0.9
Oct. 6–Dec. 2	37.54	99.9	0.0	0.1
Mean	34.14	68.6	30.5	1.0

Source: After Farrell and Tesar (1982).

Phytoplankton Production

Prior to the completion of the two downstream dams (Fort Randall Dam in 1953 and Gavins Point Dam in 1955), phytoplankton cell densities were low. From April to October 1945, the mean filtered water cell density in a channelized reach within the state of Missouri averaged only 67 cells L^{-1} (Berner, 1951). Total water cell densities in the channelized river between Nebraska City and Kansas City averaged only 50 cells mL^{-1} (Damann, 1951, as cited in Cross and Moss, 1987). Total cell densities were higher (1200 to 2000 cells mL^{-1}) in the unchannelized river near Yankton, South Dakota (river km 1297) (Damann, 1951, as cited in Hesse et al., 1982c). Even these cell densities, however, were low relative to those recorded in less turbid rivers, which suggests that turbidity was the primary factor limiting phytoplankton production (Berner, 1951; Hesse et al., 1982c).

Phytoplankton cell densities have increased by more than an order of magnitude since the completion of the main-stem impoundments. From July 1960 to July 1961, total water cell densities at Omaha averaged 1508 cells mL^{-1} (Williams and Scott, 1962). Cell densities at St. Joseph, Missouri (km 721.2), averaged 5957 cells mL^{-1} during water year 1977 (USGS, 1978) and 28,000 cells mL^{-1} during water year 1981 (USGS, 1982, as cited in Cross and Moss, 1987). Increased riverine cell densities are primarily the result of phytoplankton discharges from the main-stem impoundments, and reductions in cell density are related directly to distance downsteam from the dam. The annual

TABLE 3.9.   *Chlorophyll* a *and Total Photosynthetic Pigment Concentrations (mg m^{-2}) for Reference Station Periphyton Collected on Glass Slides in the Channelized Missouri River (river km 1000) near the Fort Calhoun Nuclear Station, Nebraska, 1974–1975*

	1974		1975	
	Chl. *a*	Total	Chl. *a*	Total
July 14–July 21	—	—	37.44	77.76
Aug. 4–Aug. 29	16.58	30.01	16.13	39.14
Sept. 2–Sept. 29	43.66	77.18	33.74	63.38
Oct. 4–Oct. 31	57.99	100.44	116.35	193.25
Nov. 3–Nov. 24	26.08	33.34	32.70	58.55
Mean	30.08	60.24	47.27	86.42

Source: After Farrell and Tesar (1982).

phytoplankton discharge from Lewis and Clark Lake was estimated to be 9058 metric tons wet weight, most of which occurred in spring and summer (Benson and Cowell, 1968, as cited in Hesse et al., 1989c).

Although riverine phytoplankton are derived primarily from the mainstem impoundments, they appear to be more abundant within backwaters than they are in the main channel. For example, total chlorophyll *a* from a backup site at an unchannelized station located downstream from Fort Randall Dam averaged 20.8 mg L^{-1}, while that from a main-channel site averaged only 8.5 mg L^{-1}; mean total chlorophyll concentrations for two nearby chute sites averaged 15.9 and 17.9 mg L^{-1} (Hesse et al., 1989b).

River phytoplankton were studied in detail at the water intake of the Fort Calhoun Nuclear Power Station, Nebraska (river km 1000). From 1974 to 1977, phytoplankton cell densities ranged from <1000 to >25,000 units mL^{-1}, although most (98%) density values were less than 10,000 units mL^{-1}. Variability between sample dates within years and variability from year to year obscured any seasonal trends. Winter densities were low during 1974, 1976, and 1977, but not in 1975. Density maxima occurred in late winter and spring during 1977, in spring during 1974, and in summer during 1976. During 1975, density maxima occurred throughout the year, except in December, March, and April. Chlorophyll *a* concentrations, which ranged as high as 33.7 mg m^{-2} but usually ranged from 2 to 20 mg m^{-2}, were also highly variable. As with densities, winter concentrations were low for 1974, 1976, and 1977 but not for 1975. Concentration maxima occurred in spring and early summer during 1974 and 1976, in late spring and late summer for 1977, and throughout the year in 1975. On the other hand, seasonality was clearly evident for carbon fixation rates, which are strongly dependent on stream temperatures. Rates were consistently less than 20 mg C m^{-3} h^{-1} during December, January, and February. Maxima greater than 50 mg C m^{-3} h^{-1} occurred from March through

November but were most frequent from April through September (Reetz, 1982).

Despite a distance of more than 300 km, the phytoplankton assemblage at the Fort Calhoun water intake was determined primarily by discharges from Lewis and Clark Lake. Relatively minor modifications to the downstream assemblage were made by inputs from tributary streams, from pools behind trail dikes, from backwater areas in the unchannelized reaches, and from the entrainment of periphytic algae. Diatoms were abundant throughout the year and almost completely dominated winter and spring samples. *Asterionella formosa,* either alone or in combination with *Stephanodiscus* spp., dominated the diatoms. *Cyclotella* spp., *Melosira granulata, Skeletonema potamos, Fragillaria* spp., and *Nitzschia* spp. were occasionally abundant but were not seasonally consistent. A diverse assemblage of green algae, of which *Actinastrum hantzschii, Ankistrodesmus spiralis, Dictyosphaerium pulchellum,* and *Scenedesmus* spp. were the most representative, was frequently numerous in mid- and late summer. The blue-green alga *Merismopedia tenuissima* was occasionally abundant during summer (Reetz, 1982).

Macrophyte Production
Submerged vascular macrophytes are extremely rare in the Missouri River. High sediment loads, unstable substrates, and high stream power had probably prevented their growth in the precontrol river. High sediment loads and fluctuating water levels prevent their development in the main-stem impoundments (Hesse et al., 1989b).

On the other hand, emergent macrophytes formed extensive growths in backwater marshes and along the banks of the precontrol river. These stands were dominated by cattails (*Typha latifolia* and *T. angustifolia*), while reed grass (*Phragmites communis*) and sedges (*Carex* spp.) were common (Volesky, 1969). Channel meandering and flooding have helped to maintain these freshwater marshes by providing a multitude of backwater habitats and keeping floodplain vegetation in an early successional stage. However, channelization, flow regulation, and channel degradation have disrupted these maintenance processes. Stands of emergent vegetation were still relatively extensive in the unchannelized river during the 1960s and 1970s (Kallemeyn and Novoty, 1977; Schmulbach et al., 1975; Volesky, 1969), but they have since been greatly diminished. Remnants of this vegetation persist in the unchannelized reach below Fort Randall Dam, with the most extensive stand located at the confluence of the Niobrara River (Hesse et al., 1989b,c).

Zooplankton Production
The rapid currents and high sediment loads were probably not conducive to the development of significant assemblages of zooplankton in the main channel of the uncontrolled Missouri River. On the other hand, the zooplankton may have been well developed in the chutes, backups, and marshes. These

backwater assemblages, as well as zooplankton assemblages from tributaries, would probably have been characterized by *Alona, Bosmina, Chydorus* (Cladocera), littoral cyclopoid copepods, and rotifers (Repsys and Rogers, 1982).

No studies of zooplankton in the precontrol river were found in the literature, but riverine zooplankton were investigated in a channelized reach of the lower Missouri River prior to the completion of most of the main-stem impoundments. Although this study was conducted during a time when much of the riverine backwater habitat was lost to channelization, the zooplankton was still probably dominated by inputs from tributaries and backwaters from unchannelized reaches upstream. From April through October 1945, zooplankton densities from 34 collections averaged 23.3 zooplankters L^{-1}. Interestingly, most of these (46.3%) were nematodes, which are not normally collected in planktonic samples. One possibility is that these nematodes were entrained along with sediments and actually represent allochthonous inputs. True planktonic forms were dominated by rotifers (20.4%), copepod nauplii (19.3%), other copepods (3.0%), and protozoans (10.5%). Cladocera accounted for only 0.5% of the zooplankton (Berner, 1951).

Following the construction of the main-stem impoundments, the abundance, seasonality, and taxonomic composition of the riverine zooplankton have been dominated by discharges of reservoir assemblages (Hesse et al., 1989c; Kallemeyn and Novotny, 1977; Morris et al., 1968; Repsys and Rogers, 1982; Schmulbach, 1974; Williams, 1971). Discharges from Lake Francis Case exert the strongest influence over downstream zooplankton since residence time in Lewis and Clark Lake (9 days during the navigation season) is too short for the development of most zooplankters. In fact, inputs into Lewis and Clark Lake exceed that exported downstream, making it a net zooplankton sink (Cowell, 1970, as cited in Hesse et al., 1989c; Repsys and Rogers, 1982). Loss of backwater habitats in the degraded unchannelized reaches as well as in the channelized reaches has increased the relative importance of the reservoir releases.

The influence of discharges on reservoir zooplankton is demonstrated by the longitudinal decline in zooplankton abundance below the dams. Williams (1971) calculated that of the zooplankton discharged from Gavins Point Dam, there was a mean decrease in density of 51% for the first 16 km of river, which amounts to a mean rate of 3% km^{-1}. The rates of decrease diminish further downstream to 1% km^{-1} for the next 18 km and 0.2%/km for the following 107 km. Kallemeyn and Novotny (1977) reported longitudinal declines in zooplankton below both Fort Randall Dam (Lake Francis Case) and Gavins Point Dam (Lewis and Clark Lake). Mean biomass decline from 107 mg m^{-3} in an unchannelized site below Fort Randall Dam to 19 to 93 mg m^{-3} in two sites in the unchannelized reach below Gavins Point Dam to 41 mg m^{-3} in a channelized site 32 km downstream from Sioux City. Mean main-channel zooplankton density declined from 16,682 m^{-3} to 13,234 m^{-3} to 12,980 m^{-3} to 6084 m^{-3}, respectively.

Zooplankton discharged into smaller or shallower rivers are usually rapidly depleted, but those discharged into larger rivers such as the Missouri may persist as a recognizable, albeit reduced assemblage several hundred kilometers downstream. Mechanical damage from turbulence and sediment abrasion, as well as predation losses probably selectively reduce the larger and more fragile taxons. Smaller and/or thick-shelled taxons are probably less prone to riverine mortality (Repsys and Rogers, 1982). For example, *Leptodora kindti,* a large, fragile pelagic cladoceran, was abundant in Lewis and Clark Lake and in June drift samples from an unchannelized site below Gavins Point Dam (Morris et al., 1968) but was rare in several channelized sites farther downstream (Morris et al., 1968; Repsys and Rogers, 1982).

The seasonality of riverine zooplankton corresponds closely with that of the reservoirs. Density maxima within Lake Francis Case and Lewis and Clark Lake usually occur in late autumn–early winter and spring, while densities are usually low during summer and early autumn (Repsys and Rogers, 1982). From 1973 to 1977, densities in the channelized river near the Fort Calhoun Nuclear Power Plant (km 1039) usually exhibited density maxima from December through May or June, while densities from July through early November were consistently low. Similar patterns of seasonality were recorded from more seasonally restricted studies (April to October–November) at two other channelized sites as well as at an unchannelized site below Fort Randall Dam (Kallemeyn and Novotny, 1977; Repsys and Rogers, 1982). However, the imposition of reservoir seasonality upon riverine seasonality diminishes downstream in a fashion consistent with the downstream decline in mean zooplankton abundance. For example, April and May 1976 density maxima at Fort Calhoun Power Station (km 1039) and Cooper Power Station (km 856) become progressively more dampened with respect to the density maxima at an unchannelized station (km 1257) located 50 km below Gavins Point Dam (Repsys and Rogers, 1982).

Densities throughout the river were dominated by pelagic reservoir copepods and cladocerans. On average, copepods accounted for 91% (2895 m^{-3}) of the total microcrustacean zooplankton at the Fort Calhoun Power Station from 1974 to 1977. Calanoid and cyclopoid copepodites (immature copepods) were abundant throughout the year, but they were most abundant in December, January, and May. Similarly, *Cyclops bicuspidatus thomasi, Diaptomus ashlandi,* and copepod nauplii were abundant from December through May. Another dominant copepod, *D. siciloides,* was abundant throughout the year, but especially so during winter. Cladocera, which were dominated by *Daphnia pulicaria* and immature *Daphnia* spp., were common in winter but were most abundant in May and June (Repsys and Rogers, 1982). Copepod nauplii, *D. ashlandi, C. bicuspidatus,* and *Daphnia* spp., dominated August 1970 samples in the unchannelized reach below Gavins Point Dam (Schmulbach, 1974; Williams, 1971).

The zooplankton in the three unchannelized stations and one channelized station investigated by Kallemeyn and Novotny (1977) were dominated by calanoid copepods, cyclopoid copepods, and *Daphnia* spp. Total densities in the unchannelized reaches were highest in the main channel and chute habitats and lowest in the backups. Copepods occurred in high densities in both the main channel, main-channel border, chute, and backup habitats. Although cyclopoids tended to be less abundant in the backups, their densities at the unchannelized station upstream from Gavins Point Dam were actually highest in the backups. In contrast, Cladocera were less abundant in the chutes and backups than in the main channel. Taxon-specific densities at the channelized station were consistently higher in the main-channel borders than in the main channel itself (Table 3.10).

Populations of zooplankton in backwater habitats in the unchannelized river could be indicative of local production. However, these populations could also be the result of the concentration of reservoir taxons by the combination of slower currents and reduced turbulence-associated mortality. In a drift study conducted in the unchannelized river below Gavins Point Dam during June 1963, zooplankton biomass was more than sixfold greater in chute habitats than in the main channel (Morris et al., 1968). Although this collection apparently sampled only the larger taxons, it is evident that the chutes either served to concentrate reservoir releases or were actually sites for local production. A delicate, large-bodied pelagic cladoceran, *Leptodera kindti,* accounted for 91% and 87% of the main-channel and chute zooplankton, respectively. This indicates that the concentration of reservoir taxons rather than local chute production was responsible for the higher chute densities. On the other hand, periodic longitudinal increases in microcrustaceans and rotifers in the unchannelized reach below Gavins Point Dam, particularly in autumn, suggest that some backwater production is occurring (Schmulbach, 1974).

Macroinvertebrate Production
Flow regulation, backwater habitat loss, reduction in floodplain–riverine interactions, removal in snag habitats, and the trapping of sediments and organic matter behind reservoirs have greatly altered the extent and characteristics of macroinvertebrate production in the Missouri River. The diversity of marsh, backwater, snag, and main-channel habitats would have helped to create a diverse biota supported by substantial and seasonally predictable organic matter inputs from floodplain inundation, bank erosion, and tributary inputs. On the other hand, shifting substrates and high sediment loads could have reduced or eliminated many taxons. No studies of macroinvertebrates in the precontrol river were found in literature, but patterns in taxonomic composition and abundance in channelized and unchannelized sites can be used to reconstruct the patterns of macroinvertebrate production.

One of the earliest studies of macroinvertebrates in the Missouri River was conducted from April through October 1945 in the lower river. This study occurred prior to completion of the main-stem impoundments, and as such may

TABLE 3.10.   *Mean and Relative Zooplankton Density by Habitat for Four Stations in the Missouri River, April–October 1976*

Station:[a]	Unchannelized			Channelized
	1	2	3	4
River km:[b]	1382	1286	1253	1137
Copepoda				
Calanoida				
Main channel	7,690	5,467	5,288	2,104
Channel border	8,158	3,981	4,557	4,093
Chute	9,098	3,901	3,331	—
Backup	2,908	2,060	3,961	—
Cyclopoida				
Main channel	2,442	3,217	3,367	1,669
Channel border	2,139	2,737	2,007	2,411
Chute	2,388	3,739	2,180	—
Backup	3,269	1,489	1,978	—
Nauplii				
Main channel	143	404	507	171
Channel border	405	307	178	245
Chute	734	539	335	—
Backup	249	200	262	—
Cladocera				
Daphnia				
Main channel	6,199	3,840	3,588	2,106
Channel border	3,343	2,322	2,279	3,082
Chute	3,850	3,345	2,286	—
Backup	770	956	1,518	—
Other Cladocera				
Main channel	208	306	230	34
Channel border	184	233	235	210
Chute	216	272	116	—
Backup	83	193	116	—
Total				
Main channel	16,682	13,234	12,980	6,084
Channel border	14,229	9,577	9,326	10,041
Chute	16,286	11,796	8,248	—
Backup	7,279	4,898	7,835	—

Source: After Kallemeyn and Novotny (1977).

[a]Station 1 is located below Fort Randall Dam; stations 2 and 3 are located in the unchannelized reach below Gavins Point Dam; and station 4 is located in the channelized reach 32 km downstream from Sioux City, Iowa.

[b]River km is the midpoint of the range presented by the author.

have conditions relating to turbidity and detritus that resembled those characteristic of the precontrol river. On the other hand, the site had already been channelized for a number of years, so that habitat characteristics were substantially modified. In any case, Peterson grab samples indicated that benthic biomass in the main channel was extremely low [0.01 lb/acre; 0.1 mg wet weight (WW) m^{-2}]. In fact, there was some evidence that even this meager amount may have originated from another habitat. Benthic biomass was considerably higher downstream from a pile dike (1.27 lb/acre; 11.3 mg WW m^{-2}), near a sandbar (0.67 lb/acre; 6.0 mg WW m^{-2}), and near a steep bank (2.17 lb/acre; 19.4 mg WW m^{-2}), but even these values are low relative to most streams. These benthic samples were dominated by Chironomidae (38.3%), Annelida (21.6%), Trichoptera (18.0%), and other Diptera (12.1%) (Berner, 1951).

A number of studies were conducted in channelized and unchannelized reaches of the Missouri River following the completion of the main-stem impoundments in the mid-1950s. All of these studies were conducted under conditions of regulated flow and greatly reduced loads of suspended sediments, and as such represent substantially altered conditions. On the other hand, many of the precontrol habitats (i.e., chutes, marshes, snags, sandbars, and backups) were still present, albeit less extensive, during these studies. Therefore, they offer some indication of the precontrol partitioning of production and distribution of taxons among these habitats. Comparisons between unchannelized and channelized sites also reveal some interesting aspects of macroinvertebrate production.

A series of Peterson grab samples were collected during 1962 to 1963 from a variety of habitats from channelized (from Sioux City to Rulo, Nebraska), bank-stabilized (upstream from Sioux City), and unchannelized (downstream from Gavins Point Dam) river in Middle Missouri River below Gavins Point Dam. As with the 1945 study by Berner (1951) in the lower river, the main-channel habitats in the Middle Missouri River contained substantially lower mean standing stocks than did chute, mud bank, and pile dike habitats. The mean main-channel standing stock for the channelized and bank-stabilized stations was only 0.06 lb/acre (0.5 mg WW m^{-2}). At 0.43 lb/acre (3.8 mg WW m^{-2}), the mean main-channel standing stock for the unchannelized stations was almost sixfold higher than that for the channelized and bank-stabilized stations. One probable factor contributing to the greater macroinvertebrate biomass in the unchannelized main channel is a greater variety of habitats (i.e., pools and sandbars). In any case, the prevalence of shifting sand substrates contributed to lower standing stocks in both the channelized-stabilized and unchannelized rivers. In contrast to the main-channel habitats, mean standing stocks in the more productive mud bank and chute habitats were substantially higher in the channelized and bank-stabilized stations than in the unchannelized stations. Mud bank standing stocks averaged 7.17 lb/acre (64.0 mg WW m^{-2}) and 2.38 lb/acre (21.2 mg WW m^{-2}), respectively, while chute standing stocks averaged 7.28 lb/acre (65.0 mg WW m^{-2}) and 1.36 lb/acre (12.1 mg WW m^{-2}), respectively. Higher sediment loads in the stabilized and channelized river have resulted in increases in slit deposits in these habitats, which in turn stabilizes sediments and increases benthic populations. However, increases in chute standing stocks in the channelized reach were offset by the loss of chute habitats. On a habitat-weighted basis, the mean benthic standing stock was 0.63 lb/acre (5.6 mg WW m^{-2}) for the unchannelized stations and 0.67 lb/acre (6.0 mg WW m^{-2}) for the (combined) bank stabilized and channelized stations (Morris et al., 1968).

TABLE 3.11.   *Mean Relative Macroinvertebrate Biomass (%) for Unchannelized, Bank Stabilized, and Channelized Stations in the Middle Missouri River, April to October 1962 and June to August 1963*

	Unchannelized		Stabilized		Channelized	
Year:	1962	1963	1962	1963	1962	1963
Number of Stations:	2	1	3	0	4	1
Oligochaeta						
Total	13.0	10.2	29.4	—	46.5	58.0
Odonata						
Gomphidae	2.7	—	0.8	—	15.7	2.3
Ephemeroptera						
Hexagenia	2.2	45.6	36.2	—	0.9	—
Pentagenia	26.1	7.2	0.6	—	0.1	—
Other Ephemeroptera	1.2	4.1	—	—	0.3	—
Total	29.4	56.9	36.8	—	1.3	—
Trichoptera						
Cheumatopsyche	3.8	7.1	<0.1	—	0.2	2.1
Other Trichoptera	4.5	1.0	0.5	—	0.4	—
Total	8.3	8.1	0.6	—	0.6	2.1
Diptera						
Chironomidae	44.1	11.9	13.0	—	33.7	36.1
Other Diptera	2.4	—	0.6	—	2.1	1.5
Total	46.5	11.9	13.6	—	35.8	37.6
Gastropoda						
Total	—	—	0.5	—	<0.1	—
Bivalvia						
Total	—	12.9	18.6	—	—	—
Other						
Total	—	—	<0.1	—	0.1	—

Source: After Morris et al. (1968).

Oligochaeta and Chironomidae were abundant in unchannelized, channelized, and bank-stabilized stations. Progressive downstream increase in the relative biomass of oligochaetes was apparently a response to increasing silt deposition along mud banks and in chutes. Ephemeroptera, primarily *Hexagenia* and *Pentagenia,* were also relatively abundant, but only in the unchannelized and bank-stabilized stations. Trichoptera, especially *Cheumatopsyche,* were fairly common in the unchannelized river, but were rare farther downstream. Gomphidae (Odonata) were abundant only in one of the channelized stations, while bivalves were relatively abundant in one station each of the unchannelized and bank-stabilized river (Morris et al., 1968) (Table 3.11).

The patterns in benthic macroinvertebrate abundance reported in subsequent studies are in general agreement with those reported by Morris et al. (1968). Benthic densities (Ponar grab and Eckman dredge) in a June to August 1971 study at a channelized station near Whiting, Iowa, averaged 34 m^{-2} in the main channel and 317 m^{-2} in the mud banks. Chironomidae accounted for 55.9% of the density in the main channel and 80.4% in the mud bank. Oligochaetes accounted for 14.7% and 11.0%, respectively (Wolf et al., 1972). From June though October 1973 to 1977, benthic densities (Ponar grab) from a reference site behind a dike near the Cooper Nuclear Power Station, Nebraska, averaged 641.7 m^{-2}. Densities were almost always dominated by Tubificidae (Oligochaeta), which on average accounted for 78.5% of the total density. Most tubificids were immature and could not be identified to genus, but adults were dominated by *Limnodrilus cervix, L. claparedianus,* and *L. hoffmeisteri.* Chironomidae accounted for only 10.6% of the total density, probably because unstable substrates limited their abundance. Their densities were usually dominated by *Chironomus* spp. and *Cryptochironomus* spp. (Carter et al., 1982).

Patterns of benthic macroinvertebrate abundance reported in subsequent studies of the unchannelized river below Gavins Point Dam were also generally consistent with the observations of Morris et al. (1968). For example, during a June to August 1971 study, mean benthic densities from an unchannelized site near Vermillion, South Dakota, were lower in the main channel (94 m^{-2}) than they were in a variety of other unchannelized habitats, but they were higher than the mean density (34 m^{-2}) of a corresponding main-channel site in the channelized river near Whiting, Iowa. Interestingly, the mean density in the mud bank habitat of the unchannelized river (308 m^{-2}) was similar to that from the channelized river (317 m^{-2}) (Wolf et al., 1972).

Benthic macroinvertebrate abundance in the unchannelized river near Vermillion, South Dakota, was found to vary considerably from habitat to habitat. Mean standing crop for a main-channel site averaged 11.0 mg DW m^{-2} during August and September 1968 (Namminga, 1969, as cited in Modde and Schmulbach, 1973). From October 1971 through September 1972, benthic standing stocks in another main-channel site ranged from 1.3 to 30.1 mg DW m^{-2} and averaged 9.0 mg DW m^{-2} (Modde and Schmulbach, 1973). Standing crops in nearby chutes were similarly low in a June to November 1968 study, averaging 5.9 mg DW m^{-2} and ranging from 1.1 to 16.1 mg DW m^{-2}. [In this case chutes were defined as unvegetated, shallow, and sandy side channels, whereas Morris et al., (1968) included vegetated areas in their chutes.] Reduced currents and increased silt deposition apparently enhanced macroinvertebrate abundance in the unvegetated backups, which had standing crops averaging 44.2 mg DW m^{-2} and ranging from 38.0 to 47.7 mg DW m^{-2}. However, standing crops were highest in the *Typha* marshes. Marshes adjacent to the open chutes had standing crops averaging 92.7 mg DW m^{-2} (57.2 to 153.6 mg DW m^{-2}), while those adjacent to the backups averaged 106.8 mg DW m^{-2} (79.2 to 146.9 mg DW m^{-2}) (Volesky, 1969). Similar results were obtained in a later (1971) study in which a somewhat different assortment of habitats were sampled. Mean densities were low in the main channel (94 m^{-2}), intermediate in both sandbar (203 m^{-2}) and sand bank (171 m^{-2}) habitats, high in the mud bank habitats (308 m^{-2}), and highest in the *Typha* marsh (635 m^{-2}) (Wolf et al., 1972). In both studies, increased benthic macroinvertebrate abundance was

TABLE 3.12.   *Mean Benthic Macroinvertebrate Density and Standing Crops for Chutes (Ch), Backups (Bk), and Their Respective Cattail Marshes (ChM and BkM) in the Unchannelized Middle Missouri River near Vermillion, South Dakota, June– November 1968*

	Density (number m^{-2})				Biomass (mg DW m^{-2})			
	Ch	Bk	ChM	BkM	Ch	Bk	ChM	BkM
Oligochaeta								
Total	—	11	14	8	—	1.1	1.8	1.1
Isopoda								
Asellus sp.	—	2	5	8	—	1.1	4.8	6.7
Odonata								
Total	—	<1	4	1	—	0.4	13.0	7.6
Ephemeroptera								
Caenis sp.	—	26	180	141	—	4.7	32.8	15.1
Hexagenia limbata	—	3	1	1	—	11.8	5.7	21.1
Hemiptera								
Sigara sp.	—	2	48	34	—	0.4	11.0	8.1
Coleoptera								
Total	—	<1	1	2	0.1	<0.1	2.1	3.4
Trichoptera								
Total	4	7	8	15	1.1	2.8	2.3	4.8
Diptera								
Ceratopogonidae	—	2	16	30	—	0.1	0.7	1.4
Chironomidae								
Chironomus	—	17	3	4	—	4.8	0.5	1.1
Cricotopus	30	2	8	20	0.7	<0.1	0.1	0.4
Cryptochironomus[a]	48	46	18	33	2.5	3.4	1.5	2.6
Dicrotendipes	—	5	17	23	—	0.3	1.3	2.2
Harnischia	—	21	12	4	—	1.4	0.3	0.1
Polypedilum	2	124	84	85	1.0	5.2	3.6	3.7
Procladius	—	23	26	20	—	2.4	1.8	4.8
Tanytarsus	—	57	64	106	—	2.5	2.8	4.6
Other	—	1	3	4	—	1.0	0.3	0.4
Total Chironomidae	80	297	235	299	4.2	21.0	12.2	19.9
Other Diptera								
Total	<1	1	19	8	0.5	0.1	6.3	12.1
Other aquatic taxons								
Total	—	<1	<1	2	—	0.7	<0.1	5.5
Total density and biomass	84	351	531	549	5.9	44.8	93.2	106.8

Source: After Volesky (1969).
[a]Probably *Demicryptochironomus*

associated with reduced currents, increased sediment stability, and decreased silt content. Increased abundance was probably also associated with increased benthic particulate organic matter.

Chironomidae were dominant in all of the benthic habitats sampled in the unchannelized river near Vermillion. Chironomidae accounted for an average

TABLE 3.13. *Habitat-Specific Benthic Density (number m⁻¹) of Macroinvertebrates from an Unchannelized Site in the Middle Missouri River near Vermillion, South Dakota, June–August 1971*

	Main Channel	Sand bar	Sand Bank	Mud Bank	Typha Marsh
Oligochaeta	8	35	16	65	130
Odonata	—	4	—	—	—
Ephemeroptera	—	4	—	—	3
Coleoptera	1	4	—	3	—
Trichoptera	—	—	—	—	—
Diptera					
Chironomidae	75	140	154	227	487
Chironomus	—	4	—	—	46
Coleotanypus	—	—	—	3	15
Cricotopus	—	—	31	6	22
Cryptochironomus	—	12	4	22	26
Cryptotendipes	1	4	4	37	46
Demicryptochironomus A	29	20	—	—	4
Demicryptochironomus B	24	43	27	40	96
Demicryptochironomus C	—	4	—	—	—
Harnischia	—	—	4	9	—
Limnophytes	—	—	—	—	22
Microcricotopus	2	4	—	18	—
Paratanytarsus	—	4	—	—	37
Polypedilum	11	16	61	74	92
Smittia	4	16	—	3	22
Tanytarsus	1	—	—	—	18
Other Chironomidae	3	13	23	15	41
Other Diptera	10	16	—	6	15
Total density	94	203	171	308	635

Source: After McMahon et al. (1972) and Wolf et al. (1972).

of 89.9% of the biomass in one main-channel site (Modde and Schmulbach, 1977) and 78.9% of the density from another (Wolf et al., 1972). Chironomidae similarly dominated benthic densities in open chutes (95.0%), sandbars (69.0%), sand banks (90.1%), and backups (84.6%). Relative chironomid densities in the *Typha* marshes were more variable, ranging from 44.3 to 76.7%. Chironomids were generally represented by fewer taxons. They were primarily genera near *Demicryptochironomus* spp., *Cryptochironomus* spp., *Cricotopus* spp., and/or *Paratanytarsus* sp., in the predominantly sandy (main channel, chute, and sand bank) habitats, while more diverse assemblages occurred in muddier (mud bank and backup) and/or *Typha* marsh habitats (McMahon et al., 1972; Modde and Schmulbach, 1973; Volesky, 1969; Wolf et al., 1972) (Tables 3.12 and 3.13). An exception to this trend of low taxonomic richness in sandy habitats is the relatively diverse chironomid assemblage that was collected in the sandbar habitat (Table 3.13). However, several terrestrial taxons, including Arachnida and *Dermaptera,* were also collected in this habitat (Wolf et al., 1972), which raises the possibility that some of the aquatic taxons were imported from elsewhere.

Oligochaetes appeared to be considerably less dominant in the unchannelized river than they were in the channelized river. They were not collected in the open chute habitat and never accounted for more than 3.1% of the mean density for other habitats sampled during 1968 (Volesky, 1969) (Table 3.12). Mean relative densities for oligochaetes were considerably higher during the 1971 study, but they were still substantially lower than those for Chironomidae. Oligochaetes from this later study were most abundant in mud bank and marsh habitats, but they were also common in sandbars (McMahon et al., 1972) (Table 3.13).

Taxa other than Chironomidae and Oligochaeta were either absent or uncommon in the 1971 benthic habitats sampled by McMahon et al. (1972) (Table 3.13). They were also unimportant in the 1968 open chute habitat sampled by Volesky (1969). However, a number of other taxa were important in backup and marsh habitats. *Caenis* sp. (Ephemeroptera) accounted for 33.9% and 25.7% of the total density of chute marsh and backup marsh habitats, respectively. Although not important in terms of density, the large-bodied *Hexagenia limbata* (Ephemeroptera) accounted for 26.7% and 19.8% of the backup and backup marsh habitats, respectively. Other taxons, including Hirudinea, *Asellus* (Isopoda), *Gomphus* sp. and *Libellula* sp. (Odonata), *Sigara* sp. (Hemiptera), *Berosus* sp. (Coleoptera), and *Palpomyia* sp., *Chrysops* sp., and *Dolichopus* sp. (other Diptera), were common in the chute marsh and/or backup marsh habitats. Trichoptera were found in all four habitats (Volesky, 1969) (Table 3.12).

A number of studies from both the channelized and unchannelized reaches of the Middle Missouri River indicated that there were significant differences in taxonomic composition and relative abundances between macroinvertebrates collected in benthic and drift samples. In general, the relative abundances of Ephemeroptera and Trichoptera were substantially greater in the drift than they were in the benthos, whereas Chironomidae, although often an important drifter, was considerably less abundant in the drift than in the benthos (Carter et al., 1982; Kallemeyn and Novotny, 1977; Morris et al., 1968; Modde and Schmulbach, 1973; Schmulbach, 1974). The differences between drift and benthos become even more pronounced when one compares genera. Many common and abundant drifters, such as *Ameletus, Baetis, Isonychia, Ephoron* (*Ephemeroptera*), *Hydropsyche,* and *Neureclipsis* (Trichoptera), were either absent or much less common in benthic samples (Morris et al., 1968; McMahon et al., 1972; Namminga, 1969; Novotny, 1978).

This disparity between the benthic and drift faunas is explained by the fact that most Missouri River drifters originate from hard substrates (i.e., aufwuchs) rather than the sand, silt, and mud that characterize the benthos. Snags provided considerable amounts of hard substrates for the Missouri prior to extensive snagging operations and channelization. In fact, several presettlement accounts report of massive "snag islands" in the river (L. W. Hesse, personal communication). Snags were moderately extensive in the unchannelized river in the first two decades following the closing of the Fort Randall and Gavins Point Dams (Kallemeyn and Novotny, 1977; Schmulbach, 1974), but channel degradation has largely eliminated them in recent years (Hesse, 1987). Snags have also been largely eliminated in the channelized river, but assorted wood and stone channelization structures continue to provide extensive hard substrate habitat (Carter et al., 1982; Funk and Robinson, 1974).

From July to September 1970, modified Hester–Dendy multiplate artificial substrates were placed in unchannelized, bank-stabilized, and channelized reaches of the Middle Missouri River. Samplers within each station were suspended either in the main channel (fast water; 0.83 to 1.23 m s^{-1}) or in backwater (slow water; 0.01 to 0.09 m s^{-1}) sites in chutes or behind channelization structures. Mean densities and standing stocks for the fast-water sites were highest in the unchannelized station, while slow-water densities and standing stocks were highest in the downstream bank-stabilized station, possibly because of tributary influence from the Big Sioux River. Macroinvertebrate abundance within each station was consistently greater in the fast-water sites, but taxonomic richness was often greater in the slow-water sites. A total of 22 taxons were identified for both the fast- and slow-water sites in the unchannelized river, but slow-water sites in the channelized and bank-stabilized sites consistently yielded more taxons than did their corresponding fast-water sites (Nord and Schmulbach, 1973) (Table 3.14).

Hydropsyche spp., accounting for more than 80% of the standing stock, overwhelmingly dominated the fast-water sites at each station and were also abundant in the slow-water sites. Station and/or current speed was associated with the abundance of several taxa. *Baetis, Heptagenia, Stenonema,* and *Isonychia* (Ephemeroptera) were more abundant in the bank-stabilized and channelized stations, with the first two being consistently more abundant in fast water, while *Stenonema* was similarly abundant in both fast- and slow-water sites. *Neureclipsis* (Trichoptera) were most abundant in the slow-water sites. Chironomidae, which were dominated by *Cricotopus, Orthocladius,* and *Polypedilum,* were most abundant in the unchannelized station and in the slow-water site of the bank-stabilized station downstream from the Big Sioux River. Simuliidae were abundant in the fast-water sites from the unchannelized and channelized stations (Nord and Schmulbach, 1973) (Table 3.14).

Differences between macroinvertebrate aufwuchs from fast- and slow-water sites were also investigated during a July to November 1973 study in an unchannelized station near Vermillion. In this case, artificial substrates made of cottonwood stakes were employed to simulate the natural snag habitat. Mean densities on these wood stakes were higher in the slow-water sites, but mean standing stocks were higher in the fast-water sites. Although its relative biomass (62.2%) was lower than that reported for the multiplate samplers (>80%), *Hydropsyche* sp. still dominated the biomass of the fast-water substrates, but it was uncommon in slow waters. Three mayflies, *Baetis* sp., *Heptagenia* sp., and *Ameletus* sp., were more abundant in faster water, while

TABLE 3.14. *Mean Macroinvertebrate Standing Crop and Density Sampled with Hester–Dendy Artificial Substrates from Four Stations in the Middle Missouri River, July–September 1970*

Station:[a] Flow:[b]	Unchannelized 1		Bank Stabilized 2		3		Channelized 4	
	Fast	Slow	Fast	Slow	Fast	Slow	Fast	Slow
Standing Crop (mg DW m^{-2})								
Ephemeroptera								
Baetis	28	—	32	3	52	30	47	3
Heptagenia	19	1	38	1	51	34	66	—
Isonychia	2	—	131	—	11	34	4	2
Stenonema	5	<1	44	29	19	81	4	24
Caenidae	<1	8	3	6	<1	3	<1	10
Trichoptera								
Hydropsyche	2864	349	1529	80	1443	618	1441	330
Neureclypsis	19	223	28	67	—	115	—	113
Other Trichoptera	<1	<1	1	<1	3	<1	6	—
Diptera								
Chironomidae	29	36	6	4	2	21	4	7
Simuliidae	162	<1	<1	1	<1	1	213	<1
Other Diptera	3	1	<1	—	—	—	—	—
Other taxons	24	40	3	185	2	1	—	59
Density (number m^{-2})								
Ephemeroptera								
Baetis	160	—	320	40	315	140	300	30
Heptagenia	20	<10	50	<10	50	30	50	—
Isonychia	<10	—	90	—	<10	20	<10	<10
Stenonema	20	10	110	50	50	80	10	40
Caenidae	<10	40	20	30	<10	20	<10	70
Trichoptera								
Hydropsyche	5790	280	2540	260	3540	1650	3420	640
Neureclypsis	30	390	130	290	—	1050	—	420
Hydroptilidae	30	<10	100	<10	90	20	130	—
Diptera								
Chironomidae								
Cricotopus	360	170	80	30	30	400	100	40
Orthocladius	100	90	30	30	—	40	—	—
Polypedilum	40	610	110	40	40	200	20	100
Other Chironomidae	20	170	<10	40	<10	80	<10	80
Simuliidae	700	30	110	—	170	10	670	—
Other Diptera	10	20	<10	—	—	—	—	—
Other taxons	20	20	<10	10	<10	<10	<10	10

Source: After Nord and Schmulbach (1973).
[a]Stations 2 and 3 are upstream and downstream from a major tributary, the Big Sioux River.
[b]Fast water, 0.83 to 1.23 m s^{-1}; slow water, 0.01 to 0.09 m s^{-1}.

Caenis sp., which was abundant in *Typha* marshes (Volesky, 1969), was abundant only in slow water. Trichoptera other than *Hydropsyche* were also more abundant in fast water, including *Neureclipsis,* which was reported by Nord and Schmulbach (1973) to be more abundant in slow water. As a group, Chironomidae were more abundant in slow water, but some genera, including *Cricotopus* and *Polypedilum,* were more abundant in fast water. Of the other Diptera, Ceratopogonidae were more common in slow water, while *Simulium* and *Limnophora* were more abundant in faster water (Gould, 1975) (Table 3.15).

The macroinvertebrate aufwuchs was also investigated at a reference station near the Cooper Nuclear Power Station in the channelized river. In this case, aufwuchs macroinvertebrates were sampled in sites below wing dikes with both a modified Hester–Dendy multiplate sampler and a rock basket sampler. Densities from the multiplate samplers ranged from 5140 to 63,385 m^{-2} and averaged 20,962 m^{-2} during 1975 to 1977. Rock basket densities ranged from 225 to 3412 per basket and averaged 2264.7 per basket. As they did in other studies of Missouri River aufwuchs, Ephemeroptera, Hydropsychidae, and Chironomidae dominated multiplate and rock basket samplers. However, there were some important differences in the relative densities of each group between samplers. On average, Ephemeroptera (27.0%) and Hydropsychidae (39.6%) were more numerous than Chironomidae (19.7%) on the multiplate samplers, while Chironomidae (32.2%) and Ephemeroptera (20.0%) were more numerous than Hydropsychidae (4.7%) in the rock baskets. Hydropsychidae were probably more abundant on the multiplate samplers because they were positioned near the surface, which would expose them to increased current velocities and decreased sedimentation. Hydropsychidae were represented primarily by *Hydropsyche frisoni, H. orris,* and *Potamyia flava.* Chironomidae were dominated by *Rheotanytarsus, Tanytarsus, Micropsectra, Polypedilum convictum,* and *Thienemannimyia* group. Ephemeroptera were dominated by *Baetis, Stenonema, Isonychia,* and *Caenis* (Carter et al., 1982).

Several patterns emerge from the numerous studies of Missouri River macroinvertebrates. As indicated in Table 3.16, abundance (density and/or biomass) varies considerably among habitats. For example, benthic abundance within the unchannelized reaches is lowest in the main channel and unvegetated chutes, intermediate in sandbars, and along sandy banks, higher along muddy banks and silty backups, and highest in *Typha* marshes. Biomass in the marshes is approximately an order of magnitude greater than that in the main channel. In general, benthic abundance increases with substrate stability, reduced currents, and increasing silt content. Abundance may also increase with increasing accumulations of benthic particulate organic matter. The increase in macroinvertebrate abundance on hard substrates (aufwuchs) is even more dramatic. Biomass in the main channel (fast water) aufwuchs was 200- to 300-fold greater than that of the main-channel benthos. The differences between aufwuchs and benthic biomass were less pronounced in backwater (slow water) sites, but the aufwuchs was still two- to sixfold greater than

TABLE 3.15.   *Mean Macroinvertebrate Densities (number m^{-2}) and Standing Stocks (mg DW m^{-2}) on Wood Artificial Substrates Located in Fast-Water (>0.8 m s^{-1}) and Slow-water (<0.2 m s^{-1}) Sites in the Unchannelized Middle Missouri River near Vermillion, South Dakota, July–November 1973*

	Density		Standing Stock	
	Fast	Slow	Fast	Slow
Oligochaeta				
Total	20.2	125.7	4.7	27.3
Odonata				
Chromagrion sp.	—	1.4	—	1.5
Ischnura sp.	—	114.4	—	158.3
Ephemeroptera				
Ameletus sp.	15.5	—	5.3	—
Baetis sp.	44.5	5.8	15.2	2.0
Caenis sp.	—	255.7	—	83.2
Heptagenia sp.	36.4	—	12.4	—
Other Ephemeroptera	—	<0.1	—	<0.1
Coleoptera				
Dineutes sp.	—	1.4	—	38.6
Trichoptera				
Agraylea sp.	259.8	35.5	182.1	25.2
Hydropsyche sp.	1317.0	2.9	1412.9	0.1
Mayatrichia sp.	44.2	11.2	30.5	34.5
Other Hydroptilidae	144.7	—	39.1	—
Neureclypsis sp.	35.1	—	9.5	—
Other Trichoptera	—	1.4	—	1.0
Diptera				
Atrichopogon sp.	—	21.0	—	42.1
Probezzia sp.	—	42.3	—	63.5
Chironomidae				
Ablabesmyia sp.	—	68.9	—	14.5
Cricotopus sp.	789.5	39.5	20.2	9.5
Dicrotendipes sp.	2.1	427.6	0.5	100.7
Endochironomus sp.	—	257.7	—	63.4
Glyptotendipes sp.	—	2023.1	—	435.5
Polypedilum sp.	56.1	22.3	11.8	4.7
Tanytarsus sp.	35.8	317.2	7.5	81.4
Other Chironomidae	28.9	127.7	4.2	49.2
Total	912.4	3284.7	44.2	758.9
Limnophora sp.	180.1	1.4	418.3	0.8
Simulium sp.	31.9	—	18.4	—
Other Diptera	2.6	—	1.4	—
Other invertebrates				
Total	—	8.6	—	2.5
Total density and standing stock	3044.5	3913.4	2272.9	1239.5

Source: After Gould (1975).

TABLE 3.16. *Mean Benthic and Aufwuchs Macroinvertebrate Densities and Biomass in the Missouri River*

	Density (number m^{-2})	Biomass (mg m^{-2})	Source
Unchannelized stations			
Benthos			
Main channel	—	5	Morris et al. (1968)
Main channel	—	11	Namminga (1969)
Main channel	94	—	McMahon et al. (1972)
Main channel	—	9	Modde and Schmulbach (1977)
Mud bank	—	27	Morris et al. (1968)
Mud bank	308	—	McMahon et al. (1972)
Sand bank	171	—	McMahon et al. (1972)
Sandbar	203	—	McMahon et al. (1972)
Chute	—	15	Morris et al. (1968)
Chute	84	6	Volesky (1969)
Backup	351	45	Volesky (1969)
Marsh (chute)	531	92	Volesky (1969)
Marsh (backup)	549	107	Volesky (1969)
Marsh (bank)	635	—	McMahon et al. (1972)
Aufwuchs			
Multiplate (fast)	7,290	3,155	Nord and Schmulbach (1973)
Wood stake (fast)	3,044	2,273	Gould (1975)
Multiplate (slow)	1,380	208	Nord and Schmulbach (1973)
Wood stake (slow)	3,913	1,240	Gould (1975)
Channelized stations			
Benthos			
Main channel	—	<1	Berner (1951)
Main channel	—	1	Morris et al. (1968)
Main channel	34	—	McMahon et al. (1972)
Steep bank	—	24	Berner (1951)
Mud bank	—	80	Morris et al. (1968)
Mud bank	317	—	McMahon et al. (1972)
Behind pile dike	—	14	Berner (1951)
Behind pile dike	—	6	Morris et al. (1968)
Behind pile dike	642	—	Carter et al. (1982)
Chute	—	82	Morris et al. (1968)
Aufwuchs			
Multiplate (fast)	4,700	1,785	Nord and Schmulbach (1973)
Multiplate (slow)	1,430	548	Nord and Schmulbach (1973)
Multiplate (dike)	20,926	—	Carter et al. (1982)

the most productive benthic habitats, *Typha* marshes. A similar pattern emerges from studies conducted in the channelized river. Benthic abundance is lowest in the benthic main-channel sites and substantially higher in protected habitats behind pile dikes, along mud banks, and in chutes. Again, however, aufwuchs macroinvertebrates are far more abundant than those from any benthic habitat.

The patterns of macroinvertebrate abundance observed in the Missouri River are similar to those observed in some Southeastern Coastal Plain rivers. For example, macroinvertebrate biomass on aufwuchs (snag) habitats in the Satilla River (Georgia) averaged 4611 mg DW m^{-2}, while main-channel (sandy) habitats averaged 125 mg DW m^{-2}, and backwater (muddy) habitats averaged 610 mg DW m^{-2}. In addition, these respective habitats exhibited similar patterns for most of the dominant taxa (i.e., Hydropsychidae, Chironomidae, Ephemeroptera, and Oligochaeta) (Benke et al., 1984). However, the disparity between benthic and aufwuchs habitats was not as great in the Satilla as it was in the Missouri. In part, this may result from methodological differences, since Benke et al. (1984) commented that the majority of their benthic taxons were small and prone to being overlooked by standard methods. However, these differences may be indicative of actual differences in benthic abundance since the higher gradient and faster currents of the Missouri River would result in less stable substrates.

Inferences on the patterns of macroinvertebrate abundance in the natural river based on these studies of the altered river are problematic. It is reasonable to infer that the loss of backwater and marsh habitats to channelization and channel degradation has resulted in a considerable loss of benthic macroinvertebrate production. This would be reasonable even if one considers only the loss of total habitat area. However, flow regulation and the prevention of floodplain inundation may have greatly reduced the benthic productivity. Prior to regulation, benthic populations in spring would have experienced increased allochthonous inputs via floodplain inundation combined with increasing temperatures. These potentially productive conditions have been greatly modified by the impoundments. Currently, autumn and winter drawdown usually results in desired reservoir levels by early spring, after which discharges are sharply reduced. The spring dewatering of backwater and marsh habitats resulting from this reduced flow would have also depressed benthic production. This effect was evident in the seasonal pattern of benthic biomass reported for a station in the unchannelized river near Vermillion. During spring (April, May, and June) benthic standing stocks from a main-channel site averaged only 1.9 mg DW m^{-2}. In contrast, standing stocks from July through October averaged 18.2 mg DW m^{-2}. In fact, standing stocks for the remaining autumn and winter samples were never less than 3.1 mg DW m^{-2} (Modde and Schmulbach, 1973, 1977).

The effects of anthropogenic modifications on the aufwuchs could also have been profound. Reduced sediment loads and the import of reservoir plankton may have substantially altered the aufwuchs by favoring those taxons that feed on algae and/or are less tolerant of silt. Carter et al. (1982) speculated that greater relative densities of Hydropsychidae on (suspended) multiplate samplers relative to (benthic) rock basket samplers at the Cooper Nuclear Power Station may have been a result of reduced sedimentation in the suspended sampler. However, intolerance of sedimentation does not preclude hydropsychid abundance since much of the natural snag habitat would have also been relatively free from siltation. In addition, there is no clear indication that Hydropsychidae are less abundant in the more turbid channelized river. Hydropsychids were abundant (and dominant) in the artificial substrate and drift samples from sites near the Cooper and Fort Calhoun Nuclear Power Stations (Carter et al., 1982). In fact, several studies reported greater relative and absolute abundance for Hydropsychidae in drift samples from channelized stations than unchannelized stations, possibly because of a greater availability of aufwuchs habitats (Kallemeyn and Novotny, 1977; Morris et al., 1968; Novotny, 1978). Finally, Berner (1951) reported that Trichoptera and Ephemeroptera were abundant on pile dikes during his 1945 preimpoundment, high-turbidity study.

A survey of freshwater mussels (Unionidae: Bivalvia) exemplifies some of what is known about Missouri River macroinvertebrates. A recent survey indicated that the river contained a moderately rich fauna containing 13 species. Twelve of these species were recorded from unchannelized sites, while only five were recorded from the channelized river; another species was recorded only in an oxbow. Historically, unionid distribution in North America has been relatively well studied, but the characterization of the Missouri River as a poor unionid habitat by a number of late nineteenth- and early twentieth-century investigators was apparently based more on their impressions of the river than on actual survey work. Consequently, it is impossible to determine whether the present unionid fauna is comparable to that of the natural river or was enhanced by anthropogenic changes (i.e., species introductions or post-impoundment reductions in turbidity) (Hoke, 1983).

Fish Production

Missouri River fishes have been studied more extensively than either invertebrates or primary producers, and it is with them that the changes in the river's biota are most strongly documented. In general, the precontrol river supported a relatively limited and specialized fish fauna that was well adapted to the Missouri's persistently high turbidity and seasonal flooding. In fact, several of these species were limited to the turbid rivers west of the Mississippi. Subsequently, many of the native species have declined and many sight-feeding and pelagic species, both native and introduced, have increased (Cross and Moss, 1987; Pflieger and Grace, 1987). Changes in the overall productivity of the fauna have also occurred.

Fisheries data give some indication of the abundance of selected species and may indicate abundance patterns for the entire fauna. Several accounts from the second half of the nineteenth century mention catches of large catfish ranging from 200 to 500 kg. These large catfishes, which were probably blue catfish (*Ictalurus furcatus*), are now rare in the Missouri River, probably because of a combination of overfishing and loss of snag habitat (Funk and Robinson, 1974; Pflieger, 1975; Pflieger and Grace, 1987). Late nineteenth- and early twentieth-century fisheries data from the Lower Missouri indicate considerable changes in the abundance of several other species. One of the most highly prized species in the early fishery was lake sturgeon (*Acipenser fluvescens*), but it has declined dramatically since 1900, probably because of overfishing. Overfishing also probably contributed to the early twentieth-century declines in the catches of two other highly valued species, shovelnose sturgeon (*Scaphirhynchus platorynchus*) and paddlefish (*Polydon spathula*). *Cyprinus carpio,* which was introduced to the lower river in 1880, accounted for 12% of fisheries catches in 1894 but accounted for 53% of the total reported catch during 1908 and 39 to 65% of the catches reported from 1922 to 1970 (Funk and Robinson, 1974).

In addition to changes in the relative catches of selected species, there were substantial changes in the total catches for the Lower Missouri River fishery. From 1894 through 1931, reported catch data were apparently limited to the larger, organized markets, and the data are not sufficient for the estimation of total catches. Despite probable underreporting and apparently less fishing effort, the 1894, 1899, and 1908 reported catches were substantially higher than most subsequent catches (Figure 3.2). Reported catches were substantially lower in 1922 and 1931 because of a decline in the more valuable species (i.e., sturgeon, paddlefish, and blue catfish) and reduced effort. Reported catch data from 1945 to 1970 was more systematic and probably represented a greater proportion of the actual total catch. The more reliable data from this later period indicates a substantial decline in total reported and estimated catches. The major exception to this decline is the increased reported catches during 1968 to 1970. In part, this late increase was the result of increased reporting enforcement, but improvements in water quality as pollution controls took effect may have also been involved (Funk and Robinson, 1974). Throughout this period, the fishery was dominated by catfish, buffalo (*Ictiobus* spp.), and *Cyprinus carpio.* Channel catfish (*Ictalurus punctatus*), *I. furcatus,* and flathead catfish (*Pylodictis olivaris*) accounted for almost all of the catfish catch, but the latter two species are in decline. In fact, *I. punctatus* and *C. carpio* are the only two commercial species that have not seriously declined. Overfishing appears to have contributed to the decline of some species, but habitat loss caused by channelization and impoundment is the primary reason for the decline in the total fishery (Funk and Robinson, 1974; Hesse, 1987; L. W. Hesse, personal communication).

A 1972–1973 study in the Middle Missouri River contrasted fish populations from the unchannelized river below Gavins Point Dam and the channelized river downstream from Sioux City. By the time of this study, the unchannelized reach had been affected by flow regulation and reduced sediment loads for at least two decades, but much of the backwater, sandbar, and pool habitats were still intact. As such, it would give some indication of the productivity of the precontrol river. Significantly, three separate sampling methods indicated that catch per unit efforts (CPUEs) were higher in the unchannelized reach than they were in the channelized river. Gill-netting CPUEs averaged 10.31 fish per net unit in the unchannelized river and 5.25

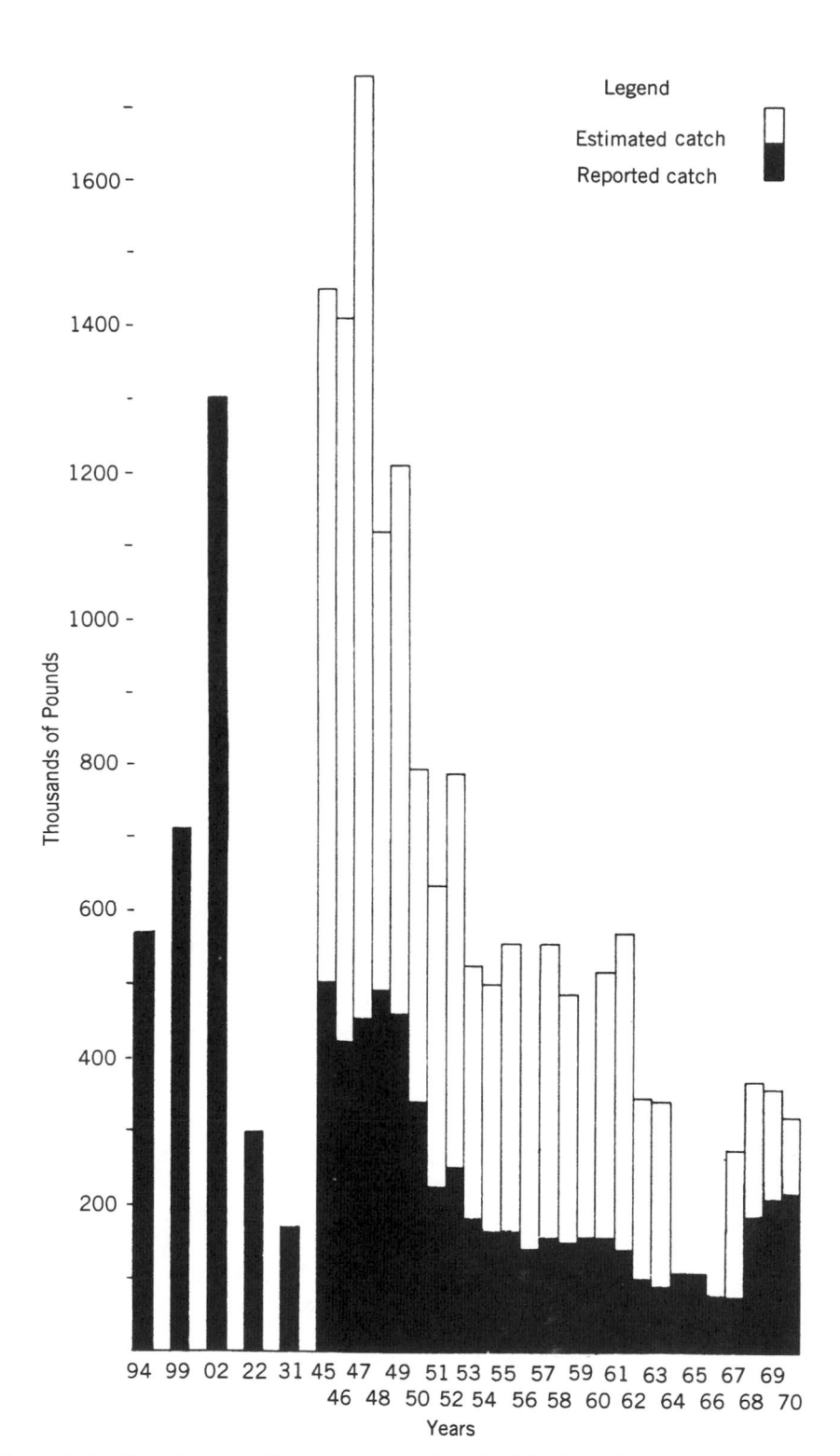

FIGURE 3.2. Reported and estimated commercial catch of fish from the Lower Missouri River, 1894 to 1970. (Modified from Funk and Robinson, 1974.)

TABLE 3.17. *Habitat-Specific Larval Fish Densities (larvae m^{-3}) from Four Stations in the Middle Missouri River, May to September 1976*

	Main Channel	Main-Channel Border	Chute	Backup
Unchannelized stations				
Below Fort Randall Dam (km 1382)				
Mean	0.02	0.03	<0.01	0.41
Maximum	0.21	0.27	0.03	3.92
Below Gavins Point Dam (km 1286)				
Mean	0.20	0.05	0.08	3.67
Maximum	1.48	0.17	0.30	16.36
Below Gavins Point Dam (km 1253)				
Mean	0.12	0.13	0.19	0.27
Maximum	4.54	0.75	1.94	2.29
Channelized station				
Below Sioux City, Iowa (km 1137)				
Mean	0.06	0.09	—	—
Maximum	0.16	0.29	—	—

Source: After Kallemeyn and Novotny (1977).

fish per net unit in the channelized river. Similarly, electrofishing yielded mean CPUEs of 59.2 and 51.0 fish h^{-1}, respectively, and angling yielded 0.72 and 0.34 fish h^{-1}, respectively (Schmulbach et al., 1975).

Additional evidence for the detrimental effects of channelization on fish populations came from a 1976 comparison of CPUEs recorded from selected channel (main-channel border, pool, and sandbar) and backwater (chute and backup) habitats in the unchannelized river. It was found that mean CPUEs for each of the three unchannelized stations were higher in the backwater habitats than in the channel habitats. In addition, backwater habitats in the two stations downstream from Gavins Point Dam almost always yielded higher CPUEs than the corresponding channel habitats during each sample period. On the other hand, channel CPUEs in the station upstream from Gavins Point Dam (below Fort Randall Dam) exceeded CPUEs from the backwaters from mid-July through late October. The frequency of higher channel CPUEs in this upstream station may be the result of unfavorable conditions in the backwaters; mean pooled backwater CPUE from the upstream station (113.6) is approximately half of the pooled backwater means recorded from the two downstream stations (223.1 and 212.1), while pooled channel means were similar for all three stations (Table 3.17). Unfavorable backwater conditions at this station are probably the result of diurnal and seasonal dewatering caused by hydroelectric generation and flood control activities at Fort Randall Dam (Kallemeyn and Novotny, 1977).

Nearshore fish populations in the channelized Middle Missouri River were sampled at preoperational and ambient temperature stations near the Fort

Calhoun Nuclear Power Station (FCS) and the Cooper Nuclear Station (CNS) from 1971 to 1977. Annual mean electrofishing CPUEs along trail dikes near FCS averaged 102 fish per 800 m of dike and ranged from 41 to 160 fish per 800 m. Trail dike electrofishing CPUEs at CNS averaged 99 fish per 800 m and ranged from 69 to 127 fish per 800 m. Electrofishing CPUEs from the downstream ends of wing dikes averaged 35 fish per 30 m. Seining CPUEs at wing dikes near FCS averaged 32 fish per 30 m haul, while they averaged 76 fish per 30 m (Hesse et al., 1982a).

One of the problems in estimating fish abundance in large rivers is that many species travel considerable distances during the warmer months. For example, several *Scaphirhynchus platorynchus* were captured at a distance of more than 450 km from their initial tagging locations (Schmulbach, 1974). An attempt to overcome this difficulty was made by sampling overwintering concentrations of fish in the pools downstream from trail dikes in the channelized Middle Missouri. A total of 28 species were collected, of which *Hiodon alosoides, Carpiodes carpio, Cyprinus carpio, Ictiobus* spp., *Ictalurus punctatus,* and *Aplodinotus grunniens* were dominant. During the winter of 1979 to 1980 the density of these dominants in a reach near Blair, Nebraska, was estimated to be 1100 fish km^{-1}. During the winter of 1980 to 1981, sampling was conducted downstream of wing dikes near Tekamah, Nebraska, but this time methods were modified to also sample the deeper (>12 m) pools favored by *I. punctatus.* This resulted in an estimated density of 11,558 fish km^{-1}, of which 81% were *I. punctatus* (Hesse and Newcomb, 1982). Biomass estimates for three of the dominant species, *Carpiodes carpio, Cyprinus carpio,* and *I. punctatus,* averaged 474, 324, and 1552 kg km^{-1}, respectively (Hesse et al., 1982a). In the unchannelized river downstream from Gavins Point Dam, tagging studies of gill-netted *Scaphirhynchus platorynchus* yielded a mean density of 2500 fish km^{-1}, which is more than double that obtained for this species in the Upper Mississippi (Schmulbach, 1974).

By using a combination of census techniques, mean specific weights, and age-class regression equations, the standing stock for the channelized Missouri River near Blair, Nebraska, was estimated to be 240 lb/acre (214 kg ha^{-1}). This estimate combined with the nearly 80% decline in commercial catches between 1947 and 1963, means fish standing stocks in the uncontrolled river were probably at least 1200 lb/acre (1071 kg ha^{-1}) and possibly much higher (Hesse, 1990). As stated before, most of this decline is attributable to habitat loss and degradation. Further indications of the importance of changes in habitat quality to fish populations come from studies on larval populations, from changes in adult assemblages, and from adult habitat preferences.

A number of researchers (e.g., Fuchs, 1967) speculated that much of the larval ichthyoplankton collected in the Middle Missouri originated from Lewis and Clark Lake since the dominant riverine ichthyoplankters, *Aplodinotus grunniens, Cyprinus carpio,* emerald shiner (*Notropis atherinoides*), and unidentified Catostomidae/Cyprinidae, are also abundant in the impoundment. A 1976 study of Middle Missouri River ichthyoplankton indicated that larval densities did, in fact, decline with distance from Gavins Point Dam. Mean main-channel densities (May to September) were highest (0.20 larvae m^{-3}) at an unchannelized station 10 km below the dam, lower at a downstream unchannelized station (0.12 larvae m^{-3}), and lower still at a channelized station 32 km downstream from Sioux City (0.06 larvae m^{-3}). Larval densities were substantially higher, and the longitudinal decline even more pronounced in the backups. Backup densities averaged 3.67 larvae m^{-3} in the unchannelized station closest to the dam and 0.45 larvae m^{-3} in the one downstream. Mean larval densities were low in the main-channel border and chute habitats, although they were somewhat higher in the downstream unchannelized station (Table 3.17). Seasonal density maxima for most sites were dominated by *A. grunniens* and *N. atherinoides* and generally coincided with their seasonal maxima in Lewis and Clark Lake (Kallemeyn and Novotny, 1977). While the longitudinal trend evident in both the main channel and the backups indicates that the reservoir was the primary source for larvae, the consistently higher densities in backups indicated that these habitats served as sites for larval production and/or concentration.

In a 1978 study, longitudinal changes in main-channel larval densities were monitored at seven transects extending from Gavins Point Dam to Leavenworth, Kansas. Instead of a longitudinal decline from Gavins Point Dam, mean larval densities from two stations located upstream (0.39 larvae m^{-3}) and downstream (0.37 larvae m^{-3}) from Sioux City were more than double that of the discharge from Gavins Point Dam (0.14 larvae m^{-3}). This indicates that the unchannelized reach between Gavins Point Dam and Sioux City was a major source of ichthyoplankton. Mean larval densities for the four channelized stations ranged from 0.21 to 0.31 larvae m^{-3} (Table 3.18). When expressed in terms of larval transport, the biggest change occurred after passage through the unchannelized reach. Mean transport from June 17 to July 9 (when data were available from all seven transects) was 689.5 larvae s^{-1} at the Gavins Point Dam outfall, but increased to 1417.6 larvae s^{-1} at the transect upstream from Sioux City. Mean transport increased to 1572.4 and 1598.4 larvae s^{-1} at the

TABLE 3.18.   *Mean and Maximum Larval Fish Densities in the Middle Missouri River, April–August 1978*

River km	Location	Density (number m^{-3})	
		Mean	Maximum
1301	Gavins Point Dam tailwaters	0.14	0.88
1186	Upstream from Sioux City, Iowa	0.39	3.85
1155	Downstream from Sioux City, Iowa	0.37	3.46
1040	Near Blair, Nebraska	0.31	2.88
923	Near Nebraska City, Nebraska	0.30	2.57
857	Near Brownville, Nebraska	0.21	1.70
662	Near Leavenworth, Kansas	0.28	3.22

Source: After Hergenrader et al. (1982).

next two (channelized) transects and then ranged between 783.6 and 1062.2 larvae s^{-1} for the remaining three transects (Hergenrader et al., 1982). Since these studies, however, habitat loss caused by channel degradation has resulted in a sharp decline in larval fish recruitment from the unchannelized river below Gavins Point Dam. By the 1980s, this reach was no longer a significant contributor to larval recruitment. Larval densities averaged only 0.06 and 0.08 larvae m^{-3} during 1983 and 1984, respectively (Hesse et al., 1988). This loss has apparently resulted in a considerable decline in larval fish densities in the channelized river. During 1975, larval densities near Fort Calhoun Station and Cooper Nuclear Station averaged approximately 0.30 fish m^{-3}. By 1989 they averaged only 0.05 fish m^{-3} (L. W. Hesse, personal communication).

The taxonomic composition of the ichthyoplankton differed significantly among habitats. During a 1976 study of the unchannelized river, *Aplodinotus grunniens* were collected primarily in the main channel, while unidentified Catostomidae/Cyprinidae and sunfish (*Lepomis* spp.) were collected primarily in the backups. *Stizostedion* spp. were most often collected along the main-channel border and backups. *Dorosoma cepedianum* and *Cyprinus carpio* were more widely distributed than the other taxons, but *D. cepedianum* was rare in the main channel (Kallemeyn and Novotny, 1977). Within the channelized river, main-channel ichthyoplankton were dominated by *A. grunniens* and Catostomidae, while *D. cepedianum*, Cyprinidae, and *A. grunniens* dominated backwater ichthyoplankton (Hergenrader et al., 1982).

In addition to being a significant source of ichthyoplankton, backwaters also served as important nursery sites for several species. The importance of backwater habitats for immature fishes was further indicated in another study from the unchannelized river below Gavins Point Dam during 1972–1973. Collections using the combination of seining and electrofishing yielded mean standing crops in marshy backwaters that averaged 48.2 kg ha^{-1} and ranged from 403.9 kg ha^{-1} in summer to no fish in late autumn. Production estimates of young-of-the-year (YOY) of the four dominant species yielded an estimated annual production of 105.7 kg ha^{-1} yr^{-1}. If extrapolated to the remaining 31 species, this would amount to a total of 121 kg ha^{-1} yr^{-1}. These standing crop and production estimates are probably very conservative; rotenone sampling indicated that the electrofishing sampling underrepresented the assemblage by a factor of 3 to 10 (Schmulbach, 1974). Sandbars were another important nursery habitat in the unchannelized river (Kallemeyn and Novotny, 1977). Mean annual standing crops for immature fishes in sandbars were 25 kg ha^{-1} (Schmulbach, 1974). Within the channelized river, backups and tributaries served as significant, albeit limited nurseries. On the other hand, postlarvae and juveniles were essentially absent in notch revetment–dike habitats and rare in chutes (Hergenrader et al., 1982).

The composition and relative abundances of Missouri River fish assemblages indicate substantial changes over time and differences between channelized and unchannelized reaches. The first important surveys of Missouri River fishes were conducted by Jordan and Meek (1885) and Meek (1892) at sites near St. Josephs, Missouri, and Sioux City, Iowa. They collected about

28 species, all of which have been recorded in a later (1945), more extensive study by Fisher (1962) in the channelized Lower Missouri River. The similarity between the two sets of surveys suggests that changes in taxonomic composition during the more than 54 intervening years may have been modest despite some channelization. However, limited evidence suggest that there have been some significant changes in the relative abundance of some species. For example, carpsuckers (*Carpiodes* spp.) were rare and the introduced common carp (*Cyprinus carpio*) was absent from the Sioux City survey, but both taxons have been dominant throughout most of the twentieth century. Another species, sturgeon chub (*Hybopsis gelida*), was abundant in the Sioux City collections but has been rare since at least 1945 (Pflieger and Grace, 1987).

The first extensive survey of fishes in the Missouri River was conducted in 1945. The survey was conducted in the channelized Lower Missouri River prior to closure of the main-stem impoundment. The survey yielded a total of 60 species. The most abundant of these were shortnose gar (*Lepisosteus platostomus*), *Dorosoma cepedianum*, *Carpiodes* spp., *Ictiobus bubalus*, bigmouth buffalo (*I. cyprinellus*), *Cyprinus carpio*, flathead chub (*Hybopsis gracilis*), western silvery minnow (*Hybognathus nuchalis*), plains minnow (*H. placitus*), red shiner (*Notropis lutrensis*), black bullhead (*Ictalurus melas*), *I. punctatus*, *Pylodictis olivaris*, and *Aplodinotus grunniens* (Fisher, 1962).

Subsequent surveys (1962 to 1972) in the Lower Missouri indicated that there were significant changes in relative abundance for several species. Flow regulation and turbidity reduction resulting from the completion of the main-stem impoundments were associated with an increase in the relative abundance of pelagic and sight-feeding species such as *Dorosoma cepedianum*, white bass (*Morone chrysops*), *Notropis atherinoides*, sand shiner (*N. stramineus*), and white crappie (*Pomoxis annularis*). Some species that are adapted to turbid conditions, including pallid sturgeon (*Scaphirhynchus albus*), *Hybopsis gracilis*, and *Ictalurus melas*, declined in abundance. *Ictiobus cyprinellus* also declined. Although still a dominant species, *Cyprinus carpio* exhibited some decline, possibly because pollution controls reduced its competitive advantage over native species (Pflieger and Grace, 1987).

A 1972–1973 study in the Middle Missouri River revealed that there were major differences between fish assemblages collected in the channelized and unchannelized reaches. Goldeye (*Hiodon alosoides*), *Dorosoma cepedianum*, river carpsucker (*Carpiodes carpio*), *Cyprinus carpio*, *Notropis atherinoides*, *N. lutrensis*, *N. stramineus*, and *Ictalurus punctatus* were abundant in both reaches. However, relative abundances for *Scaphirhynchus platorynchus*, blue sucker (*Cycleptus elongatus*), shorthead redhorse (*Moxostoma macrolepidotum*), sauger (*Stizostedium canadense*), *Roccus chrysops*, and *Aplodinotus grunniens* were greater in the unchannelized river, whereas the relative abundances of *Pylodictis olivaris*, several cyprinids, and *Ictalurus melas* was greater in the channelized reach (Schmulbach et al., 1975) (Table 3.19).

Comparisons of the fish assemblages from channelized and unchannelized reaches during a 1976 study yielded somewhat different results (Table 3.20). Many of the same dominants from previous studies were also collected in

TABLE 3.19. *Catch per Unit Effort (CPUE) for Gill Netting (fish/net unit), Electrofishing (fish h^{-1}), and Angling (fish h^{-1}) in Unchannelized (U) and Channelized (C) Reaches of the Missouri River*

	Gill Net		Electro-Fishing		Angling	
	U	C	U	C	U	C
CPUE (number)	10.31	5.24	59.2	51.0	0.72	0.34
Distribution (%)						
Acipenseridae						
Scaphirynchus platorynchus	35.8	0.6	—	—	2.9	0.4
Polydontidae						
Polydon spathula	0.1	0.6	—	—	0.5	0.4
Lepisosteidae						
Lepisosteus platostomus	0.1	5.1	1.8	1.4	0.8	1.5
Hiodontidae						
Hiodon alosoides	31.7	36.5	1.6	12.5	8.5	14.6
Clupeidae						
Dorosoma cepedianum	—	9.4	14.8	25.7	—	—
Catostomidae						
Carpiodes carpio	11.6	17.7	44.4	32.1	0.3	0.3
Cycleptus elongatus	1.8	0.9	0.5	—	0.1	0.1
Ictiobus bubalus	—	0.6	0.3	3.0	1.5	0.5
I. cyprinellus	0.3	1.4	1.8	2.7	0.7	0.5
Moxostoma macrolepidotum	5.9	1.7	2.3	—	2.3	1.8
Cyprinidae						
Cyprinus carpio	—	7.4	19.7	15.9	16.5	19.2
Ictaluridae						
Ictalurus melas	—	1	—	—	0.9	5.8
I. punctatus	1.4	2.0	—	0.3	9.5	25.0
Pylodictis olivaris	—	1.7	—	1.7	0.3	1.4
Esocidae						
Esox lucius	4.0	1.4	—	—	0.1	0.1
Centrarchidae						
Pomoxis nigromaculatus	—	0.3	1.6	—	0.7	4.6
Percidae						
Stizostedium canadense	5.5	3.7	1.8	0.3	28.9	5.5
S. vitreum	0.8	1.4	2.1	0.3	1.2	0.5
Percithydae						
Roccus chrysops	0.1	0.9	3.6	0.7	14.4	1.4
Sciaenidae						
Aplodinotus grunniens	0.4	1.7	1.6	1.4	0.1	14.9
Other taxons	1.3	5.1	2.6	2.0	0.9	1.0

Source: Schmulbach et al. (1975).

TABLE 3.20.   *Total Fish Catches from Three Unchannelized Stations Below Fort Randall Dam (1) and Below Gavins Point Dam (2,3), and a Channelized Station (4) 32 km Downstream from Sioux City, Iowa*

	Unchannelized			Channelized
	1	2	3	4
Acipenseridae				
Scaphirhynchus albus	1	—	—	—
S. platorynchus	20	131	96	—
Polydontidae				
Polydon spathula	—	25	14	4
Lepisosteidae				
Lepisosteus platostomus	47	39	42	58
Other Lepisosteidae	—	5	7	4
Hiodontidae				
Hiodon alosoides	36	375	316	239
Clupeidae				
Dorosoma cepedianum	128	548	383	824
Other Clupediae	—	5	1	—
Catostomidae				
Carpiodes carpio	372	1095	785	528
Cycleptus elongatus	1	96	40	20
Ictiobus bubalus	240	53	35	113
I. cyprinellus	87	67	29	99
Moxostoma macrolepidotum	712	208	305	166
Other Catostomidae	2	12	6	5
Cyprinidae				
Cyprinus carpio	265	206	229	537
Notropis atherinoides	887	2615	3109	863
N. lutrensis	338	228	323	802
N. stramineus	3	105	207	224
Other Cyprinidae	15	8	4	47
Ictaluridae				
Ictalurus punctatus	219	532	296	1286
Other Ictaluridae	22	4	5	76
Centrarchidae				
Lepomis macrochirus	3	417	181	265
Other *Lepomis* spp.	3	8	117	34
Pomoxis annularis	2	12	32	234
P. nigromaculatus	4	16	32	82
Micropterus spp.	10	15	9	89
Percidae				
Etheostoma spp.	84	28	78	14
Perca flavescens	1012	82	119	44
Stizostedion canadense	36	71	61	16
Stizostedion vitreum	61	16	17	16
Percithyidae				
Morone chrysops	27	42	17	74
Sciaenidae				
Aplodinotus grunniens	15	11	7	57

Source: After Kallemeyn and Novotny (1977).

large numbers in this study, but several taxons, including *Ictiobus bubalus,* bluegill (*Lepomis macrochirus*), other sunfish (*Lepomis* spp.), largemouth bass (*Micropterus salmoides*), yellow perch (*Perca flavescens*), and walleye (*Stizostedion vitreum*), were also collected in large numbers in one or more stations. The large number of *Perca flavescens* and *S. vitreum* collected at the unchannelized station downstream from Fort Randall Dam may have originated in Lewis and Clark Lake (Kallemeyn and Novotny, 1977).

One of the most extensive surveys of the channelized Middle Missouri River was conducted in the vicinity of the Fort Calhoun and Cooper Nuclear Power Plants, Nebraska. Electrofishing and seining CPUEs yielded many of the same dominant species as have been reported by Kallemeyn and Novotny (1977) and Schmulbach et al. (1975) (Table 3.21). Major exceptions include

TABLE 3.21. *Mean (1%) Catch per Unit Effort (CPUE) at Two Stations, Fort Calhoun Station (FCS) and Cooper Nuclear Station (CNS), in the Channelized Middle Missouri River, 1971–1974*

	Electrofishing		Seining	
	FCS	CNS	FCS	CNS
CPUE (number)	21.7	36.1	18.3	97.1
Distribution (%)				
Hiodontidae				
Hiodon alosoides	3.7	6.9	—	—
Clupediae				
Dorosoma cepedianum	18.4	20.8	4.4	2.2
Catostomidae				
Carpiodes carpio	15.2	28.8	4.4	6.3
Cycleptus elongatus	0.9	0.3	—	—
Ictiobus bubalus	0.9	1.1	—	—
Moxostoma macrolepidotum	3.2	0.6	—	—
Cyprindiae				
Cyprinus carpio	37.3	14.7	—	—
Hybopsis storeriana	—	—	12.6	4.2
Hybognathus spp.	—	—	0.5	41.6
Notropis atherinoides	—	—	27.9	14.0
N. blennius	—	—	1.6	12.3
N. lutrensis	—	—	14.7	7.9
N. stramineus	—	—	20.8	3.4
Ictaluridae				
Ictalurus punctatus	—	—	5.5	2.5
Pylodictis olivaris	1.8	1.7	—	—
Percidae				
Stizostedium canadense	2.8	2.5	—	—
Sciaenidae				
Aplodinotus grunniens	7.3	5.8	—	—

Source: After Hesse et al. (1982a).

TABLE 3.22.   *Habitat Utilization by Selected Fish Species in the Unchannelized Middle Missouri River[a]*

	Habitat[b]						
	MC	MCB	P	SB	Ch	BU	M
Acipenseridae							
Scaphirhynchus platorynchus	X	—	P	—	—	—	—
Polydontidae							
Polydon spathula	—	—	P	—	—	P	—
Lepisosteidae							
Lepisosteus platostomus	—	—	X	—	—	P	X
Hiodontidae							
Hiodon alosoides	X	X	X	—	X	X	—
Clupeidae							
Dorosoma cepedianum	—	X	X	—	X	P	X
Catostomidae							
Carpiodes carpio	—	X	X	X	X	X	X
Cycleptus elongatus	X	P	—	—	P	—	—
Ictiobus bubalus	X	X	P	—	X	P	X
I. cyprinellus	—	X	P	—	X	P	X
Moxostoma macrolepidotum	X	X	X	X	X	X	X
Cyprinidae							
Cyprinus carpio	—	X	X	—	X	P	P
Notropis atherinoides	—	X	—	X	X	X	X
N. lutrensis	—	—	—	—	—	P	X
N. stramineus	—	—	—	X	—	X	—
Ictaluridae							
Ictalurus punctatus	X	X	X	—	X	X	—
Centrarchidae							
Lepomis cyanellus	—	—	—	—	—	P	P
L. humilis	—	—	—	—	—	P	X
L. macrochirus	—	—	—	—	—	P	P
Pomoxis annularis	—	—	—	—	—	P	—
P. nigromaculatus	—	—	—	—	—	P	—
Percidae							
Perca flavescens	—	—	X	X	—	P	P
Stizostedion canadense	X	X	X	X	X	X	—
Percithyidae							
Morone chrysops	—	X	X	X	X	X	—
Sciaenidae							
Aplodinotus grunniens	X	X	X	X	X	X	—

Source: After Kallemeyn and Novotny (1977).

[a]X, found; —, not found; P, preferred habitat.

[b]MC, main channel; MCB, main-channel border; P, pool; SB, sandbar; Ch, chute; BU, backup; M, marsh.

high relative CPUEs for silver chub (*Hybopsis storeriana*), *Hybognathus* spp. (primarily *H. nuchalis*), and river shiner (*Notropis blennius*) (Hesse et al., 1982a). In another survey of the channelized river near Sioux City, *Hiodon alosoides, Carpiodes carpio, Ictiobus bubalus, Cyprinus carpio, Moxostoma macrolepidotum*, and *Ictalurus punctatus* accounted for 90% of the fish collected by electrofishing over a 10-year period (Trondreau et al., 1983, as cited in Hesse et al., 1989c).

Habitat preferences for many Missouri River fishes were examined by both Kallemeyn and Novotny (1977) and Schmulbach et al. (1975) (Tables 3.22 and 3.23). Although there are some disagreements between the two studies (e.g., with *Ictiobus* spp. and *Aplodinotus grunniens*), they concur on the importance of backup, chute, pool, and sandbar habitats for many species. In fact, the largest catches of fish by Kallemeyn and Novotny (1977) at their channelized station came from notched revetments, notched spur dikes, and notched wing dikes. This includes over 90% of *Dorosoma cepedianum, Notropis lutrensis,* Centrarchidae, and *Perca flavescens,* and over 80% of *Ictiobus bubalus* and *I. cyprinellus*. These notched channelization structures represent efforts at mitigating the loss of backwater habitat, but they still comprise only a tiny fraction of the total habitat area.

The channelized and degraded reaches of the Middle Missouri River exhibit a taxonomic richness comparable to that recorded in the unchannelized river during the 1970s, but the fauna is dominated by only a few species (Hesse et al., 1989c). Of these, *Dorosoma cepedianum, Carpiodes carpio, Ictiobus* spp., *Cyprinus carpio,* and *Aplodinotus grunniens* are found in a wide range of habitats but are usually most abundant in quiet and relatively deep waters. This preference is reflected in the greater concentration of these species in the protected areas downstream from wing dikes. Three other abundant species, *Hiodon alosoides, Moxostoma macrolepidotum,* and *Ictalurus punctatus,* are abundant in swift, deep water, which is plentiful in the channelized river (Cross, 1967; Hesse et al., 1982a; Kallemeyn and Novotny, 1977; Pflieger, 1975; Schmulbach et al., 1975).

Changes in total abundance and the abundance of particular species have been attributed to the loss of backwater habitats, main-channel degradation, reduction in turbidity, and overfishing. Another factor, flow regulation, is also probably seriously affecting the fish fauna (Cross and Moss, 1987; Hesse et al., 1989a). Under the natural hydrological regime, flow maxima usually occurred in March and June. These floods would have imported considerable amounts of organic matter into the river and expanded the amount of shallow and backwater habitat available to spring spawners. Presently, flow regulation policies usually result in a dewatering of backwaters during spring (Modde and Schmulbach, 1973) and prevent the inundation of floodplains. Many of the species characteristic of the precontrol fauna, including *Scaphirhynchus platorynchus, Polydon spathula, Hiodon alosoides, Cycleptus elongatus, Ictiobus* spp., *Moxostoma macrolepidotum,* sturgeon chub (*Hybopsis meeki*), *H. storeriana, Stizostedion canadense,* and *Aplodinotus grunniens,* spawn primar-

TABLE 3.23. *Abundant and Common Fishes Among Habitats[a] from Unchannelized (Below Gavins Point Dam, South Dakota) Stations and Channelized (from Sioux City, Iowa, to Rulo, Nebraska) Stations in the Middle Missouri River*

	Unchannelized					Channelized			
	MC	SB	Ch	Bk	TC	MC	WD	FD	TC
Acipenseridae									
Scaphirhynchus platorynchus	X	X							
Polydontidae									
Polydon spathula	X								
Lepisosteidae									
Lepisosteus platostomus		X	X		X		X		X
Hiodontidae									
Hiodon alosoides	X	X			X	X	X	X	X
Clupeidae									
Dorosoma cepedianum	X		X	X	X	X	X	X	X
Catostomidae									
Carpiodes carpio	X	X	X	X	X	X	X	X	X
Cycleptus elongatus		X							
Ictiobus bubalus			X	X			X	X	
I. cyprinellus							X		
Moxostoma macrolepidotum		X							
Cyprinidae									
Cyprinus carpio	X	X	X	X	X	X	X	X	X
Hybognathus placitus							X		X
Notropis atherinoides			X	X	X				
N. lutrensis			X	X	X				
N. stramineus			X	X	X				
Ictaluridae									
Ictalurus punctatus	X	X			X	X	X		X
Pylodictis olivaris							X	X	
Percidae									
Etheostoma nigrum			X	X					
Stizostedium canadense	X	X		X	X		X		X
Sciaenidae									
Aplodinotus grunniens								X	

Source: After Schmulbach et al. (1975).

[a]MC, main channel; SM, sandbar; Ch, chute; Bk, backup; TC, tributary confluence; WD, wing dike; FD, finger dike.

ily or exclusively in the spring (Cross, 1967; Pflieger, 1975). Low spring flows are believed to be particularly harmful to *P. spathula*, which normally spawns in shallow beds of gravel (Pfleiger, 1975). It may be significant that three currently abundant spring spawners, *H. alosoides, M. macrolepidotum,* and *A. grunniens,* often spawn in tributaries; *A. grunniens* will also spawn pelagically in main-stem rivers. Several other abundant species spawn either later in the year or have extended spawning seasons. *Carpiodes carpio, Hybognathus* spp., *Notropis atherinoides, N. blennius,* and *N. lutrensis* have protracted breeding seasons, which extend from late spring through summer. *Cyprinus carpio* is an intermittent spawner that often spawns in response to rising water levels (Cross, 1967; Pflieger, 1975).

Angling CPUEs (Schmulbach et al., 1975) and hoop-net CPUEs (Hesse et al., 1982a) indicated that *Ictalurus punctatus* was actually more abundant in the channelized river than in the unchannelized river. Its preference for swift currents and clean substrates has probably contributed to its abundance in the Missouri River. Another factor in its success may be the extensive use of tributaries by riverine populations. More than half (59%) of the riverine *I. punctatus* (fish initially caught in the river) in the Lower Missouri were found to move into or out Perche Creek (river km 273). In contrast, only 21% of the tributary population moved into the river. Smaller *I. punctatus* tended to remain in the river, while those entering the tributary were of the size to spawn and to feed on the abundant tributary populations of *Dorosoma cepedianum.* On the other hand, riverine *Pylodictis olivaris,* which appears to be considerably less numerous than *I. punctatus,* was less likely to use tributary habitats (Dames et al., 1989).

COMMUNITIES OF AQUATIC LIFE

Functional Relationships

Allochthonous inputs of dissolved and fine-particulate organic matter originating from floodplain and tributary sources probably contributed most of the trophic support for the precontrol Missouri River. Terrestrial insects and freshwater marshes could have supplied additional significant inputs, but high sediment concentrations probably limited autochonous primary production via high light extinction, sedimentation, and abrasion. Seasonal pulses of floodplain and wetland organic matter may have accompanied the March and June floods. There are indications (e.g., spring spawning by some fishes) that the life cycles of some species are adapted to these pulses.

The modified Missouri River is also heavily dependent on allochthonous inputs, although the inputs are somewhat different. Channelization and channel degradation have isolated the river from the floodplains and reduced the freshwater marshes. In addition, most of the floodplain forests have been converted to agriculture. Instead of originating from floodplains and wetlands, much of the allochthonous input originates via surface runoff from agricultural lands in both the floodplains and tributary watersheds. Flow regulation has probably resulted in a less pulsed seasonality to these inputs, but the increased importance of local precipitation events may also make them less predictable. Little is known as to how these changes have altered the quantity and quality of allochthonous inputs.

In addition to changes in the sources and timing of allochthonous inputs, modification of the Missouri has probably increased the relative contribution of autochthonous inputs. Sediment trapping and flow regulation by the main-stem impoundments and the proliferation of channelization structures have probably increased periphytic production. In addition, substantial populations of phytoplankton and zooplankton are discharged from these reservoirs, although the magnitude of these exports diminish with distance.

Collector-gatherers (gatherers or deposit feeders) were a dominant component of the macroinvertebrate assemblages collected in benthic samples from both the unchannelized and channelized river (Carter et al., 1982; McMahon et al., 1972; Morris et al., 1968; Schmulbach, 1974; Volesky, 1969), and it is likely that this group dominated the macroinvertebrate fauna of the pre-control river. These organisms probably fed primarily on fine detritus but may also have eaten epipeltic algae and microbial ooze.

Most gatherers collected in the unchannelized sites are tolerant of turbidity, and as such one would expect them to have also been abundant in the precontrol river. Gatherers exhibited patterns of distribution and abundance among unchannelized habitats that were consistent with the expected benthic distribution of fine detritus. In addition to being unstable, the sandy substrates of the main channel and open chutes probably contained reduced quantities of benthic detritus. These habitats contained low numbers of only a few taxons, the most important of which was a genus near *Demicryptochironomus*. Sandbars and sandy banks contain a greater number and variety of deposit feeders than do main-channel and open chute habitats, but the abundance and diversity of deposit feeders are greatest in backup and marsh habitats, where silt, mud, and fine detritus accumulate. These habitats are characterized by a diverse assemblage of deposit-feeding Chironomidae, which included *Chironomus, Cryptotendipes, Dicrotendipes, Harnischia,* and a genus near *Demicryptochironomus;* worms (Oligochaeta); and mayflies *Hexagenia limbata;* and *Caenis* sp. were also abundant deposit feeders in backup and marsh habitats (McMahon et al., 1972; Volesky, 1969).

In addition to feeding on fine detritus, *Cricotopus* (Chironomidae), *Asellus* (Isopoda), and *Hyalella* (Amphipoda) may also feed on periphytic algae, filamentous algae, living macrophytes, and/or larger fragments of detritus. Another chironomid, *Polypedilum,* is known to feed on a variety of detrital, algal, macrophyte, and invertebrate material. All of these taxa were abundant in the marsh and backup habitats, but the two chironomids were also common in main channel, open chute, sandbar, and bank habitats. Herbivorous *Sigara* (Corixidae) were abundant in the *Typha* marshes (Volesky, 1969).

Several of the abundant benthic gatherers were also abundant in aufwuchs samples (wood stakes and multiplate samplers). With the exceptions of two taxons, *Cricotopus* and *Polypedilum,* they were more abundant on backwater samplers than they were on samplers in the main channel. Snags provided the primary aufwuchs habitat in the precontrol river, while dikes and revetments provided aufwuchs habitat in the channelized river. In addition to being offered a stable substrate, snag-dwelling gatherers could have fed on decaying wood, periphytic algae, and accumulations of fine detritus. Aufwuchs collections also yielded high densities for some gatherers that were not common in benthic samples. For example, *Glyptotendipes* (Chironomidae) was abundant on backwater samplers, while *Ameletus* (Ephemeroptera) and *Orthocladius* (Chironomidae) were common on fast-water sites (Gould, 1975; Nord and Schmulbach, 1973).

Aufwuchs samples also yielded several abundant gatherer-scrapers, including *Baetis, Heptagenia, Stenonema* (Ephemeroptera), and *Hydroptila* sp. (Trichoptera) (Carter et al., 1982; Gould, 1975; Nord and Schmulbach, 1973). Taxons belonging to this group can scrape periphytic algae and microbial films as well as gather accumulations of fine detritus. Another taxon, *Agraylea* (Trichoptera), which is a piercing herbivore as well as a gatherer, was also abundant on aufwuchs samplers (Gould, 1975). Characteristically, fast-water aufwuch samplers yielded high densities of these herbivore-detritivores, while backwater aufwuchs and benthic samplers did not. Most of these gatherer-scrapers require the stable substrates provided by snags and channelization structures, but their preferences for fast-water sites may occur in response to the detrimental effects of sedimentation on filamentous and periphytic algae. Faster currents would minimize sedimentation, even in high-turbidity regimes.

Unlike benthic habitats, which are dominated by fine-particulate detritivores, the aufwuchs of the modified Missouri River is dominated largely by filter feeders. The dominance of filter feeders was affected by both current speeds and sampling methods. The relative abundance of filter feeders varied with sampling methods and current. For example, filter feeders in the unchannelized river accounted for 97% and 87% of the aufwuchs macroinvertebrate biomass on multiplate samplers from fast-water and backwater sites, respectively (Nord and Schmulbach, 1973). On the other hand, they accounted for 63% of the biomass on wooden stakes from fast-water sites, but with the exception of some possible filter-feeding chironomids, they accounted for less than 1% of the wood stakes biomass from backwater sites (Gould, 1975). Fast-water aufwuchs samples in the unchannelized river were overwhelmingly dominated by *Hydropsyche* spp., but filter-feeding *Neureclipsis* (Trichoptera), Simuliidae (Diptera), and *Tanytarsus* sp. (Chironomidae) were also common to abundant. *Hydropsyche* were considerably less common in backwater aufwuchs samples, but *Neureclipsis* and Tanytarsini were abundant (Gould, 1975; Modde and Schmulbach, 1973). *Hydropsyche* spp., *Isonychia* (Ephemeroptera), Tanytarsini, and Simuliidae were abundant in fast-water aufwuchs samples from channelized and bank-stabilized stations. Aufwuchs samples in slower-water sites of the channelized river were dominated by *Hydropsyche* spp., *Potamyia flava, Neureclipsis,* and Tanytarsini (Carter et al., 1982; Modde and Schmulbach, 1973). Filter feeders are also found in benthic habitats, but not in the numbers encountered in the aufwuchs. Benthic filter feeders were probably concentrated in habitats that contained relatively stable substrates and were probably dominated by Unionidae (Bivalvia) and Tanytarsini.

Considering the abundance of organic material in the water column, it is not surprising that filter feeders are abundant in the modified river. However, their abundance in the precontrol river is uncertain. Low sediment loads and plentiful plankton make for very favorable conditions in the unchannelized river below Gavins Point Dam, but reduced plankton inputs and greater sediment loads may have made the precontrol river less favorable. Nonetheless, filter feeders are abundant in the plankton-poor and more turbid reaches of the channelized river. But at least two filter feeders, Hydropsychidae and *Isonychia,* were strongly limited by sedimentation; both taxons were abundant on multiplate samplers near the surface but uncommon in rock basket samplers subject to severe sedimentation (Carter et al., 1982).

Missouri River filter feeders will trap a variety of food from the water column, including detritus, phytoplankton, zooplankton, and drifting macro-invertebrates. Microfilterers such as *Isonychia,* Tanytarsini, Simuliidae, and Unionidae are probably most dependent on fine detritus, bacteria, algae, and possibly some of the smaller zooplankters. Hydropsychidae filter larger particles than do the microfilterers and both *Hydropsyche* spp. and *Potamyia flava* probably feed on a variety of detrital, algal, and animal material. In a comparison of hydropsychids in the Upper Mississippi, Fremling (1960) reported that *Hydropsyche orris* preferred faster currents and had larger capture net mesh sizes than *P. flava.* Larger mesh sizes and preferences for faster currents have been associated with greater carnivory by other hydropsychids in other streams (e.g., Ross and Wallace, 1983), which suggests that Missouri River populations of *H. orris* are also highly carnivorous. Another filter feeder, *Neureclipsis,* which appeared to be more common in slower water, is primarily carnivorous.

A number of carnivorous macroinvertebrates were found in benthic and aufwuchs habitats. Carnivorous taxons such as Odonata, *Probezzia* (Ceratopogonidae: Diptera), and Tanypodinae (Chironomidae) were most abundant either in marshes, backups, or in backwater aufwuchs. *Limnophora* sp. was the only abundant carnivore collected in fast-water aufwuchs samples (Carter et al., 1982; Gould, 1975; McMahon et al., 1972; Nord and Schmulbach, 1973; Volesky, 1969).

Fish in the Missouri River feed on a wide range of materials, ranging from benthic algae to other fish. While several species are omnivorous, macro-invertebrates and zooplankton appear to be the primary food items for most species. Changes in the river have probably affected the status of several species and the diets of others. Increases in water transparency and plankton would enhance feeding by sight feeders and planktivores. Reductions in main-channel and backwater macroinvertebrates would impair feeding by bottom feeders.

Benthic accumulations of fine detritus and diatoms are probably the primary food items for *Hybognathus nuchalis* and *H. placitus.* These accumulations may also be important for three abundant omnivores, *Carpiodes carpio, Cyprinus carpio,* and *Ictalurus punctatus.* Filamentous algae or other plant material may also be a common food item for *Dorosoma cepedianum,* *Cyprinus carpio,* and *I. punctatus* (Cross, 1967; Pflieger, 1975). Plant material accounted for 80.5% of the stomach contents of *Cyprinus carpio* and 12.6% of the stomach contents of *I. punctatus* in ambient-temperature collections in the channelized river near Fort Calhoun Station (Hesse et al., 1982a). Berner (1951) reported that plant seeds and plant fragments accounted for most of the gut volume for *Cyprinus carpio* and *Ictiobus bubalus* in the Lower Missouri River. Both Cross (1967) and Smith (1979) report that *I. bubalus* feeds primarily on benthic invertebrates, which suggests that its intake of plant material was incidental. However, young-of-the-year *I. bubalus* in Lewis and Clark Lake fed primarily on zooplankton and attached algae (McComish, 1967).

Benthic macroinvertebrates were probably a major prey item for many native Missouri River fishes (e.g., sturgeons, buffalos, chubs, and catfish), but the role of benthic macroinvertebrates in the trophic structure of the Missouri River may have been subsantially altered by channelization and impoundment. The loss of backwater habitats and degradation of the main channel have reduced the extent and productivity of benthic habitats. A decline in fish abundance and a shift away from benthic feeding are two possible responses to these changes. A decline in overall fish abundance has apparently occurred, but it is unclear how much of this decline is attributable to a reduction in benthic prey.

A dietary shift away from the less extensive or less productive benthos may have occurred with *Scaphirhynchus platorhynchus,* which is morphologically adapted to benthic feeding. In a study of its diet in the unchannelized river below Gavins Point Dam, it was discovered that its maximum food intake (i.e., gut volume) and condition occurred during late autumn, while reduced intake and deteriorating condition occurred during most of the normal growing season (May to September). Significantly, this seasonal pattern of food intake and condition did not correspond to the seasonal abundance of macroinvertebrates. Instead, the late autumn maximum was the result of selective feeding on drifting Hydropsychidae, which were concentrated in main-channel pools by the late autumn reduction in flow. On the other hand, the increased flow and current speeds that occur from late spring through summer prevented *S. platorhynchus* from feeding successfully on the drift. Instead, it fed, less efficiently, on widely dispersed benthic chironomids (Modde and Schmulbach, 1977).

Diet shifts away from benthic sources may also occur in a number of other species. *Ictiobus bubalus* is reported by a number of authors (Cross, 1967; Miller and Robinson, 1971; Smith, 1979) to feed primarily on benthic invertebrates, but in Lewis and Clark Lake, young-of-the-year fed primarily on zooplankton and attached algae; benthic invertebrates were eaten only rarely (McComish, 1967). Several other abundant bottom feeders, including *Carpiodes carpio, Cyprinus carpio, Notropis lutrensis,* and *Ictalurus punctatus,* are omnivorous. Benthic invertebrates may be less important to the diets of two other bottom feeders. *Ictiobus cyprinellus* is also known to feed on zooplankton (Cross, 1967; McComish, 1967; Pflieger, 1975), while gut analysis of *Aplodinotus grunniens* in the channelized Middle Missouri indicates that it is heavily dependent on macroinvertebrate drift (Hesse et al., 1982c).

In contrast to the possibly declining importance of benthic macroinvertebrates, aufwuch macroinvertebrates are central to the trophic structure of the modified Missouri River. In fact, the use of limestone revetments and dikes has partially offset the loss of benthic productivity by providing macroinvertebrate attachment sites (Hesse et al., 1982b). A number of studies (Carter et al., 1982; Kallemeyn and Novotny, 1977; Modde and Schmulbach, 1973; Morris et al., 1968; Namminga, 1969; Nord and Schmulbach, 1973; Novotny, 1978) have demonstrated that most of the macroinvertebrate drift in the channelized and unchannelized Missouri River originated from the aufwuchs. Consequently, these macroinvertebrates are available to fish both in the aufwuchs and in the drift.

Sampling of macroinvertebrate drift during 1963 and 1976 indicated that estimates of drift biomass and density from channelized reaches were approximately double those from corresponding unchannelized reaches. In addition, drift in both the channelized and unchannelized river tended to be more abundant in the main-channel habitat than in chutes, backups, and the main-channel border (Kallemeyn and Novotny, 1977; Morris et al., 1968). However, drift biomass near a pile dike was nearly double that at a nearby main-channel site (Morris et al., 1968). Drift densities also vary with the time of day and within the water column. In a study of diurnal patterns in drift densities, Novotny (1978) reported that nearshore drift samples exhibited significant nighttime maxima, while those collected in the main channel exhibited no diel differences even though the two sets of samples were similar in taxonomic composition. One possibility for the absence of diel periodicity in the main channel is that these drifters have been entrained for extended periods and in essence become lost to the currents. With time these entrained drifters may accumulate in the reduced current zone near the bottom, as was observed by Berner (1951) in the channelized Lower Missouri.

A number of fishes depend heavily on aufwuch macroinvertebrates. Populations of *Hiodon alosoides, Ictalurus punctatus, Pylodictis olivaris, Pomoxis nigromaculatus,* and *Aplodinotus grunniens* collected in the channelized river were found to be strongly dependent on aufwuchs macroinvertebrates either by feeding directly on them or by feeding on them after they enter the drift. Drifting macroinvertebrates were especially important prey items for *H. alosoides* and *A. grunniens* (Hesse et al., 1982c). Macroinvertebrate drift may also be important prey items for *Dorosoma cepedianum, Ictiobus* spp., *Hybopsis* spp., *Notropis* spp., and *Lepomis* spp. Speckled chub (*Hybopsis aestivalis*), sturgeon chub (*H. gelida*), and sicklefin chub (*H. meeki*) inhabit open channels with swift currents and firm substrates (Pflieger and Grace, 1987), and it is possible that they depend on drift that concentrates near the bottom.

Terrestrial insects are another potentially important prey item for Missouri River fishes. Terrestrial drift was found in a variety of Missouri River habitats but was most abundant in chutes and backwaters (Kallemeyn and Novotny, 1977). Several fishes were present, including *Hiodon alosoides,* flathead chub (*Hybopsis gracilis*), *Notropis atherinoides, N. blennius, N. lutrensis,* and *Lepomis spp. (Cross, 1967; Pflieger, 1975; Smith, 1979). H. gracilis* was the principal surface-feeding minnow in the turbid precontrol river, but it may have been in direct competition with surface-feeding *Notropis* spp. following the reductions in turbidity that resulted from mainstem impoundment (Pflieger and Grace, 1987).

The importance of zooplankton and phytoplankton to Missouri River fishes is suggested from diet studies conducted in Lewis and Clark Lake. *Notropis atherinoides* fed heavily on both phytoplankton and zooplankton (Fuchs, 1967). Lewis and Clark Lake zooplankton were important food items for immature *Ictiobus bubalus, I. cyprinellus* (McComish, 1967), and *Stizostedion canadense* (Nelson, 1968), and both immature and adult *Aplodinotus grunniens* (Sweedburg, 1968). Zooplankton was an important food item in the diet of *Pomoxis annularis* and *P. nigromaculatus* sampled from the channelized Missouri (Hesse et al., 1982a). Mature and immature *Polydon spathula, Dorosoma cepedianum, I. cyprinellus, N. atherinoides,* as well as immature *Lepomis* spp., *Pomoxis* spp., and *Morone chrysops,* have been reported to be planktivores in a number of other streams and lakes (Cross, 1967; Pflieger, 1975).

Low zooplankton and phytoplankton densities suggest that planktivory is insignificant in most of the channelized river. On the other hand, plankton may have been particularly important to fish populations in the unchannelized reaches below Fort Randall and Gavins Point Dams. These reaches were important sources of larval fishes, many of which are planktivorous (Hesse et al., 1982c). In addition, several planktivores, including *Polydon spathula, Dorosoma cepedianum,* and *Notropis atherionides,* were abundant in the tailwaters of Gavins Point Dam (Groen and Schmulbach, 1978; Kallemeyn and Novotny, 1977; Schmulbach et al., 1975). However, the importance of planktivory in the unchannelized river may have been greatly diminished following the loss of backwater habitats via channel degradation.

Minnows and *Dorosoma cepedianum* are important prey items for *Lepisosteus osseus, Ictalurus punctatus, Pylodictis olivaris, Pomoxis annularis, Morone chrysops, Stizostedion canadense,* and *Aplodinotus grunniens* (Cross, 1967; Hesse et al., 1982a; Pflieger, 1975). In particular, an ontogenic shift from feeding on macroinvertebrates to feeding on fish may influence the movement of *I. punctatus* from the channelized river into tributaries; *D. cepedianum* were considerably more abundant in the tributaries (Dames et al., 1989). Finally, crayfish, which were not collected in any of the benthic and aufwuchs studies contributed significantly to the diets of several Missouri River fishes, including *I. punctatus, P. olivaris,* and *A. grunniens* (Berner, 1951; Hesse et al., 1982a).

Structure of Aquatic Communities

The structuring of the aquatic communities in the main stem of the Missouri River is difficult. The reason is that the river has been dammed and channelized in so many areas so that a truly natural ecosystem is difficult to structure. However, a number of habitats and unchanneled portions of the river do support communities of aquatic life. For example, there are marshes and pools in backwaters or in areas where the flow is almost cut off from the main stem. There are also snag bars that contain a great deal of debris, in some cases plants, and fine sand and silt. Backwaters are occasionally present and are associated with the channelized portion. Therefore, the structure of the communities in the main stem of the Missouri is postulated from the species that have been found and the habitats in which they would probably live.

The unchannelized portions that were studied were below Gavins Point Dam, in association with the Fort Randall Dam and the Calhoun Power Plant. Fairly rich plankton and fish populations are found in some portions of the channelized Missouri River. These are, no doubt, largely seeded by the backwaters, the marshes, the pools, and areas where these species can breed. In the Missouri River one recognizes in general certain types of habitats. They are habitats associated with vegetation where the flow of the water is usually moderate or slow; lentic habitats, which are pools or backwaters where the substrate is largely mud or sand; and faster-water habitats, often in chutes and below dams, where the substrate is largely sand and gravel or wood or rocks.

Vegetative Habitats. The vegetation that forms the main substrates for this community were unidentified species of *Carex, Phragmites communis,* and *Typha angustifolia,* and *T. latifolia.* All of these are emergent plants, and their leaves and roots together with plant debris would constitute the main characteristics of the habitat. Here one would find such protozoans as the unidentified species of the genus *Mallomonas,* which is a primary producer, and *Dinobryon* sp., also a primary producer. In and among the debris of the vegetation were found unidentified species of *Amoeba,* which are omnivores, and unidentified species of *Chilodonella,* also an omnivore. Also present were two species of *Colpoda,* which are omnivores; *Strobilidium* sp., an omnivore; and *Epistylis* sp., an omnivore. These omnivorous protozoans feed on bacteria, small algae, and small flagellates. Also present in this habitat was an unidentified species of *Vaginicola* and one of *Vorticella.* Both of these are believed to be omnivores. Attached to the vegetation and sometimes to the debris were unidentified specimens of a *Hydra* species, *Hydra* sp., probably an omnivore.

Rotifers were fairly common in this habitat. They are listed in Table 3.24, and all of them are omnivores. Thirteen omnivorous taxons were found associated with the vegetation. Various Crustacea were also present in and among the vegetation. They were three species of *Daphnia,* two species of *Monia,* one species of *Scapholeberis,* and a single species of *Leptodora, L. kindti.* Other Crustacea found in and among the vegetation were *Diaphanosoma*

(text continues on page 345)

TABLE 3.24. *Species List: Missouri River*

Taxon	V	Lentic M,S	Lotic G,R	Site[b]	Source[c]
SUPERKINGDOM PROKARYOTAE					
KINGDOM MONERA					
Division Cyanophycota					
Class Cyanophyceae					
Order Chroococcales					
Family Chroococcaceae					
Merismopedia tenuissima			X	Mc	p
Order Nostocales					
Family Oscillatoriaceae					
Lyngbya sp.			X	Mc	a
Oscillatoria sp.		X		Mc	a
Schizothrix calcicola		X		Mc	a
Family Scytonemataceae					
Plectonema notatum			X	Mc	a
SUPERKINGDOM EUKARYOTAE					
KINGDOM PLANTAE					
Subkingdom Thallobionta					
Division Chlorophycota					
Class Chlorophyceae					
Order Chlorococcales					
Family Characiaceae					
Characium sp.		X		Mc	a
Family Oocystaceae					
Ankistrodesmus hantzschii		X		Mc	p
A. spiralis		X		Mc	p
Dictyosphaerium pulchellum		X		Mc	p
Family Scenedesmaceae					
Scenedesmus spp.				Mc	p
Order Chaetophorales					
Family Chaetophoraceae					
Chaetophora sp.		X	X	Mc	a
Stigeoclonium tenue		X	X	Mc	a
Stigeoclonium sp.		X		Mc	a
Order Oedogoniales					
Family Oedogoniaceae					
Oedogonium sp.	X	X	X	Mc	a
Order Siphonocladales					
Family Cladophoraceae					
Cladophora glomerata	X	X	X	Mc	a
Cladophora sp.		X		Mc	a
Order Zygnematales					
Family Zygnemataceae					
Spirogyra sp.	X	X		Mc	a

Continued

TABLE 3.24.   (Continued)

Taxon	V	Lentic M,S	Lotic G,R	Site[b]	Source[c]
Division Chromophycota					
Class Bacillariophyceae					
Order Eupodiscales					
Family Coscinodiscaceae					
*Cyclotella meneghiniana	X		X	Mc	a
*Cyclotella spp.	X		X	M,Mc,Mu	d,a,p,h
*Melosira granulata	X		X	Mc	a,p
*M. varians	X		X	Mc	a
Melosira sp.		X		M,Mu	d,h
*Stephanodiscus astraea		X		Mc	p
*S. hantzschii		X		Mc	p
*S. invisitatus		X		Mc	p
*S. minutus		X		Mc	p
*Stephanodiscus sp.		X		M,Mc,Mu	d,a,h
Order Biddulphiales					
Family Biddulphiaceae					
*Biddulphia laevis		X		Mc	a
Order Fragilariales					
Family Fragilariaceae					
Asterionella formosa	X		X	Mc	a,p
Asterionella sp.	X		X	M	h
*Diatoma vulgare	X	X		Mc	a
*Diatoma sp.	X	X		M,Mu	d,h
Fragilaria brevistriata	X			Mc	a
F. capucina		X		Mc	a
*F. construens		X		Mc	a
*F. pinnata		X		Mc	a
Fragilaria spp.		X		M,Mc,Mu	d,p,h
Meridion sp.	X	X		M	h
*Ophephora sp.	X	X		M	h
Synedra sp.		X		M,Mc,Mu	d,a,h
Order Eunotiales					
Family Eunotiaceae					
*Eunotia sp.		X		M	h
Order Achnanthales					
Family Achnanthaceae					
*Achnanthes lanceolata	X		X	Mc	a
*Achnanthes sp.	X		X	M	h
*Cocconeis diminuta	X		X	Mc	a
*C. pediculus	X		X	Mc	a
*C. placentula	X		X	Mc	a
*C. placentula var.					
euglypta	X		X	Mc	a
Cocconeis sp.	X		X	M,Mu	d,h
*Rhoicosphenia curvata		X		Mc	a
*Rhoicosphenia sp.		X		M,Mu	d,h

TABLE 3.24. *(Continued)*

Taxon	V	Lentic M,S	Lotic G,R	Site[b]	Source[c]
Order Naviculales					
Family Cymbellaceae					
Amphora sp.	X			Mu	d
Cymbella sp.	X			M,Mu	d,h
Family Gomphonemaceae					
*Gomphonema angustatum	X		X	Mc	a
*G. bohemicum	X		X	Mc	a
*G. intricatum	X		X	Mc	a
*G. olivaceum	X	X		Mc	a
*G. parvulum	X	X		Mc	a
Gomphonema sp.				M,Mc,Mu	d,a,h
Family Naviculaceae					
Amphipleura sp.		X		M	h
Amphiprora sp.		X		M	h
Anomoeoneis sp.		X		M	h
Caloneis sp.			X	M,Mu	d,h
Diploneis sp.		X	X	M	h
Frustulia sp.		X		M	h
Gyrosigma sp.		X	X	M	h
Mastogloia sp.		X	X	M,Mu	h,d
*Navicula cryptocephala		X	X	Mc	a
*N. graciloides			X	Mc	a
*N. luzonensis	X	X		Mc	a
*N. radiosa	X	X		Mc	a
*N. tripunctata	X	X		Mc	a
*N. tripunctata var. schizonemoides	X	X		Mc	a
*N. viridula		X		Mc	a
*N. vitabunda		X		Mc	a
Navicula sp.				M,Mc,Mu	d,a,h
Neidium sp.				M,Mu	d,h
Pinnularia sp.				M,Mu	d,h
Pleurosigma sp.		X		M,Mc	a
Stauroneis sp.		X		M	h
Order Epithemiales					
Family Epithemiaceae					
Denticula sp.		X	X	M	h
Epithemia sp.		X	X	M	h
Rhopalodia sp.		X	X	M,Mu	d,h
Order Bacillariales					
Family Nitzschiaceae					
Hantzschia sp.			X	M	h
*Nitzschia acicularis		X		Mc	a
*N. dissipata	X	X		Mc	a
*N. filiformis		X		Mc	a

Continued

TABLE 3.24. *(Continued)*

Taxon	V	Lentic M,S	Lotic G,R	Site[b]	Source[c]
Family Nitzschiaceae *(cont.)*					
N. frustulum var. *perpusilla*		X		Mc	a
N. palea		X		Mc	a
N. tryblionella		X		Mc	a
Nitzschia spp.		X		M,Mc,Mu	d,a,p,h
Order Surirellales					
Family Surirellaceae					
Surirella sp.		X		M	h
Class Dinophyceae					
Order Gymnodiniales					
Family Gymnodiniaceae					
Amphidinium sp.		X		M	h
Gymnidinium sp.		X		M	h
Order Peridinales					
Family Peridiniaceae					
Ceratium sp.			X	M	h
Peridinium sp.			X	M	h
Subkingdom Embryobionta					
Division Magnoliophyta					
Class Monocotyledoneae					
Order Cyperales					
Family Cyperaceae					
Carex sp.	X			Mu	v
Family Poaceae					
Phragmites communis	X	X		Mu	v
Order Typhales					
Family Typhaceae					
Typha angustifolia	X			Mu	v
T. latifolia	X			Mu	v
KINGDOM ANIMALIA					
Subkingdom Protozoa					
Class Mastigophora					
Order Chrysomonadida					
Family Chromulinidae					
Mallomonas sp.	X	X		M	h
Family Ochromonadidae					
Dinobryon sp.	X	X		M	h
Order Cryptomonadida					
Family Cryptomonadidae					
Chilomonas sp.	X			M	h
Cryptomonas sp.	X			M	h
Rhodomonas sp.	X			M	h
Order Euglenoidida					
Family Euglenidae					
Lepocinclis sp.		X		M	h
Euglena sp.		X		M	h
Trachelomonas sp.		X		M	h

TABLE 3.24. *(Continued)*

Taxon	V	Substrate[a] Lentic M,S	Lotic G,R	Site[b]	Source[c]
Class Sarcodina					
Order Amoebida					
Family Amoebidae					
*Amoeba sp.	X	X		M	h
Order Heliozoida					
Family Actinophryidae					
Actinosphaerium sp.	X	X		M	h
Class Ciliata					
Order Gymnostomatida					
Family Amphileptidae					
Amphileptus sp.	X			M	h
Chlamydodontidae					
*Chilodonella sp.	X			M	h
Family Didiniidae					
Didinium sp.	X			M	h
Family Holophryidae					
Enchelys sp.	X			M	h
Family Nassulidae					
Nassula sp.	X			M	h
Order Trichostomatida					
Family Coelosomididae					
Pseudoprorodon sp.	X			M	h
Family Colpodidae					
*Colpoda steini	X			M	h
*Colpoda sp.	X			M	h
Order Hymenostomatida					
Family Frontoniidae					
Frontonia sp.		X		M	h
Family Parameciidae					
*Paramecium aurelia		X		M	h
Order Heterotrichida					
Family Spirostomatidae					
*Spirostomum sp.		X		M	m
Order Oligotrichida					
Family Halteriidae					
*Strombidium sp.		X		M	h
Family Strobilidiidae					
*Strobilidium sp.	X	X		M	h
Order Tintinnida					
Family Tintinnidae					
Codonella sp.		X		M	h
Order Hypotrichida					
Family Oxytrichidae					
*Oxytricha sp.		X		M	h

Continued

TABLE 3.24.   (Continued)

Taxon	V	Lentic M,S	Lotic G,R	Site[b]	Source[c]
Order Peritrichida					
Family Epistylidae					
Epistylis sp.	X	X		M	h
Family Vaginicollidae					
Vaginicola sp.	X			M	h
Family Vorticellidae					
Vorticella sp.	X			M	h
Subkingdom Eumetazoa					
Phylum Cnidaria					
Class Hydrozoa					
Order Hydroida					
Family Hydridae					
Hydra sp.	X			Mu	i,b,n
Phylum Platyhelminthes					
Class Turbellaria					
Order Tricladida					
Family Planariidae					
*unident. spp.		X		Mu	i
Phylum Rotifera					
Class Digonota					
Order Bdelloidea					
Family Philodonidae					
Rotaria spp.	X	X		Mc	z
Class Monogononta					
Order Ploima					
Family Asplanchnidae					
Asplanchna spp.	X	X		Mc	z
Family Brachionidae					
Brachionus spp.	X	X		Mc	z
Euchlanis spp.	X	X		Mc	z
Keratella spp.	X	X		Mc	z
Lecane spp.		X		Mc	z
Monostyla spp.		X		Mc	z
Notholca spp.	X	X		Mc	z
Platyais spp.	X	X		Mc	z
Trichotria spp.	X	X		Mc	z
Family Notommatidae					
Cephalodella spp.	X	X		Mc	z
Dicranophorus spp.	X	X		Mc	z
Encentrum spp.	X	X		Mc	z
Notommata spp.	X	X		Mc	z
Family Synchaetidae					
Polyartha spp.	X	X		Mc	z
Synchaeta spp.		X		Mc	z
Family Trichoceridae					
Trichotria spp.		X		Mc	z

TABLE 3.24. *(Continued)*

		Substrate[a]			
		Lentic	Lotic		
Taxon	V	M,S	G,R	Site[b]	Source[c]
Order Collotheceae					
Family Collothecidae					
Collotheca spp.	X			Mc	z
Cupelopagis spp.	X			Mc	z
Order Flosculariacea					
Family Conochilidae					
Conochiloides spp.	X			Mc	z
Conochilus spp.	X			Mc	z
Family Hexarthridae					
Hexarthra spp.	X			Mc	z
Family Testudinellidae					
Filinia spp.	X			Mc	z
Testudinella spp.	X			Mc	z
Phylum Nemata					
unident. spp.				Mu	e
Phylum Mollusca					
Class Gastropoda					
unident. spp.				Mu	m
Order Mesogastropoda					
Family Hydrobiidae					
unident. sp.	X	X			
Family Pleuroceridae					
unident. sp.	X	X			
Family Valvatidae					
unident. sp.					
Family Viviparidae					
unident. sp.	X				
Order Basommatophora					
Family Ancylidae					
unident. sp.	X	X			
Family Lymnaeidae					
unident. sp.	X		X		
Family Physidae					
unident. sp.	X	X	X		
Family Planorbidae					
unident. sp.	X	X	X		
Class Bivalvia					
unident. spp.				Mu	m
Order Unioniida					
Family Unionidae					
*Anodonta grandis corpulenta		X	X	Mu	u
*A. grandis grandis		X	X	Mc,Mu	u
*A. suborbiculata		X	X	Mu	u
*Lampsilis teres teres		X	X	Mu	u
*Lasmigona complanata		X	X	Mu	u

Continued

TABLE 3.24.   (*Continued*)

Taxon	V	Substrate[a] Lentic M,S	Lotic G,R	Site[b]	Source[c]
Family Unionidae (*cont.*)					
*Leptodea fragilis		X	X	Mc,Mu	u
*L. lepodon		X	X	Mu	u
*Potamilus atatus		X	X	Mu	u
*P. ohiensis		X	X	Mc,Mu	u
*Tritogonia verrucosa		X	X	Mu	u
*Truncilla donaciformis		X	X	Mu	u
*T. truncata		X	X	Mu	u
Order Veneroida					
Family Corbiculidae					
unident. sp.	X	X			
Family Sphaeriidae					
unident. sp.	X	X			
Plylum Annelida					
Class Hirudinoidea					
unident. spp.	X	X		Mu	v
Order Rhynchobdellida					
Family Glossiphoniidae					
unident. sp.	X	X			
Family Ozobranchidae					
unident. sp.					
Family Piscicolidae					
unident. sp.	X	X			
Order Arhynchobdellida					
Family Erpobdellidae					
unident. sp.		X			
Family Hirudinidae					
unident. sp.		X			
Class Oligochaeta					
unident. spp.	X	X		Mu	v,e,i,m
Order Lumbriculida					
Family Lumbriculidae					
unident. sp.	X	X			
Order Haplotaxida					
Family Enchytraeidae					
unident. sp.	X	X			
Family Glossoscolecidae					
unident. sp.	X	X			
Family Lumbricidae					
unident. sp.	X	X			
Family Megascolecidae					
unident. sp.	X	X			
Family Naididae					
unident. sp.	X				
Family Tubificidae					
unident. sp.	X	X			

TABLE 3.24. *(Continued)*

Taxon	V	Lentic M,S	Lotic G,R	Site[b]	Source[c]
Phylum Arthropoda					
Class Arachnida					
Order Acariformes					
unident. spp.		X		Mu	k,b
Class Crustacea					
Subclass Cephalocarida					
(Branchiopoda)					
Order Cladocera					
Family Bosminidae					
*Bosminia longirostris		X		Mc,Mu	c,z
Family Chydoridae					
*Acropterus harpae		X		Mc	z
*Alona spp.		X		Mc	z
*Camptocercus oklahomensis		X		Mc	z
*C. rectirostris		X		Mc	z
*Ceriodaphnia laucustris		X		Mc	z
*C. quadrangula		X		Mc	z
*C. reticulata		X		Mc	z
*C. rigaudi		X		Mc	z
*Ceriodapnia sp.		X		Mu	c
*Chydorus sphaericus		X		Mc	z
*Disparolona rostrata		X		Mc	z
Dunhevidia serata		X		Mc	z
Eurycercus lamellatus		X		Mc	z
Kurzia latissima		X		Mc	z
Leydigia acanthocercoides		X		Mc	z
L. leydigi		X		Mc	z
Pleuroxus denticulatus		X		Mc	z
P. hamulatus		X		Mc	z
P. procurvus		X		Mc	z
Family Daphinidae					
*Daphnia ambigua	X	X		Mc	z
*D. galeata	X			Mu	c
*D. galeata medotae	X	X		Mc	z
*D. parvula		X		Mc,Mu	c,z
*D. pulex		X		Mu	c
*D. pulicaria		X		Mc	z
*D. retrocurva		X		Mc,Mu	c,z
*Daphnia spp.		X		Mu	c
*Monia micrura	X	X		Mc	z
*M. wierzejskii	X	X		Mc	z
*Monia spp.		X		Mc,Mu	c,z
*Scapholeberis kingi	X	X		Mc	z
*Simocephalus exspinosus		X		Mc	z
S. serrulatus		X		Mc	z
*S. vetulus		X		Mc	z
unident. spp.				Mu	m

Continued

TABLE 3.24.   (Continued)

Taxon	V	Lentic M,S	Lotic G,R	Site[b]	Source[c]
Family Leptodoridae					
*Leptodora kindti	X	X		Mc,Mu	m
Family Macrothricidae					
*Ilyocryptus sordidus		X		Mc	z
I. spinifer		X		Mc	z
*Macrothrix laticornis		X		Mc	z
Family Sididae					
*Diaphanosoma brachyurum	X	X		Mc,Mu	c,z
*D. leuchtenbergianum	X	X		Mc	z
*Latona setifera		X		Mc	z
*Sida crystallina		X		Mc	z
*Sida sp.		X		Mu	c
Subclass Copepoda					
unident. spp.	X	X		Mu	m
Order Calanoida					
Family Diaptomidae					
*Diaptomus ashlandi	X	X		Mc,Mu	c,z
*D. clavipes	X	X		Mc,Mu	c,z
*D. forbesi	X			Mc,Mu	c,z
*D. oregonensis	X			Mc	z
*D. pallidus	X			Mc	z
*D. sicilis	X			Mc,Mu	c,z
*D. siciloides	X			Mc,Mu	c,z
Order Harpacticoida					
unident. spp.	X	X		Mc,Mu	c,z
Order Cyclopoida					
Family Cyclopodae					
*Cyclops bicuspidatus	X	X		Mu	c
*C. bicuspidatus thomasi	X	X		Mc	z
*C. crassicaudus brachycercus		X		Mc	z
*C. varicans rubellus		X		Mc	z
*C. vernalis	X			Mc,Mu	c,z
*Eucyclops agilis	X			Mc,Mu	c,z
*E. prionophorus	X			Mc	z
*E. speratus	X	X		Mc	z
*Macrocyclops albidus	X	X		Mc	z
*Mesocyclops edax		X		Mc,Mu	c,z
*Paracyclops fimbriatus	X	X		Mc	z
*P. fimbriatus poppei		X		Mc	z
*Tropocyclops prasinus		X		Mc	z
*T. prasinus mexicanus		X		Mc	z
*Tropocyclops sp.		X		Mu	c
Family Ergasilidae					
Ergasilus chautauguaensis	X	X		Mc	z
E. megaceros	X	X		Mc	z

TABLE 3.24.   (Continued)

Taxon	V	Lentic M,S	Lotic G,R	Site[b]	Source[c]
Subclass Malacostraca					
Order Isopoda					
*unident. spp.			X	Mu	n,m
Family Asellidae					
*Asellus sp.			X	Mu	k,e,v,b
Order Amphipoda					
unident. spp.	X	X		Mu	n
Family Gammaridae					
*Gammarus sp.	X		X	Mu	b
unident. spp.	X		X	Mu	e
Family Talitridae					
*Hyalella sp.	X		X	Mu	k
Class Insecta					
Order Collembola					
*unident. spp.			X	Mu	b,m
Order Odonata					
Suborder Zygoptera					
Family Coenagrionidae					
*Argia sp.	X	X		Mu	k
*Chromagrion sp.	X	X		Mu	i
*Enallagma sp.	X			Mu	b
*Ischnura sp.	X			Mu	k,i
unident. spp.				Mu	m
Suborder Anisoptera					
Family Gomphidae					
*Gomphus sp.	X	X		Mu	k,v,b,m
Family Libellulidae					
*Libellula sp.	X	X		Mu	v
*Perithemis sp.	X	X		Mu	v
Order Ephemeroptera					
Suborder Schistonota					
Family Ametropodidae					
*Ametropus sp.		X	X	Mu	b
Family Baetidae					
*Baetis spp.	X	X	X	Mu	k,j,b,i,n
*Callibaetis sp.	X			Mu	k
*Centroptilum sp.	X	X	X	Mu	w
Neocloeon (= Cloeon?) sp.			X	Mu	w
Family Ephemeridae					
*Ephemera sp.		X	X	Mu	e
*Hexagenia limbata		X	X	Mu	v
*Hexagenia sp.		X	X	Mu	k,j,e, b,w,m
Family Heptageniidae					
*Anepeorus sp.	X	X	X	Mu	j

Continued

TABLE 3.24.   (Continued)

Taxon	V	Lentic M,S	Lotic G,R	Site[b]	Source[c]
Family Heptageniidae (cont.)					
*Cinygma sp.	X	X	X	Mu	b
*Heptagenia sp.	X	X	X	Mu	k,j,e,b, i,w,n
*Iron (= Epeorus?) sp.	X	X	X	Mu	b
*Stenacron sp.	X	X	X	Mu	j
*Stenonema sp.	X	X	X	Mu	k,w,n,m
Family Leptophlebiidae					
*Leptophlebia sp.	X	X		Mu	k,j
Family Metretopodidae					
*Siphoplectron sp.	X	X	X	Mu	i
Family Oligoneuriidae					
*Homoeoneuris sp.	X	X		Mu	b,j
*Isonychia sp.			X	Mu	k,b,w,n,m
Family Palingeniidae					
*Pentagenia sp.		X		Mu	e,m
Family Polymitarcydae					
*Ephoron sp.		X	X	Mu	w,m
Family Potamanthidae					
*Potamanthus sp.	X	X		Mu	w
Family Siphlonuridae					
*Ameletus sp.	X	X	X	Mu	e,m
Suborder Pannota					
Family Baetiscidae					
*Baetisca sp.		X		Mu	k,j
Family Caenidae					
*Brachycerus sp.	X	X		Mu	m,w
*Caenis sp.	X	X	X	Mu	k,j,e,b, i,w,m,v
unident. spp.				Mu	n
Family Tricorythidae					
*Tricorythodes sp.		X		Mu	k,n,j,w
Order Plecoptera					
unident. spp.				Mu	e,n
Family Perlidae					
*Acroneuria sp.	X	X	X	Mu	n
Neophasganophora sp.			X	Mu	n
Family Perlodidae					
*Isoperla sp.	X	X	X	Mu	k
Order Hemiptera					
Family Corixidae					
*Sigara sp.	X	X		Mu	v,b
unident. spp.	X	X		Mu	k,e,b,m
Family Gerridae					
unident. spp.	X	X	X	Mu	b
Family Notonectidae					
*unident. spp.	X	X		Mu	b

TABLE 3.24.   (*Continued*)

Taxon	V	Lentic M,S	Lotic G,R	Site[b]	Source[c]
Family Saldidae					
*unident. spp.	X	X		Mu	b
Order Coleoptera					
Suborder Adephaga					
Family Dytiscidae					
Bidessus sp.	X	X	X	Mu	v
Rhantus sp.	X	X		Mu	v
Family Gyrinidae					
Dineutes sp.	X	X		Mu	v,i
Family Haliplidae					
unident. spp.	X	X		Mu	b
Suborder Polyphaga					
Family Elmidae					
*unident. spp.	X		X	Mu	b
Family Hydrophilidae					
Berosus sp.	X	X		Mu	v
unident. spp.	X	X	X	Mu	b
Order Trichoptera					
Family Hydropsychidae					
Cheumatopsyche spp.	X	X		Mu	k,b,m
Hydropsyche orris	X	X		Mu	n,e,b
Hydropsyche spp.	X	X		Mu	k,v,j,b, i,s,n,m,w
Macronemum transversum	X	X		Mu	w
Potamyia sp.	X	X		Mu	k,j
Family Hydroptilidae					
Agraylea sp.	X	X		Mu	n,b,i
Hydroptila sp.	X	X	X	Mu	k,v,j
Mayatrichia sp.			X	Mu	n,i
Ochrotrichia sp.	X	X	X	Mu	n,w
Family Leptoceridae					
Leptocella (= *Nectopsyche*?) sp.	X			Mu	b
Leptocerus sp.	X			Mu	w
Mystacides sp.	X	X		Mu	b
Nectopsyche sp.	X			Mu	k
Family Philopotamidae					
Wormaldia sp.	X	X	X	Mu	k
unident. spp.				Mu	b
Family Phryganeidae					
Ptilostomis sp.	X	X		Mu	m
Family Polycentropodidae					
Neureclipsis sp.	X			Mu	k,j,i, w,n,m
Polycentropis sp.			X	Mu	v,b,w,m

Continued

TABLE 3.24. *(Continued)*

Taxon	V	Lentic M,S	Lotic G,R	Site[b]	Source[c]
Family Psychomyiidae					
Psychomyia sp.	X	X	X	Mu	i,w
Family Rhyacophilidae					
Rhyacophila sp.	X	X	X	Mu	w
Order Lepidoptera					
Family Gelechiidae					
unident. spp.	X			Mu	v
Order Diptera					
Suborder Nematocera					
Family Ceratopogonidae					
Atrichopogon sp.		X		Mu	i
Culicoides sp.		X		Mu	v
Palpomyia sp.	X	X		Mu	v
Probezzia sp.	X	X	X	Mu	v,i
unident. spp.				Mu	k,n,j,b
Family Chaoboridae					
unident. spp.	X	X		Mu	k
Family Chironomidae					
Ablabesmyia sp.	X	X	X	Mu	k,n,e,i,w
Chernovskiia sp.				Mu	k
Chironomus sp.	X	X		Mu	v,n,b,i,w
Cladotanytarsus sp.	X	X		Mu	k
Coelotanypus sp.	X	X		Mu	k,b,w
Corynoneura sp.	X	X		Mu	k,n
Cricotopus sp.	X	X	X	Mu	k,v,i,n,w
Cryptochironomus spp.	X	X		Mu	k,v,e,b, i,s,w
Cryptotendipes sp.	X	X		Mu	k,w
Cyphomella sp.				Mu	k
Diamesa sp.	X	X	X	Mu	b
Dicrotendipes sp.	X	X		Mu	i,w,v
Einfeldia sp.	X	X	X	Mu	i
Endochironomus sp.		X		Mu	i
Glyptotendipes sp.	X	X	X	Mu	k,n,i
Harnischia sp.	X			Mu	v,e,s,w,b
Kiefferulus sp.	X	X		Mu	k,i
Lasiodiamesa sp.	X	X		Mu	w
Lenziella cruseula	X	X		Mu	w
Lenziella sp.	X	X		Mu	k
Leptochironomus sp.				Mu	k
Limnophyes sp.	X	X	X	Mu	w
Mesosmittia sp.				Mu	k
Microcricotopus sp.			X	Mu	w
Micropsectra sp.	X	X		Mu	n,i
Microtendipes sp.	X	X		Mu	w,b
Nanocladius sp.	X	X	X	Mu	k

TABLE 3.24. (Continued)

Taxon	V	Lentic M,S	Lotic G,R	Site[b]	Source[c]
Family Chironomidae (cont.)					
*Orthocladius sp.	X	X	X	Mu	k,e,i,n,w
*Parachironomus sp.	X	X		Mu	k,w
*Paracladopelma sp.	X	X		Mu	k,e
*Paralauterborniella sp.	X			Mu	w,b
*Paratanytarsus sp.	X	X	X	Mu	k,w
*Paratendipes sp.		X		Mu	k,e,w,b
*Pentaneura sp.	X	X	X	Mu	b
*Phaenopsectra sp.	X	X		Mu	k,u,e
*Polypedilum sp.	X			Mu	k,v,b, i,n,s,w
*Procladius sp.	X	X		Mu	k,v,e, b,i,w
*Psectrocladius sp.	X	X		Mu	n,i,b
*Pseudochironomus sp.	X	X	X	Mu	n,k,w,b
Psilotanypus bellus				Mu	b
*Rheotanytarsus sp.	X	X	X	Mu	k
Rhovackia sp.				Mu	k
*Smittia sp.	X	X	X	Mu	k,w
*Stenochironomus sp.	X			Mu	k,b,i,w
*Tanypus sp.	X	X		Mu	k,w
*Tanytarsus sp.	X		X	Mu	k,v,n, i,w,b
*Thienemanniella sp.	X	X	X	Mu	e
*Tribelos sp.	X	X		Mu	i
*Trissocladius sp.	X	X	X	Mu	k,e
*Xenochironomus sp.	X	X		Mu	k,v,e,i,b
*Zavrelia sp.			X	Mu	b
*n. nr. Demicryptochironomus	X	X		Mu	e,s,w
n. nr. Omisus				Mu	e,s
*unident. Chironominae	X	X		Mu	b
unident. Diamesinae			X	Mu	b
unident. Orthocladiinae			X	Mu	b
*unident. Tanypodinae	X	X	X	Mu	b
*unident. spp.	X	X	X	Mu	j,n,m
Family Culicidae					
*unident. spp.	X	X		Mu	k,m
Family Psychodidae					
*unident. spp.	X	X	X	Mu	k,m
Family Simuliidae					
Simulium sp.			X	Mu	v,n,i
unident. spp.			X	Mu	k,j,n,m
Family Tanyderidae					
unident. spp.			X	Mu	b
Family Tipulidae					
*unident. spp.	X	X	X	Mu	k,b

Continued

TABLE 3.24.   (Continued)

Taxon	V	Substrate[a] Lentic M,S	Substrate[a] Lotic G,R	Site[b]	Source[c]
Suborder Brachycera					
Family Dolichopodidae					
Dolichopus sp.	X	X	X	Mu	v
unident. spp.	X	X	X	Mu	k
Family Empididae					
Hemerodromia sp.	X	X	X	Mu	i
unident. spp.	X	X	X	Mu	k,n
Family Ephydriadae					
Ephydra sp.	X	X	X	Mu	v
unident. spp.	X	X		Mu	k,b
Family Muscidae					
Limnophora sp.			X	Mu	i
Family Tabanidae					
Chrysops sp.		X	X	Mu	v
unident. spp.				Mu	k
Phylum Bryozoa					
Class Ectoprocta					
Order Phylactolaemata					
Family Plumatellidae					
Plumatella sp.			X	Mu	i
Phylum Chordata					
Subphylum Vertebrata					
Class Cephalaspidomorphi					
Order Petromyzontiformes					
Family Petromyzontidae					
Ichthyomyzon castaneus		X	X	M	f
I. unicuspis		X	X	M	f
Class Osteichthyes					
Order Acipenseriformes					
Family Acipenseridae					
Acipenser fulvescens		X	X	M	f
Scaphirhynchus albus		X	X	Mu	f
S. platorhynchus		X	X	Mu	f,k
Family Polydontidae					
Polydon spathula	X	X	X	Mu	f,k
Order Lepisosteiformes					
Family Lepisosteidae					
Lepisosteus osseus	X	X	X	Mu	k,f
L. platostomus	X	X	X	Mu	f,k
Order Amiiformes					
Family Amiidae					
Amia calva	X	X		M	f
Order Osteoglossiformes					
Family Hiodontidae					
Hiodon alosoides		X	X	Mu	k,f,g

TABLE 3.24.   *(Continued)*

Taxon	V	Lentic M,S	Lotic G,R	Site[b]	Source[c]
		Substrate[a]			
Order Anguilliformes					
Family Anguillidae					
Anguilla rostrata		X	X	M	k,f
Order Clupeiformes					
Family Clupeidae					
Alosa chrysochloris		X	X	Mu	k,f
Dorosoma cepedianum	X	X	X	Mu	f,k
Order Cypriniformes					
Family Catostomidae					
Carpiodes carpio	X	X		Mu	f,k
C. velifer		X	X	Mu,M	f,k
Catostomus commersoni	X		X	Mu,M	f,k
Cycleptus elongatus		X	X	Mu	f,k
Ictiobus bubalus		X	X	Mu	f,k
I. cyprinellus	X	X		Mu	f,g,k
I. niger		X	X	M	f
Moxostoma macrolepidotum			X	Mu	f,g,k
Family Cyprinidae					
Carassius auratus	X	X		M	f
Cyprinus carpio	X	X		Mu	k,f,g
Hybognathus nuchalis	X	X		M	k,f
H. placitus		X		M	f
Hybopsis aestivalis		X		M	f
H. gelida		X	X	M	f
H. gracilis		X		M	f
H. meeki		X	X	M	f
H. storeriana	X	X		Mu	f,k
Notropis atherinoides		X		Mu	f,k
N. blennius		X	X	Mu	f
N. cornutus		X	X	M	f
N. dorsalis		X		M	f,k
N. lutrensis		X	X	Mu	f,k
N. shumardi		X	X	M	f
N. stramineus		X	X	Mu	f,k
N. topeka		X	X	M	f
Pimephales promelas	X	X		Mu	f
Semotilus atromaculatus		X	X	M	f
Order Siluriformes					
Family Ictaluridae					
Ictalurus furcatus		X	X	Mu	f
I. melas	X	X		Mu	f,g,k
I. natalis	X	X	X	Mu	f
I. nebulosus	X	X		Mu	f
I. punctatus		X	X	M	f,g,k
Noturus flavus		X	X	M	f

Continued

TABLE 3.24.   *(Continued)*

Taxon	Substrate[a] V	Lentic M,S	Lotic G,R	Site[b]	Source[c]
Family Ictaluridae *(cont.)*					
*N. gyrinus	X	X		M	f
*Pylodictus olivaris	X	X		Mu	f,g,k
Order Salmoniformes					
Family Esocidae					
*Esox lucius	X	X		Mu	k,f
Order Gadiformes					
Family Gadidae					
*Lota lota	X	X	X	Mu	f,k
Order Perciformes					
Family Centrarchidae					
*Lepomis cyanellus	X	X		Mu,M	f,k
*L. humilis	X	X		Mu,M	f,k
*L. macrochirus	X	X		Mu	f,k
*Micropterus salmoides	X	X	X	Mu	f,k
*Pomoxis annularis	X	X		Mu	f,k
*P. nigromaculatus	X	X		Mu	f,k
Pomoxis spp.				Mu	g
Family Percidae					
*Etheostoma exile	X	X		Mu	k
*E. nigrum		X	X	Mu	k,f
*Perca flavescens	X	X	X	Mu	k,f
*Stizostedion canadensis	X	X	X	Mu	k,f,g
*S. vitreum	X	X	X	Mu	k,f,g
Family Percithyidae					
*Morone chrysops		X	X	Mu	k,f,g
Family Sciaenidae					
*Aplodinotus grunniens		X		Mu	k,f,g

*Species discussed in the section "Structure of Aquatic Communities" based on knowledge of R. Patrick.

[a]V, vegetation; M, mud; S, sand; G, gravel; R, rock.

[b]Mc, channelized reaches; Mu, unchannelized reaches; M, recorded in main river, but not specified whether it was found in channelized or unchannelized reaches.

[c]a, Farrell and Tesar (1982) (channelized nuke algae); b, Namminga (1969) (invertebrate drift, Mu); c, Williams (1971) (unchannel zooplankton); d, Nelson (1974) (unchannelized diatoms); e, Modde and Schmulbach (1977) (sturgeon prey); f, Schmulbach et al. (1975) (unchannelized fish); g, Groen and Schmulbach (1978) (unchannelized fish); h, Hansen and Dillon (1974) (diatoms and invertebrates); i, Gould (1975) (unchannelized invertebrates); j, Novotny (1978) (unchannelized drift); k, Kallemeyn and Novotny (1977) (invertebrates and fish); m, Morris et al. (1968) (invertebrates from unchannelized sites); n, Nord and Schmulbach (1973) (invertebrates); p, Reetz (1982) (phytoplankton); s, Modde and Schmulbach (1973) (invertebrates); u, Hoke (1983) (unionids); v, Volesky (1969) (invertebrates and plants); w, McMahon et al. (1972) (invertebrates); z, Repsys and Rogers (1982) (nuke zooplankton).

brachyurum and *D. leuchtenbergianum.* These are omnivores feeding mainly on algae and bacteria.

Copepods, particularly calanoids, were found in this habitat. They are omnivorous, but feeding largely on algae and bacteria. There were seven species of *Diaptomus* found in and among the vegetion. The genus *Cyclops,* which is believed to be an omnivore, was represented by three species; the genus *Eucyclops* by three species; the genus *Macrocyclops* by one species; and there was one species of *Paracyclops.* All of these are omnivores (Table 3.24). The amphipods found associated with the vegetation were an unidentified species of *Gammarus,* which is an omnivore, and an unidentified species of the genus *Hyalella,* also an omnivore.

Various insects were present in and among the vegetation. They were taxons belonging to the suborder Zygoptera and were unidentified species of the genera *Argia, Chromagrion, Enallagma,* and *Ischnura,* all of which are carnivores. Other species found in and among the vegetation were *Gomphus* sp., a carnivore; *Libellula,* a carnivore; and *Perithemis,* a carnivore. Mayflies were also present in this habitat. They were unidentified species of the genus *Baetis,* an omnivore; and *Callibaetis* and *Centroptilum,* which are also omnivores. The family Heptageniidae was represented by the carnivorous *Anepeorus* sp. and the omnivorous *Cinygma* sp., and *Heptagenia,* also an omnivore. Other taxons belonging to the family Heptageniidae were *Iron* sp., *Stenacron* sp., and *Stenonema* sp., all omnivores. Other mayflies found were unidentified species of *Leptophlebia,* which is an omnivore; *Siphoplectron* sp., a carnivore; and *Homoeoneuris* sp., an omnivore. Mayflies associated with the vegetation were an unidentified species of the genus *Potamanthus,* an omnivore, and *Ameletus* sp., a detritivore. The caenids were represented by two species, *Brachycerus* sp. and *Caenis* sp., both of which are omnivores. Stoneflies were also present in and among the vegetation. The genus *Acroneuria* sp. was fairly common. *Isoperla* sp., an omnivore, was also present.

Several true bugs were present. They were the omnivorous *Sigara* sp. and an unidentified species each of the families Gerridae; Notonectidae, which is known to be carnivorous; as are species belonging to the family Saldidae, which were also present. Beetles were fairly common in and among the vegetation in the vegetation habitats, and they were represented by the genera *Bidessus* sp., *Rhantus* sp., both carnivores, and the genus *Dineutes* sp., also a carnivore. The elmid beetles, which are omnivores, were represented by unidentified species. The genus *Berosus* sp., an omnivore, was in and among the vegetation.

A few Hydropsychids were found in and among the vegetation habitats. They were species belonging to the genera *Cheumatopsyche* and *Hydropsyche,* both omnivores. Also present where the current was more rapid in and among the vegetation were *Macronemum transversum,* an omnivore; *Potamyia* sp., an omnivore; and *Agraylea* sp., an omnivore-herbivore. Other Hydropsychids found in and among the vegetation where the current was moderate to fairly swift were unidentified species of the genera *Agraylea,*

Hydroptila, and *Ochrotrichia,* all omnivore-herbivores. The family Leptoceridae was represented by four species in this habitat. They belong to the genera *Leptocella* sp., an omnivore; *Leptocerus* sp., a herbivore; *Nectopsyche* sp., an omnivore; and *Mystacides* sp., an omnivore that prefers herbivorous material. Also present was an unidentified species of the genus *Wormaldia,* an omnivore. The family Phryganidae was represented by a single taxon belonging to the genus *Ptilostomis,* an omnivore. The family Polycentropodidae was represented by a single taxon belonging to the genus *Neureclipsis,* which is an omnivore. Other species found in and among the vegetation were an unidentified species of the genus *Psychomyia,* an omnivore, and *Rhyacophila* sp., an omnivore. The true flies were also present in and among the vegetation. They were an unidentified species of the genus *Palpomyia,* a carnivore-omnivore, and *Probezzia* sp., a carnivore.

The family Chironomidae was very common in and among the vegetation, particularly in the debris formed by the dead leaves and roots of the plants. A total of 45 taxons belonging to the family Chironomidae were found, and most of these are believed to be omnivorous. One chironomid species was found, which is believed to be a carnivore. It is the genus *Xenochironomus* sp. The family Culicidae was represented by one undetermined species in and among the vegetation, as was the family Psychodidae. These species are believed to be omnivores. The family Tipulidae was represented by one or more unidentified species in and among the vegetation, and they are believed to be omnivorous. The family Dolichopodidae was represented by an unidentified species belonging to the genus *Dolichopus,* which is a carnivore. The family Empididae was represented by an unidentified species of the genus *Hemerodromia,* which is a carnivore-omnivore, and the family Ephydridae by a species of the genus *Ephydra,* an omnivore.

Several fish were found in and among the vegetation: *Polydon spathula,* a carnivore; *Lepisosteus osseus,* a carnivore; and *L. platostomus,* a carnivore. Also present in and among the vegetation was *Amia calva,* a carnivore. In this habitat was *Dorosoma cepedianum,* an omnivore, and feeding in this habitat *Carpiodes carpio,* an omnivore. *Catostoma commersoni,* an omnivore, was also present in and among the vegetation, as was the omnivorous *Ictiobus cyprinellus.* Several cyprinids were found in this habitat. They were *Carassius auratus,* an omnivore; *Cyprinus carpio,* an omnivore; and *Hybognathus nuchalis,* a herbivore. The carnivorous, *Hybopsis storeriana,* was also in and among the vegetation. Other fish found in this habitat were the omnivorous *Pimephales promelas,* and *Ictalurus melas, I. natalis,* and *I. nebulosus.* All three of these are omnivorous. Also present were the carnivorous *Noturus gyrinus* and *Pylodictus olivaris.* These vegetative habitats, which were in backwaters, marshes, or sloughs, supported a high diversity of fish. Also present besides those listed above were *Esox lucius,* a carnivore; *Lota lota,* a carnivore; several centrarchids, *Lepomis cyanellus* and *L. humilis,* both carnivores; *L. macrochirus,* an omnivore; *Micropterus salmoides,* an omnivore; and *Pomoxis annularis* and *P. nigromaculatus,* both carnivores. The Percidae were represented by several species in this vegetative habitat: the carnivorous *Etheostoma exile; Perca flavescens,* also a carnivore; *Stizostedion canadense,* a carnivore; and *S. vitreum,* a carnivore.

Lentic Habitats. The lentic habitats were typically found in sloughs and backwaters and pools that may be present in the main river. In these areas the current was relatively slow. Mud and sand and sometimes only sand were the substrates. A covering of debris accumulated in these areas. The blue-green algae, *Oscillatoria* sp. and *Schizothrix calcicola,* were often found on the surface of the mud. Living among the debris, often floating above the debris, were *Ankistrodesmus hantzschii* and *A. spiralis. Dictyosphaerium pulchellum* was also found in this habitat. Attached to the debris were filaments of *Chaetophora* sp. and *Stigeoclonium tenue* and an unidentified species of *Stigeoclonium. Oedogonium* sp. filaments might be found here. These lentic areas were also favorable habitats for *Cladophora glomerata* and *Cladophora* sp. Some filaments of *Spirogyra* were also present.

In this habitat where the current was moderate were filaments of the diatom, *Melosira* sp. On the surface of the substrate were five species of the genus *Stephanodiscus.* Also in and among the debris was the diatom *Biddulphia laevis.* Where the current was moderate and perhaps associated with some vegetation were filaments of the diatom *Diatoma vulgare* and also an unidentified species of the same genus. *Fragilaria construens* and *F. pinnata* were also here. These lentic habitats were also suitable for the growth of the diatom, *Rhoicosphenia curvata,* and an unidentified species of the same genus. *Gomphonema olivaceum* and *G. parvulum* were also present. Other diatoms that were encountered in these lentic habitats were *Amphipleura* sp., *Amphiprora* sp., *Anomoeoneis* sp., *Diploneis* sp., *Frustulia* sp., *Gyrosigma* sp., *Mastogloia* sp., and seven species of the genus *Navicula* (Table 3.24). Usually associated with debris and sometimes attached to it were *Denticula* sp., *Epithemia* sp., and *Rhopalodia* sp. Seven taxons belonging to the genus *Nitzschia* were also found here, as was one taxon belonging to the genus *Surirella.* The Gymnodiniaceae were represented by two taxons. They were unidentified species of the genus *Amphidinium* and *Gymnodinium.*

Various protozoans were found in and among the debris in these lentic habitats. They were *Mallomonas* sp. and *Dinobryon* sp., both of which are primary producers, as were species of *Euglena,* and *Trachelomonas* sp. Crawling over the debris was a species of the genus *Amoeba,* an omnivore. Also present living in and among the bed material was *Paramecium aurelia,* an omnivore; that is, it lives on bacteria and small protozoans and other invertebrates. It may also eat algae and debris. Other protozoans found in this habitat were the omnivorous *Spirostomum, Strombidium, Strobilidium, Oxytricha* sp., and *Epistylis* sp. All of these species are omnivorous in that they eat the bacteria, other small protozoans and invertebrates, and algae. Crawling over the debris in these habitats might be found unidentified species of the family Planariidae.

Rotifers were very common in these lentic habitats. They were typically omnivores and belong to the genera *Rotaria, Asplanchna, Brachionus, Euchlanis, Keratella, Lecane, Monostyla, Notholca, Platyais, Trichotria.* Other rotifers that were present were the omnivorous *Cephalodella* spp., *Dicranophorus* spp., *Encentrum* spp., *Notommata* spp., *Polyartha* spp., *Synchaeta* spp., and *Trichotria* spp. Living in the sandy mud where small amounts of current were present were the detritivore-herbivore mollusc, Unionidae. Present were three species of *Anodonta* that are detritivore-herbivores, *Lampsilis teres teres, Lasmigona complanata,* and *Leptodea fragilis; L. lepodon; Potamilus,* which was represented by two taxons; *Tritogonia verrucosa; Truncilla donaciformis;* and *T. truncata.* Several Cladocera were found in these lentic habitats. They were *Bosminia longirostris,* which is an omnivore. Also present were species of chydorids, which are mainly algae and bacterial feeders but might also be considered omnivorous. They were one taxon belonging to the genus *Acropterus; Alona* sp.; two taxons belonging to the genus *Camptocercus;* four taxons belonging to the genus *Ceriodaphnia* and one unidentified species of this same genus; *Chydorus sphaericus;* and *Disparolona rostrata.* Eight species of *Daphnia,* which are omnivorous but feed primarily on algae and bacteria, were also present, as were three taxons belonging to the genus *Monia.* Other protozoans that were present were *Simocephalus exspinosus,* and *S. vetulus.* All of these are omnivorous species feeding largely on algae and bacteria. Other species of the same feeding type were *Leptodora kindti, Ilyocryptus sordidus,* and *Macrothrix laticornis.* Other omnivorous taxons were two species belonging to the genus *Diaphanosoma,* one species belonging to the genus *Latona,* and two species belonging to the genus *Sida.*

Copepods were also present in this habitat. They were *Diaptomus ashlandi* and *D. clavipes,* which were omnivores feeding primarily on algae and detritus. The family Cyclopodae were well represented in this habitat. There were four taxons belonging to the genus *Cyclops,* all of which are omnivores; one taxon belonging to the genus *Eucyclops;* one taxon belonging to each of the following genera: *Macrocyclops* and *Mesocyclops;* two taxons belonging to the genus *Paracyclops;* and three taxons belonging to the genus *Tropocyclops.*

Several odonates were found in these lentic habitats. They were an unidentified species of the genus *Argia* and an unidentified species of the genus *Chromagrion.* Both of these are carnivores. Other carnivorous species in this habitat were an unidentified species of the genus *Gomphus,* a carnivore; *Libellula* sp., a carnivore; and *Perithemis* sp., a carnivore.

Various mayflies were found in and among the debris and associated with algae in this habitat. They were the omnivorous *Ametropus* sp., usually in the sandy habitats. Other mayflies were the omnivorous *Baetis* spp. and *Centroptilum* sp. The family Ephemeridae was represented by three taxons, two of which belong to the genus *Hexagenia,* and one to the genus *Ephemera.* All of these are believed to be omnivores, as are unidentified species belonging to the genera *Anepeorus, Cinygma,* and *Heptagenia.* Other species present belonging to the family Heptageniidae were *Iron* sp., an omnivore; one species belonging to the genus *Stenacron,* an omnivore; and one belonging to the genus *Stenonema* sp. In and among the sandy mud was an unidentified species of the genus *Leptophlebia* sp. and an unidentified species of the genus *Siphoplectron* sp., which is a carnivore. Also present was an unidentified species of the omnivorous genus *Homoeoneuria.* Other omnivorous mayflies that were present in this habitat were an unidentified species of the genus *Pentagenia,* an omnivore; and *Ephoron* sp., an omnivore; and *Potamanthus* sp., an omnivore; and *Ameletus* sp., an omnivore. The family Baetiscidae was represented by a single taxon, which was an unidentified species of the genus *Baetisca,* which was living primarily in the sandy substrates and is an omnivore. An unidentified species of the omnivorous genus *Brachycerus* sp. was also present. An unidentified species of the genus *Caenis,* an omnivore, was present, as was an unidentified species of the genus *Tricorythodes.*

A few stoneflies were also found in this habitat. They were an unidentified species of the genus, *Acroneuria,* a carnivore, and an unidentified species of the genus *Isoperla,* an omnivore. True bugs were present. They are believed to be omnivores and belong to the genera *Sigara* sp., an unidentified species belonging to the family Notonectidae, which is believed to be a carnivore, and an unidentified species belonging to the family Saldidae, a carnivore. Several beetles were found in and among the muddy sand and the debris, sometimes associated with algae in this habitat and various invertebrates. They were two species belonging to the family Dytiscidae. They were an unidentified species of the carnivorous genus *Bidessus* and *Rhantus* sp. Also present was an unidentified species, *Dineutes* sp., of the family Gyrinidae. Also present was an unidentified species belonging to the genus *Berosus,* which belongs to the family Hydrophilidae.

Caddisflies or Trichoptera were represented by several species in this habitat. They were unidentified species of the genus *Cheumatopsyche,* omnivores; *Hydropsyche orris;* and other species of the genus *Hydropsyche,* which were unidentified. All of these are omnivorous, as are *Macronemum transversum* and an unidentified species of the genus *Potamyia.* Other species in this habitat were an omnivore that is mainly an unidentified species of the genus *Agraylea,* an unidentified species of the genus *Hydroptila* and of the genus *Ochrotrichia,* an unidentified species of the genus *Mystacides,* which is omnivorous but mainly herbivorous, and *Wormaldia* sp., which is an omnivore, as is an unidentified species of the genus *Ptilostomis* sp. One taxon belonging to the family Psychomyiidae, *Psychomyia* sp., which is omnivorous was present in these lentic habitats, as was an unidentified species of the genus *Rhyacophila,* belonging to the family Rhyacophilidae. Various species belonging to the family Ceratapogonidae were present. They were *Atrichopogon; Culicoides* sp., an omnivore-carnivore; *Palpomyia* sp., an omnivore-carnivore; and *Probezzia* sp., a carnivore.

Chironomids were fairly common in this habitat. These are typically omnivores and belong to the genera *Ablabesmyia, Chironomus, Cladotanytarsus, Coelotanypus, Corynoneura, Cricotopus,* and *Cryptochironomus.* All of these are omnivorous, but the last taxon may also be carnivorous. Other species found in this habitat were unidentified species of the genera *Cryptotendipes* and *Diamesa*, which are omnivores. These lentic habitats were indeed favorite places for the chironomids to live. Other genera found in these lentic habitats were unidentified species of the omnivorous *Einfeldia, Endochironomus, Glyptotendipes, Kiefferulus, Lasiodiamesa, Lenziella, Limnophyes, Micropsectra, Microtendipes, Nanocladius, Orthocladius, Parachironomus, Paracladopelma, Paratanytarsus, Paratendipes, Pentaneura, Phaenopsectra, Procladius, Psectrocladius, Pseudochironomus, Rheotanytarsus, Smittia, Tanypus, Thienemanniella, Tribelos, Trissocladius, Xenochironomus,* and *Demicryptochironomus.*

Other Diptera that were present were an unidentified species belonging to the family Culicidae, which is probably an omnivore; an unidentified species belonging to the family Psychodidae, which is an omnivore; one taxon belonging to the family Tipulidae, which are craneflies; one taxon belonging to the genus *Dolichopus*, a carnivore; one taxon belonging to the genus *Hemerodromia*, which is carnivorous but may be omnivorous; one taxon belonging to the genus *Ephydra*, an omnivore; and one taxon belonging to the genus *Chrysops*, an omnivore.

Several species of fish were found in and among the mud and sand, where the current was moderate to very slow. These areas existed in pools and backwaters and in some cases along the edges of the channelized river. Here one found *Ichthyomyzon castaneus* and *I. unicuspis*, both of which were carnivores probably feeding off the variety of invertebrates that were present. Other carnivores that were present in this habitat were *Acipenser fluvescens, Scaphirhynchus albus,* and *S. platorhynchus.* Also present were *Polydon spathula*, a carnivore; *Lepisosteus osseus*, a carnivore, as was *L. platostomus.* Other carnivores that were present were *Amia calva, Hiodon alosoides,* and the eel, *Anguilla rostrata.*

In the pool area, particularly where there was a moderate flow and sandy bottom to the stream, was a carnivore, *Alosa chrysochloris.* Below the releases of the dams were *Dorosoma cepedianum*, an omnivore. Several cyprinids were found in these lentic habitats: the omnivorous *Carpiodes carpio, C. velifer, Cycleptus elongatus, Ictiobus bubalus, I. cyprinellus,* and *I. niger,* all omnivores. Among the cyprinids that were found in these habitats where the current was very slow were *Carassius auratus* and *Cyprinus carpio,* both omnivores. Others present were two herbivores, *Hybognathus nuchalis* and *H. placitus.* Omnivores that were present were *Hybopsis aestivalis,* which preferred areas where there was some current, as did *H. gelida, H. gracilis,* and *H. meeki.* Carnivorous species in this habitat were *Hybopsis storeriana* and *Notropis atherinoides,* along with other *Notropis* species that are carnivorous, such as *N. blennius.* Omnivorous species in this habitat in the genus *Notropis* were *N. cornutus, N. dorsalis, N. lutrensis, N. shumardi,* and *N. stramineus.* Other omnivorous species in this habitat, particularly in and among the pool-like areas, were *Pimephales promelas* and *Semotilus atromaculatus.*

Several catfish were found in these areas where the current was very slow. Present were the carnivorous *Ictalurus furcatus* and four other species belonging to this genus, all were omnivores (Table 3.24). Carnivorous species present were *Noturus flavus, N. gyrinus,* and *Pylodictus olivaris.* Other carnivores present were *Esox lucius* and *Lota lota.* The centrarchids were represented by various carnivores and omnivores. The genus *Lepomis,* which is carnivorous, was represented by *Lepomis cyanellus* and *L. humilis.* Omnivorous species were *Lepomis macrochirus* and *Micropterus salmoides.* Two carnivores present in this habitat were *Pomoxis annularis* and *P. nigromaculatus.* The Percidae were represented by several carnivores in this habitat: *Etheostoma exile, E. nigrum, Perca flavescens, Stizostedion canadensis,* and *S. vitreum.* Two other carnivores were present in these lentic areas: *Morone chrysops* and *Aplodinotus grunniens.*

Lotic Habitats. In those areas, particularly in the main channel, where there was relatively swift flow and the substrate was mostly sand, gravel, and in a few cases rocks, the flora and fauna were not as plentiful but often well developed. Attached to the rocks were the blue-green algae, *Merismopedia tenuissima, Lyngbya* sp., and *Plectonema notatum.* The green algae attached to the rocks were *Chaetophora* sp. and *Stigeoclonium tenue.* An unidentified species of *Oedogonium* was also found attached to the rocks. Among the gravel and rocks were filaments of the green algae, *Cladophora glomerata.* This was a suitable habitat for some diatoms. In and among the gravel and sand were *Cyclotella meneghiniana* and unidentified species of *Cyclotella.* Two species of *Melosira* were found attached to the rocks in areas where the flow was not very swift. Closely appressed to rocks and gravel, particularly gravel, and in some cases sand grains, were two species of *Achnanthes* and four taxons belonging to the genus *Cocconeis.* Other species found attached to the gravel and rock where the current was not as rapid were *Gomphonema angustatum, G. bohemicum,* and *G. intricatum.* Several naviculoid diatoms were found in and among the gravel: an unidentified species of *Caloneis,* of *Diploneis,* of *Gyrosigma,* and of *Mastogloia.* Two species of *Navicula* were found in this habitat: *Navicula cryptocephala* and *N. graciloides.* These areas in between the rocks and gravel where the current was less rapid was a favorable habitat for unidentified species of the genera *Denticula, Epithemia,* and *Rhopalodia.* Two species of the Peridinalies were found in and among the gravel: *Ceratium* sp. and *Peridinium.* In the gravel and sand where the current was moderately rapid were many species of unionids: the bacterivorous-herbivorous *Anodonta grandis corpulenta, Lampsilis teres, Leptodea fragilis, L. lepodon, Potamilus atatus,* and *P. ohiensis.* These species might be considered omnivorous. However, they seemed to prefer bacteria and algae. There were three other species in this category: *Tritogonia verrucosa* and *T. truncata.*

Isopods and amphipods were found in and among the gravel. They were an unidentified species belonging to the order Isopoda, the omnivorous *Asellus* sp., the omnivorous *Gammarus* sp., and the omnivorous *Hyalella* sp. There were also unidentified species belonging to the order Collembola in and among the gravel. This seems to be a fairly favorable habitat for mayflies that were mainly in and among the gravel and in the areas often under rock surfaces, where the current was perhaps not as rapid. They were *Ametropus,* which is an omnivore, an unidentified species of *Baetis,* and of *Centroptilum,* both of these are omnivores. Other species found in and among the gravel were an unidentified species of the genus *Ephemera,* an omnivore, and two species belonging to the genus *Hexagenia,* both omnivores. These species, together with *Ephemera,* were often found on the undersides of rocks. Other species found in this habitat were *Anepeorus* sp., *Cinygma* sp., and *Hepta-genia* sp., an omnivore, as were unidentified species of the genera *Iron, Stenacron,* and *Stenonema.* A carnivorous species belonging to the genus *Siphoplectron* was found associated with the rocks, as was an unidentified species of the genus *Isonychia.* Other omnivores present were unidentified species of the genus *Ephoron* and *Ameletus* sp.

Certain stoneflies were found on the undersides of rocks and between rocks. They were the carnivorous *Acroneuria* sp. and the omnivorous *Isoperla* sp. The Hemiptera were represented by an unidentified species of the family Gerridae which was also found in this habitat. It is probably a carnivore. Several beetles were found in the lotic habitats. A carnivorous species of the genus *Bidessus* was here. Other beetles in this habitat were unidentified species of Elmidae and of the Hydrophilidae. Caddisflies (Trichoptera) were represented by the genera *Hydroptila,* a herbivore and *Ochrotrichia,* an omnivore that probably prefers algae. Other hydropsychids found were unidentified species of the genus *Wormaldia,* an omnivore; *Psychomyia,* an omnivore; and *Rhyacophila,* which probably is an omnivore with carnivorous tendencies. The ceraptogonid, *Probezzia* sp. (a dipteran), which is carnivorous, was also found in this habitat.

Also here were several chironomids. They were the omnivorous carnivore *Ablabesmyia,* the omnivorous *Cricotopus* sp., and an unidentified species of the omnivorous *Diamesa.* Other chironomids in this habitat were an unidentified species of the genus *Einfeldia* and of the genus *Glyptotendipes,* both of which are omnivores. Other omnivorous chironomids in this habitat were an unidentified species of *Limnophyes, Orthocladius,* and of *Nanocladius* which are omnivores. In and among the gravel were unidentified species of the omnivorous *Paratanytarsus, Pentaneura, Pseudochironomus,* and *Rheotany-tarsus.* Other taxons found in this habitat were the omnivorous *Smittia* and *Tanytarsus* sp. and the omnivorous *Thienemanniella* sp. Also present among the gravel and rocks associated with the rocks were the omnivorous species of *Trissocladius* and *Zavrelia* sp. Also found in these lotic habitats were several unidentified species of the genera *Dolichopus,* an omnivore; *Hemerodromia,* an omnivore; and *Ephydra* an omnivore. *Chrysops* sp. was also found.

Several species of fish seemed to prefer the more rapidly flowing water associated with the dam releases or other areas where the gradient produced more rapid flow. In these lotic areas were the species *Ichthyomyzon castaneus,* a carnivore, and *I. unicuspis,* also a carnivore. Other carnivorous species found in this habitat were *Acipenser fluvescens, Scaphirhynchus albus, S.*

platorhynchus, and *Polydon spathula.* Also present were *Lepisosteus osseus* and *L. platostomus. Anguilla rostrata,* a carnivore, was found associated with the rocks. Other species living particularly associated with the rocks and the gravel were the omnivorous *Catostomus commersoni* and *Cycleptus elongatus.* Associated mainly with the gravel were two species of the genus *Ictiobus,* both of which are omnivores. In and among the rocks was the carnivorous *Moxostoma macrolepidotum.* Found where the current was not quite as rapid were the omnivorous *Hybopsis gelida* and *H. meeki.* The genus *Notropis* was represented by several species: the carnivorous *Notropis blennius; N. cornutus,* an omnivore; *N. lutrensis,* also an omnivore; *N. shumardi; N. stramineus,* an omnivore; and *N. topeka,* an omnivore. The omnivorous *Semotilus atromaculatus* was in and among the gravel. Several species of *Ictalurus* were found in and among the gravel, sometimes among the gravel and rocks. Such species were the carnivorous *Ictalurus furcatus; I. natalis,* an omnivore; *I. punctatus,* an omnivore; and *Noturus flavus,* a carnivore; whereas in the less rapid water were *Ictalurus natalis* and *I. punctatus,* both omnivorous. Also present were *Lota lota* and *Micropterus salmoides.* Associated with the gravel in the less rapidly flowing water were the carnivorous *Etheostoma nigrum* and *Perca flavescens.* In and among the gravel and rocks were the carnivorous *Stizostedion canadensis, S. vitreum,* and the carnivorous *Morone chrysops.*

SUMMARY

The Missouri River is the longest river in North America. It originates in southwestern Montana with the confluence of the Gallatin, Madison, and Jefferson Rivers and flows 3678 km to the east and southeast, where it joins the Mississippi near St. Louis, Missouri. It drains an area of 1,354,564 km^2, which is approximately one-sixth of contiguous United States, and it encompasses four major physiographic regions. The westernmost 10.5% of the basin includes parts of Saskatchewan, Montana, Wyoming, and Colorado and lies within the Rocky Mountains. Most of the basin (68.8%) lies within the semiarid Great Plains and encompasses portions of Montana, North and South Dakota, Nebraska, Colorado, and Kansas; 16.8% of the basin lies in more mesic conditions and includes parts of eastern Dakota, Nebraska, and Kansas as well as portions of Missouri, Iowa, and Minnesota. The remaining basin drains portions of the Great Uplands in Missouri.

Today, most of the river has been inundated by six main-stem impoundments, and approximately 95% of the floodplain forests in the lower river have been inundated by agricultural, industrial, or urban land use. Approximately half of the land use within the entire basin is pasture and rangeland, while another third is cropland. Most of the remaining is either forest or woodland. Today, most of the main stem of the Missouri River has been channelized, and there are six main-stem impoundments in the upper river for flood control, irrigation, hydroelectric generation, water supply, and navigational controls. The lower part of the river (1202 km) has been channelized.

This area is mainly between Kansas City and St. Louis. Due to channelization, most of the backwater habitats of the lower river have been eliminated. Four reaches of tributaries are the primary remaining back water habitats in the Lower Missouri. Because of channelization, many of the natural habitats have been lost in the main channel. Despite channelization of the lower river, flooding remains a major problem.

The temperature of the Missouri River is variable. In the unchannelized reach below Gavins Point Dam, the main-channel temperature ranged from 3 to 29.5°C during an April–October study. The temperature in the channelized river near Blair, Nebraska, ranged from 0 to 27°C. Vegetation of the watershed ranges from a semiarid short-grass prairie and shrubland in the western Great Plains to a mosaic of tallgrass prairies and oak–hickory woodlands in the east.

The Missouri is a hard to very hard alkaline river with high conductivity and high total dissolved solids. The hardness is dominated by calcium and magnesium hardness. The hardness is caused primarily by carbonates and alkaline sulfates. There is also a fair amount of chloride present in certain reaches. In reaches of the river, for example at Hermann, Missouri, the hardness averages 208 mg L^{-1}. Nitrates and phosphates are variable along the course of the river, depending primarily on watershed use. There is a greater percentage of organic matter in winter and spring. Organic matter input is primarily dependent on allochthonous inputs from the floodplain and/or its tributaries.

The main stem supports a fairly rich plankton. The riverine phytoplankton are primarily derived from the main-stem impoundments. However, they appear to be more abundant in backwaters than in the main channel. Vegetation in the Missouri River is highly variable. Submerged aquatic macrophytes appear to be relatively rare, whereas emergent macrophytes form extensive growths in the backwater marshes and along the banks of the precontrolled river in the channelized portions. These stands of vegetation are relatively rare.

Although zooplankton is not very plentiful in the main river, it is apparent that zooplankton may be well developed in some of the chutes, backups, and marshes. The main plankton organisms throughout the river are pelagic reservoir copepods and cladoceran. This development of zooplankton is in the unchannelized portions of the river.

Where the banks of the river had been stabilized, oligochaetes and chironomids were abundant. Oligochaetes and chironomids are abundant in both the unchannelized and channelized portions. Mayflies, particularly *Hexagenia* and *Pentagenia,* were relatively abundant in the unchannelized and bank-stabilized areas. Trichoptera, especially the *Cheumatopsyche,* were fairly common in the unchannelized river but were rare downstream. Odonates were abundant primarily in one of the channelized stations, while bivalves were relatively abundant in one station in each of the unchannelized and bank-stabilized areas. Chironomids are often abundant in the unchannelized areas. However, some species were also fairly common in the channelized habitats.

Oligochaetes often appeared to be less dominant in the unchannelized river than in the channelized river. Marsh habitats and backwaters were excellent habitats for many species of insects and some of the other invertebrates, such as clams and worms.

Further studies indicate that there were considerable differences in the composition and relative abundance of macrophytes collected in the benthic and drift samples. In general, the Ephemeroptera and Trichoptera were substantially greater in the drift than they were in the benthos. Whereas the chironomids were often an important drifter, they were considerably less abundant in the drift than in the benthos. An examination of the fauna indicates that this disparity between benthic and drift faunas is explained by the fact that most Missouri River drift originates from hard substrates rather than from the sand, silt, and mud that characterizes the benthos in the main river.

Snags, where present, are an important habitat for the fauna. It is interesting to note that the pattern of macroinvertebrate abundance in the Missouri River is similar to those observed in some of the Eastern Coastal Plain rivers. However, the disparity between benthic and aufwuchs habitats was not as great in the southeastern rivers (e.g., the Satilla) as it was in the Missouri. There are probably many causes of this difference.

It is very probable that the loss of backwater and marsh habitats to channelization and channel degradation has resulted in a considerable loss in benthic macroinvertebrate production. This would be reasonable if one only considered loss of total habitat area. However, flow regulations and the prevention of floodplain inundation may have greatly reduced the benthic productivity. Prior to regulation, benthic populations in the spring would have experienced increased allochthonous inputs via floodplain inundation combined with increasing temperatures. These potential productive conditions have been greatly modified by the impoundments.

The effects of anthropogenic modifications on the aufwuchs would also have been profound. Reduced sediment loads and the import of reservoir plankton may have substantially altered the aufwuchs by favoring those taxa that feed on algae and are less tolerant of silt. They seem to be about as abundant in the more turbid channelized river as in the natural river.

Trichoptera and Ephemeroptera were abundant on pile dikes during high-turbidity studies according to Berner (1951). Mollusc fauna is relatively rich in the river. Fish fauna in the precontrolled Missouri River supported a relatively limited and specialized fish fauna that was well adapted to the Missouri's persistently high turbidity and seasonal flooding. In fact, several of these species were limited to turbid rivers west of the Mississippi. Subsequently, many of the native species have declined, and many sight-feeding and pelagic species, both native and introduced, have increased. The fish fauna has changed greatly over the years. The large catfish catches that existed in the prechannelized river are now relatively rare. While the lake sturgeon has declined dramatically since 1900, probably because of overfishing, fishing has also probably been the cause of the decline of the shovelnose sturgeon and the paddlefish. In contrast, carp have increased in recent times.

There has not only been a change in kinds of species caught but also in the total catch. Since the early part of the twentieth century there has been a decided decline in the fishes caught in this section of the Missouri River. The only commercial species that have not seriously declined are *Ictalurus punctatus* and *Cyprinus carpio.* Overfishing and habitat loss seem to be the causes of this decline in fisheries. The disposition and relative abundance of Missouri fish assemblages indicate substantial changes over time and differences between channelized and unchannelized reaches. There may not have been very much change in the taxonomic composition over 54 years in the unchannelized and channelized areas. There is limited evidence that there have been some significant changes in the relative abundance of some species. For example, the carp suckers were rare and the introduced common carp was absent from the Sioux City survey, but both taxa have been dominant throughout most of the twentieth century. Another species, *Sturgeon chub,* was abundant in Sioux City collections but has been rare since at least 1945.

Those species analyzed in degraded reaches of the middle Missouri River exhibited a taxonomic richness comparable to that recorded in the unchannelized river during the 1970s, but the fauna is dominated by only a few species. Notched rivetments, notched spur dikes, and notched wind dikes seemed to be preferable habitats and increased the fisheries in the river in the channelized portions.

The aquatic life in the Missouri River is very dependent on allochthonous inputs. The fauna consists primarily of species very tolerant of turbidity. In the unchannelized portions, filter feeders were very common, accounting for 87 to 97% of the aufwuchs macroinvertebrate biomass on multiplate samplers in fast-water and backwater sites. Multiplate samplers on wooden stakes accounted for 63% of the biomass in fast-water sites. The most productive aquatic communities were in vegetative and lentic habitats where the current was relatively slow and where mud, silt, and organic matter formed the substrates. Habitats in swifter waters where the substrate was hard—wood, rocks, and gravel—were less productive. Each habitat supported a great variety of species representing all the major stages of nutrient and energy transfer in the foodweb. The most productive habitats seemed to be those in backwaters and pools and along the edges of the channel in vegetative habitats where the current was reduced. However, productivity in fast waters was fairly large for certain groups.

BIBLIOGRAPHY

Benke, A. L., and J. L. Meyer. 1988. Structure and function of a blackwater river in the southeastern U.S.A. Int. Verein. Limnol. Verh. 23(1): 1209–1218.

Benkw, A. C., T. C. Van Arsdall, Jr., D. M. Gillespie, and F. K. Parrish. 1984. Invertebrate productivity in a subtropical blackwater river: the importance of habitat and life history. Ecol. Monogr. 54(1): 25–63.

Benson, N. G., and B. C. Cowell. 1968. The environment and plankton density in Missouri River reservoirs. pp. 358–373. *In* Reservoir rishery resources symposium. Reservoir Committee, Southern Division, American Fisheries Society, Bethesda, Md.

Berner, L. M. 1951. Limnology of the Lower Missouri. Ecology 32: 1–12.

Bragg, T. B., and A. K. Tatschi. 1977. Changes in floodplain vegetation and land use along the Missouri River from 1826–1972. Environ. Manage. 1(4): 343–348.

Carter, S. R., K. R. Bazata, and D. L. Andersen. 1982. Macroinvertebrate communities of the channelized Missouri River near two nuclear power stations. pp. 147–182. *In* L. W. Hesse, G. L. Hergenrader, H. S. Lewis, S. D. Reetz, and A. B. Schlesinger, eds., The Middle Missouri River: a collection of papers on the biology with special reference to power station effects. Missouri River Study Group, Norfolk, Neb., 301 pp.

Cowell, B. C. 1970. The influence of plankton discharge from an upstream reservoir on standing crops in a Missouri River reservoir. Limno. Oceanogr. 15: 427–441.

Cross, F. B. 1967. Handbook of fishes of Kansas. Misc. Publ. 45. Museum of Natural History, Univ. Kansas, Lawrence, Kans. 357 pp.

Cross, F. B., and R. E. Moss. 1987. Historic changes in communities and aquatic habitats of plains streams in Kansas. pp. 155–165. *In* W. J. Matthews and D. C. Heins, eds., Community and evolutionary ecology of North American stream fishes. University of Oklahoma Press, Norman, Okla. 309 pp.

Damann, K. E. 1951. Missouri River Basin plankton study. Public Health Service, Environmental Health Center, Cincinnati, Ohio. 100 pp.

Dames, H. R., T. G. Coon, and J. W. Robinson. 1989. Movement of channel and flathead catfish between the Missouri River and a tributary, Perche Creek. Trans. Am. Fish. Soc. 118(6): 670–679.

Farrell, J. R., and M. A. Tesar. 1982. Periphytic algae in the channelized Missouri River with special emphasis on apparent optimal temperature. pp. 85–123. *In* L. W. Hesse, G. L. Hergenrader, H. S. Lewis, S. D. Reetz, and A. B. Schlesinger, eds., The Middle Missouri River: a collection of papers on the biology with special reference to power station effects. Missouri River Study Group, Norfolk, Neb., 301 pp.

Fisher, H. J. 1962. Some fishes of the Lower Missouri River. Am. Midl. Nat. 68(2): 424–429.

Ford, J. C. 1982. Water quality of the Lower Missouri River, Gavins Point Dam to mouth. Misc. Publ. Missouri Department of Natural Resources, Jefferson City, Mo. 35 pp.

Fremling, C. R. 1960. Biology and possible control of nuisance caddisflies on the Upper Mississippi River. Agric. Home Econ. Exp. Stn. Iowa State Univ. Res. Bull. 483: 856–879.

Fuchs, E. H. 1967. Life history of the emerald shiner, *Notropis atherinoides,* in Lewis and Clark Lake, South Dakota. Trans. Am. Fish. Soc. 96(3): 247–256.

Funk, J. L., and J. W. Robinson. 1974. Changes in the channel of the Lower Missouri River and effects on fish and wildlife. Aquat. Ser. 11. Missouri Department of Conservation, Jefferson City, Mo. 52 pp.

Gould, G. R. 1975. Macroinvertebrate aufwuchs communities on natural substrates in the unchannelized Missouri River, South Dakota. Unpublished master's thesis. Univ. South Dakota, Vermillion, S. Dak.

Groen, C. L., and J. C. Schmulbach. 1978. The sport fishery of the unchannelized and channelized Middle Missouri River. Trans. Am. Fish. Soc. 107: 412–418.

Hansen, M. D., and R. D. Dillon. 1974. The diversity of microorganisms in channelized and unchannelized portions of the Missouri River. Proc. S. Dak. Acad. Sci. 53: 254–259.

Hergenrader, G. L., L. G. Harrow, R. G. King, G. F. Cada, and A. B. Schlesinger. 1982. Larval fishes in the Missouri River and the effects of entrainment. pp. 185–223. *In* L. W. Hesse, G. L. Hergenrader, H. S. Lewis, S. D. Reetz, and A. B. Schlesinger, eds., The Middle Missouri River: a collection of papers on the biology with special reference to power station effects. Missouri River Study Group, Norfolk, Neb. 301 pp.

Hesse, L. W. Personal communication. Nebraska Game and Parks Commission, Norfolk, Neb.

Hesse, L. W. 1987. Taming the wild Missouri River: what has it cost? Fisheries 12(2): 2–9.

Hesse, L. W. 1990. Missouri River mitigation: river channel morphology, and its relationship to fish and wildlife habitat, and common sense restoration. Federal Aid in Fish Restoration, Dingell–Johnson Project F-75-R-7 Job 1. Missouri Department of Conservation. 29 pp.

Hesse, L. W., and B. A. Newcomb. 1982. On estimating the abundance of fish in the upper channelized Missouri River. North Am. J. Fish. Manage. 2: 80–83.

Hesse, L. W., Q. P. Bliss, and G. J. Zuerlein. 1982a. Some aspects of the ecology of adult fishes in the channelized Missouri River with special reference to the effects of two nuclear power generating stations. pp. 225–276. *In* L. W. Hesse, G. L. Hergenrader, H. S. Lewis, S. D. Reetz, and A. B. Schlesinger, eds., The Middle Missouri River: a collection of papers on the biology with special reference to power station effects. Missouri River Study Group, Norfolk, Neb., 301 pp.

Hesse, L. W. , G. L. Hergenrader, H. S. Lewis, S. D. Reetz, and A. B. Schlesinger. 1982b. The Middle Missouri River: a collection of papers on the biology with special reference to power station effects. Missouri River Study Group, Norfolk, Neb., 301 pp.

Hesse, L. W., A. B. Schlesinger, G. L. Hergenrader, S. D. Reetz, and H. S. Lewis. 1982c. The Missouri River Study: ecological perspectives. pp. 287–300. *In* L. W. Hesse, G. L. Hergenrader, H. S. Lewis, S. D. Reetz, and A. B. Schlesinger, eds. The Middle Missouri River: a collection of papers on the biology with special reference to power station effects. Missouri River Study Group, Norfolk, Neb., 301 pp.

Hesse, L. W., C. W. Wolfe, and N. C. Cole. 1988. Some aspects of energy flow in the Missouri River ecosystem and rationale for recovery. pp. 13–29. *In* N. G. Benson, ed., The Missouri River: the resources, their uses and values. Spec. Publ. 8. North Central Division, American Fisheries Society, Bethesda, Md.

Hesse, L. W., G. R. Chaffin, and J. Barbander. 1989a. Missouri River mitigation: a system approach. Fisheries 14(1): 11–15.

Hesse, L. W., G. E. Mestl, and M. J. Rohrke. 1989b. Chemical and physical characteristics of the Missouri River, Nebraska. Trans. Nebr. Acad. Sci. 17: 103–109.

Hesse, L. W., J. C. Schmulbach, J. M. Carr, K. D. Keenlyne, D. G. Unkenholz, J. W. Robinson, and G. E. Mestl. 1989c. Missouri River fishery resources in relation to past, present, and future stresses. pp. 352–371. *In* D. P. Dodge, ed., Proceedings of the international large river symposium. Can. Spec. Publ. Fish. Aquat. Sci. 106. Canadian Government Publications Centre, Ottawa, Canada.

Hoke, E. 1983. Unionid molluscs of the Missouri River on the Nebraska border. Am. Malacol. Union Bull. 1(1983): 71–74.

Jewell, M. E. 1927. Aquatic biology of the prairie. Ecology 8(3): 289–298.

Jordon, D. S., and S. E. Meek. 1885. List of fishes collected in Iowa and Missouri in August, 1884, with descriptions of three new species. Proc. U.S. Natl. Mus. 8: 1–17.

Kallemeyn, L. W., and J. F. Novotny. 1977. Fish and fish food organisms in various habitats of the Missouri River in South Dakota, Nebraska, and Iowa. FWS/OBS-77/25. U.S. Fish and Wildlife Service, Biological Services Program, Washington, D.C. 100 pp.

Malcolm, R. L., and W. H. Durum. 1976. Organic carbon and nitrogen concentrations and annual organic carbon load of six selected rivers of the United States. Water-Supply Pap. 1817-F. U.S. Geological Survey, Washington, D.C. 21 pp.

Martin, D. B., and J. F. Novotny. 1975. Nutrient limitation of summer phytoplankton in two Missouri River reservoirs. Ecology 56(1): 199–205.

McComish, T. S. 1967. Food habits of bigmouth and smallmouth buffalo in Lewis and Clark Lake and the Missouri River. Trans. Am. Fish. Soc. 96(1): 70–74.

McMahon, J., J. Wolf, and Sister M. Diggins. 1972. Chironomidae, Ephemeroptera, and Trichoptera in the benthos of unchannelized and channelized portions of the Missouri River. Proc. S. Dak. Acad. Sci. 51: 168–181.

Meek, S. E. 1892. A report upon the fishes of Iowa, based upon observations and collections made during 1889, 1890, and 1891. Bull. U.S. Fish. Comm. 10: 217–248.

Miller, R. J., and H. W. Robinson. 1971. The fishes of Oklahoma. Oklahoma State Univ. Press, Stillwater, Okla. 246 pp.

Modde, T. C., and J. C. Schmulbach. 1973. Seasonal changes in the drift and benthic macroinvertebrates in the unchannelized Missouri River. Proc. S. Dak. Acad. Sci. 52: 118–126.

Modde, T., and J. C. Schmulbach. 1977. Food and feeding behavior of the shovelnose sturgeon, *Scaphirhynchus platorhynchus,* in the unchannelized Missouri River, South Dakota. Trans. Am. Fish. Soc. 106(6): 602–608.

Morris, L. A., R. N. Langemeier, T. R. Russell, and A. Witt, Jr. 1968. Effect of main stem impoundments and channelization upon the limnology of the Missouri River, Nebraska. Trans. Am. Fish. Soc. 97(4): 380–388.

Namminga, H. E. 1969. An investigation of the macroscopic drift of the Missouri River. Unpublished Master's thesis. Univ. South Dakota, Vermillion, S. Dak.

Nelson, G. L. 1974. A limnological investigation of the periphyton community in the unchannelized Missouri River, with emphasis on the diatoms. Unpublished Master's thesis. Univ. South Dakota, Vermillion, S. Dak.

Nelson, W. R. 1968. Reproduction and early life history of sauger, *Stizostedion canadense,* in Lewis and Clark Lake. Trans. Am. Fish. Soc. 97(2): 159–166.

Nord, A. E., and J. C. Schmulbach. 1973. A comparison of the macroinvertebrate aufwuchs in the unstablized and stabilized Missouri River. Proc. S. Dak. Acad. Sci. 52: 127–139.

Novotny, J. F. 1978. Diurnal characteristics of macroinvertebrates in the Missouri River. Proc. S. Dak. Acad. Sci. 57: 144–153.

Pflieger, W. L. 1975. The fishes of Missouri. Missouri Department of Conservation, Jefferson City, Mo. 343 pp.

Pflieger, W. L., and T. B. Grace. 1987. Changes in the fish fauna of the Lower Missouri River, 1940–1983. pp. 166–177. *In* W. J. Matthews and D. C. Heins, eds., Community and evolutionary ecology of North American stream fishes. Univ. Oklahoma Press, Norman, Okla. 310 pp.

Reetz, S. D. 1982. Phytoplankton studies in the Missouri River at Fort Calhoun and Cooper Nuclear Station. pp. 71–83. *In* L. W. Hesse, G. L. Hergenrader, H. S. Lewis, S. D. Reetz, and A. B. Schlesinger, eds., The Middle Missouri River: a collection of papers on the biology with special reference to power station effects. Missouri River Study Group, Norfolk, Neb., 301 pp.

Repsys, A. J., and G. D. Rogers. 1982. Zooplankton studies in the channelized Missouri River. pp. 125–145. *In* L. W. Hesse, G. L. Hergenrader, H. S. Lewis, S. D. Reetz, and A. B. Schlesinger, eds., The Middle Missouri River: a collection of papers on the biology with special reference to power station effects. Missouri River Study Group, Norfolk, Neb., 301 pp.

Ross, D. H., and J. B. Wallace. 1983. Longitudinal patterns of production, food consumption and seston utilization by net-spinning caddisflies (Trichoptera) in a Southern Appalachian stream. U.S.A. Holarct. Ecol. 6(3): 270–284.

Schmulbach, J. C. 1974. An ecological study of the Missouri River prior to channelization. B-024-SDAK. Water Resource Institute, South Dakota State Univ., Brookings, S. Dak. 34 pp.

Schmulbach, J. C., G. Gould, and C. L. Goen. 1975. Relative abundance and distribution of fishes in the Missouri River, Gavins Points Dam to Rulo Nebraska. S. Dak. Acad. Sci. 54: 194–222.

Slizeski, J. J., J. L. Andersen, and W. G. Dorough. 1982. Hydrologic setting, system operation: present and future stress. pp. 15–37. *In* L. W. Hesse, G. L. Hergenrader, H. S. Lewis, S. D. Reetz, and A. B. Schlesinger, eds., The Middle Missouri River: a collection of papers on the biology with special reference to power station effects. Missouri River Study Group, Norfolk, Neb., 301 pp.

Smith, P. W. 1979. The fishes of Illinois. Univ. Illinois Press, Urbana, Ill. 314 pp.

Sweedburg, D. V. 1968. Food and growth of freshwater drum in Lewis and Clark Lake, South Dakota. Trans. Am. Fish. Soc. 97(4): 442–447.

Todd, R. D., and J. F. Bender. 1982. Water quality characteristics of the Missouri River near Fort Calhoun and Cooper nuclear stations. pp. 39–68. *In* L. W. Hesse, G. L. Hergenrader, H. S. Lewis, S. D. Reetz, and A. B. Schlesinger, eds., The Middle Missouri River: a collection of papers on the biology with special reference to power station effects. Missouri River Study Group, Norfolk, Neb., 301 pp.

Tondreau, R. L., J. Hey, and E. Shane. 1983. Missouri River aquatic ecology studies ten year summary (1972–1982). Morningside College, Sioux City, Iowa. 71 pp.

U.S. Geological Survey. 1970. The national atlas of the United States. USGS, Washington, D.C. 417 pp.

U.S. Geological Survey. 1975. Quality of surface waters of the United States, 1970. Part 6. Missouri River Basin. Water-Supply Pap. 2155. USGS, Washington, D.C.

U.S. Geological Survey. 1978. Water resources data for Missouri, water year 1977. Water-Data Rep. MO-77-1. USGS, Washington, D.C.

U.S. Geological Survey. 1982. Water resources data for Missouri, water year 1981. Water-Data Rep. MO-81-1. USGS, Washington, D.C.

Vanden Berge, R. J., and P. A. Vohs, Jr. 1977. Population status of beaver on the free-running Missouri in southeastern South Dakota. Pro. S. Dak. Acad. Sci. 56: 230–236.

Volesky, D. F. 1969. A comparison of the macrobenthos from selected habitats in cattail marshes of the Missouri River. Unpublished master's thesis. Univ. South Dakota. Vermillion, S. Dak. 42 pp.

Whitley, J. R., and R. S. Campbell. 1974. Some aspects of the water quality and biology of the Missouri River. Trans. Mo. Acad. Sci. 7–8: 60–72.

Williams, L. G., and C. Scott. 1962. Principal diatoms of major waterways of the United States. Limnol. Oceanogr. 7(3): 365–379.

Williams, M. C., H. G. Nagel, and C. E. True. 1985. Water quality of a limited segment of the Big Blue River in Nebraska. Trans. Nebr. Acad. Sci. 13: 59–73.

Williams, R. E. 1970. Succession in stands of *Populus deltoides* along the Missouri River in southeastern South Dakota. Am. Midl. Nat. 83: 330–342.

Williams, W. D. 1971. Horizontal and vertical distribution and taxonomic composition of net zooplankton in a large lotic ecosystem, the Missouri River. Unpublished master's thesis, Univ. South Dakota, Vermillion, S. Dak.

Wolf, J., J. McMahon, and Sister M. Diggins. 1972. Comparison of benthic organisms in semi-natural and channelized portions of the Missouri River. Proc. S. Dak. Acad. Sci. 51: 160–167.

CHAPTER 4

Kansas River

INTRODUCTION

The Kansas River, sometimes known as the Kaw River, and its tributary the Smoky Hill Branch traverses the state of Kansas from Colorado to the Missouri state line. Perennial springs are important in maintaining the flow of the river. (Figure 4.1)

PHYSICAL CHARACTERISTICS

The watershed area for the Kansas River Basin occupies 156,547 km^2 and covers most of northern Kansas and much of southern Nebraska and northeastern Colorado. The basin extends 774 km from west to east and about 210 km from north to south. Most of the major tributaries arise from the High Plains and flow in an easterly direction toward the Missouri River (Colby et al., 1956).

The Kansas Basin is subdivided into four main subbasins. The largest two subbasins, the Republican River (to the north) and Smoky Hill (to the south), cover all the western and most of the central portion of the basin. The Big Blue Subbasin occupies a northern portion of the central and eastern part of the basin and the Main-Stem Kansas Subbasin occupies the remaining portion of the eastern basin. The dominant landforms of the Republican and Smoky Hill Subbasins are High Plains and Dissected High Plains. Three major patches of Sand Hills are also found within the Republican Subbasin, and East Central Kansas Plains are prevalent in the lower reaches of both subbasins.

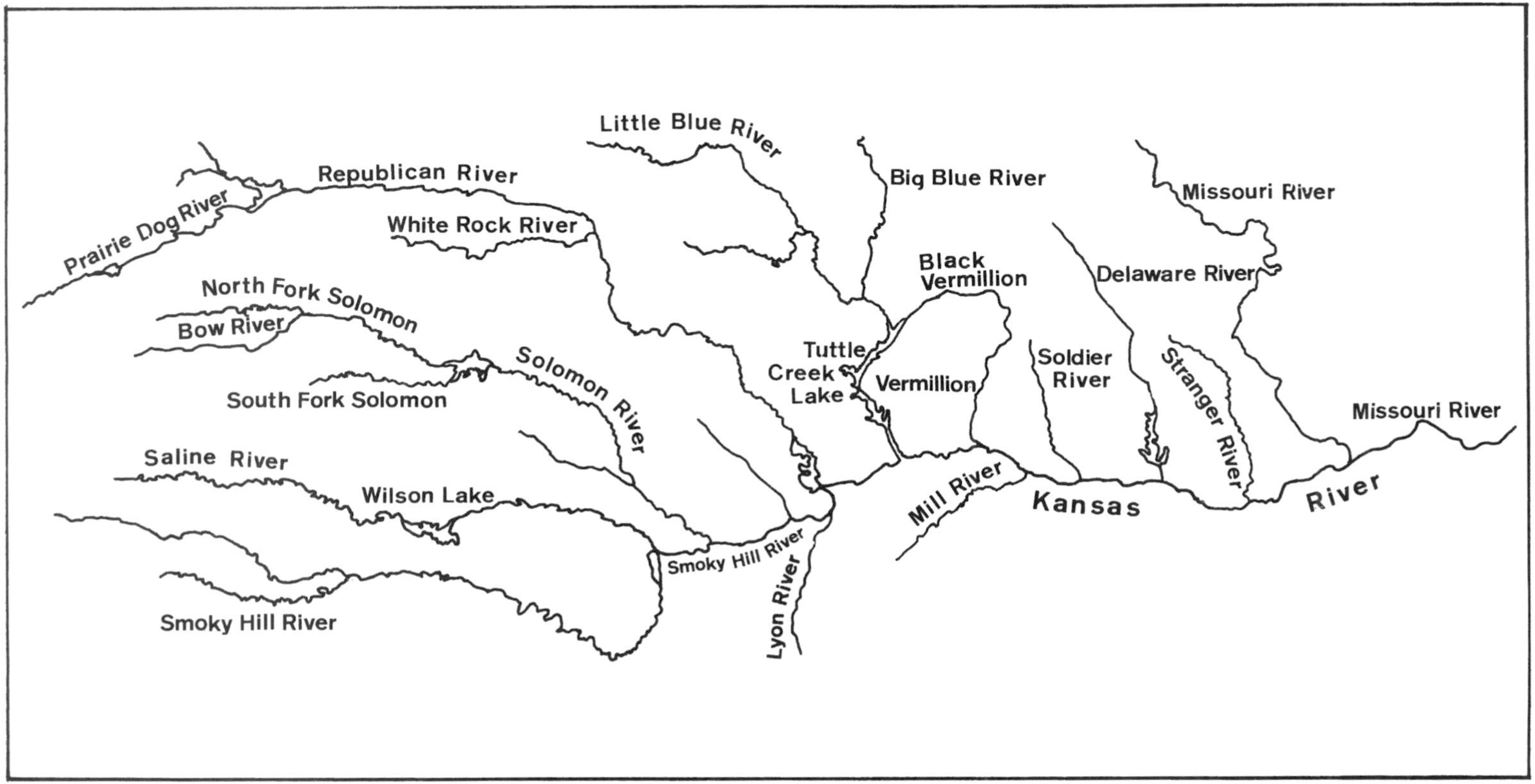

FIGURE 4.1. Map of the Kansas River.

The dominant landforms in the Big Blue Subbasin are Eastern Nebraska Loess Plains, Flint Hills, and Dissected Till Plains, while Dissected Till Plains, Osage Cuestas, and Flint Hills dominate the Main-Stem Kansas Subbasin (Colby et al., 1956).

Most of the basin is moderately sloped to nearly level. A total of 30.5% of the watershed area is essentially level (slope <2%), and about one-third of this level land (10.9%) is bottomland. An additional 30.9% of the total watershed topography is undulating to gently rolling (slope = 2 to 7%). Rolling uplands (21.1%) and hilly uplands (17.5%) occupy the remaining watershed area (Colby et al., 1956).

The bedrock of the Kansas River Basin consists of Pennsylvanian through Tertiary sedimentary deposits with the newer deposits prevalent in the western portion of the basin (USGS, 1970). Because of mid-Pleistocene glaciation, till and outwash materials are the predominant surface deposits over much of the Main-Stem Kansas Subbasin. The river valleys in this subbasin cut into Pennsylvanian and Permian bedrock composed of alternating layers of shale, sandstone, and limestone. The soils in the Main-Stem Kansas Subbasin are loess, alluvium, or derived from local weathered bedrock, and are easily erodible (Kansas FF&G, 1977). Impermeable clay or claypan subsoils are distributed extensively in the eastern portion of the Kansas River Basin (Colby et al., 1956).

Land use for the Kansas River Basin is about 90% agriculture. Grain and livestock are predominant in the upland areas, and row crops dominate the fertile bottomlands. Stream banks are occupied by adjacent farmland or mature or semimature riparian habitats dominated by cottonwoods, elm, and willows (Colby et al., 1956; Kansas FF&G, 1977). Natural vegetation in the uplands was dominated by bluestem prairies. In the eastern third of the basin, the bluestem prairie formed a mosaic with an oak–hickory forest, and in the western half, the bluestem graded into semiarid prairies (USGS, 1970).

The annual mean precipitation ranges from about 40 to 50 cm yr^{-1} in the semiarid western portion of the Kansas River Basin to 75 to 90 cm yr^{-1} in the semihumid eastern portion. Precipitation can vary greatly from year to year, and in most years it deviates wildly from the average. Seasonal patterns in precipitation are also highly variable, but winter is typically the season of lowest precipitation, and about 70% of the total precipitation will occur from April through September; June and July are commonly the two wettest months, but maxima can occur at any time during this period. Most of the precipitation comes as rain, often as localized thunderstorms, but periods of extended rainfall occur on occasion (Colby et al., 1956).

Most of the stream flow for the Kansas River Basin originiates as precipitation, but perennial springs and some groundwater from the adjacent Platte Basin percolates into portions of the Republican and Bil Blue Subbasins. Most of the precipitation is lost through evapotranspiration, especially in the drier western half of the basin. For example, evapotranspiration loss accounted for 98% of the precipitation occurring in a western Kansas site (53 cm

yr^{-1}) and accounted for 89% (75 cm yr^{-1}) of the precipitation (84 cm yr^{-1}) in an eastern Kansas site (Colby et al., 1956).

Runoff, which is usually less than 2.5 cm yr^{-1} in the western half of the Kansas River Basin, is concentrated in the eastern third (including the Main-Stem Kansas Subbasin and the lowermost reaches of the other subbasins), where it averages between 10 and 18 cm yr^{-1}. As an example of the importance of the lower mainstem to stream flow, the watershed below Topeka accounts for between one-fifth and one-sixth of the river's total discharge. As with precipitation, runoff is highly variable from year to year and from month to month. Monthly totals commonly show one or two months contributing a large portion of the annual runoff. Runoff maxima usually occur in June or July but can also occur anytime between March and October (Colby et al., 1956).

One obvious reason for the greater runoff in the eastern third of the Kansas River Basin is the increased precipitation found there. In addition, the eastern third of the basin has a greater concentration of rolling and hilly uplands, and it has the greatest concentrations of clay and claypan subsoils. The greater slopes and reduced permeability combined with soils that are more likely to be saturated with previous rainfall result in reduced infiltration, thereby increasing runoff (Colby et al., 1956).

Because these rivers depend so heavily on surface runoff for their flow, water levels can change rapidly. For example, the daily discharge at the U.S. Geological Survey gaging station for the Kansas River at Topeka (water year 1966) ranged from 650 to 13,600 ft^3/s (USGS, 1972). For water year 1958, the daily discharge at the Kansas River Wemago gaging station (approximately 65 km upstream from Topeka) ranged from 860 to 51,000 ft^3/s. Daily discharge at Wemago was consistently less than 2000 from December through mid-February, and discharges below 5000 ft^3/s were common in late spring and early autumn. Daily discharges in excess of 20,000 ft^3/s occurred from mid-July until early August and during early September (USGS, 1962). During the same year, the Topeka gaging station recorded two peak flood stages. The first occurred on July 18 (gage height = 17.72 ft, discharge of 55,300 ft^3/s). The second occurred on September 8 (gage height = 17.99 ft, discharge = 56,900 ft^3/s) (Matthai, 1968), about a week prior to the beginning of the sampling period for the Topeka vicinity sites. During this sampling period, average gage height was 7.51 ft and the average discharge was 11,104 ft^3/s (ANSP, 1959).

Under normal flow conditions, the main stem of the Kansas River averaged 165 m in width and 1 m in depth (Kansas FF&G, 1977). In the Topeka vicinity sites, depths were either moderate or shallow and small islands were present. The banks ranged from steep to gradual, and at least one had collapsed after being undercut (ANSP, 1959). In the Smoky Hill River site near Junction City, the width averaged 97 m and the depth averaged 0.4 m. Pools were uncommon and the banks were formed by earthen levees (Summerfelt, 1967).

Substrates in the Main-Stem Kansas Subbasin are dominated by unstable sand and have very few areas of bedrock outcrops or boulders (Kansas

FF&G, 1977). Shifting sand dominated the substrate at the study sites in the Topeka vicinity, but logs and submerged shrubs presented some snag habitat, and mud was found in protected areas (ANSP, 1959). Sand and fine gravel dominated the Smoky Hill River site and logs were common (Kansas FF&G, 1979; Summerfelt, 1967). Sand was the predominant substrate for the Big Blue River study sites of Williams et al. (1985).

The rivers of the Kansas Basin are turbid and high in suspended sediments. For example, during water year 1958 the U.S. Geological Survey station in the Main-Stem Kansas near Wamego recorded a range for the concentrations of suspended sediments from 87 to 8650 ppm. Concentrations were consistently below 200 ppm from late November through January and were rarely less than 500 ppm for the rest of the year. Concentrations exceeding 5000 ppm occurred in March, May, June, July, and September (USGS, 1962). In the Topeka sites, the mid- to late September turbidity was consistently greater than 72,000 ppm (ANSP, 1959). Turbidity at a Smoky Hill River site 10 km upstream from its confluence with the Republican River averaged 2100 JTU (Jackson turbidity units) and ranged from 80 to 6000 JTU (Summerfelt, 1967). Sediment loads are high because of moderate to severe sheet and gully erosion aggravated by agriculture (Colby et al., 1956), but periodic high turbidity was a characteristic of these rivers prior to agricultural development (Metcalf, 1966).

Extensive modifications to the natural flow of the Kansas River have occurred in recent decades. Numerous flood control and water storage impoundments have been constructed. In the Kansas Main-Stem subbasin, there are two large impoundments, the Perry on the Delaware River and the Clinton on the Wakarusa River, both of which are downstream of Topeka. Within the river itself, numerous artificial levees and riprap piers direct the flow of the main channel, permanently altering the river's geomorphology (Kansas FF&G, 1977).

Impoundments in the Missouri River have reduced turbidity and have improved fish production in their tailwaters, probably because of plankton export. In the channelized area the habitat diversity, has been reduced and this has reduced the production of in-stream plankton and benthos and resulted in a serious loss of fish habitats (Whitley and Campbell, 1973). In the main stem of the Kansas River, turbidity has not been noticeably reduced; suspended sediments at Wamego reached 2680 mg L^{-1} at least once during water year 1984 (USGS, 1985). The detrimental effects of channelization found in the Missouri were also probably present in the Kansas.

Water temperatures in the larger rivers of the Kansas Basin are warm. For example, the annual range of the Kansas River near Wamego was 0 to 31°C (USGS, 1974), and the late September temperatures near Topeka ranged from 20 to 23°C (ANSP, 1959). Temperatures at the Smoky Hill River site near Junction City reached 31°C during at least one collection period (Summerfelt, 1967). August stream temperatures for the Big Blue River sites near Beatrice averaged 27.0°C (Williams et al., 1985).

CHEMICAL CHARACTERISTICS

During water year 1969, the total hardness in the main stem of the Kansas River near Wamego varied from 128 to 246 mg L^{-1} as $CaCO_3$. Concentrations of calcium varied from 40 to 74 mg L^{-1}, magnesium varied from 6.8 to 18 mg L^{-1}, sulfate varied from 13 to 83 mg L^{-1} and bicarbonate varied from 139 to 224 mg L^{-1}. Chloride concentrations varied from 6 to 80 mg L^{-1}. pH varied from 7.4 to 8.2 (USGS, 1974). During water year 1958, the carbonate hardness averaged 187 ppm, noncarbonate hardness averaged 48 ppm, and specific conductance averaged 533 μS cm^{-1} (USGS, 1962).

The mean total hardness at the four mid- to late September Kansas River sites near Topeka ranged from 177 to 194 mg L^{-1} as $CaCO_3$. The mean methyl orange alkalinity ranged from 124 to 130 mg L^{-1} and the mean pH ranged from 7.7 to 7.8. The mean concentrations of calcium ranged from 50.7 to 57.2 mg L^{-1}, mean magnesium ranged from 12.1 to 13.2 mg L^{-1}, and mean sulfate ranged from 39 to 44 mg L^{-1} (ANSP, 1959) (Table 4.1). At the Smoky River site, the alkalinity varied from 94 to 310 mg L^{-1} and averaged 288 mg L^{-1} over four spring and summer collection periods. The pH averaged 7.9 and varied from 7.4 to 8.4 (Summerfelt, 1967). At the nearby Smoky Hill River site, the late August total hardness was 280 mg L^{-1}, the alkalinity was 210 mg L^{-1}, and

TABLE 4.1.   *Chemical Characteristics of the Kansas River (Station 1), 1959*

Turbidity (ppm)	>72,000
Total solids (ppm)	2395.6
Total organic matter (ppm)	266.4
Fixed residue (ppm)	2129.2
Alkalinity (ppm)	
Phenolphthalein	3.44
Methyl orange	129.88
Temperature ($^{\circ}$ C)	21.16
Dissolved oxygen (ppm)	7.83
Sulfide (ppm)	0.00
pH	7.76
Total hardness as $CaCO_3$ (ppm)	192.80
Calcium (ppm)	57.20
Magnesium (ppm)	12.14
Phosphate (ppm)	0.3038
NO_2-N (ppm)	0.0022
NH_4-N (ppm)	0.0242
NO_3-N (ppm)	0.3592
Sulfate (ppm)	43.89
Iron (ppm)	0.002
Chloride (ppm)	55.96
Silica (ppm)	6.09

Source: ANSP (1959).

the pH was 8.6 (Kansas FF&G), 1979). August specific conductance for the Big Blue River sites near Beatrice averaged 594 μS cm^{-1} and the pH averaged 8.5 (Williams et al., 1985).

The annual mean NO$_3$-N concentration for the Kansas River site at Wamego was 0.784 mg L^{-1} and that of PO$_4$-P was 0.246 mg L^{-1} (USGS, 1974). The mean NO$_3$-N/PO$_4$-P ratio was 3.2, but individual ratios ranged from 0.6 to 11.5, with the majority of them ranging between 4.2 and 6.8. Ratios tended to be greatest in late winter and early spring. During water year 1958, the mean concentration of NO$_3$-N was 0.98 ppm (USGS, 1962).

Mean NO$_3$-N concentrations at the four mid- to late September Kansas River sites near Topeka ranged from 0.290 to 0.505 ppm and averaged 0.392 ppm. The mean NH$_4$-N concentration ranged from 0.007 to 0.035 ppm and averaged 0.018 ppm. The mean PO$_4$-P concentrations ranged from 0.093 to 0.109 ppm, with an overall mean of 0.104 ppm (ANSP, 1959). The N/P ratios at the Topeka vicinity sites ranged from 2.8:1 to 5.1:1 and averaged 3.6:1.

The late September dissolved oxygen concentrations for the Kansas River sites near Topeka ranged from 7.7 to 7.9 mg L^{-1} at about 21°C (approximately 86% saturation) (ANSP, 1959). Late spring and summer dissolved oxygen concentrations at the Smoky Hill River site averaged 8.2 mg L^{-1} and ranged from 6.8 to 9.2 mg L^{-1} (Summerfelt, 1967). August concentrations in the Big Blue River near Beatrice averaged 8.2 mg L^{-1} (Williams et al., 1985).

ECOSYSTEM DYNAMICS

Detritus

Narrow stands of well-developed riparian vegetation were present at both the Topeka vicinity Kansas River sites and the Smoky Hill River site, but on an areal basis, leaf-litter inputs from the riparian zone are probably not substantial. The lack of retention devices (e.g., riffles) probably results in the diminution of any leaf input. One author (Jewell, 1927) reported that in contrast to some from two Illinois rivers, sediment samples from the Kansas River had very little organic content, and in the sandy main stem of the Big Blue River, Williams et al. (1985) found only traces of organic matter. Fallen trees and seasonally submerged shrubs may be important organic matter sources at the river's margin, but their contribution as snag habitat may be more important.

Because of the substantial runoff and erosion, particularly in the productive croplands, the input of terrestrially processed fine-particulate organic matter (e.g., crop residue) may be significant. If so, such inputs would be associated with increases in suspended sediments. Mature prairies, which probably reduced surface runoff, may also have retained much of their detrital pool.

Two sets of measurements of organic matter were found in the literature. The late September mean concentrations of organic matter for the Kansas River sites in the vicinity of Topeka ranged from 222 to 266 ppm (ANSP, 1959). In the Kansas River near De Soto, the concentrations of organic carbon from two water quality samples were 3.3 and 20.0 mg L^{-1} (Briggs and Ficke, 1977).

Benthic Primary Production
High loads of suspended sediments precluded quantitative sampling of the periphyton at the four Kansas River sites near Topeka (late September 1958). However, qualitative assessments indicated that algal abundance was low. Only small patches of attached green and blue-green algae were found. Attached diatoms, of which *Navicula gracilis* var. *schizonemoides, N. pelliculosa, Nitzschia palea*, and *N. palea* var. *kuetzingiana* were most numerous, were well represented only in the diatometer samples (artificial substrates situated near the surface). Scattered patches of unidentified vascular hydrophytes were found in protected backwaters (ANSP, 1959). At the Smoky Hill site, only a small amount of filamentous algae, attached to submerged brush, was noted; no comment was made with respect to periphyton (Kansas FF&G, 1979).

Quantitative estimates of periphyton abundance were obtained from the Kansas River near De Soto, about 80 km downstream from Topeka and from the Republican River near Clay Center. The periphyton biomass in one sample from the Kansas River was 7 g m^{-2} (ash-free dry weight) and those from two samples from the Republican River were 0.5 and 3.0 g m^{-2}. The chlorophyll *a* concentration from the Kansas River site was 0.2 mg m^{-2}, and those from the Republican River were 0.0 and 5.1 mg L^{-1} (Briggs and Ficke, 1977).

Because the periphyton sampling for the Topeka vicinity sites took place shortly after unusually high river stages, it is unclear whether algal populations increase during periods of low water or are suppressed throughout the year. On the one hand, turbidity greatly reduces benthic illumination, and sedimentation can cover much of the new growth. In addition, algal populations would be reduced by the abrasion from suspended sediments and burial by shifting sands. On the other hand, the relatively cloudless climatic conditions and ample concentrations of macronutirents suggest that large algal populations could develop. The diversity of the diatom assemblage collected near Topeka suggests that under conditions of lower flow and reduced turbidity, periphyton biomass could be much higher.

In the Des Moines River (Iowa), Starrett and Patrick (1952) reported that bottom ooze, consisting almost entirely of diatoms, was largely confined to the shallow and clear portions of the river, where flow was reduced. Visual observations indicated that this ooze fluctuated in abundance in accordance with river stage and stream temperature. The largest increases occurred when decreases in river levels were accompanied by stream temperatures above 21°C. Although turbidity is not as extreme and the flow regime is somewhat more seasonally predictable in the Des Moines River than in the Kansas River, it is probable that benthic diatom ooze is important in the Kansas River. That many of the dominant fish in the Kansas River feed on this benthic ooze (Cross, 1967) provides additional circumstantial evidence that benthic algal production, at least at certain times and in certain microhabitats, is significant.

Plankton Primary Production

The high concentrations of suspended sediment that were encountered in the Kansas River sites near Topeka precluded plankton tow estimates of phytoplankton abundance. Qualitative sampling indicated that phytoplankton were scarce but diverse (ANSP, 1959). As with the periphyton, the phytoplankton may have been flushed away by the early September floodwaters. Jewell (1927) also reported suspended sediment-related problems with collecting plankton tow samples from sites within the Kansas and Big Blue Rivers.

Staurastrum gracile was the most frequent green alga in the Kansas River plankton tows near Topeka. *Biddularia laevis, Gyrosigma scalproides, Navicula gracilis* var. *schizonemoides, Nitzschia sigma, Pinnularia microstauron, Pleurosigma* sp., *Surirella palmerii, S. stratula,* and *Synedra ulna* were the more frequent planktonic diatoms. Because of the shallowness of the river and the relatively fast flow, the mixing of the water was extensive, resulting in similar sublittoral and midchannel planktonic communities. The diversity of the phytoplankton suggests that aside from the high concentrations of suspended sediment, conditions were generally favorable for primary production (ANSP, 1959).

Phytoplankton densities from August (1973) plankton tows from five sites in the Big Blue River near Beatrice averaged 890 individuals L^{-1} and ranged from 760 to 1050. *Coelastrum, Crucigenia, Oocystis, Scenedesmus* (green algae), *Cyclotella, Fragilaria, Gomphonema, Melosira, Navicula, Nitzschia, Surirella* (diatoms), and *Trachelomonas* (Phytomamastigia) were the more frequently collected taxons (Williams et al., 1985).

Estimates of phytoplankton densities from the National Stream Quality Accounting Network (NASQAN) contrast with this estimate. For water year 1975, the annual mean total water phytoplankton counts for most of the river sites in Kansas, Nebraska, and eastern Colorado exceeded 10,000 cells mL^{-1} and many exceeded 20,000 cells mL^{-1}; only about one-fourth of the 345 stations across the United States reported an excess of 10,000 cells mL^{-1}. For the station in the Kansas River near De Soto (Kansas), the annual mean for 10 samples was 19,010 cells mL^{-1}, with a range of 1200 to 82,000. Cell density was even higher for the station on the Republican River at Clay Center (Kansas), where the annual mean was 41,058 cells mL^{-1} and the range was 550 to 220,000. The annual mean from the Missouri River at St. Joseph (Missouri) was 5909 cells mL^{-1}, with a range of 1300 to 13,000 (Briggs and Ficke, 1977).

Benthic Secondary Production

No quantitative estimates of Kansas River invertebrate abundance or production were found in the literature, but qualitative collections in the Topeka vicinity sites indicated that invertebrate abundance is low (ANSP, 1959). These invertebrate populations may have been greatly reduced by the early September (1958) flooding, but secondary production may be chronically low. Jewell (1927) characterized the sandy bottom of the Kansas River as an aquatic desert.

Low macroinvertebrate standing crops have been reported from the predominantly sandy substrates in the Big Blue River near Beatrice. August (1973) benthic core samples from five stations averaged 0.038 g m^{-2} (dry weight) and ranged from 0.0001 to 0.103. Eckman dredge samples from three stations taken in May (1974) averaged 0.199 g m^{-2} and ranged from 0.006 to 0.576. Oligochaeta and Chironomidae, especially *Chironomus* sp., dominated the samples numerically, but at one station the biomass was dominated by Ephemeroptera (Williams et al., 1985).

Estimates of macroinvertebrate abundance from other prairie rivers are also low. The standing crops from the sandy channels of the swiftly flowing Platte River averaged only 0.010 g m^{-2}, and a higher estimate of 0.580 g $^{-2}$ was reported for Platte River pool habitats (Chapman, 1972, as cited in Williams et al., 1985). Two sets of macroinvertebrate standing crop estimates have been recorded for the Missouri River. Volesky (1969) reported approximately 0.010 g m^{-2} for the main channel and 0.10 g m^{-2} in backwater habitats. In the dredge samples of Berner (1951), the main channel yielded only 0.001 g m^{-2}. Samples near a sandbar yielded 0.067 g m^{-2}, and samples near steep banks yielded 0.217 g m^{-2}. Overall, the benthic standing crop was 0.04 g m^{-2}.

Protozoan populations at the Kansas River sites near Topeka were generally low but diverse, with the populations dominated by Phytomonagia. The lack of algal food and the heavy silt load were probably detrimental to the development of the ciliate fauna, the Sarcodina were probably severely limited by the unstable substrates, and the fast currents were detrimental to most protozoans. Most protozoans were collected only from log surfaces, debris, and quiet backwater sediments (ANSP, 1959).

Very few noninsect macroinvertebrates were collected in the Kansas River sites near Topeka (ANSP, 1959). In the Smoky Hill River site near Junction City, two unidentified species of clams and one unidentified species of crayfish were collected (Kansas FF&G, 1979). The high silt load may be detrimental for many macroinvertebrates, but the scarcity of suitable habitats is also important. For example, unionid mussels in Kansas are generally tolerant of high turbidity, but they are rare in shifting sand (Murry and Leonard, 1962).

The high silt load and shifting sand bottoms severely limit the insect fauna. Over 90% of the insect fauna at the Kansas River sites near Topeka were collected in the scattered accumulations of debris found in snag habitats. Sheltered backwaters with mud bottoms were the only other important insect habitats (ANSP, 1959).

Zooplankton Production
No measures of zooplankton abundance or production for rivers in the Kansas Basin were found in the literature.

Fish Production

Poor sampling conditions hampered fish collection in the Kansas River sites near Topeka, but the fish population in the main river was apparently limited and the main concentrations of captured fish occurred in relatively quiet side pockets and tributaries, where the suspended sediments were lower and food more abundant. Included among the more frequently collected fish were gizzard shad *(Dorosoma cepedianum)*, river carpsucker *(Carpiodes carpio)*, carp *(Cyprinus carpio)*, central silvery minnow *(Hybognathus nuchalis)*, speckled chub *(Hybopsis aestivalis)*, *(Notropis deliciosus)*, red shiner *(N. lutrensis)*, fathead minnow *(Pimephales promelas)*, bluntnose minnow *(P. notatus)*, *N. percobromus*, channel catfish *(Ictalurus punctatus)*, flathead catfish *(Pylodictis olivaris)*, green sunfish *(Lepomis cyanellus)*, orange-spotted sunfish *(L. humilis)*, bluegill *(L. macrochirus)*, white crappie *(Pomoxis annularis)*, and freshwater drum *(Aplodinotus grunniens)* (ANSP, 1959).

The estimated fish standing crop at the Smoky Hill River site near Junction City was only 0.11 kg ha^{-1}. Because of the relatively large size of the river, the reduced efficiency of the electroshock sampling may have resulted in an underestimation of fish abundance, but fish abundance was still probably low. Upstream Smoky Hill River sites, with a greater variety of substrates and much less turbidity, yielded standing crops that ranged from 1.4 to 30.9 kg ha^{-1}. The most numerous fishes at the Junction City site were plains minnow *(Hybognathus placitus)* and sand shiner *(Notropis stramineus)*. Red minnow *(N. lutrensis)*, suckermouth minnow *(Phenacobius mirabilis)*, fathead minnow *(Pimephales promelas)*, and river carpsucker *(Carpiodes carpio)* were other common fish (Summerfelt, 1967). Channel catfish *(Ictalurus punctatus)* and flathead catfish *(Pylodictis olivaris)* are, along with some carp *(Cyprinus carpio)* and drum *(Aplodinotus grunniens)*, the more commonly caught sportfish from the lower Smoky Hill River (Kansas FF&G, 1979).

The more common fish in the sand-bottomed main stem of the Big Blue Subbasin were *Lepisosteus osseus, Dorosoma cepedianum, Carpiodes carpio, Notropis lutrensis, N. deliciosus, Hybognathus nuchalis, Hybopsis aestivalis, Ictalurus punctatus, Pylodictis olivaris,* and *Lepomis humilis.*

Taxonomic and nomenclatural questions exist for some of the most abundant fish species. The sand shiner, *Notropis deliciosus,* is considered synonomous with *N. stramineus* by Becker (1983), Cross (1967), and Metcalf (1966). *Notropis percobromus* is considered synonomous with the emerald shiner *(N. atherinoides)* by Cross (1967) and Metcalf (1966). The taxonomy of *Hybognathus nuchalis* and *H. placitus* is more problematic. According to Lee et al. (1980), the range of *H. nuchalis* is centered on the Mississippi River and does not extend into the Missouri Drainage, whereas that of *H. placitus* is concentrated in the western tributaries of the Mississippi, especially the Missouri. Cross (1967) noted that Kansas distribution for *H. nuchalis* is restricted to the lowermost portion of the Kansas River (below Lawrence) and the Missouri River. He also noted that its extension up into the Kansas River was most pronounced during 1951 to 1952, two years of protracted flooding, and that all of the collections of *H. nuchalis* he studied contained more *H. placitus* than *H. nuchalis.* Metcalf (1966) considers *H. nuchalis* and *H. placitus* to be closely related but distinct species, with the former's Kansas distribution limited to the lowermost portion of the Kansas River.

High silt load is a major environmental factor affecting fish populations in the Kansas River and its major tributaries. Siltation and turbidity limit potential food sources, hinder sight feeding, reduce the efficiency of filter feeding, and blanket spawning sites (ANSP, 1959).

One factor that is important in determining the abundance of fish in turbid rivers is the timing of reproduction. For example, the high turbidity and scouring currents that accompany late spring and early summer high water levels in the Des Moines River (Iowa) result in poor reproduction for most of the early spawning minnows. Consequently, late (July and August) and intermittent spawning (spring through summer) minnows are usually dominant (Starrett, 1951).

Extended spawning may be a particularly adaptive life-history attribute for fish confronted with the highly variable flow regimes characteristic of rivers in the Kansas Basin. Indeed, many of the dominant species have long spawning periods. The breeding seasons for *Notropis stramineus missuriensis* and *Hybognathus placitus* extend from April through August, that of *N. lutrensis* extends from May through October, and that of *Hybopsis aestivalis* extends from late May through August. *Cyprinus carpio* spawns intermittently from as early as March until after July, and *Carpiodes carpio* spawns from late May to July or later (Cross, 1969).

Changes in the available habitat area caused by the substantial variation in water level is another important factor affecting fish populations. When the water level is lowered, crowding pressures are increased. For example, low water levels combined with high initial populations contributed to the poor spawning success of several minnows, including *Notropis stramineus* and *Hybopsis aestivalis,* in the Des Moines River (Starrett, 1951). In the Smoky Hill River, the decline in population of *N. stramineus* has been attributed to postspawning variations in the water level (Summerfelt, 1967). One common minnow, *N. lutrensis,* increases in abundance during periods of drought (Cross, 1967).

The paucity of favorable habitats is another major contributor to low fish populations. As mentioned with respect to the Kansas River sites near Topeka, most fish were found in backwaters and tributaries (ANSP, 1959). Several species (e.g., *Hybopsis aestivalis, Pimephales promelas, Ictalurus melas,* and *Lepomis* spp.) are physiologically hardy, tolerant of turbidity, and/or have prolonged spawning seasons, but prefer riffle, muddy, or weedy habitats, which are poorly developed in these rivers. The most abundant species are usually those that can inhabitat open areas over sand (e.g., *Cyprinus carpio, Hybognathus placitus, Notropis lutrensis, N. stramineus,* and *Carpiodes carpio*) (Cross, 1967).

A number of morphological features characterize plains races of wide-

spread species, and these features may represent adaptations to the environmental conditions prevalent in prairie rivers. The eye size is usually smaller in
plains races, apparently in response to the abrasion associated with turbidity,
and many have a marked development of ventral and oral cutaneous sensory
organs, probably in response to poor visibility. Several plains races have a
decurved anterior dorsal profile, which probably helps the fish swim and feed
over the open bottoms despite fast currents. The reduction in scale size characteristic in many plains races may also be an adaptation for the swifter currents
(Metcalf, 1966).

COMMUNITIES OF AQUATIC LIFE

Functional Relationships

This discussion on the functional relationships of Kansas Basin river organisms is structured around three habitat types: unstable sand, other benthic
habitats (including river margins, mouths of tributaries, backwaters, and snag
habitats), and the pelagic zone.

The predominance of unstable sand substrates means that most of the
benthos is unsuitable for most protozoans and macroinvertebrates. Burrowing
deposit feeders such as oligochaetes and *Chironomus* (chironomids) may be
the most important macroinvertebrates in the sandy substrates. Filter-feeding
unionid bivalves, abundant in most large rivers, are either absent or rare. In
contrast to the apparent paucity of invertebrate consumers, several species of
fish, including the most abundant, depend on the sand habitats for much of
their trophic support. Presumably, unlike invertebrates, fish can avoid being
buried by shifting sand.

One of the most abundant fish in Kansas Basin rivers is *Hybognathus
placitus,* a herbivorous cyprinid that probably feeds on films of diatoms that
accumulate on sandy substrates in shallow water. Its ecological counterpart,
Carpiodes carpio, is a common omnivorous catostomid that feeds on similar
accumulations in deeper water (Cross, 1967). *Cyprinus carpio, Notropis
lutrensis,* and *N. stramineus* are other common to abundant omnivorous fish
that may feed on algal accumulations over sand.

Despite the apparent lack of prey, several feeders of invertebrates frequent
the shifting sands. In addition to the omnivores mentioned previously, several
common carnivores, including *Hybopsis aestivalis, H. storeriana, Scaphirhynchus platyrhynchus,* and *Aplodinotus grunniens,* are typical of sandy habitats. Other carnivores, including piscivorous *Lepisosteus osseus, Ictalurus
punctatus,* and *Pylodictus olivaris,* extend onto the sand during their feeding
forays, and older individuals of *Dorosoma cepedianum* apparently feed on
benthic invertebrates (Cross, 1967).

While densities of macroinvertebrates are probably very low on the shifting
sands, the quantity of prey supplied by drift may provide a sufficient, and
energetically efficient, food base. In the main stem of the Missouri River,

terrestrial organisms accounted for 68% of the total benthic biomass (0.14 g m^{-2}) near a sandbar and 95% of the biomass (0.02 g m^{-2}) in the main channel. Drift samples for the Missouri River were similar to the benthic composition except that there was a bias in favor of Ephemeroptera and Plecoptera and against Annelida. The biomass of one 24-hour drift collection in April was approximately 10% (0.006 g per square meter of surface) of the average annual benthic biomass (0.04 g m^{-2}). Under most flow conditions, drift tended to be concentrated near the bottom. During sharp rises in the river level, most of the drift is concentrated near the surface (Berner, 1951).

The debris accumulations of snag habitats, and the mud bottoms and vegetation in quieter backwaters in the Kansas River near Topeka, hosted a variety of invertebrates, including many species of saprophytic and holozoic protozoans and most of the invertebrates. Prominent among the macroinvertebrates collected in the debris accumulations in snag habitats were two primarily detritivorous collector-gatherers, *Caenis* sp. and *Tricorythodes* sp., and one herbivore-detritivore, *Stenonema* near *ares* (Ephemeroptera). Low densities of other herbivorous and detritivorous mayflies, Elmidae (Coleoptera) and Chironomidae, were also found in the debris accumulations. The detritivorous *Limnodrillus* (Oligochaeta) was found in mud on the bank of one island. A few species of shredder-collectors were collected from accumulated debris and in muddy backwaters with marginal vegetation (ANSP, 1959).

Since unionid mussels are virtually absent, the major sites for filter feeders are snag habitats. Snag-dwelling filter feeders are typically situated where they are exposed to the force of the current and the abrasion caused by the suspended sediments. Consequently, the populations of these filter feeders are expected to be low, especially after floods. Indeed, the populations of *Isonychia* (Ephemeroptera), Hydropsychidae (Trichoptera), Simuliidae (Diptera), and Tanytarsini (Chironomidae) collected from the snag habitats in the Kansas River appeared to be low (ANSP, 1959).

The most frequent macroinvertebrate carnivores collected in the Kansas River near Topeka belonged to the Odonata. All of the damselflies (Zygoptera), *Macromia,* and *Neurocordulia* were found in among the snagged debris. The burrowing Gomphidae were located in muddy sites. Carnivores from the Hemiptera, Coleoptera, and Diptera appeared to be most common in the scattered muddy habitats, usually with marginal vegetation (ANSP, 1959).

A number of omnivorous and carnivorous fish frequent muddy backwaters and snag habitats. *Cyprinus carpio* and *Pimephales promelas* are two of the more common omnivores, often feeding on filamentous algae and vascular plants as well as invertebrates. The omnivorous *Notropis lutrensis* also frequents quiet backwaters. Carnivores such as *Ictalurus punctatus, Pylodictis olivaris,* and *Lepomis* spp. require cover in the form of deeper pools, macrophytes, or snags and are therefore more common near the margins.

The abundance of several planktivorous fish suggests that the plankton is a major source of food in the Kansas River. *Dorosoma cepedianum* and

Notropis atherinoides feed on both phytoplankton and zooplankton. In addition, the young of *Lepomis* spp. and *Pomoxis annularis* feed on zooplankton, usually in shallow water. The pelagic and possibly migratory *Morone chrysops* commonly feeds on *D. cepedianum* (Becker, 1983; Cross, 1967).

Structure of Aquatic Communities
Like the Missouri River in its main channel, the Kansas River has been channelized. As a result, a relatively few natural habitats exist. These are found in the mouths of small streams that enter the main channel; in pools and backwaters that, under flood conditions, connect with the main channel; and along the margins of the main channel, where vegetation and lentic habitats may be found.

Vegetative Habitats. Here were found two members of the bacterial phylum Bacteriophycea: *Asterothrix raphidoides* and *Cladothrix dichotoma*. These belong to the Cyanophyceae. They were found in and among the vegetation along the margins of the channel. Attached to vegetation were *Cyclotella atomus, C. glomerata,* and *C. kutzinghiana,* as were *Achnanthes lanceolata* and *A. minutissima.* One identified species of *Caloneis* was also found in these habitats. The vegetation was a fairly suitable habitat for seven taxons belonging to the genus *Navicula* (Table 4.2). Attached to the vegetation were *Amphora submontana, Cymbella ventricosa,* and six taxons belonging to the genus *Gomphonema.* Associated with the debris produced by the vegetation and, in some cases, attached to the vegetation were 11 taxons belonging to the genus *Nitzschia.*

The vegetation was also a suitable habitat for several of the protozoans. The autotrophs found associated with the vegetation were two taxons belonging to the genus *Cryptomonas* and one of the genus *Cyathomonas.* Present was the autotroph *Gonium pectorale,* two taxons belonging to the genus *Phacus,* and *Strombomonas gibberosa.* Living in and among the vegetation were five taxons belonging to the genus *Bodo* (Table 4.2). Crawling over the vegetation were the detritivore-omnivore, *Halteria grandinella; Physa* sp.; *Pseudosuccinea columella;* and the carnivorous leech, *Erpobdella punctata.*

Several insects were found in these vegetative habitats. They were the omnivorous mayfly, *Pentagenia* prob. *vittigera.* Also present were two taxons belonging to the genus *Baetis,* which are omnivore-herbivores; *Stenonema* near *carolina* and *S.* near *ares,* which are omnivores. Several stoneflies were found in and among the vegetation living in areas where there was a moderate current. They were *Togoperla* sp., an omnivore. A few true bugs were found in this habitat. They were the species *Trichocorixa calva,* a carnivore, and the megalopteran *Corydalis cornutus.* Several beetles were in and among the vegetation. They were the omnivorous *Laccophilus proximus, Helichus lithophilus,* and the hydrophilid, *Enochrus perplexus,* which is an omnivore-herbivore. Also present was the omnivorous *Helichus lithophilus.* Several caddisflies were found in and among the vegetation. They were the omnivo-

(text continues on page 383)

TABLE 4.2.   *Species List: Kansas River*

| | | Substrate[a] | |
| | | Lent. | Lot. |
Taxon	V	M,S	G,R
SUPERKINGDOM PROKARYOTAE			
KINGDOM MONERA			
Division Cyanophycota			
Class Cyanophyceae			
Order Nostocales			
Family Oscillatoriaceae			
Oscillatoria subtilissima			
Phormidium tenue			
Division Bacteriophyta			
Asterothrix raphidioides	X	X	X
Cladothrix dichotoma	X	X	X
SUPERKINGDOM EUKARYOTAE			
KINDGOM PLANTAE			
Subkingdom Thallobionta			
Division Chlorophycota			
Class Chlorophyceae			
Order Tetrasporales			
Family Gleocystaceae			
Palmogloea protuberans	X		
Order Chlorococcales			
Family Oocystaceae			
Ankistrodesmus falcatus		X	
Division Chromophycota			
Class Bacillariophyceae			
Order Eupodiscales			
Family Coscinodiscaceae			
Cyclotella atomus	X		X
C. glomerata	X	X	
C. kutzinghiana	X	X	X
C. meneghiniana		X	
C. nana		X	
C. pseudostelligera		X	X
C. stelligeroides		X	X
Melosira granulata	X		X
var. *angustissima*			
Stephanodiscus alpinus		X	
S. astraea var. *minutula*		X	
Family Thalassiosiraceae			
Thalassiosira fluviatilis			
Order Achnanthales			
Family Achnanthaceae			
Achnanthes lanceolata	X		X
A. minutissima	X		X
Order Naviculales			
Family Cymbellaceae			
Amphora submontana	X		X
Cymbella ventricosa	X		X

TABLE 4.2. *(Continued)*

Taxon	V	Lent. M,S	Lot. G,R
Family Gomphonemaceae			
*Gomphonema affine	X	X	
*G. angustatum	X	X	
*G. angustatum var. intermedia	X	X	
*G. angustatum var. obesa	X		
*G. olivaceum	X		X
*G. parvulum	X	X	
Gomphonema sp.			
Family Naviculaceae			
*Caloneis bacillum	X		X
*Caloneis sp.			
*Diploneis sp.		X	X
*Gyrosigma scalproides		X	
*Navicula accomoda	X	X	
*N. aszellus	X	X	
*N. caduca	X	X	
*N. cryptocephala var. veneta		X	X
N. gracilis var. schizonemoides		X	
*N. lanceolata		X	X
*N. menisculus	X	X	
N. menisculus var. obtusa		X	
*N. mutica	X	X	X
*N. mutica var. cohnii		X	X
*N. pelliculosa	X	X	X
N. pupula forma. minutula		X	
*N. symmetrica	X		X
N. tantula		X	
*N. vaucheriae var. densistriata			X
N. viridula var. argunensis		X	
N. viridula var. rostrata		X	
Navicula spp.			
Order Bacillariales			
Family Nitzschiaceae			
*Nitzschia acicularis		X	
*N. amphibia	X	X	
*N. apiculata	X	X	
*N. capitellata		X	X
*N. dissipata	X	X	
*N. fonticola	X	X	
*N. frustulum	X	X	X
*N. gracilis	X		X
*N. hungarica	X		X
*N. invicta var. lanceolata	X		
*N. palea		X	
*N. palea var. kutzingiana		X	
*N. romana		X	

Continued

TABLE 4.2.   (Continued)

Taxon	V	Lent. M,S	Lot. G,R
Family Nitzschiaceae (cont.)			
*N. stagnorum		X	
*N. subcapitellata		X	X
*N. tarda	X	X	
*N. umblicata	X		X
*N. valdestriata	X	X	
Nitzschia spp.			
Order Surirellales			
Family Surirellaceae			
Surirella angustata		X	
S. ovata		X	
S. ovata var. salina		X	
Class Dinophyceae			
Order Gymnodiniales			
Family Gymnodiniaceae			
*Gymnodinium sp.		X	
KINGDOM ANIMALIA			
SUBKINGDOM PROTOZOA			
Class Mastigophora			
Order Chrysomonadida			
Family Ochromonidida			
Anthophysa vegetans			
Monas dangeardii			
M. socialis			
Monas sp.			
Order Cryptomonadida			
Family Cryptomonadidae			
*Cryptomonas erosa	X		
*C. marssonii	X		
*Cyathomonas truncata	X		
Order Phytomonadida			
Family Carteriidae			
Collodictyon sparsevacuolatum			
Mesostigma viride			
Family Chlamydomonadidae			
Chlamydomonas reinhardii			
Family Phacotidae			
*Phacotus lenticularis		X	
Family Volvocidae			
*Gonium pectorale	X		
Order Euglenoidina			
Family Anisonemidae			
Peranema pleururum			
Family Euglenidae			
Euglena acus			
E. anabaena			
E. chadefaudii			

TABLE 4.2. *(Continued)*

Taxon	V	Lent. M,S	Lot. G,R
Family Euglenidae (*cont.*)			
E. intermedia			
E. pisciformis			
E. sociabilis			
E. tripteris			
E. viridis		X	
*Lepocinclis acuta		X	
L. texta		X	
*Phacus pyrum	X	X	
*P. tortus	X	X	
*Strombomonas gibberosa	X	X	
Trachelomonas hispida			
T. scabra			
T. stokesiana			
T. varians			
T. verrucosa			
T. volvocina			
Order Protomonadina			
Family Bodonidae			
*Bodo angustatus	X	X	
*B. caudatus	X	X	
*B. obovatus	X	X	
*B. repens	X	X	
*B. saltans	X	X	
Pleuromonas nasuta			
Rhynchomonas nasutum			
Class Ciliata			
Order Gymnostomatida			
Family Amphileptidae			
*Dipleptus americanus		X	
*Loxophyllum helus			X
Family Didiniidae			
*Askenasia sp.		X	
*Didinium balbianii var. nanum		X	
Suborder Hymenostomata			
Family Frontoniidae			
*Cinetochilum margaritaceum		X	
*Cyrtolophosis mucicola		X	
Glaucoma sp.			
Family Pleuronematidae			
*Ctedoctema acanthocrypta		X	
*Cyclidium citrullus		X	
*C. glaucoma		X	
*C. lanuginosum		X	

Continued

TABLE 4.2.   (Continued)

Taxon	V	Lent. M,S	Lot. G,R
Order Oligotrichida			
Family Halteriidae			
Halteria grandinella	X	X	
Order Tintinnida			
Family Euplotidae			
Euplotes eurystomus		X	X
Family Tintinnidae			
Tintinnopsis sp.			
Order Peritrichida			
Family Vorticellidae			
Vorticella sp.		X	X
Subkindgom Eumetazoa			
Phylum Mollusca			
Class Gastropoda			
Order Basommatophora			
Family Lymnaeidae			
Pseudosuccinea columella	X	X	
Family Physidae			
Physa sp.	X	X	X
Phylum Annelida			
Class Hirudinoidea			
Order Arhynchobdellidae			
Family Erpobdellidae			
Erpobdella punctata	X		
Phylum Arthropoda			
Class Crustacea			
Subclass Copepoda			
Family Argulidae			
Argulus sp.			
Class Insecta			
Order Odonata			
Suborder Zygoptera			
Family Coenagrionidae			
Argia apicalis		X	X
A. translata		X	X
Suborder Anisoptera			
Family Gomphidae			
Gomphus amnicola		X	
G. externus		X	
Gomphus sp.		X	
Order Ephemeroptera			
Suborder Schistonota			
Family Baetidae			
Baetis sp. 1	X	X	X
Baetis sp. 2	X	X	X
Heterocloeon spp.			X

TABLE 4.2.   (*Continued*)

Taxon	V	Lent. M,S	Lot. G,R
Family Ephemeridae			
Pentagenia prob. *vittigera*	X	X	X
Family Heptageniidae			
Heptagenia flavescens?			X
Stenonema nr. *ares*	X	X	X
Stenonema nr. *carolina*	X	X	X
Family Oligoneuridae			
Isonychia nr. *bicolor*			X
Suborder Pannota			
Family Caenidae			
Caenis sp.		X	
Tricorythodes sp.		X	X
Order Plecoptera			
Family Perlidae			
Togoperla spp.	X	X	X
Order Hemiptera			
Family Corixidae			
Trichocorixa calva	X	X	
Family Gerridae			
Metrobates hesperius			X
Family Veliidae			
Rhagovelia sp.			X
Order Megaloptera			
Family Corydalidae			
Corydalis cornutus	X	X	
Order Coleoptera			
Suborder Adephaga			
Family Dytiscidae			
Laccophilus proximus	X	X	
Suborder Polyphaga			
Family Dryopidae			
Helichus lithophilus	X		X
Family Elmidae			
Macronychus glabratus		X	X
Stenelmis crenata		X	X
S. sexlineata		X	X
Family Hydrophilidae			
Enochrus perplexus	X	X	
Order Trichoptera			
Family Hydropsychidae			
Cheumatopsyche spp.			X
Hydropsyche frisoni	X		X
Family Leptoceridae			
Leptocella nr. *candida*	X	X	X
Leptocella nr. *diarina*	X	X	X

Continued

TABLE 4.2.   (Continued)

Taxon	V	Lent. M,S	Lot. G,R
Order Diptera			
Suborder Nematocera			
Family Chaoboridae			
Chaoborus punctipennis		X	X
Family Chironomidae			
Calopsectra exigua			X
Calopsectra nr. *longiradius*			X
Calopsectra sp.			X
Harnischia sp.	X		
Pentaneura (Melanops gr.) sp.	X	X	X
Pentaneura (Melanops gr.) sp. - pupa			
Polypedilum cinctum?	X		
P. halterale	X		
P. illinoense	X		
P. nr. illinoense	X		
Tanytarsus nigricans	X		X
*unident. Tendipedini sp.		X	
Family Simuliidae			
Simulium sp.			X
Phylum Chordata			
Subphylum Vertebrata			
Class Osteichthyes			
Order Lepisosteiformes			
Family Lepisosteidae			
Lepisosteus osseus	X	X	X
Order Clupeiformes			
Family Clupeidae			
Subfamily Dorosomatinae			
Dorosoma cepedianum	X	X	X
Order Cypriniformes			
Family Catostomidae			
Carpiodes carpio	X	X	
Carpiodes forbesi		X	X
(*C. cyprinus*)			
Family Cyprinidae			
Carassius auratus	X	X	X
Cyprinus carpio		X	X
Hybognathus nuchalis		X	
Hybopsis aestivalis		X	X
Hybopsis storeriana		X	
Notropis camurus			X
N. deliciosus (*N. stramineus*)		X	X
N. lutrensis		X	X
N. percobromus?			
Notropis sp.			X

TABLE 4.2.   (Continued)

Taxon	V	Lent. M,S	Lot. G,R
Family Cyprinidae (*cont.*)			
*Pimephales notatus	X	X	
*P. promelas	X	X	
Order Siluriformes			
Family Ictaluridae			
*Ictalurus melas	X	X	
*I. punctatus		X	X
*Pylodictis olivaris	X	X	
Order Perciformes			
Family Centrarchidae			
*Lepomis cyanellus	X	X	
*L. humilis	X	X	
*L. macrochirus	X	X	
Lepomis sp.	X	X	X
Pomoxis annularis	X	X	
Family Moronidae			
Morone chrysops			
Family Sciaenidae			
*Aplodinotus grunniens		X	

Sources: Becker (1983), Cross (1967), and Lee et al. (1980).
*Species discussed in the section "Structure of Aquatic Communities" based on knowledge of R. Patrick.
^{a}V, vegetation; M, mud; S, sand; G, gravel; R, rock.

rous *Hydropsyche frisoni* and an omnivore-herbivore, *Leptocella* prob. *diarina* and *L.* prob. *candida.*

Several tendipeds were found in and among the vegetation. They were the omnivorous, *Pentaneura* group. Other omnivorous tendipeds were *Harnischia* sp., *Polypedilum cinctum?, P. halterale, P. illinoenses, P.* near *illinoenses,* and *Tanytarsus nigricans.*

A few fish were found among the vegetation. They were the carnivorous *Lepisosteus osseus,* the omnivorous *Dorosoma cepedianum,* and the omnivorous *Carpiodes carpio.* Other omnivores present in and among the vegetation were *Pimephales notatus; P. promelas;* the omnivorous catfish, *Ictalurus melas;* and *Pylodictis olivaris.* The centrarchids were represented by three species: the carnivorous *Lepomis cyanellus* and *L. humilis* and the omnivorous *L. macrochirus.*

Lentic Habitats.   Many of the lentic habitats contained mud and fine sand. They might occur along the edges of the channel in temporary pools or in backwaters where there was very little current. In some areas where small streams entered the main channel, this habitat occurred. Here one might find the green alga, *Ankistrodesmus falcatus,* and two taxons belonging to a division of the plant kingdom known as the Bacteriophyta (Table 4.2). Diatoms were fairly common growing on the surface of the mud or in and among vegetation and debris found in these lentic habitats. Six taxons belonging to the diatom genus *Cyclotella* were found here. Also present were the two taxons belonging to the genus *Stephanodiscus*. This was a favorite habitat for several species belonging to the family Naviculaceae. They were an unidentified species of *Diploneis*, *Gyrosigma scalproides*, and 11 taxa belonging to the genus *Navicula*. Attached to the debris or the vegetation in these habitats were four taxons belonging to the genus *Gomphonema*. As one might expect, this was a favorite habitat for the genus *Nitzschia*. Fourteen taxons belonging to this genus were found here (Table 4.2). The dinoflagellate *Gymnodinium* sp. was also found.

Several protozoans were found in these lentic habitats. *Phacotus lenticularis*, *Lepocinclis acuta*, *Phacus pyrum*, *P. tortus*, and *Strombomonas gibberosa*. Moving in and among the detritus was an unidentifed species of the genus *Gymnodinium*. The genus Bodo was quite common in these lentic habitats, where mud and sand were dominant. Five taxons were found (Table 4.2).

Several ciliates were found in these lentic habitats. They were an unidentified species of the genus *Askenasia*, *Didinium balbianii* var. *nanum*, *Dileptus americanus*, *Cinetochilum margaritaceum*, *Cyrtolophosis mucicola*, *Ctedoctema acanthocrypta*, *Cyclidium citrullus*, *C. glaucoma*, and *C. lanuginosum*. An oligotrich, *Halteria grandinella*, was also found here, as was *Euplotes eurystomus*. Attached to the debris was an unidentified species of *Vorticella*, which is a detritivore-omnivore.

This was a favorite habitat for a few molluscs. They were the detritivore-omnivore, *Physa* sp., and *Pseudosuccinea columella*. This was a favorite habitat, where the current was slow to moderate, for several odonates. They were the carnivorous *Argia apicalis*, *A. translata*, and three species belonging to the carnivorous genus *Gomphus*. A few mayflies were found in this habitat. They were the omnivorous *Pentagenia* prob. *vittigera*, the omnivorous *Caenis*, an unidentified species of the genus *Tricorythodes*, two unidentifed species of the omnivorous-herbivorous genus *Baetis*, the omnivorous *Stenonema* near *carolina*, and *S.* near *ares*. A few stoneflies were found in these lentic habitats. They were two unidentified species of the omnivorous genus *Togoperla*. A few corixids were found here: the carnivorous *Trichocorixa calva* and a carnivorous megalopteran, *Corydalis cornutus*. Beetles were found in this habitat. They were the omnivorous *Laccophilus proximus* and the hyrophilid *Enochrus perplexus*. A few elmids were found in these lentic habitats. They were the omnivore-detritivore, *Macronychus glabratus*, and the omnivorous *Stenelmis crenata* and *S. sexlineata*. The Trichoptera, commonly known as caddisflies, were also present. They were the omnivorous-herbivorous species *Leptocella* prob. *diarina* and *L.* prob. *candida*. The family Chaoboridae was represented by one species, *Chaoborus punctipennis*. The tendipeds were represented by a species of *Pentaneura* of the group *Melanops*. If it is not this group, it is probably an omnivore-herbivore. Also present was an unidentified species of the genus *Tendipedini.*

Several fish were found in these lentic habitats. They were the carnivorous *Lepisosteus osseus,* the omnivorous *Dorosoma cepedianum,* and the omnivorous *Carpiodes carpio,* and *Hybopsis aestivalis,* and omnivore. Other species found in the lentic habitats were the carnivore *Notropis lutrensis* and the omnivorous *Pimephales notatus* and *P. promelas.* The catfish, *Ictalurus melas,* and *I. punctatus* which are omnivores, were found here, as was the omnivorous *Pylodictis olivaris.* The centrarchids were represented by several species: the carnivorous *Lepomis cyanellus, L. humilis,* the omnivorous *L. macrochirus,* and the carnivorous *Aplodinotus grunniens.*

Lotic Habitats.   Habitats where the current was relatively swift were found in the main channel. Here the substrate was often gravel and hard mud or wooden snags and other debris. These habitats were not very common, but where they did exist there was often a well-developed community of aquatic life. In the crevices of the rocks one found *Asterothrix raphidoides* and *Cladothrix dichotoma.* In among the gravel were six taxons belonging to the genus *Cyclotella.* Attached to the hard substrates were *Achnanthes lanceolata* and *A. minutissima.* Among the gravel was *Caloneis bacillum* and an unidentified species of the genus *Caloneis.* Eight taxons belonging to the genus *Navicula* were also found in and among the gravel. Attached to the hard substrates were *Amphora submontana, Cymbella ventricosa,* and *Gomphonema olivaceum.* A few *Nitzschias* occurred in and among the gravel or attached to the hard substrates. They were *Nitzschia capitellata, N. frustulum, N. gracilis,* and *N. hungarica.* Also present were *N. subcapitellata* and *N. umblicata.*

A few protozoans were found in these lotic habitats. However, most of the protozoans seemed to be scuffed-up plankton. They were *Loxophyllum helus, Euplotes eurystomus,* and *Vorticella* sp.

Crawling over the hard substrates were an unidentified species of snail belonging to the genus *Physa,* probably a detritivore-omnivore. Crawling over the rocks were several species of insects. They were the odonates *Argia apicalis* and *A. translata,* both of which are carnivores. Also present in this habitat were the mayflies *Pentagenia* prob. *vittigera,* which is an omnivore, and an unidentifed species of the genus *Tricorythodes,* which is probably an omnivore. Other mayflies found in this habitat were the omnivore, sometimes carnivore, *Isonychia* near *bicolor.* Other mayflies present were the genus *Baetis* sp., which is a detritivore-herbivore. Two species of this genus were found. Also present were two unidentified species of the genus *Heterocloeon,* detritivore-omnivores. *Heptagenia* was found crawling over the rocks. The species was the omnivorous *Heptagenia flavescens.* Also found were *Stenonema* prob. *carolina* and *S.* nr. *ares,* which are omnivores.

This was a habitat for a few stoneflies. They were the omnivores *Togoperla* sp. A few gerrids were found in this habitat. They were the carnivorous *Metrobates hesperius* and an unidentified species of the carnivorous genus

Rhagovelia sp. A few beetles were found: *Helichus lithophilus,* probably an omnivore; *Macronychus glabratus,* a detritivore-omnivore; and two species of the genus *Stenelmis, S. crenata* and *S. sexlineata,* both omnivores.

These lotic habitats were suitable for several species of hydropsychids. They were two unidentified species of the genus *Cheumatopsyche,* which are probably omnivores and *Hydropsyche frisoni,* an omnivore. Other hydropsychids found in this habitat were the omnivorous, sometimes carnivorous, *Leptocella* near *diarina* and *L.* near *candida.* Also present was the omnivorous species *Chaoborus punctipennis.* Found living in and among the gravel was an unidentified species of the omnivorous-herbivorous genus *Pentaneura* of the *Melanops* group. Other tendipeds found were *Tanytarsus nigricans,* an omnivore; *Calopsectra exigua,* an omnivore; *Calopsectra* near *longiradius,* probably an omnivore; and an unidentified species of the same genus. On the rocks and sometimes in and among the gravel was an unidentified species of blackfly.

Several fish seemed to prefer these lotic habitats. They were the carnivorous *Lepisosteus osseus* and the omnivorous *Dorosoma cepedianum.* Several cyprinids were found in and among the sand and gravel, where the current was moderate, or among the gravel and rocks, where the current was more rapid. They were the omnivorous *Hybopsis aestivalis* and the carnivorous *Notropis camurus,* and *N. lutrensis,* which is an omnivore. A catfish, the omnivorous *Ictalurus punctatus,* was found in these lotic habitats.

SUMMARY

The watershed area of the Kansas River Basin occupies 156,542 km^2 and covers most of the northern half of Kansas and part of southern Nebraska and northeastern Colorado. Most of the major tributaries arise from the high plains and flow in an easterly direction toward the Missouri River. The basin is divided into four main subbasins. The Republican River to the north, the Solomon River and the Smoky Hill River to the south cover all the western and most of the central portion of the basin. The Solomon River and the Smoky Hill River are the main riverine basins in the western northern half of Kansas. The Arkansas River is the main river draining the western and southern half of Kansas. The Big Blue Subbasin occupies the northern portion of the eastern part of the basin, and the Main-Stem Kansas occupies the remaining portion of the eastern basin. The dominant landforms of the Republican and Smoky Hill Subbasins are High Plains and Dissected High Plains. Dominant landforms such as the Sand Hills are also found within the Republican Subbasin. Eastern Central Kansas Plains are prevalent in the lower reaches of both subbasins. Most of the basin is moderately sloped to nearly level.

The bedrock of the Kansas River Basin consists of Pennsylvanian through Tertiary sedimentary deposits, with the newer deposits prevalent in the western portion of the basin. Because of mid-Pleistocene glaciation, till and outwash materials are the predominant surface deposits over much of the

Main-Stem Kansas Subbasin. The river valleys in this subbasin cut into Pennsylvanian and Permean rock composed of alternating layers of shale, sandstone, and limestone. The soils of the Main-Stem Kansas Subbasin are loess, aluvium, or derived from local weathered bedrock and are easily erodible. Impermeable clay or claypan subsoils are distributed extensively in the eastern portion of the Kansas River Basin.

Most of the Kansas River Basin is agriculture; grain and livestock are predominant in the upland areas, and row crops dominate the fertile bottomlands. Common trees along the banks are cottonwood, elm, and willow. The uplands are dominated by bluestem pairies. In the eastern half of the basin, bluestem prairies form a mosaic with oak–hickory forests. In the western half, the bluestem grades into semiarid prairies.

Most of the stream flow of the Kansas River Basin originates as precipitation, but perennial springs and some groundwater from the adjacent Platte Basin percolate into portions of the Republic River and Big Blue Subbasins. Most of the runoff is from rain and falls in the eastern third of the Main-Stem Kansas Subbasin. In the watershed flow, Topeka accounts for between one-fifth and one-sixth of the river's total discharge. The main stem of the Kansas River averages 165 m in width and 1 m in depth. In the area of study of the aquatic life, the depths of the river are moderate or shallow and small islands are present. The banks range from steep to gradual.

In the main stem of the Kansas River near Wamego, the hardness varied from 128 to 146 mg L^{-1} as calcium carbonate, chloride concentrations varied from 6 to 80 mg L^{-1}, and the pH from 7.4 to 8.2 in water year 1958. The total drainage basin consists of hard water rich in calcium and magnesium. Probably due to agricultural activities, the nitrates and phosphates are relatively high. However, the productivity of the river is greatly reduced because of its turbidity. Detritus in many parts of the river is relatively low. However, where agriculture is important, the input of detritus increases. For example, in late September in the vicinity of Topeka, mean concentrations of organic matter from Kansas River sites ranged from 222 to 266 ppm, whereas in two water quality samples taken near De Soto, the organic carbon ranged from 3.3 to 20 mg L^{-1}.

The periphyton is relatively low in the main stem of the Kansas River. This is caused by the high turbidity and unstable bed and banks, and by the high suspended-solids load. However, the diversity of the diatom assemblage collected near Topeka suggests that under conditions of lower flow and reduced turbidity, periphyton biomass could be much higher. In a protected area where the turbidity was reduced, the diatom flora was relatively well developed. It is no doubt that the high load of suspended solids reduces the primary productivity, which otherwise might be relatively large. It is interesting to note that in the Big Blue River, one of the headwaters, the phytoplankton productivity is relatively high. In areas where the suspended solids were relatively low, the phytoplankton greatly increased in rivers comprising the Kansas River watershed.

The macroinvertebrate standing crop in this riverine system is usually relatively low. The high silt load and shifting sand bottoms severly limit the insect fauna in the areas of study. Most of the insect fauna in the areas studied near Topeka were collected from sheltered backwaters. As with other aquatic life, the fish populations are relatively low in the Kansas River and were found primarily in relatively quiet side pockets and tributaries where the suspended solids are lower and food was more abundant. Near Junction City, the estimated fish standing crop at the Smoky Hill River site was only 0.11 kg/ha^{-1}. Downstream from the Smoky Hill River site, where there was a greater variety of substrates and much less turbidity, the standing crop ranged from 1.4 to 10.9 kg/ha^{-1}.

The most abundant fish at the Junction City site were plains minnow *(Hybognathus placitus),* sand shiner *(Notropis stramineus),* red minnow *(N. lutrensis),* suckermouth minnow *(Phenacobius mirabilis),* fathead minnow *(Pimephales promelas),* and river carpsucker *(Carpiodes carpio).* The high silt load is a major environmental factor affecting the size of populations of fish in the Kansas River and its major tributaries. The lack of favorable habitats and changing water levels probably were partially responsible for the low fish populations in these rivers, as they probably affected spawning success.

The abundance of aquatic life is relatively low in the Kansas River. This is due to many environmental factors, such as unstable silt–sand substrates, high turbidity affecting light penetration and hence algae production, and the shifting substrate, all of which affected the productivity of aquatic life. The most productive areas for invertebrates were in mud buttom areas with vegetation that was present in quiet backwaters of the Kansas River. Probably because of the high turbidity and unstable beds, the mussel fauna is relatively limited. It should be noted that several planktivorous fish were abundant, such as *Dorosoma cepedianum* and *Notropis atherinoides.* Most of the aquatic life was found where there was vegetation. The vegetation and mud and sand habitats in small pools and backwaters were the most productive for aquatic life. The lotic habitats, which consist of substrates of gravel, hard mud, wood, and other debris, were the most productive for aquatic life. These supported a variety of aquatic life, and the various stages of nutrient and energy transfer were evident by the kinds of species that occurred in these habitats. Compared with other rivers, productivity is relatively low in the main stem of the Kansas River.

BIBLIOGRAPHY

Academy of Natural Sciences of Philadelphia. 1959. Kansas River survey for the Tecumseh plant of the E.I. DuPont de Nemours and Company. ANSP, Philadelphia, Pa.

Becker, G. C. 1983. Fishes of Wisconsin. Univ. Wisconsin Press, Madison, Wis. 1052 pp.

Berner, L. M. 1951. Limnology of the Lower Missouri River. Ecology 32(1): 1–12.

Briggs, J. C., and J. F. Ficke. 1977. Quality of rivers of the United States, 1975 water year—based on the National Stream Quality Accounting Network (NASQAN). Open-File Rep. 78–200. U.S. Geological Survey, Washington, D.C.

Chapman, J. 1972. Effects of a diversion dam on the benthos and macroinvertebrate drift of the Platte River. Masters thesis. Kearney State College, Kearney, Nebr. 43 pp.

Colby, C. C., H. L. Dillingham, E. G. Erickson, G. F. Jenks, J. O. Jones, and R. Sinclair. 1956. Tha Kansas Basin: pilot study of a watershed. Univ. Kansas study. Univ. Kansas, Lawrence, Kans.

Cross, F. B. 1967. Handbook of fishes of Kansas. Misc. Publ. 45. State Biological Survey and Univ. Kansas Museum of Natural History, Lawrence, Kans.

Jewell, M. E. 1927. Aquatic biology of the prairie. Ecology 8(3): 289–298.

Kansas Forestry, Fish and Game Commission. 1977. Kansas River Basin, Kansas: preliminary stream survey. KFF&G, Topeka, Kans.

Kansas Forestry, Fish and Game Commission. 1979. Smoky Hill River Basin: Kansas stream survey. KFF&G, Topeka, Kans.

Lee, D. C., C. R. Gilbert, C. H. Hocutt, R. E. Jenkins, D. E. McAllister, and J. R. Stauffer, Jr. 1980. Atlas of North American freshwater fishes. North Carolina State Museum of Natural History, Raleigh, N.C., 854 pp.

Matthai, H. F. 1968. Magnitude and frequency of floods in the United States. Part 6-B. Missouri River Basin below Sioux City, Iowa. Water-Supply Pap. 1680. U.S. Geological Survey, Washington, D.C.

Metcalf, A. L. 1966. Fishes of the Kansas River System in relation to zoogeography of the Great Plains. Univ. Kans. Publ., Mus. Nat. Hist. 17: 23–189.

Morris, L. A., R. N. Langmeier, and A. Witt, Jr. 1968. Trans. Am. Fish. Soc. 97(4): 380–388.

Murry, H. D., and A. B. Leonard. 1962. Handbook of unionid mussels in Kansas. Misc. Publ. 28. State Biological Survey and Univ. Kansas Department of Zoology, Lawrence, Kans.

Starrett, W. C. 1951. Some factors affecting the abundance of minnows in the Des Moines River, Iowa. Ecology 32(1): 13–27.

Starrett, W. C., and R. Patrick. 1952. Net plankton and bottom microflora of the Des Moines River, Iowa. Proc. Acad. Nat. Sci. Phila. 104: 219–243.

Summerfelt, R. C. 1967. Fishes of the Smoky Hill River, Kansas. Trans. Kans. Acad. Sci. 70(1): 102–139.

U.S. Geological Survey. 1962. Quality of surface waters of the United States, 1958. Parts 5 and 6. Hudson Bay and Upper Mississippi River Basins, and Missouri River Basin. Water-Supply Pap. 1572. USGS, Washington, D.C.

U.S. Geological Survey. 1970. The national atlas of the United States of America. USGS, Washington, D.C. 417 pp.

U.S. Geological Survey. 1972. Surface water supply of the United States, 1966–1970. Part 6. Missouri River Basin. Water-Supply Pap. 2119. USGS, Washington, D.C.

U.S. Geological Survey. 1974. Quality of surface waters of the United States, 1969. Part 6. Missouri River Basin. Water-Supply Pap. 2145. USGS, Washington, D.C.

U.S. Geological Survey. 1985. Water resource data, Kansas, water year 1984. Water-Data Rep. KS-84-1. USGS, Washington, D.C.

Volesky, D. F. 1969. A comparison of the macrobenthos from selected habitats in cattail marshes of the Missouri River. Unpublished Master's thesis. Univ. South Dakota, Vermillion, S. Dak. 42 pp.

Whitley, J. R., and R. S. Campbell. 1973. Some aspects of water quality and biology of the Missouri River. Trans. Mo. Acad. Sci. 7–8: 60–72.

Williams, M. C., H. G. Nagel, and C. E. True. 1985. Water quality of a limited segment of the Big Blue River in Nebraska. Trans. Nebr. Acad. Sci. 13: 59–73.